DUMP
D DUMP
UMP

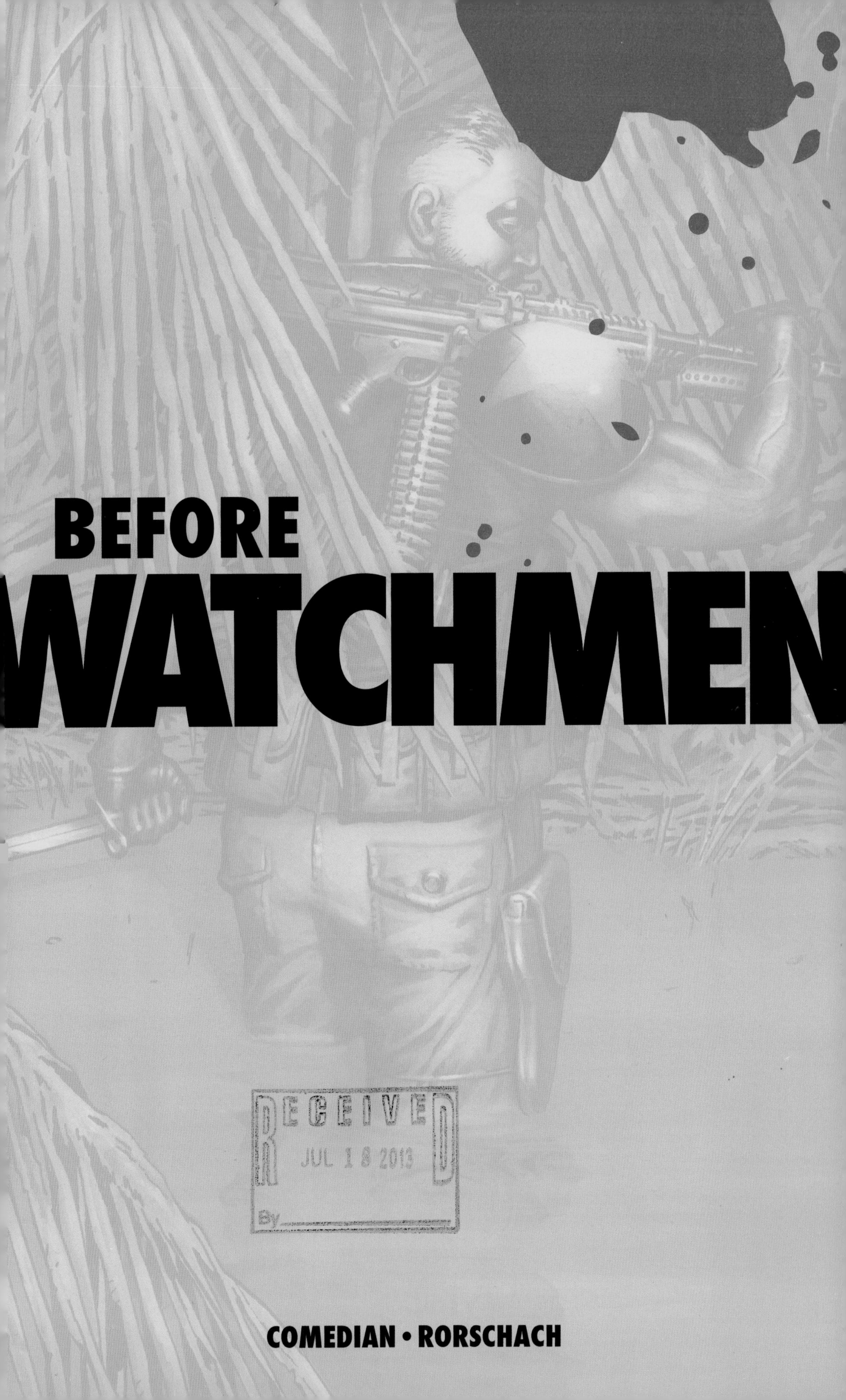

BEFORE WATCHMEN

COMEDIAN • RORSCHACH

BEFORE

WATC

COMEDIAN • RORSCHACH

BRIAN AZZARELLO
writer

J.G JONES
LEE BERMEJO
artists

ALEX SINCLAIR
TONY AVINA
LEE LOUGHRIDGE
BARBARA CIARDO
colorists

CLEM ROBBINS
ROB LEIGH
letterers

J.G. JONES and **LEE BERMEJO**
with **ALEX SINCLAIR** and **BARBARA CIARDO**
cover artists

Watchmen created by
ALAN MOORE and **DAVE GIBBONS**

WILL DENNIS Editor – Original Series
MARK DOYLE Associate Editor – Original Series
CAMILLA ZHANG Assistant Editor – Original Series
PETER HAMBOUSSI Editor
RACHEL PINNELAS Assistant Editor
ROBBIN BROSTERMAN Design Director – Books
ROBBIE BIEDERMAN Publication Design

BOB HARRAS Senior VP – Editor-in-Chief, DC Comics

DIANE NELSON President
DAN DIDIO and JIM LEE Co-Publishers
GEOFF JOHNS Chief Creative Officer
JOHN ROOD Executive VP – Sales, Marketing & Business Development
AMY GENKINS Senior VP – Business & Legal Affairs
NAIRI GARDINER Senior VP – Finance
JEFF BOISON VP – Publishing Planning
MARK CHIARELLO VP – Art Direction & Design
JOHN CUNNINGHAM VP – Marketing
TERRI CUNNINGHAM VP – Editorial Administration
ALISON GILL Senior VP – Manufacturing & Operations
HANK KANALZ Senior VP – Vertigo & Integrated Publishing
JAY KOGAN VP – Business & Legal Affairs, Publishing
JACK MAHAN VP – Business Affairs, Talent
NICK NAPOLITANO VP – Manufacturing Administration
SUE POHJA VP – Book Sales
COURTNEY SIMMONS Senior VP – Publicity
BOB WAYNE Senior VP – Sales

Cover design by CHIP KIDD

DC COMICS, 1700 BROADWAY, NEW YORK, NY 10019
A WARNER BROS. ENTERTAINMENT COMPANY.
PRINTED BY RR DONNELLEY, SALEM, VA, USA. 6/14/13. FIRST PRINTING.

SUSTAINABLE FORESTRY INITIATIVE
Certified Chain of Custody
At Least 20% Certified Forest Content
www.sfiprogram.org
SFI-01042
APPLIES TO TEXT STOCK ONLY

Library of Congress Cataloging-in-Publication Data

Azzarello, Brian.
Before Watchmen : Comedian/Rorschach / Brian Azzarello, J.G. Jones, Lee Bermejo.
pages cm. — (Before Watchmen)
"Originally published in single magazine form in Before Watchmen: Comedian 1-6, Before Watchmen: Rorschach 1-4."
ISBN 978-1-4012-3893-3
1. Graphic novels. I. Jones, J. G. II. Bermejo, Lee. III. Title. IV. Title: Comedian/Rorschach.
PN6728.W386A97 2013
741.5'973 — dc23

2013009154

BEFORE WATCHMEN

COMEDIAN
writer – BRIAN AZZARELLO
artist – J.G. JONES
colorists – ALEX SINCLAIR, TONY AVINA & LEE LOUGHRIDGE
letterer – CLEM ROBBINS

RORSCHACH
writer – BRIAN AZZARELLO
artist – LEE BERMEJO
colorist – BARBARA CIARDO
letterer – ROB LEIGH

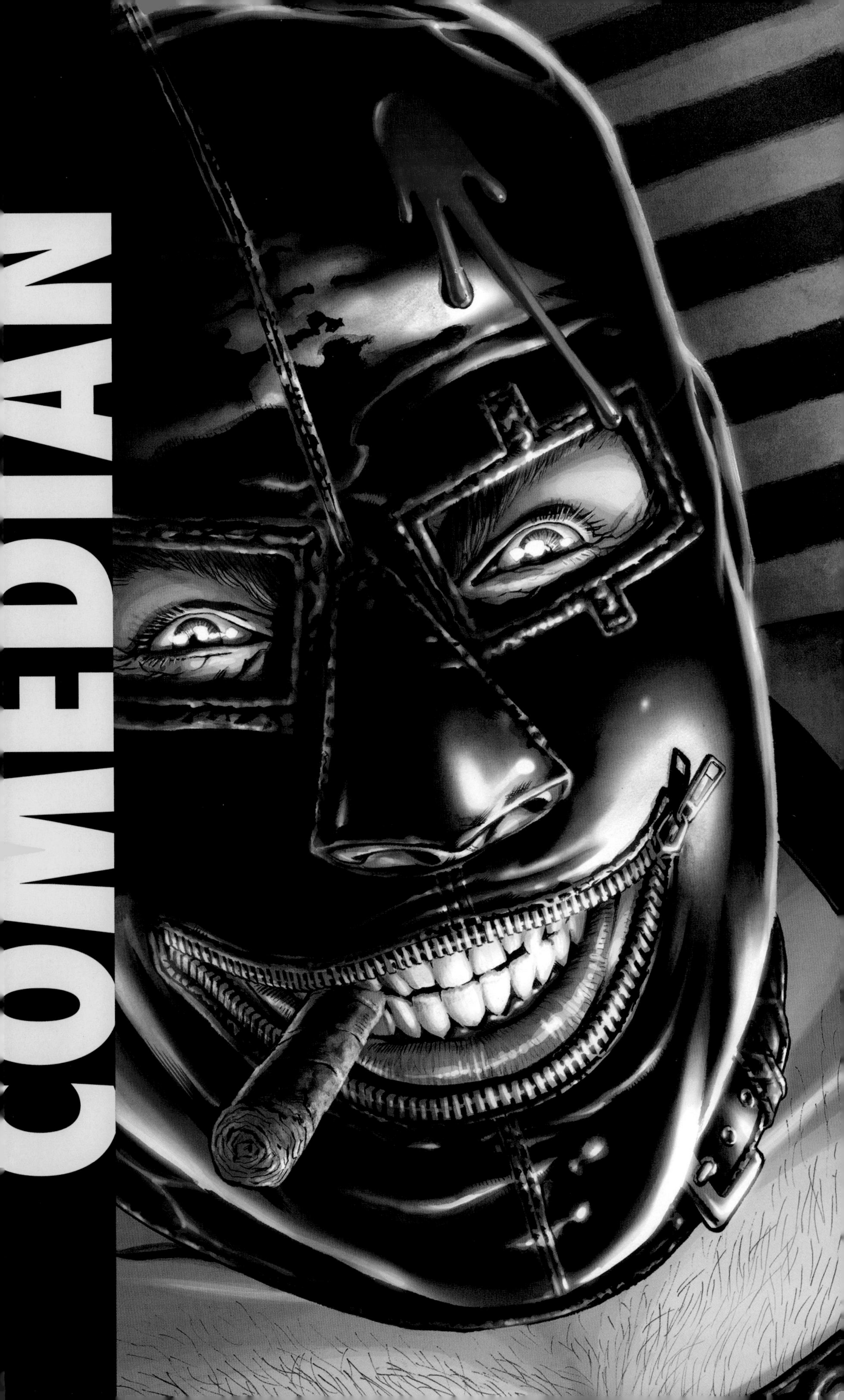
COMEDIAN

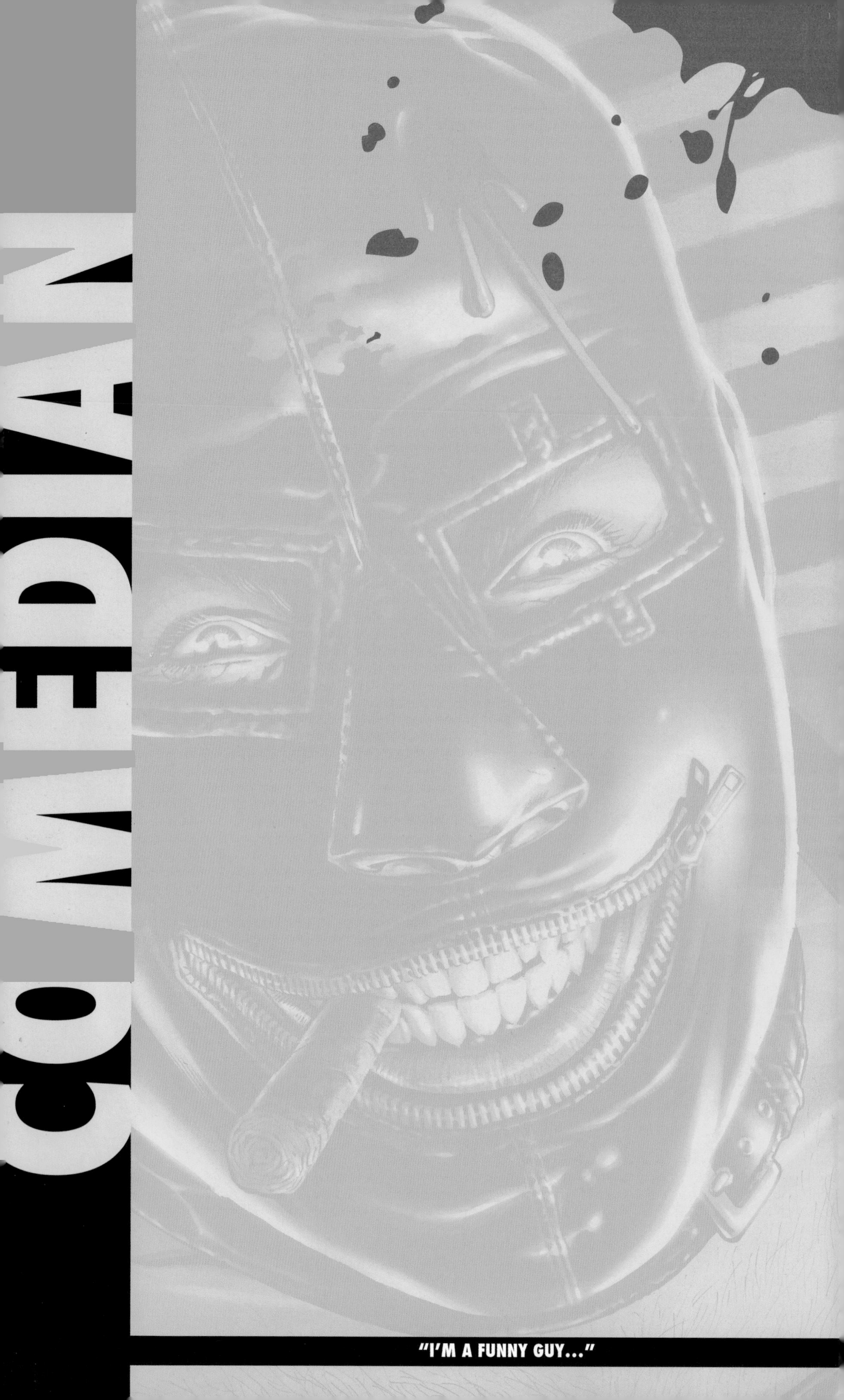
COMEDIAN
"I'M A FUNNY GUY..."

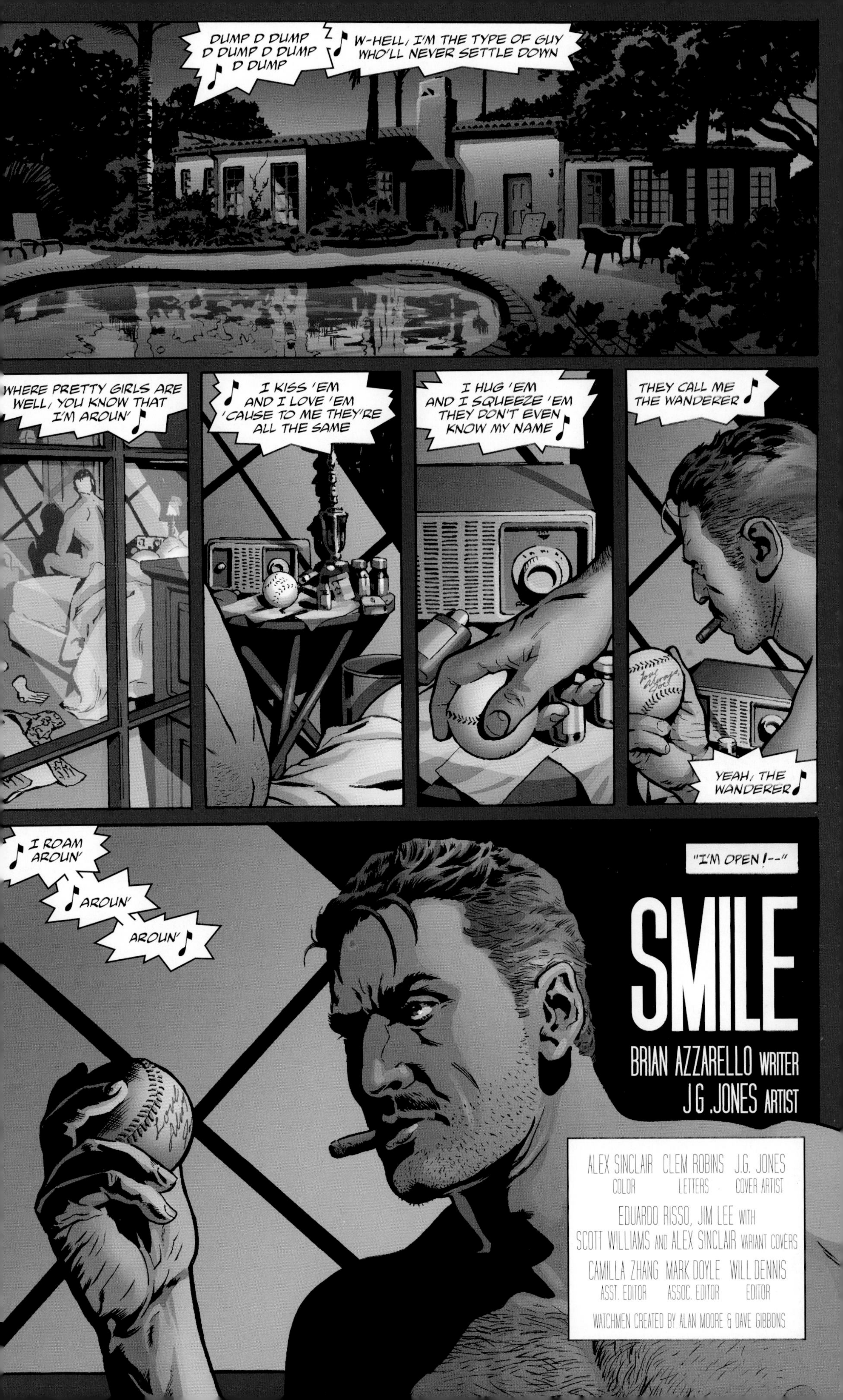
DUMP D DUMP D DUMP D DUMP D DUMP
W-HELL, I'M THE TYPE OF GUY WHO'LL NEVER SETTLE DOWN
WHERE PRETTY GIRLS ARE WELL, YOU KNOW THAT I'M AROUN'
I KISS 'EM AND I LOVE 'EM 'CAUSE TO ME THEY'RE ALL THE SAME
I HUG 'EM AND I SQUEEZE 'EM THEY DON'T EVEN KNOW MY NAME
THEY CALL ME THE WANDERER
YEAH, THE WANDERER
I ROAM AROUN'
AROUN'
AROUN'
"I'M OPEN!--"
SMILE
BRIAN AZZARELLO WRITER
J G .JONES ARTIST
ALEX SINCLAIR COLOR
CLEM ROBINS LETTERS
J.G. JONES COVER ARTIST
EDUARDO RISSO, JIM LEE WITH SCOTT WILLIAMS AND ALEX SINCLAIR VARIANT COVERS
CAMILLA ZHANG ASST. EDITOR
MARK DOYLE ASSOC. EDITOR
WILL DENNIS EDITOR
WATCHMEN CREATED BY ALAN MOORE & DAVE GIBBONS

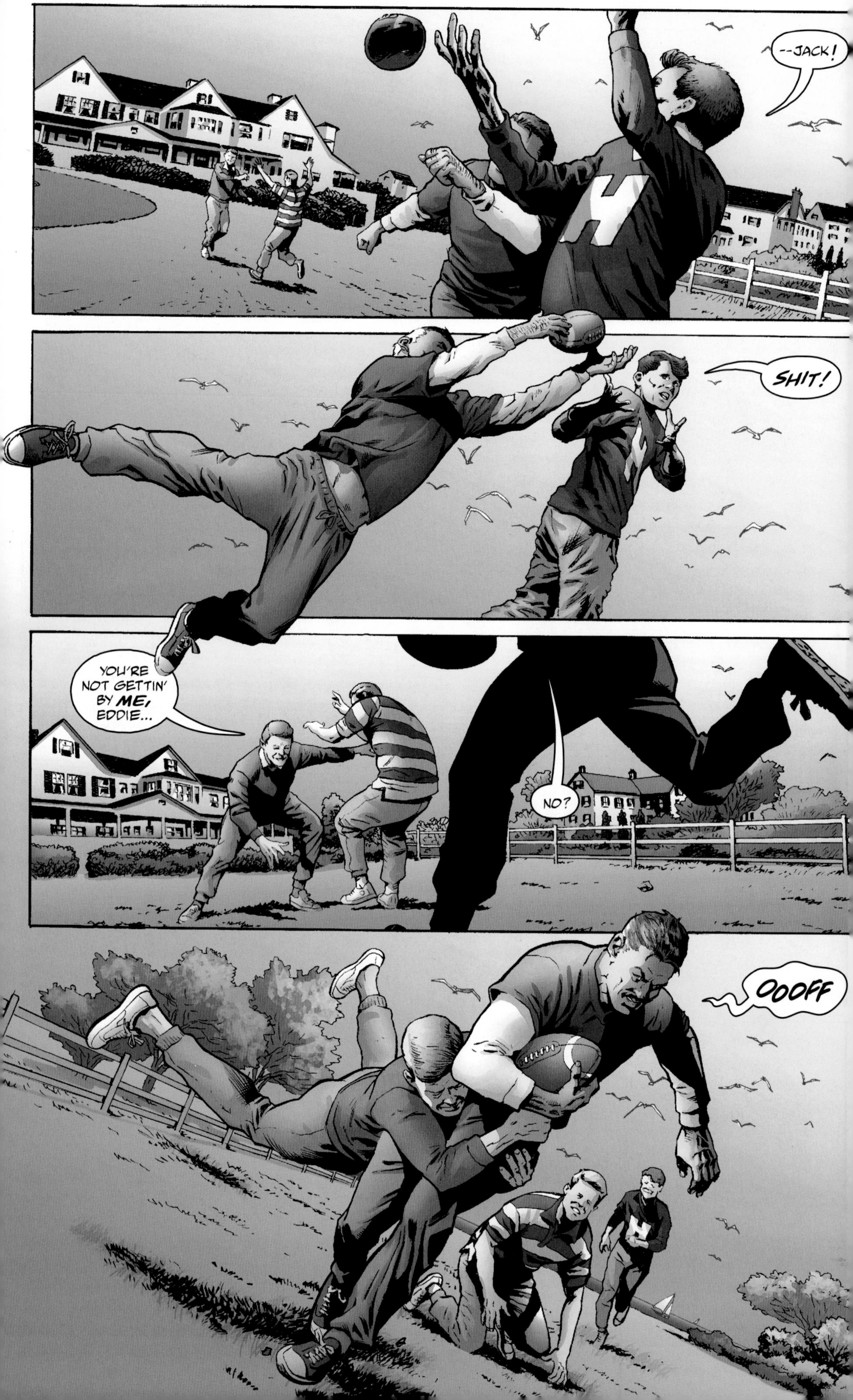
--JACK!
SHIT!
YOU'RE NOT GETTIN' BY ME, EDDIE...
NO?
OOOFF

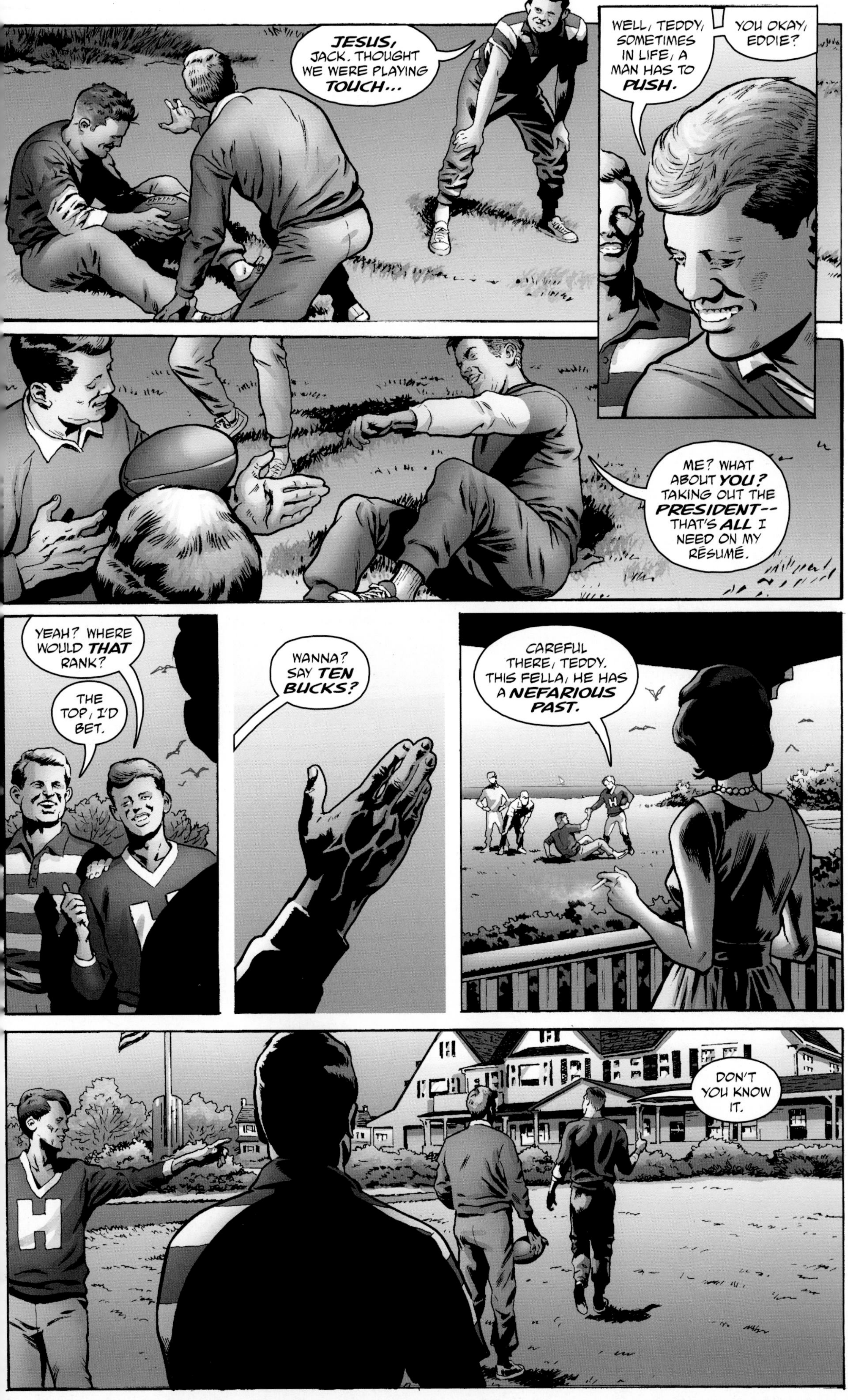
JESUS, JACK. THOUGHT WE WERE PLAYING TOUCH...
WELL, TEDDY, SOMETIMES IN LIFE, A MAN HAS TO PUSH.
YOU OKAY, EDDIE?
ME? WHAT ABOUT YOU? TAKING OUT THE PRESIDENT-- THAT'S ALL I NEED ON MY RÉSUMÉ.
YEAH? WHERE WOULD THAT RANK?
THE TOP, I'D BET.
WANNA? SAY TEN BUCKS?
CAREFUL THERE, TEDDY. THIS FELLA, HE HAS A NEFARIOUS PAST.
DON'T YOU KNOW IT.

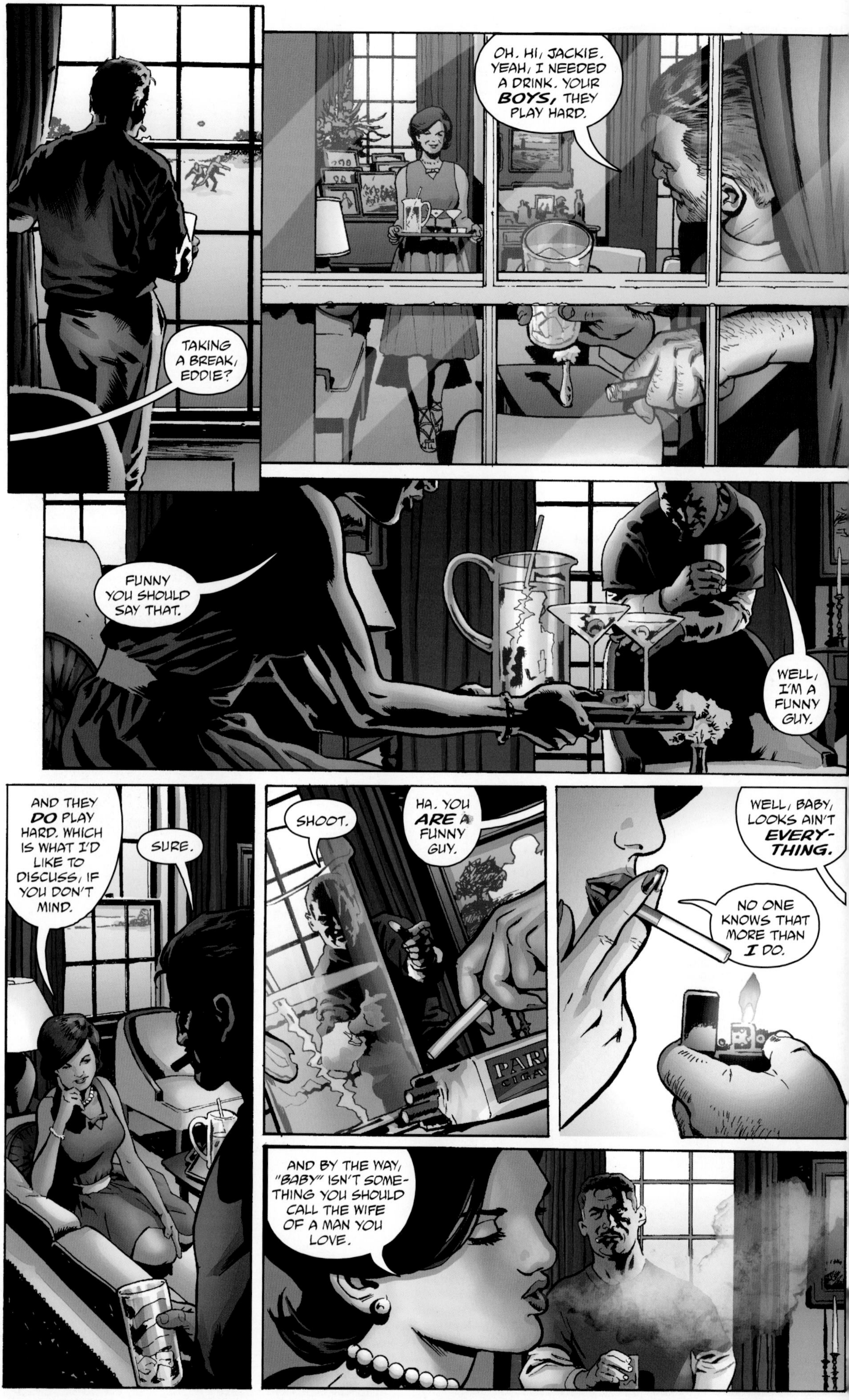
OH. HI, JACKIE. YEAH, I NEEDED A DRINK. YOUR BOYS, THEY PLAY HARD.
TAKING A BREAK, EDDIE?
FUNNY YOU SHOULD SAY THAT.
WELL, I'M A FUNNY GUY.
AND THEY DO PLAY HARD. WHICH IS WHAT I'D LIKE TO DISCUSS, IF YOU DON'T MIND.
SURE.
SHOOT.
HA. YOU ARE A FUNNY GUY.
WELL, BABY, LOOKS AIN'T EVERYTHING.
NO ONE KNOWS THAT MORE THAN I DO.
AND BY THE WAY, "BABY" ISN'T SOMETHING YOU SHOULD CALL THE WIFE OF A MAN YOU LOVE.

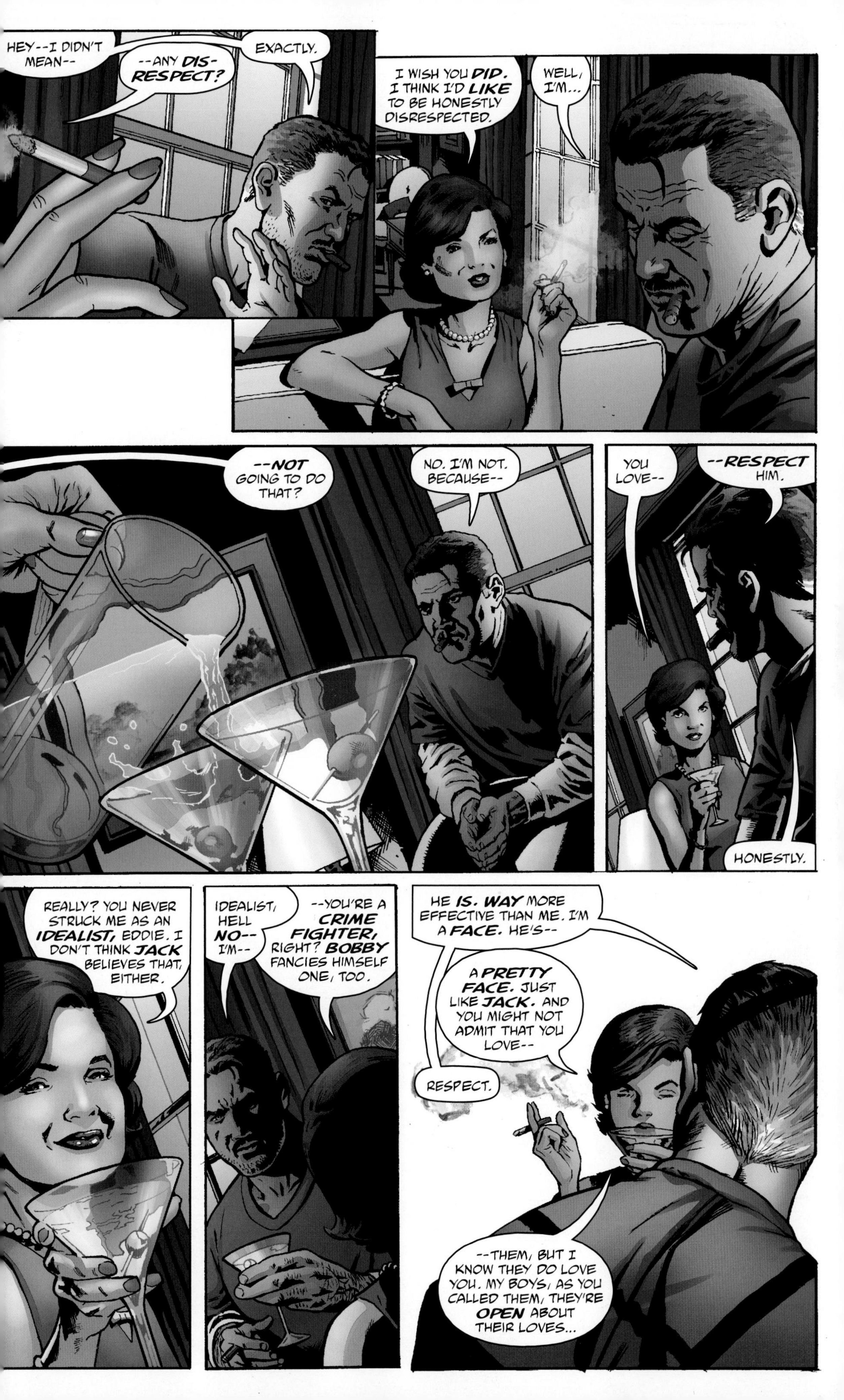

HEY--I DIDN'T MEAN--
--ANY DIS-RESPECT?
EXACTLY.
I WISH YOU DID. I THINK I'D LIKE TO BE HONESTLY DISRESPECTED.
WELL, I'M...
--NOT GOING TO DO THAT?
NO. I'M NOT. BECAUSE--
YOU LOVE--
--RESPECT HIM.
HONESTLY.
REALLY? YOU NEVER STRUCK ME AS AN IDEALIST, EDDIE. I DON'T THINK JACK BELIEVES THAT, EITHER.
IDEALIST, HELL NO-- I'M--
--YOU'RE A CRIME FIGHTER, RIGHT? BOBBY FANCIES HIMSELF ONE, TOO.
HE IS. WAY MORE EFFECTIVE THAN ME. I'M A FACE. HE'S--
A PRETTY FACE. JUST LIKE JACK. AND YOU MIGHT NOT ADMIT THAT YOU LOVE--
RESPECT.
--THEM, BUT I KNOW THEY DO LOVE YOU. MY BOYS, AS YOU CALLED THEM, THEY'RE OPEN ABOUT THEIR LOVES...

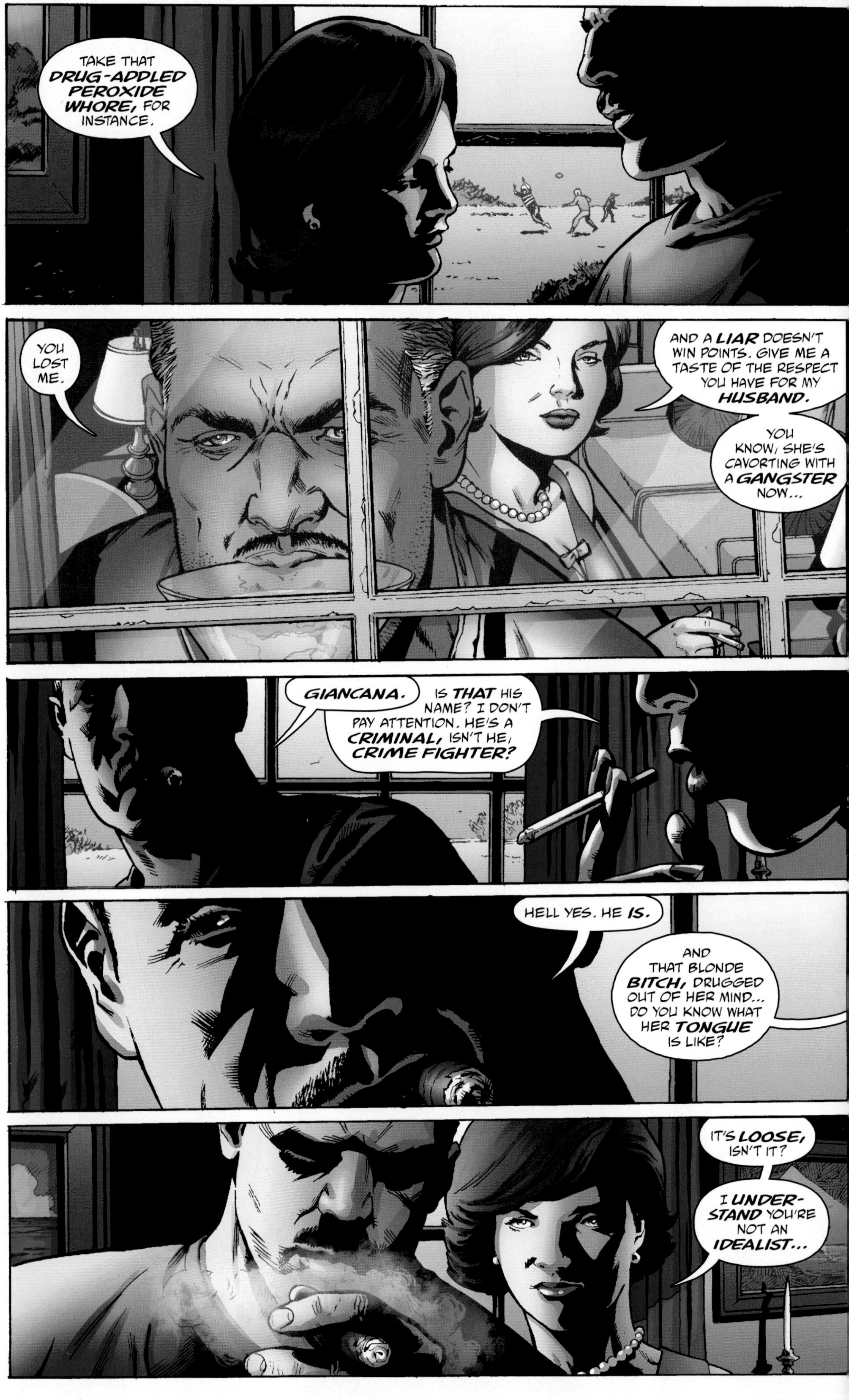
TAKE THAT DRUG-ADDLED PEROXIDE WHORE, FOR INSTANCE.
YOU LOST ME.
AND A LIAR DOESN'T WIN POINTS. GIVE ME A TASTE OF THE RESPECT YOU HAVE FOR MY HUSBAND.
YOU KNOW, SHE'S CAVORTING WITH A GANGSTER NOW...
GIANCANA.
IS THAT HIS NAME? I DON'T PAY ATTENTION. HE'S A CRIMINAL, ISN'T HE, CRIME FIGHTER?
HELL YES. HE IS.
AND THAT BLONDE BITCH, DRUGGED OUT OF HER MIND... DO YOU KNOW WHAT HER TONGUE IS LIKE?
IT'S LOOSE, ISN'T IT?
I UNDER-STAND YOU'RE NOT AN IDEALIST...

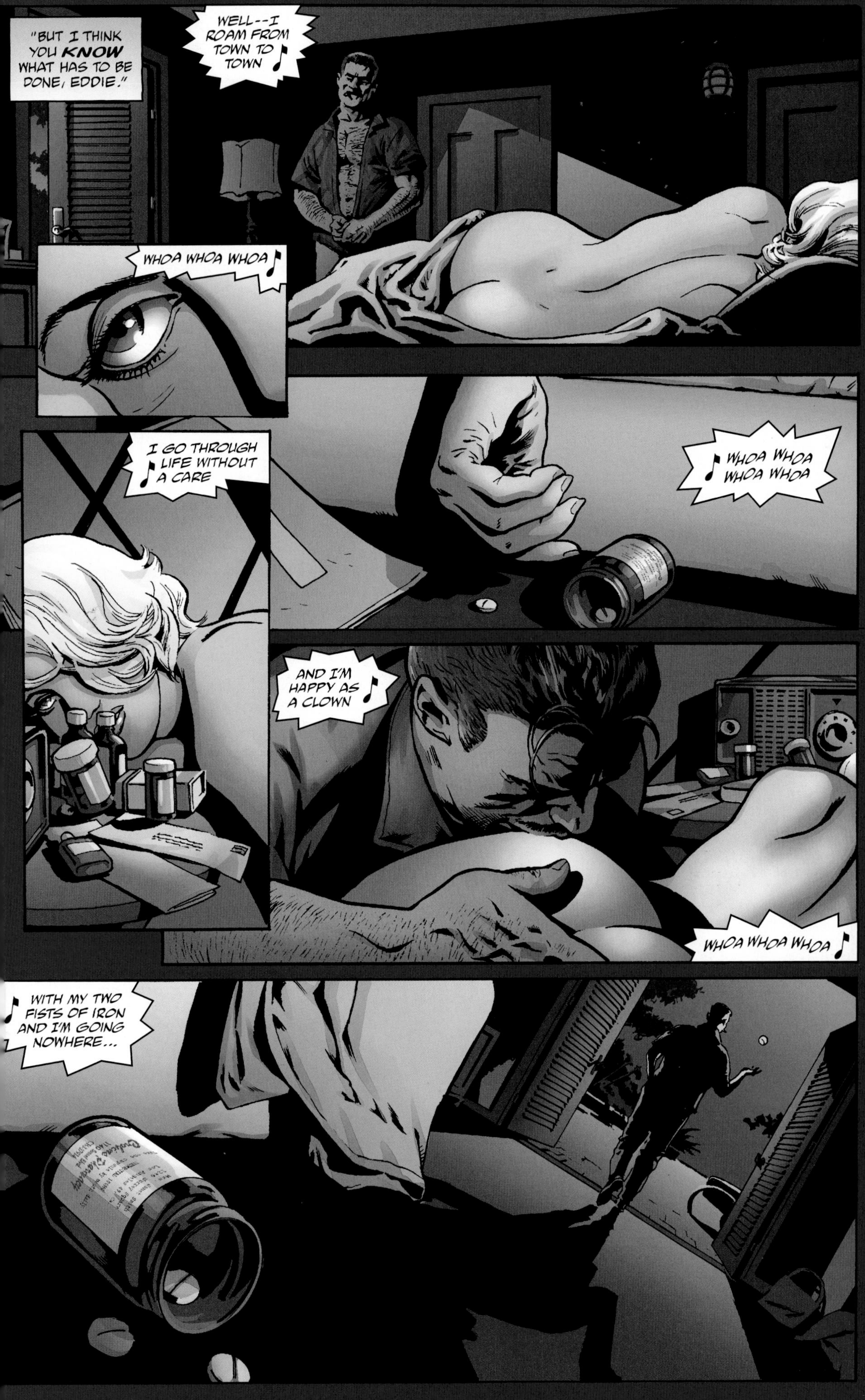
"BUT I THINK YOU **KNOW** WHAT HAS TO BE DONE, EDDIE."
WELL--I ROAM FROM TOWN TO TOWN ♪
WHOA WHOA WHOA ♪
♪ I GO THROUGH LIFE WITHOUT A CARE
♪ WHOA WHOA WHOA WHOA
AND I'M HAPPY AS A CLOWN ♪
WHOA WHOA WHOA ♪
♪ WITH MY TWO FISTS OF IRON AND I'M GOING NOWHERE...

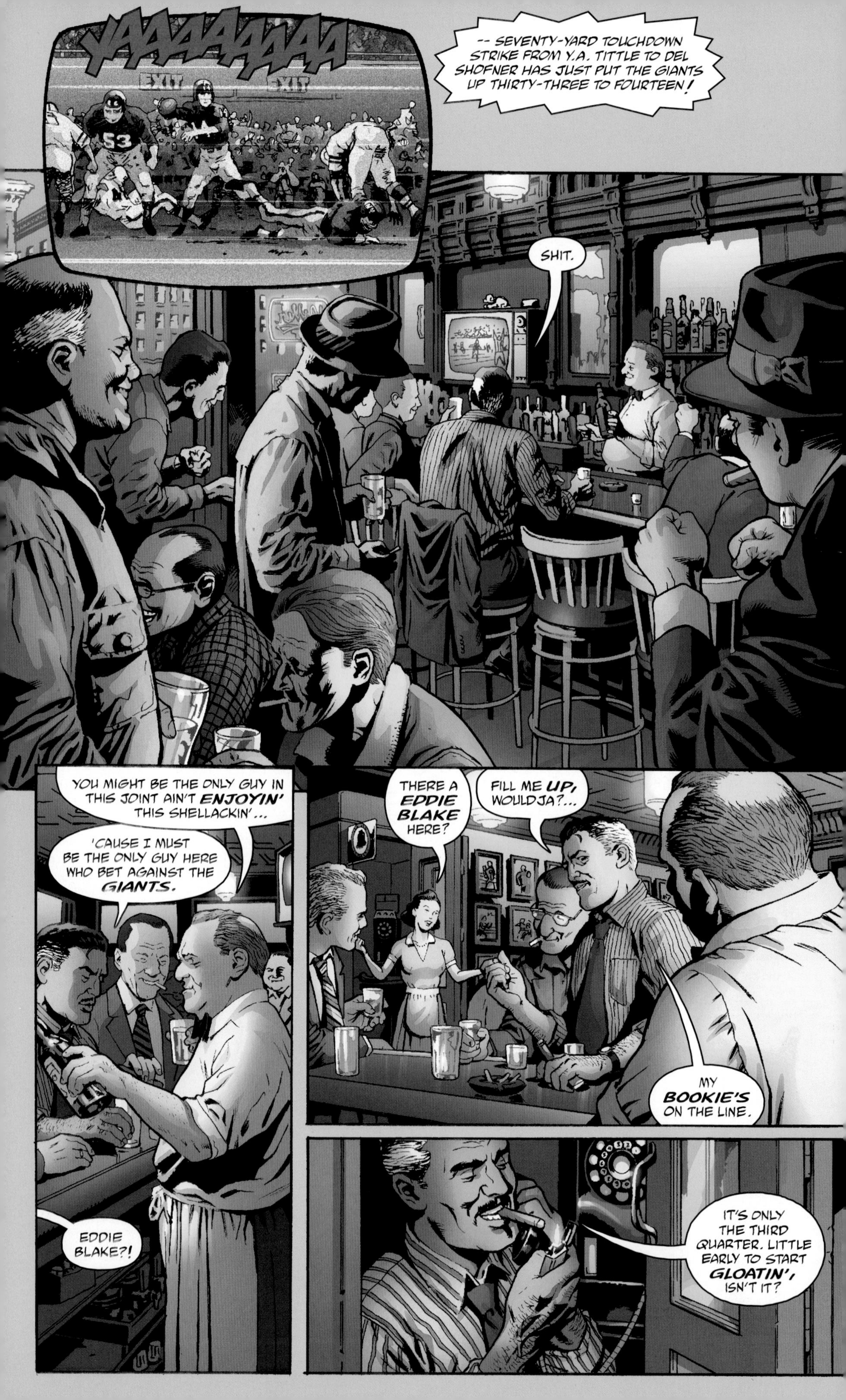
YAAAAAAAAA
-- SEVENTY-YARD TOUCHDOWN STRIKE FROM Y.A. TITTLE TO DEL SHOFNER HAS JUST PUT THE GIANTS UP THIRTY-THREE TO FOURTEEN!
SHIT.
YOU MIGHT BE THE ONLY GUY IN THIS JOINT AIN'T ENJOYIN' THIS SHELLACKIN'...
'CAUSE I MUST BE THE ONLY GUY HERE WHO BET AGAINST THE GIANTS.
EDDIE BLAKE?!
THERE A EDDIE BLAKE HERE?
FILL ME UP, WOULDJA?...
MY BOOKIE'S ON THE LINE.
IT'S ONLY THE THIRD QUARTER. LITTLE EARLY TO START GLOATIN', ISN'T IT?

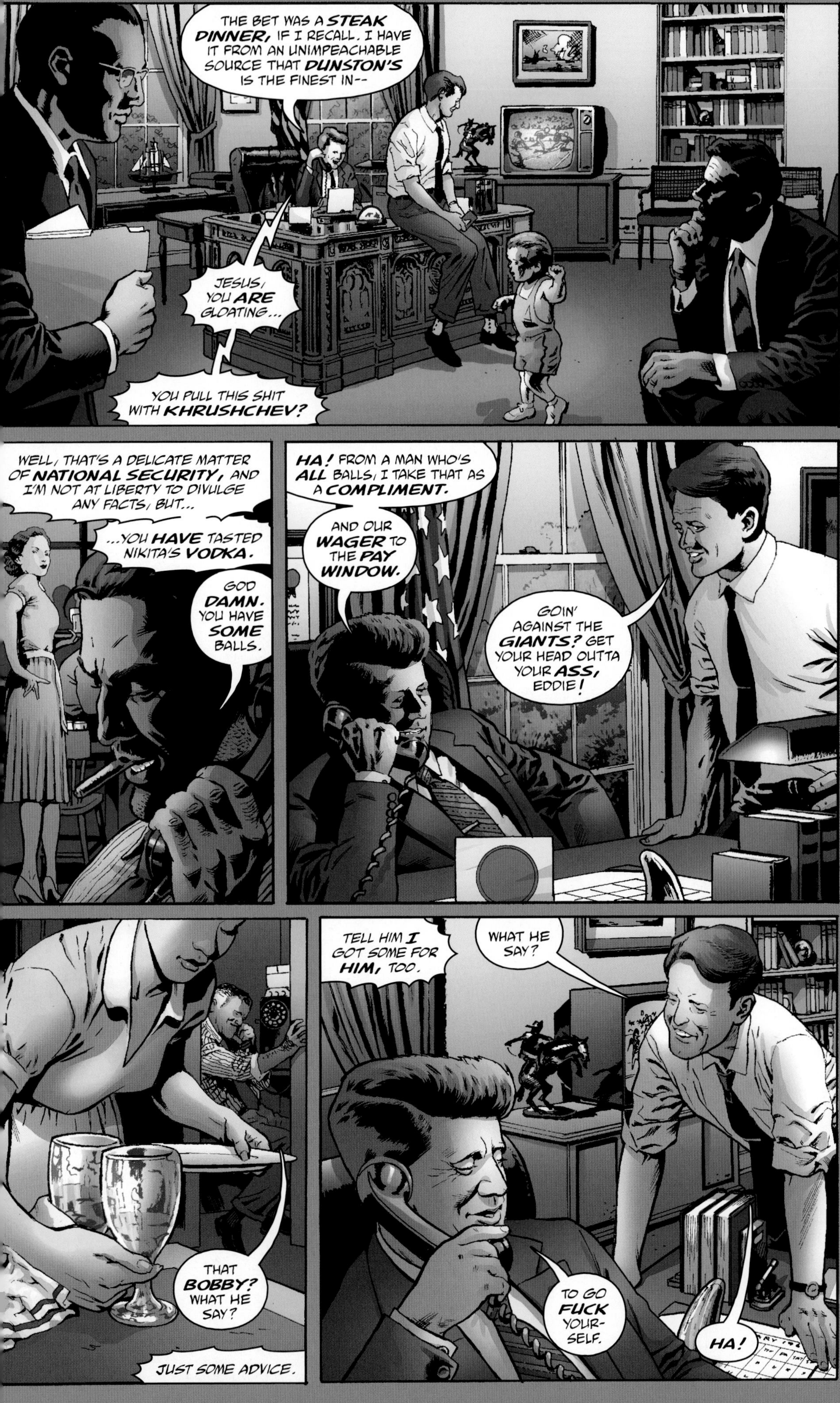
THE BET WAS A STEAK DINNER, IF I RECALL. I HAVE IT FROM AN UNIMPEACHABLE SOURCE THAT DUNSTON'S IS THE FINEST IN--
JESUS, YOU ARE GLOATING...
YOU PULL THIS SHIT WITH KHRUSHCHEV?
WELL, THAT'S A DELICATE MATTER OF NATIONAL SECURITY, AND I'M NOT AT LIBERTY TO DIVULGE ANY FACTS, BUT...
...YOU HAVE TASTED NIKITA'S VODKA.
GOD DAMN. YOU HAVE SOME BALLS.
HA! FROM A MAN WHO'S ALL BALLS, I TAKE THAT AS A COMPLIMENT.
AND OUR WAGER TO THE PAY WINDOW.
GOIN' AGAINST THE GIANTS? GET YOUR HEAD OUTTA YOUR ASS, EDDIE!
THAT BOBBY? WHAT HE SAY?
JUST SOME ADVICE.
TELL HIM I GOT SOME FOR HIM, TOO.
WHAT HE SAY?
TO GO FUCK YOUR-SELF.
HA!

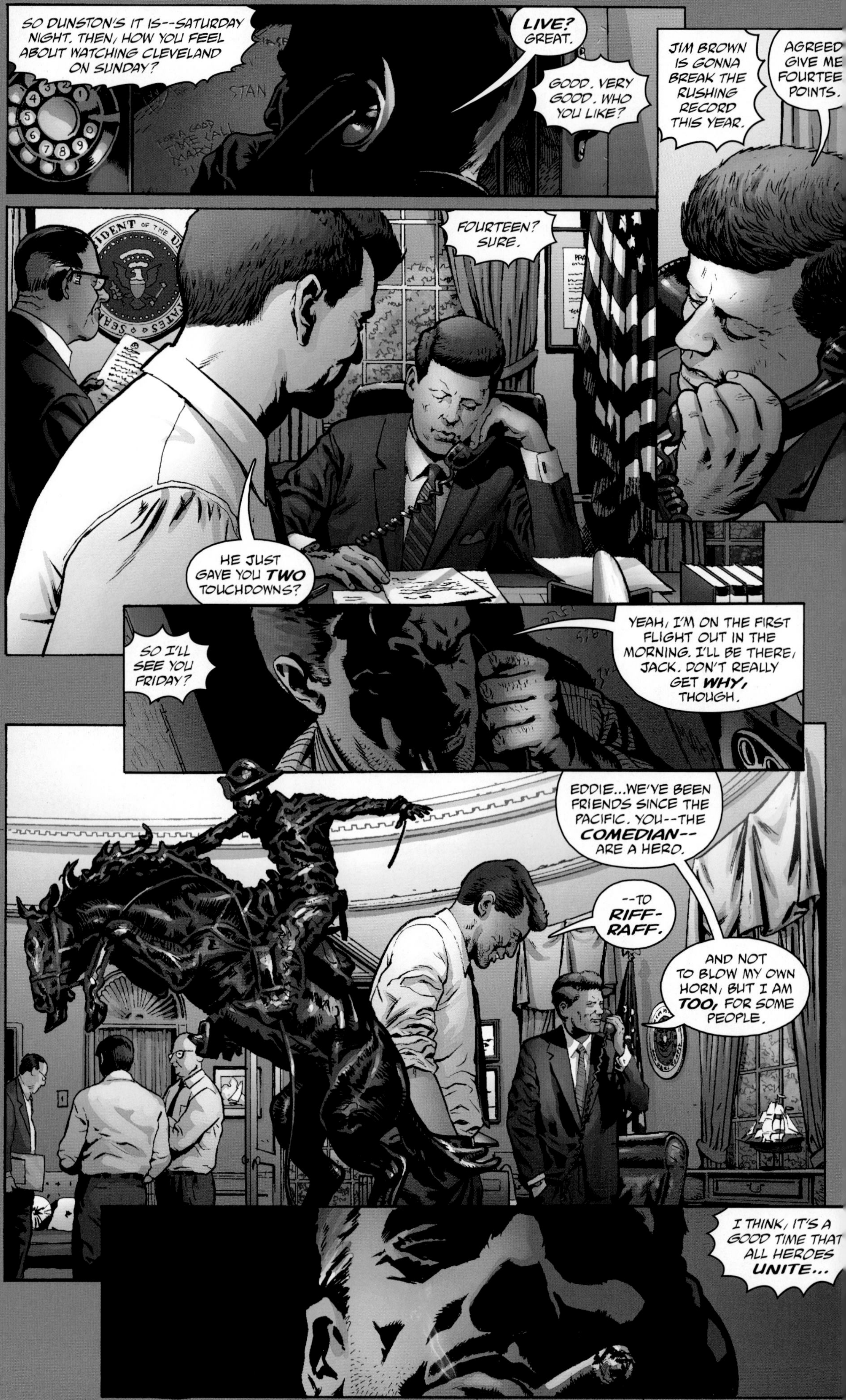
SO DUNSTON'S IT IS--SATURDAY NIGHT. THEN, HOW YOU FEEL ABOUT WATCHING CLEVELAND ON SUNDAY?
LIVE? GREAT.
GOOD. VERY GOOD. WHO YOU LIKE?
JIM BROWN IS GONNA BREAK THE RUSHING RECORD THIS YEAR.
AGREED GIVE ME FOURTEE POINTS.
FOURTEEN? SURE.
HE JUST GAVE YOU TWO TOUCHDOWNS?
SO I'LL SEE YOU FRIDAY?
YEAH, I'M ON THE FIRST FLIGHT OUT IN THE MORNING. I'LL BE THERE, JACK. DON'T REALLY GET WHY, THOUGH.
EDDIE...WE'VE BEEN FRIENDS SINCE THE PACIFIC. YOU--THE COMEDIAN-- ARE A HERO.
--TO RIFF-RAFF.
AND NOT TO BLOW MY OWN HORN, BUT I AM TOO, FOR SOME PEOPLE.
I THINK, IT'S A GOOD TIME THAT ALL HEROES UNITE...

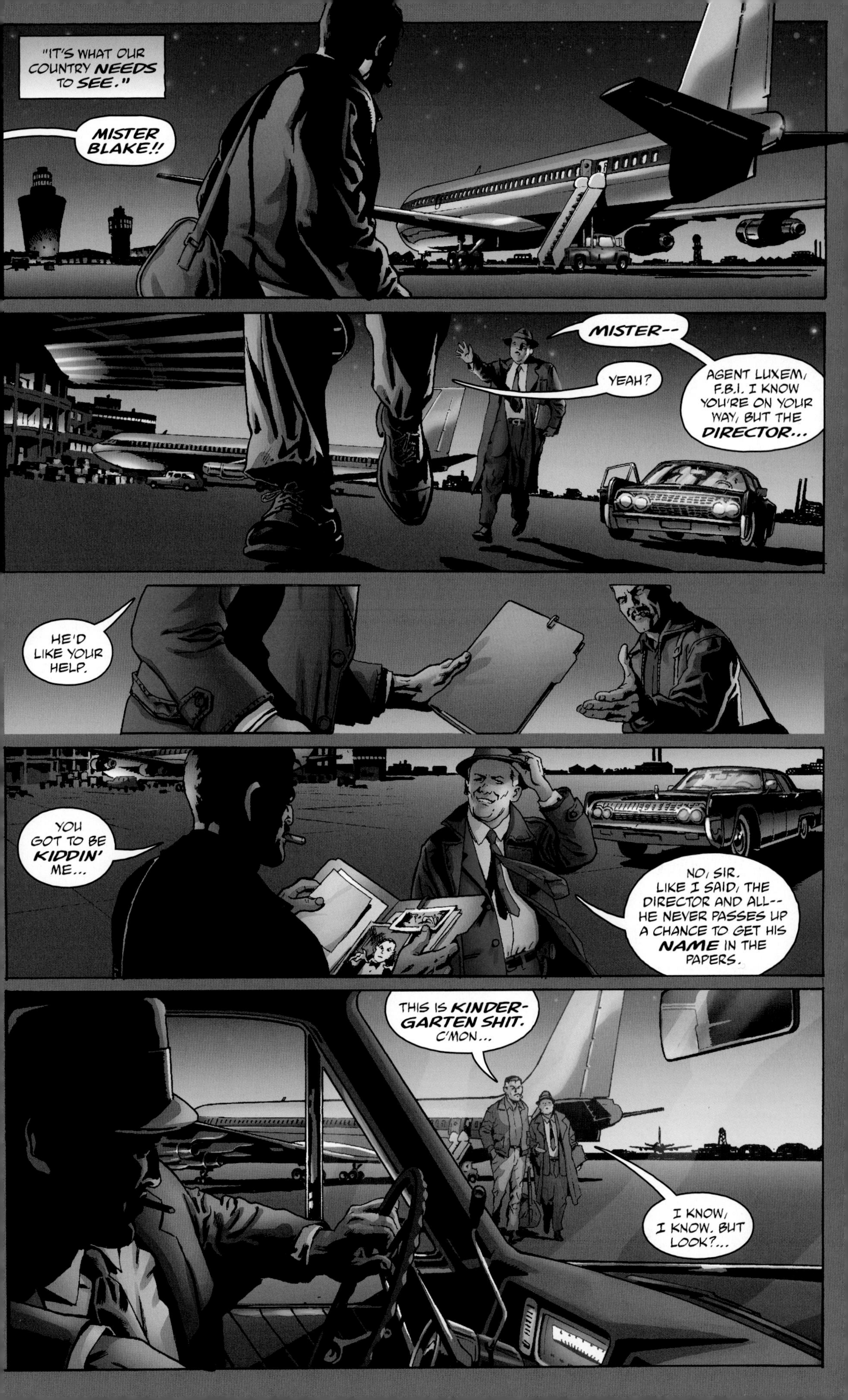
"IT'S WHAT OUR COUNTRY NEEDS TO SEE."
MISTER BLAKE!!
MISTER--
YEAH?
AGENT LUXEM, F.B.I. I KNOW YOU'RE ON YOUR WAY, BUT THE DIRECTOR...
HE'D LIKE YOUR HELP.
YOU GOT TO BE KIDDIN' ME...
NO, SIR. LIKE I SAID, THE DIRECTOR AND ALL-- HE NEVER PASSES UP A CHANCE TO GET HIS NAME IN THE PAPERS.
THIS IS KINDER-GARTEN SHIT. C'MON...
I KNOW, I KNOW. BUT LOOK?...

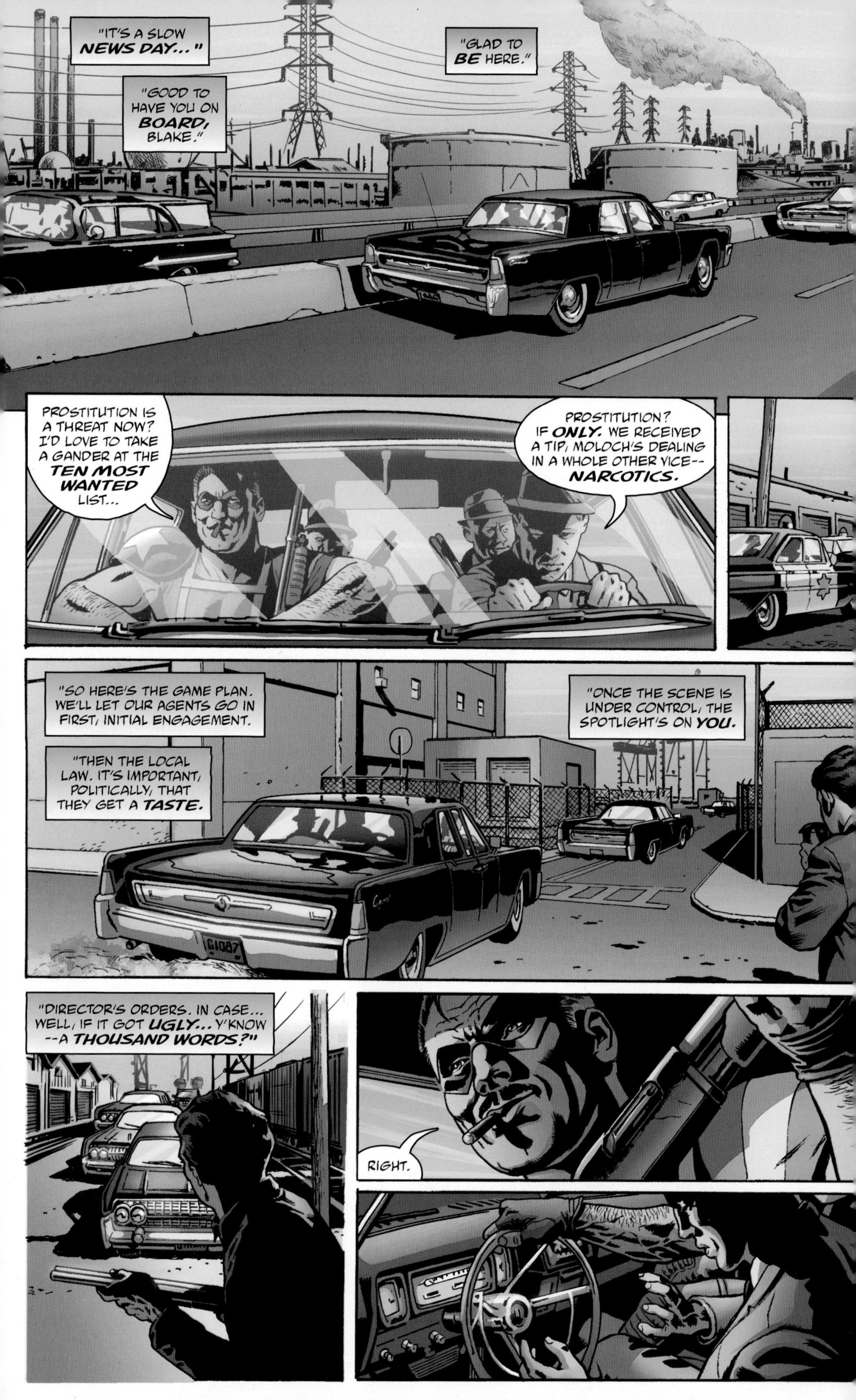

"IT'S A SLOW NEWS DAY..."
"GOOD TO HAVE YOU ON BOARD, BLAKE."
"GLAD TO BE HERE."
PROSTITUTION IS A THREAT NOW? I'D LOVE TO TAKE A GANDER AT THE TEN MOST WANTED LIST...
PROSTITUTION? IF ONLY. WE RECEIVED A TIP, MOLOCH'S DEALING IN A WHOLE OTHER VICE-- NARCOTICS.
"SO HERE'S THE GAME PLAN. WE'LL LET OUR AGENTS GO IN FIRST, INITIAL ENGAGEMENT.
"THEN THE LOCAL LAW. IT'S IMPORTANT, POLITICALLY, THAT THEY GET A TASTE.
"ONCE THE SCENE IS UNDER CONTROL, THE SPOTLIGHT'S ON YOU.
"DIRECTOR'S ORDERS. IN CASE... WELL, IF IT GOT UGLY... Y'KNOW --A THOUSAND WORDS?"
RIGHT.

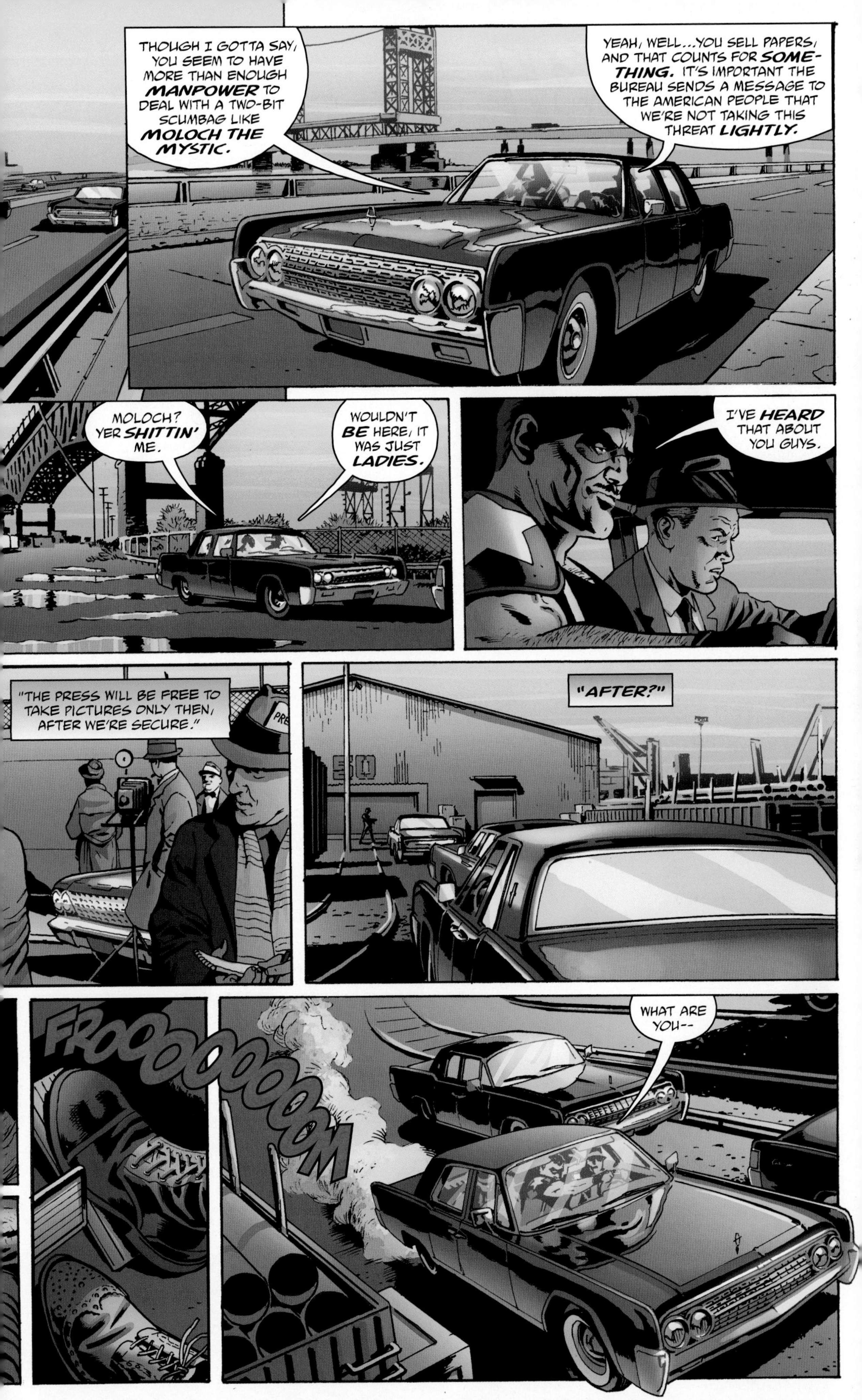
THOUGH I GOTTA SAY, YOU SEEM TO HAVE MORE THAN ENOUGH MANPOWER TO DEAL WITH A TWO-BIT SCUMBAG LIKE MOLOCH THE MYSTIC.
YEAH, WELL...YOU SELL PAPERS, AND THAT COUNTS FOR SOME-THING. IT'S IMPORTANT THE BUREAU SENDS A MESSAGE TO THE AMERICAN PEOPLE THAT WE'RE NOT TAKING THIS THREAT LIGHTLY.
MOLOCH? YER SHITTIN' ME.
WOULDN'T BE HERE, IT WAS JUST LADIES.
I'VE HEARD THAT ABOUT YOU GUYS.
"THE PRESS WILL BE FREE TO TAKE PICTURES ONLY THEN, AFTER WE'RE SECURE."
"AFTER?"
FROOOOOOOOOM
WHAT ARE YOU--

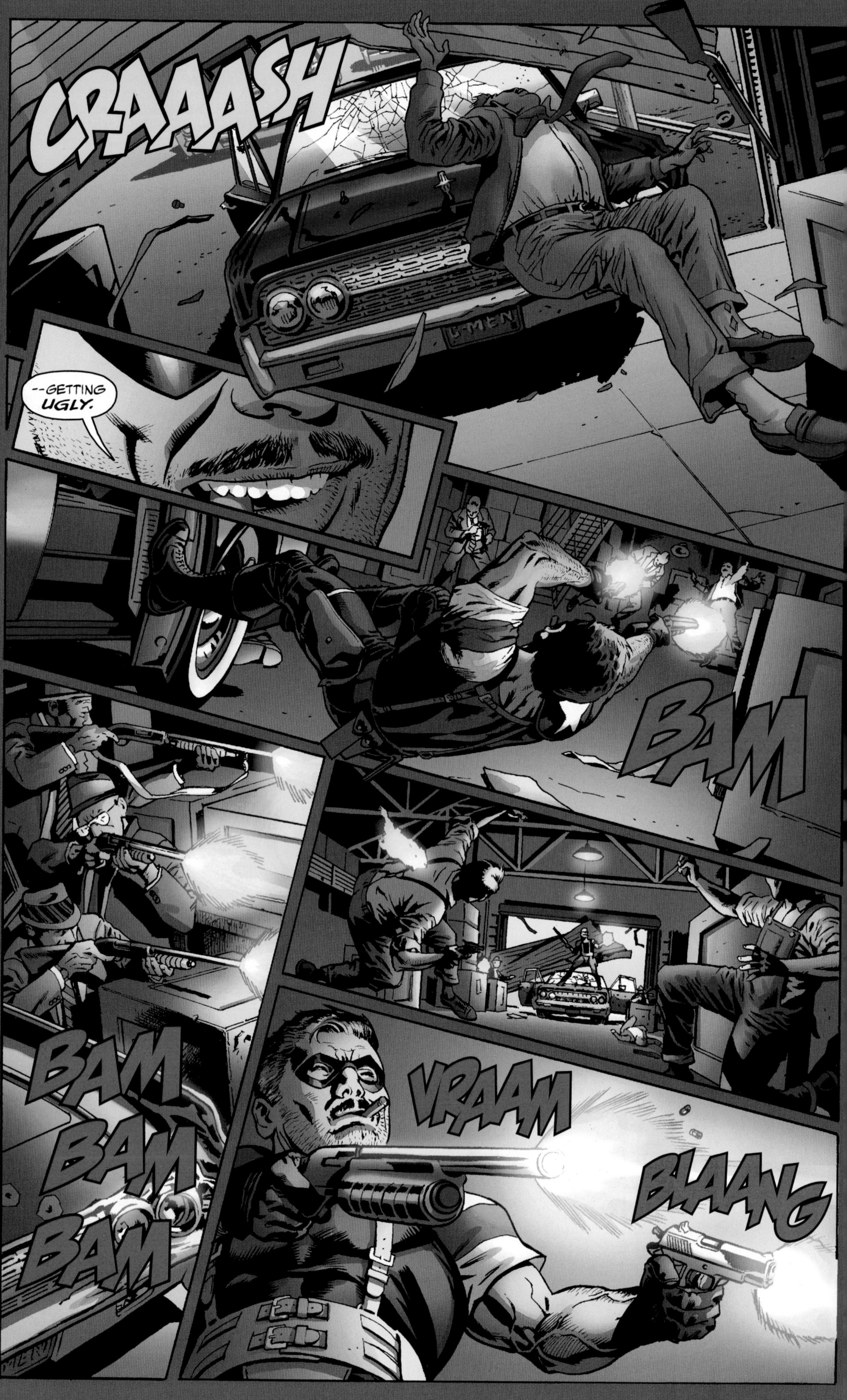
CRAAASH
G-MEN
--GETTING UGLY.
BAM
BAM
BAM
BAM
VRAAM
BLAANG

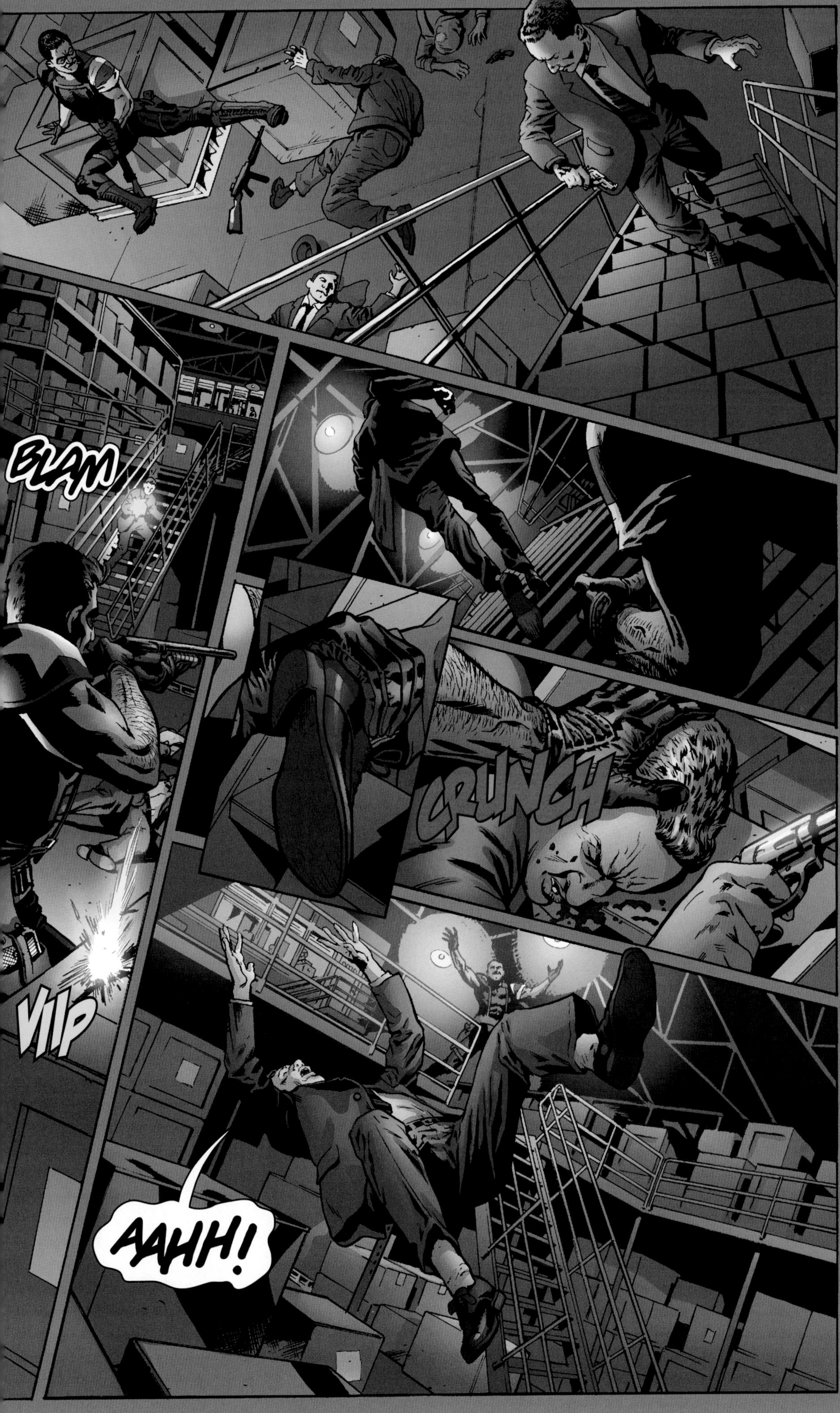
BLAM
CRUNCH
VIIP
AAHH!

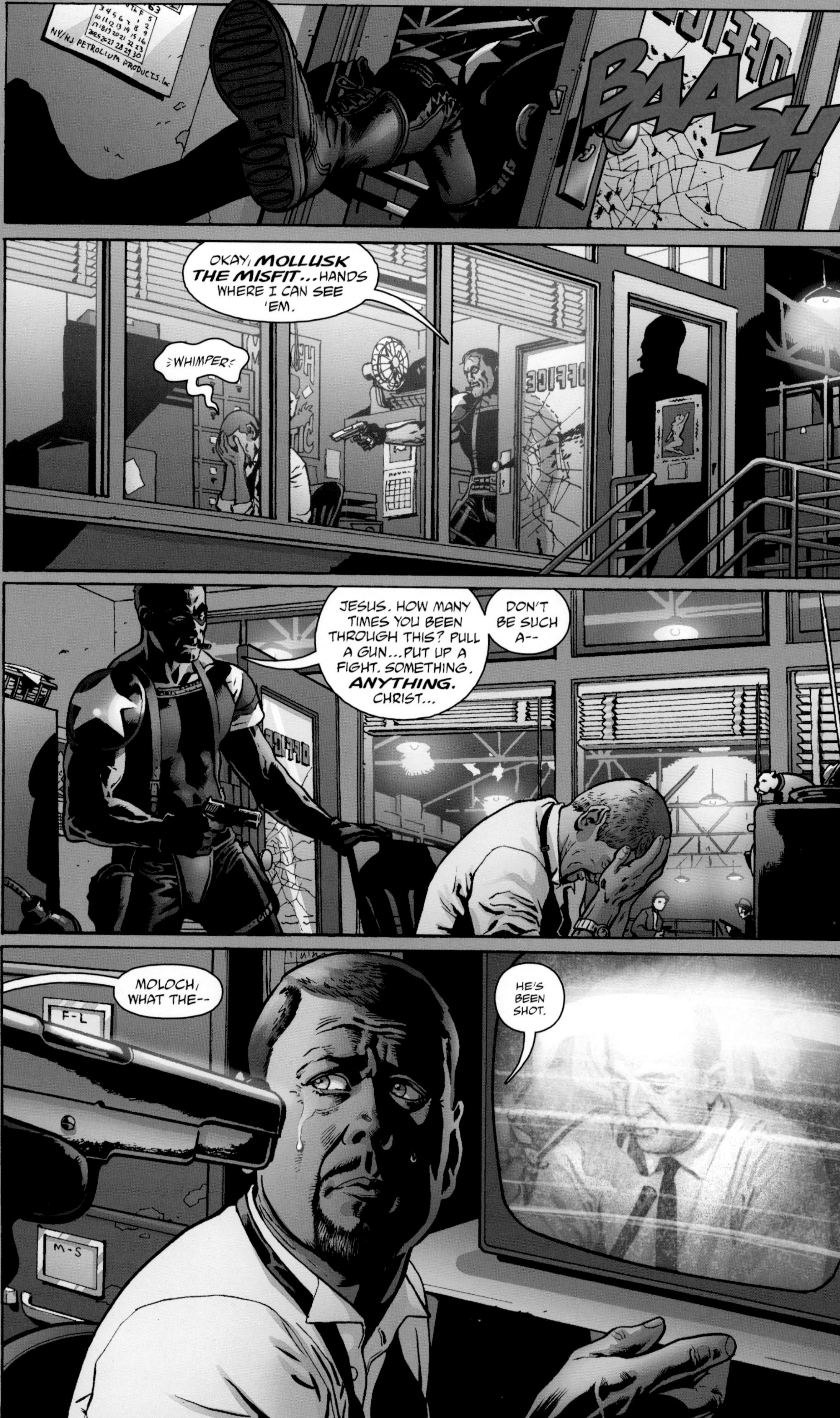
NY/NJ PETROLEUM PRODUCTS, Inc
BAASH
OKAY, MOLLUSK THE MISFIT...HANDS WHERE I CAN SEE 'EM.
WHIMPER
JESUS. HOW MANY TIMES YOU BEEN THROUGH THIS? PULL A GUN...PUT UP A FIGHT. SOMETHING. ANYTHING. CHRIST...
DON'T BE SUCH A--
MOLOCH, WHAT THE--
HE'S BEEN SHOT.
F-L
M-S

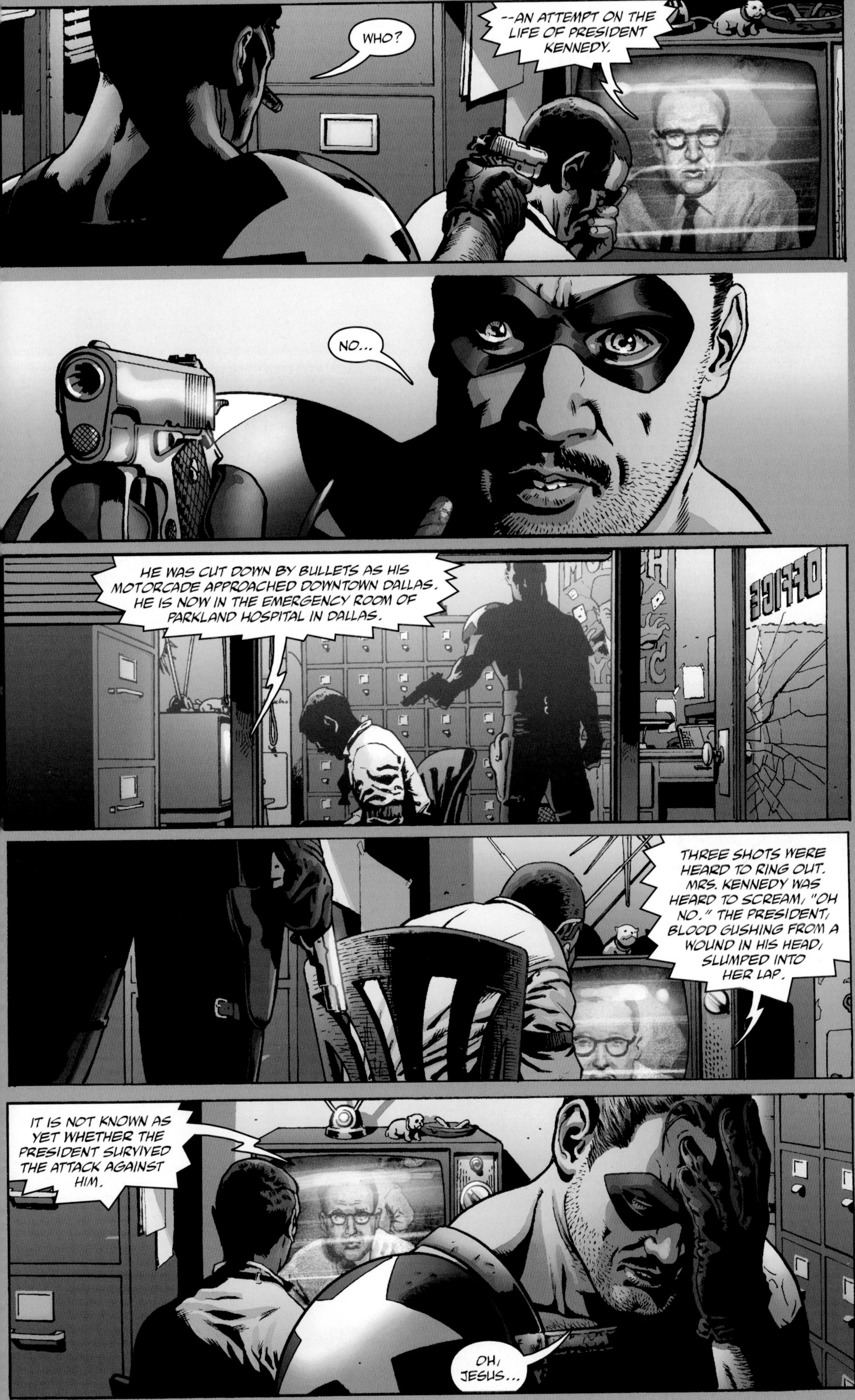
WHO?
--AN ATTEMPT ON THE LIFE OF PRESIDENT KENNEDY.
NO...
HE WAS CUT DOWN BY BULLETS AS HIS MOTORCADE APPROACHED DOWNTOWN DALLAS. HE IS NOW IN THE EMERGENCY ROOM OF PARKLAND HOSPITAL IN DALLAS.
THREE SHOTS WERE HEARD TO RING OUT. MRS. KENNEDY WAS HEARD TO SCREAM, "OH NO." THE PRESIDENT, BLOOD GUSHING FROM A WOUND IN HIS HEAD, SLUMPED INTO HER LAP.
IT IS NOT KNOWN AS YET WHETHER THE PRESIDENT SURVIVED THE ATTACK AGAINST HIM.
OH, JESUS...

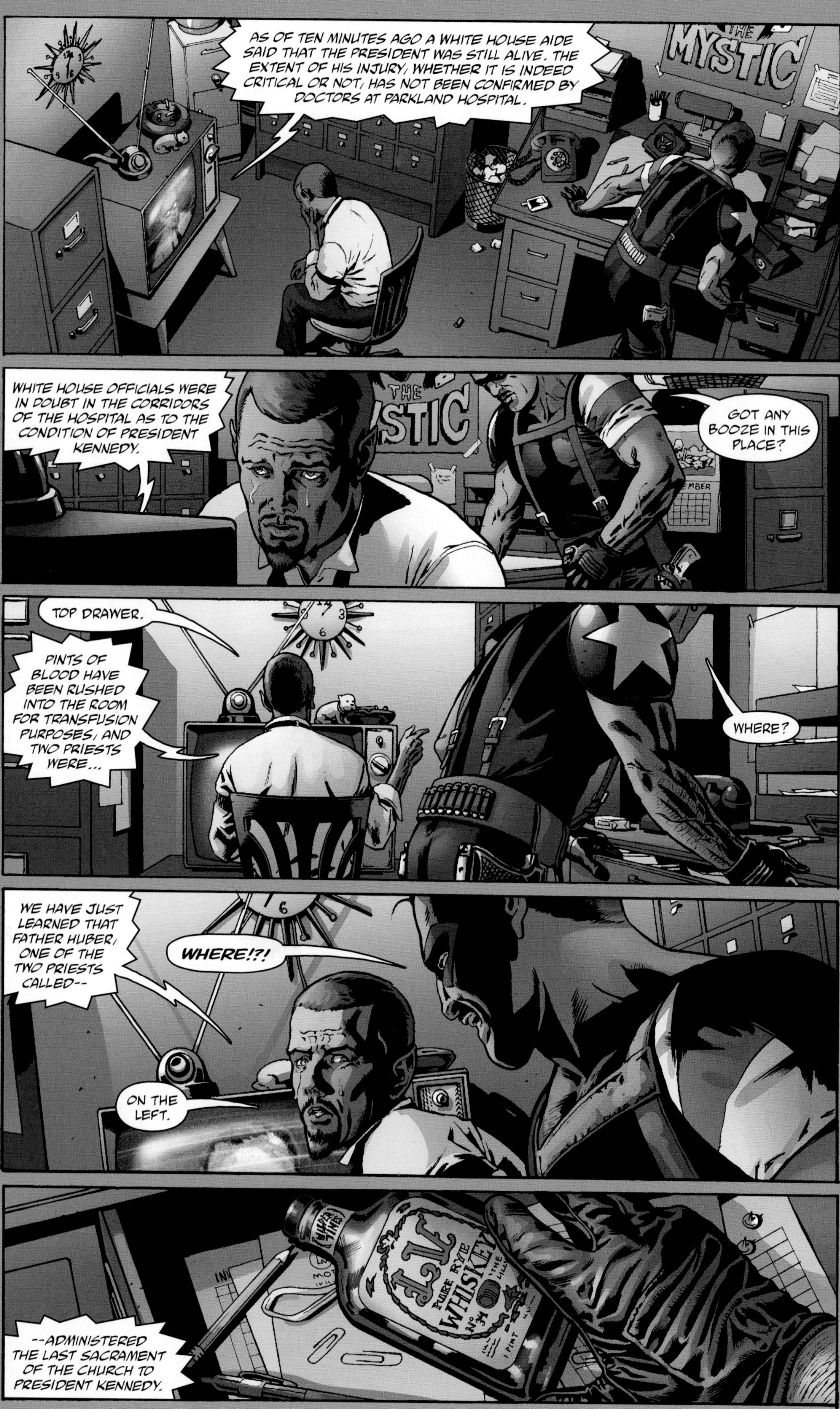

THE MYSTIC
AS OF TEN MINUTES AGO A WHITE HOUSE AIDE SAID THAT THE PRESIDENT WAS STILL ALIVE. THE EXTENT OF HIS INJURY, WHETHER IT IS INDEED CRITICAL OR NOT, HAS NOT BEEN CONFIRMED BY DOCTORS AT PARKLAND HOSPITAL.
WHITE HOUSE OFFICIALS WERE IN DOUBT IN THE CORRIDORS OF THE HOSPITAL AS TO THE CONDITION OF PRESIDENT KENNEDY.
GOT ANY BOOZE IN THIS PLACE?
TOP DRAWER.
PINTS OF BLOOD HAVE BEEN RUSHED INTO THE ROOM FOR TRANSFUSION PURPOSES, AND TWO PRIESTS WERE...
WHERE?
WE HAVE JUST LEARNED THAT FATHER HUBER, ONE OF THE TWO PRIESTS CALLED--
WHERE!?!
ON THE LEFT.
PURE RYE WHISKEY
--ADMINISTERED THE LAST SACRAMENT OF THE CHURCH TO PRESIDENT KENNEDY.

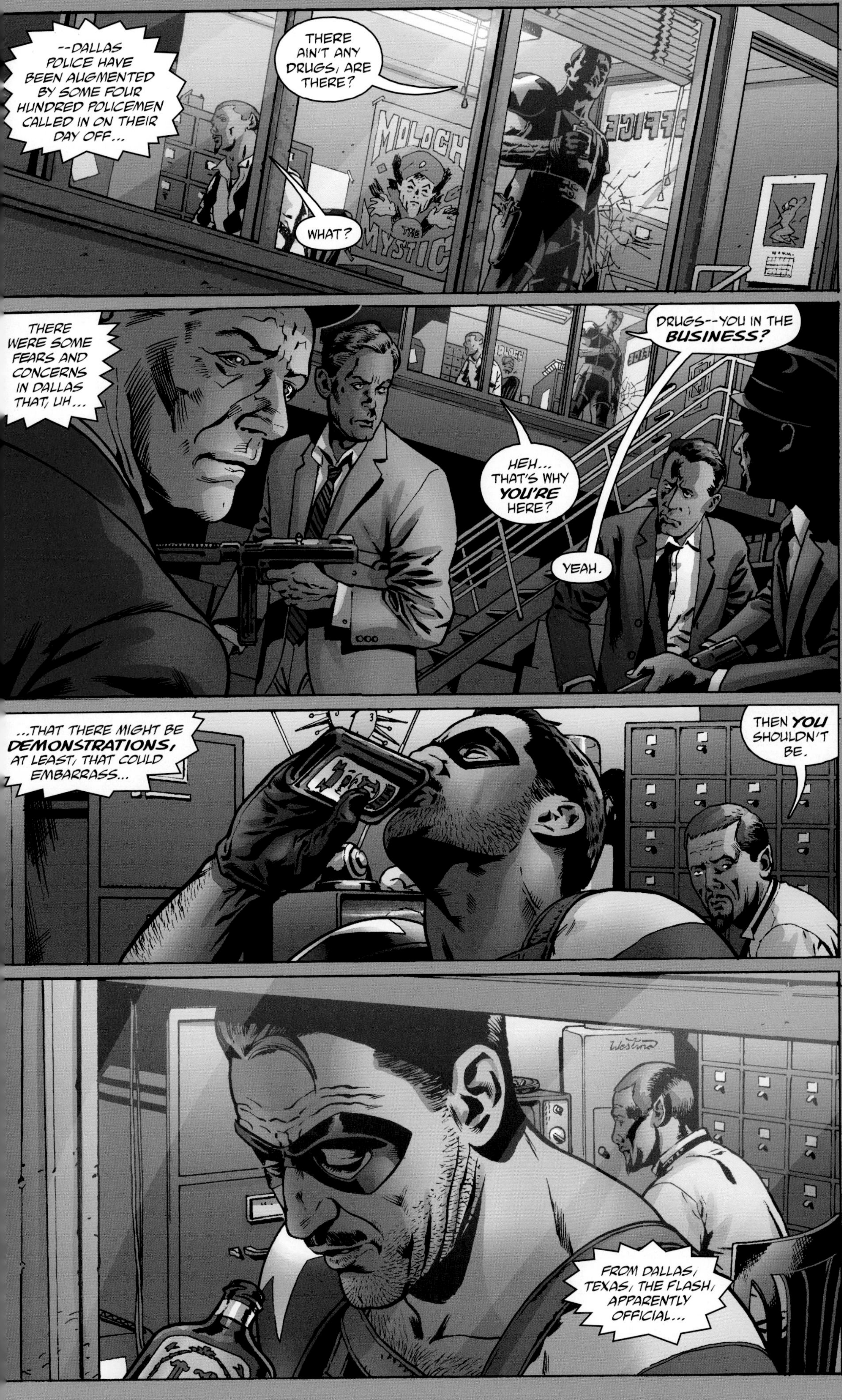
--DALLAS POLICE HAVE BEEN AUGMENTED BY SOME FOUR HUNDRED POLICEMEN CALLED IN ON THEIR DAY OFF...
THERE AIN'T ANY DRUGS, ARE THERE?
WHAT?
MOLOCH THE MYSTIC
THERE WERE SOME FEARS AND CONCERNS IN DALLAS THAT, UH...
DRUGS--YOU IN THE **BUSINESS?**
HEH... THAT'S WHY **YOU'RE** HERE?
YEAH.
...THAT THERE MIGHT BE **DEMONSTRATIONS,** AT LEAST, THAT COULD EMBARRASS...
THEN **YOU** SHOULDN'T BE.
FROM DALLAS, TEXAS, THE FLASH, APPARENTLY OFFICIAL...

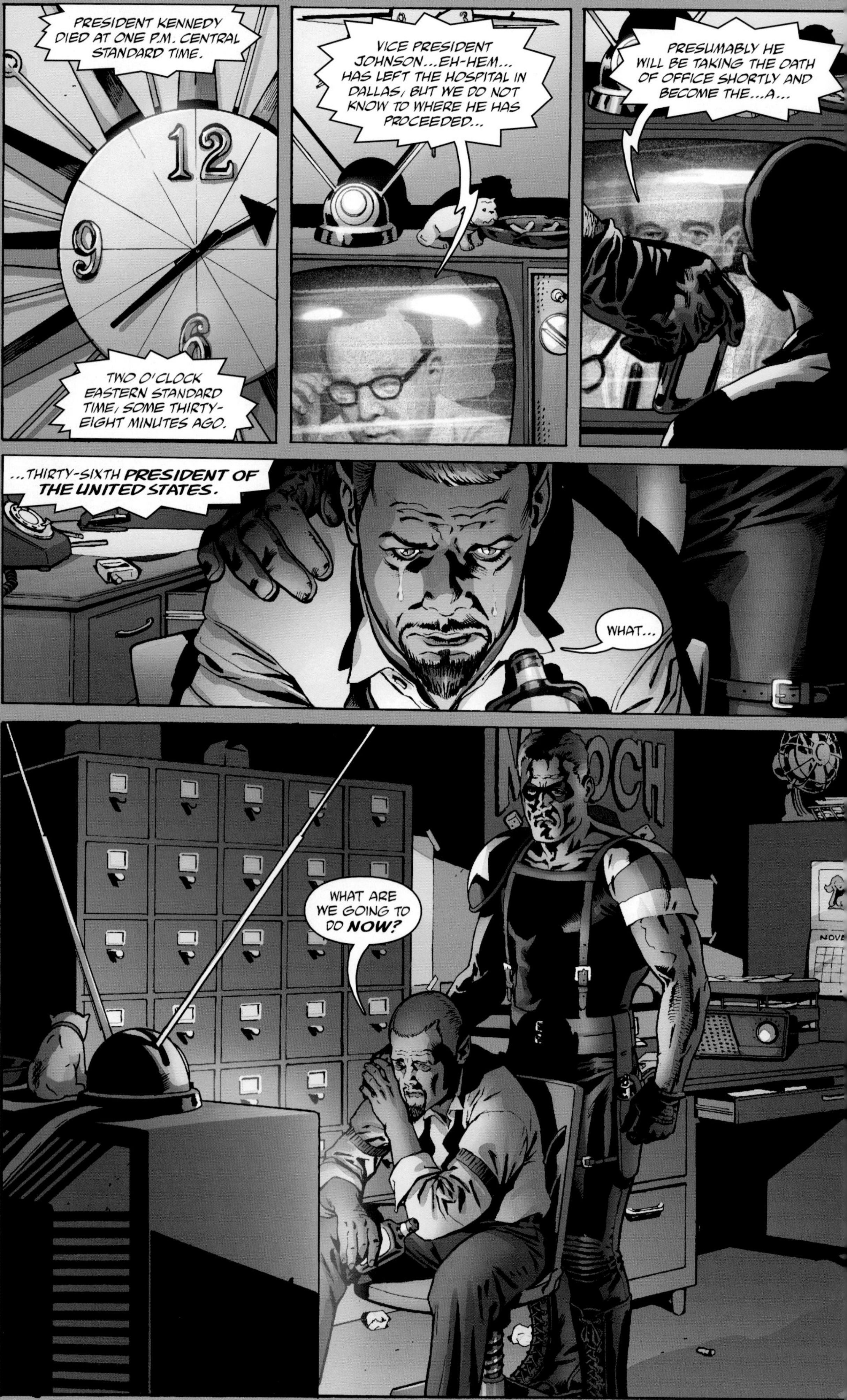

PRESIDENT KENNEDY DIED AT ONE P.M. CENTRAL STANDARD TIME.
TWO O'CLOCK EASTERN STANDARD TIME; SOME THIRTY-EIGHT MINUTES AGO.
VICE PRESIDENT JOHNSON...EH-HEM... HAS LEFT THE HOSPITAL IN DALLAS, BUT WE DO NOT KNOW TO WHERE HE HAS PROCEEDED...
PRESUMABLY HE WILL BE TAKING THE OATH OF OFFICE SHORTLY AND BECOME THE...A...
...THIRTY-SIXTH PRESIDENT OF THE UNITED STATES.
WHAT...
WHAT ARE WE GOING TO DO NOW?

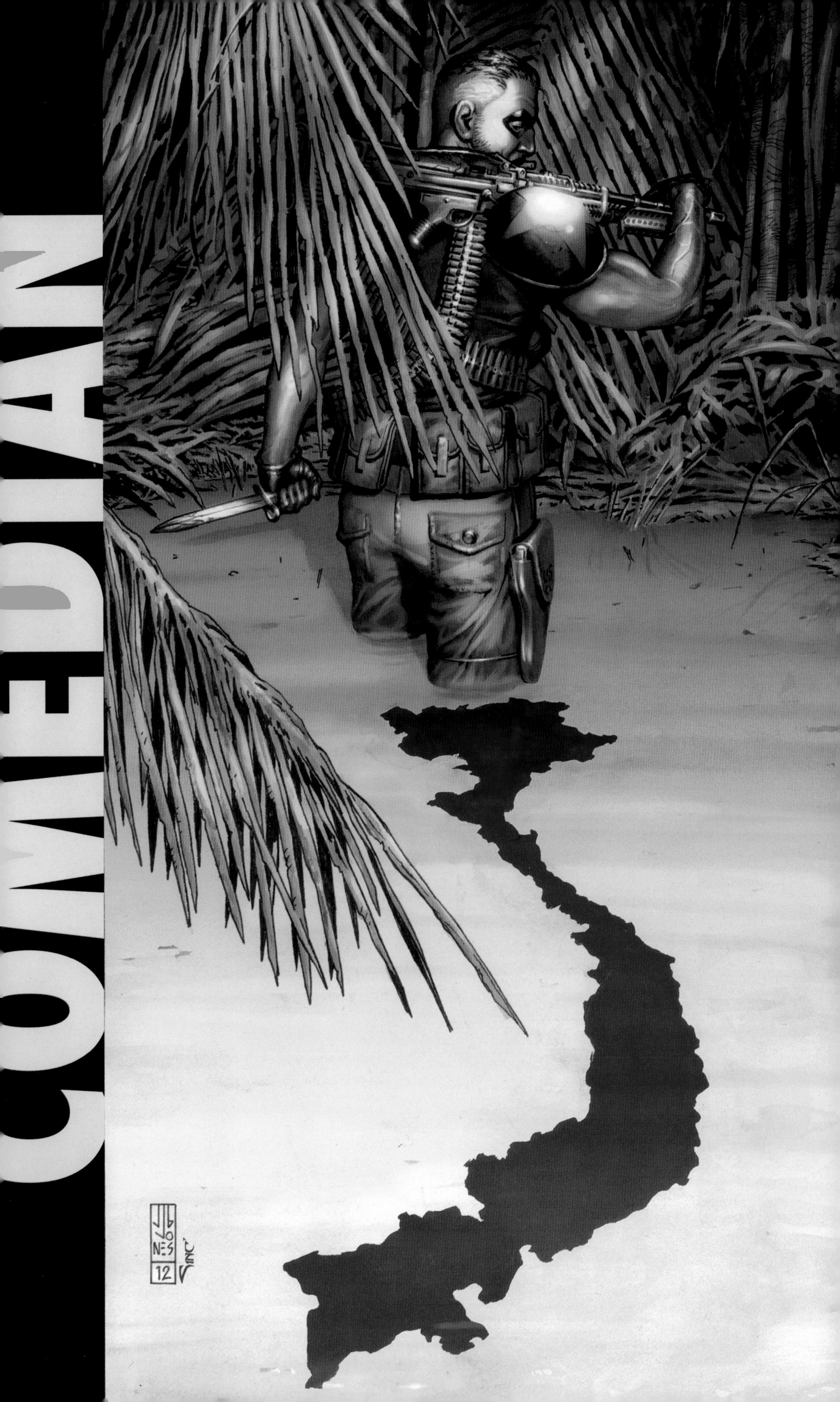
COMEDIAN

COMEDIAN

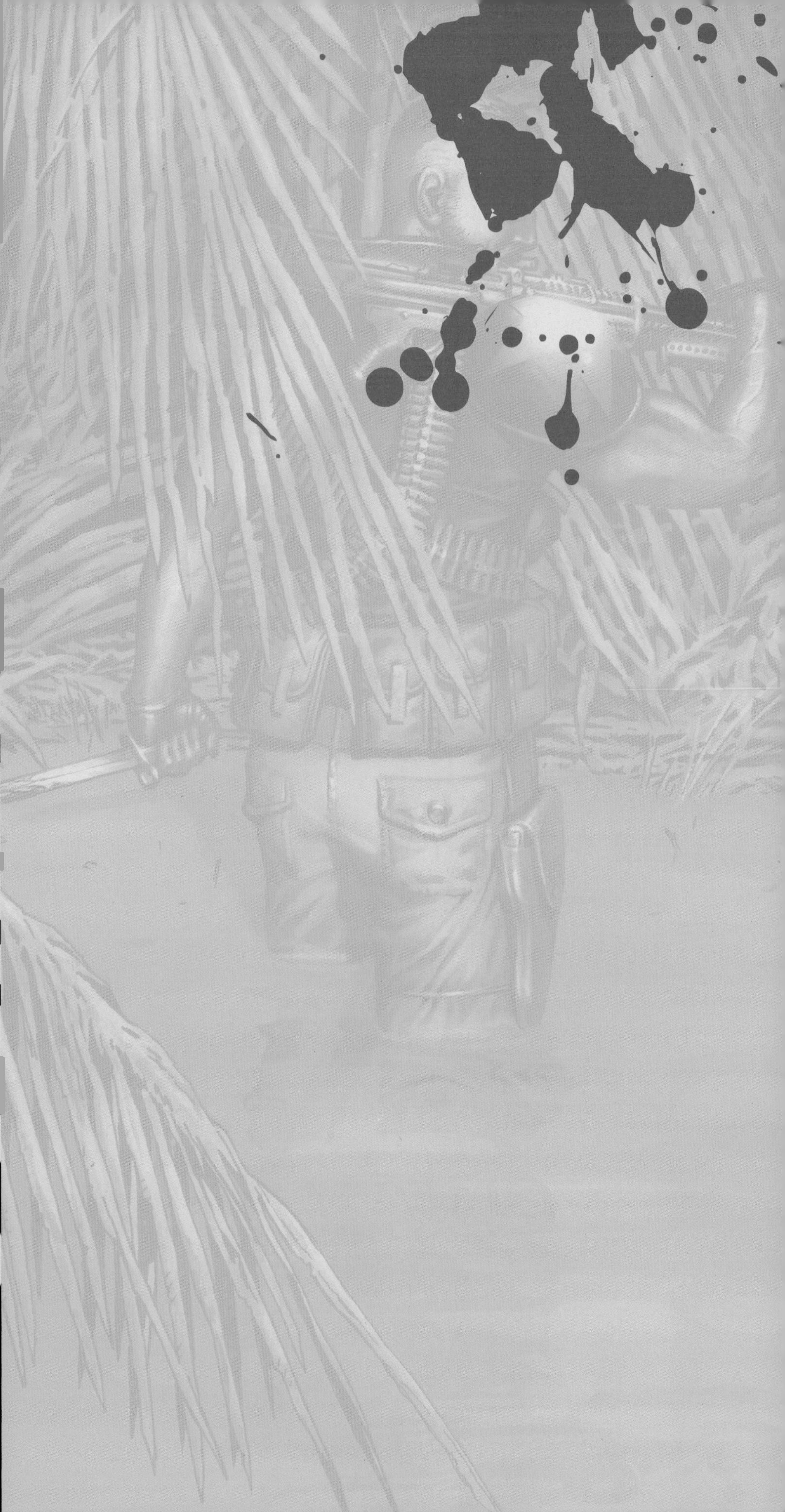

"IT'S SOMETHING I'M GOOD AT. IT'S WAR."

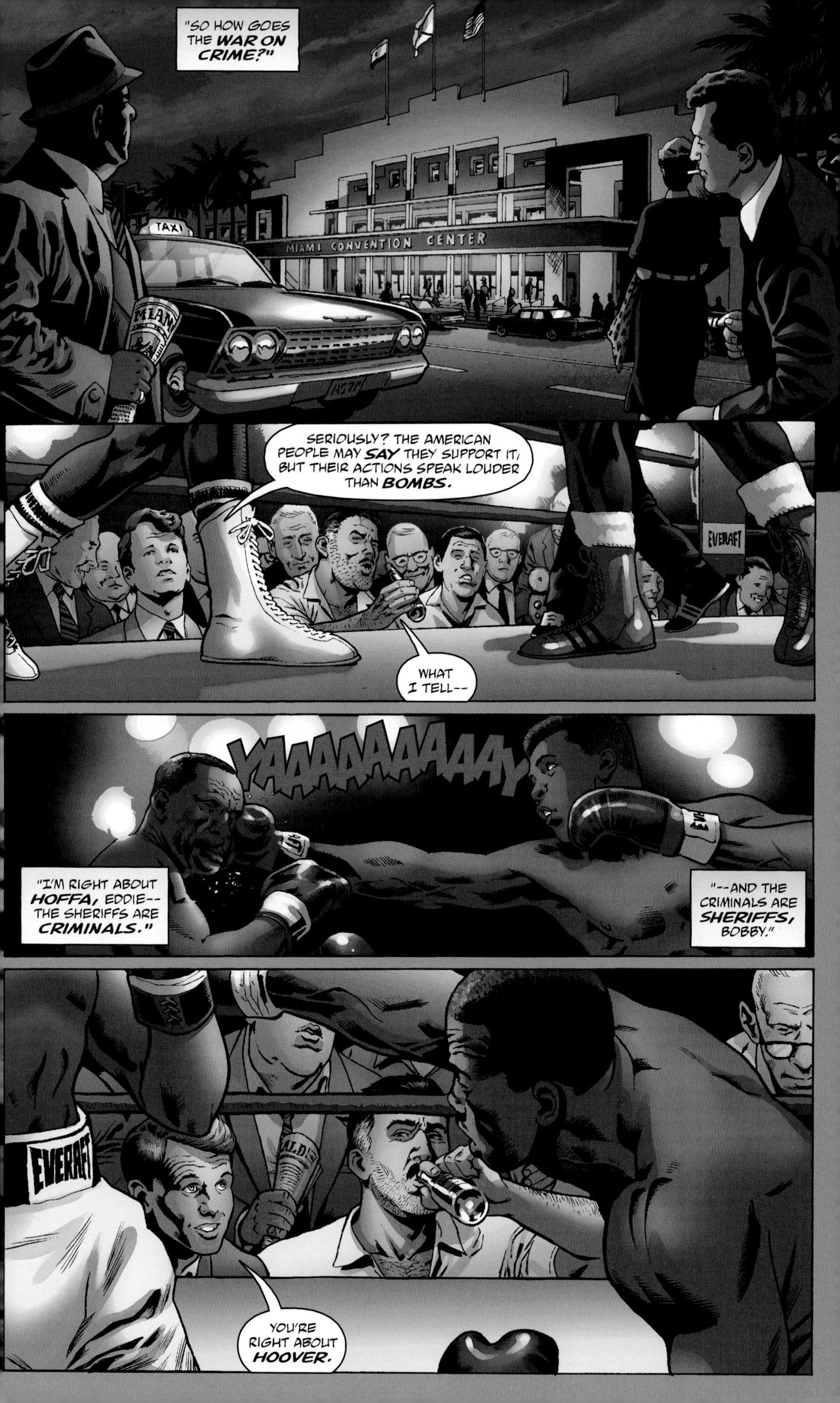

"SO HOW GOES THE WAR ON CRIME?"
TAXI
MIAMI CONVENTION CENTER
SERIOUSLY? THE AMERICAN PEOPLE MAY SAY THEY SUPPORT IT, BUT THEIR ACTIONS SPEAK LOUDER THAN BOMBS.
EVERAST
WHAT I TELL--
YAAAAAAAAAY
"I'M RIGHT ABOUT HOFFA, EDDIE-- THE SHERIFFS ARE CRIMINALS."
"--AND THE CRIMINALS ARE SHERIFFS, BOBBY."
EVERAST
YOU'RE RIGHT ABOUT HOOVER.

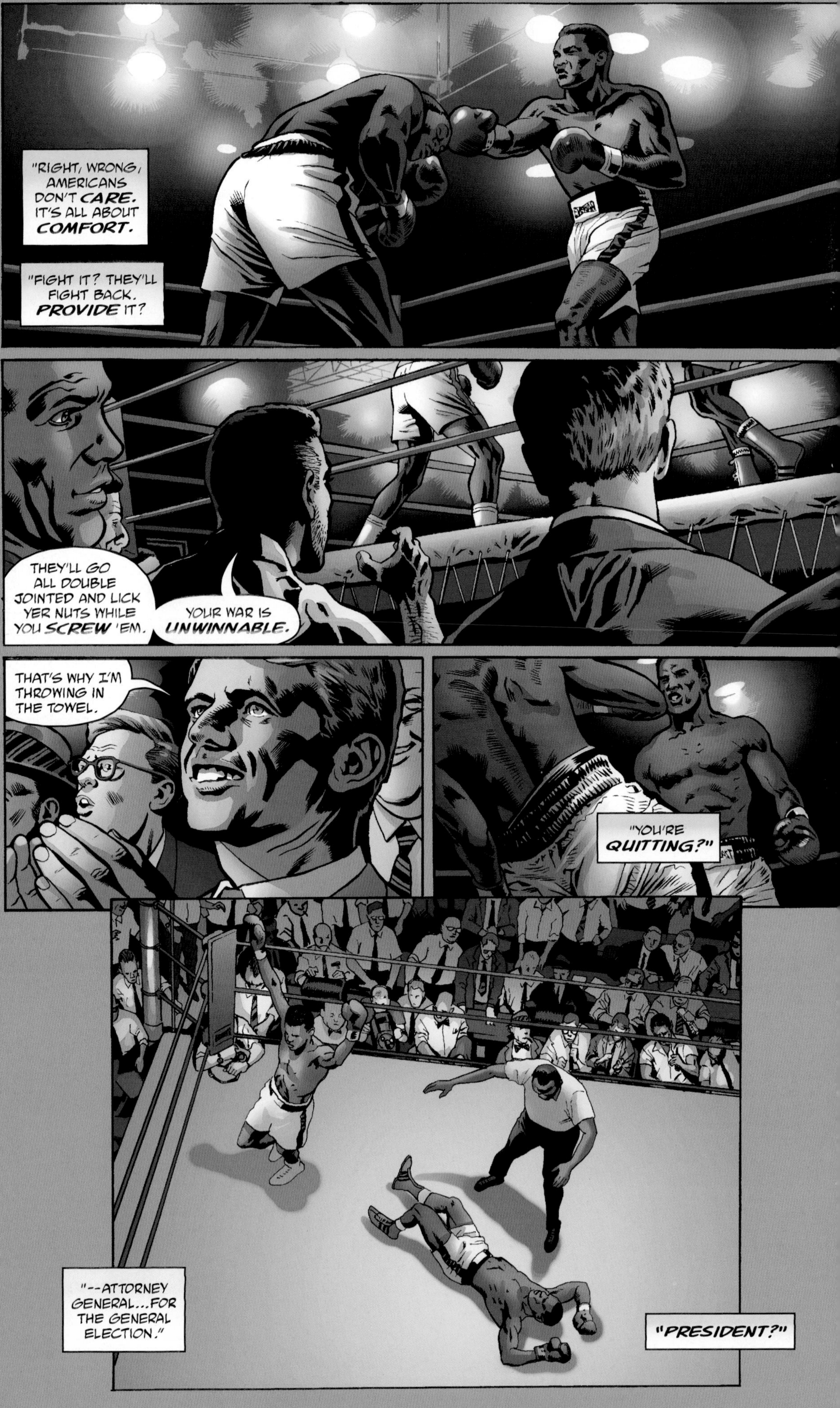
"RIGHT, WRONG, AMERICANS DON'T CARE. IT'S ALL ABOUT COMFORT.
"FIGHT IT? THEY'LL FIGHT BACK. PROVIDE IT?
THEY'LL GO ALL DOUBLE JOINTED AND LICK YER NUTS WHILE YOU SCREW 'EM.
YOUR WAR IS UNWINNABLE.
THAT'S WHY I'M THROWING IN THE TOWEL.
"YOU'RE QUITTING?"
"--ATTORNEY GENERAL...FOR THE GENERAL ELECTION."
"PRESIDENT?"

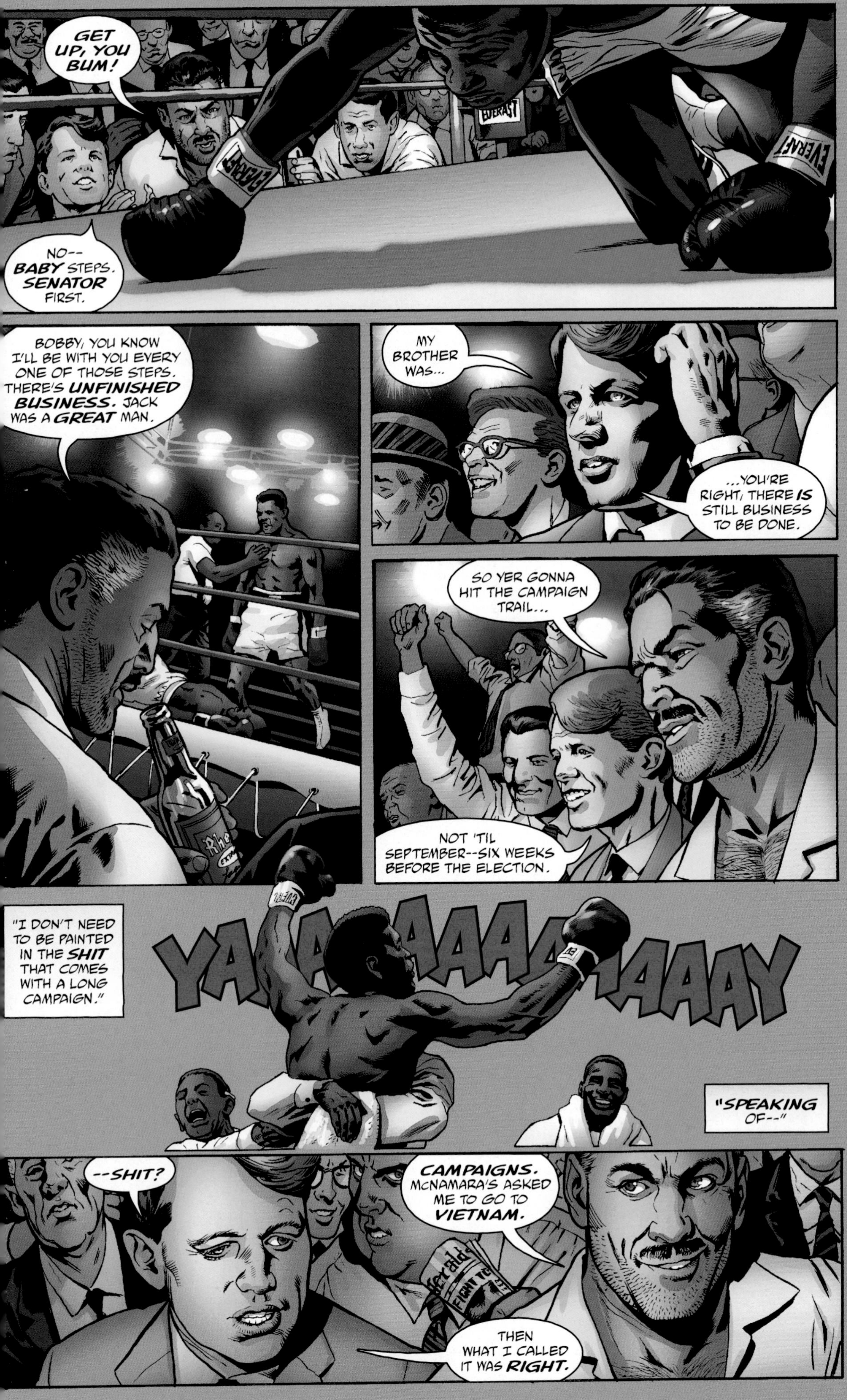
GET UP, YOU BUM!
NO-- BABY STEPS. SENATOR FIRST.
BOBBY, YOU KNOW I'LL BE WITH YOU EVERY ONE OF THOSE STEPS. THERE'S UNFINISHED BUSINESS. JACK WAS A GREAT MAN.
MY BROTHER WAS...
...YOU'RE RIGHT, THERE IS STILL BUSINESS TO BE DONE.
SO YER GONNA HIT THE CAMPAIGN TRAIL...
NOT 'TIL SEPTEMBER--SIX WEEKS BEFORE THE ELECTION.
"I DON'T NEED TO BE PAINTED IN THE SHIT THAT COMES WITH A LONG CAMPAIGN."
"SPEAKING OF--"
--SHIT?
CAMPAIGNS. McNAMARA'S ASKED ME TO GO TO VIETNAM.
THEN WHAT I CALLED IT WAS RIGHT.

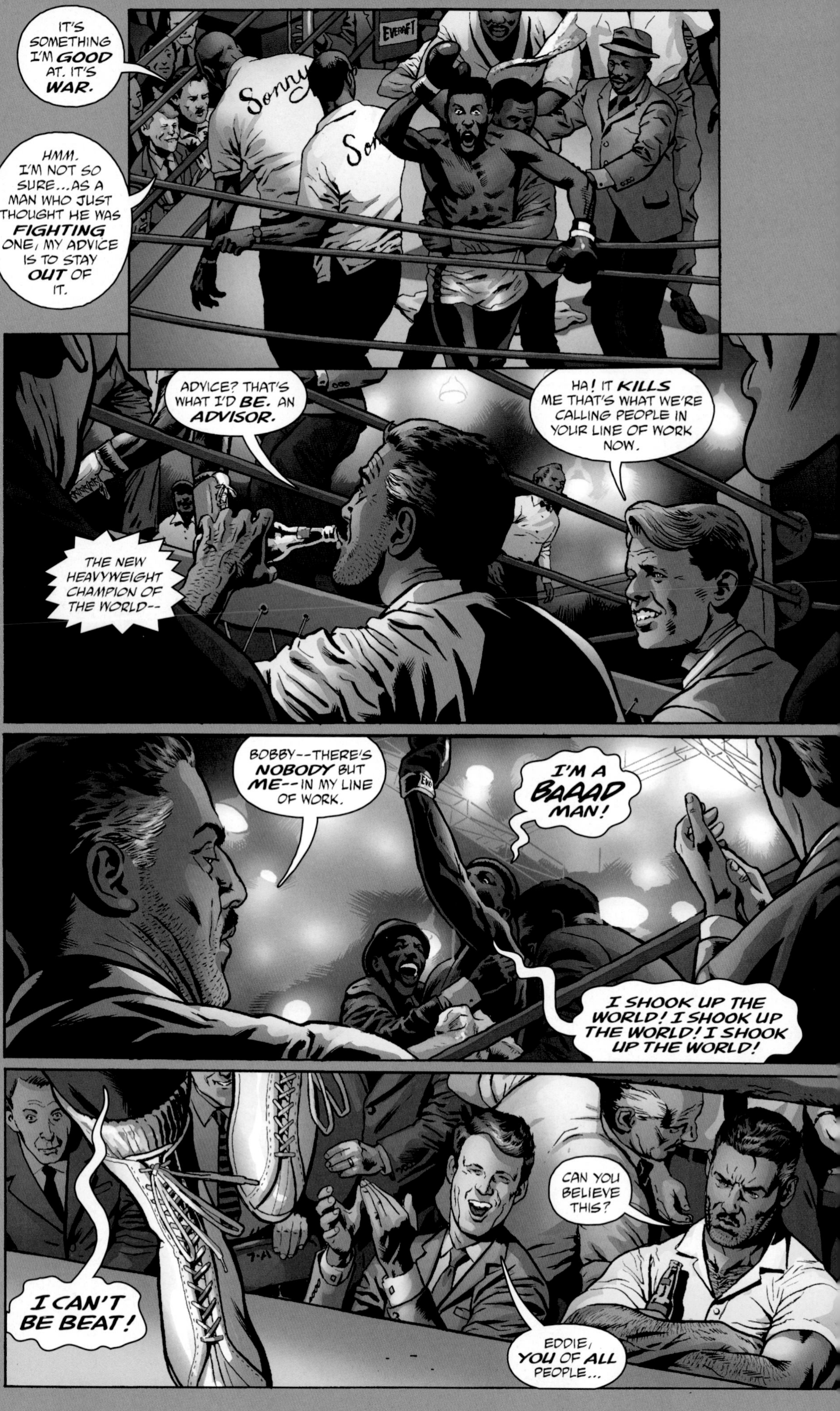
IT'S SOMETHING I'M GOOD AT. IT'S WAR.
HMM. I'M NOT SO SURE...AS A MAN WHO JUST THOUGHT HE WAS FIGHTING ONE, MY ADVICE IS TO STAY OUT OF IT.
ADVICE? THAT'S WHAT I'D BE. AN ADVISOR.
HA! IT KILLS ME THAT'S WHAT WE'RE CALLING PEOPLE IN YOUR LINE OF WORK NOW.
THE NEW HEAVYWEIGHT CHAMPION OF THE WORLD--
BOBBY--THERE'S NOBODY BUT ME--IN MY LINE OF WORK.
I'M A BAAAD MAN!
I SHOOK UP THE WORLD! I SHOOK UP THE WORLD! I SHOOK UP THE WORLD!
CAN YOU BELIEVE THIS?
I CAN'T BE BEAT!
EDDIE, YOU OF ALL PEOPLE...

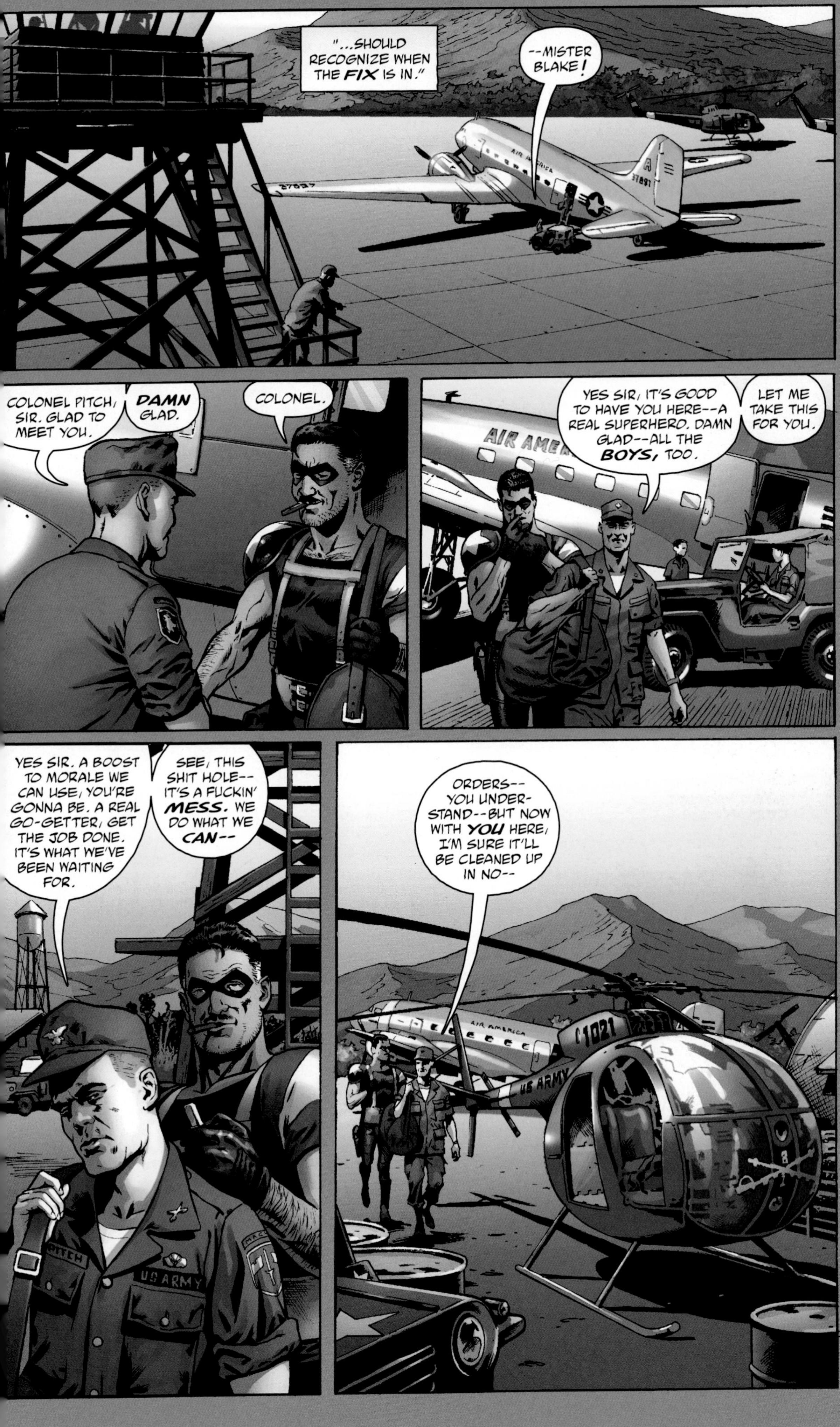
"...SHOULD RECOGNIZE WHEN THE FIX IS IN."
--MISTER BLAKE!
AIR AMERICA
COLONEL PITCH, SIR. GLAD TO MEET YOU.
DAMN GLAD.
COLONEL.
YES SIR, IT'S GOOD TO HAVE YOU HERE--A REAL SUPERHERO. DAMN GLAD--ALL THE BOYS, TOO.
LET ME TAKE THIS FOR YOU.
YES SIR. A BOOST TO MORALE WE CAN USE, YOU'RE GONNA BE. A REAL GO-GETTER, GET THE JOB DONE. IT'S WHAT WE'VE BEEN WAITING FOR.
SEE, THIS SHIT HOLE--IT'S A FUCKIN' MESS. WE DO WHAT WE CAN--
PITCH
US ARMY
ORDERS--YOU UNDERSTAND--BUT NOW WITH YOU HERE, I'M SURE IT'LL BE CLEANED UP IN NO--
1021
US ARMY

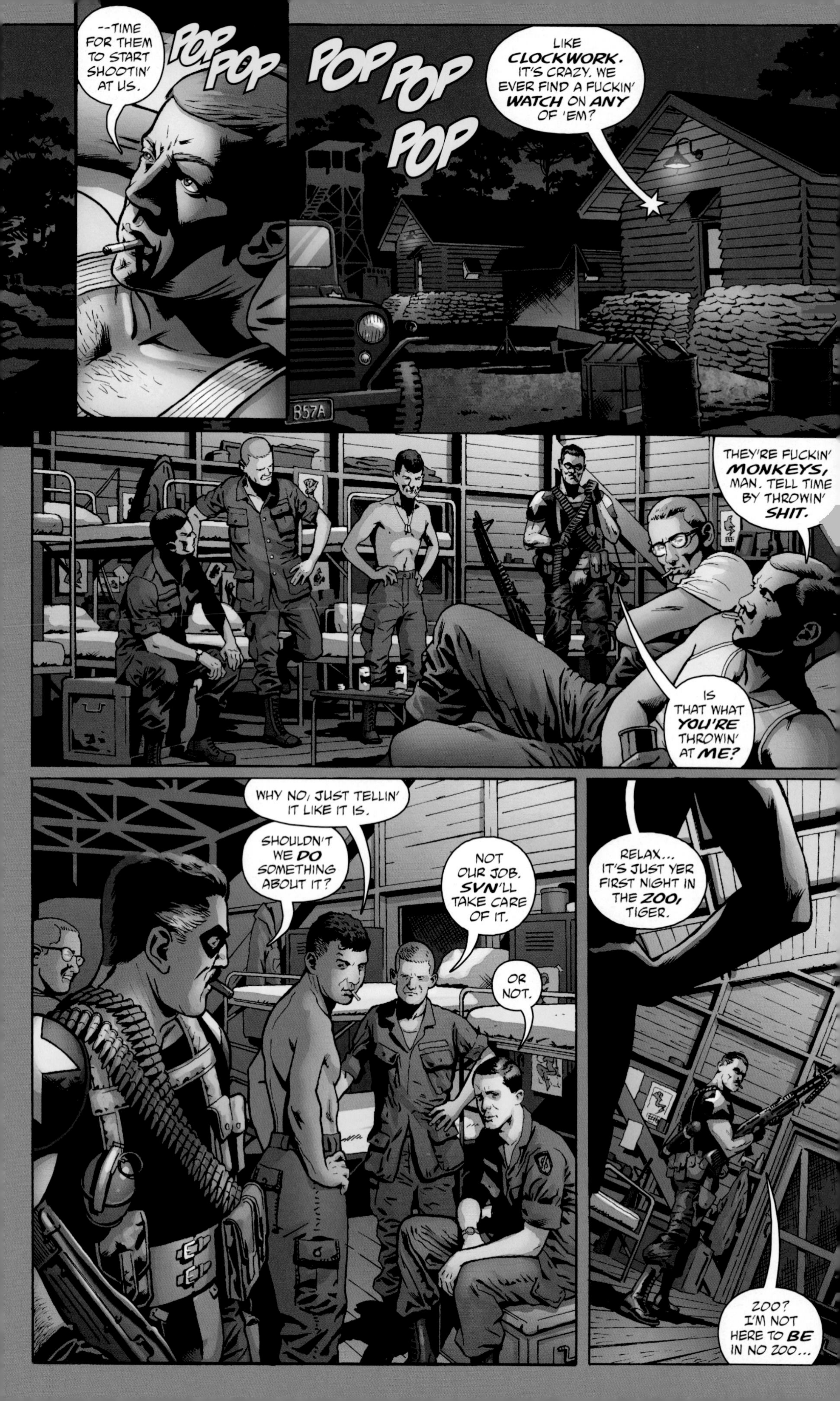

--TIME FOR THEM TO START SHOOTIN' AT US.
POP POP
POP POP POP POP
LIKE CLOCKWORK. IT'S CRAZY. WE EVER FIND A FUCKIN' WATCH ON ANY OF 'EM?
B57A
THEY'RE FUCKIN' MONKEYS, MAN. TELL TIME BY THROWIN' SHIT.
IS THAT WHAT YOU'RE THROWIN' AT ME?
WHY NO, JUST TELLIN' IT LIKE IT IS.
SHOULDN'T WE DO SOMETHING ABOUT IT?
NOT OUR JOB. SVN'LL TAKE CARE OF IT.
OR NOT.
RELAX... IT'S JUST YER FIRST NIGHT IN THE ZOO, TIGER.
ZOO? I'M NOT HERE TO BE IN NO ZOO...

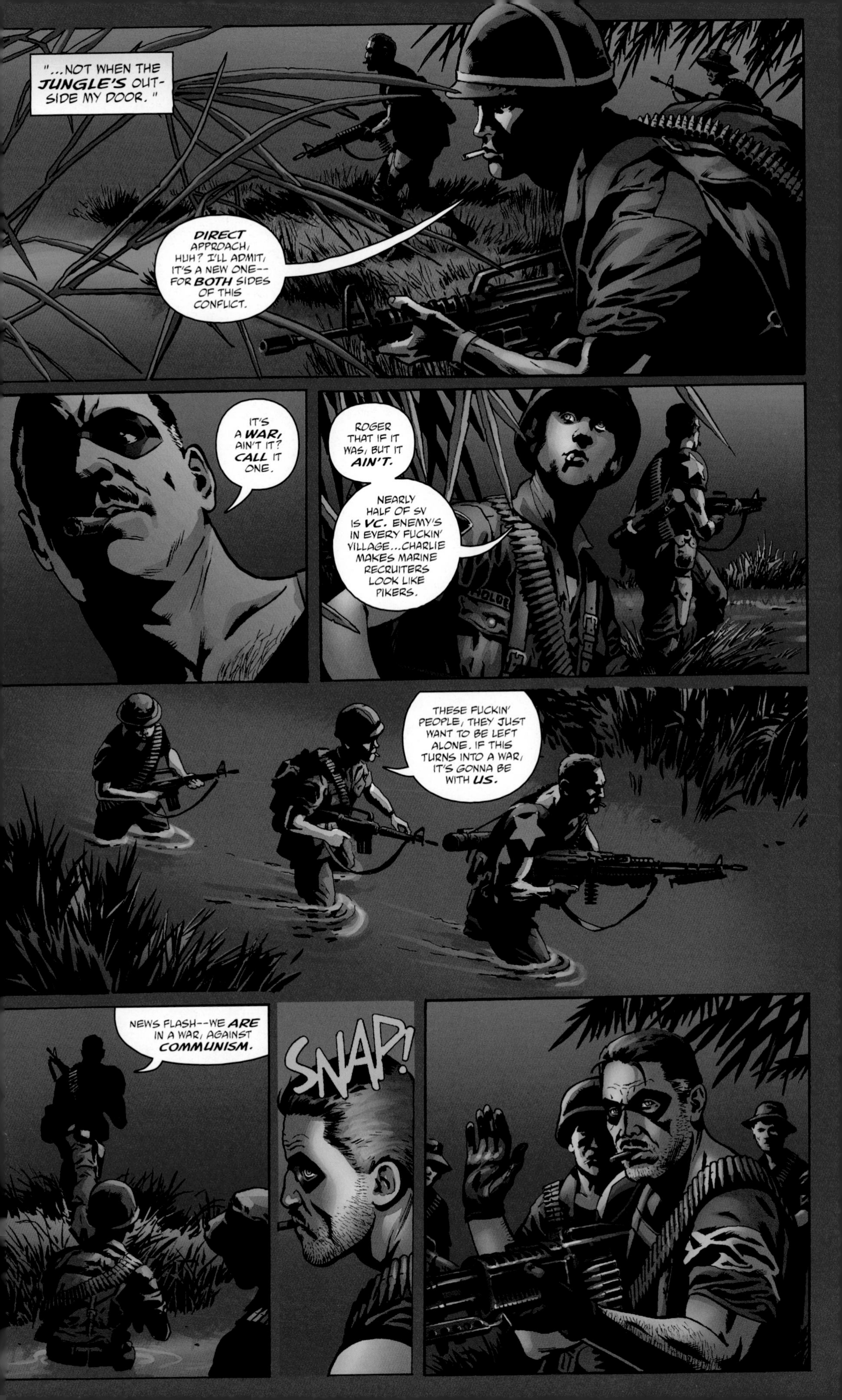
"...NOT WHEN THE JUNGLE'S OUT-SIDE MY DOOR."
DIRECT APPROACH, HUH? I'LL ADMIT, IT'S A NEW ONE--FOR BOTH SIDES OF THIS CONFLICT.
IT'S A WAR, AIN'T IT? CALL IT ONE.
ROGER THAT IF IT WAS, BUT IT AIN'T.
NEARLY HALF OF SV IS VC. ENEMY'S IN EVERY FUCKIN' VILLAGE...CHARLIE MAKES MARINE RECRUITERS LOOK LIKE PIKERS.
THESE FUCKIN' PEOPLE, THEY JUST WANT TO BE LEFT ALONE. IF THIS TURNS INTO A WAR, IT'S GONNA BE WITH US.
NEWS FLASH--WE ARE IN A WAR, AGAINST COMMUNISM.
SNAP!

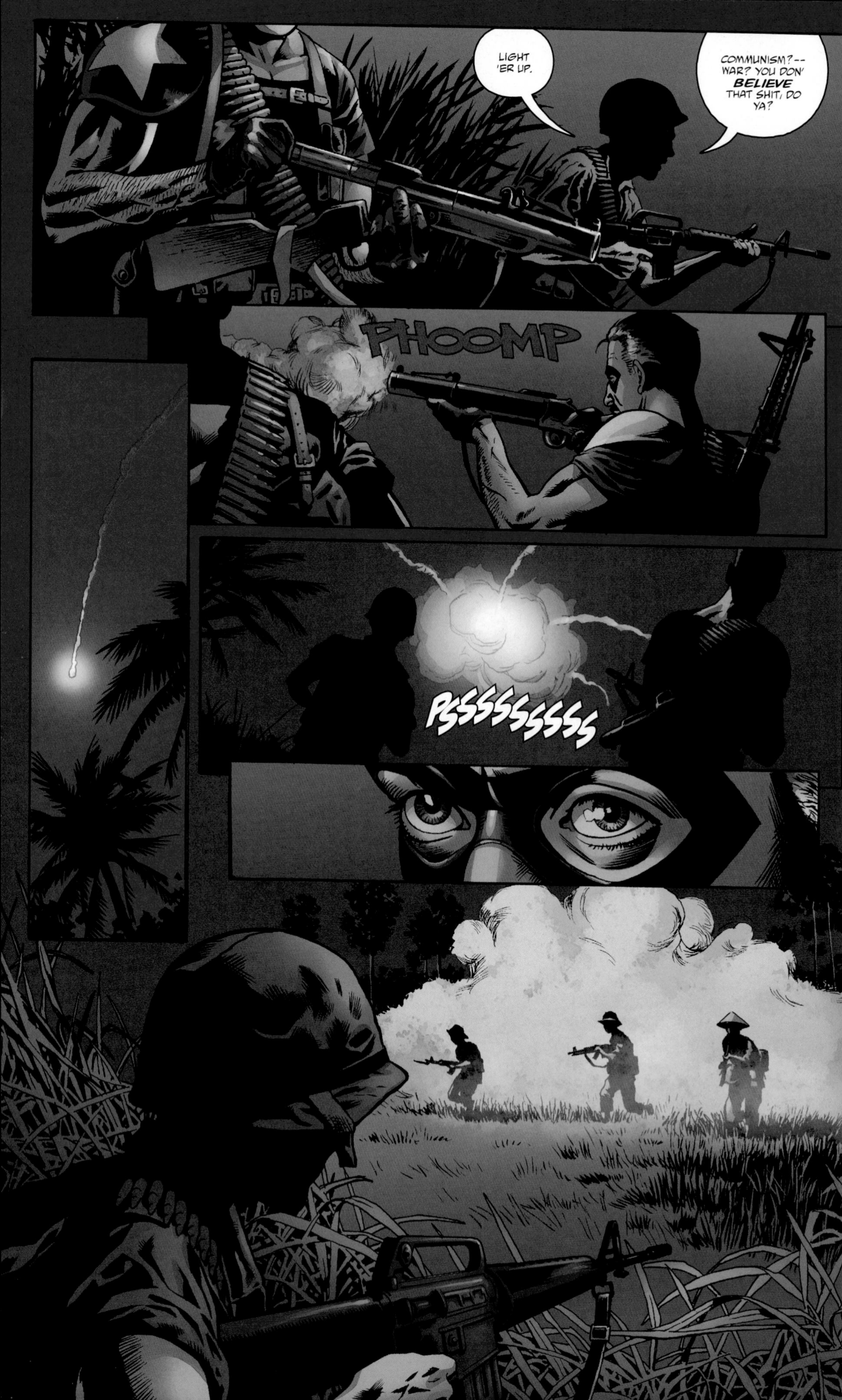
LIGHT 'ER UP.
COMMUNISM?-- WAR? YOU DON' BELIEVE THAT SHIT, DO YA?
PHOOMP
PSSSSSSSSS

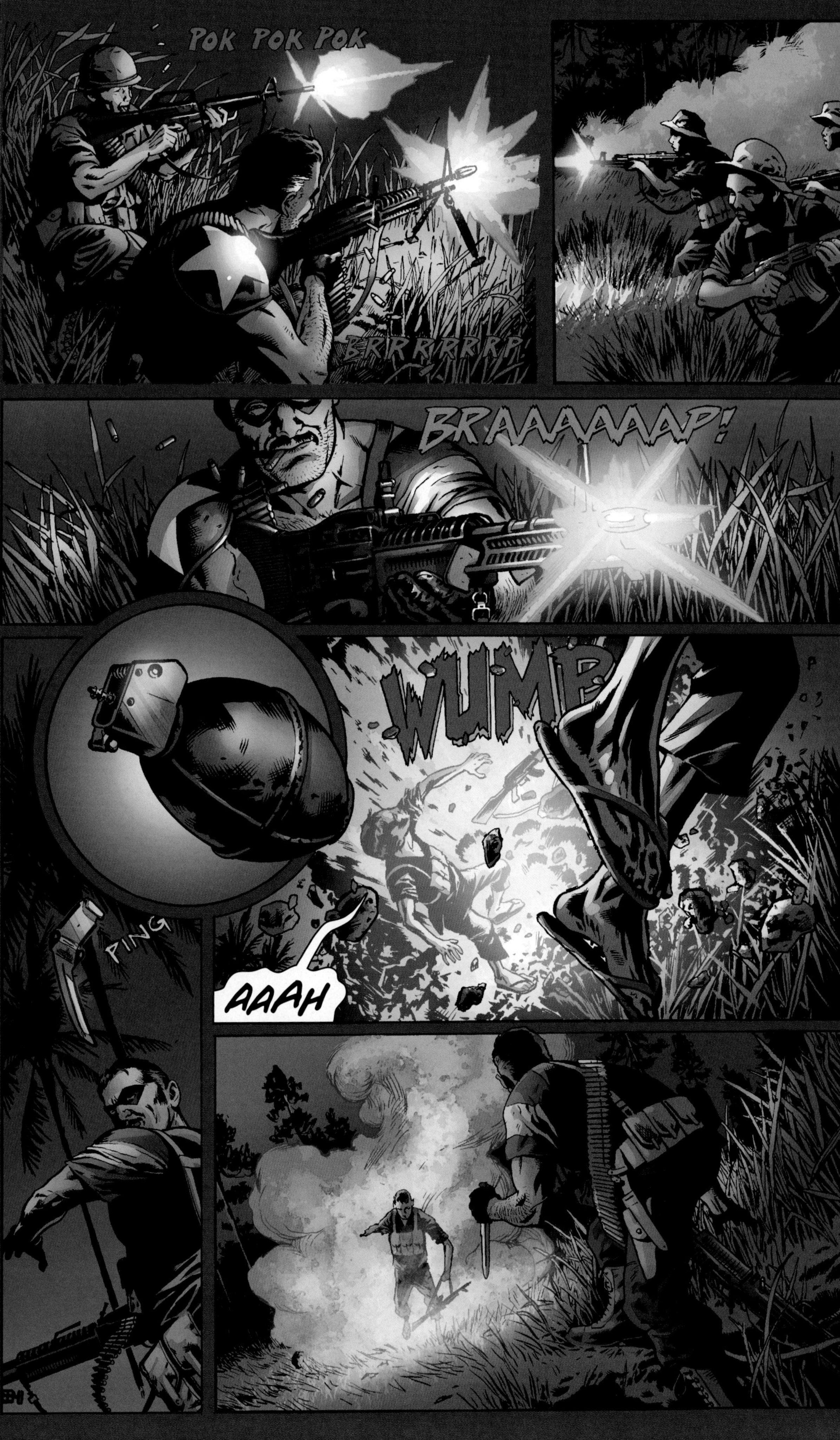
POK POK POK
BRRRRRRRP
BRAAAAAAAP!
WUMP
PING
AAAH

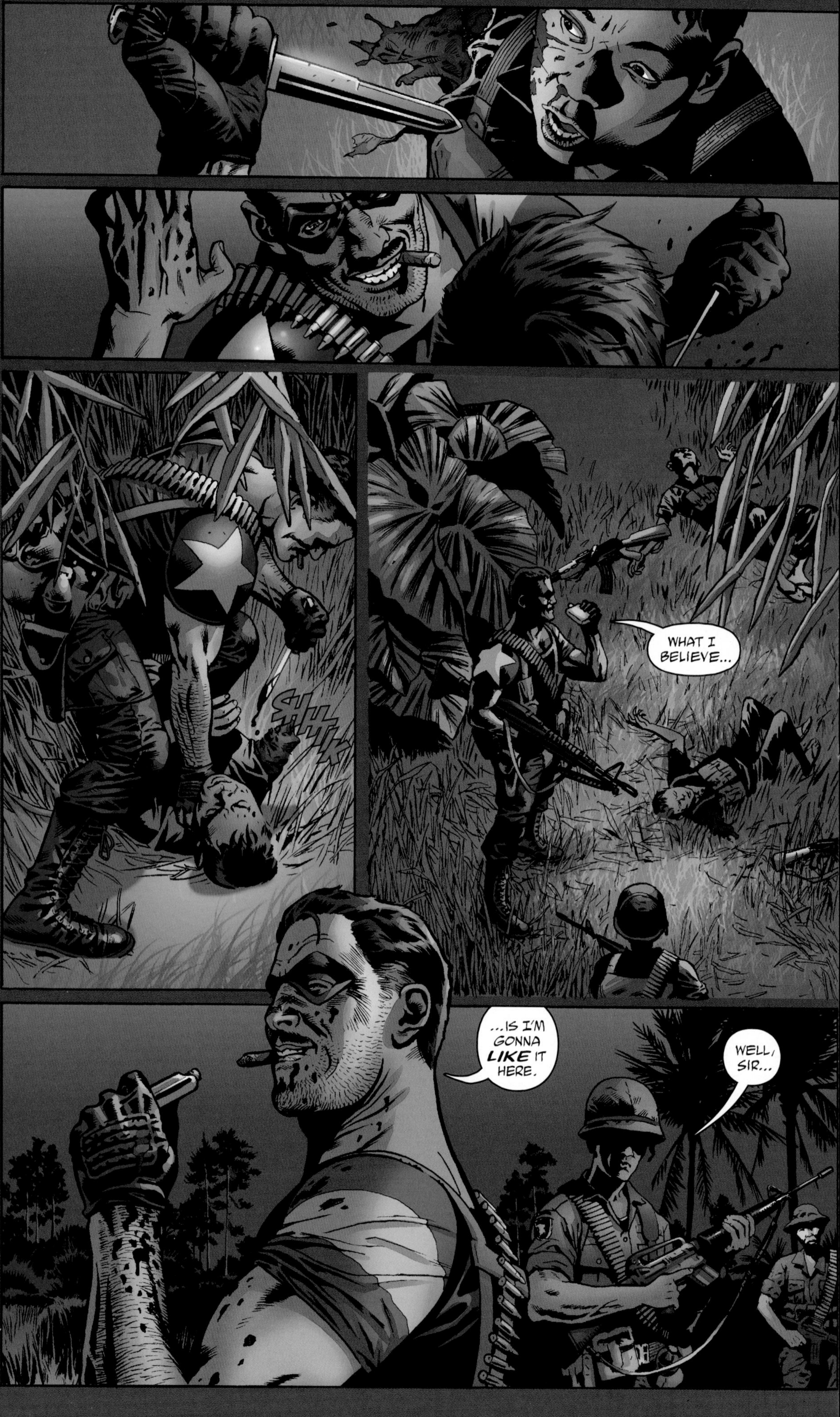
SHHHK
WHAT I BELIEVE...
...IS I'M GONNA **LIKE** IT HERE.
WELL, SIR...

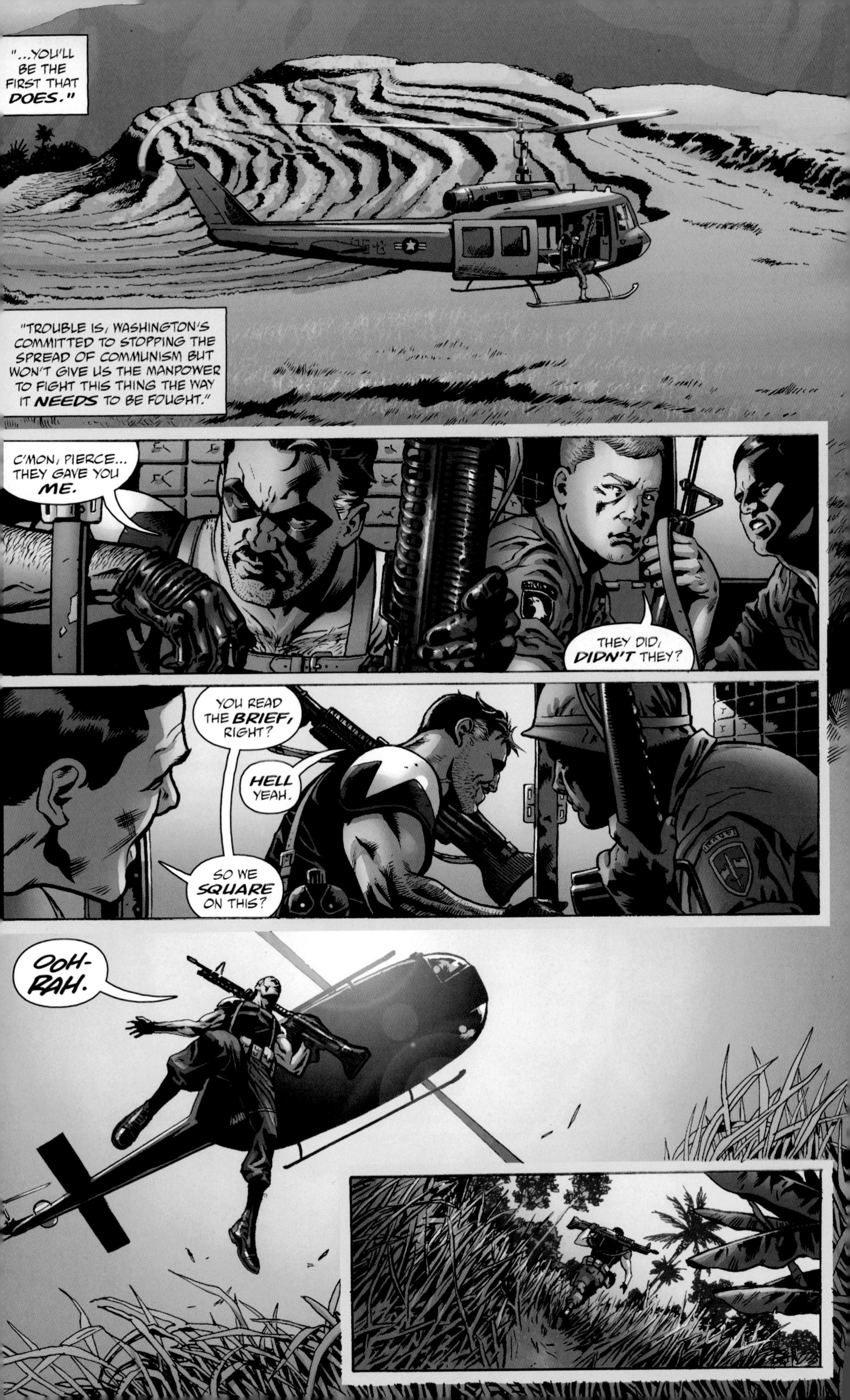
"...YOU'LL BE THE FIRST THAT DOES."
"TROUBLE IS, WASHINGTON'S COMMITTED TO STOPPING THE SPREAD OF COMMUNISM BUT WON'T GIVE US THE MANPOWER TO FIGHT THIS THING THE WAY IT NEEDS TO BE FOUGHT."
C'MON, PIERCE... THEY GAVE YOU ME.
THEY DID, DIDN'T THEY?
YOU READ THE BRIEF, RIGHT?
HELL YEAH.
SO WE SQUARE ON THIS?
OOH-RAH.

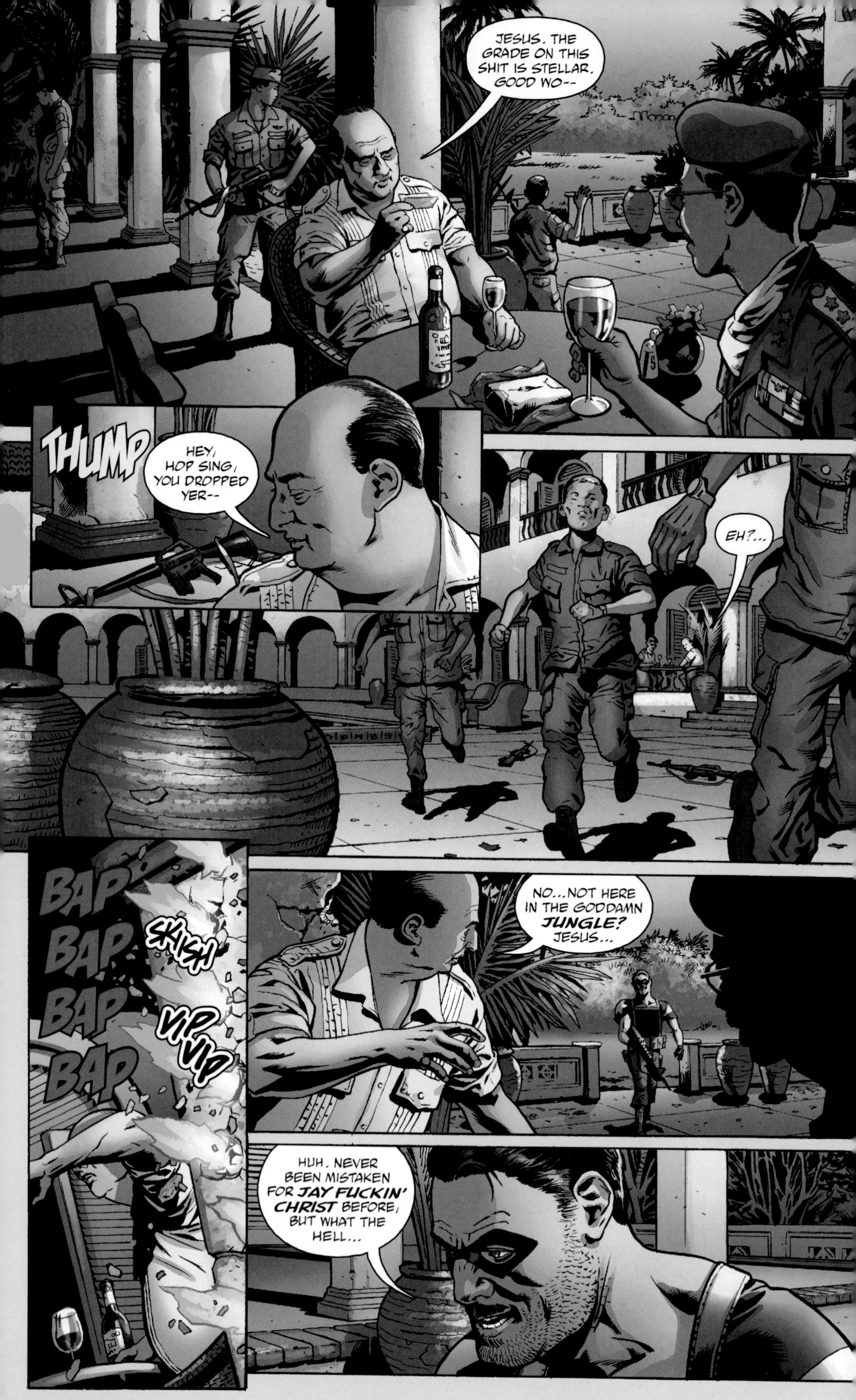
JESUS. THE GRADE ON THIS SHIT IS STELLAR. GOOD WO--
THUMP
HEY, HOP SING, YOU DROPPED YER--
EH?...
BAP BAP BAP BAP
SKISH
VIP VIP
NO...NOT HERE IN THE GODDAMN JUNGLE? JESUS...
HUH. NEVER BEEN MISTAKEN FOR JAY FUCKIN' CHRIST BEFORE, BUT WHAT THE HELL...

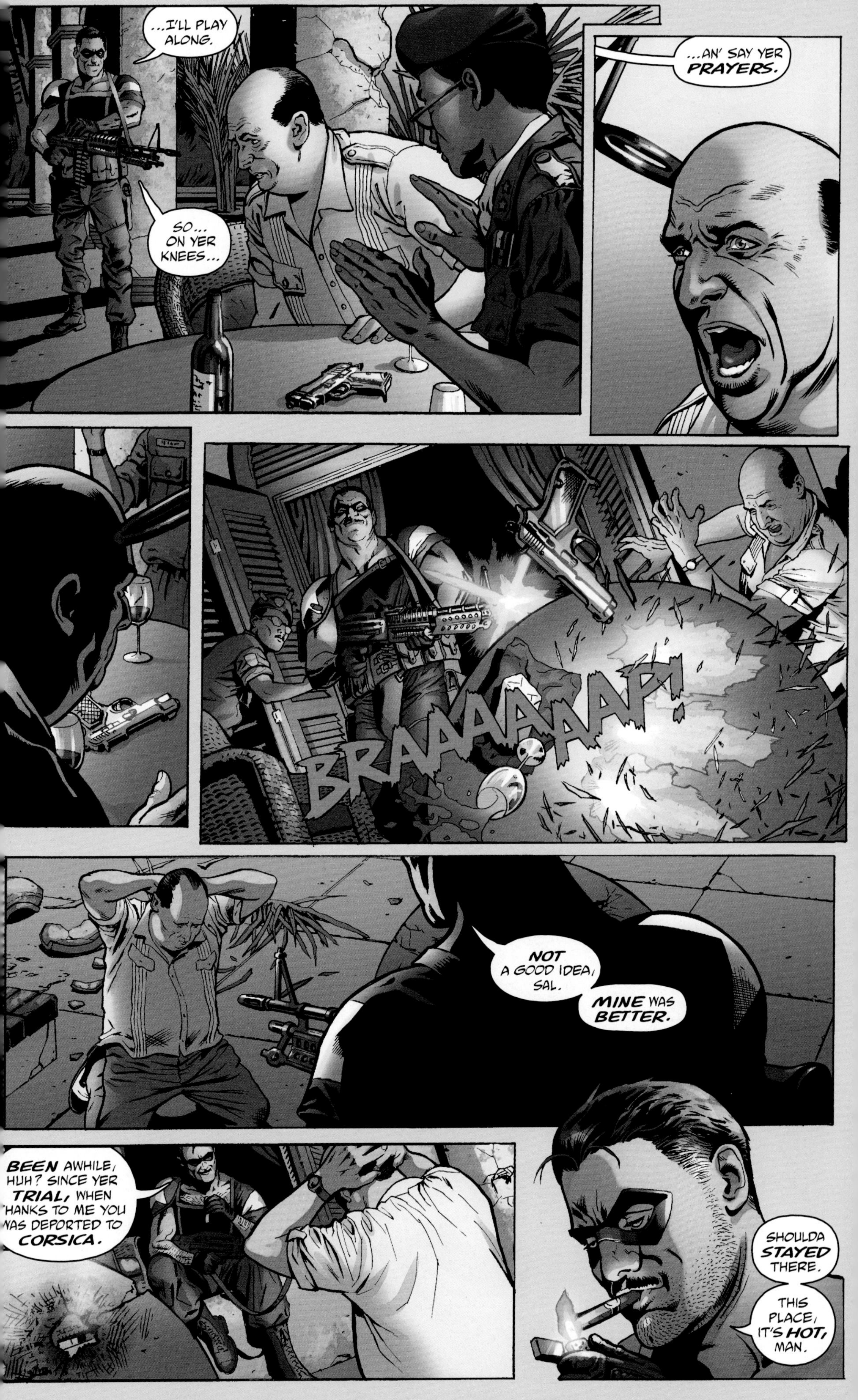

...I'LL PLAY ALONG.
SO... ON YER KNEES...
...AN' SAY YER PRAYERS.
BRAAAAAAP!
NOT A GOOD IDEA, SAL.
MINE WAS BETTER.
BEEN AWHILE, HUH? SINCE YER TRIAL, WHEN THANKS TO ME YOU WAS DEPORTED TO CORSICA.
SHOULDA STAYED THERE.
THIS PLACE, IT'S HOT, MAN.

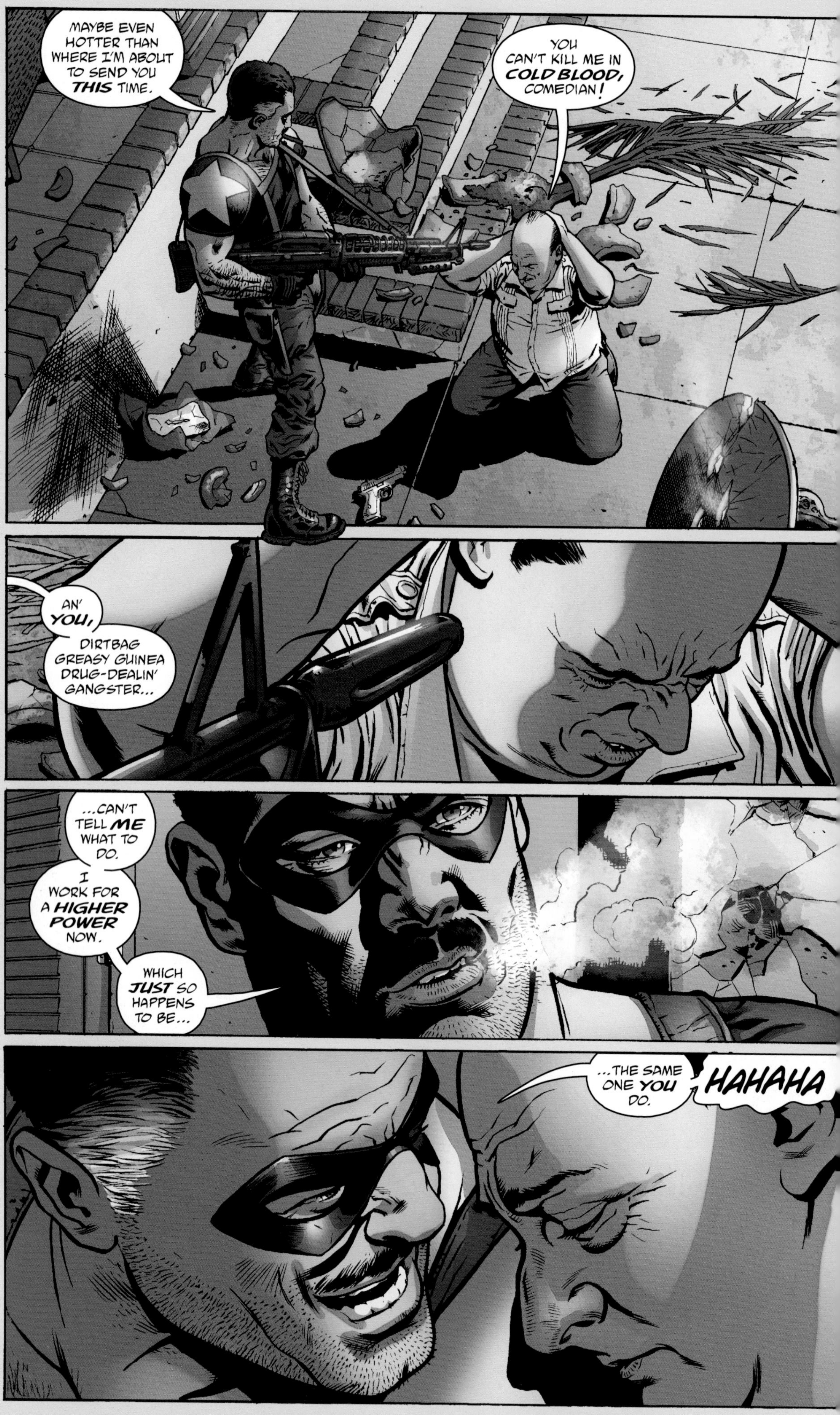
MAYBE EVEN HOTTER THAN WHERE I'M ABOUT TO SEND YOU **THIS** TIME.
YOU CAN'T KILL ME IN **COLD BLOOD**, COMEDIAN!
AN' **YOU**, DIRTBAG GREASY GUINEA DRUG-DEALIN' GANGSTER...
...CAN'T TELL **ME** WHAT TO DO.
I WORK FOR A **HIGHER POWER** NOW.
WHICH **JUST** SO HAPPENS TO BE...
...THE SAME ONE **YOU** DO.
HAHAHA

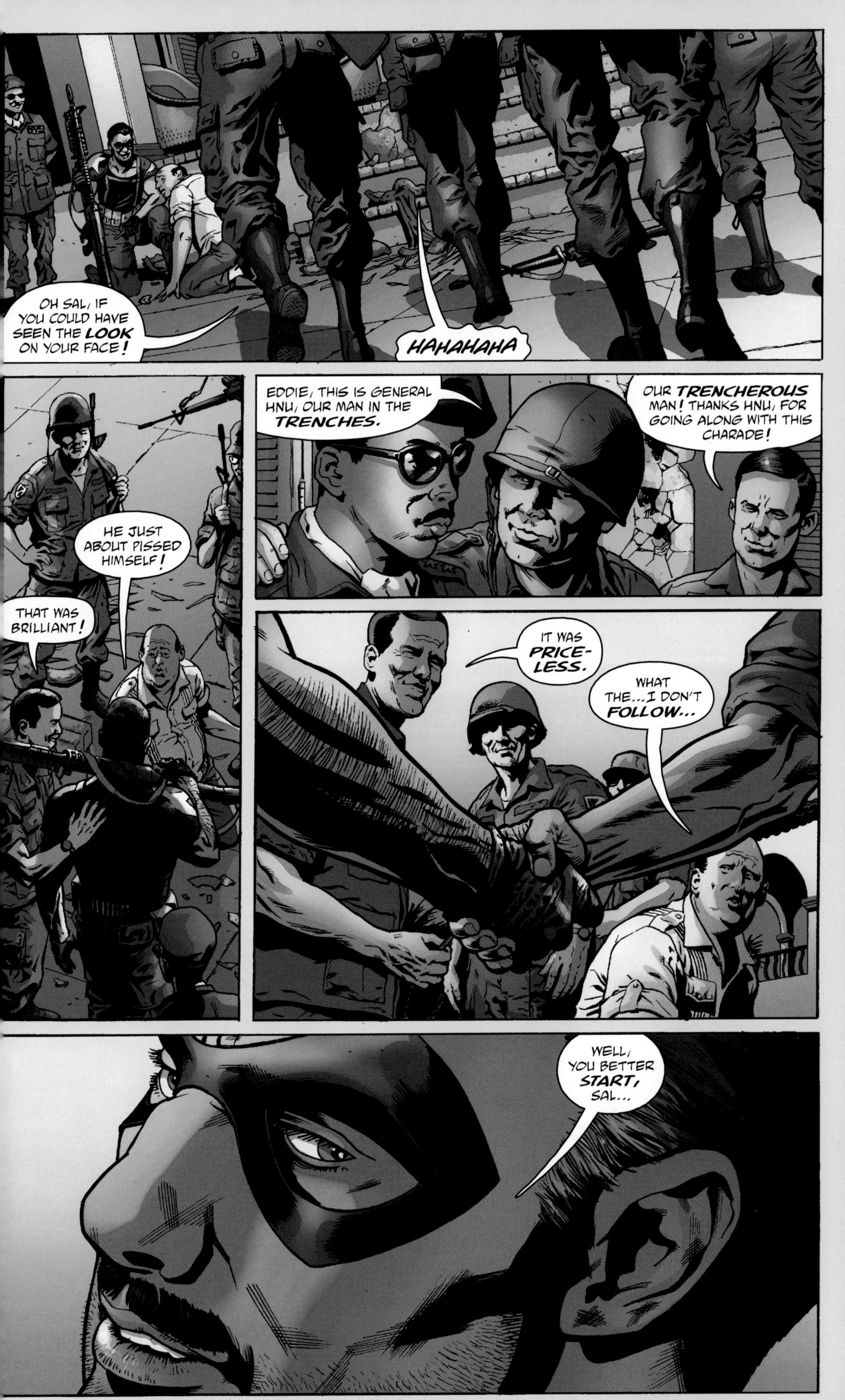
OH SAL, IF YOU COULD HAVE SEEN THE LOOK ON YOUR FACE!
HAHAHAHA
HE JUST ABOUT PISSED HIMSELF!
THAT WAS BRILLIANT!
EDDIE, THIS IS GENERAL HNU, OUR MAN IN THE TRENCHES.
OUR TRENCHEROUS MAN! THANKS HNU, FOR GOING ALONG WITH THIS CHARADE!
IT WAS PRICE-LESS.
WHAT THE...I DON'T FOLLOW...
WELL, YOU BETTER START, SAL...

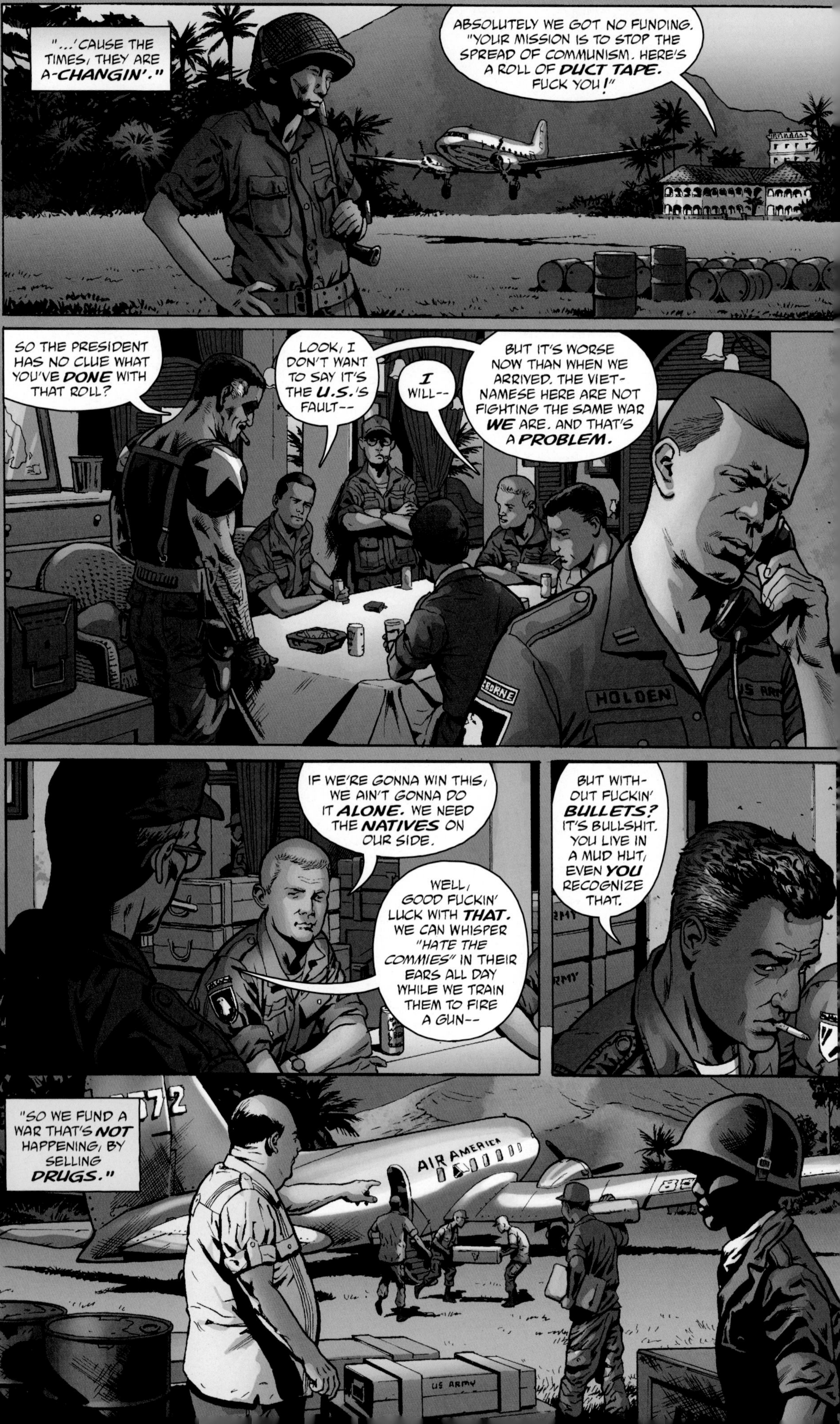
"...'CAUSE THE TIMES, THEY ARE A-CHANGIN'."
ABSOLUTELY WE GOT NO FUNDING. "YOUR MISSION IS TO STOP THE SPREAD OF COMMUNISM. HERE'S A ROLL OF DUCT TAPE. FUCK YOU!"
SO THE PRESIDENT HAS NO CLUE WHAT YOU'VE DONE WITH THAT ROLL?
LOOK, I DON'T WANT TO SAY IT'S THE U.S.'S FAULT--
I WILL--
BUT IT'S WORSE NOW THAN WHEN WE ARRIVED. THE VIETNAMESE HERE ARE NOT FIGHTING THE SAME WAR WE ARE. AND THAT'S A PROBLEM.
HOLDEN
IF WE'RE GONNA WIN THIS, WE AIN'T GONNA DO IT ALONE. WE NEED THE NATIVES ON OUR SIDE.
WELL, GOOD FUCKIN' LUCK WITH THAT. WE CAN WHISPER "HATE THE COMMIES" IN THEIR EARS ALL DAY WHILE WE TRAIN THEM TO FIRE A GUN--
BUT WITHOUT FUCKIN' BULLETS? IT'S BULLSHIT. YOU LIVE IN A MUD HUT, EVEN YOU RECOGNIZE THAT.
"SO WE FUND A WAR THAT'S NOT HAPPENING, BY SELLING DRUGS."
AIR AMERICA
US ARMY

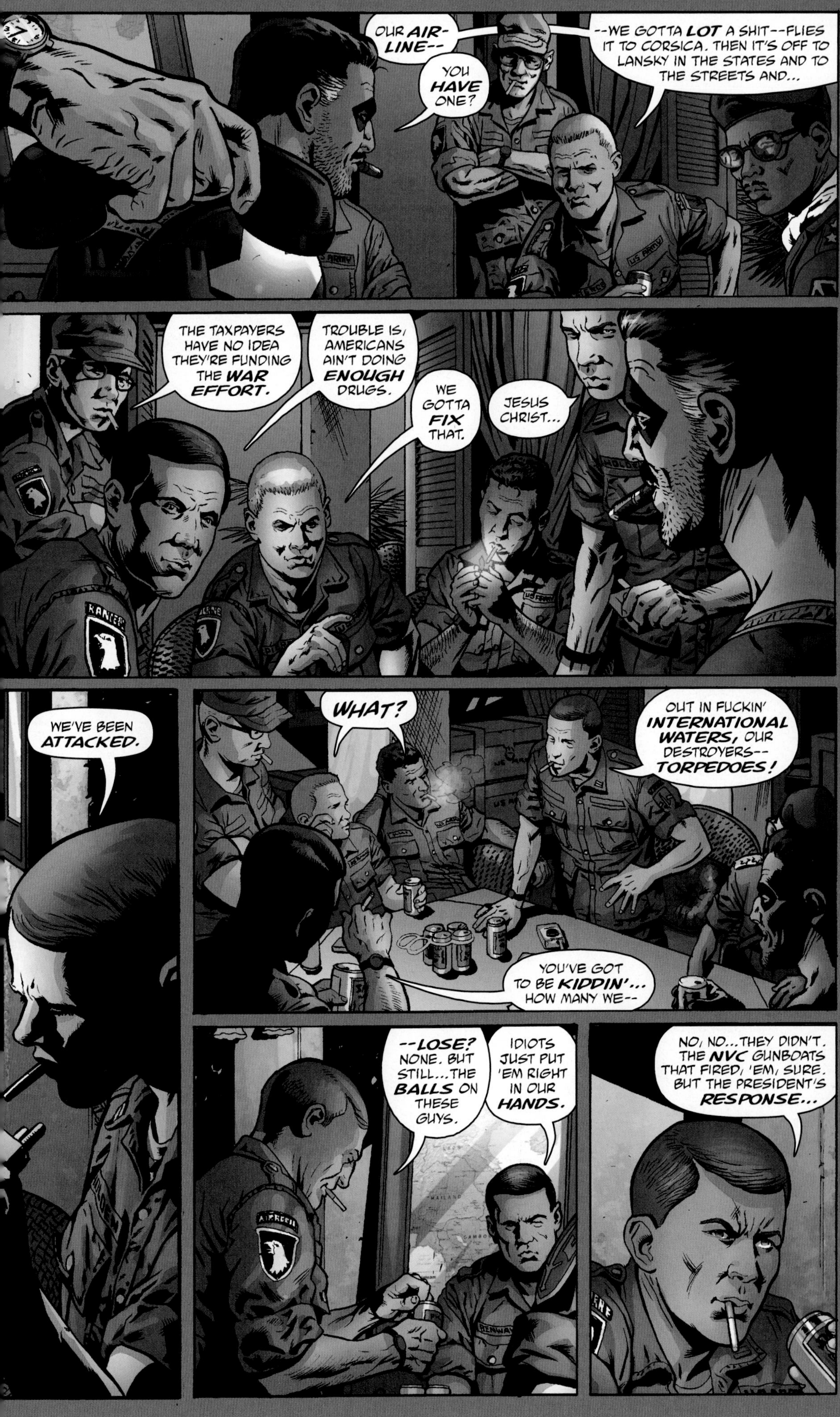

OUR AIR-LINE--
YOU HAVE ONE?
--WE GOTTA LOT A SHIT--FLIES IT TO CORSICA. THEN IT'S OFF TO LANSKY IN THE STATES AND TO THE STREETS AND...
THE TAXPAYERS HAVE NO IDEA THEY'RE FUNDING THE WAR EFFORT.
TROUBLE IS, AMERICANS AIN'T DOING ENOUGH DRUGS.
WE GOTTA FIX THAT.
JESUS CHRIST...
WE'VE BEEN ATTACKED.
WHAT?
OUT IN FUCKIN' INTERNATIONAL WATERS, OUR DESTROYERS--TORPEDOES!
YOU'VE GOT TO BE KIDDIN'... HOW MANY WE--
--LOSE? NONE. BUT STILL...THE BALLS ON THESE GUYS.
IDIOTS JUST PUT 'EM RIGHT IN OUR HANDS.
NO, NO...THEY DIDN'T. THE NVC GUNBOATS THAT FIRED, 'EM, SURE. BUT THE PRESIDENT'S RESPONSE...

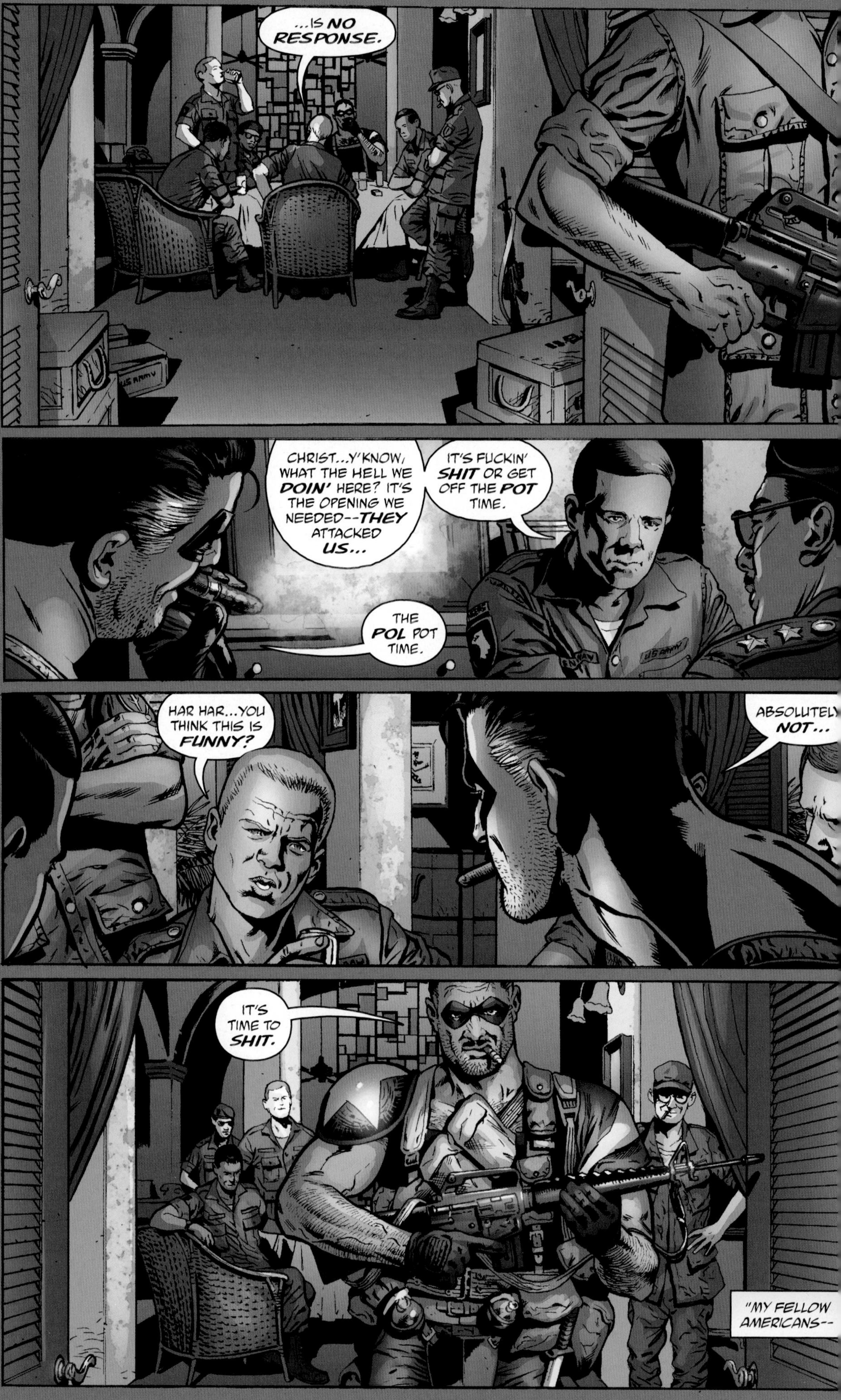
...IS NO RESPONSE.
CHRIST...Y'KNOW, WHAT THE HELL WE DOIN' HERE? IT'S THE OPENING WE NEEDED--THEY ATTACKED US...
IT'S FUCKIN' SHIT OR GET OFF THE POT TIME.
THE POL POT TIME.
HAR HAR...YOU THINK THIS IS FUNNY?
ABSOLUTELY NOT...
IT'S TIME TO SHIT.
"MY FELLOW AMERICANS--

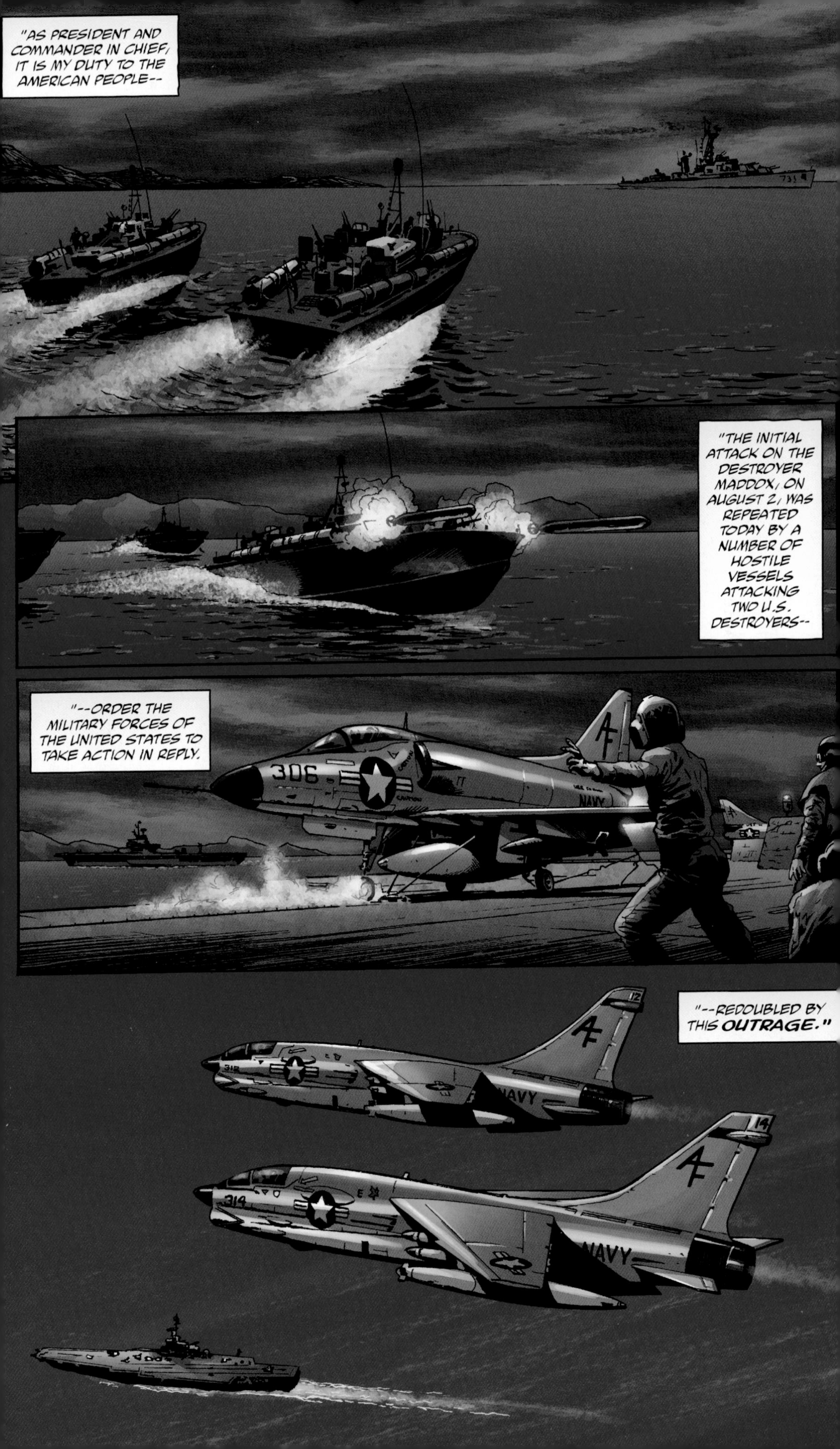
"AS PRESIDENT AND COMMANDER IN CHIEF, IT IS MY DUTY TO THE AMERICAN PEOPLE--
"THE INITIAL ATTACK ON THE DESTROYER MADDOX, ON AUGUST 2, WAS REPEATED TODAY BY A NUMBER OF HOSTILE VESSELS ATTACKING TWO U.S. DESTROYERS--
"--ORDER THE MILITARY FORCES OF THE UNITED STATES TO TAKE ACTION IN REPLY.
"--REDOUBLED BY THIS OUTRAGE."
306
NAVY
312
NAVY
314
NAVY

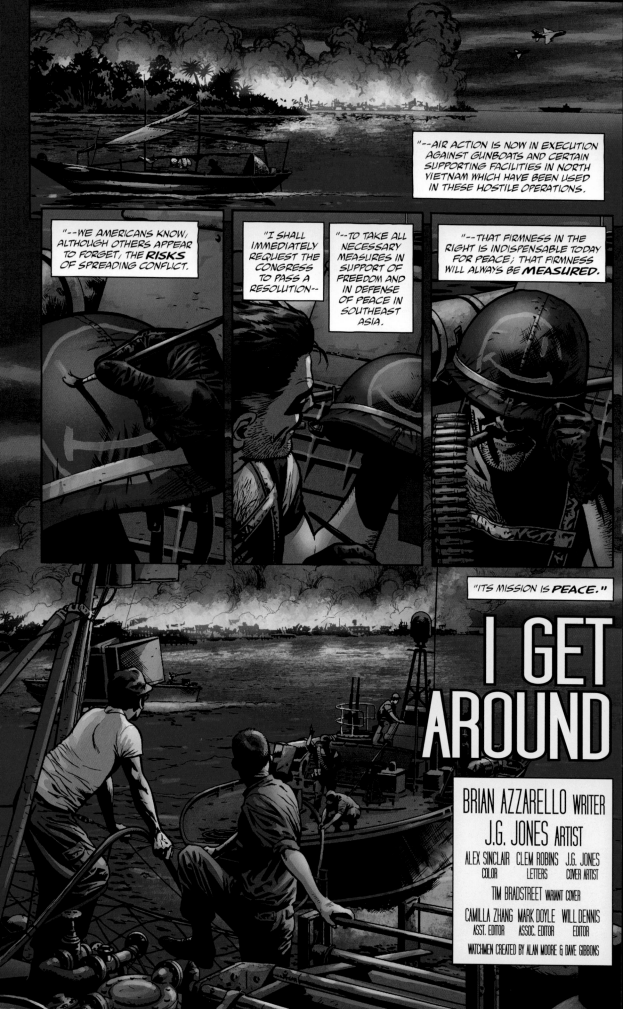

"--AIR ACTION IS NOW IN EXECUTION AGAINST GUNBOATS AND CERTAIN SUPPORTING FACILITIES IN NORTH VIETNAM WHICH HAVE BEEN USED IN THESE HOSTILE OPERATIONS.

"--WE AMERICANS KNOW, ALTHOUGH OTHERS APPEAR TO FORGET, THE **RISKS** OF SPREADING CONFLICT.

"I SHALL IMMEDIATELY REQUEST THE CONGRESS TO PASS A RESOLUTION--

"--TO TAKE ALL NECESSARY MEASURES IN SUPPORT OF FREEDOM AND IN DEFENSE OF PEACE IN SOUTHEAST ASIA.

"--THAT FIRMNESS IN THE RIGHT IS INDISPENSABLE TODAY FOR PEACE; THAT FIRMNESS WILL ALWAYS BE **MEASURED**.

"ITS MISSION IS **PEACE**."

I GET AROUND

BRIAN AZZARELLO WRITER

J.G. JONES ARTIST

ALEX SINCLAIR — CLEM ROBINS — J.G. JONES
COLOR — LETTERS — COVER ARTIST

TIM BRADSTREET VARIANT COVER

CAMILLA ZHANG — MARK DOYLE — WILL DENNIS
ASST. EDITOR — ASSOC. EDITOR — EDITOR

WATCHMEN CREATED BY ALAN MOORE & DAVE GIBBONS

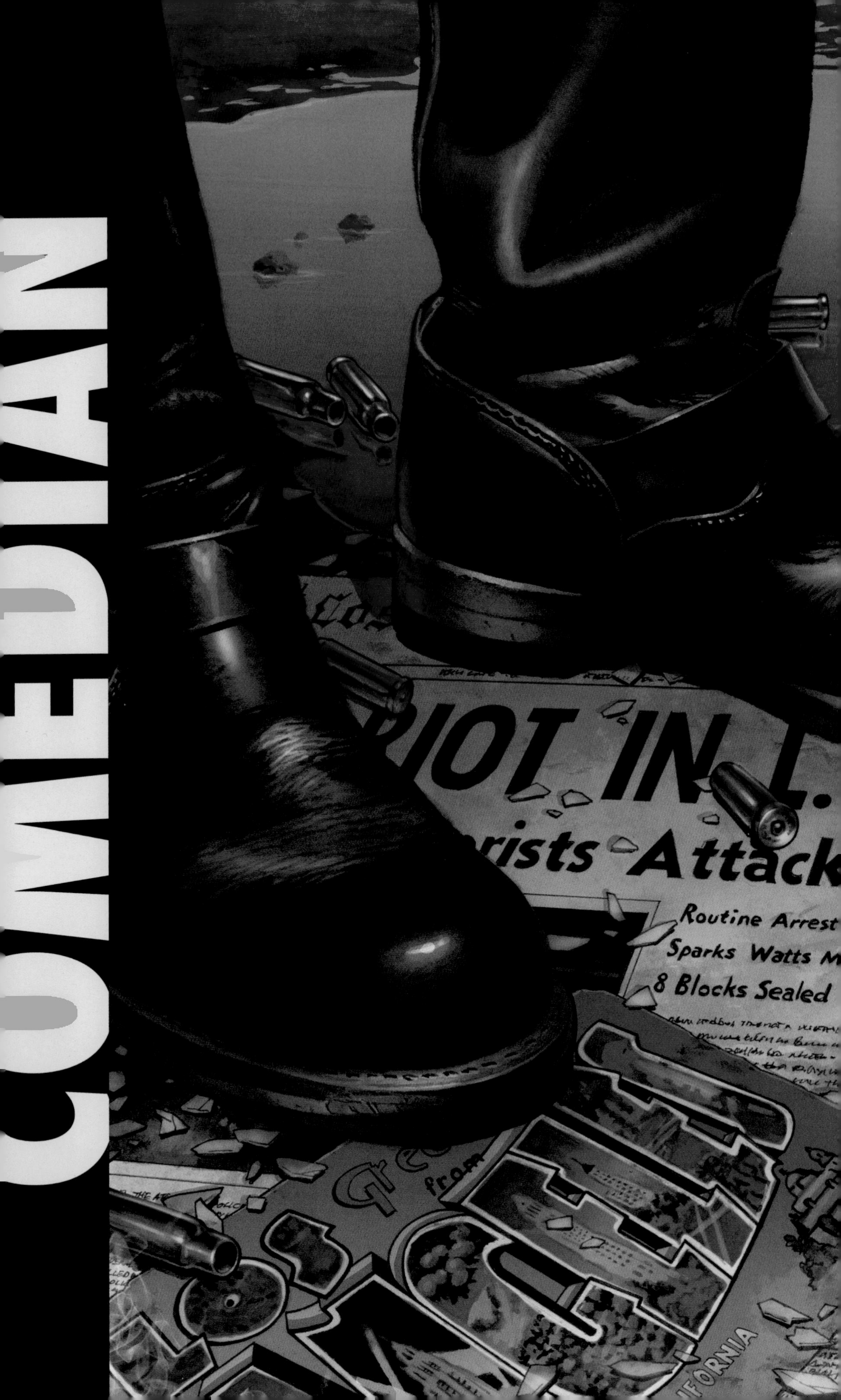
COMEDIAN
RIOT IN L.
rists Attack
Routine Arrest
Sparks Watts M
8 Blocks Sealed
CALIFORNIA

COMEDIAN

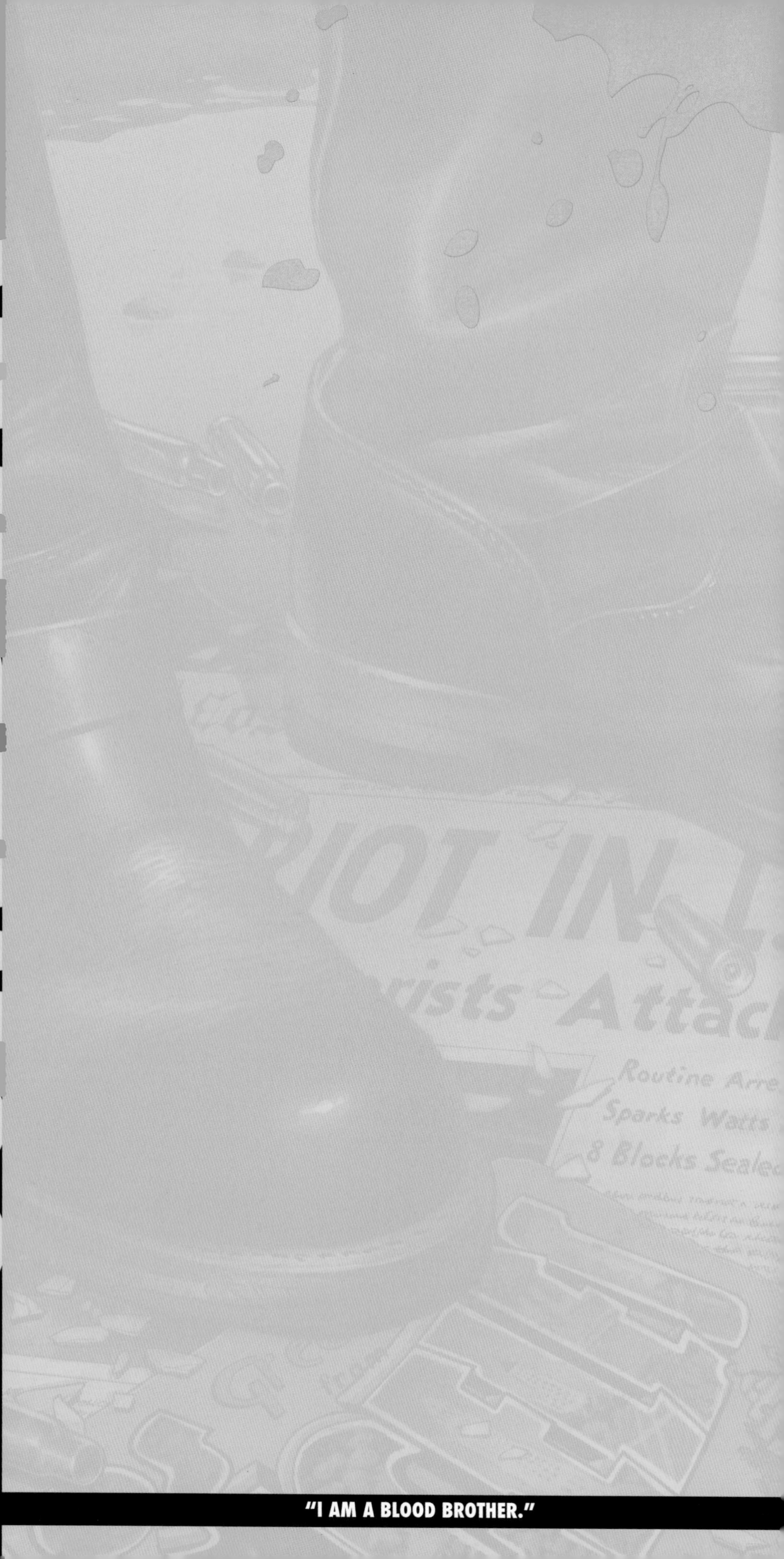

"I AM A BLOOD BROTHER."

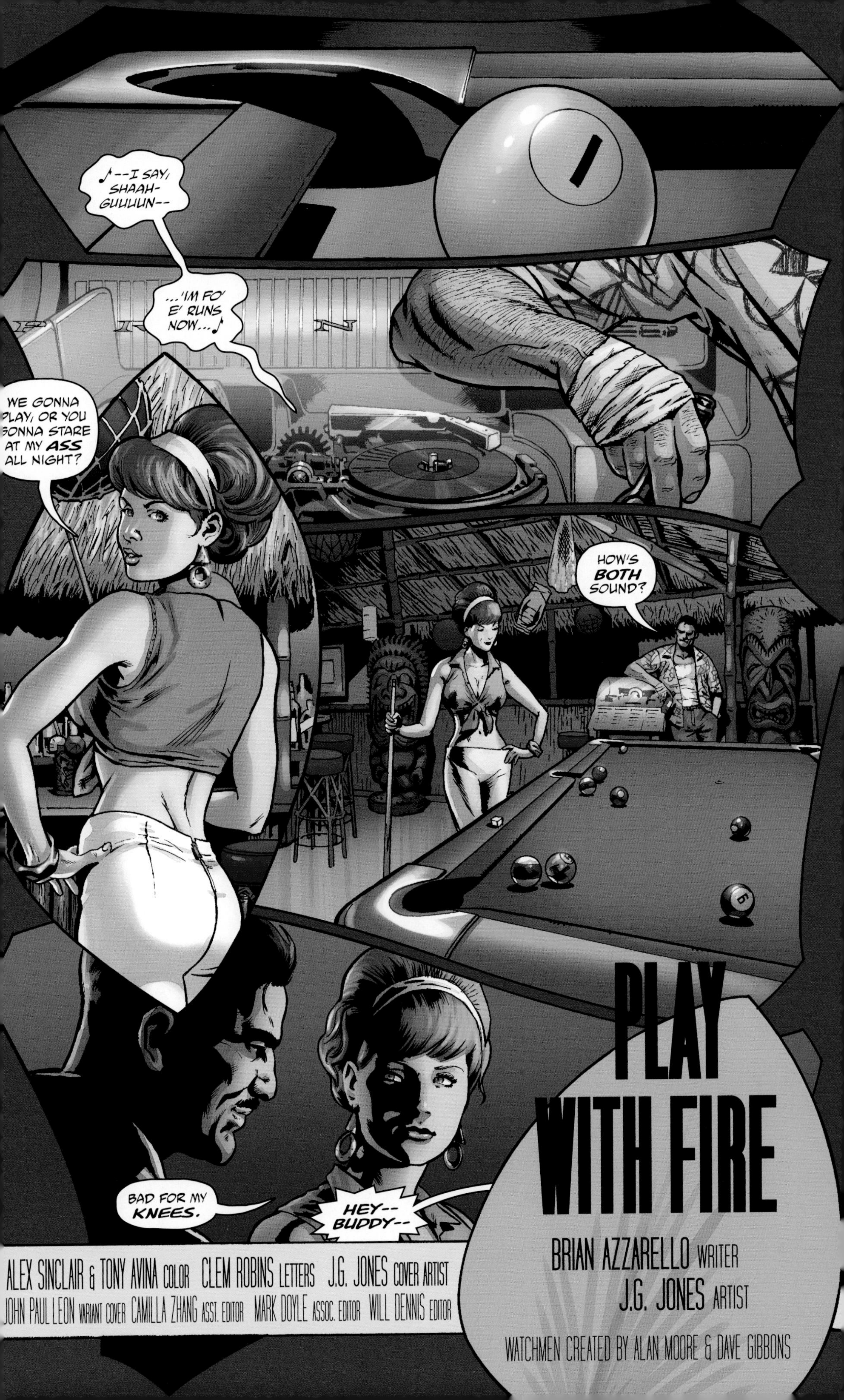

♪--I SAY, SHAAH-GUUUUN--
...'IM FO' E' RUNS NOW...♪
WE GONNA PLAY, OR YOU GONNA STARE AT MY ASS ALL NIGHT?
HOW'S BOTH SOUND?
BAD FOR MY KNEES.
HEY--BUDDY--
PLAY WITH FIRE
BRIAN AZZARELLO WRITER
J.G. JONES ARTIST
WATCHMEN CREATED BY ALAN MOORE & DAVE GIBBONS
ALEX SINCLAIR & TONY AVINA COLOR CLEM ROBINS LETTERS J.G. JONES COVER ARTIST
JOHN PAUL LEON VARIANT COVER CAMILLA ZHANG ASST. EDITOR MARK DOYLE ASSOC. EDITOR WILL DENNIS EDITOR

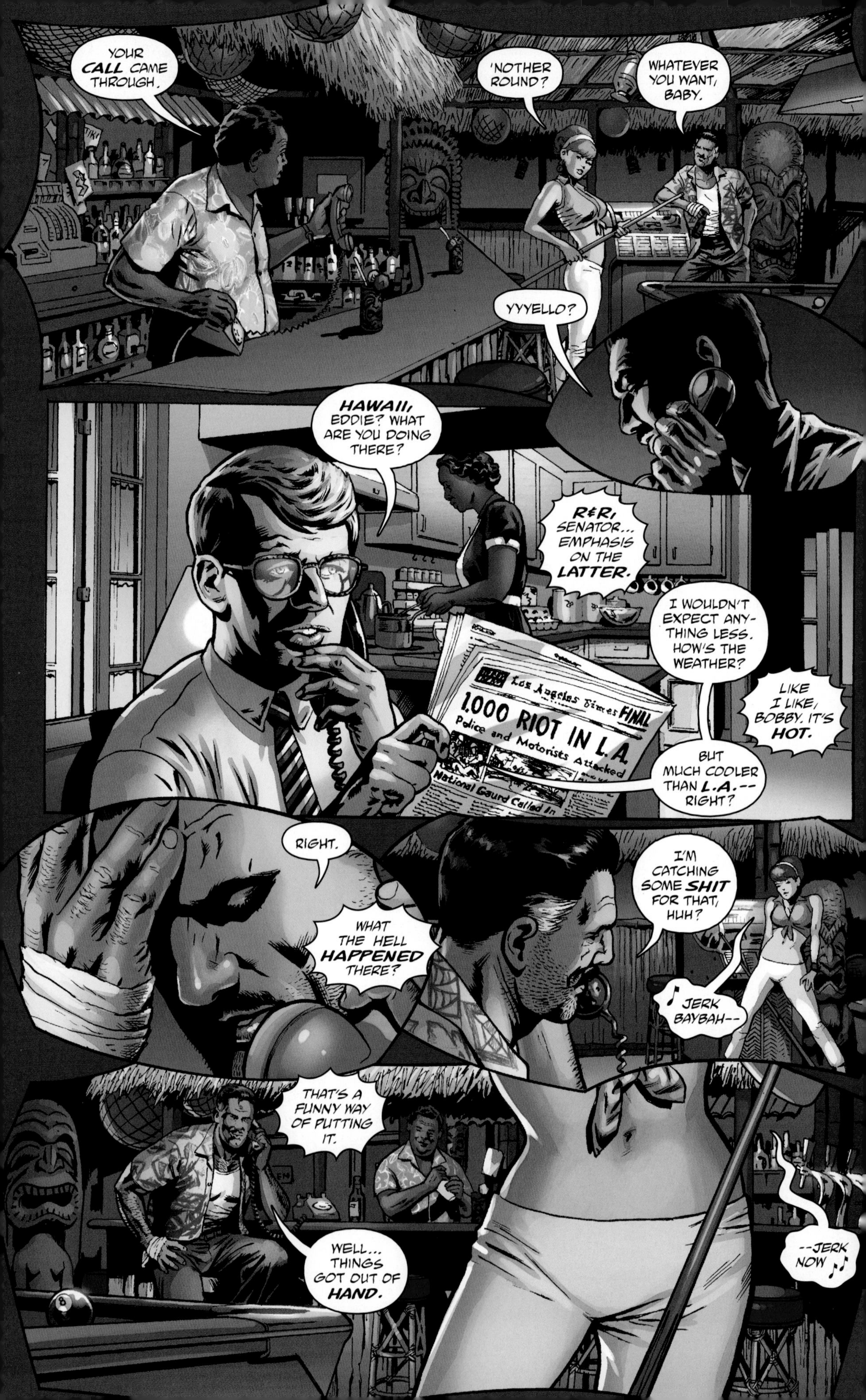

YOUR **CALL** CAME THROUGH.
'NOTHER ROUND?
WHATEVER YOU WANT, BABY.
YYYELLO?
HAWAII, EDDIE? WHAT ARE YOU DOING THERE?
R&R, SENATOR... EMPHASIS ON THE ***LATTER.***
Los Angeles Times FINAL
1,000 RIOT IN L.A.
Police and Motorists Attacked
National Gaurd Called In
I WOULDN'T EXPECT ANYTHING LESS. HOW'S THE WEATHER?
LIKE I LIKE, BOBBY. IT'S ***HOT.***
BUT MUCH COOLER THAN ***L.A.***-- RIGHT?
RIGHT.
WHAT THE HELL ***HAPPENED*** THERE?
I'M CATCHING SOME ***SHIT*** FOR THAT, HUH?
♪ JERK BAYBAH--
WELL... THINGS GOT OUT OF ***HAND.***
THAT'S A FUNNY WAY OF PUTTING IT.
--JERK NOW ♪♪

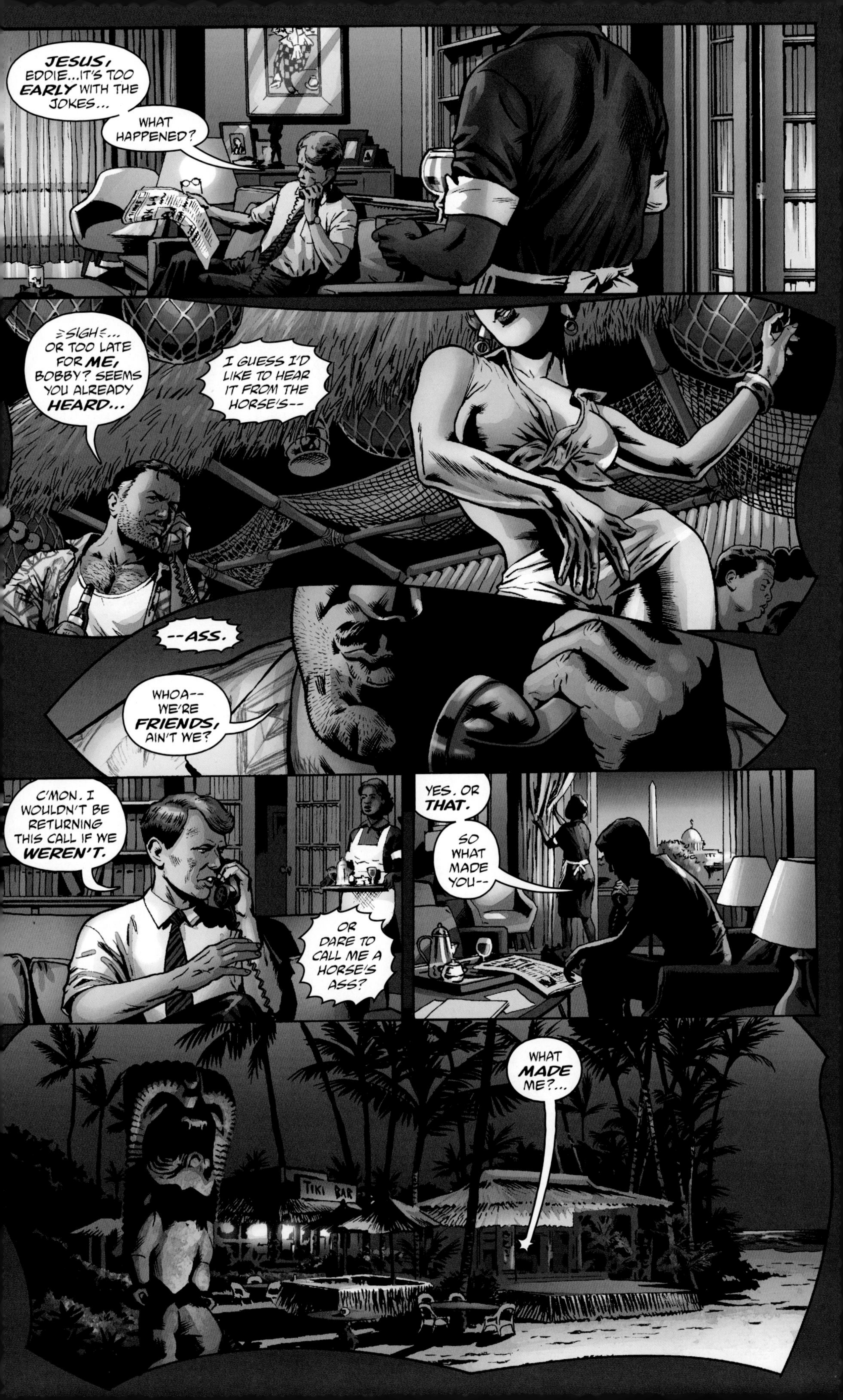
JESUS, EDDIE...IT'S TOO EARLY WITH THE JOKES...
WHAT HAPPENED?
≥SIGH≤... OR TOO LATE FOR ME, BOBBY? SEEMS YOU ALREADY HEARD...
I GUESS I'D LIKE TO HEAR IT FROM THE HORSE'S--
--ASS.
WHOA--WE'RE FRIENDS, AIN'T WE?
C'MON. I WOULDN'T BE RETURNING THIS CALL IF WE WEREN'T.
OR DARE TO CALL ME A HORSE'S ASS?
YES. OR THAT.
SO WHAT MADE YOU--
WHAT MADE ME?...
TIKI BAR

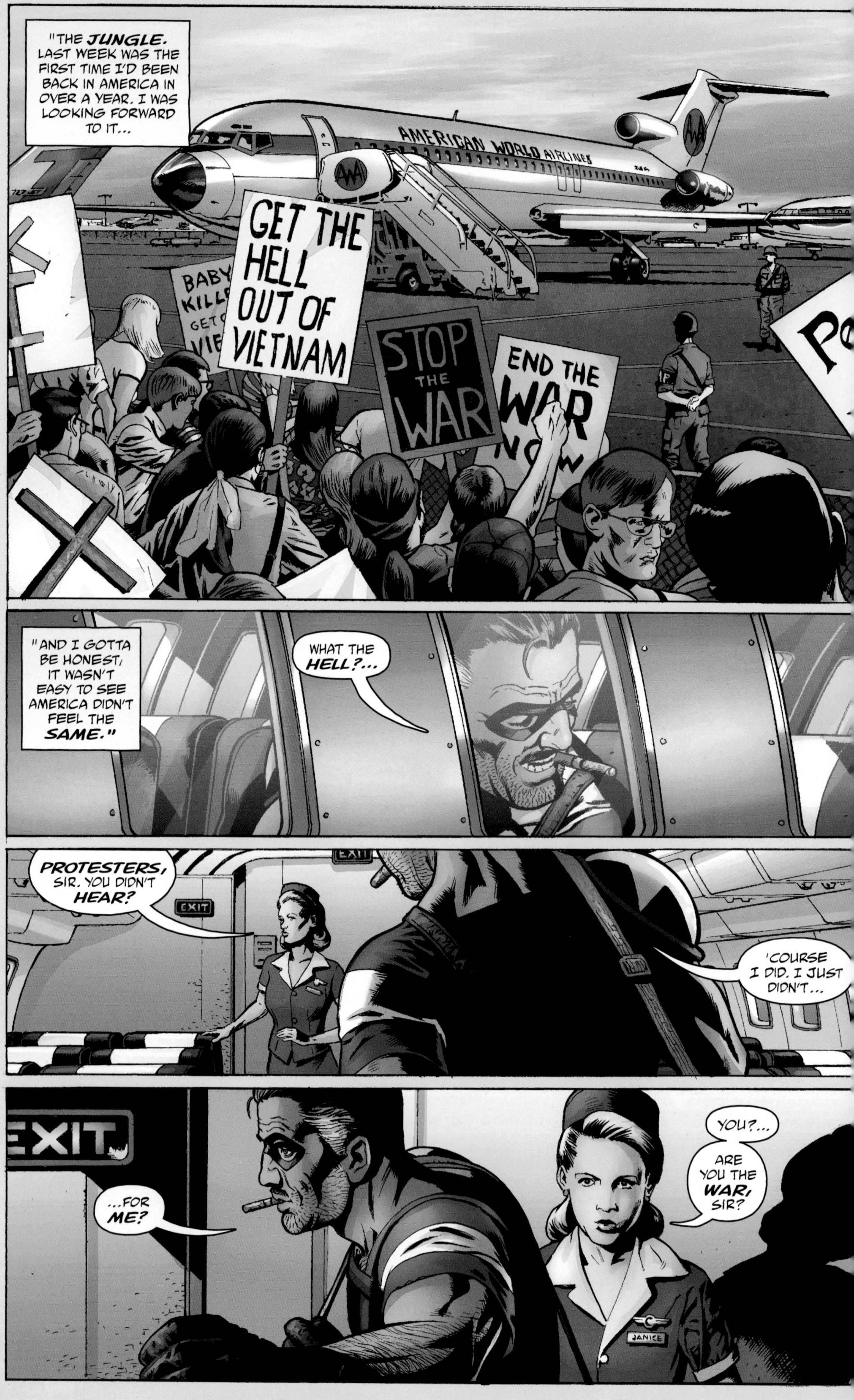
"THE JUNGLE. LAST WEEK WAS THE FIRST TIME I'D BEEN BACK IN AMERICA IN OVER A YEAR. I WAS LOOKING FORWARD TO IT...
AMERICAN WORLD AIRLINES
GET THE HELL OUT OF VIETNAM
STOP THE WAR
END THE WAR NOW
"AND I GOTTA BE HONEST, IT WASN'T EASY TO SEE AMERICA DIDN'T FEEL THE SAME."
WHAT THE HELL?...
EXIT
PROTESTERS, SIR. YOU DIDN'T HEAR?
EXIT
'COURSE I DID. I JUST DIDN'T...
EXIT
...FOR ME?
YOU?...
ARE YOU THE WAR, SIR?

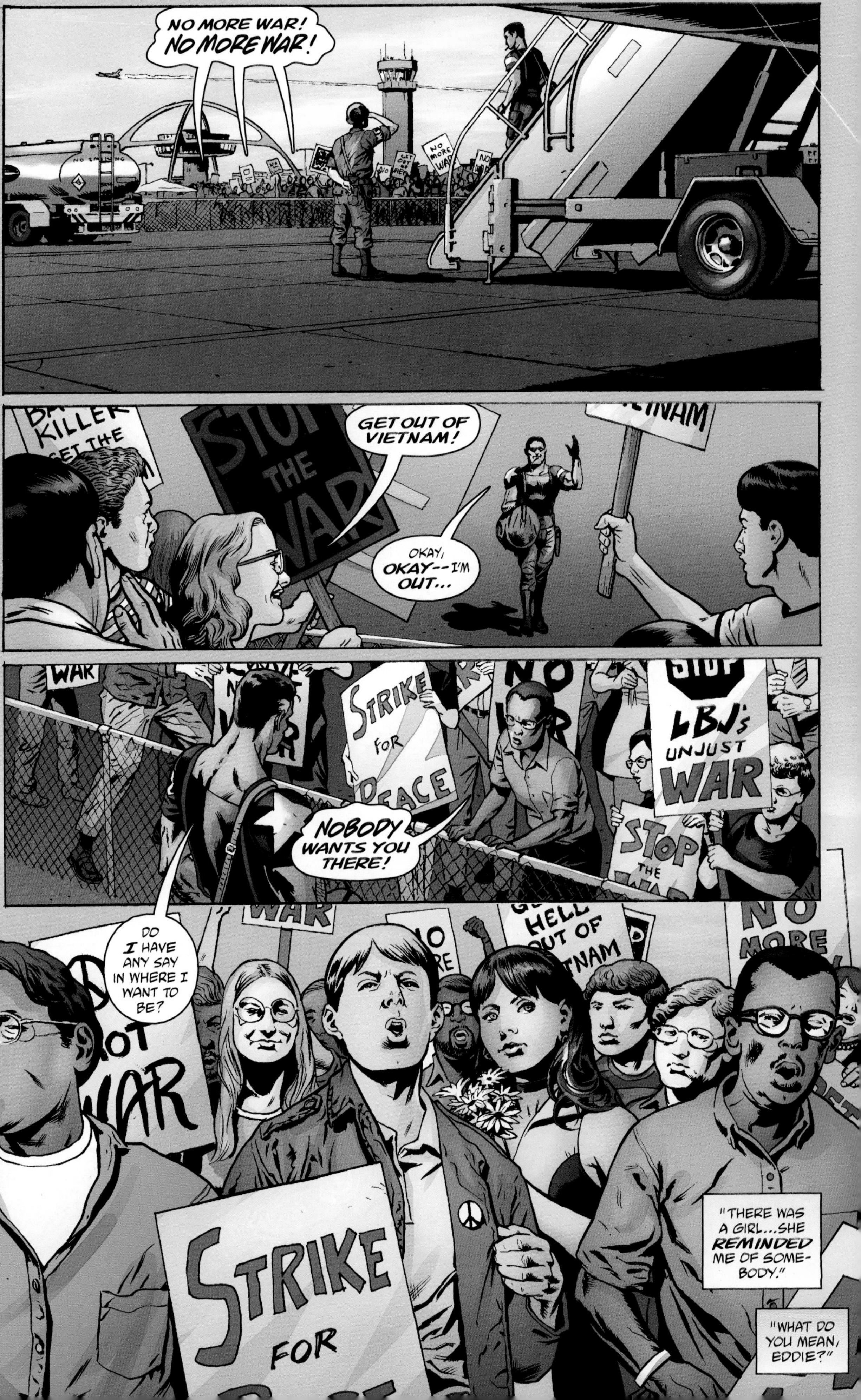
NO MORE WAR! NO MORE WAR!
GET OUT OF VIETNAM!
OKAY, OKAY--I'M OUT...
NOBODY WANTS YOU THERE!
DO I HAVE ANY SAY IN WHERE I WANT TO BE?
"THERE WAS A GIRL...SHE REMINDED ME OF SOME-BODY."
"WHAT DO YOU MEAN, EDDIE?"

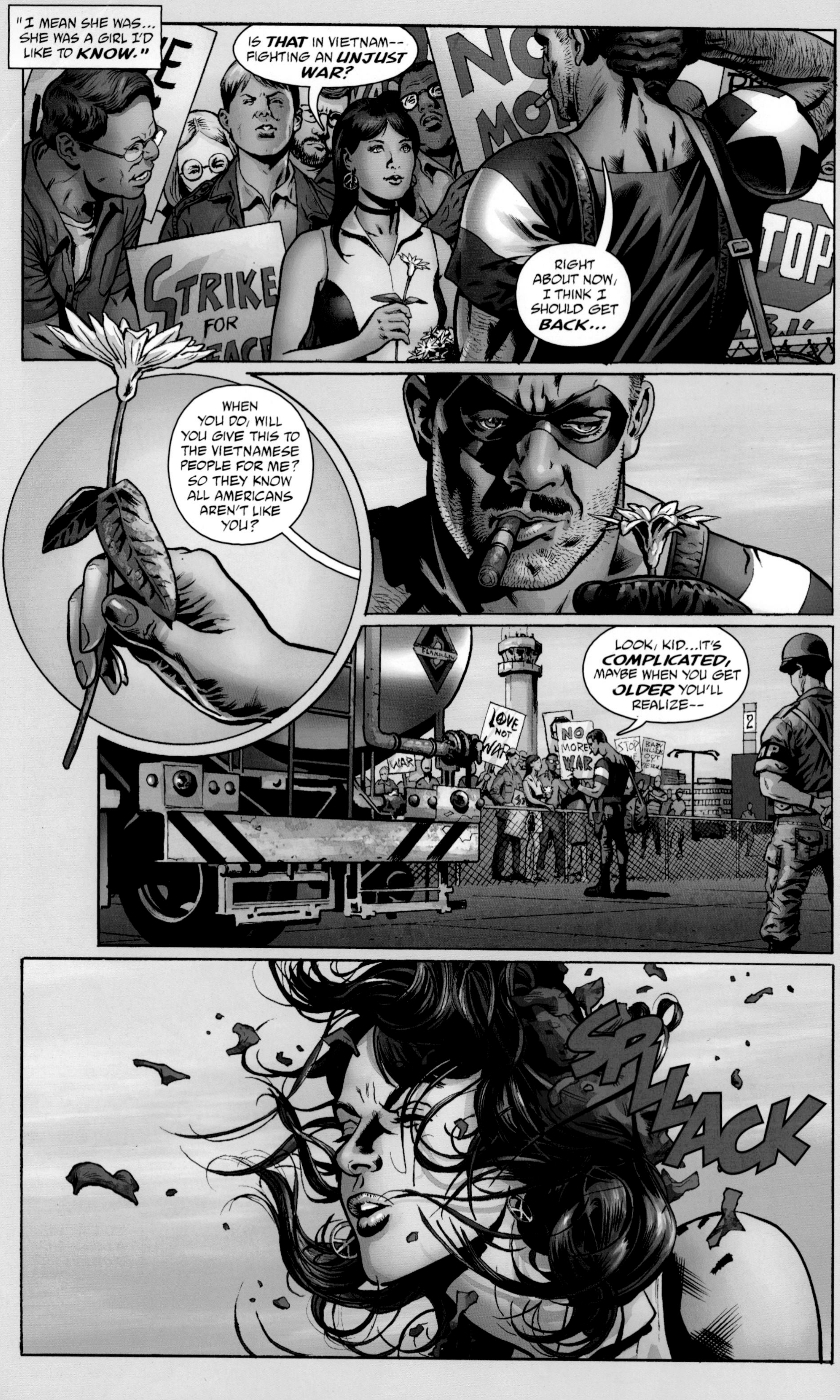

"I MEAN SHE WAS... SHE WAS A GIRL I'D LIKE TO **KNOW.**"
IS **THAT** IN VIETNAM-- FIGHTING AN **UNJUST WAR?**
NO MO
STRIKE FOR
STOP
RIGHT ABOUT NOW, I THINK I SHOULD GET **BACK...**
WHEN YOU DO, WILL YOU GIVE THIS TO THE VIETNAMESE PEOPLE FOR ME? SO THEY KNOW ALL AMERICANS AREN'T LIKE YOU?
LOOK, KID...IT'S **COMPLICATED,** MAYBE WHEN YOU GET **OLDER** YOU'LL REALIZE--
LOVE NOT WAR
NO MORE WAR
WAR
SPLLACK

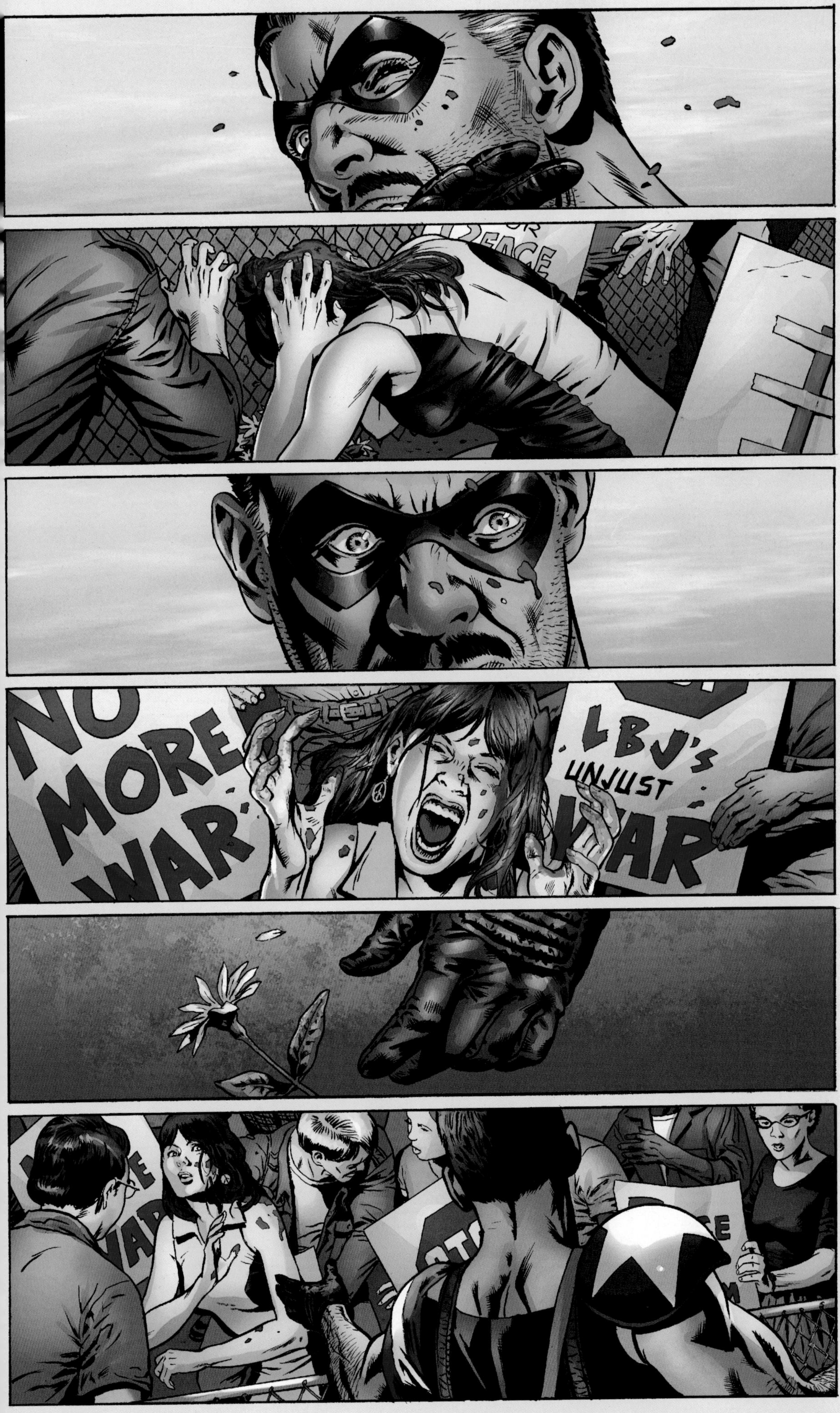
NO
MORE
LBJ's
UNJUST

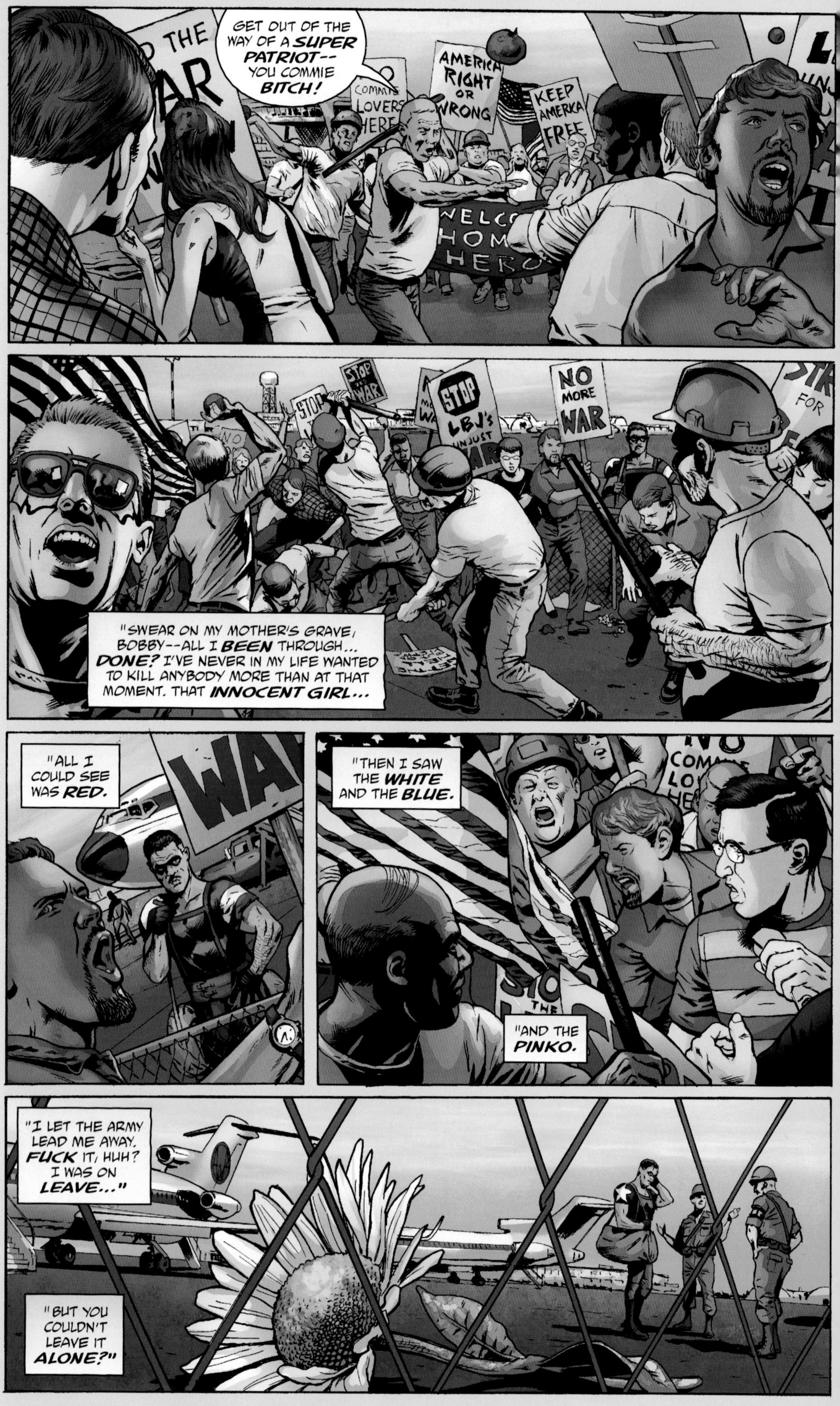

GET OUT OF THE WAY OF A SUPER PATRIOT-- YOU COMMIE BITCH!
AMERICA RIGHT OR WRONG
KEEP AMERKA FREE
COMMIE LOVERS HERE
WELCOME HOME HERO
STOP THE WAR
STOP LBJ's UNJUST WAR
NO MORE WAR
"SWEAR ON MY MOTHER'S GRAVE, BOBBY--ALL I BEEN THROUGH... DONE? I'VE NEVER IN MY LIFE WANTED TO KILL ANYBODY MORE THAN AT THAT MOMENT. THAT INNOCENT GIRL...
"ALL I COULD SEE WAS RED.
WAR
"THEN I SAW THE WHITE AND THE BLUE.
"AND THE PINKO.
"I LET THE ARMY LEAD ME AWAY. FUCK IT, HUH? I WAS ON LEAVE..."
"BUT YOU COULDN'T LEAVE IT ALONE?"

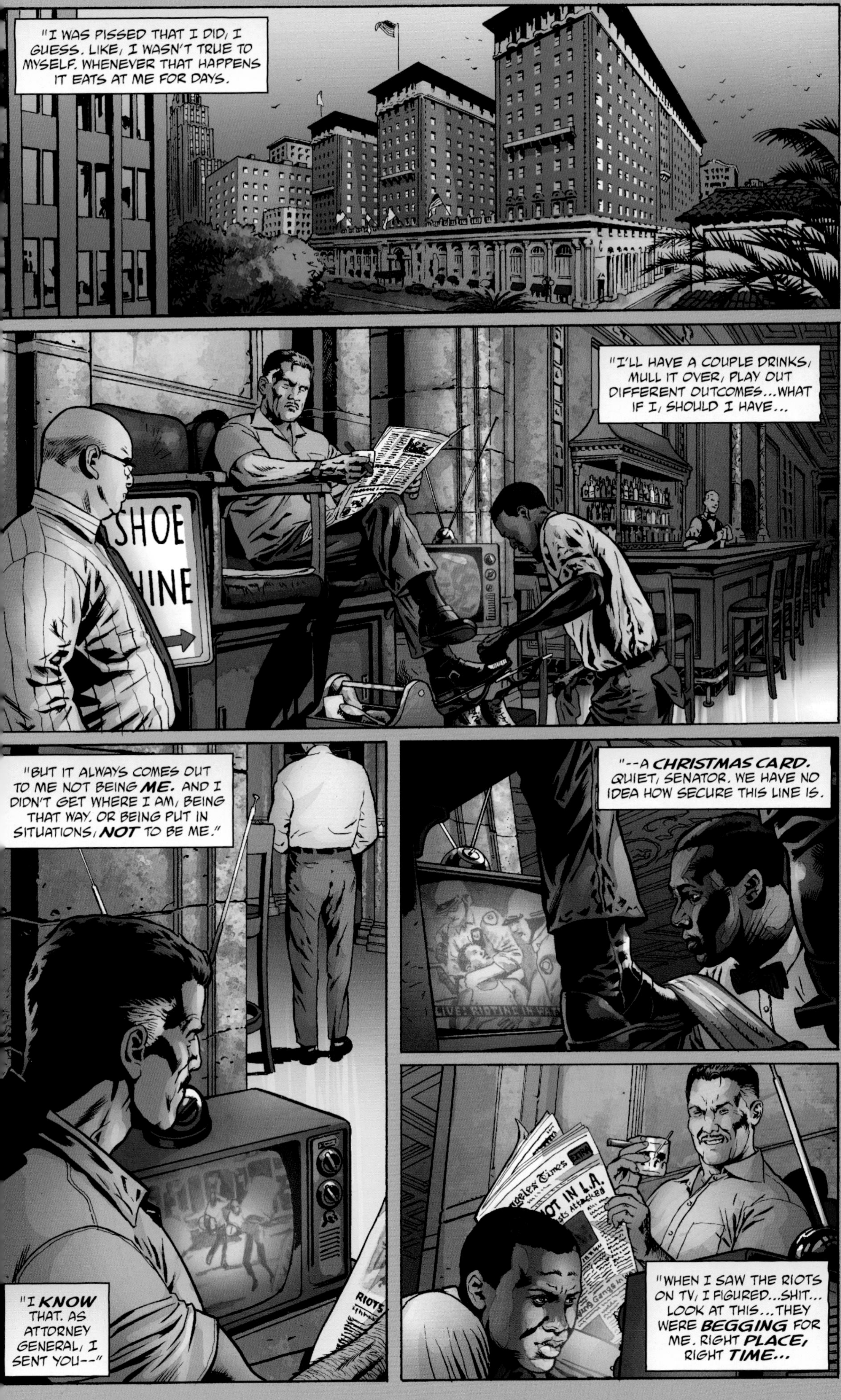
"I WAS PISSED THAT I DID, I GUESS. LIKE, I WASN'T TRUE TO MYSELF. WHENEVER THAT HAPPENS IT EATS AT ME FOR DAYS.
"I'LL HAVE A COUPLE DRINKS, MULL IT OVER, PLAY OUT DIFFERENT OUTCOMES...WHAT IF I, SHOULD I HAVE...
SHOE
HINE
"BUT IT ALWAYS COMES OUT TO ME NOT BEING ME. AND I DIDN'T GET WHERE I AM, BEING THAT WAY. OR BEING PUT IN SITUATIONS, NOT TO BE ME."
"I KNOW THAT. AS ATTORNEY GENERAL, I SENT YOU--"
"--A CHRISTMAS CARD. QUIET, SENATOR. WE HAVE NO IDEA HOW SECURE THIS LINE IS.
"WHEN I SAW THE RIOTS ON TV, I FIGURED...SHIT... LOOK AT THIS...THEY WERE BEGGING FOR ME. RIGHT PLACE, RIGHT TIME...

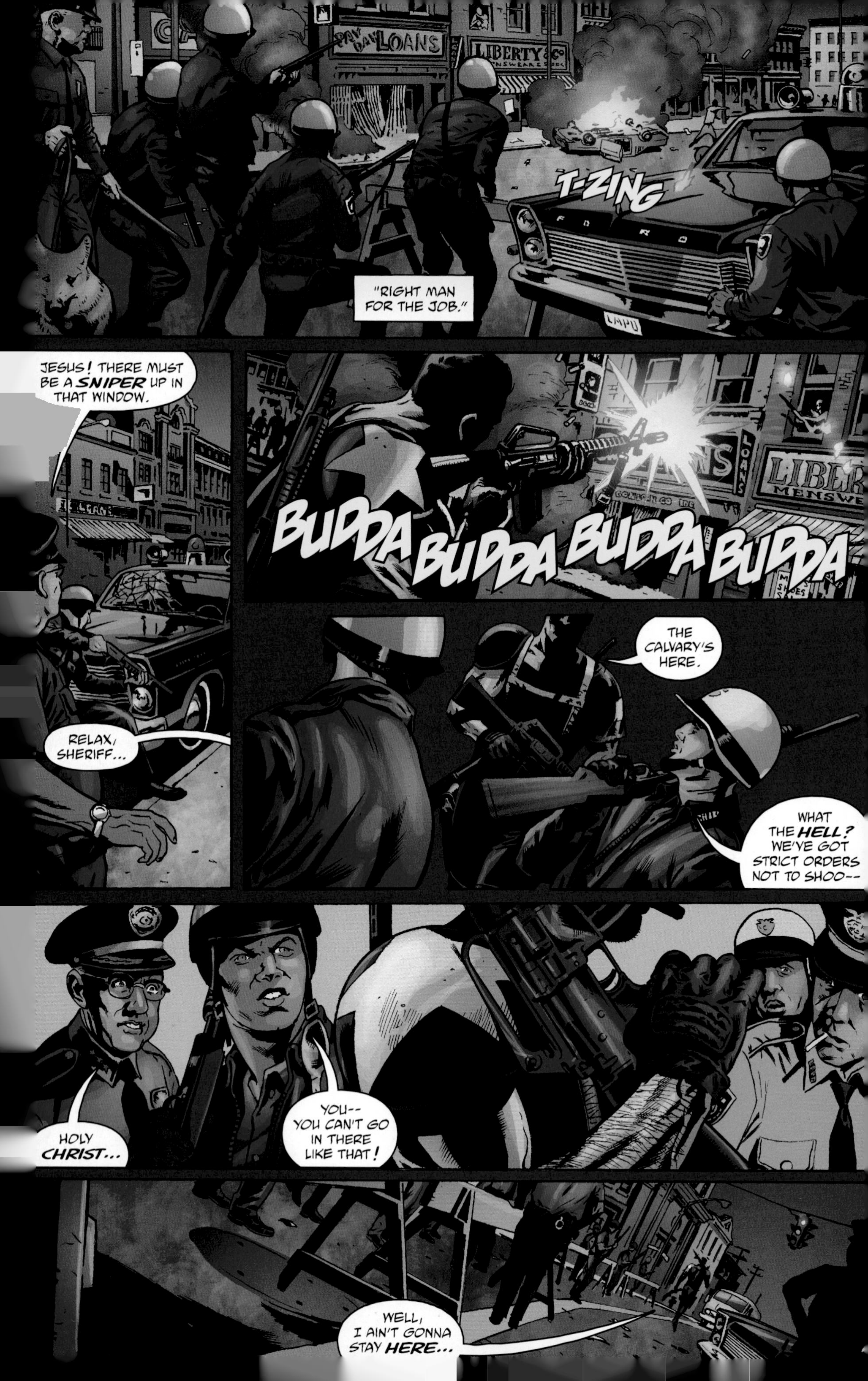

T-ZING
"RIGHT MAN FOR THE JOB."
JESUS! THERE MUST BE A SNIPER UP IN THAT WINDOW.
RELAX, SHERIFF...
BUDDA BUDDA BUDDA BUDDA
THE CALVARY'S HERE.
WHAT THE HELL? WE'VE GOT STRICT ORDERS NOT TO SHOO--
HOLY CHRIST...
YOU-- YOU CAN'T GO IN THERE LIKE THAT!
WELL, I AIN'T GONNA STAY HERE...

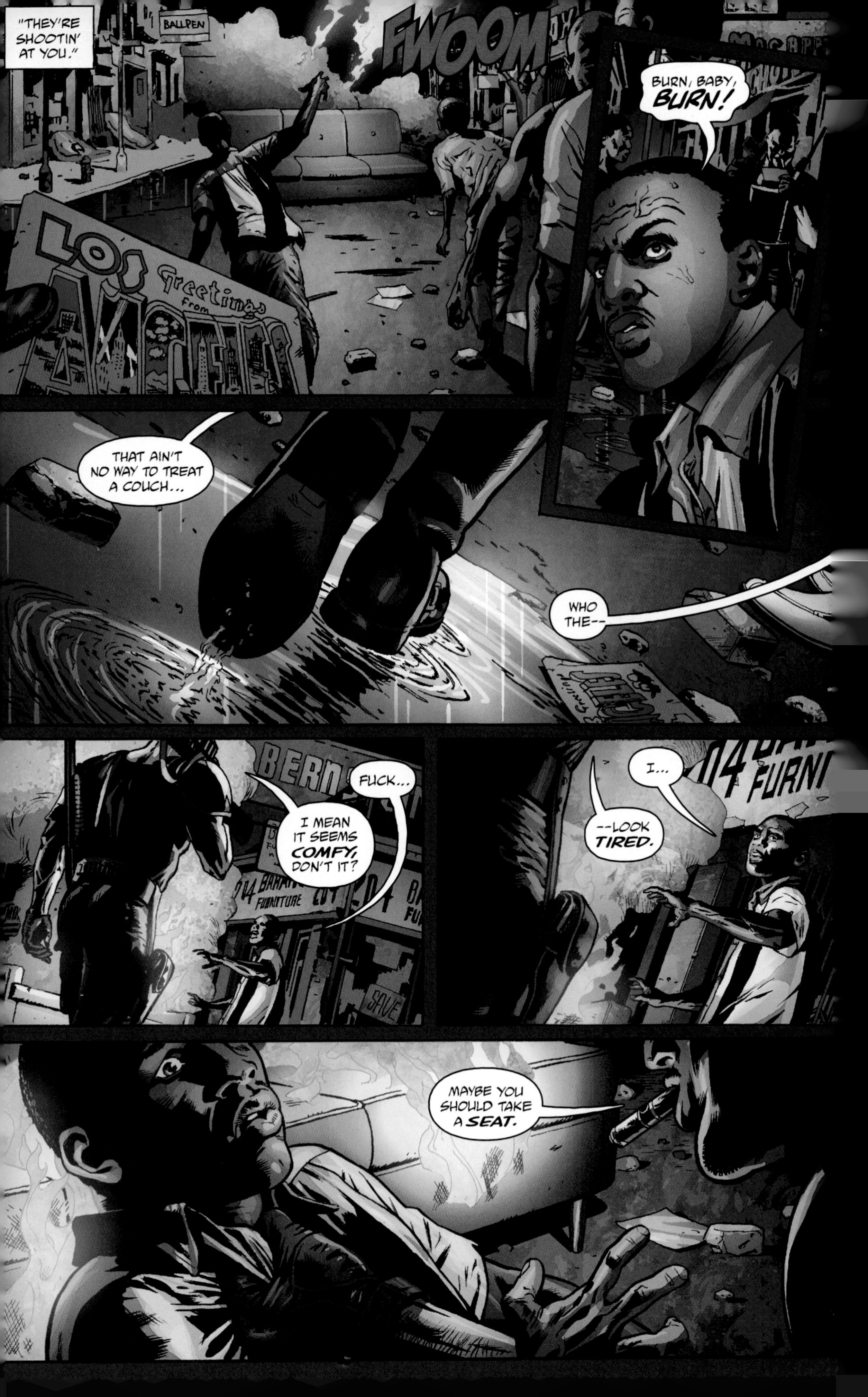
"THEY'RE SHOOTIN' AT YOU."
FWOOM
BALLPEN
BURN, BABY, BURN!
THAT AIN'T NO WAY TO TREAT A COUCH...
WHO THE--
FUCK...
I MEAN IT SEEMS COMFY, DON'T IT?
I...
--LOOK TIRED.
MAYBE YOU SHOULD TAKE A SEAT.

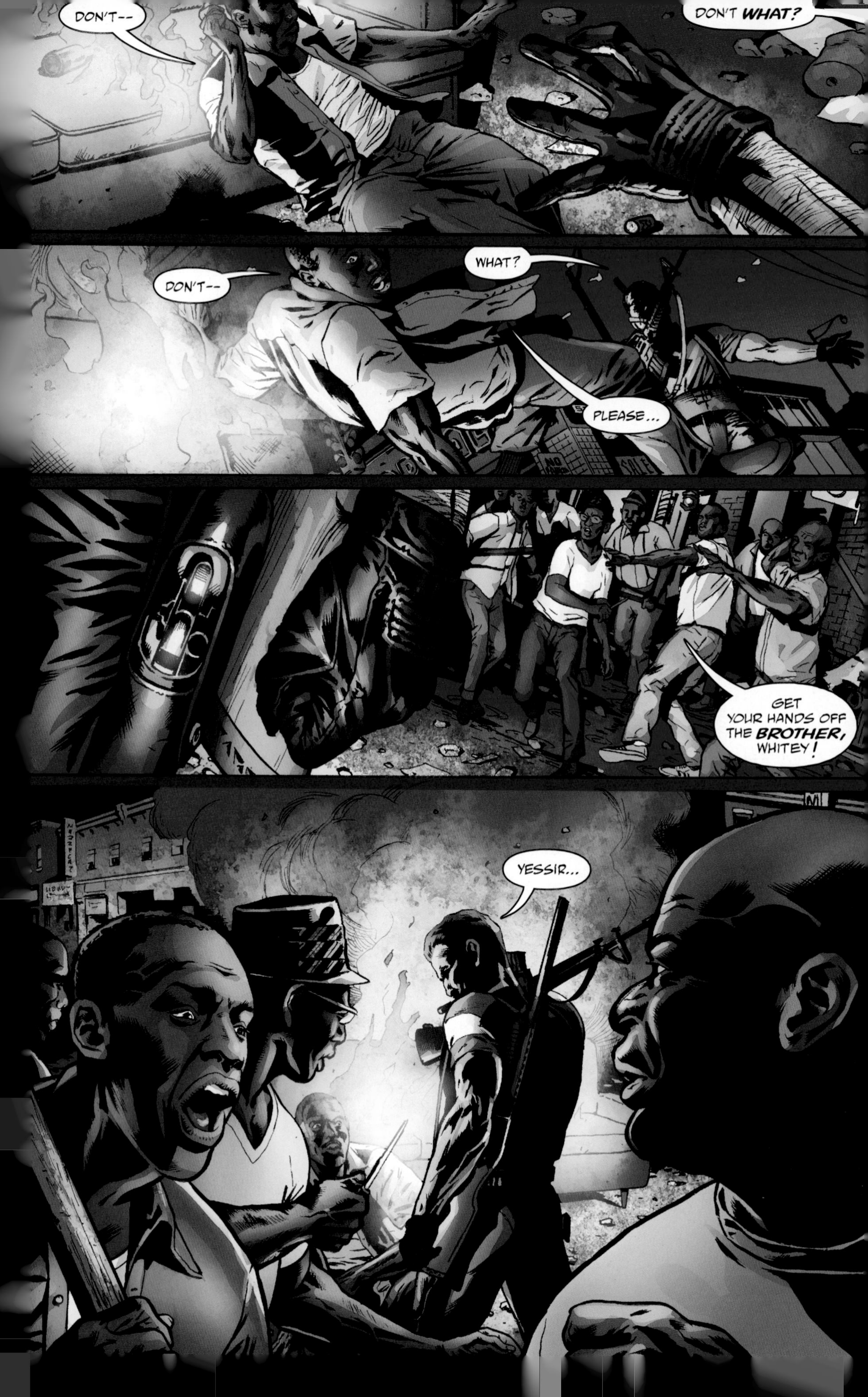
DON'T--
DON'T WHAT?
DON'T--
WHAT?
PLEASE...
GET YOUR HANDS OFF THE BROTHER, WHITEY!
YESSIR...

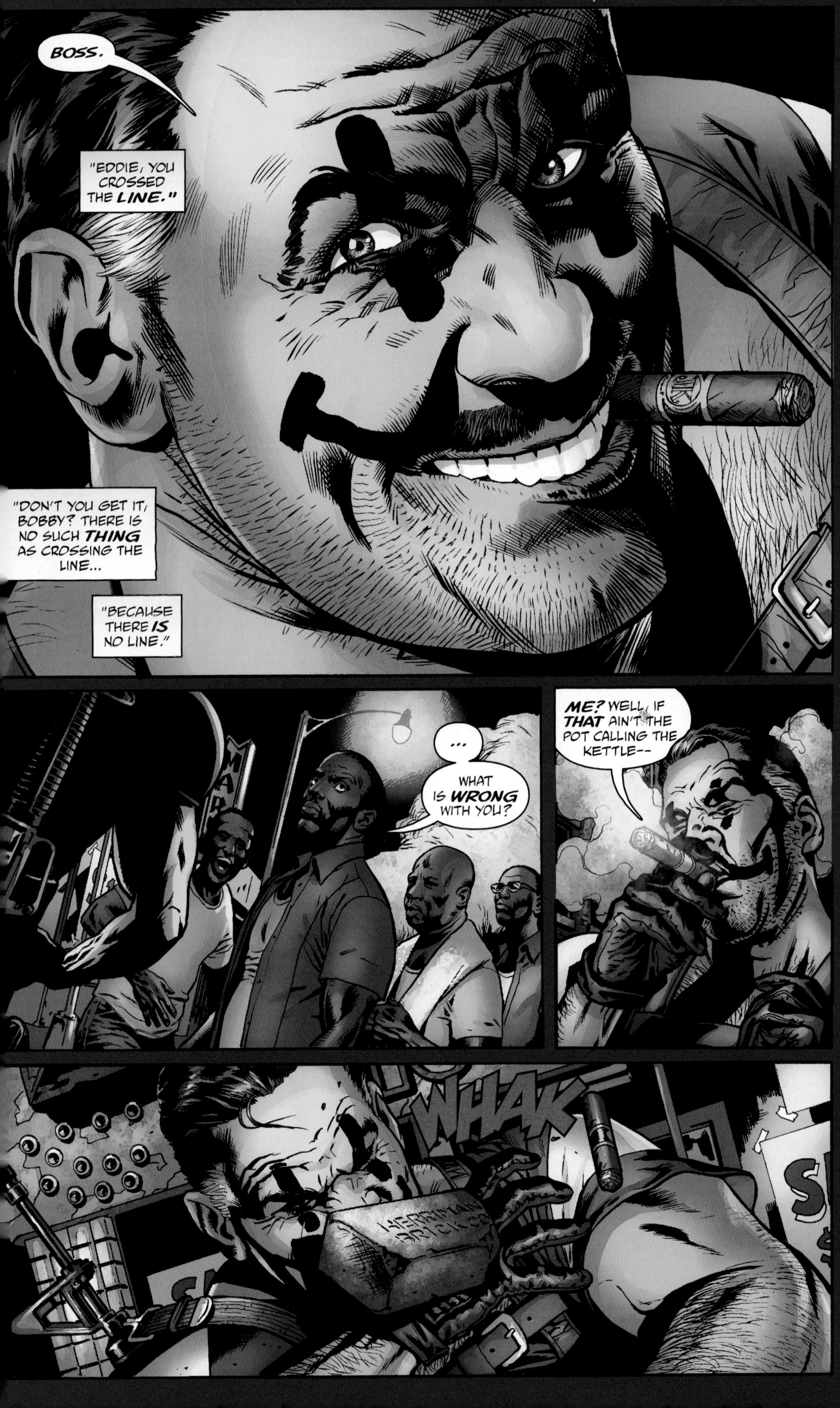
BOSS.
"EDDIE, YOU CROSSED THE LINE."
"DON'T YOU GET IT, BOBBY? THERE IS NO SUCH THING AS CROSSING THE LINE...
"BECAUSE THERE IS NO LINE."
...
WHAT IS WRONG WITH YOU?
ME? WELL, IF THAT AIN'T THE POT CALLING THE KETTLE--
WHAK

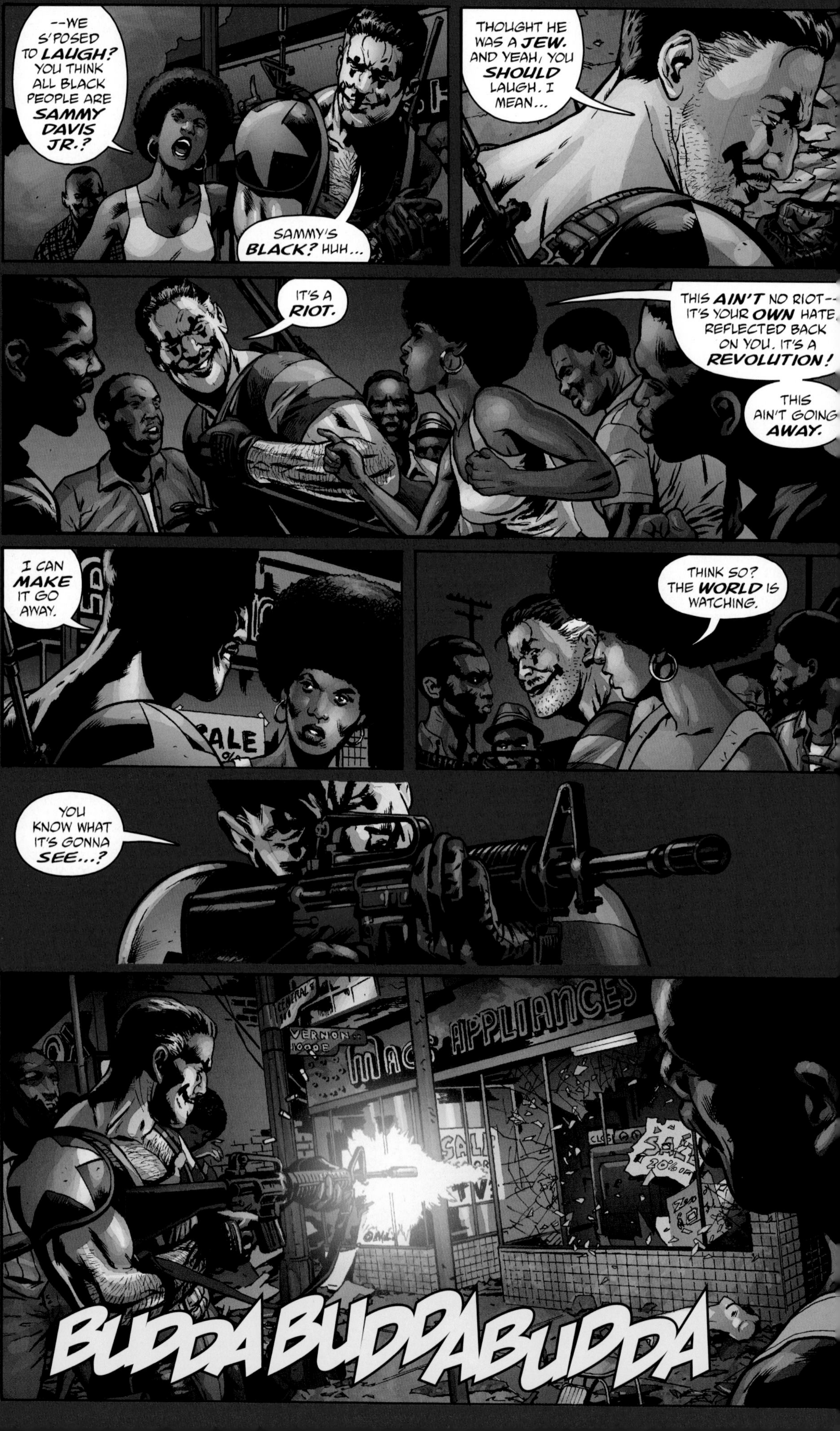

--WE S'POSED TO LAUGH? YOU THINK ALL BLACK PEOPLE ARE SAMMY DAVIS JR.?
SAMMY'S BLACK? HUH...
THOUGHT HE WAS A JEW. AND YEAH, YOU SHOULD LAUGH. I MEAN...
IT'S A RIOT.
THIS AIN'T NO RIOT-- IT'S YOUR OWN HATE REFLECTED BACK ON YOU. IT'S A REVOLUTION!
THIS AIN'T GOING AWAY.
I CAN MAKE IT GO AWAY.
SALE
THINK SO? THE WORLD IS WATCHING.
YOU KNOW WHAT IT'S GONNA SEE...?
VERNON
MAC'S APPLIANCES
BUDDABUDDABUDDA

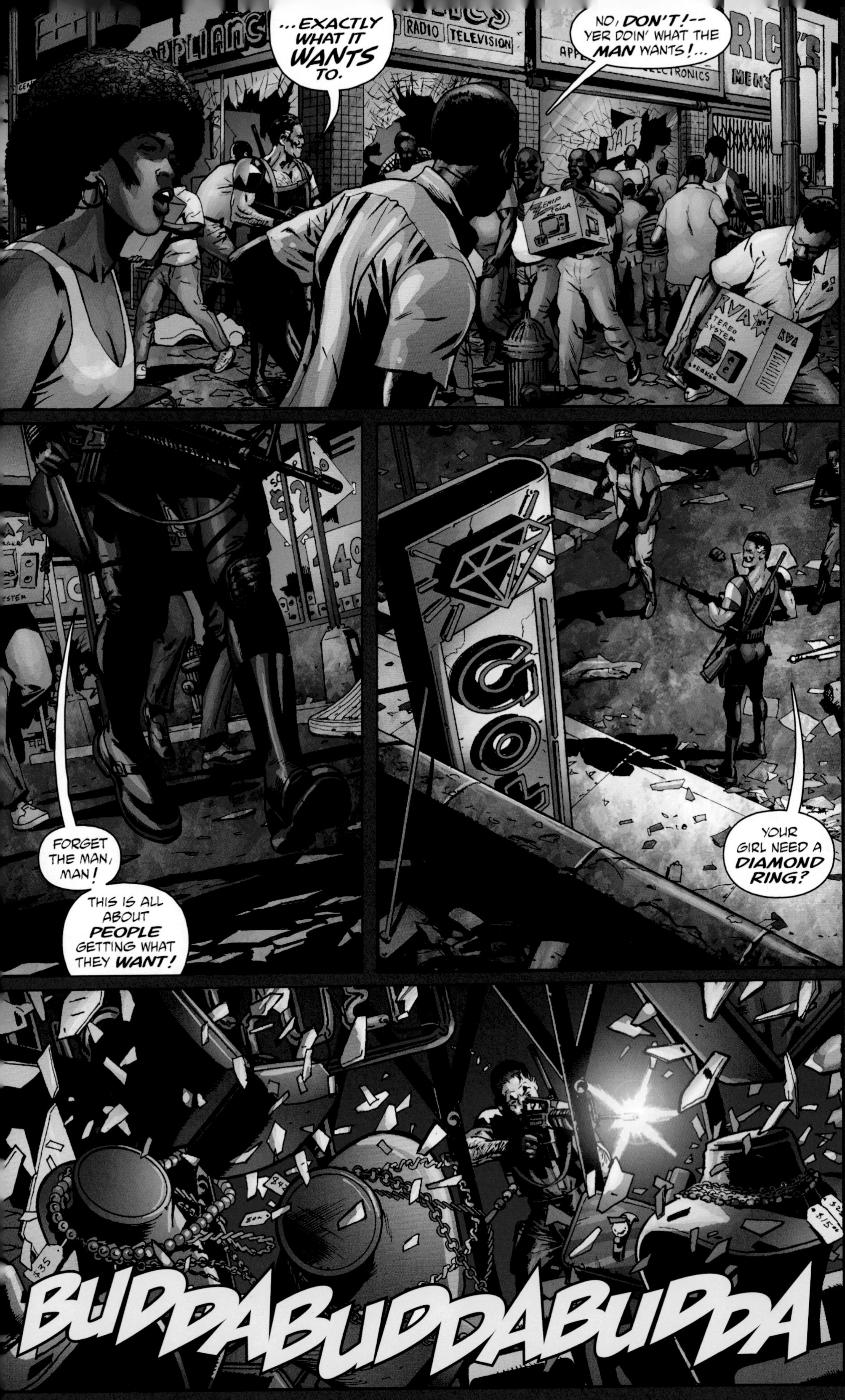
APPLIANCES
RADIO
TELEVISION
...EXACTLY WHAT IT WANTS TO.
NO, DON'T!-- YER DOIN' WHAT THE MAN WANTS!...
ELECTRONICS
RICK'S
MEN'S
SALE
RVA
STEREO SYSTEM
FORGET THE MAN, MAN!
THIS IS ALL ABOUT PEOPLE GETTING WHAT THEY WANT!
YOUR GIRL NEED A DIAMOND RING?
BUDDABUDDABUDDA

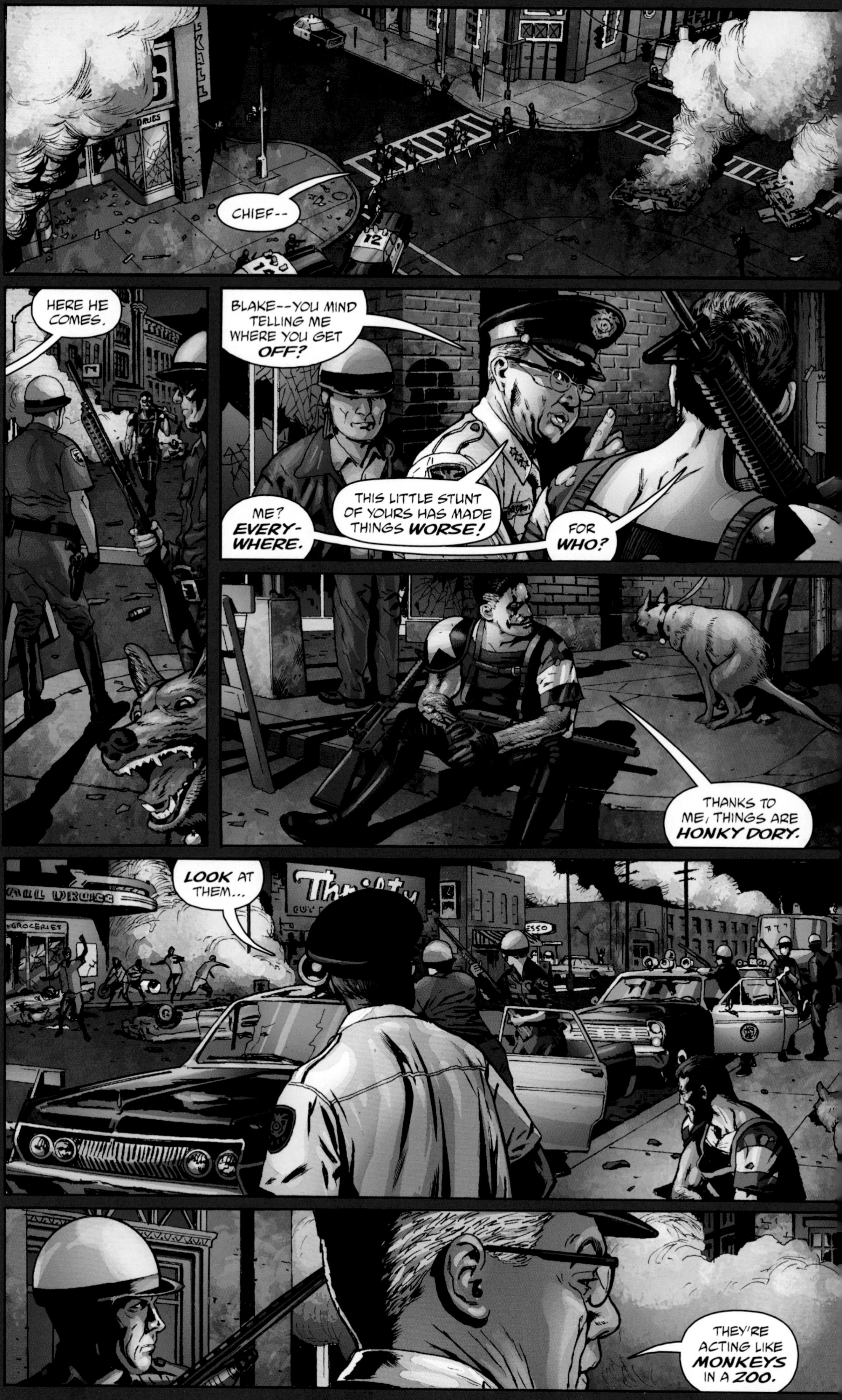

CHIEF--
HERE HE COMES.
BLAKE--YOU MIND TELLING ME WHERE YOU GET OFF?
ME? EVERYWHERE.
THIS LITTLE STUNT OF YOURS HAS MADE THINGS WORSE!
FOR WHO?
THANKS TO ME, THINGS ARE HONKY DORY.
LOOK AT THEM...
THEY'RE ACTING LIKE MONKEYS IN A ZOO.

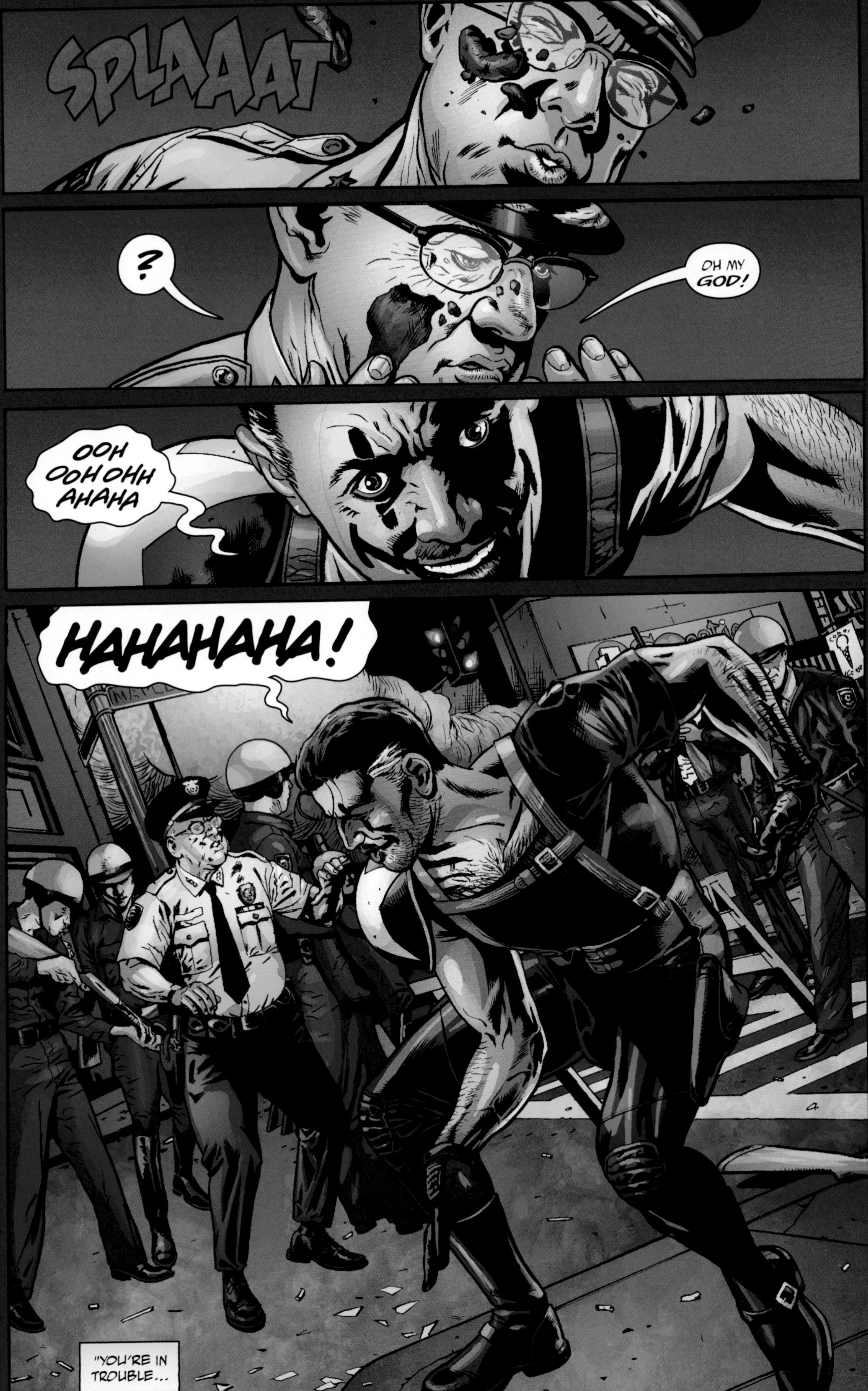
SPLAAAT
?
OH MY GOD!
OOH OOH OHH AHAHA
HAHAHAHA!
"YOU'RE IN TROUBLE...

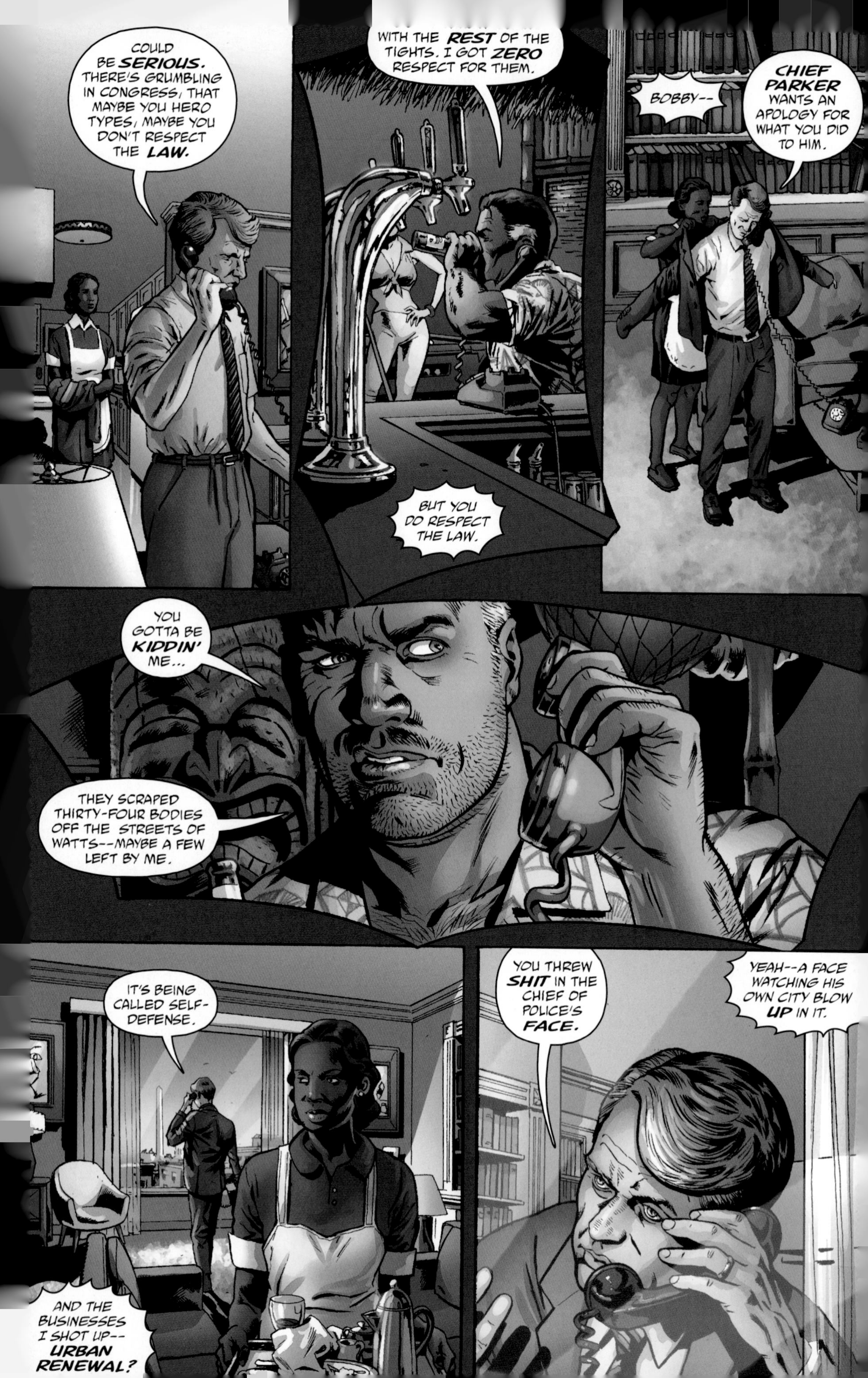

COULD BE SERIOUS. THERE'S GRUMBLING IN CONGRESS, THAT MAYBE YOU HERO TYPES, MAYBE YOU DON'T RESPECT THE LAW.
WITH THE REST OF THE TIGHTS. I GOT ZERO RESPECT FOR THEM.
BUT YOU DO RESPECT THE LAW.
BOBBY--
CHIEF PARKER WANTS AN APOLOGY FOR WHAT YOU DID TO HIM.
YOU GOTTA BE KIDDIN' ME...
THEY SCRAPED THIRTY-FOUR BODIES OFF THE STREETS OF WATTS--MAYBE A FEW LEFT BY ME.
IT'S BEING CALLED SELF-DEFENSE.
AND THE BUSINESSES I SHOT UP--URBAN RENEWAL?
YOU THREW SHIT IN THE CHIEF OF POLICE'S FACE.
YEAH--A FACE WATCHING HIS OWN CITY BLOW UP IN IT.

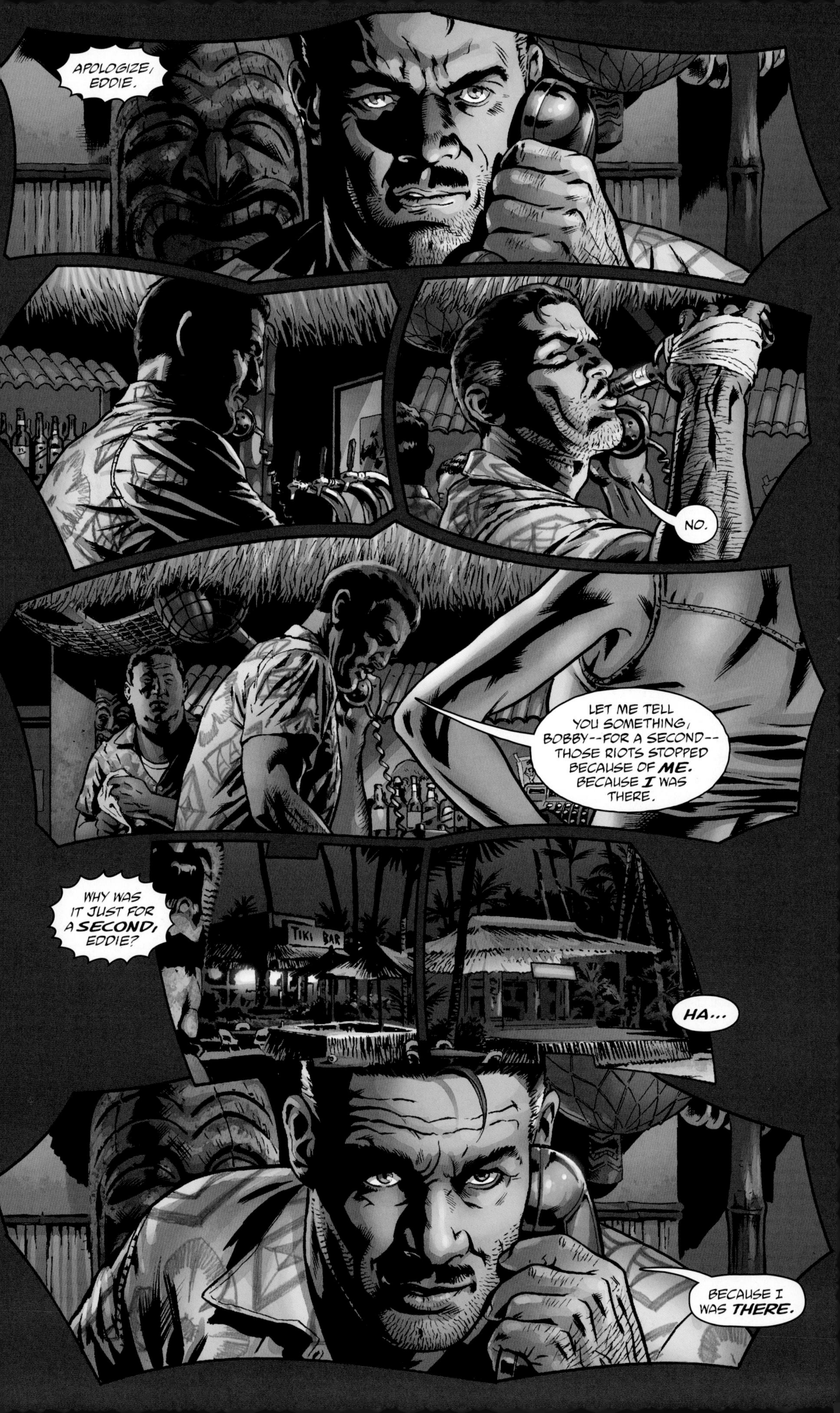

APOLOGIZE, EDDIE.
NO.
LET ME TELL YOU SOMETHING, BOBBY--FOR A SECOND--THOSE RIOTS STOPPED BECAUSE OF **ME.** BECAUSE **I** WAS THERE.
WHY WAS IT JUST FOR A **SECOND,** EDDIE?
TIKI BAR
HA...
BECAUSE I WAS **THERE.**

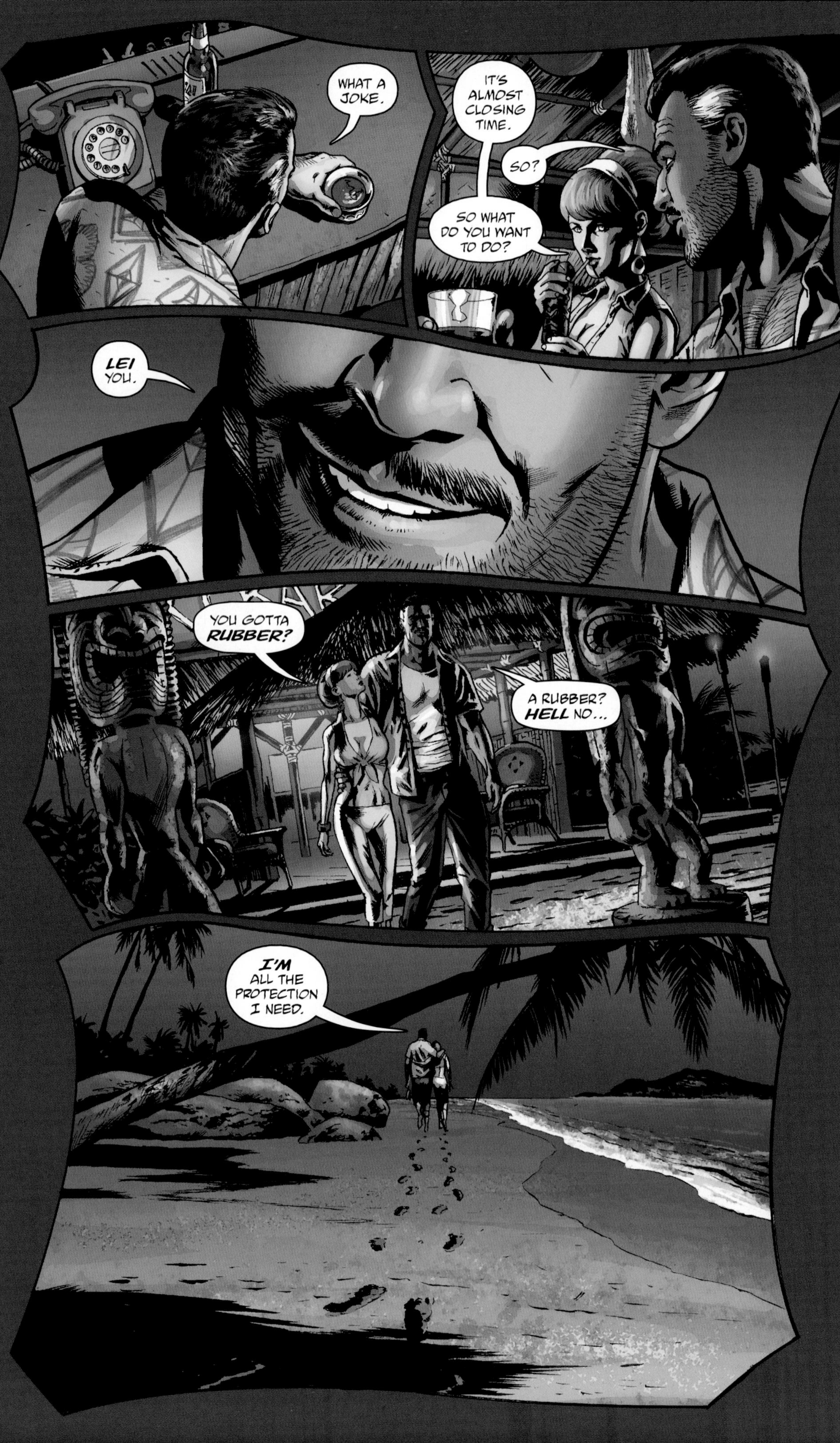
WHAT A JOKE.
IT'S ALMOST CLOSING TIME.
SO?
SO WHAT DO YOU WANT TO DO?
LEI YOU.
YOU GOTTA RUBBER?
A RUBBER? HELL NO...
I'M ALL THE PROTECTION I NEED.

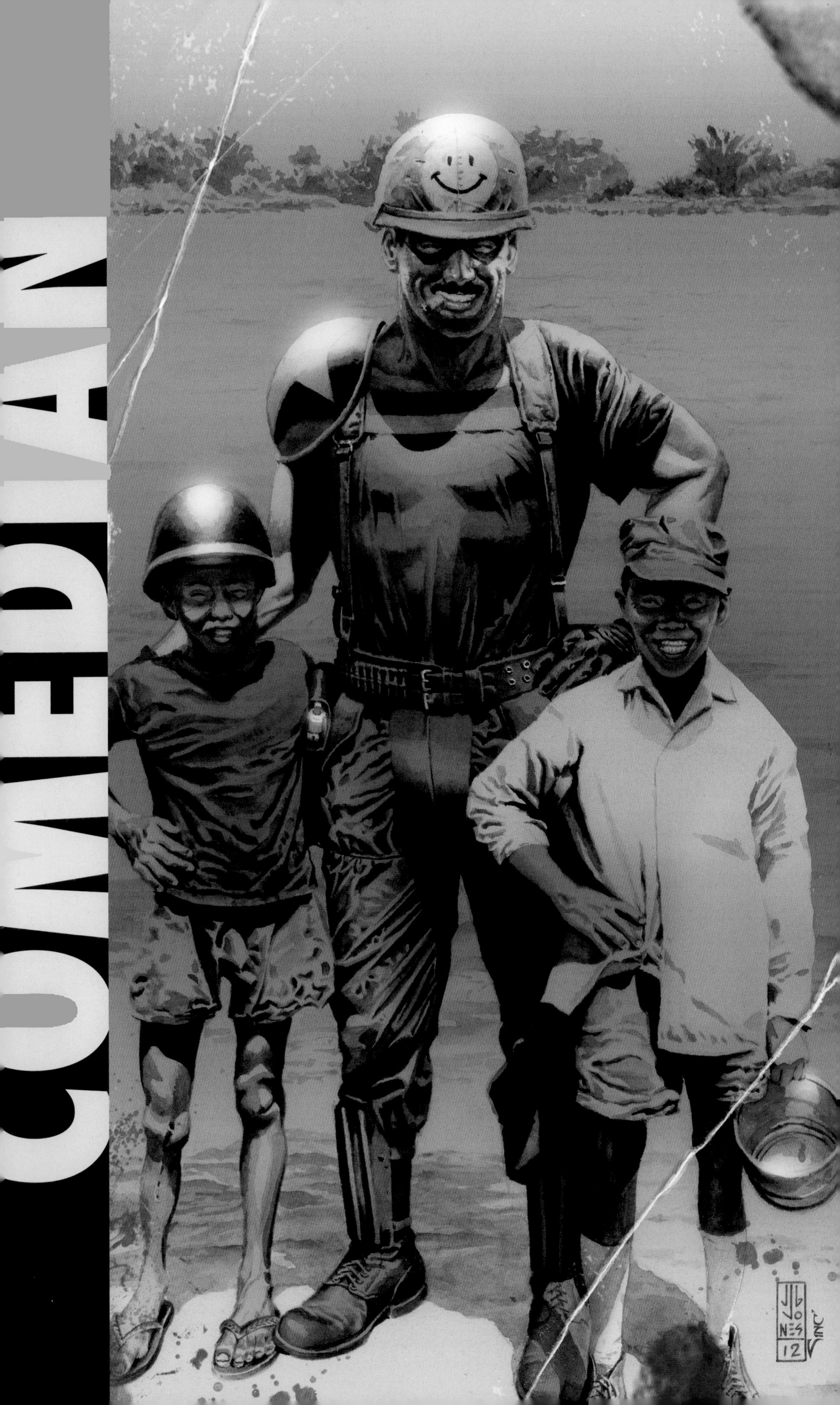
COMEDIAN

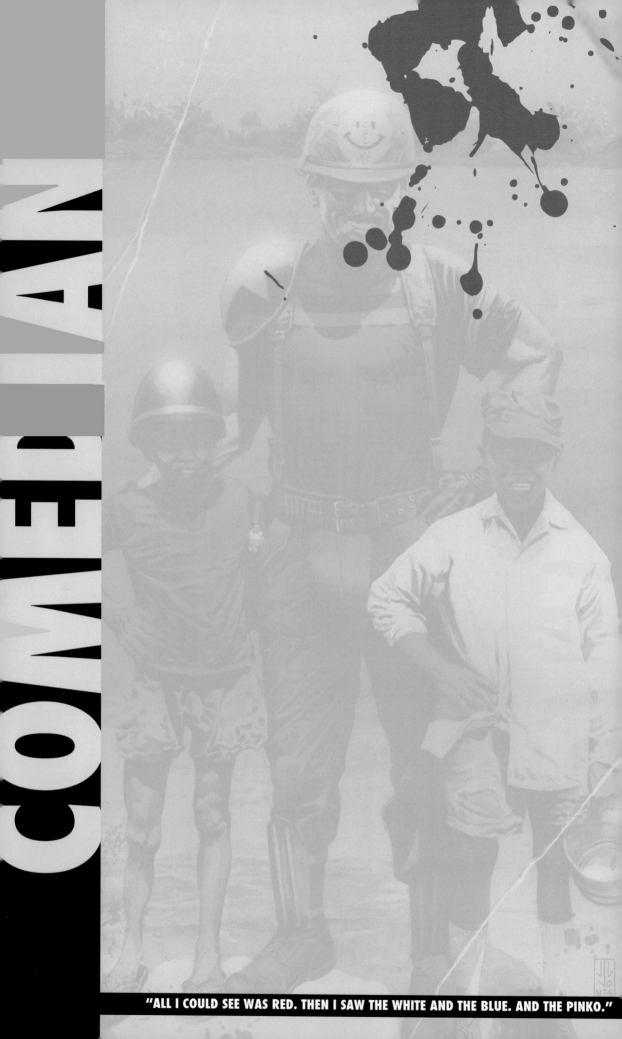

COMEDIAN

"ALL I COULD SEE WAS RED. THEN I SAW THE WHITE AND THE BLUE. AND THE PINKO."

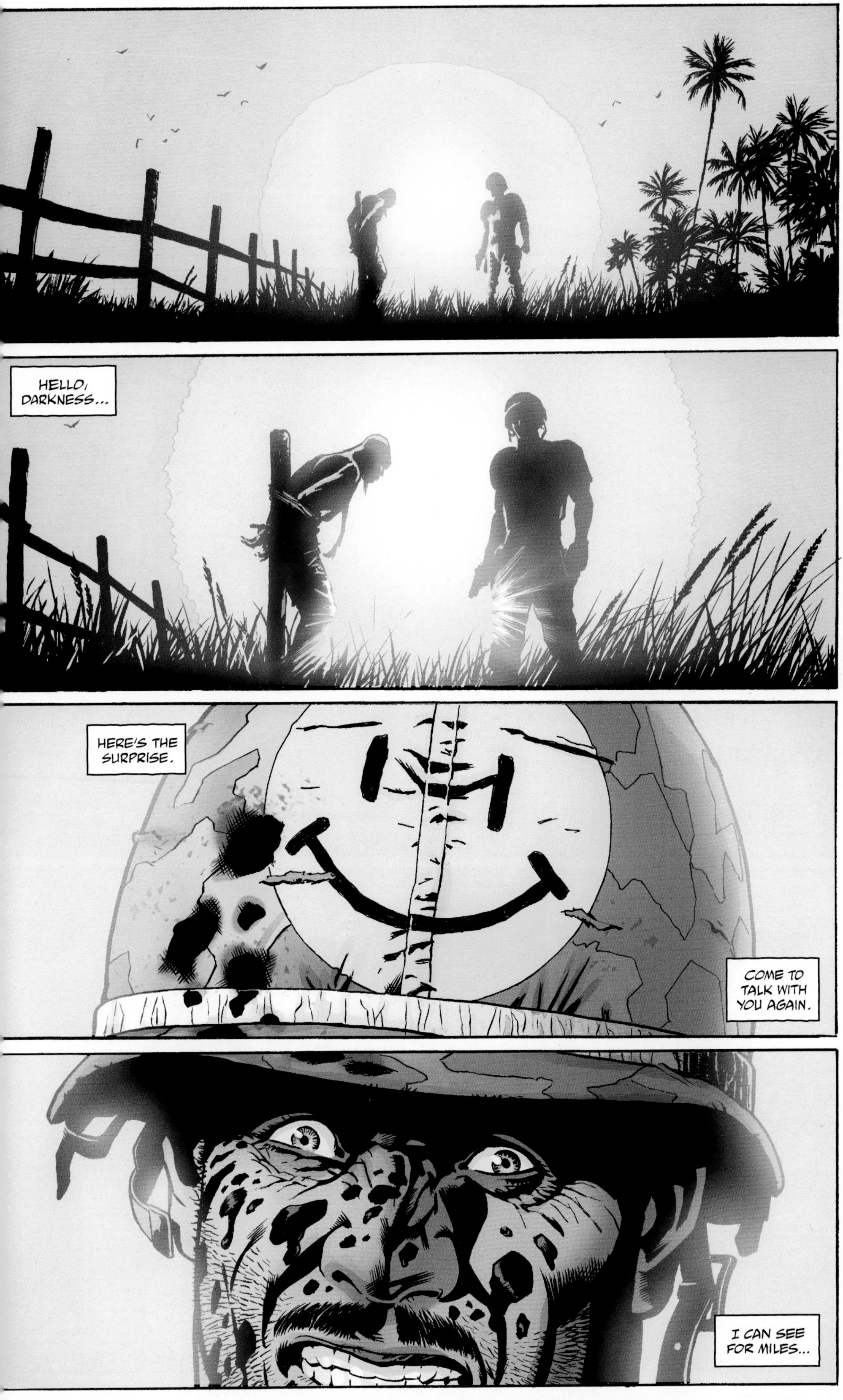
HELLO, DARKNESS...
HERE'S THE SURPRISE.
COME TO TALK WITH YOU AGAIN.
I CAN SEE FOR MILES...

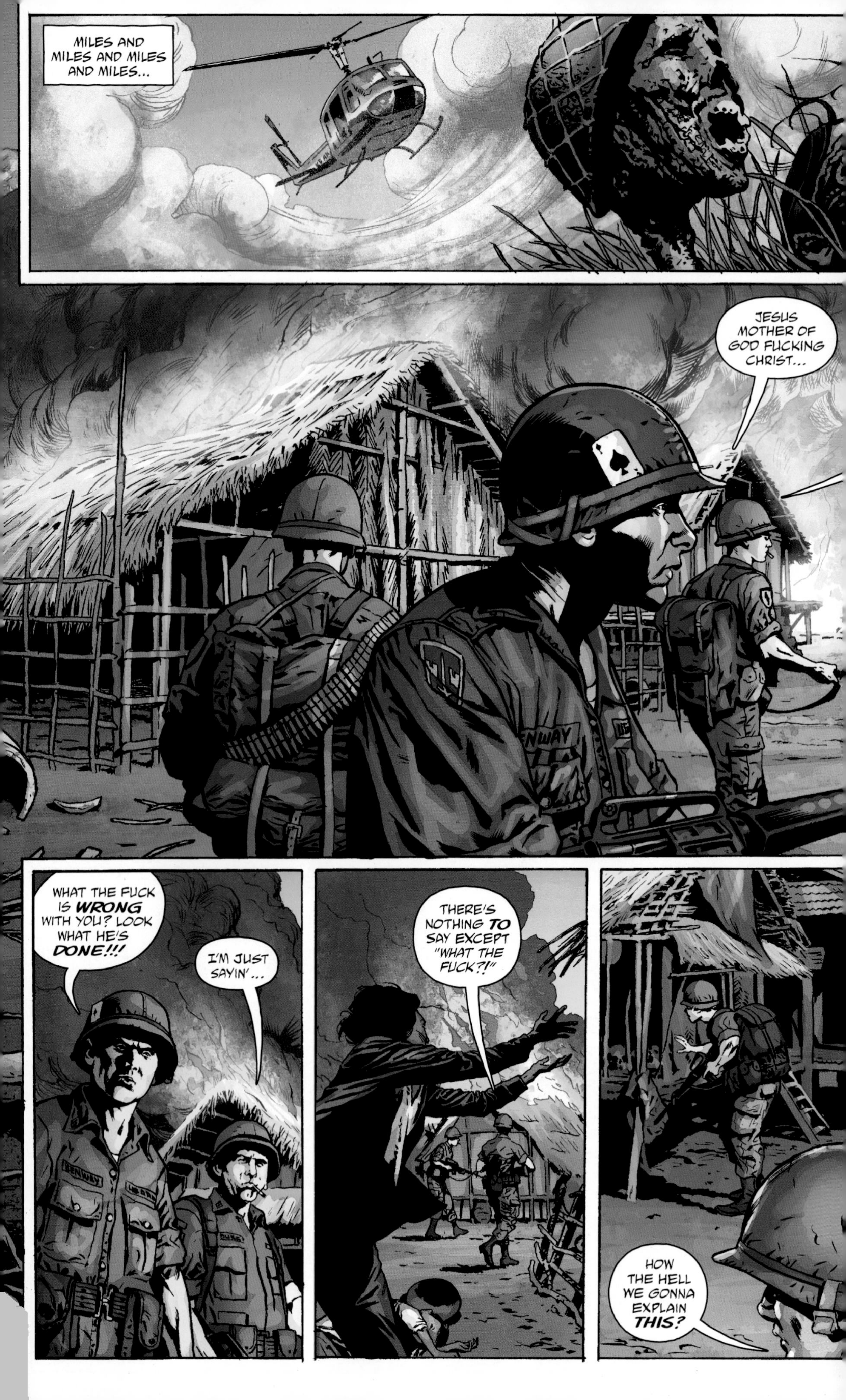
MILES AND MILES AND MILES AND MILES...
JESUS MOTHER OF GOD FUCKING CHRIST...
WHAT THE FUCK IS WRONG WITH YOU? LOOK WHAT HE'S DONE!!!
I'M JUST SAYIN'...
THERE'S NOTHING TO SAY EXCEPT "WHAT THE FUCK?!"
HOW THE HELL WE GONNA EXPLAIN THIS?

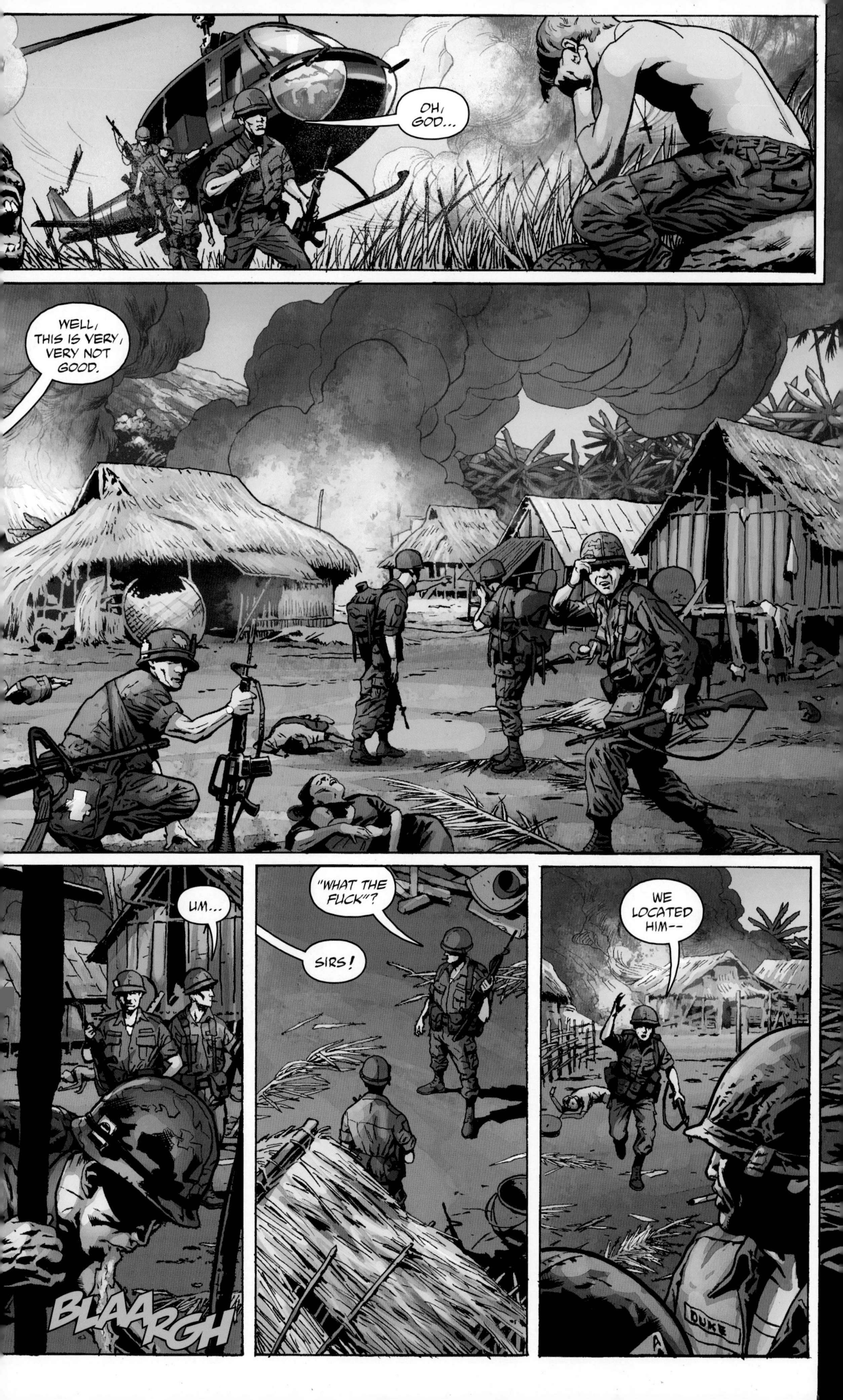
OH, GOD...
WELL, THIS IS VERY, VERY NOT GOOD.
UM...
BLAARGH
"WHAT THE FUCK"?
SIRS!
WE LOCATED HIM--
DUKE

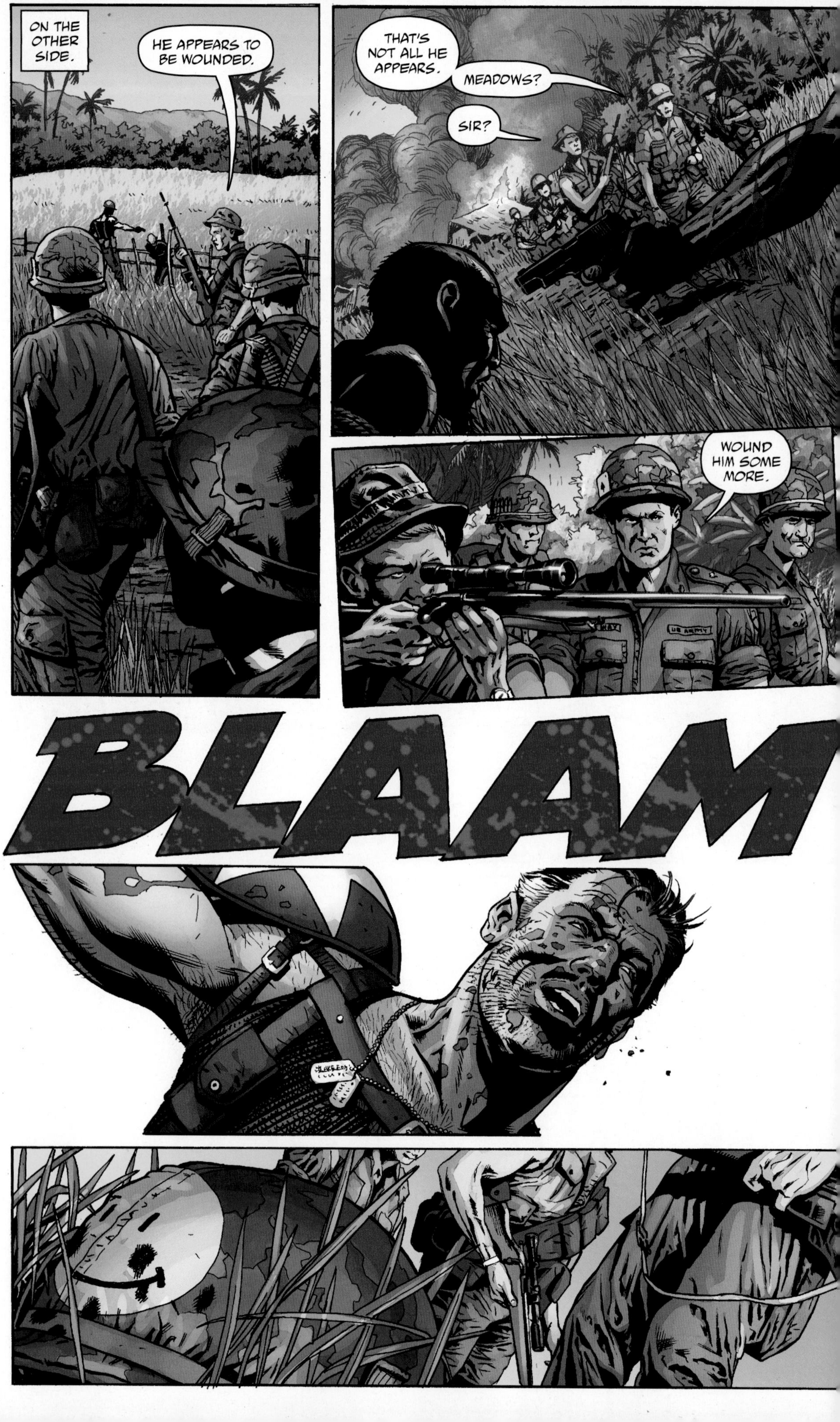
ON THE OTHER SIDE.
HE APPEARS TO BE WOUNDED.
THAT'S NOT ALL HE APPEARS.
MEADOWS?
SIR?
WOUND HIM SOME MORE.
BLAAM

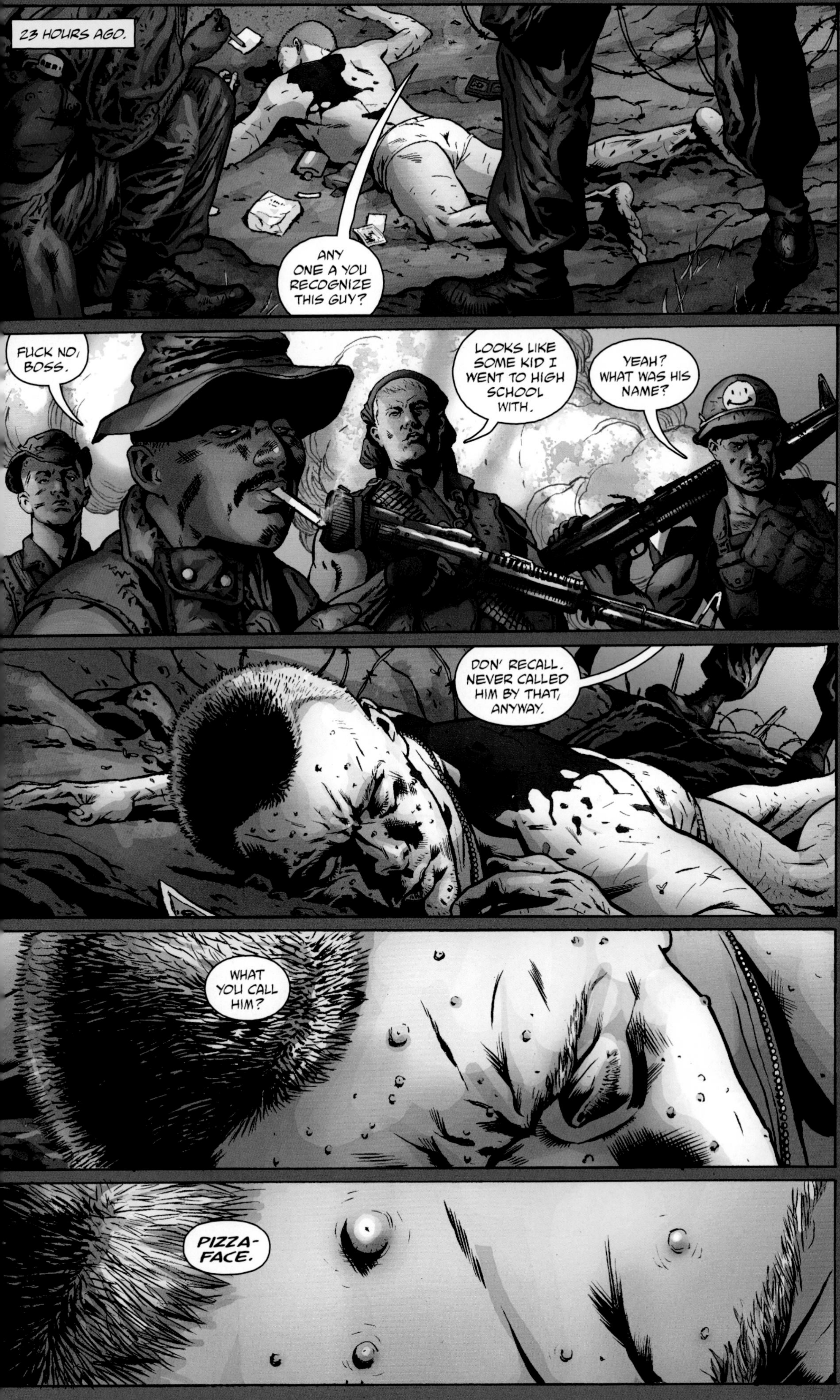
23 HOURS AGO.
ANY ONE A YOU RECOGNIZE THIS GUY?
FUCK NO, BOSS.
LOOKS LIKE SOME KID I WENT TO HIGH SCHOOL WITH.
YEAH? WHAT WAS HIS NAME?
DON' RECALL. NEVER CALLED HIM BY THAT, ANYWAY.
WHAT YOU CALL HIM?
PIZZA-FACE.

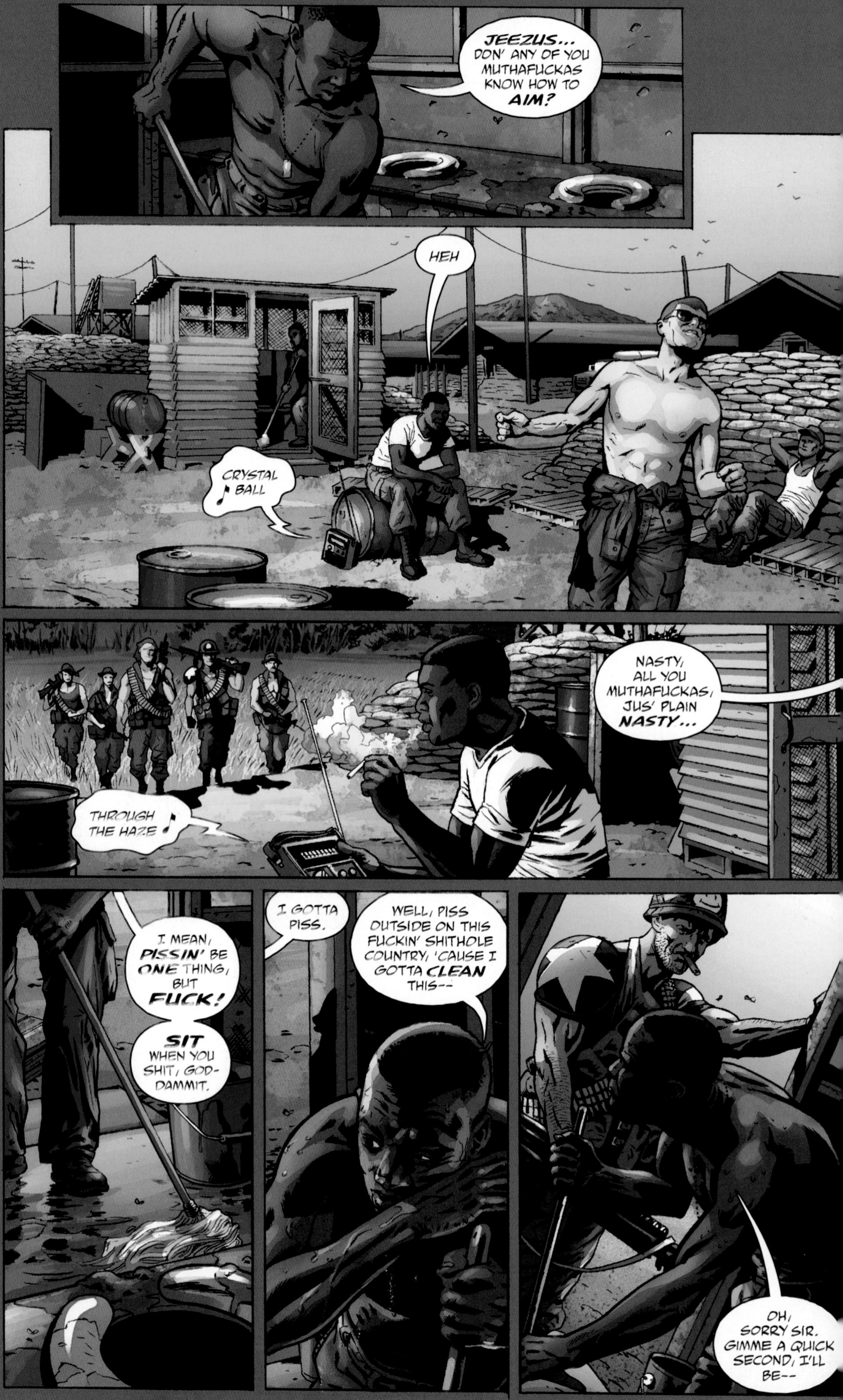

JEEZUS... DON' ANY OF YOU MUTHAFUCKAS KNOW HOW TO AIM?
HEH
CRYSTAL BALL ♪
NASTY, ALL YOU MUTHAFUCKAS, JUS' PLAIN NASTY...
THROUGH THE HAZE ♪
I MEAN, PISSIN' BE ONE THING, BUT FUCK!
SIT WHEN YOU SHIT, GOD-DAMMIT.
I GOTTA PISS.
WELL, PISS OUTSIDE ON THIS FUCKIN' SHITHOLE COUNTRY, 'CAUSE I GOTTA CLEAN THIS--
OH, SORRY SIR. GIMME A QUICK SECOND, I'LL BE--

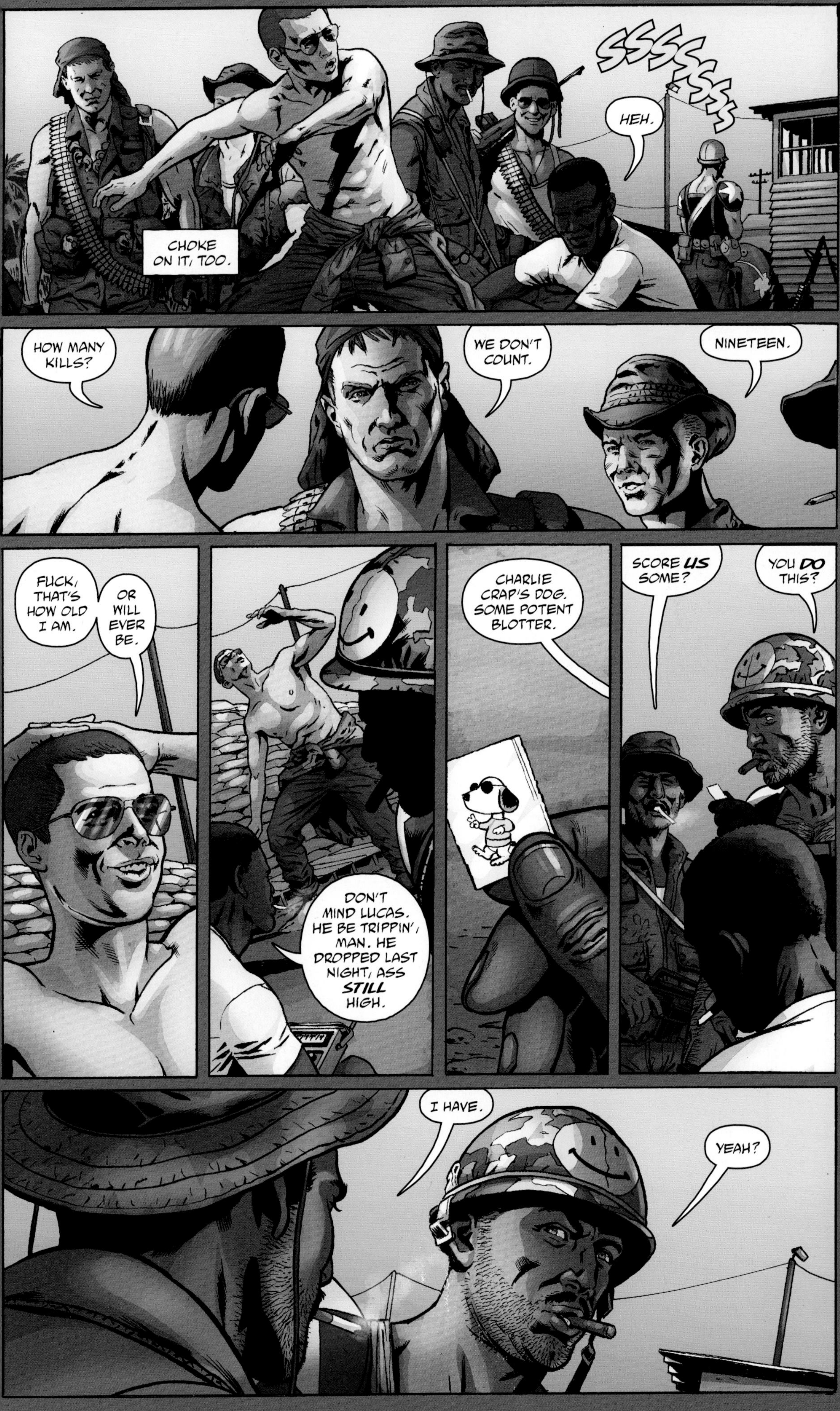
SSSSSSSS
HEH.
CHOKE ON IT, TOO.
HOW MANY KILLS?
WE DON'T COUNT.
NINETEEN.
FUCK, THAT'S HOW OLD I AM.
OR WILL EVER BE.
DON'T MIND LUCAS. HE BE TRIPPIN', MAN. HE DROPPED LAST NIGHT, ASS STILL HIGH.
CHARLIE CRAP'S DOG. SOME POTENT BLOTTER.
SCORE US SOME?
YOU DO THIS?
I HAVE.
YEAH?

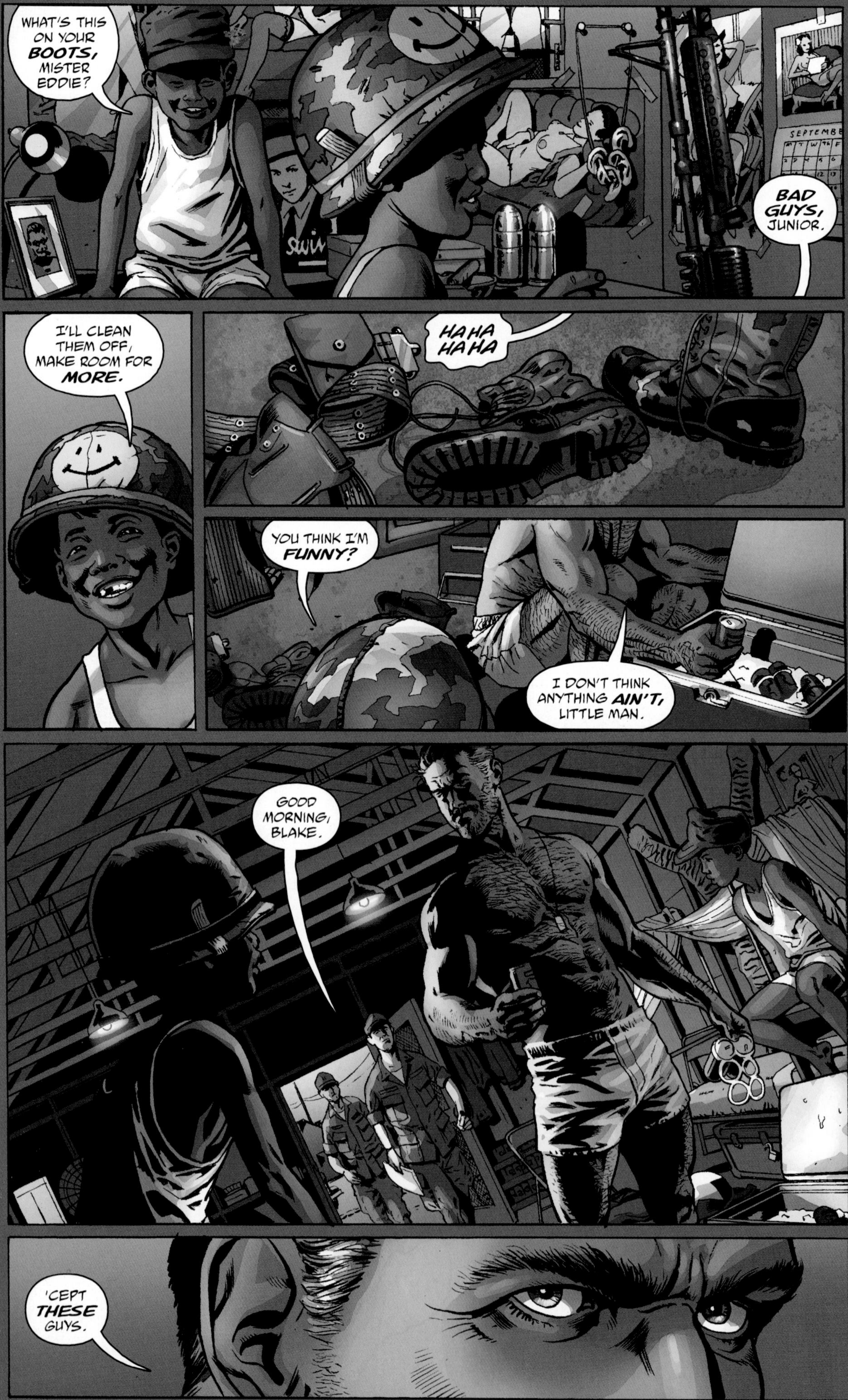
WHAT'S THIS ON YOUR BOOTS, MISTER EDDIE?
BAD GUYS, JUNIOR.
I'LL CLEAN THEM OFF, MAKE ROOM FOR MORE.
HA HA HA HA
YOU THINK I'M FUNNY?
I DON'T THINK ANYTHING AIN'T, LITTLE MAN.
GOOD MORNING, BLAKE.
'CEPT THESE GUYS.

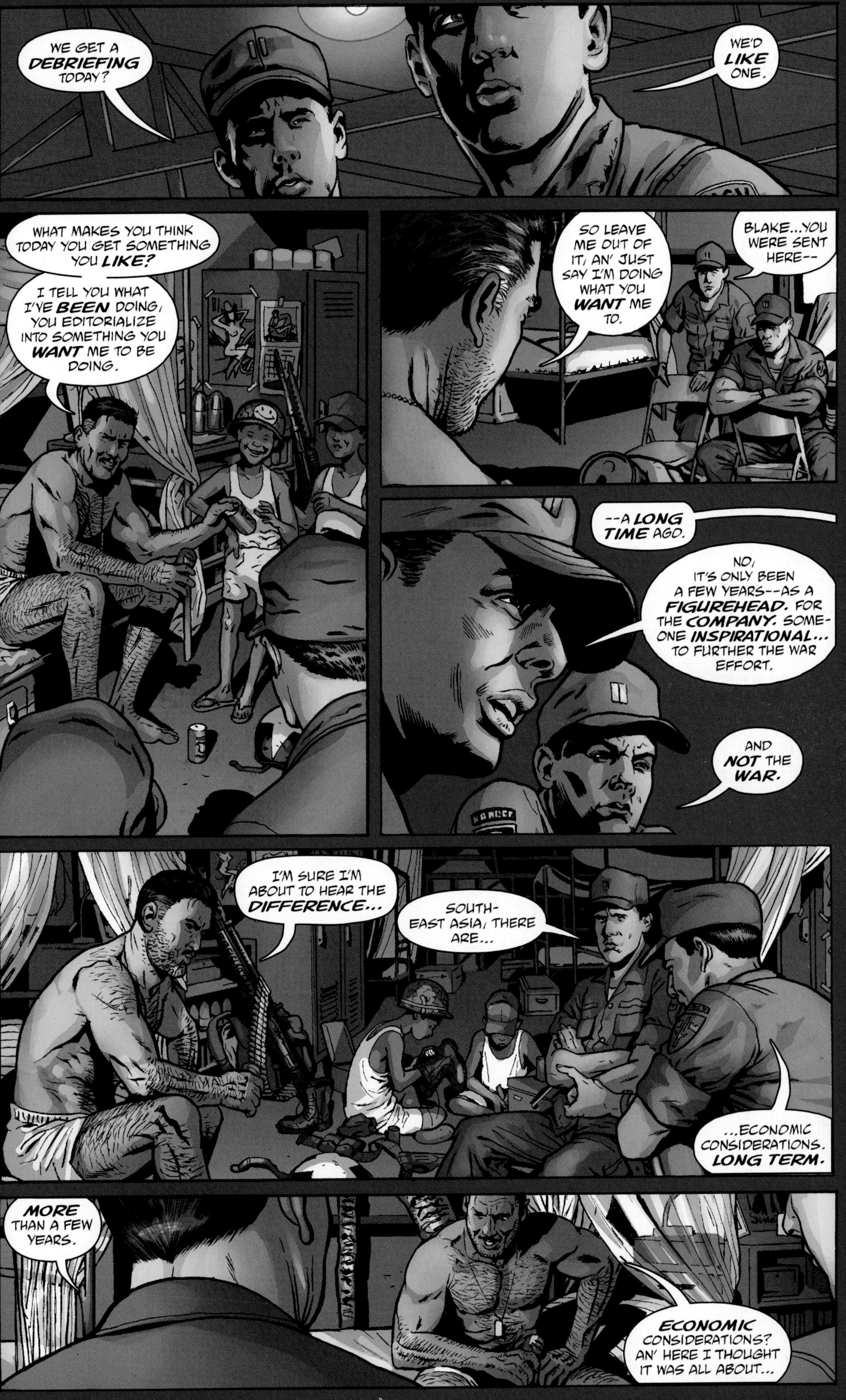
WE GET A DEBRIEFING TODAY?
WE'D LIKE ONE.
WHAT MAKES YOU THINK TODAY YOU GET SOMETHING YOU LIKE?
I TELL YOU WHAT I'VE BEEN DOING, YOU EDITORIALIZE INTO SOMETHING YOU WANT ME TO BE DOING.
SO LEAVE ME OUT OF IT, AN' JUST SAY I'M DOING WHAT YOU WANT ME TO.
BLAKE...YOU WERE SENT HERE--
--A LONG TIME AGO.
NO, IT'S ONLY BEEN A FEW YEARS--AS A FIGUREHEAD. FOR THE COMPANY. SOME-ONE INSPIRATIONAL... TO FURTHER THE WAR EFFORT.
AND NOT THE WAR.
I'M SURE I'M ABOUT TO HEAR THE DIFFERENCE...
SOUTH-EAST ASIA, THERE ARE...
...ECONOMIC CONSIDERATIONS. LONG TERM.
MORE THAN A FEW YEARS.
ECONOMIC CONSIDERATIONS? AN' HERE I THOUGHT IT WAS ALL ABOUT...

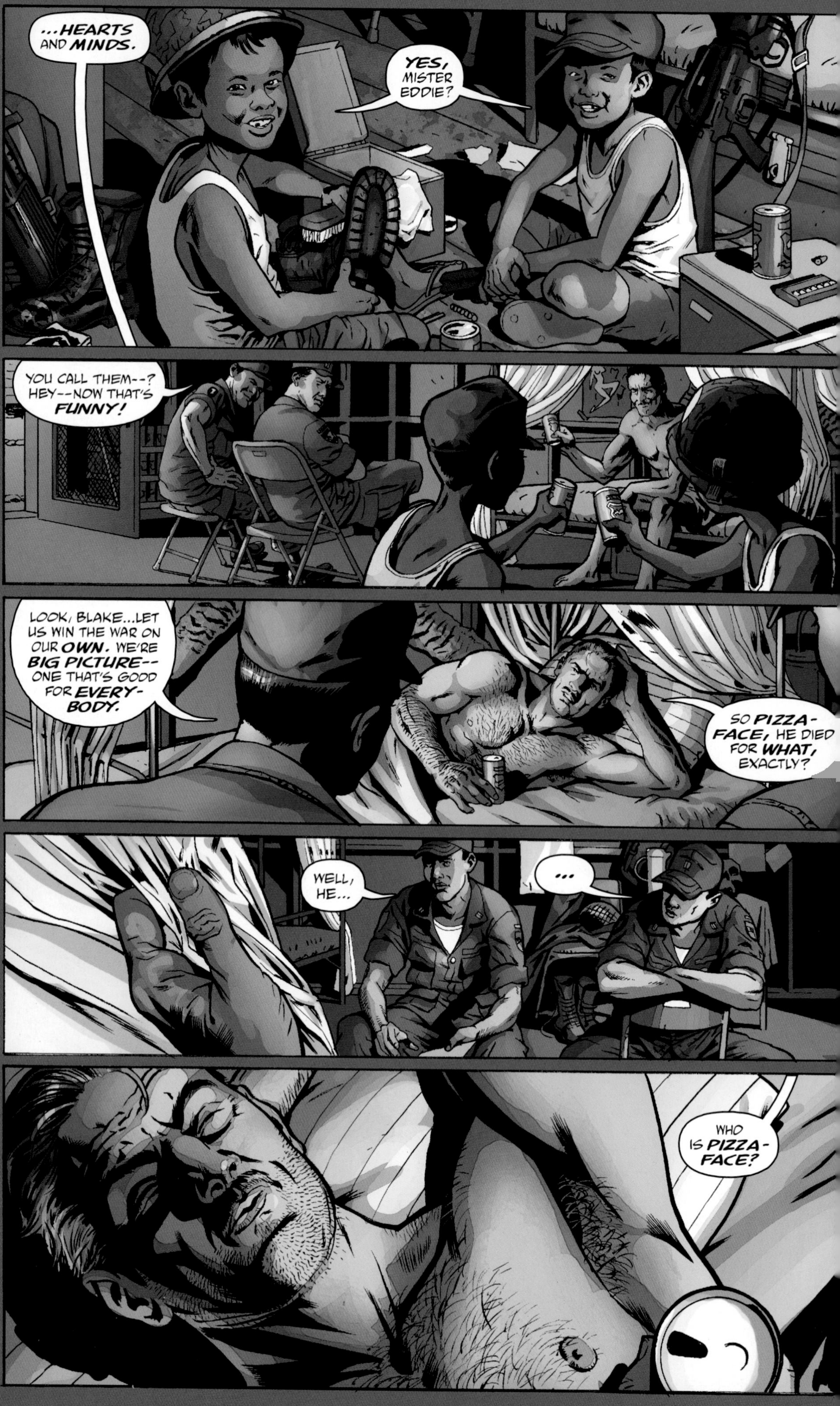
...HEARTS AND MINDS.
YES, MISTER EDDIE?
YOU CALL THEM--? HEY--NOW THAT'S FUNNY!
LOOK, BLAKE...LET US WIN THE WAR ON OUR OWN. WE'RE BIG PICTURE--ONE THAT'S GOOD FOR EVERY-BODY.
SO PIZZA-FACE, HE DIED FOR WHAT, EXACTLY?
WELL, HE...
...
WHO IS PIZZA-FACE?

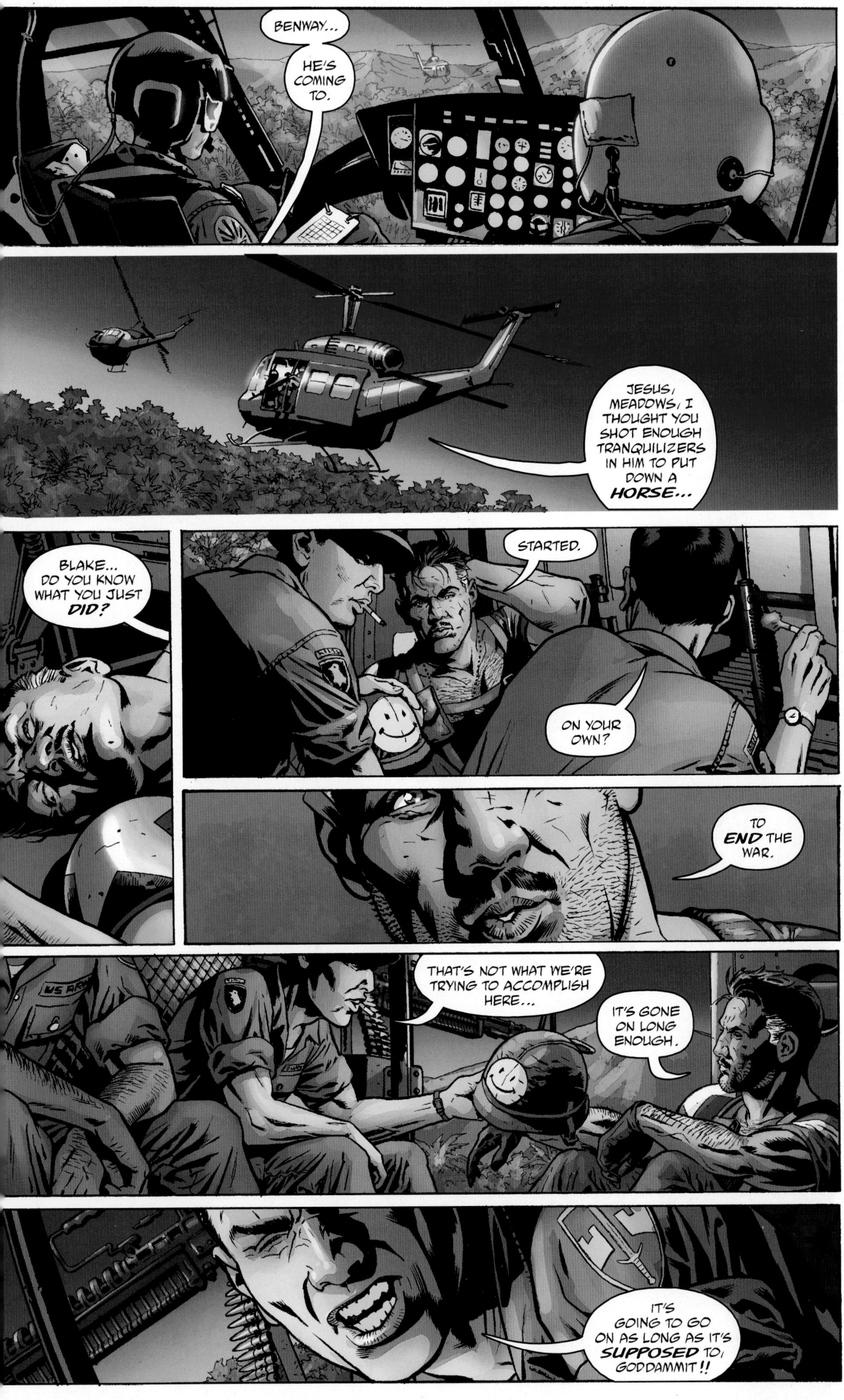
BENWAY...
HE'S COMING TO.
JESUS, MEADOWS, I THOUGHT YOU SHOT ENOUGH TRANQUILIZERS IN HIM TO PUT DOWN A **HORSE...**
BLAKE... DO YOU KNOW WHAT YOU JUST **DID?**
STARTED.
ON YOUR OWN?
TO **END** THE WAR.
THAT'S NOT WHAT WE'RE TRYING TO ACCOMPLISH HERE...
IT'S GONE ON LONG ENOUGH.
IT'S GOING TO GO ON AS LONG AS IT'S **SUPPOSED** TO, GODDAMMIT!!

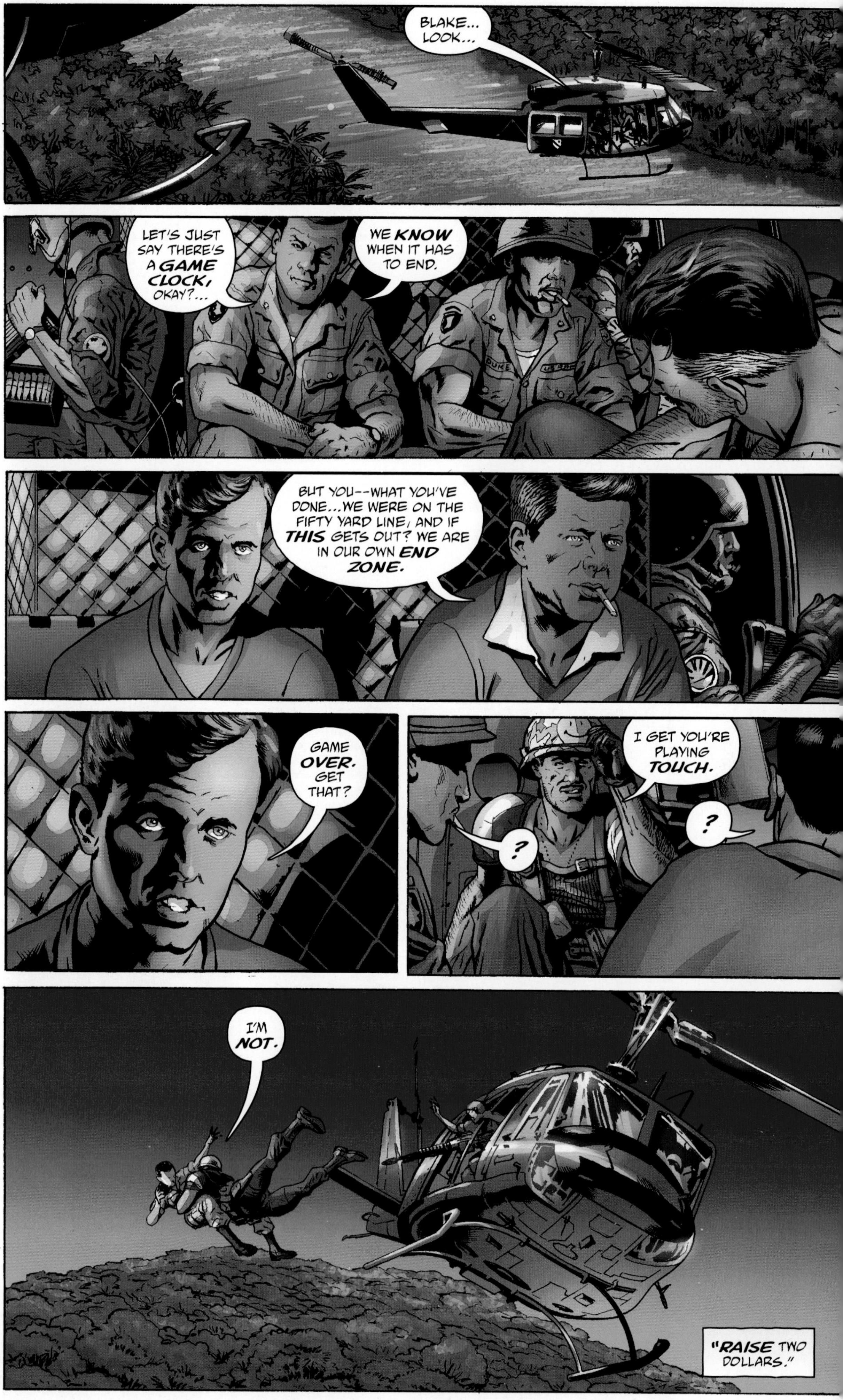
BLAKE...
LOOK...
LET'S JUST SAY THERE'S A GAME CLOCK, OKAY?...
WE KNOW WHEN IT HAS TO END.
BUT YOU--WHAT YOU'VE DONE...WE WERE ON THE FIFTY YARD LINE, AND IF THIS GETS OUT? WE ARE IN OUR OWN END ZONE.
GAME OVER. GET THAT?
I GET YOU'RE PLAYING TOUCH.
?
?
I'M NOT.
"RAISE TWO DOLLARS."

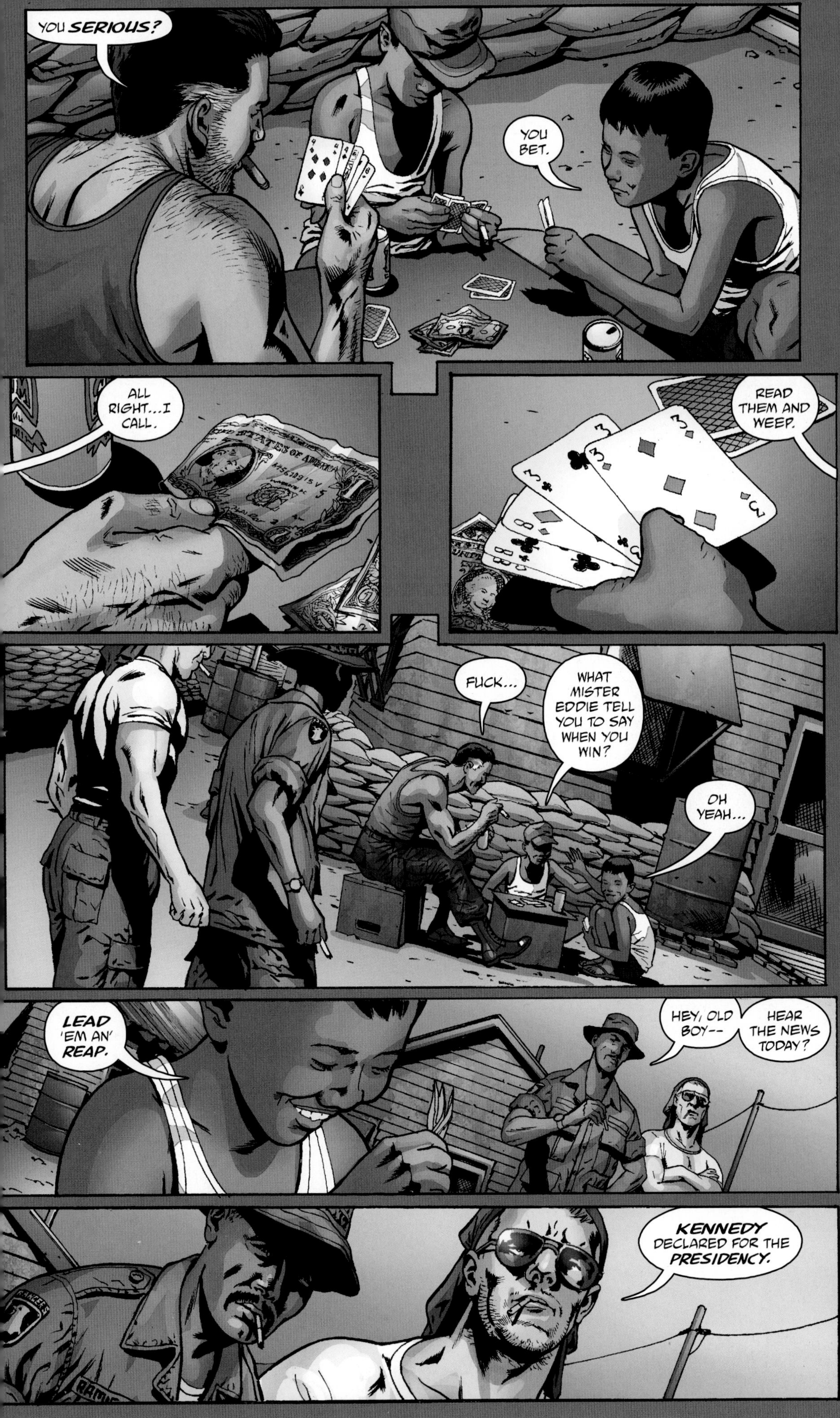

YOU SERIOUS?
YOU BET.
ALL RIGHT...I CALL.
READ THEM AND WEEP.
FUCK...
WHAT MISTER EDDIE TELL YOU TO SAY WHEN YOU WIN?
OH YEAH...
LEAD 'EM AN' REAP.
HEY, OLD BOY--
HEAR THE NEWS TODAY?
KENNEDY DECLARED FOR THE PRESIDENCY.

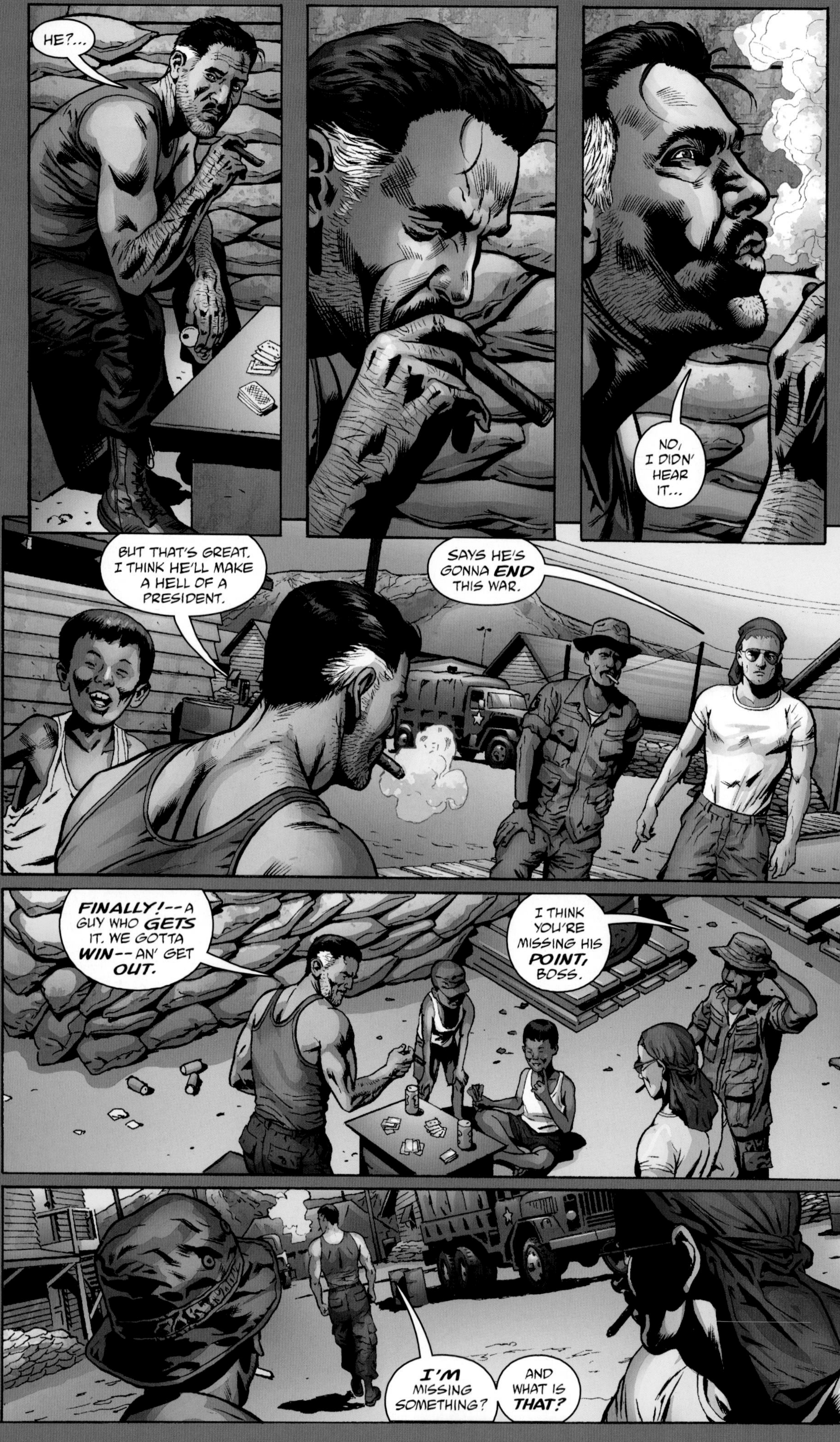
HE?...
NO, I DIDN' HEAR IT...
BUT THAT'S GREAT. I THINK HE'LL MAKE A HELL OF A PRESIDENT.
SAYS HE'S GONNA END THIS WAR.
FINALLY!--A GUY WHO GETS IT. WE GOTTA WIN--AN' GET OUT.
I THINK YOU'RE MISSING HIS POINT, BOSS.
I'M MISSING SOMETHING?
AND WHAT IS THAT?

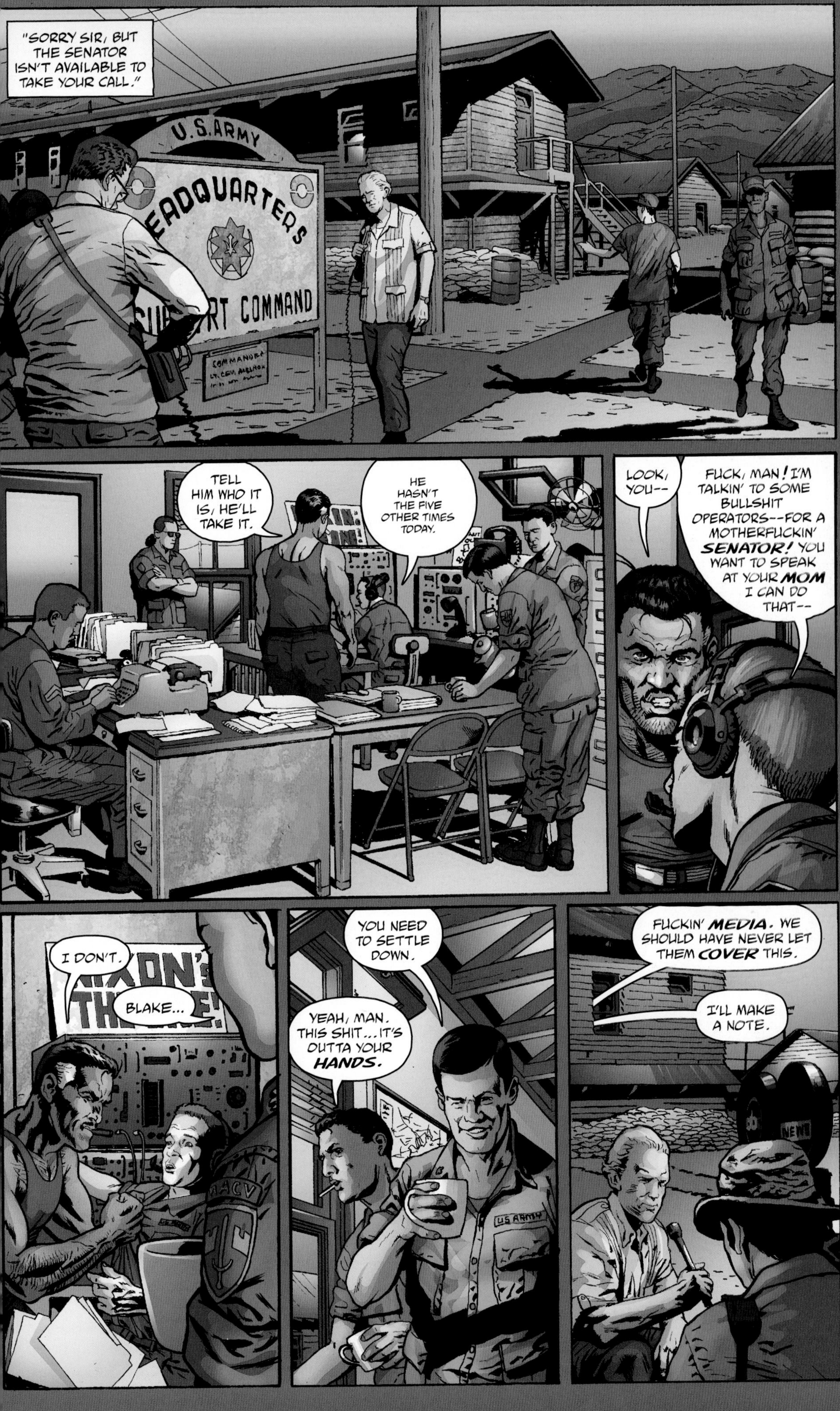
"SORRY SIR, BUT THE SENATOR ISN'T AVAILABLE TO TAKE YOUR CALL."
U.S.ARMY
EADQUARTERS
TELL HIM WHO IT IS, HE'LL TAKE IT.
HE HASN'T THE FIVE OTHER TIMES TODAY.
LOOK, YOU--
FUCK, MAN! I'M TALKIN' TO SOME BULLSHIT OPERATORS--FOR A MOTHERFUCKIN' SENATOR! YOU WANT TO SPEAK AT YOUR MOM I CAN DO THAT--
I DON'T.
BLAKE...
YOU NEED TO SETTLE DOWN.
YEAH, MAN. THIS SHIT... IT'S OUTTA YOUR HANDS.
US ARMY
FUCKIN' MEDIA. WE SHOULD HAVE NEVER LET THEM COVER THIS.
I'LL MAKE A NOTE.
NEWS

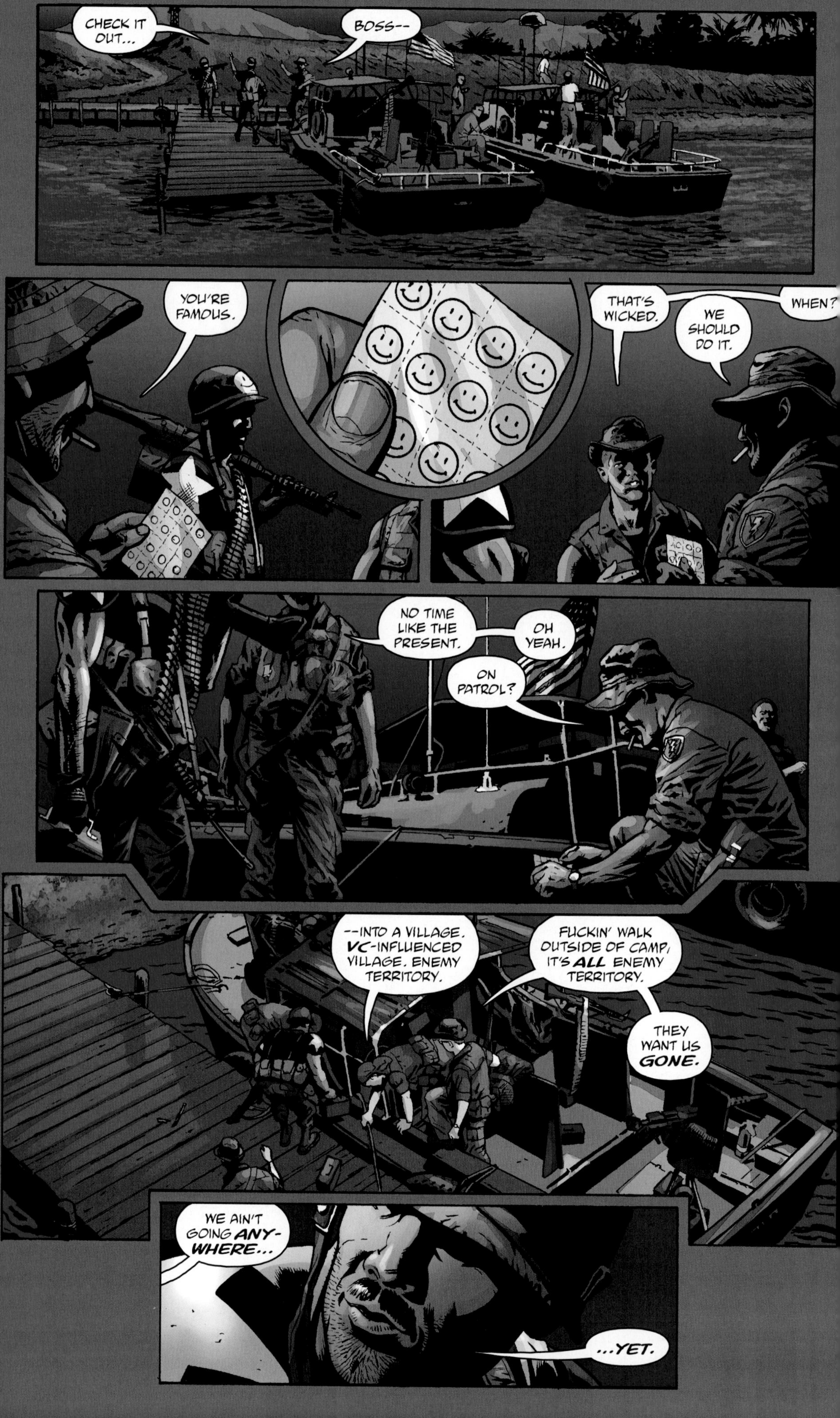
CHECK IT OUT...
BOSS--
YOU'RE FAMOUS.
THAT'S WICKED.
WE SHOULD DO IT.
WHEN?
NO TIME LIKE THE PRESENT.
OH YEAH.
ON PATROL?
--INTO A VILLAGE. VC-INFLUENCED VILLAGE. ENEMY TERRITORY.
FUCKIN' WALK OUTSIDE OF CAMP, IT'S ALL ENEMY TERRITORY.
THEY WANT US GONE.
WE AIN'T GOING ANY-WHERE...
...YET.

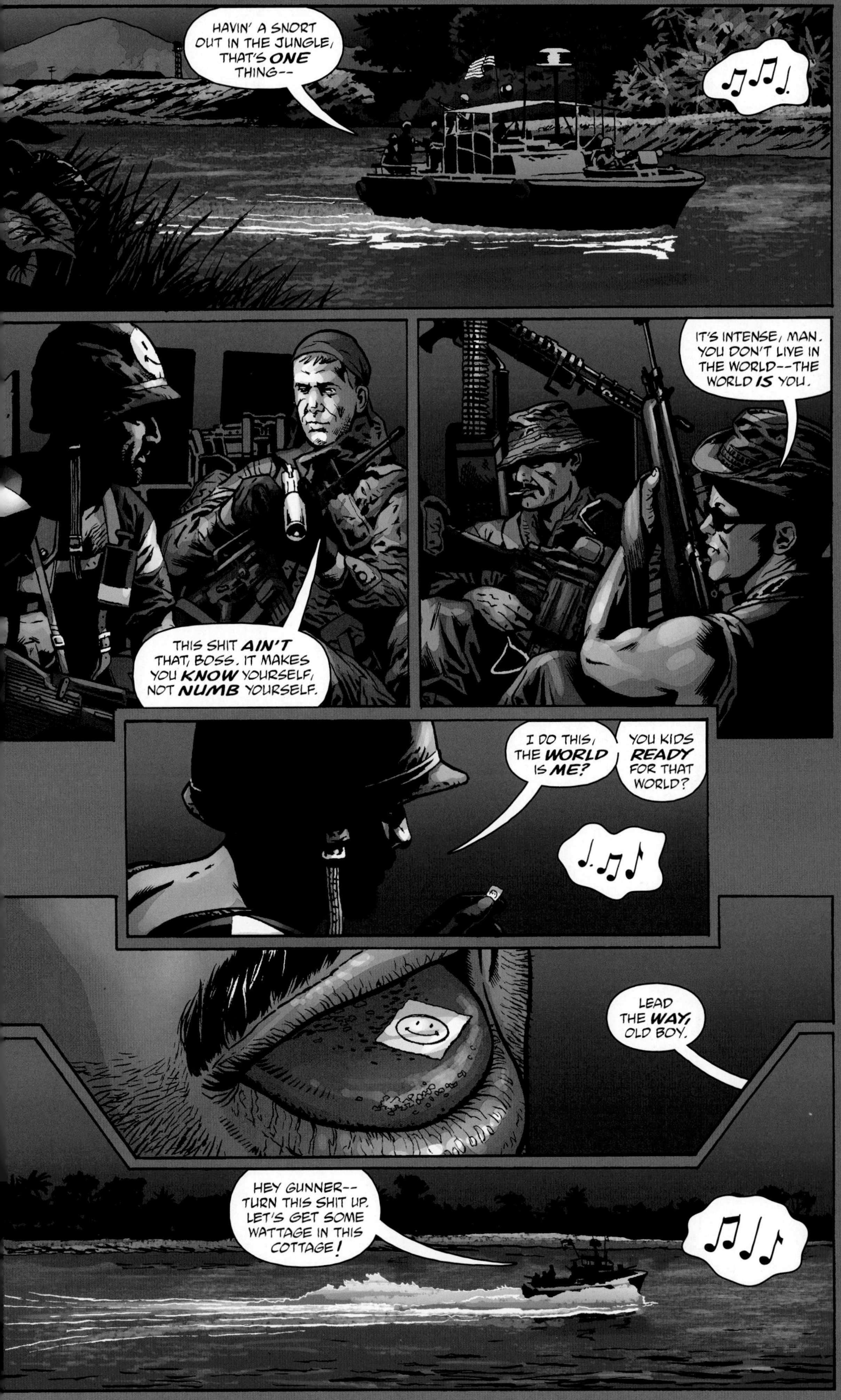
HAVIN' A SNORT OUT IN THE JUNGLE, THAT'S ONE THING--
♫♫♩
THIS SHIT AIN'T THAT, BOSS. IT MAKES YOU KNOW YOURSELF, NOT NUMB YOURSELF.
IT'S INTENSE, MAN. YOU DON'T LIVE IN THE WORLD--THE WORLD IS YOU.
I DO THIS, THE WORLD IS ME?
YOU KIDS READY FOR THAT WORLD?
♩♫♪
LEAD THE WAY, OLD BOY.
HEY GUNNER--TURN THIS SHIT UP. LET'S GET SOME WATTAGE IN THIS COTTAGE!
♫♩♪

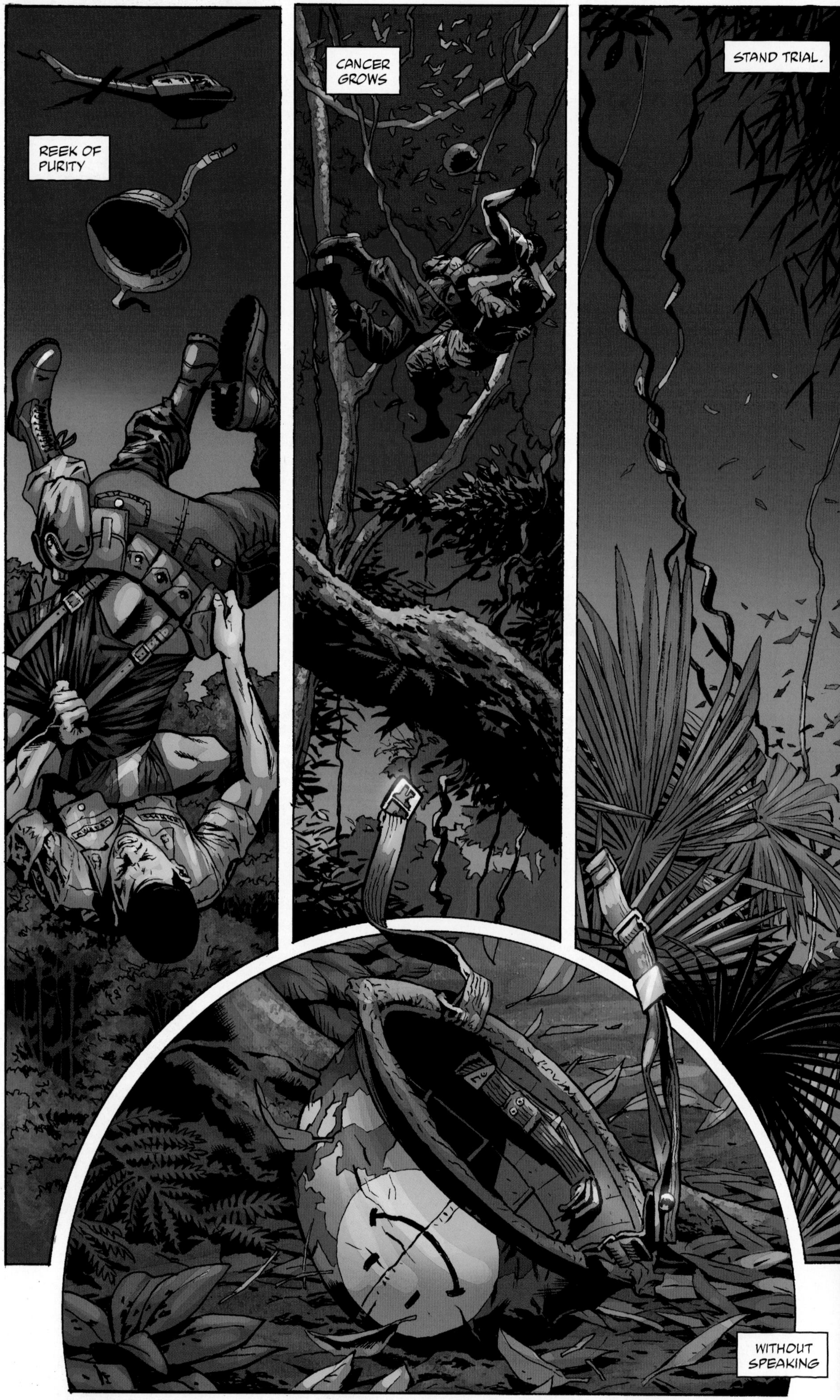
REEK OF PURITY
CANCER GROWS
STAND TRIAL.
WITHOUT SPEAKING

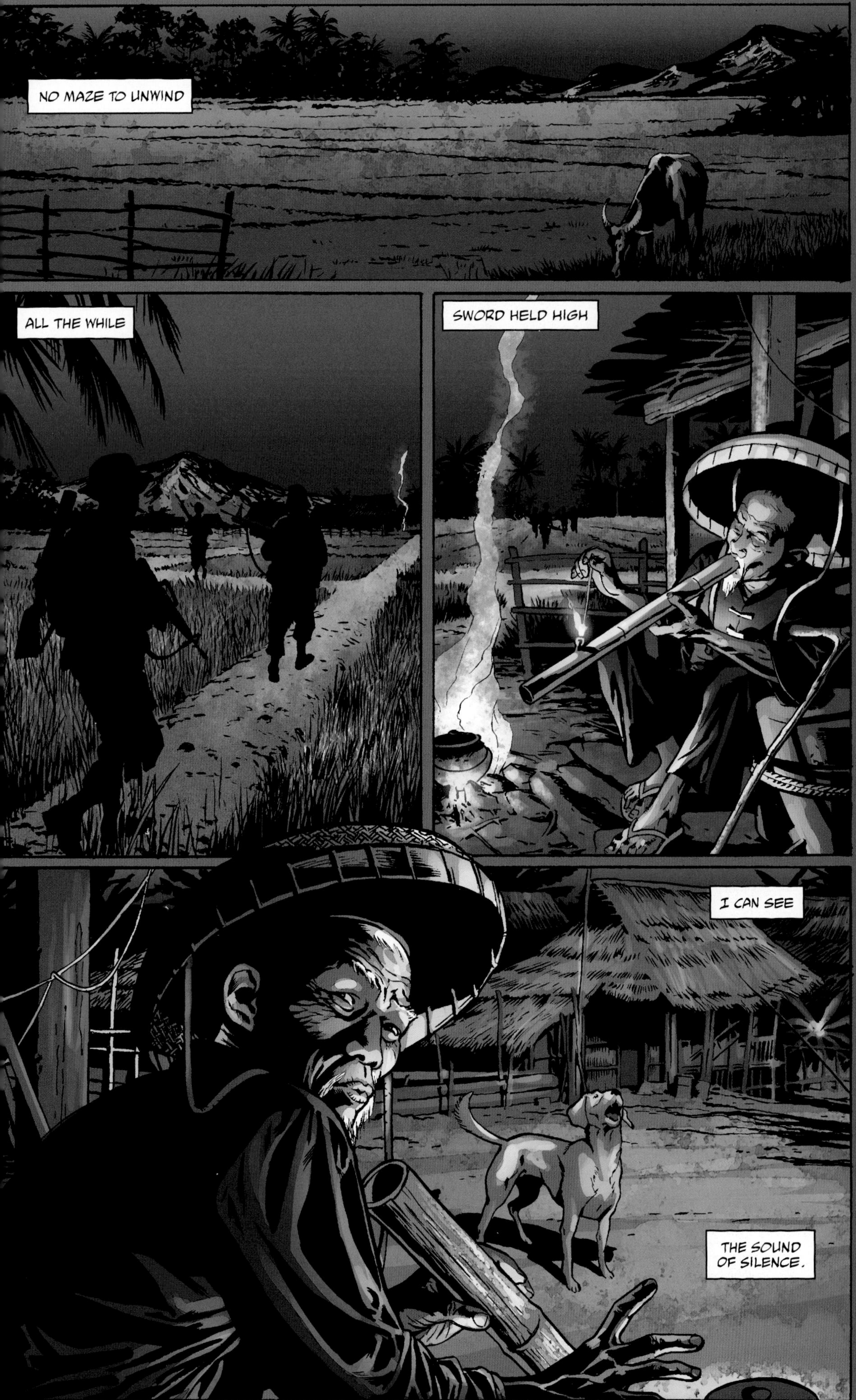
NO MAZE TO UNWIND
ALL THE WHILE
SWORD HELD HIGH
I CAN SEE
THE SOUND OF SILENCE.

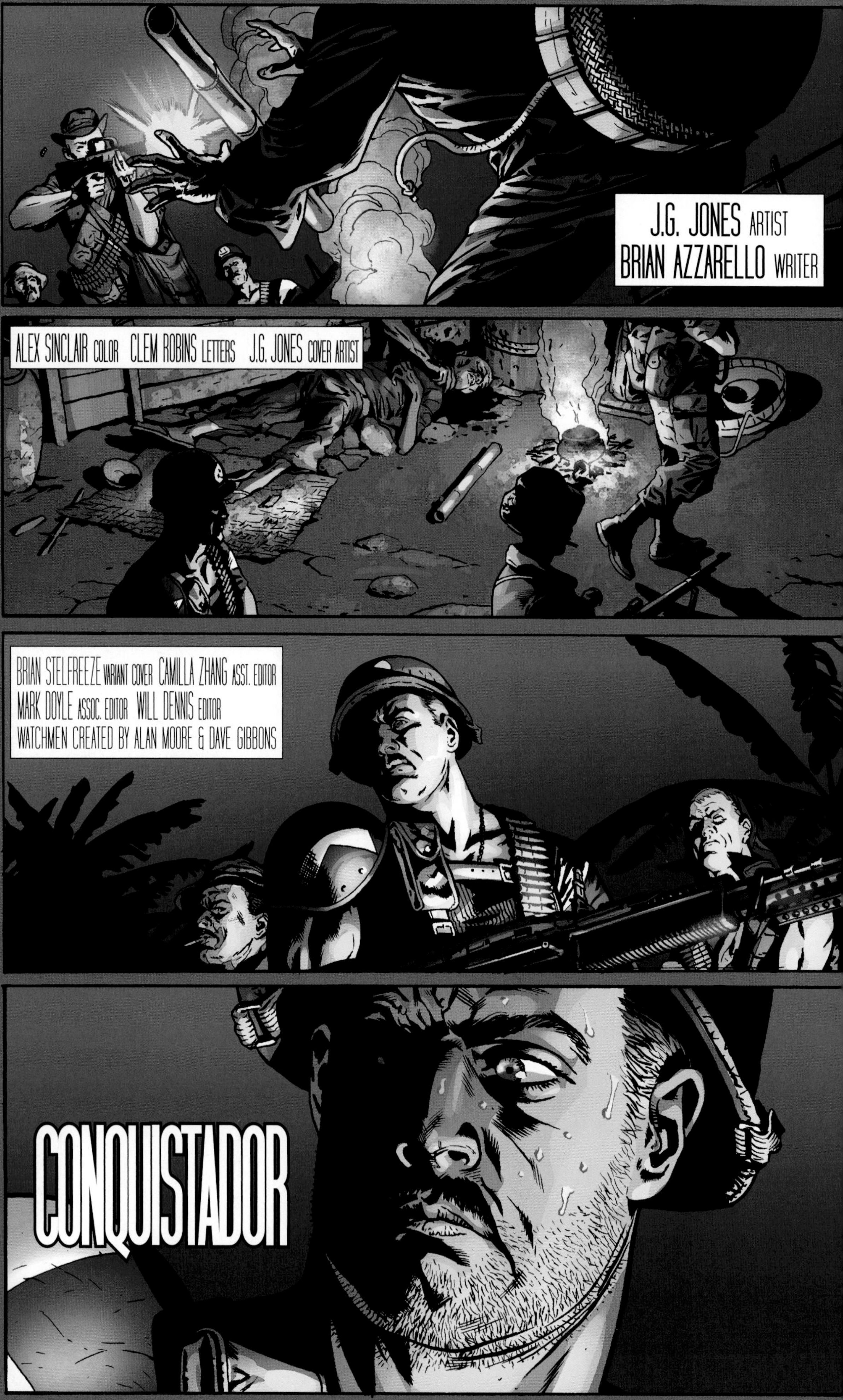
J.G. JONES ARTIST
BRIAN AZZARELLO WRITER
ALEX SINCLAIR COLOR CLEM ROBINS LETTERS J.G. JONES COVER ARTIST
BRIAN STELFREEZE VARIANT COVER CAMILLA ZHANG ASST. EDITOR
MARK DOYLE ASSOC. EDITOR WILL DENNIS EDITOR
WATCHMEN CREATED BY ALAN MOORE & DAVE GIBBONS
CONQUISTADOR

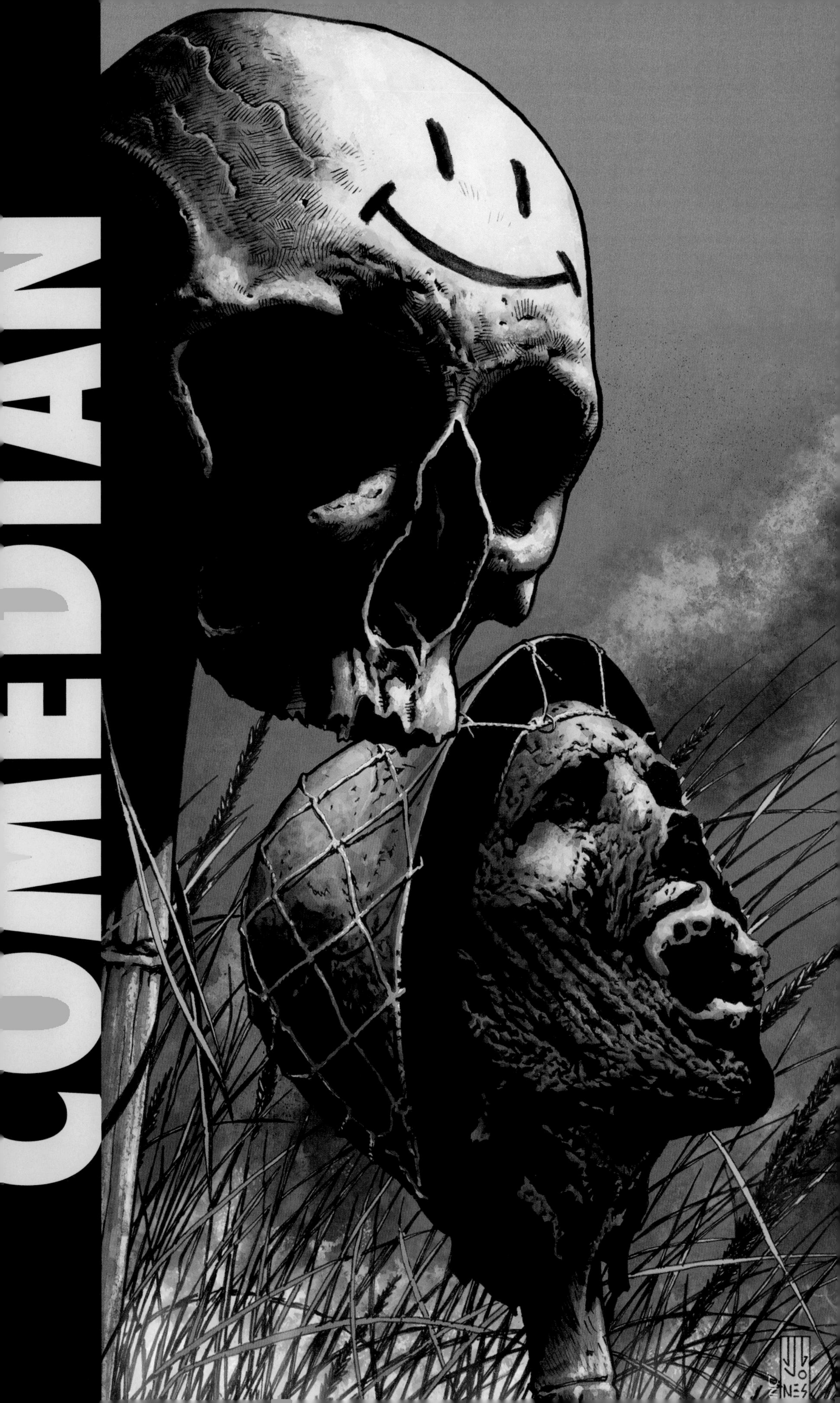
COMEDIAN

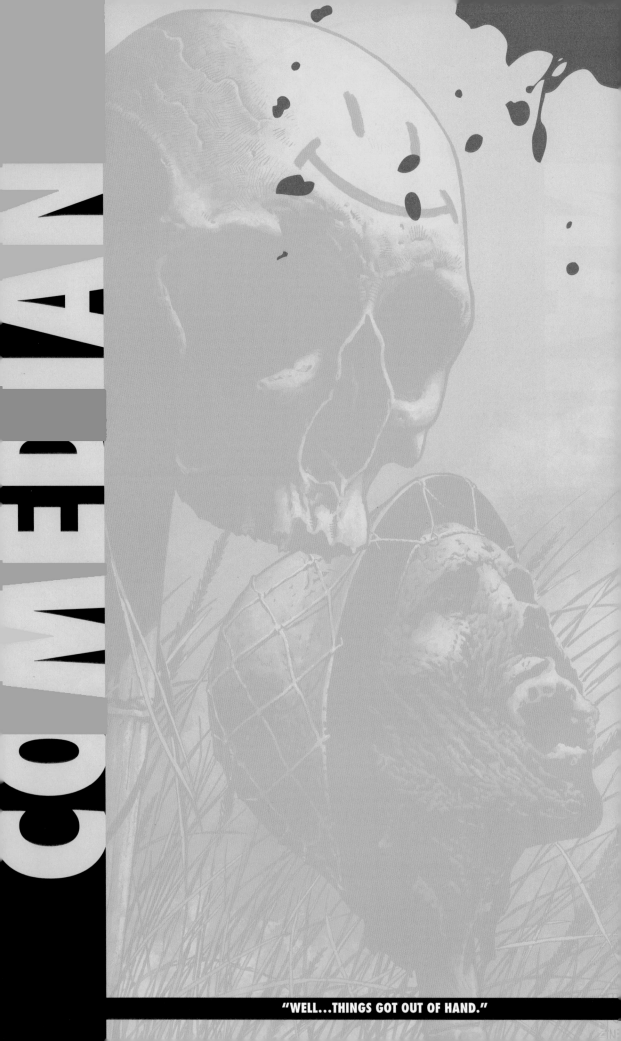

COMEDIAN

"WELL...THINGS GOT OUT OF HAND."

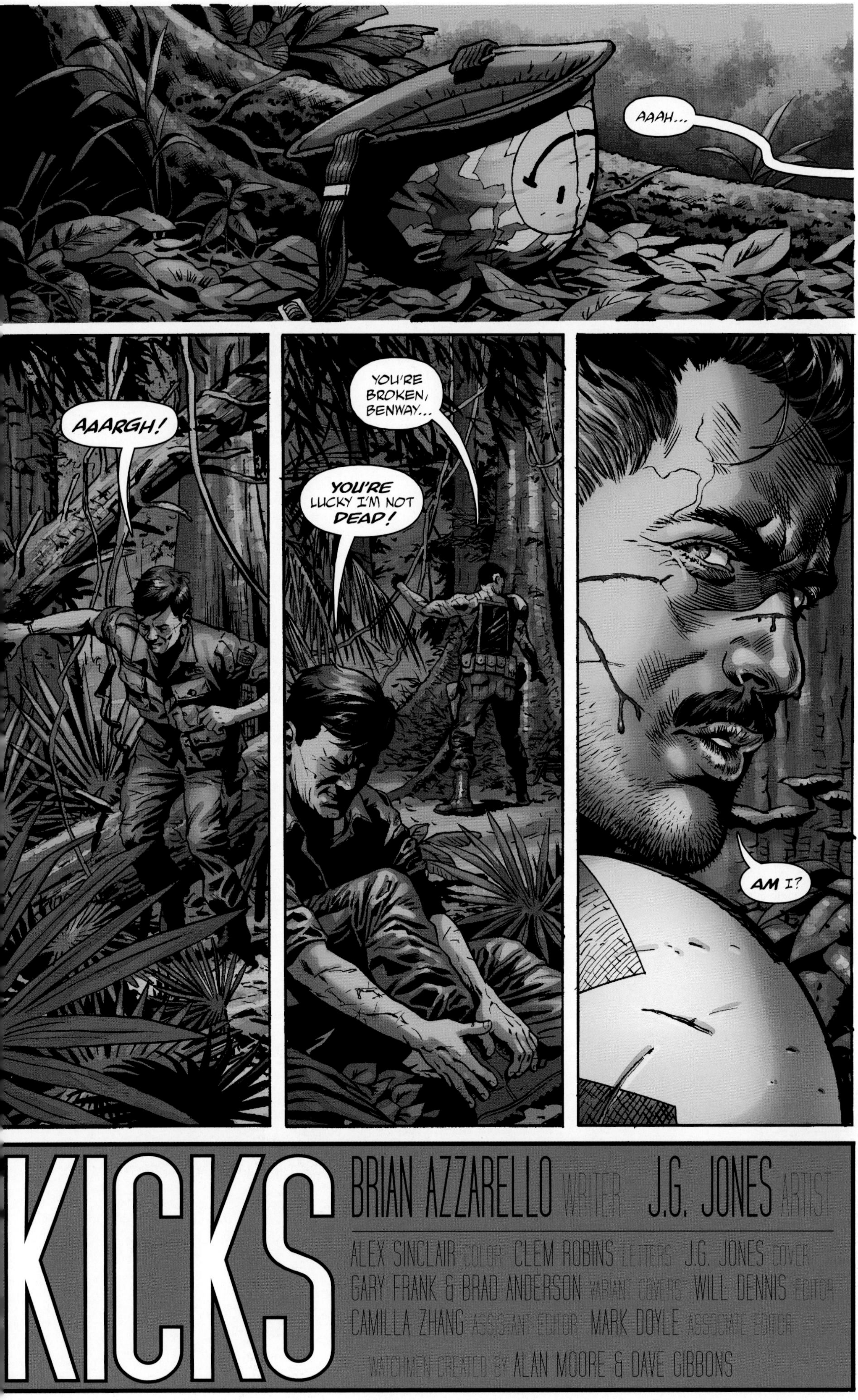
AAAH...
AAARGH!
YOU'RE BROKEN, BENWAY...
YOU'RE LUCKY I'M NOT DEAD!
AM I?

KICKS

BRIAN AZZARELLO WRITER J.G. JONES ARTIST

ALEX SINCLAIR COLOR CLEM ROBINS LETTERS J.G. JONES COVER
GARY FRANK & BRAD ANDERSON VARIANT COVERS WILL DENNIS EDITOR
CAMILLA ZHANG ASSISTANT EDITOR MARK DOYLE ASSOCIATE EDITOR

WATCHMEN CREATED BY ALAN MOORE & DAVE GIBBONS

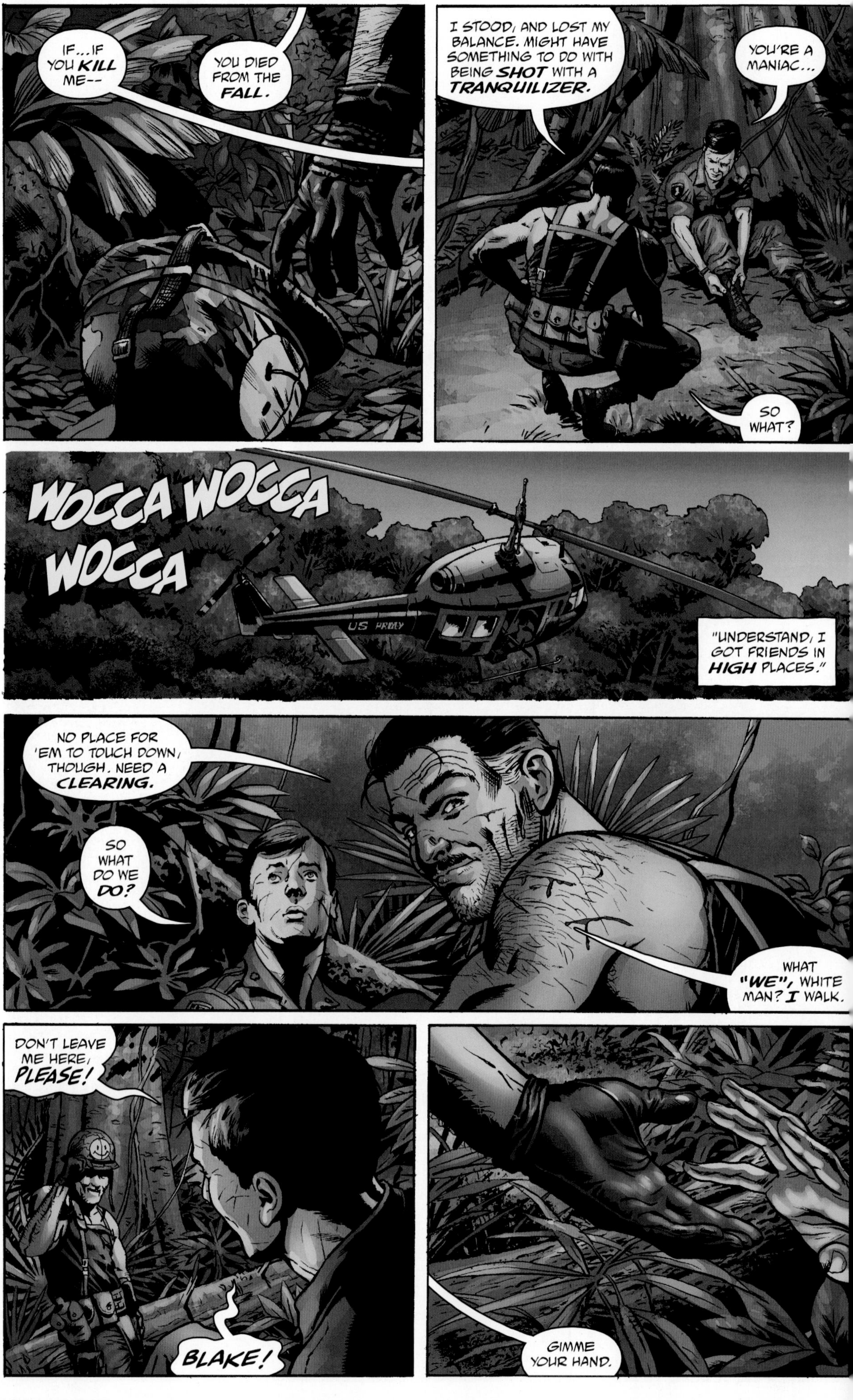

IF...IF YOU KILL ME--
YOU DIED FROM THE FALL.
I STOOD, AND LOST MY BALANCE. MIGHT HAVE SOMETHING TO DO WITH BEING SHOT WITH A TRANQUILIZER.
YOU'RE A MANIAC...
SO WHAT?
WOCCA WOCCA WOCCA
US ARMY
"UNDERSTAND, I GOT FRIENDS IN HIGH PLACES."
NO PLACE FOR 'EM TO TOUCH DOWN, THOUGH. NEED A CLEARING.
SO WHAT DO WE DO?
WHAT "WE", WHITE MAN? I WALK.
DON'T LEAVE ME HERE, PLEASE!
BLAKE!
GIMME YOUR HAND.

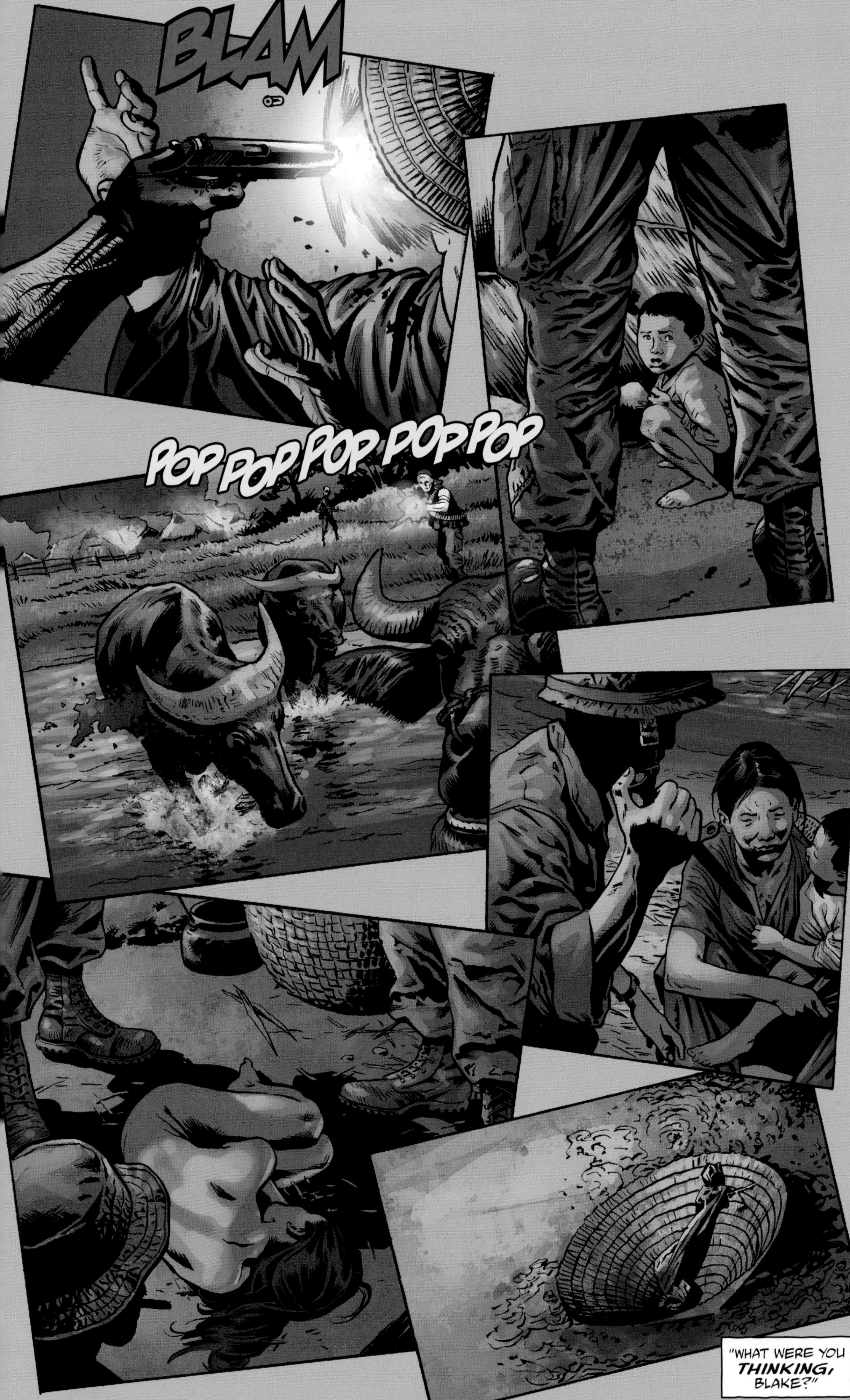
BLAM
POP POP POP POP POP
"WHAT WERE YOU THINKING, BLAKE?"

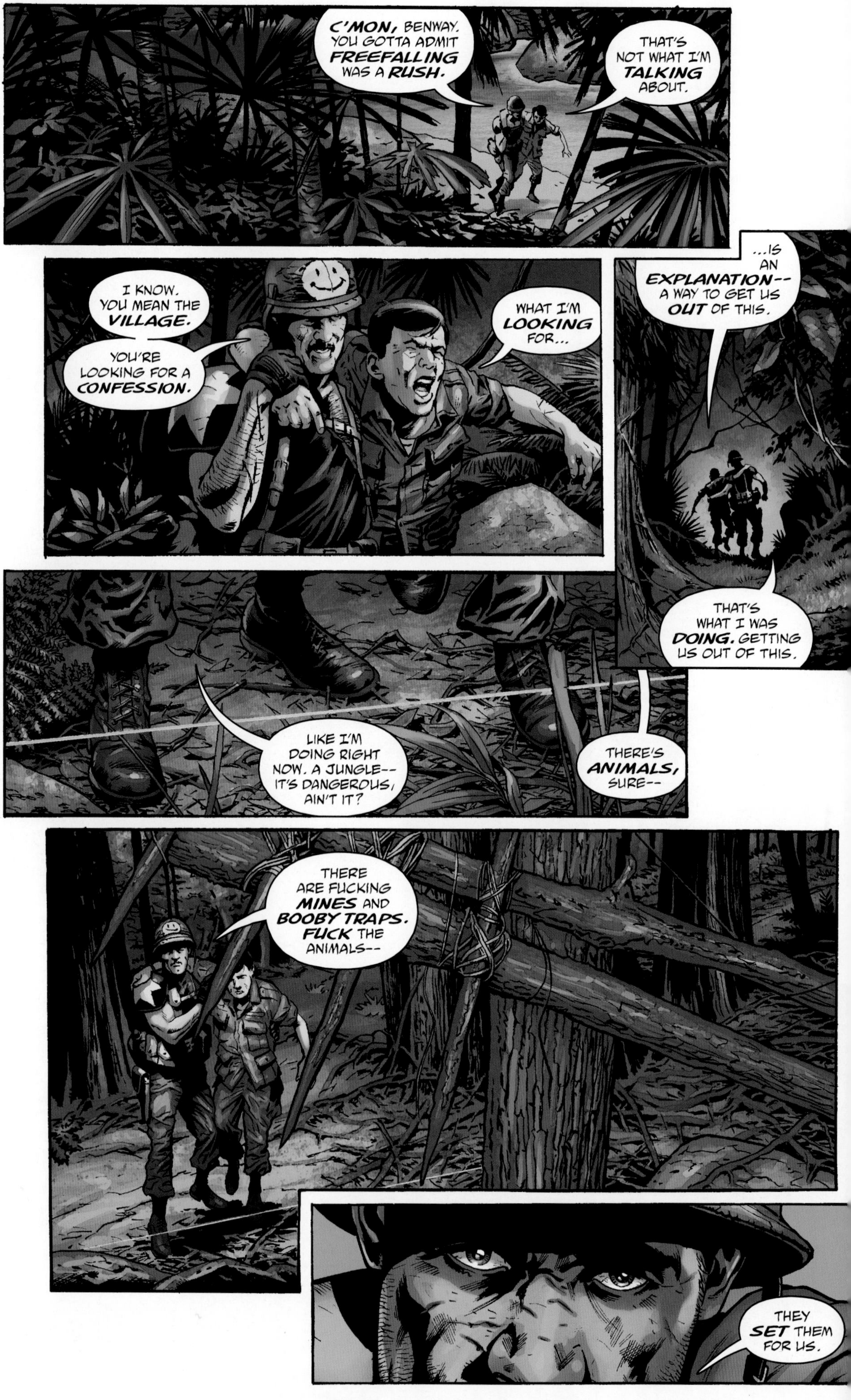
C'MON, BENWAY. YOU GOTTA ADMIT FREEFALLING WAS A RUSH.
THAT'S NOT WHAT I'M TALKING ABOUT.
I KNOW. YOU MEAN THE VILLAGE.
YOU'RE LOOKING FOR A CONFESSION.
WHAT I'M LOOKING FOR...
...IS AN EXPLANATION-- A WAY TO GET US OUT OF THIS.
THAT'S WHAT I WAS DOING. GETTING US OUT OF THIS.
LIKE I'M DOING RIGHT NOW. A JUNGLE-- IT'S DANGEROUS, AIN'T IT?
THERE'S ANIMALS, SURE--
THERE ARE FUCKING MINES AND BOOBY TRAPS. FUCK THE ANIMALS--
THEY SET THEM FOR US.

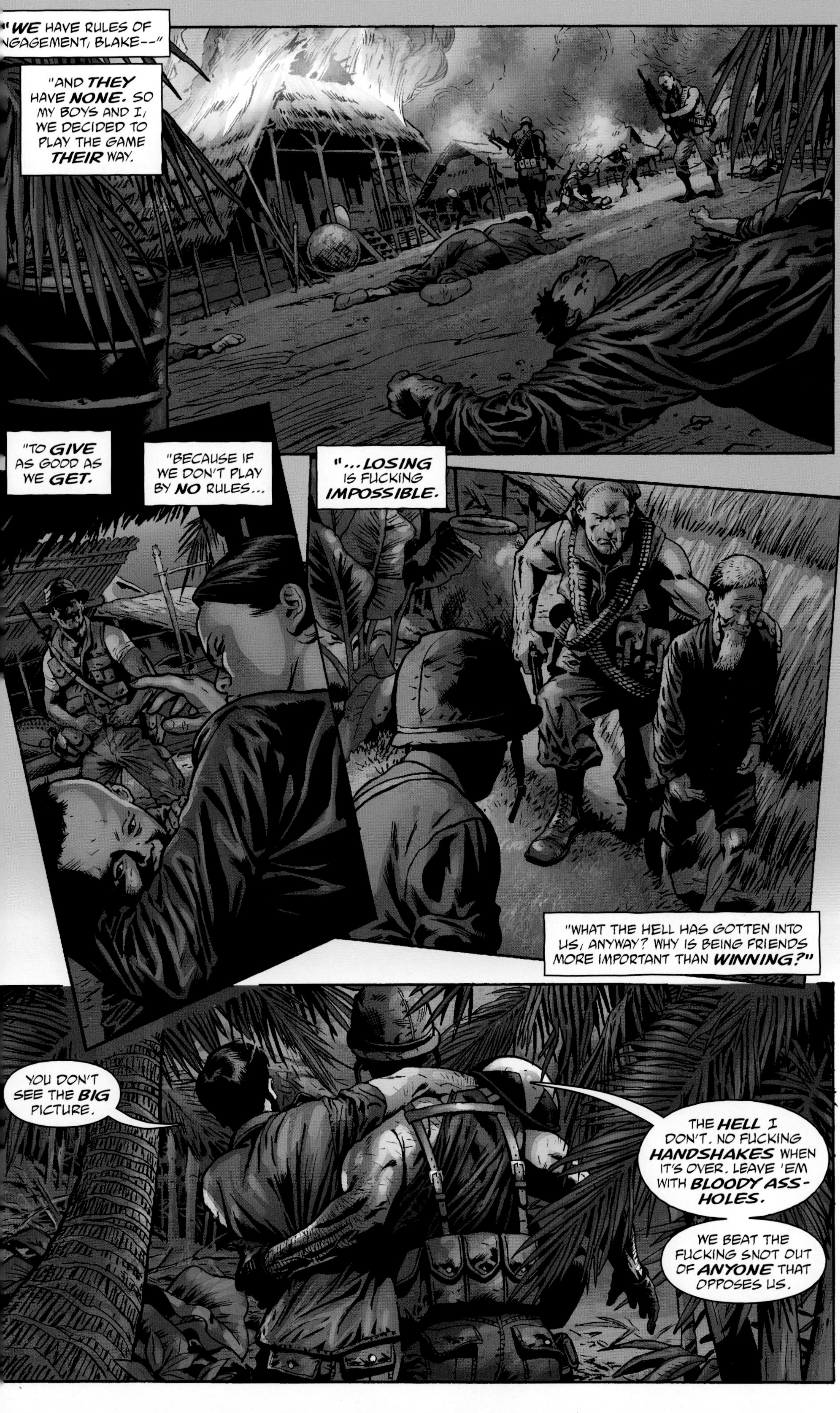
"WE HAVE RULES OF ENGAGEMENT, BLAKE--"
"AND THEY HAVE NONE. SO MY BOYS AND I, WE DECIDED TO PLAY THE GAME THEIR WAY.
"TO GIVE AS GOOD AS WE GET.
"BECAUSE IF WE DON'T PLAY BY NO RULES...
"...LOSING IS FUCKING IMPOSSIBLE.
"WHAT THE HELL HAS GOTTEN INTO US, ANYWAY? WHY IS BEING FRIENDS MORE IMPORTANT THAN WINNING?"
YOU DON'T SEE THE BIG PICTURE.
THE HELL I DON'T. NO FUCKING HANDSHAKES WHEN IT'S OVER. LEAVE 'EM WITH BLOODY ASS-HOLES.
WE BEAT THE FUCKING SNOT OUT OF ANYONE THAT OPPOSES US.

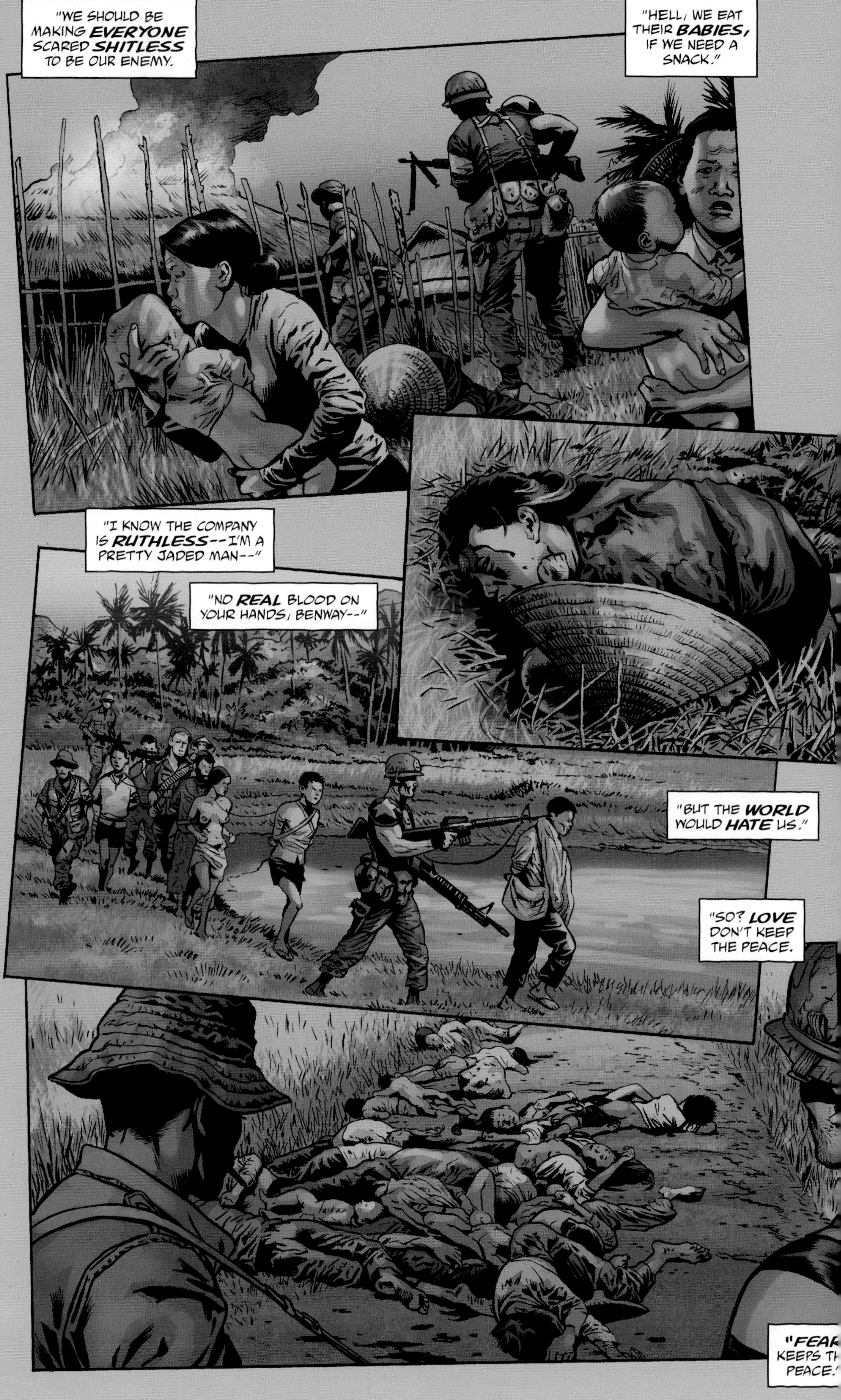
"WE SHOULD BE MAKING EVERYONE SCARED SHITLESS TO BE OUR ENEMY.
"HELL, WE EAT THEIR BABIES, IF WE NEED A SNACK."
"I KNOW THE COMPANY IS RUTHLESS--I'M A PRETTY JADED MAN--"
"NO REAL BLOOD ON YOUR HANDS, BENWAY--"
"BUT THE WORLD WOULD HATE US."
"SO? LOVE DON'T KEEP THE PEACE.
"FEAR KEEPS TH PEACE."

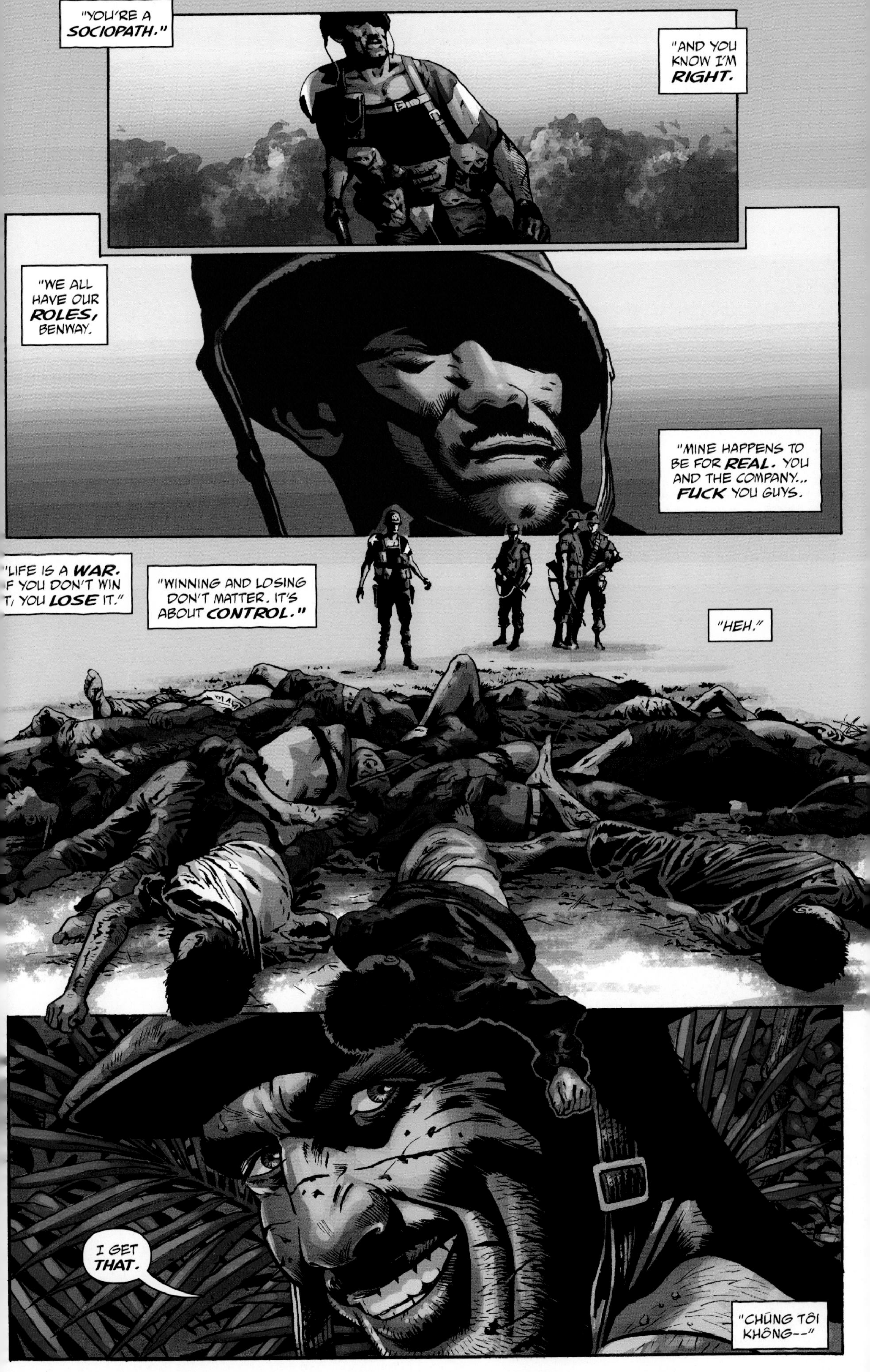
"YOU'RE A SOCIOPATH."
"AND YOU KNOW I'M RIGHT.
"WE ALL HAVE OUR ROLES, BENWAY.
"MINE HAPPENS TO BE FOR REAL. YOU AND THE COMPANY... FUCK YOU GUYS.
"LIFE IS A WAR. F YOU DON'T WIN T, YOU LOSE IT."
"WINNING AND LOSING DON'T MATTER. IT'S ABOUT CONTROL."
"HEH."
I GET THAT.
"CHÚNG TÔI KHÔNG--"

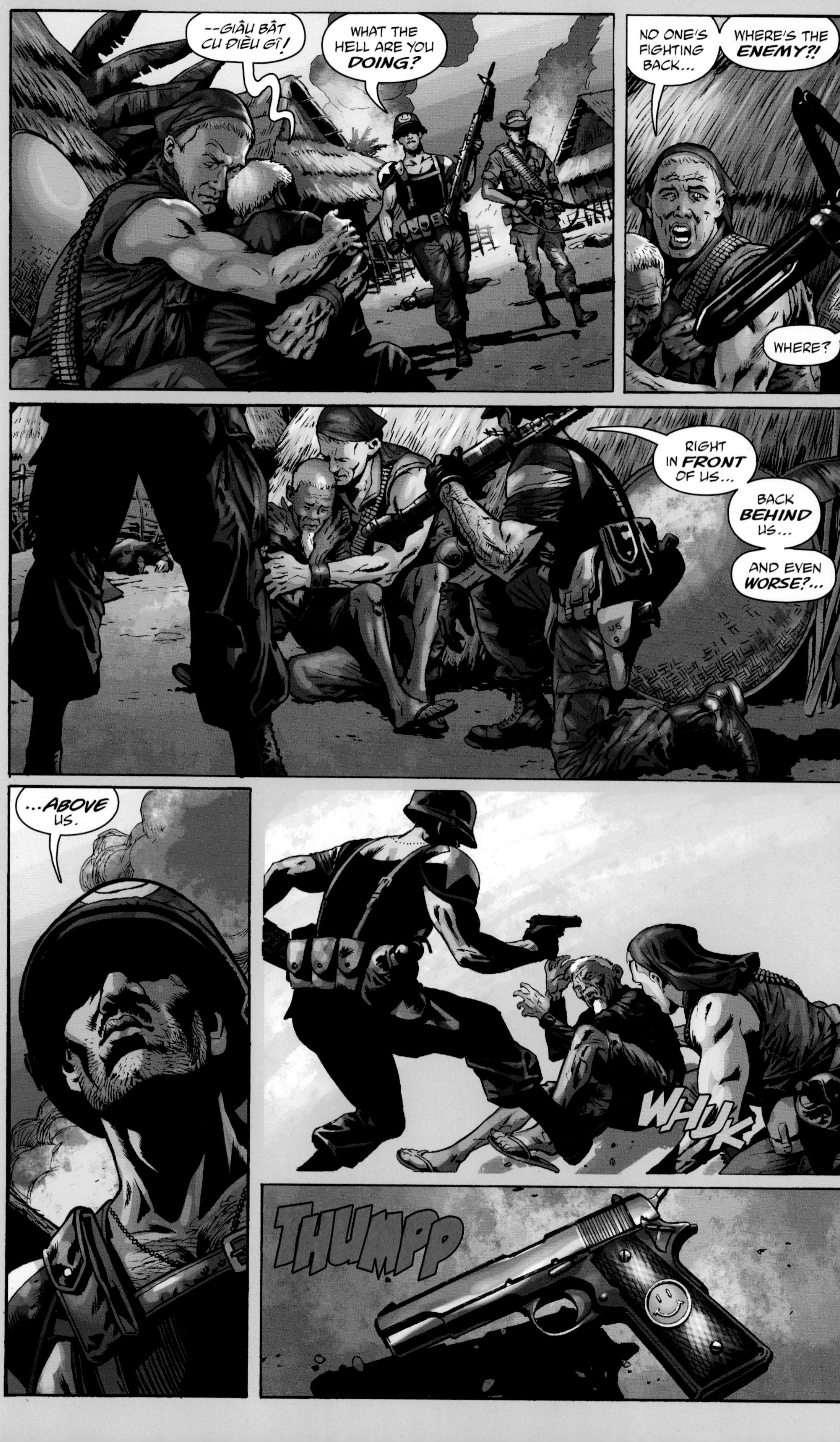
--GIẤU BẤT CỨ ĐIỀU GÌ!
WHAT THE HELL ARE YOU DOING?
NO ONE'S FIGHTING BACK...
WHERE'S THE ENEMY?!
WHERE?
RIGHT IN FRONT OF US...
BACK BEHIND US...
AND EVEN WORSE?...
...ABOVE US.
WHUK!
THUMPP

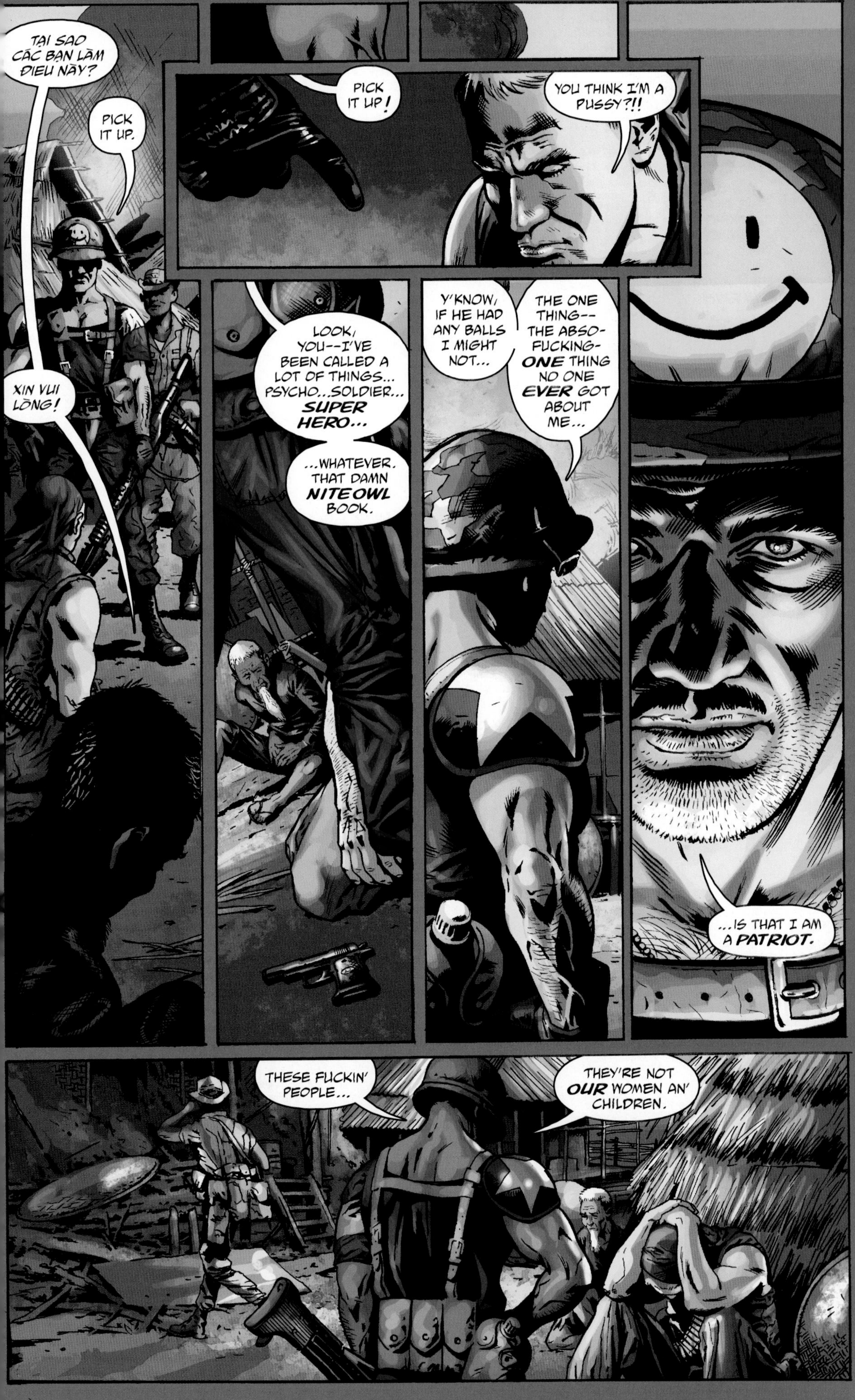
TẠI SAO CÁC BẠN LÀM ĐIỀU NÀY?
PICK IT UP.
PICK IT UP!
YOU THINK I'M A PUSSY?!!
XIN VUI LÒNG!
LOOK, YOU--I'VE BEEN CALLED A LOT OF THINGS... PSYCHO...SOLDIER... SUPER HERO...
...WHATEVER. THAT DAMN NITEOWL BOOK.
Y'KNOW, IF HE HAD ANY BALLS I MIGHT NOT...
THE ONE THING-- THE ABSO-FUCKING-ONE THING NO ONE EVER GOT ABOUT ME...
...IS THAT I AM A PATRIOT.
THESE FUCKIN' PEOPLE...
THEY'RE NOT OUR WOMEN AN' CHILDREN.

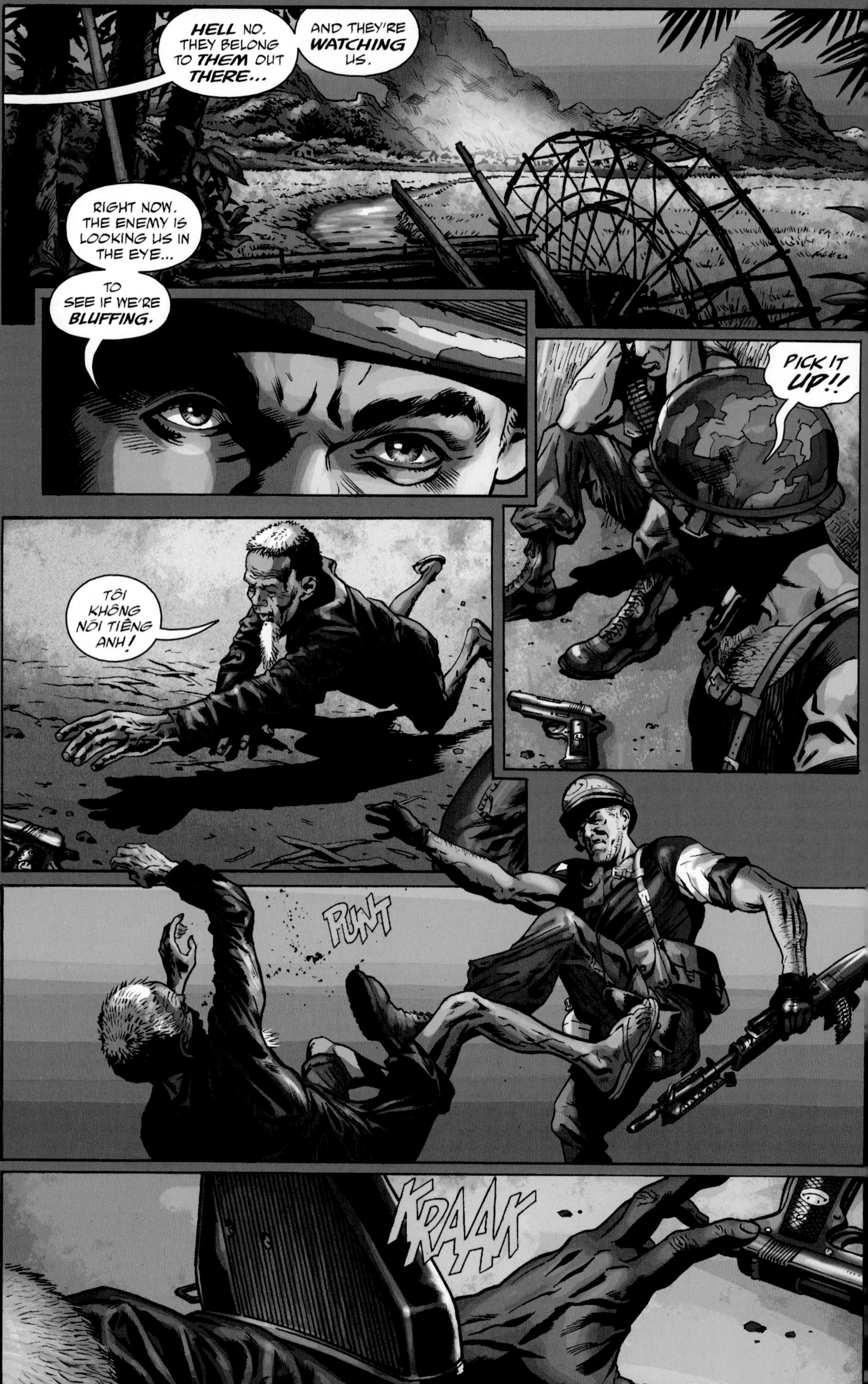
HELL NO. THEY BELONG TO THEM OUT THERE...
AND THEY'RE WATCHING US.
RIGHT NOW. THE ENEMY IS LOOKING US IN THE EYE...
TO SEE IF WE'RE BLUFFING.
PICK IT UP!!
TÔI KHÔNG NÓI TIẾNG ANH!
PUNT
KRAAK

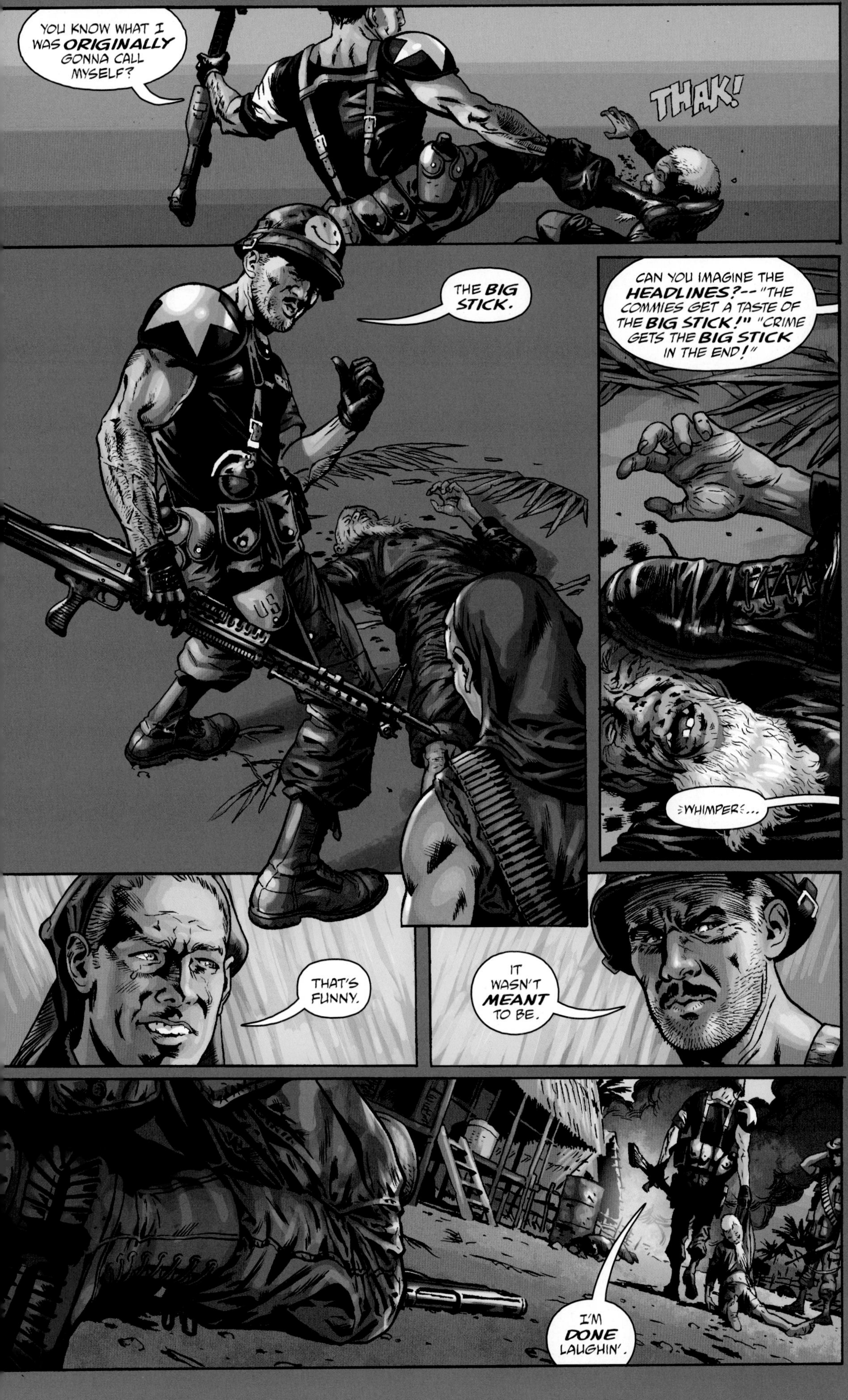
YOU KNOW WHAT I WAS ORIGINALLY GONNA CALL MYSELF?
THAK!
THE BIG STICK.
CAN YOU IMAGINE THE HEADLINES?-- "THE COMMIES GET A TASTE OF THE BIG STICK!" "CRIME GETS THE BIG STICK IN THE END!"
WHIMPER...
THAT'S FUNNY.
IT WASN'T MEANT TO BE.
I'M DONE LAUGHIN'.

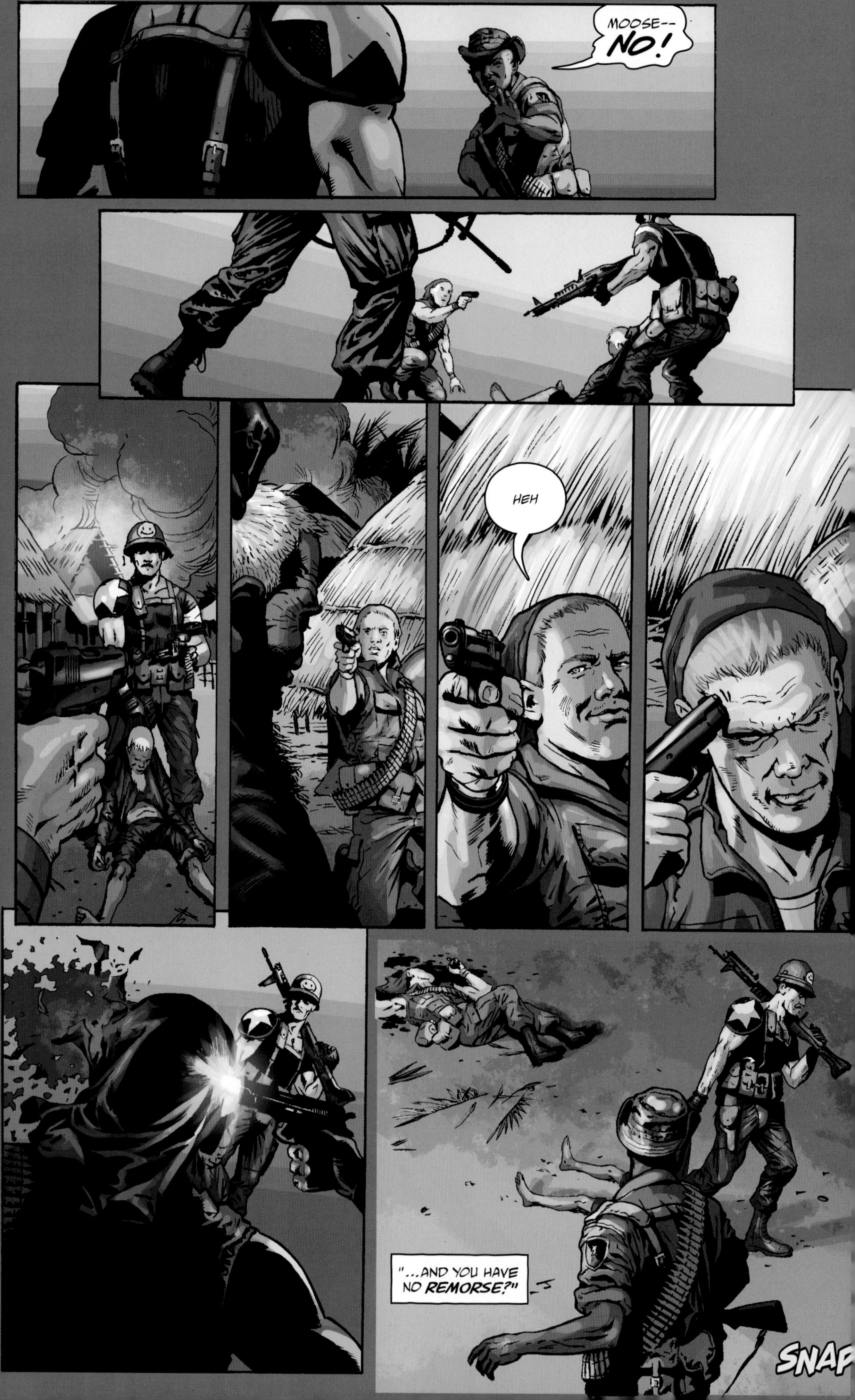
MOOSE-- NO!
HEH
"...AND YOU HAVE NO REMORSE?"
SNAP

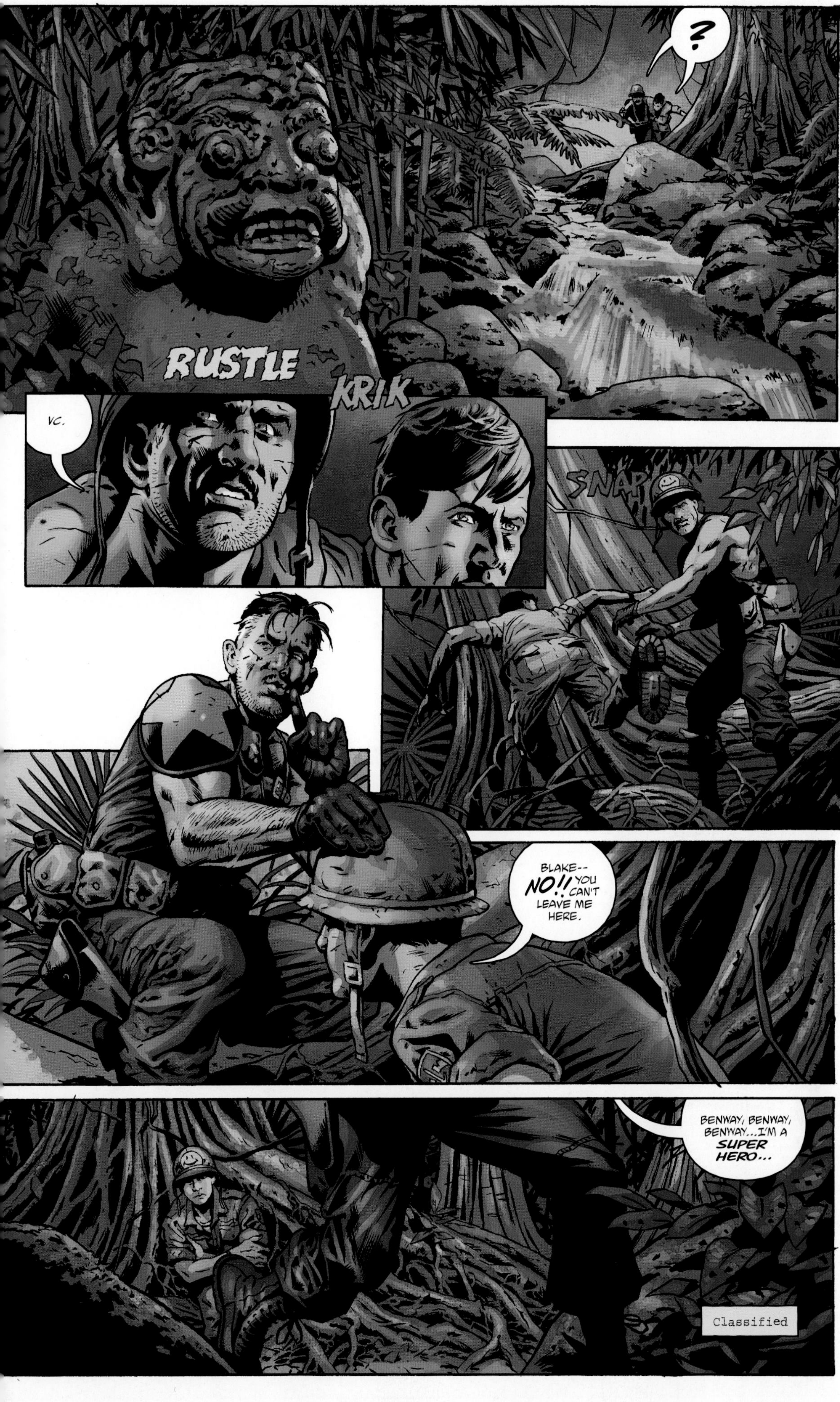
?
RUSTLE
KRIK
VC.
SNAP
BLAKE--
NO!! YOU CAN'T LEAVE ME HERE.
BENWAY, BENWAY, BENWAY...I'M A SUPER HERO...
Classified

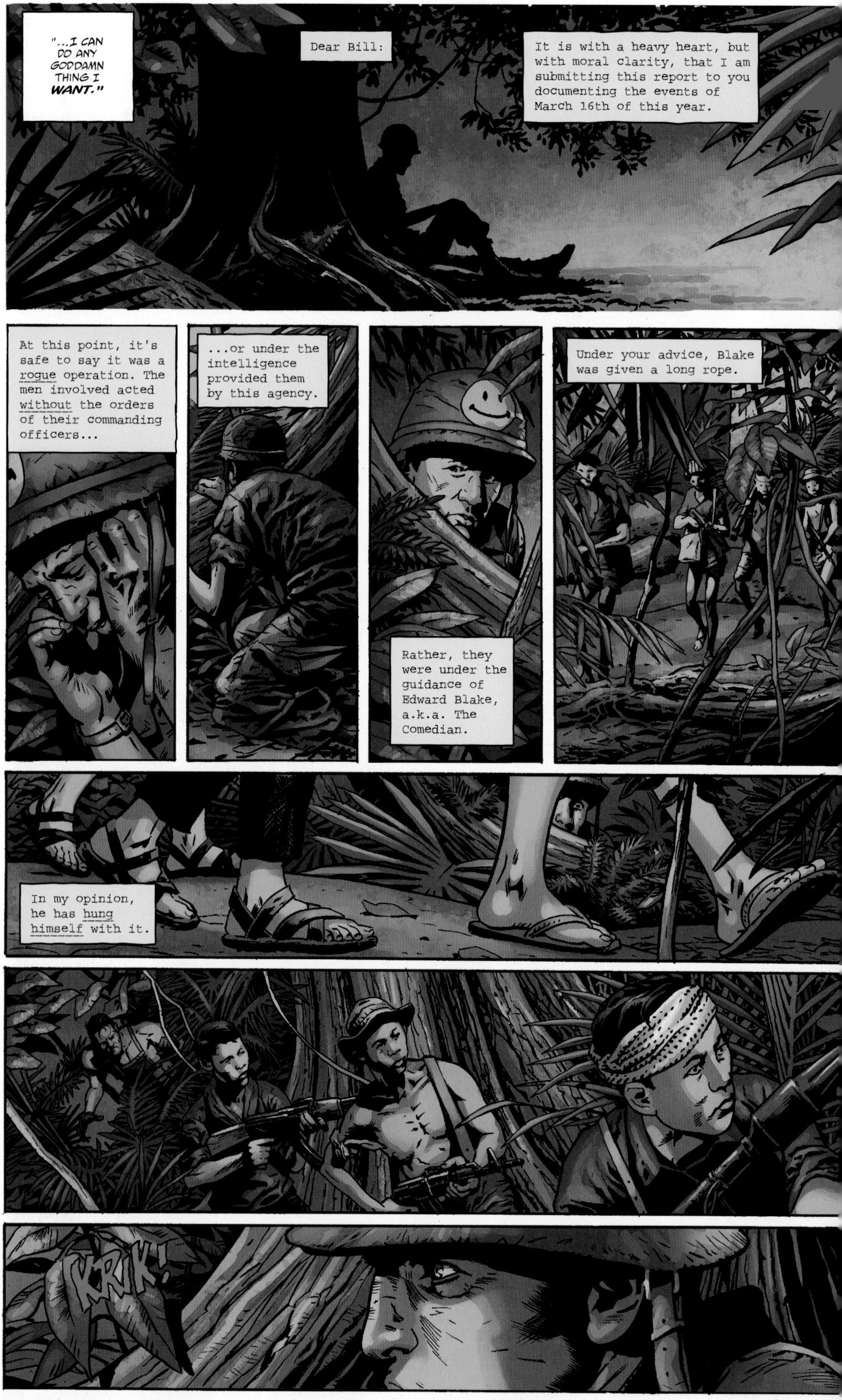

"...I CAN DO ANY GODDAMN THING I *WANT.*"
Dear Bill:
It is with a heavy heart, but with moral clarity, that I am submitting this report to you documenting the events of March 16th of this year.
At this point, it's safe to say it was a rogue operation. The men involved acted without the orders of their commanding officers...
...or under the intelligence provided them by this agency.
Rather, they were under the guidance of Edward Blake, a.k.a. The Comedian.
Under your advice, Blake was given a long rope.
In my opinion, he has hung himself with it.
KRIK!

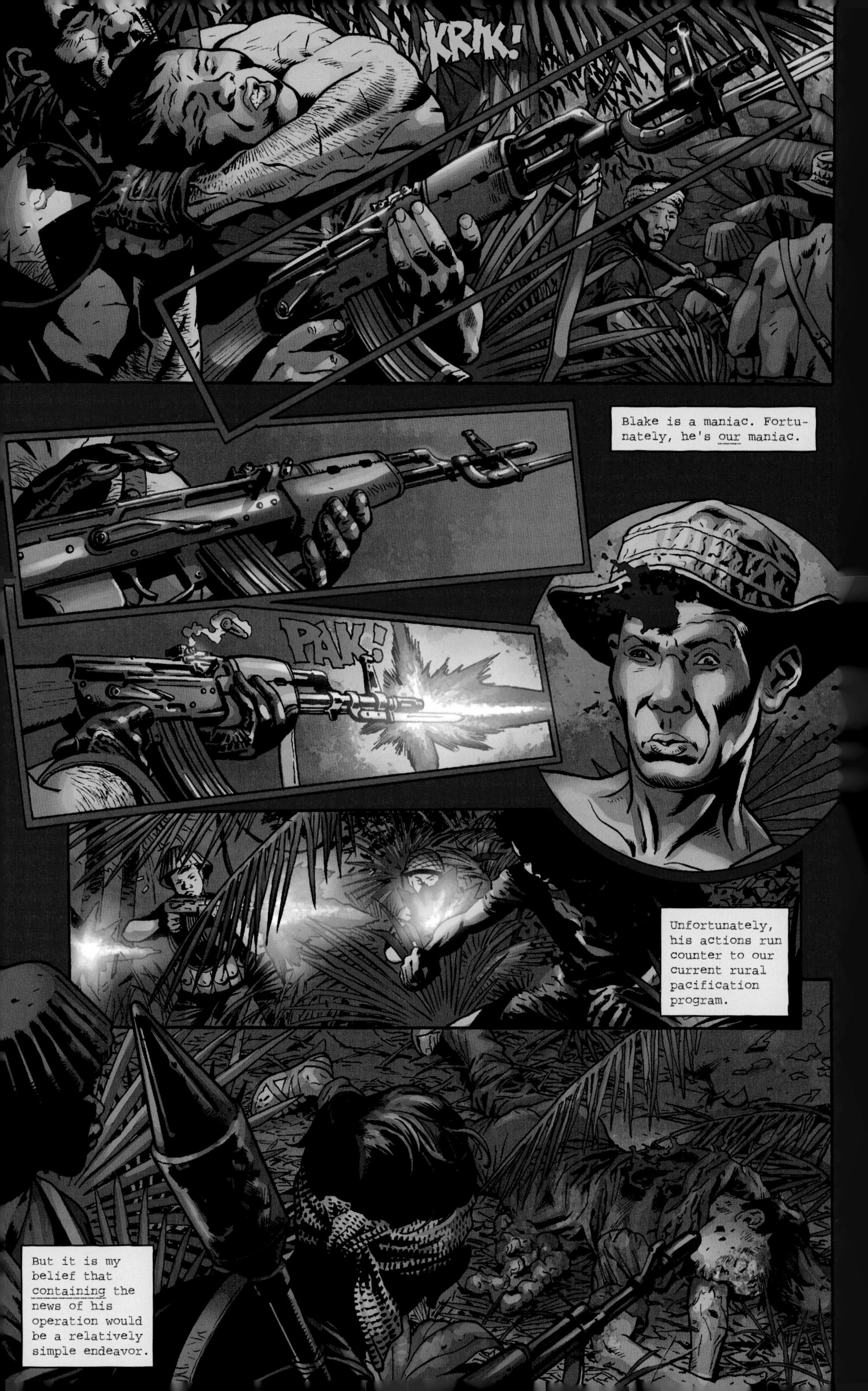
KRIK!
Blake is a maniac. Fortunately, he's our maniac.
PAK!
Unfortunately, his actions run counter to our current rural pacification program.
But it is my belief that containing the news of his operation would be a relatively simple endeavor.

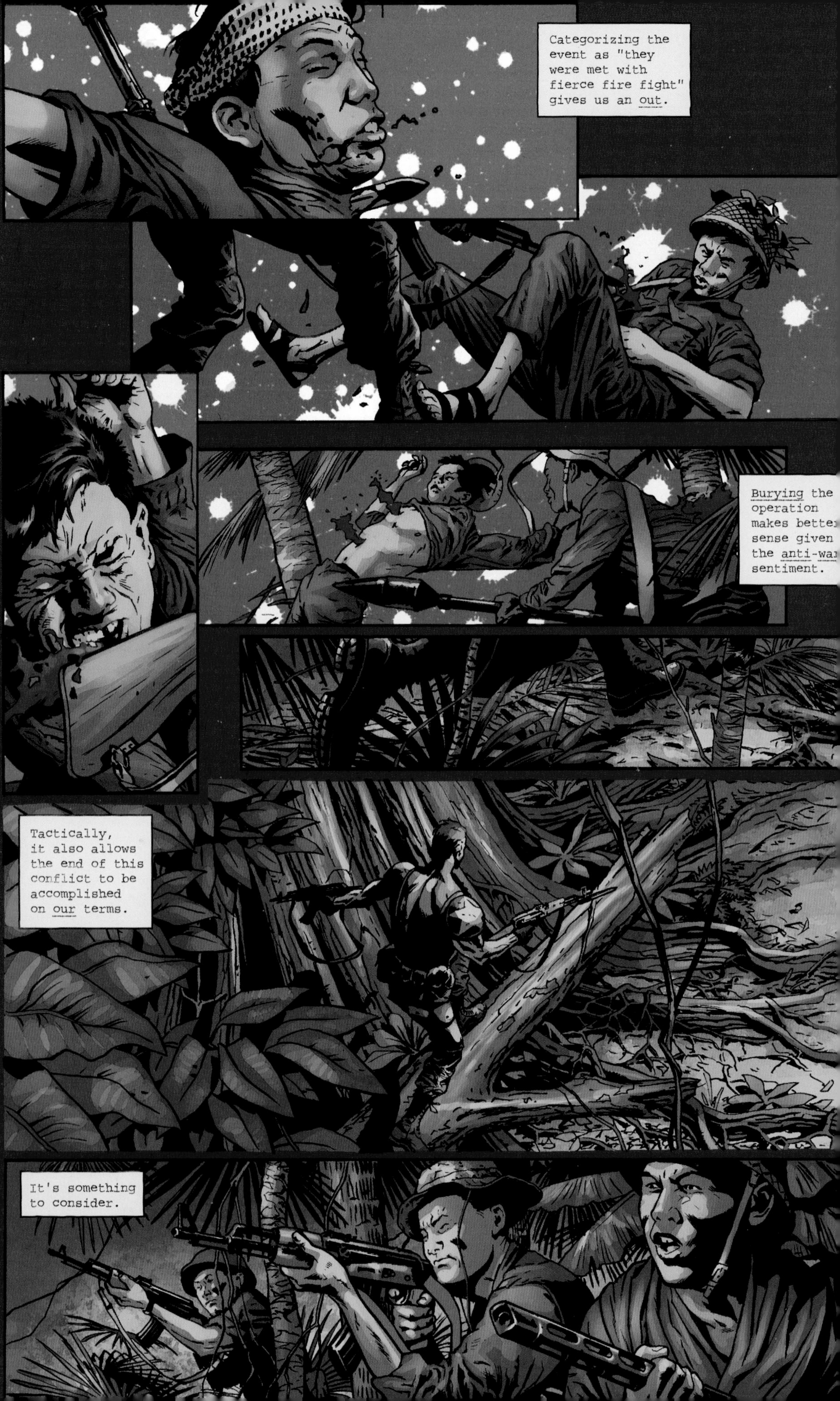
Categorizing the event as "they were met with fierce fire fight" gives us an out.
Burying the operation makes better sense given the anti-war sentiment.
Tactically, it also allows the end of this conflict to be accomplished on our terms.
It's something to consider.

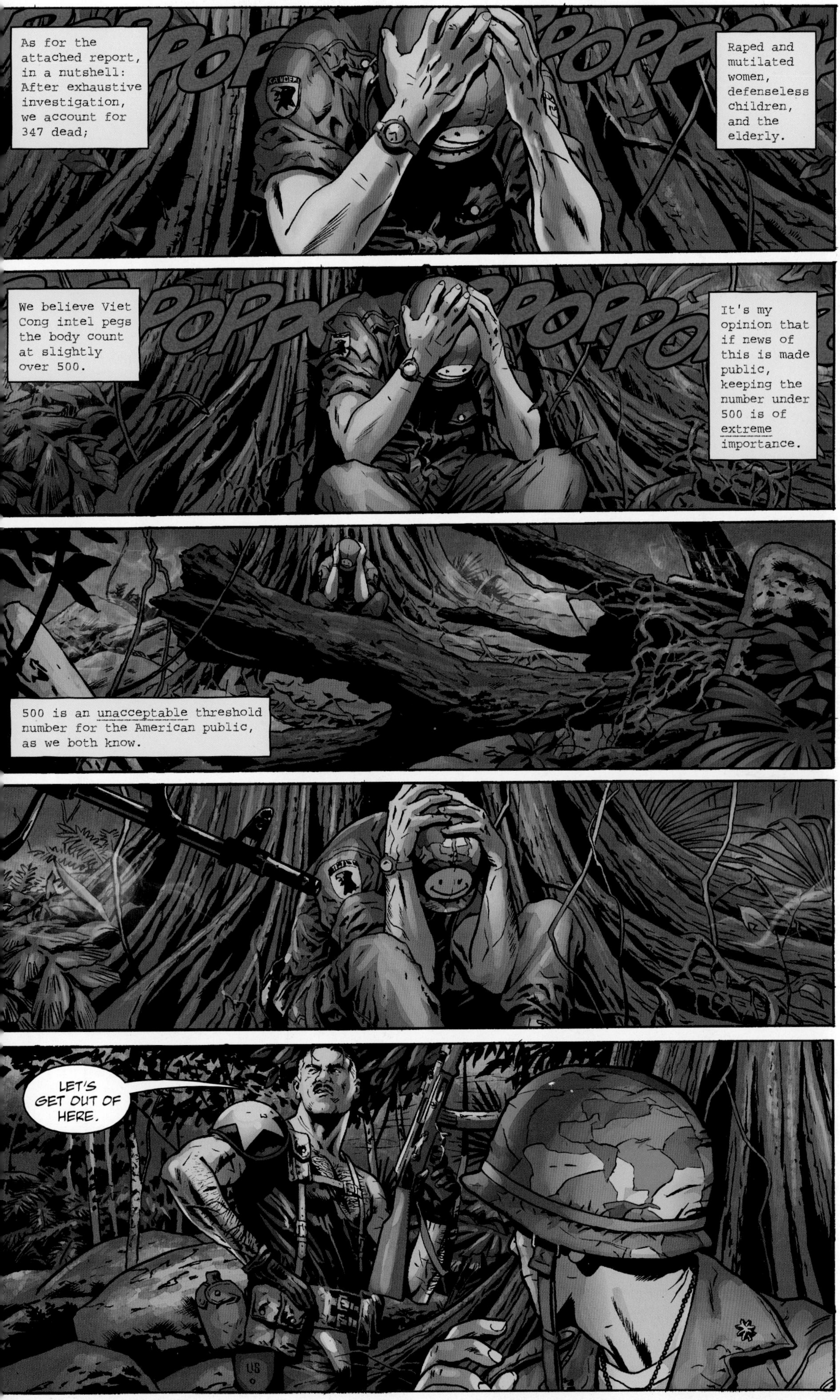
As for the attached report, in a nutshell: After exhaustive investigation, we account for 347 dead;
Raped and mutilated women, defenseless children, and the elderly.
We believe Viet Cong intel pegs the body count at slightly over 500.
It's my opinion that if news of this is made public, keeping the number under 500 is of extreme importance.
500 is an unacceptable threshold number for the American public, as we both know.
LET'S GET OUT OF HERE.

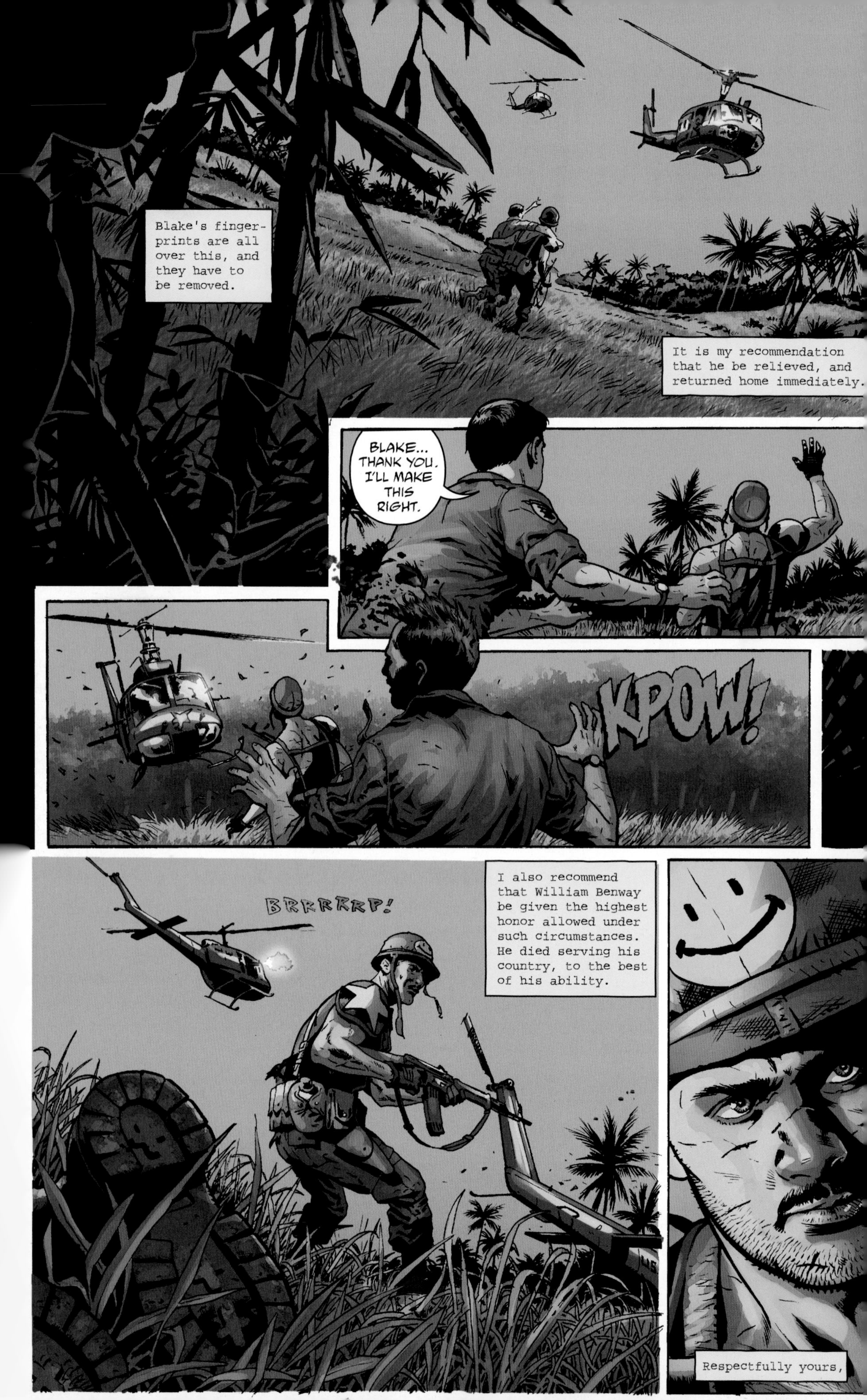

Blake's finger-prints are all over this, and they have to be removed.
It is my recommendation that he be relieved, and returned home immediately.
BLAKE... THANK YOU. I'LL MAKE THIS RIGHT.
KPOW!
BRRRRRP!
I also recommend that William Benway be given the highest honor allowed under such circumstances. He died serving his country, to the best of his ability.
Respectfully yours,

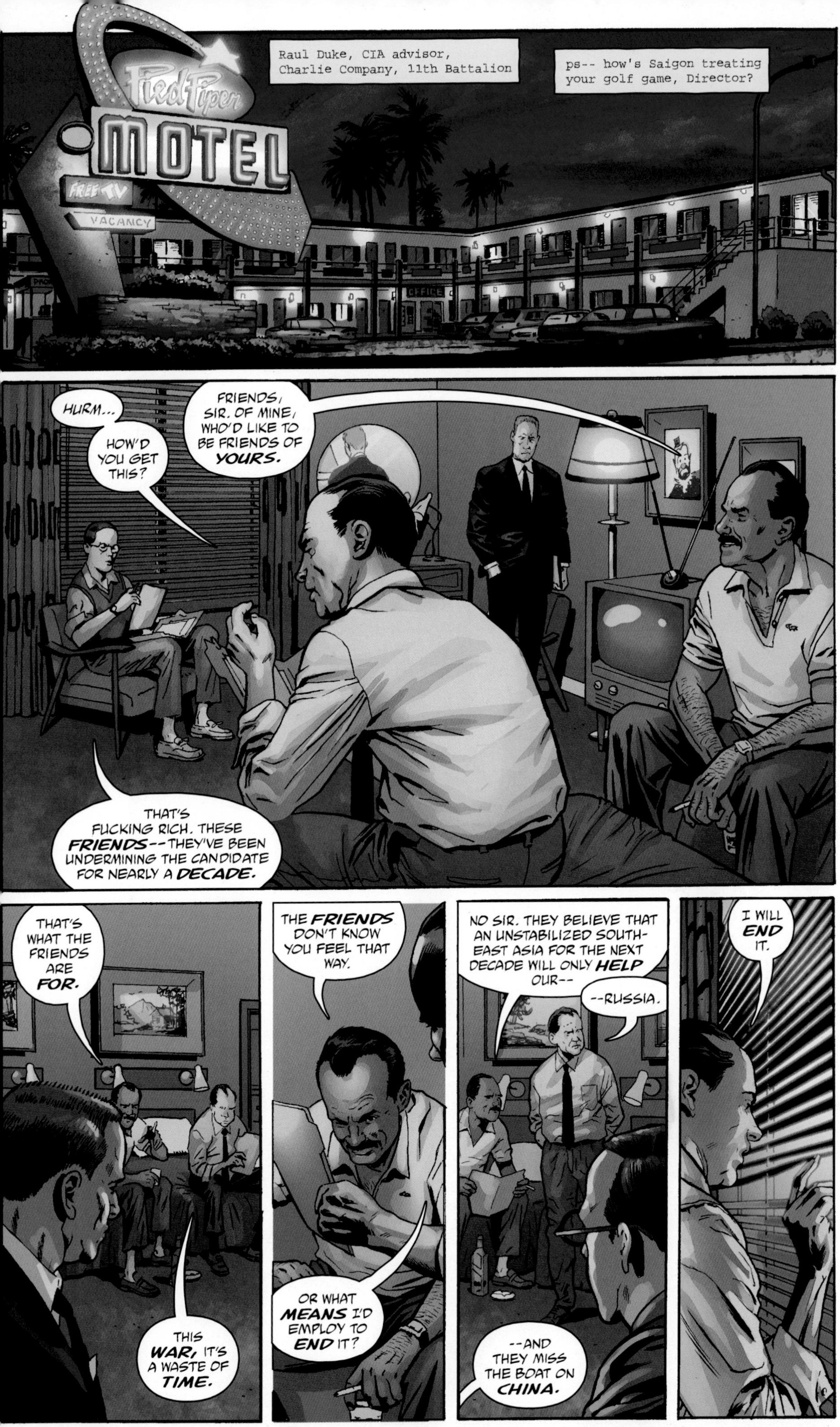
Raul Duke, CIA advisor, Charlie Company, 11th Battalion
ps-- how's Saigon treating your golf game, Director?
Fied Piper
MOTEL
FREE TV
VACANCY
OFFICE
HURM...
HOW'D YOU GET THIS?
FRIENDS, SIR. OF MINE, WHO'D LIKE TO BE FRIENDS OF YOURS.
THAT'S FUCKING RICH. THESE FRIENDS--THEY'VE BEEN UNDERMINING THE CANDIDATE FOR NEARLY A DECADE.
THAT'S WHAT THE FRIENDS ARE FOR.
THIS WAR, IT'S A WASTE OF TIME.
THE FRIENDS DON'T KNOW YOU FEEL THAT WAY.
OR WHAT MEANS I'D EMPLOY TO END IT?
NO SIR. THEY BELIEVE THAT AN UNSTABILIZED SOUTH-EAST ASIA FOR THE NEXT DECADE WILL ONLY HELP OUR--
--RUSSIA.
--AND THEY MISS THE BOAT ON CHINA.
I WILL END IT.

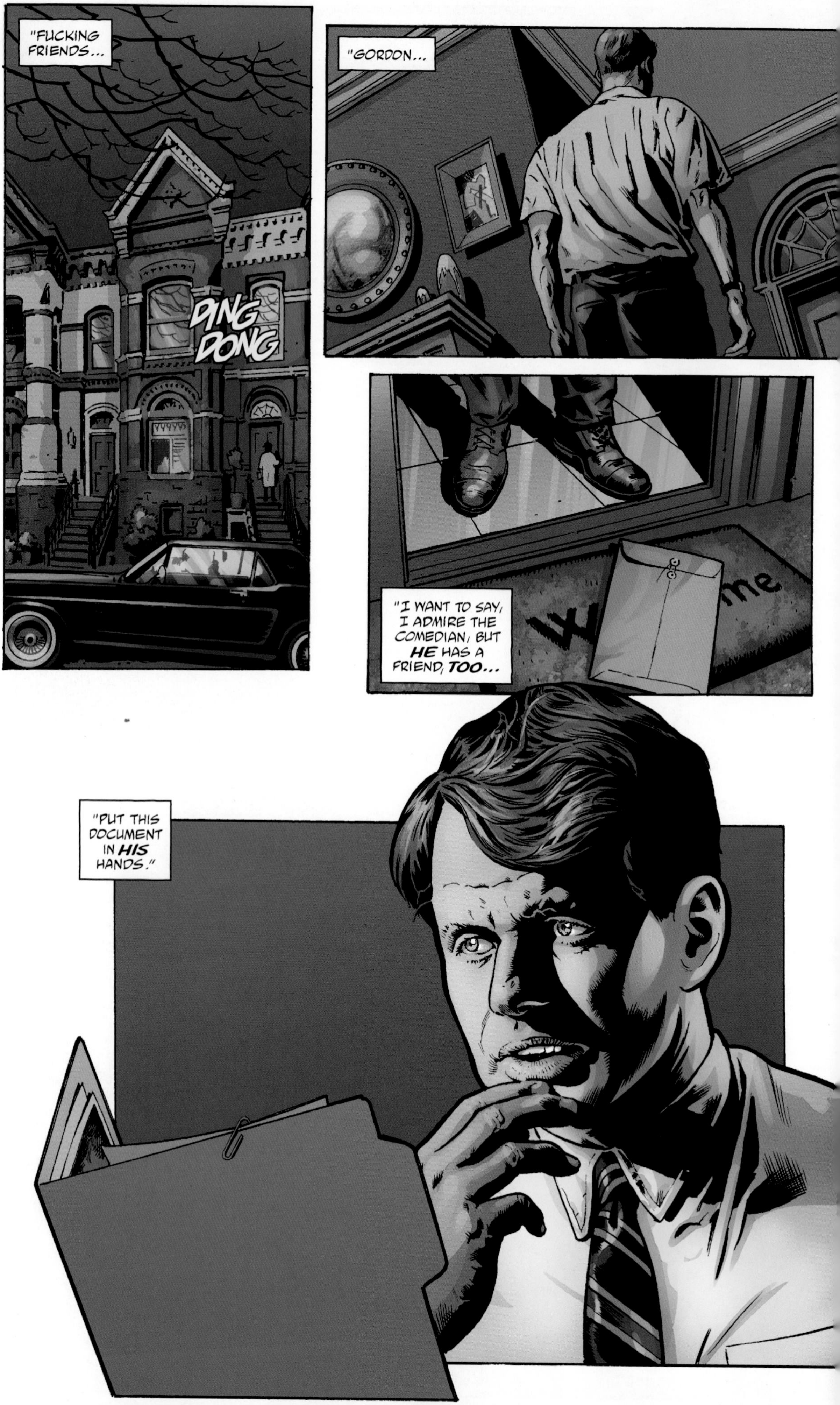
"FUCKING FRIENDS...
DING DONG
"GORDON...
"I WANT TO SAY, I ADMIRE THE COMEDIAN, BUT HE HAS A FRIEND, TOO...
"PUT THIS DOCUMENT IN HIS HANDS."

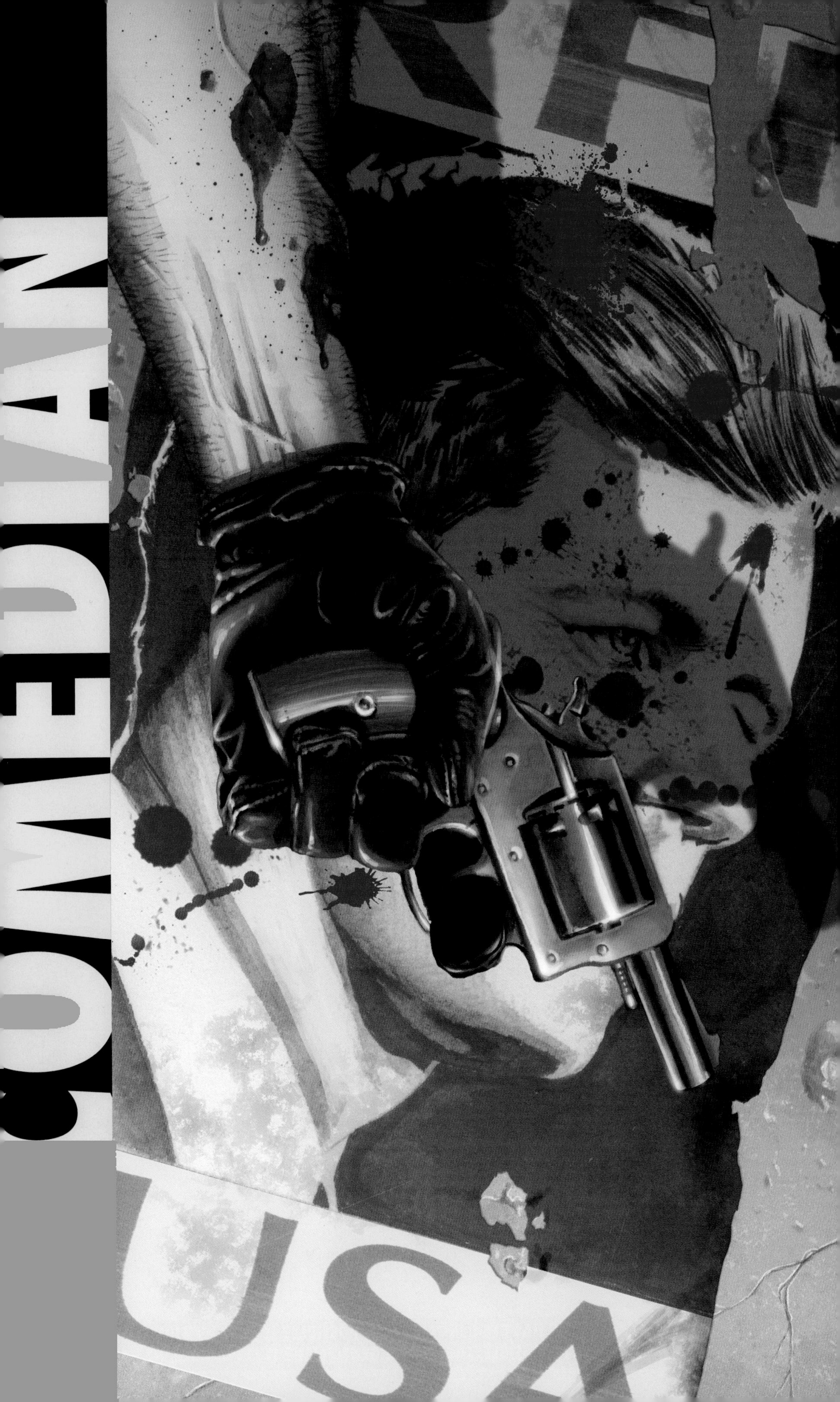
COMEDIAN
USA

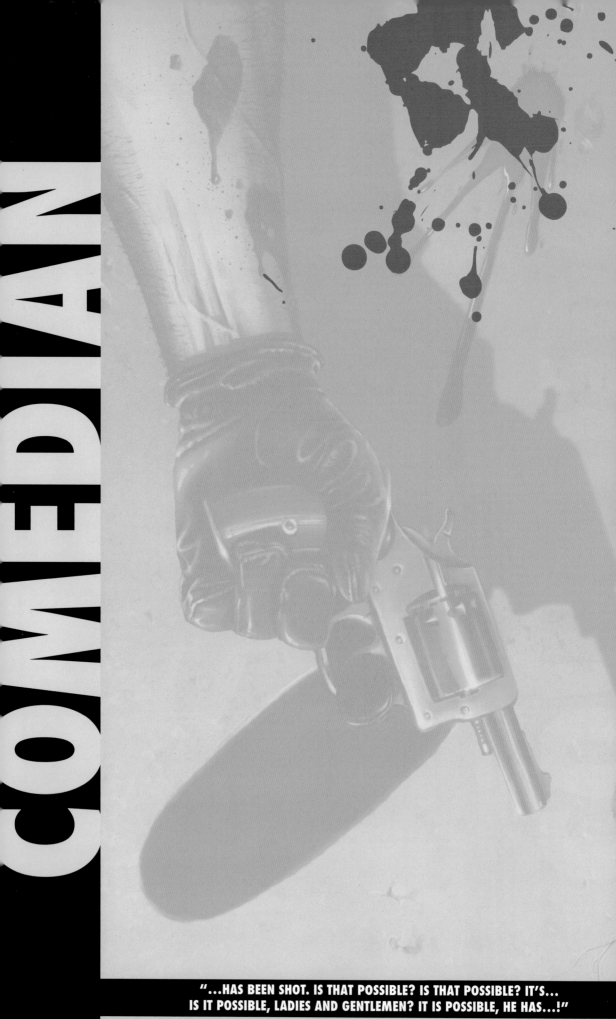

COMEDIAN

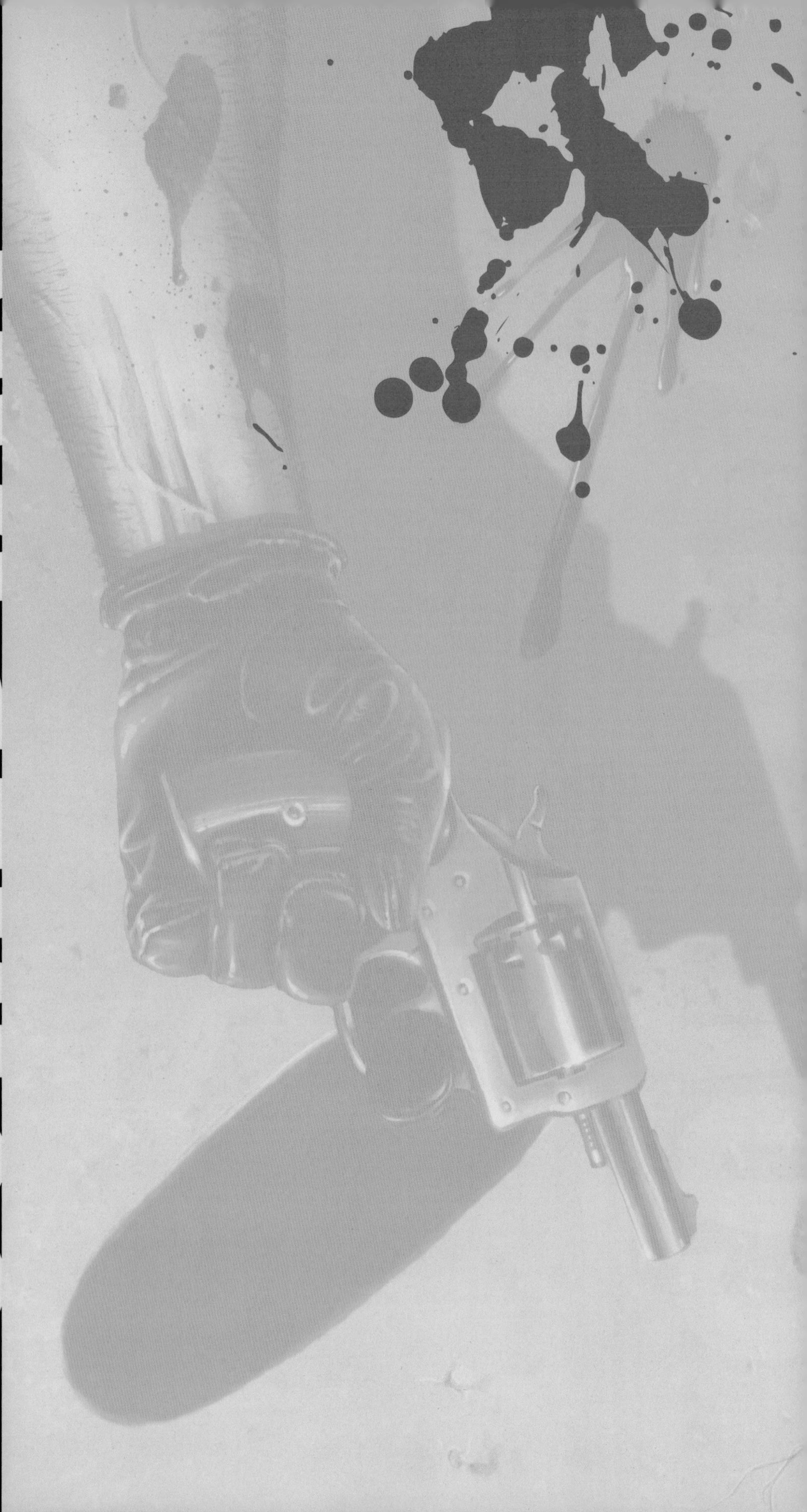

"...HAS BEEN SHOT. IS THAT POSSIBLE? IS THAT POSSIBLE? IT'S...
IS IT POSSIBLE, LADIES AND GENTLEMEN? IT IS POSSIBLE, HE HAS...!"

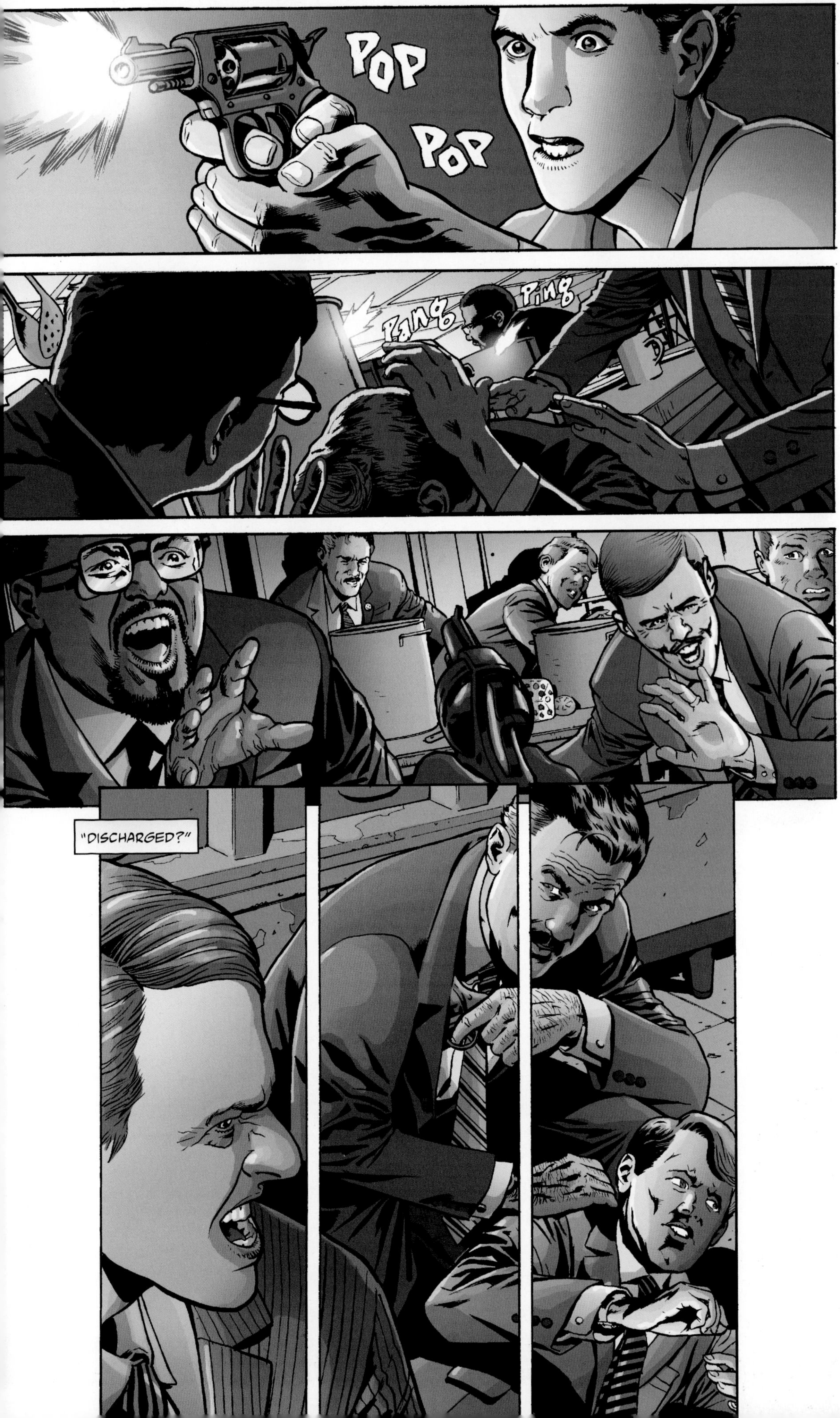
POP
POP
PANG
PING
"DISCHARGED?"

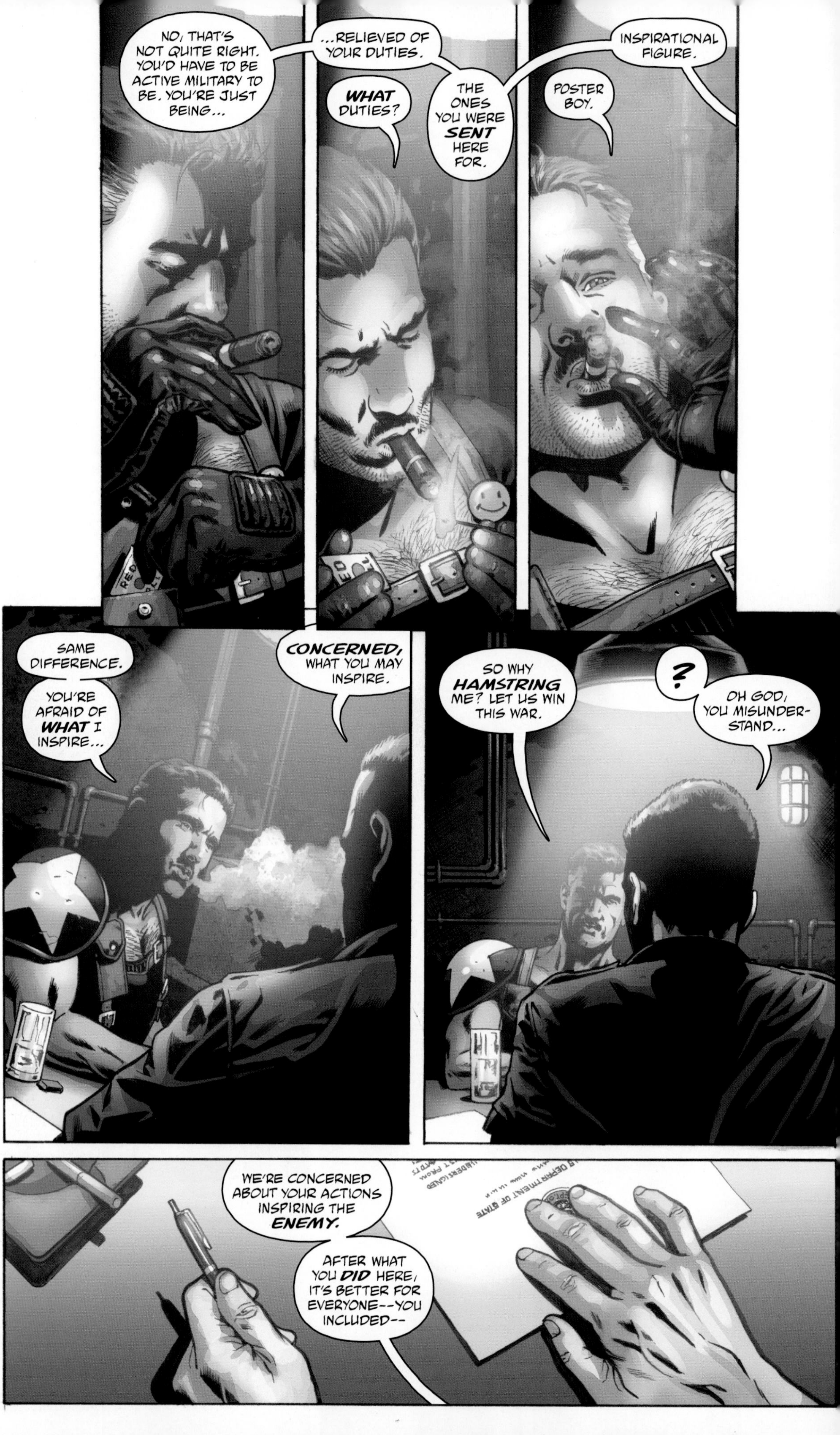
NO, THAT'S NOT QUITE RIGHT. YOU'D HAVE TO BE ACTIVE MILITARY TO BE. YOU'RE JUST BEING...
...RELIEVED OF YOUR DUTIES.
WHAT DUTIES?
THE ONES YOU WERE SENT HERE FOR.
INSPIRATIONAL FIGURE.
POSTER BOY.
SAME DIFFERENCE.
YOU'RE AFRAID OF WHAT I INSPIRE...
CONCERNED, WHAT YOU MAY INSPIRE.
SO WHY HAMSTRING ME? LET US WIN THIS WAR.
?
OH GOD, YOU MISUNDER-STAND...
WE'RE CONCERNED ABOUT YOUR ACTIONS INSPIRING THE ENEMY.
AFTER WHAT YOU DID HERE, IT'S BETTER FOR EVERYONE--YOU INCLUDED--

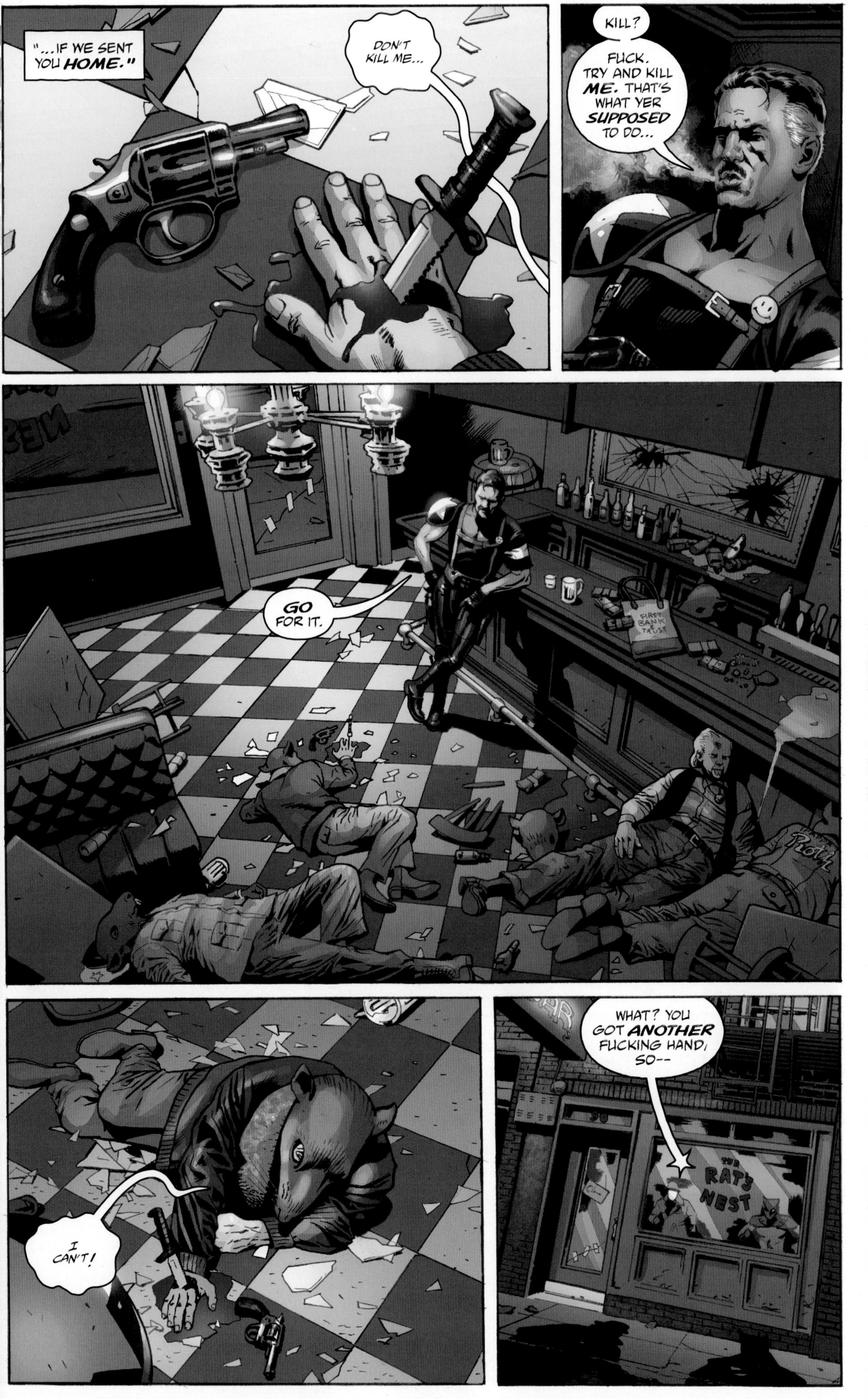
"...IF WE SENT YOU **HOME.**"
DON'T KILL ME...
KILL?
FUCK. TRY AND KILL **ME.** THAT'S WHAT YER **SUPPOSED** TO DO...
GO FOR IT.
I CAN'T!
WHAT? YOU GOT **ANOTHER** FUCKING HAND, SO--
THE RAT'S NEST

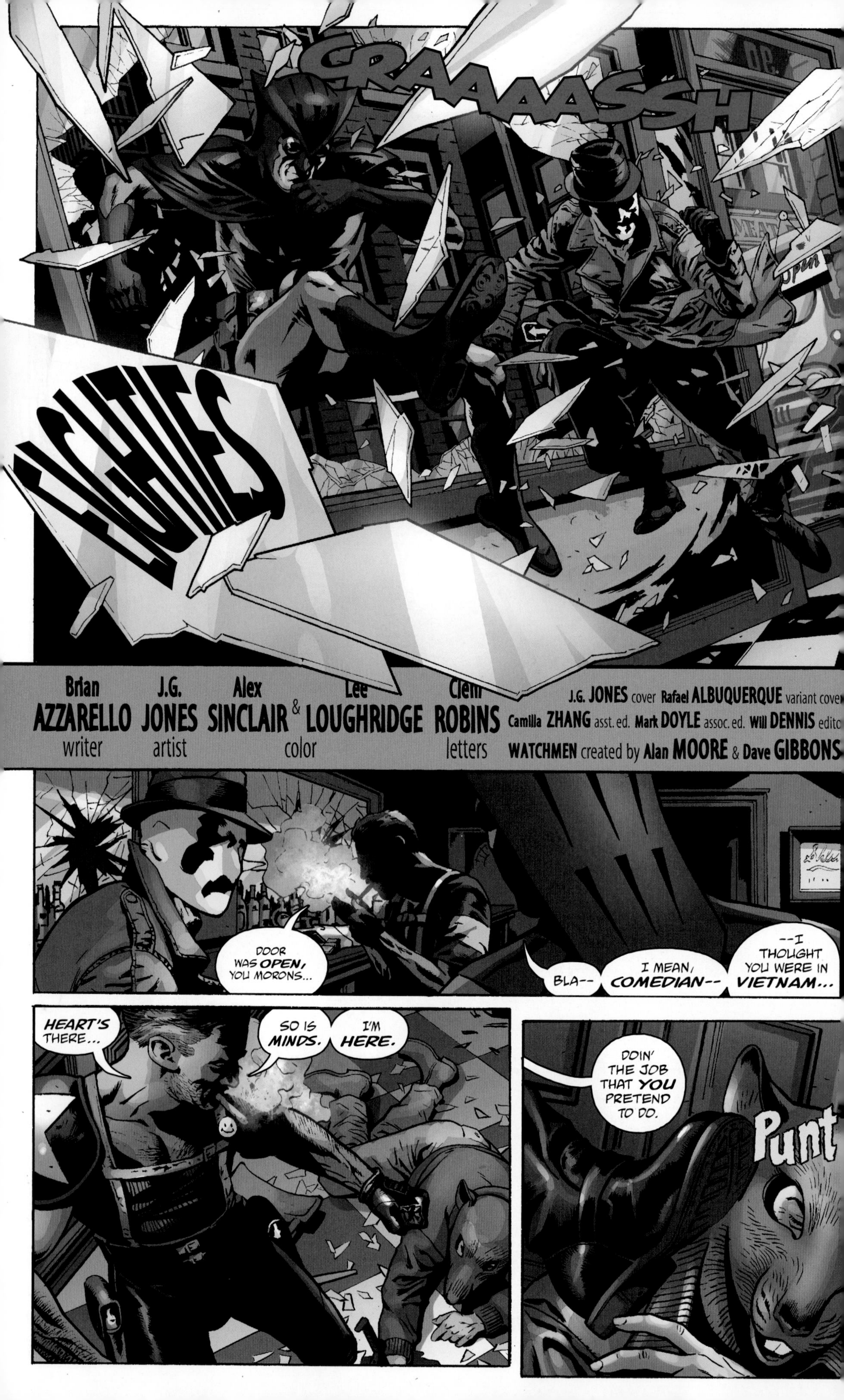

GRAAAASSH
EIGHTIES
Brian AZZARELLO writer
J.G. JONES artist
Alex SINCLAIR & Lee LOUGHRIDGE color
Clem ROBINS letters
J.G. JONES cover Rafael ALBUQUERQUE variant cover
Camilla ZHANG asst. ed. Mark DOYLE assoc. ed. Will DENNIS editor
WATCHMEN created by Alan MOORE & Dave GIBBONS
DOOR WAS OPEN, YOU MORONS...
BLA--
I MEAN, COMEDIAN--
--I THOUGHT YOU WERE IN VIETNAM...
HEART'S THERE...
SO IS MINDS.
I'M HERE.
DOIN' THE JOB THAT YOU PRETEND TO DO.
Punt

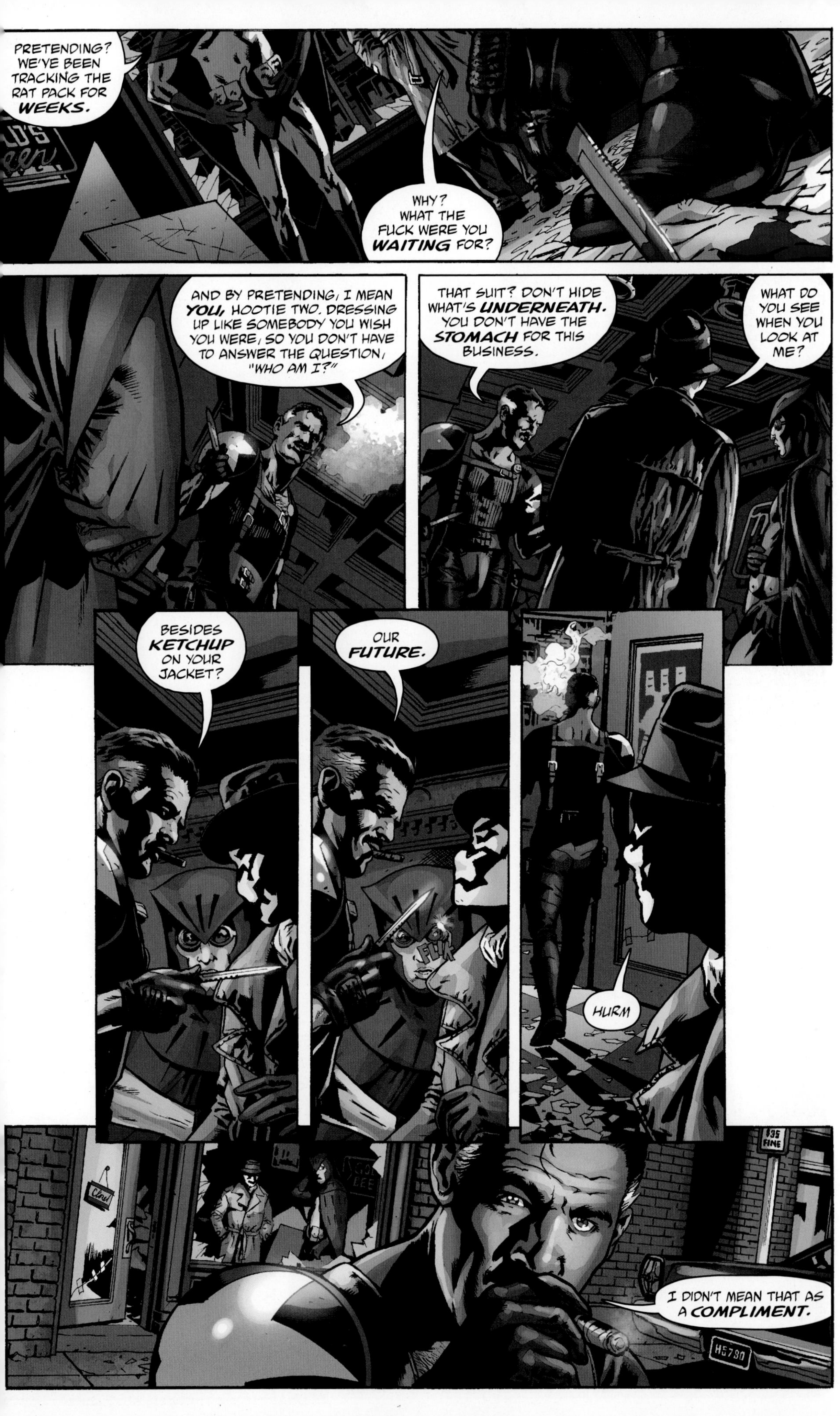
PRETENDING? WE'VE BEEN TRACKING THE RAT PACK FOR **WEEKS.**
WHY? WHAT THE FUCK WERE YOU **WAITING** FOR?
AND BY PRETENDING, I MEAN **YOU,** HOOTIE TWO. DRESSING UP LIKE SOMEBODY YOU WISH YOU WERE, SO YOU DON'T HAVE TO ANSWER THE QUESTION, "WHO AM I?"
THAT SUIT? DON'T HIDE WHAT'S **UNDERNEATH.** YOU DON'T HAVE THE **STOMACH** FOR THIS BUSINESS.
WHAT DO YOU SEE WHEN YOU LOOK AT ME?
BESIDES **KETCHUP** ON YOUR JACKET?
OUR **FUTURE.**
FLIK
HURM
$35 FINE
I DIDN'T MEAN THAT AS A **COMPLIMENT.**

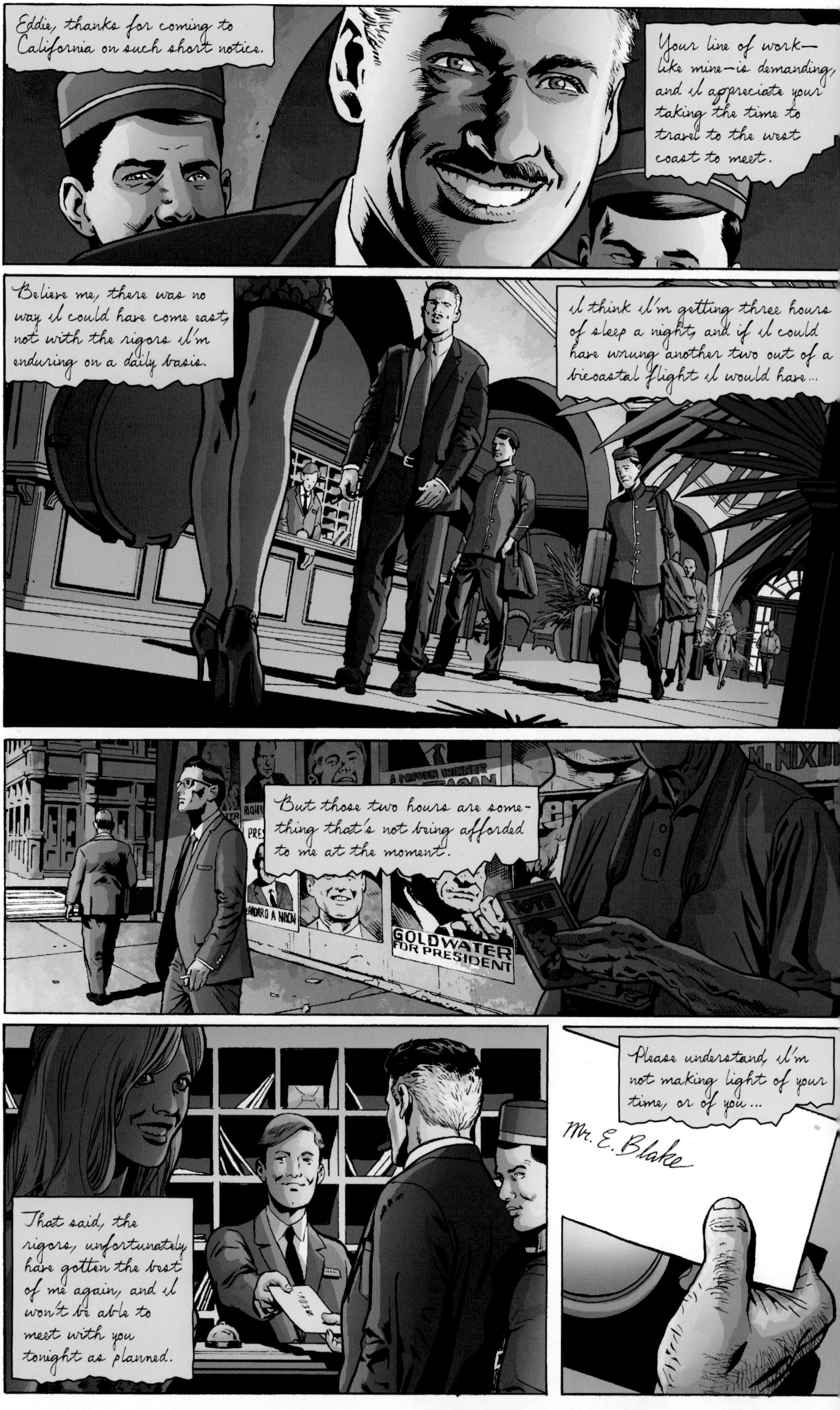

Eddie, thanks for coming to California on such short notice.
Your line of work—like mine—is demanding, and I appreciate your taking the time to travel to the west coast to meet.
Believe me, there was no way I could have come east, not with the rigors I'm enduring on a daily basis.
I think I'm getting three hours of sleep a night, and if I could have wrung another two out of a bicoastal flight I would have...
A PROVEN WINNER
But those two hours are something that's not being afforded to me at the moment.
GOLDWATER
FOR PRESIDENT
VOTE
Please understand, I'm not making light of your time, or of you...
Mr. E. Blake
That said, the rigors, unfortunately have gotten the best of me again, and I won't be able to meet with you tonight as planned.

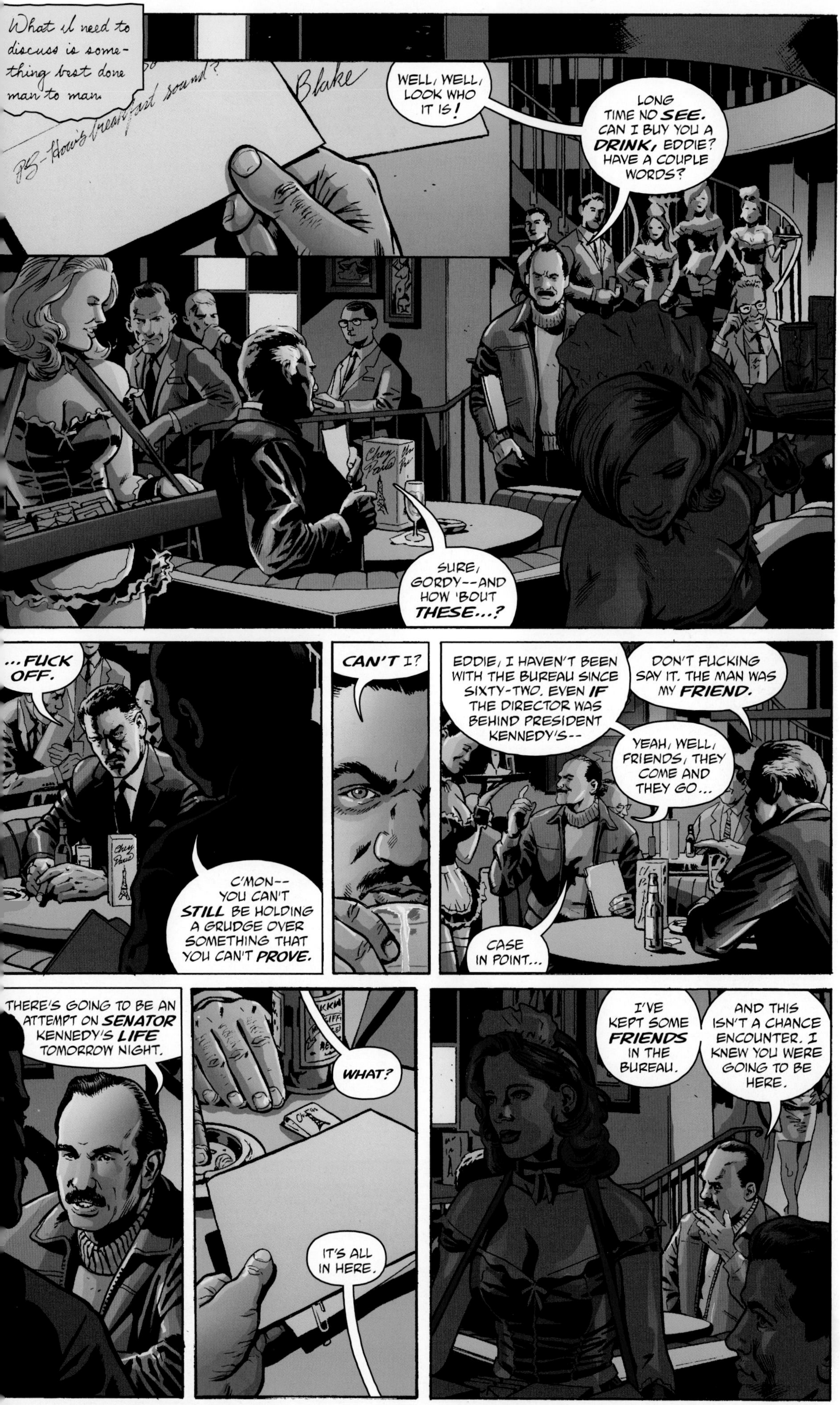
What I need to discuss is something best done man to man.
Blake
WELL, WELL, LOOK WHO IT IS!
LONG TIME NO SEE. CAN I BUY YOU A DRINK, EDDIE? HAVE A COUPLE WORDS?
SURE, GORDY--AND HOW 'BOUT THESE...?
...FUCK OFF.
C'MON-- YOU CAN'T STILL BE HOLDING A GRUDGE OVER SOMETHING THAT YOU CAN'T PROVE.
CAN'T I?
EDDIE, I HAVEN'T BEEN WITH THE BUREAU SINCE SIXTY-TWO. EVEN IF THE DIRECTOR WAS BEHIND PRESIDENT KENNEDY'S--
DON'T FUCKING SAY IT. THE MAN WAS MY FRIEND.
YEAH, WELL, FRIENDS, THEY COME AND THEY GO...
CASE IN POINT...
THERE'S GOING TO BE AN ATTEMPT ON SENATOR KENNEDY'S LIFE TOMORROW NIGHT.
WHAT?
IT'S ALL IN HERE.
I'VE KEPT SOME FRIENDS IN THE BUREAU.
AND THIS ISN'T A CHANCE ENCOUNTER. I KNEW YOU WERE GOING TO BE HERE.

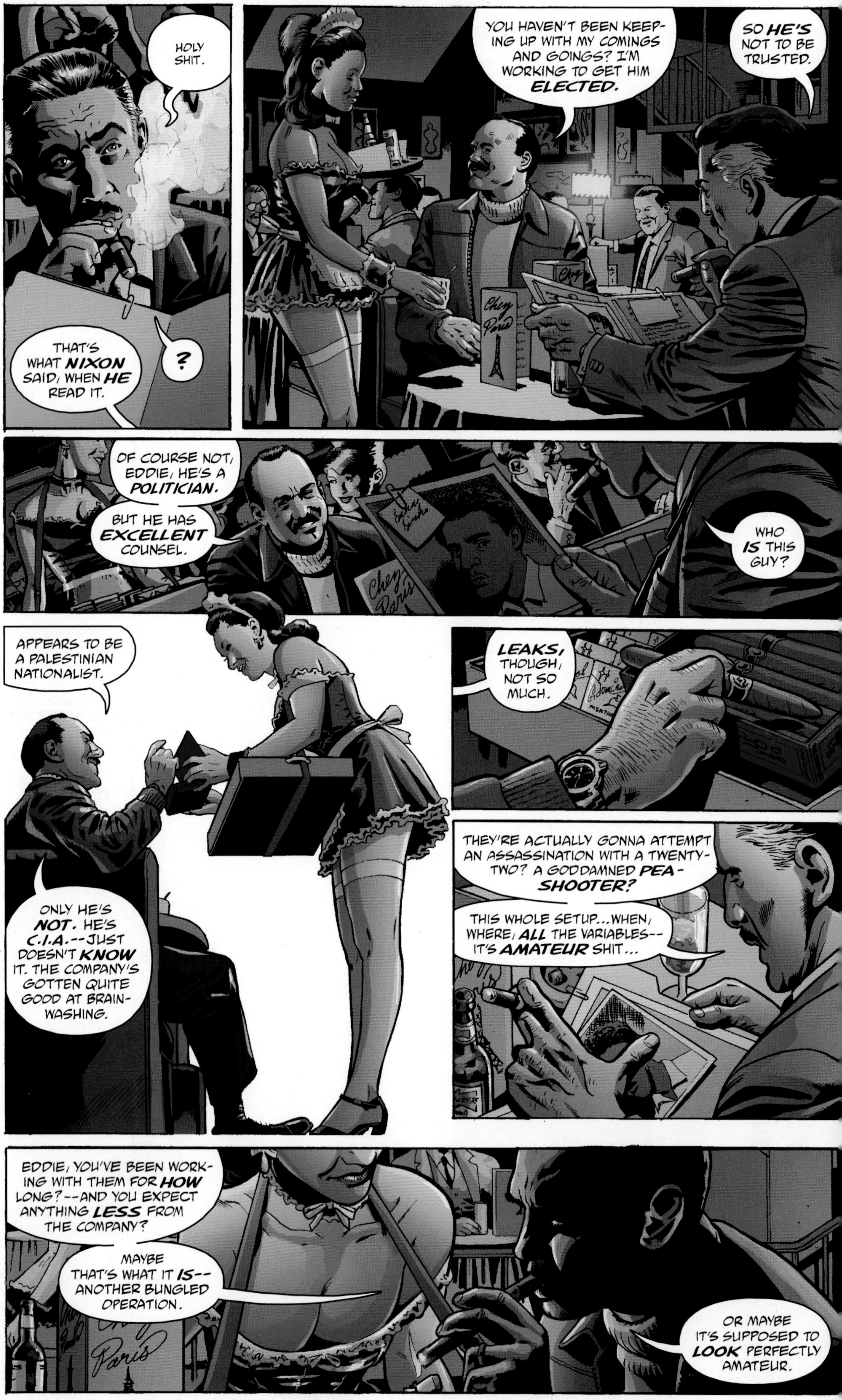
HOLY SHIT.
?
THAT'S WHAT NIXON SAID, WHEN HE READ IT.
YOU HAVEN'T BEEN KEEPING UP WITH MY COMINGS AND GOINGS? I'M WORKING TO GET HIM ELECTED.
SO HE'S NOT TO BE TRUSTED.
OF COURSE NOT, EDDIE, HE'S A POLITICIAN.
BUT HE HAS EXCELLENT COUNSEL.
WHO IS THIS GUY?
APPEARS TO BE A PALESTINIAN NATIONALIST.
ONLY HE'S NOT. HE'S C.I.A.--JUST DOESN'T KNOW IT. THE COMPANY'S GOTTEN QUITE GOOD AT BRAINWASHING.
LEAKS, THOUGH, NOT SO MUCH.
THEY'RE ACTUALLY GONNA ATTEMPT AN ASSASSINATION WITH A TWENTY-TWO? A GODDAMNED PEA-SHOOTER?
THIS WHOLE SETUP...WHEN, WHERE, ALL THE VARIABLES--IT'S AMATEUR SHIT...
EDDIE, YOU'VE BEEN WORKING WITH THEM FOR HOW LONG?--AND YOU EXPECT ANYTHING LESS FROM THE COMPANY?
MAYBE THAT'S WHAT IT IS--ANOTHER BUNGLED OPERATION.
OR MAYBE IT'S SUPPOSED TO LOOK PERFECTLY AMATEUR.

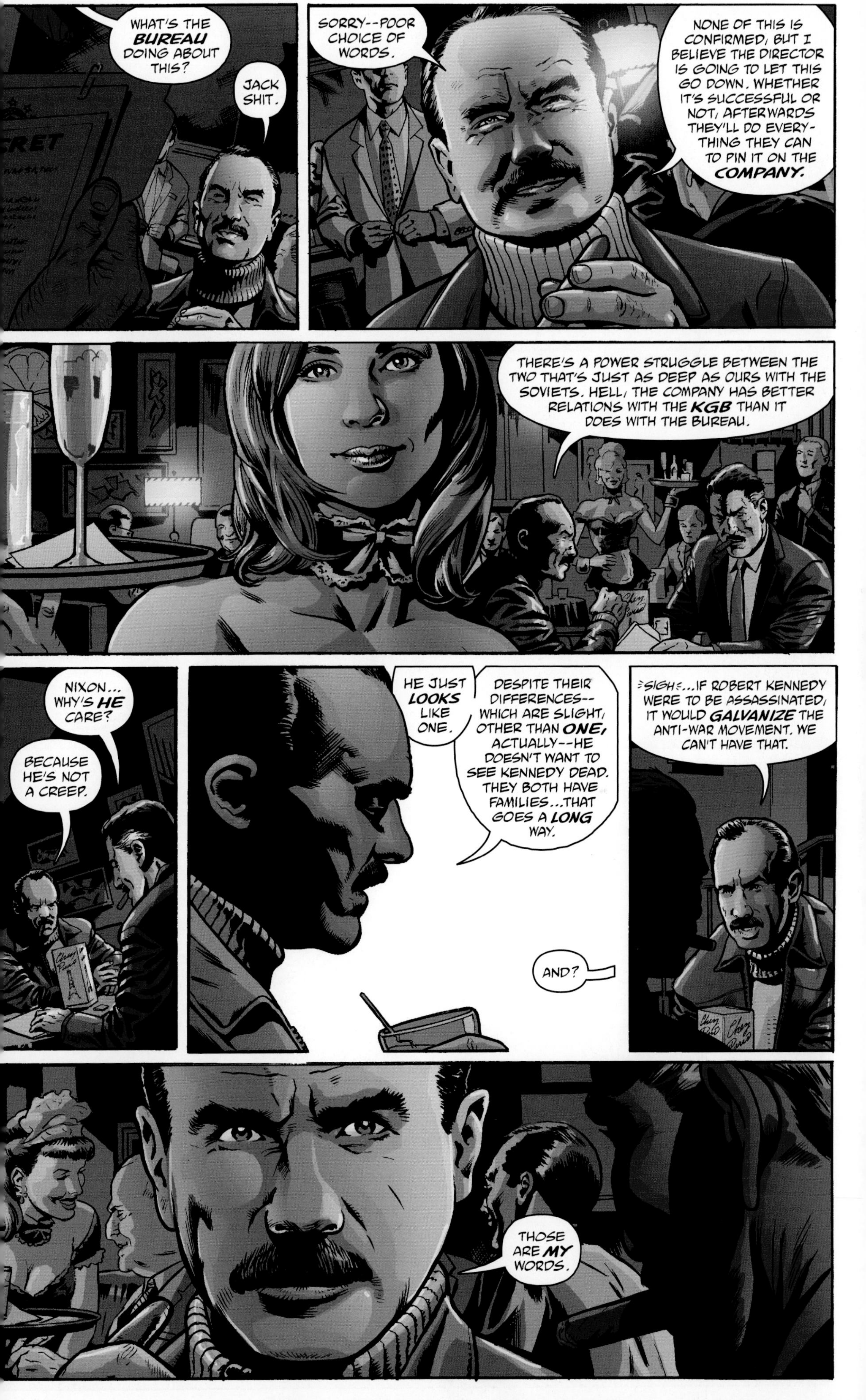
WHAT'S THE BUREAU DOING ABOUT THIS?
JACK SHIT.
SORRY--POOR CHOICE OF WORDS.
NONE OF THIS IS CONFIRMED, BUT I BELIEVE THE DIRECTOR IS GOING TO LET THIS GO DOWN. WHETHER IT'S SUCCESSFUL OR NOT, AFTERWARDS THEY'LL DO EVERYTHING THEY CAN TO PIN IT ON THE COMPANY.
THERE'S A POWER STRUGGLE BETWEEN THE TWO THAT'S JUST AS DEEP AS OURS WITH THE SOVIETS. HELL, THE COMPANY HAS BETTER RELATIONS WITH THE KGB THAN IT DOES WITH THE BUREAU.
NIXON... WHY'S HE CARE?
BECAUSE HE'S NOT A CREEP.
HE JUST LOOKS LIKE ONE.
DESPITE THEIR DIFFERENCES--WHICH ARE SLIGHT, OTHER THAN ONE, ACTUALLY--HE DOESN'T WANT TO SEE KENNEDY DEAD. THEY BOTH HAVE FAMILIES...THAT GOES A LONG WAY.
AND?
SIGH...IF ROBERT KENNEDY WERE TO BE ASSASSINATED, IT WOULD GALVANIZE THE ANTI-WAR MOVEMENT. WE CAN'T HAVE THAT.
THOSE ARE MY WORDS.

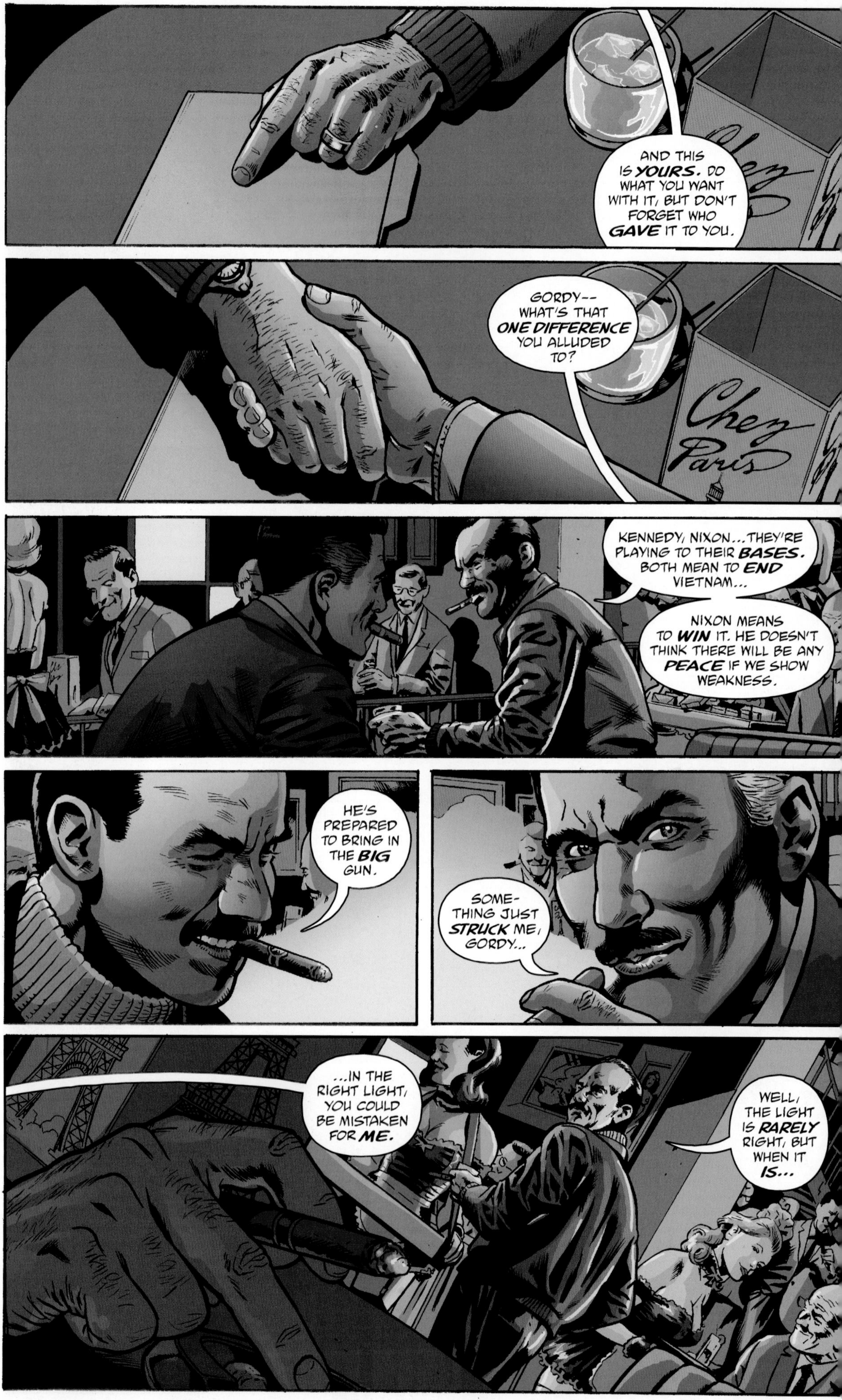
AND THIS IS YOURS. DO WHAT YOU WANT WITH IT, BUT DON'T FORGET WHO GAVE IT TO YOU.
GORDY-- WHAT'S THAT ONE DIFFERENCE YOU ALLUDED TO?
Chez Paris
KENNEDY, NIXON... THEY'RE PLAYING TO THEIR BASES. BOTH MEAN TO END VIETNAM...
NIXON MEANS TO WIN IT. HE DOESN'T THINK THERE WILL BE ANY PEACE IF WE SHOW WEAKNESS.
HE'S PREPARED TO BRING IN THE BIG GUN.
SOME-THING JUST STRUCK ME, GORDY...
...IN THE RIGHT LIGHT, YOU COULD BE MISTAKEN FOR ME.
WELL, THE LIGHT IS RARELY RIGHT, BUT WHEN IT IS...

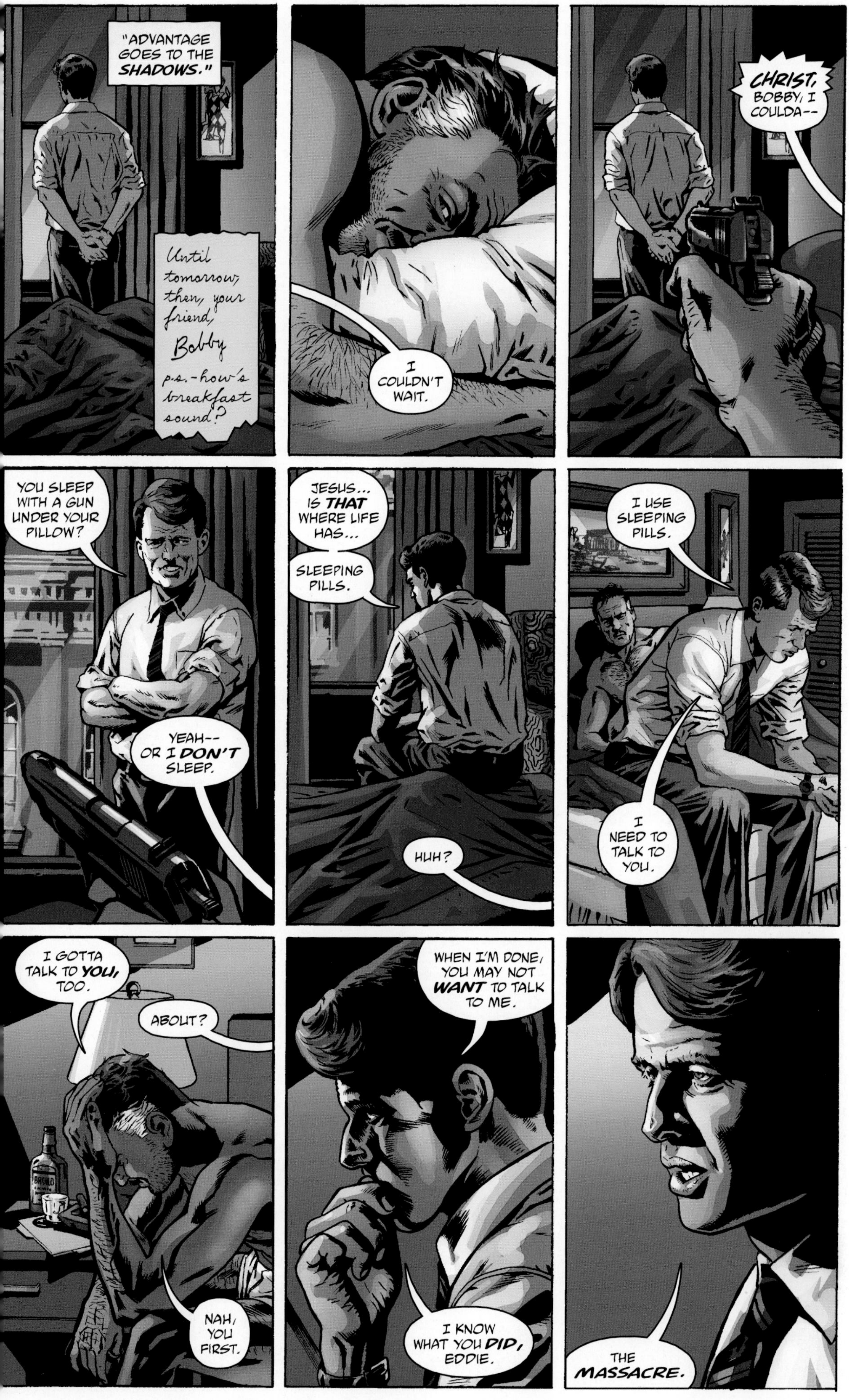
"ADVANTAGE GOES TO THE SHADOWS."
Until tomorrow, then, your friend, Bobby p.s.-how's breakfast sound?
I COULDN'T WAIT.
CHRIST, BOBBY, I COULDA--
YOU SLEEP WITH A GUN UNDER YOUR PILLOW?
YEAH-- OR I DON'T SLEEP.
JESUS... IS THAT WHERE LIFE HAS...
SLEEPING PILLS.
HUH?
I USE SLEEPING PILLS.
I NEED TO TALK TO YOU.
I GOTTA TALK TO YOU, TOO.
ABOUT?
NAH, YOU FIRST.
WHEN I'M DONE, YOU MAY NOT WANT TO TALK TO ME.
I KNOW WHAT YOU DID, EDDIE.
THE MASSACRE.

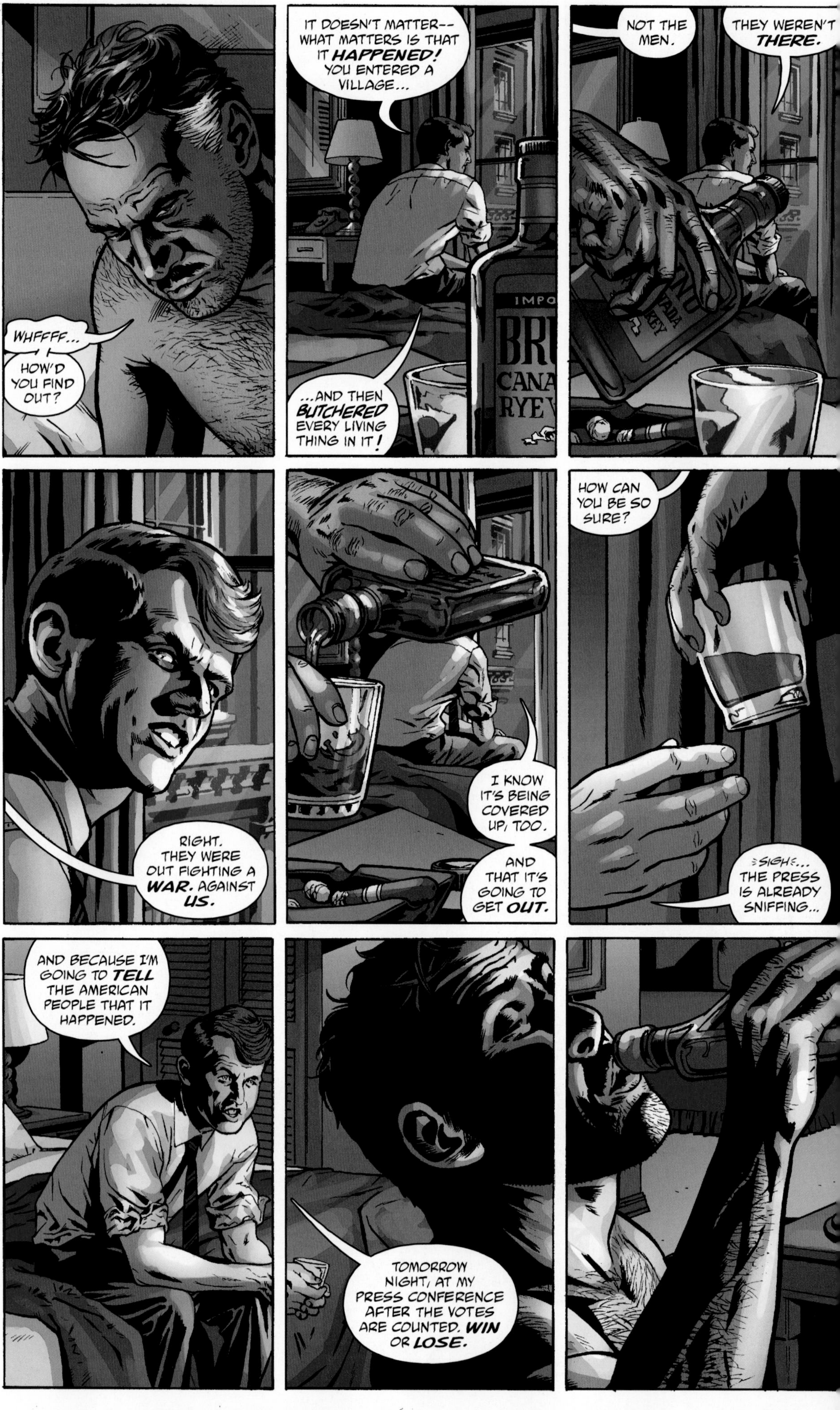
WHFFFF...
HOW'D YOU FIND OUT?
IT DOESN'T MATTER-- WHAT MATTERS IS THAT IT HAPPENED! YOU ENTERED A VILLAGE...
...AND THEN BUTCHERED EVERY LIVING THING IN IT!
IMPO
BRU
CANA
RYE W
NOT THE MEN.
THEY WEREN'T THERE.
RIGHT. THEY WERE OUT FIGHTING A WAR. AGAINST US.
I KNOW IT'S BEING COVERED UP, TOO.
AND THAT IT'S GOING TO GET OUT.
HOW CAN YOU BE SO SURE?
SIGH... THE PRESS IS ALREADY SNIFFING...
AND BECAUSE I'M GOING TO TELL THE AMERICAN PEOPLE THAT IT HAPPENED.
TOMORROW NIGHT, AT MY PRESS CONFERENCE AFTER THE VOTES ARE COUNTED. WIN OR LOSE.

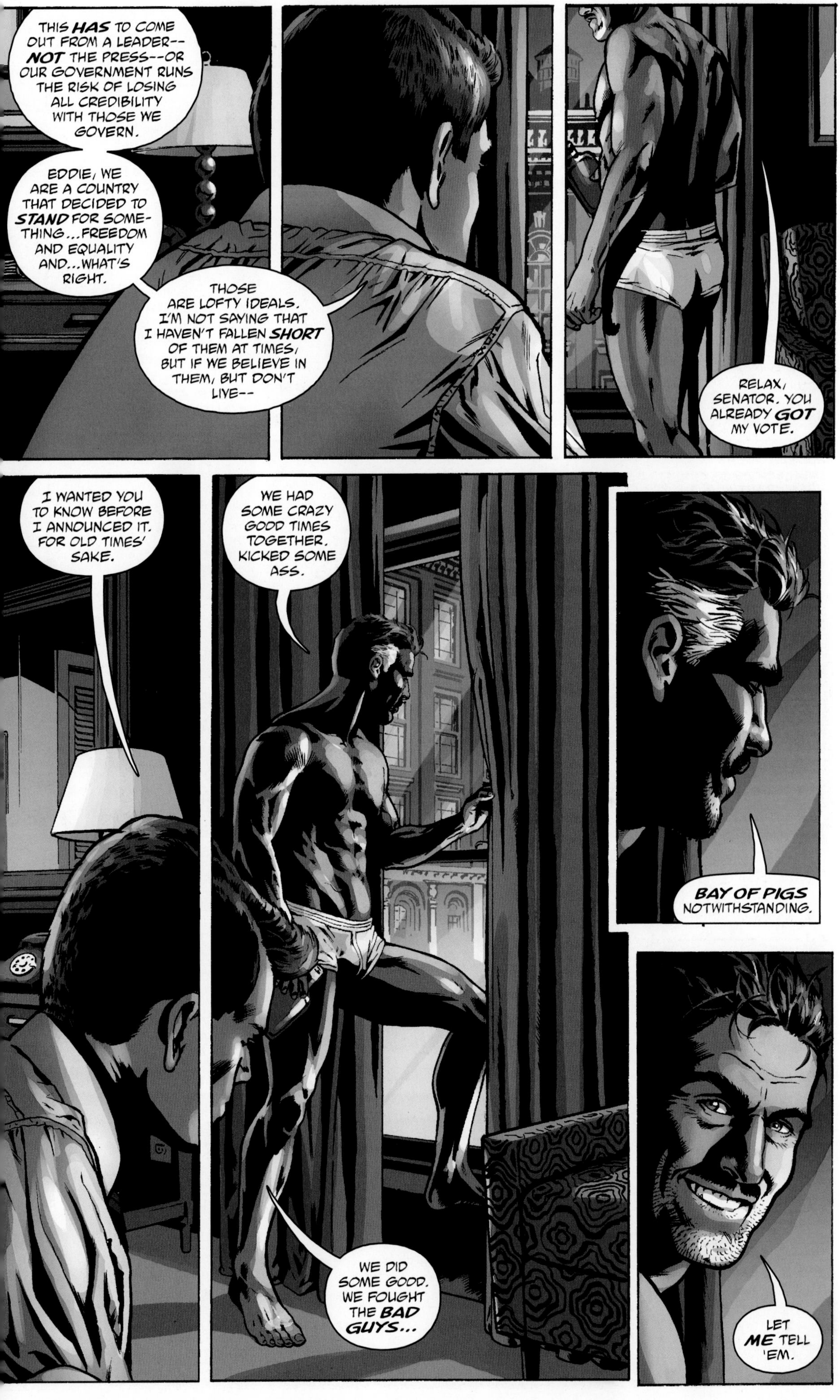
THIS HAS TO COME OUT FROM A LEADER--NOT THE PRESS--OR OUR GOVERNMENT RUNS THE RISK OF LOSING ALL CREDIBILITY WITH THOSE WE GOVERN.
EDDIE, WE ARE A COUNTRY THAT DECIDED TO STAND FOR SOME-THING...FREEDOM AND EQUALITY AND...WHAT'S RIGHT.
THOSE ARE LOFTY IDEALS. I'M NOT SAYING THAT I HAVEN'T FALLEN SHORT OF THEM AT TIMES, BUT IF WE BELIEVE IN THEM, BUT DON'T LIVE--
RELAX, SENATOR. YOU ALREADY GOT MY VOTE.
I WANTED YOU TO KNOW BEFORE I ANNOUNCED IT. FOR OLD TIMES' SAKE.
WE HAD SOME CRAZY GOOD TIMES TOGETHER. KICKED SOME ASS.
WE DID SOME GOOD. WE FOUGHT THE BAD GUYS...
BAY OF PIGS NOTWITHSTANDING.
LET ME TELL 'EM.

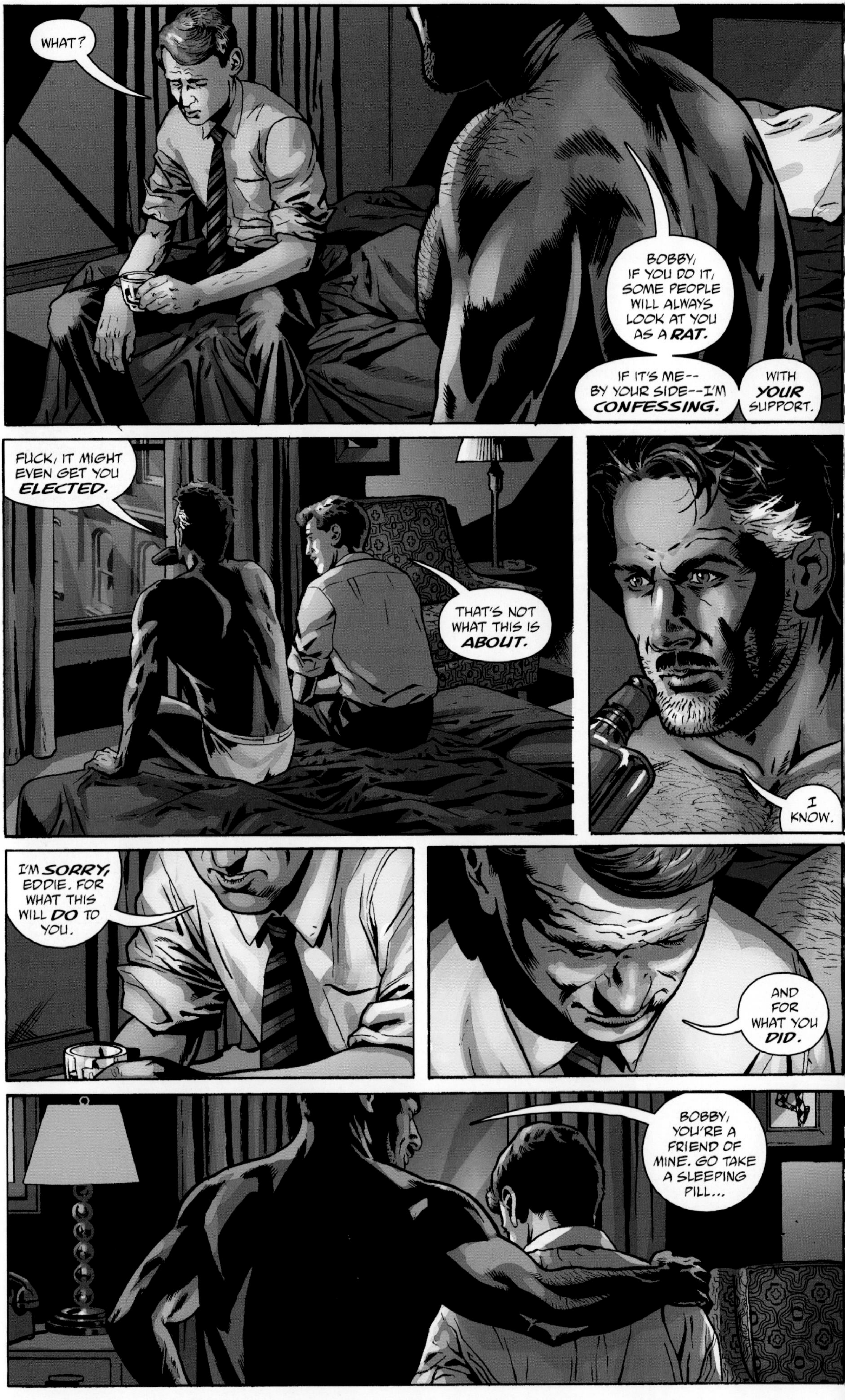
WHAT?
BOBBY, IF YOU DO IT, SOME PEOPLE WILL ALWAYS LOOK AT YOU AS A **RAT.**
IF IT'S ME-- BY YOUR SIDE--I'M **CONFESSING.**
WITH **YOUR** SUPPORT.
FUCK, IT MIGHT EVEN GET YOU **ELECTED.**
THAT'S NOT WHAT THIS IS **ABOUT.**
I KNOW.
I'M **SORRY,** EDDIE. FOR WHAT THIS WILL **DO** TO YOU.
AND FOR WHAT YOU **DID.**
BOBBY, YOU'RE A FRIEND OF MINE. GO TAKE A SLEEPING PILL...

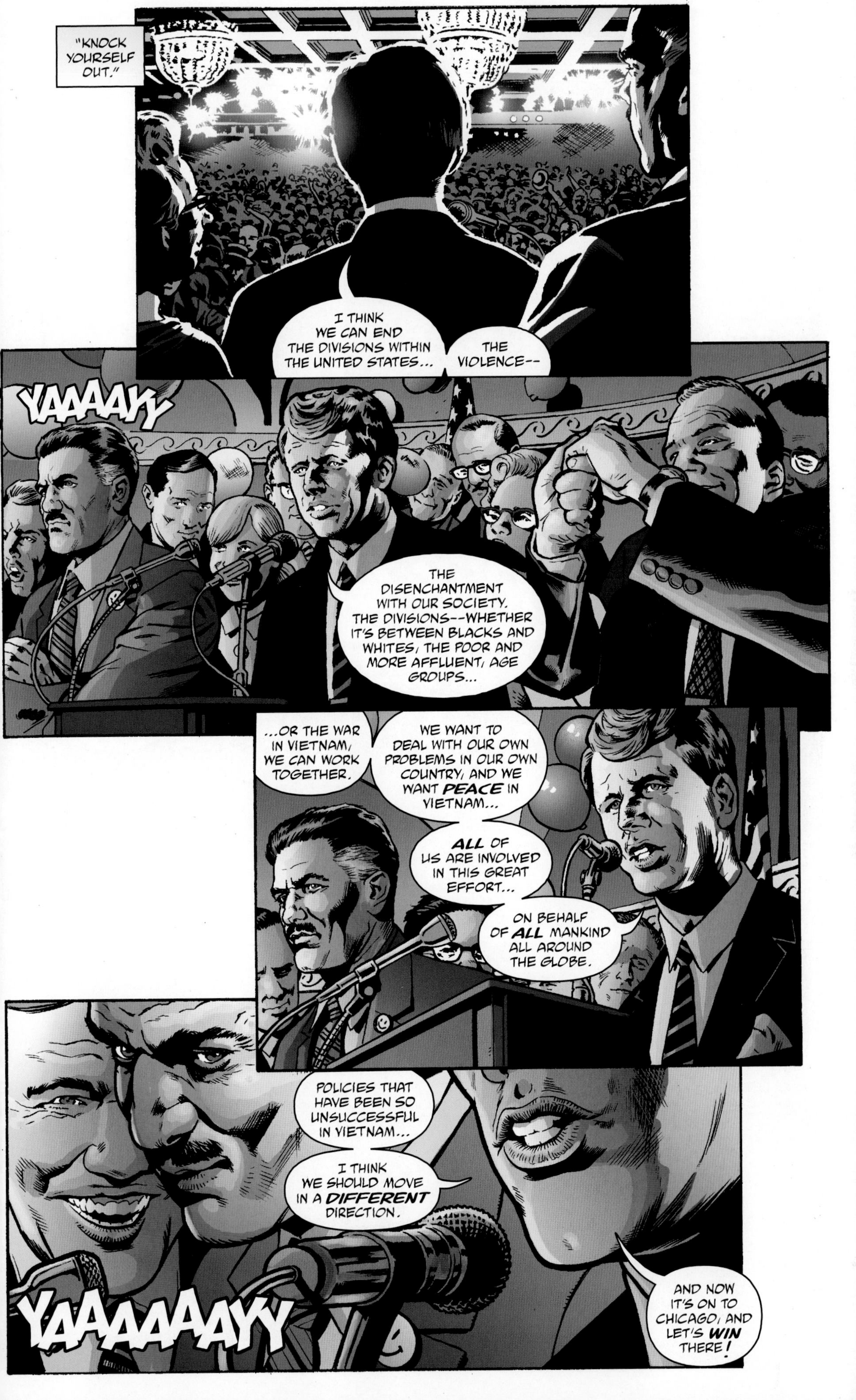
"KNOCK YOURSELF OUT."
I THINK WE CAN END THE DIVISIONS WITHIN THE UNITED STATES...
THE VIOLENCE--
YAAAAYY
THE DISENCHANTMENT WITH OUR SOCIETY. THE DIVISIONS--WHETHER IT'S BETWEEN BLACKS AND WHITES, THE POOR AND MORE AFFLUENT, AGE GROUPS...
...OR THE WAR IN VIETNAM, WE CAN WORK TOGETHER.
WE WANT TO DEAL WITH OUR OWN PROBLEMS IN OUR OWN COUNTRY, AND WE WANT PEACE IN VIETNAM...
ALL OF US ARE INVOLVED IN THIS GREAT EFFORT...
ON BEHALF OF ALL MANKIND ALL AROUND THE GLOBE.
POLICIES THAT HAVE BEEN SO UNSUCCESSFUL IN VIETNAM...
I THINK WE SHOULD MOVE IN A DIFFERENT DIRECTION.
YAAAAAAYY
AND NOW IT'S ON TO CHICAGO, AND LET'S WIN THERE!

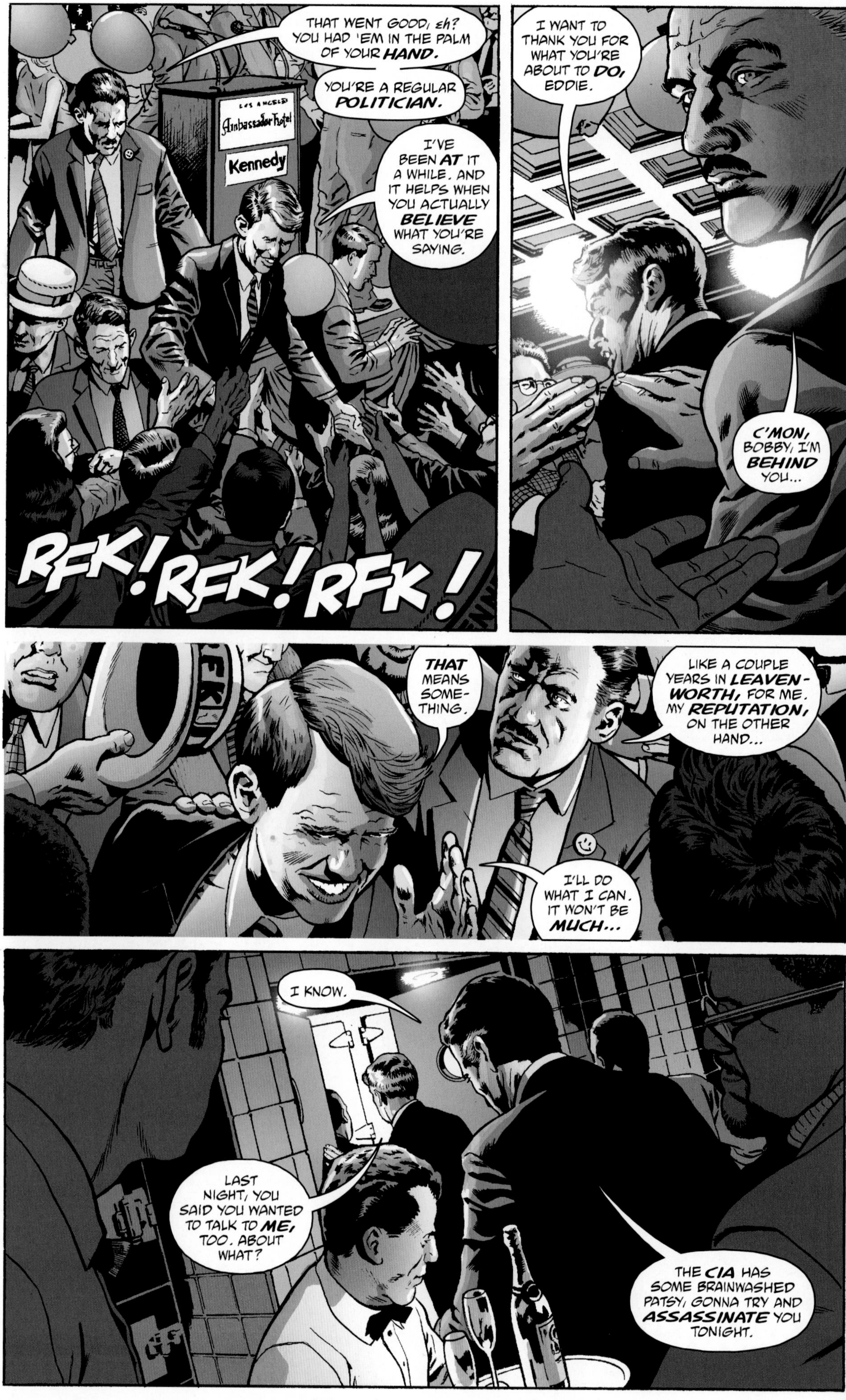
THAT WENT GOOD, eh? YOU HAD 'EM IN THE PALM OF YOUR HAND.
YOU'RE A REGULAR POLITICIAN.
Kennedy
I'VE BEEN AT IT A WHILE. AND IT HELPS WHEN YOU ACTUALLY BELIEVE WHAT YOU'RE SAYING.
RFK! RFK! RFK!
I WANT TO THANK YOU FOR WHAT YOU'RE ABOUT TO DO, EDDIE.
C'MON, BOBBY, I'M BEHIND YOU...
THAT MEANS SOMETHING.
LIKE A COUPLE YEARS IN LEAVENWORTH, FOR ME. MY REPUTATION, ON THE OTHER HAND...
I'LL DO WHAT I CAN. IT WON'T BE MUCH...
I KNOW.
LAST NIGHT, YOU SAID YOU WANTED TO TALK TO ME, TOO. ABOUT WHAT?
THE CIA HAS SOME BRAINWASHED PATSY, GONNA TRY AND ASSASSINATE YOU TONIGHT.

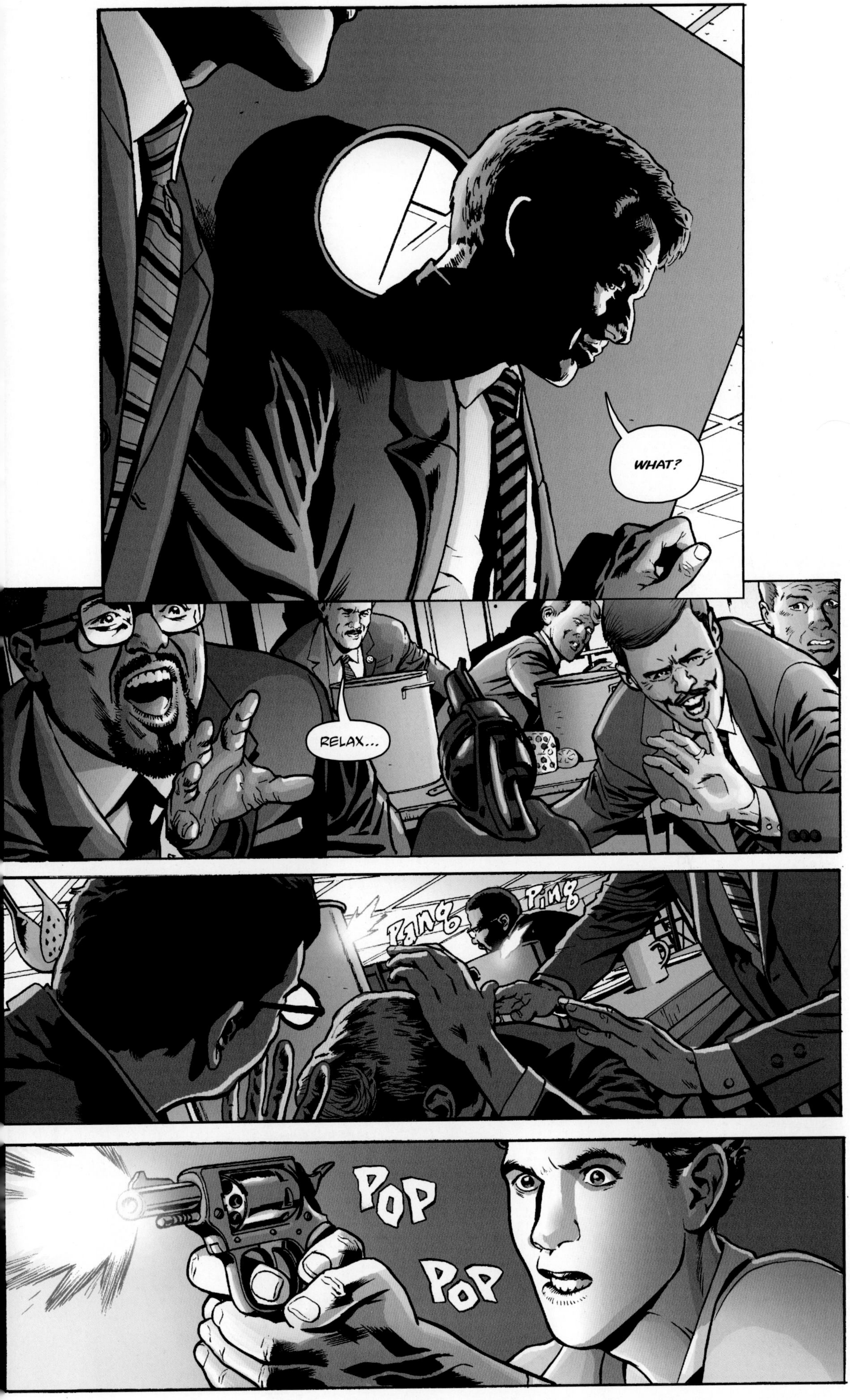
WHAT?
RELAX...
PING
PING
POP
POP

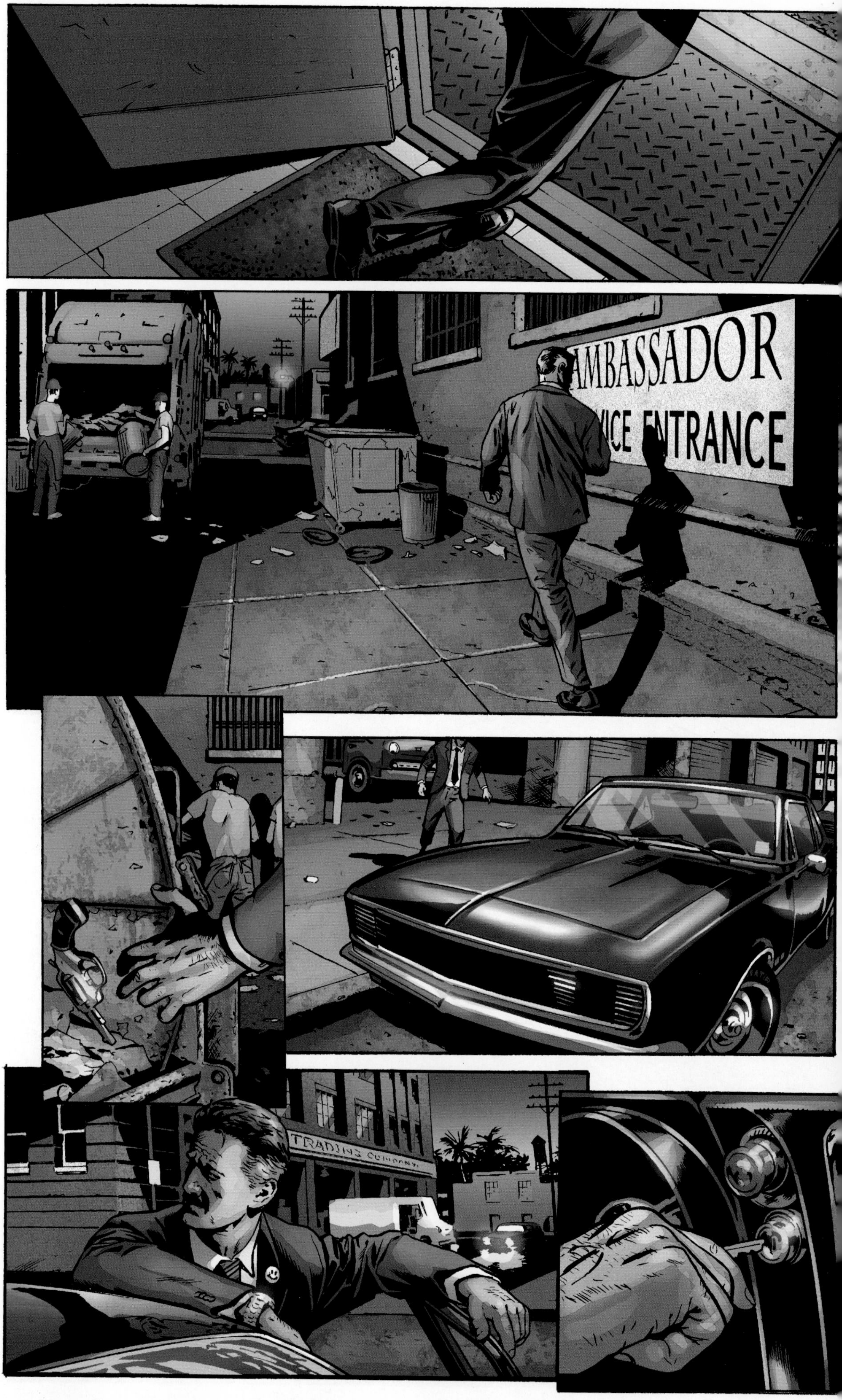
AMBASSADOR
VICE ENTRANCE
TRADING COMPANY

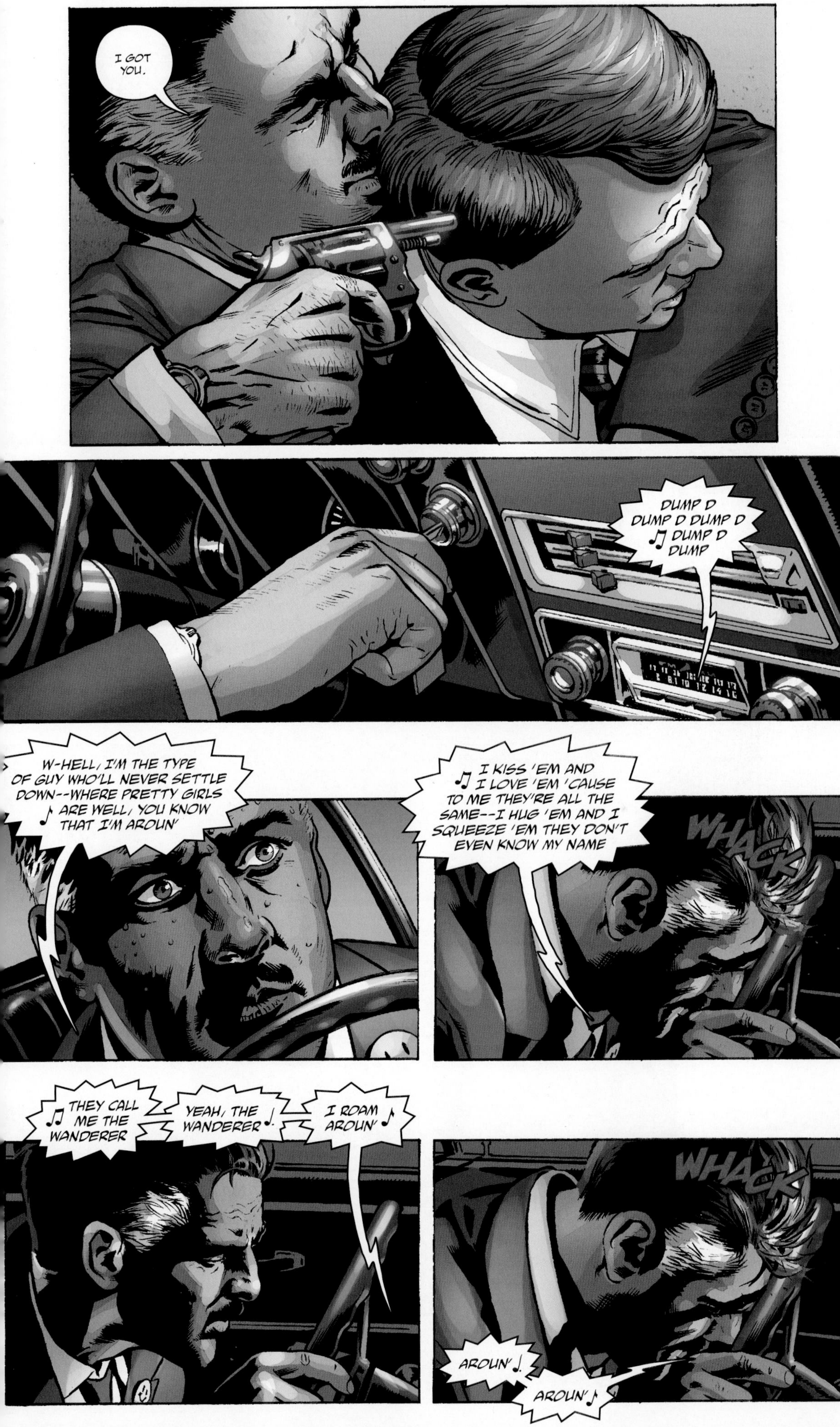

I GOT YOU.
DUMP D DUMP D DUMP D ♫ DUMP D DUMP
W-HELL, I'M THE TYPE OF GUY WHO'LL NEVER SETTLE DOWN--WHERE PRETTY GIRLS ♪ ARE WELL, YOU KNOW THAT I'M AROUN'
♫ I KISS 'EM AND I LOVE 'EM 'CAUSE TO ME THEY'RE ALL THE SAME--I HUG 'EM AND I SQUEEZE 'EM THEY DON'T EVEN KNOW MY NAME
WHACK
♫ THEY CALL ME THE WANDERER
YEAH, THE WANDERER ♩.
I ROAM AROUN' ♪
WHACK
AROUN' ♩.
AROUN' ♪

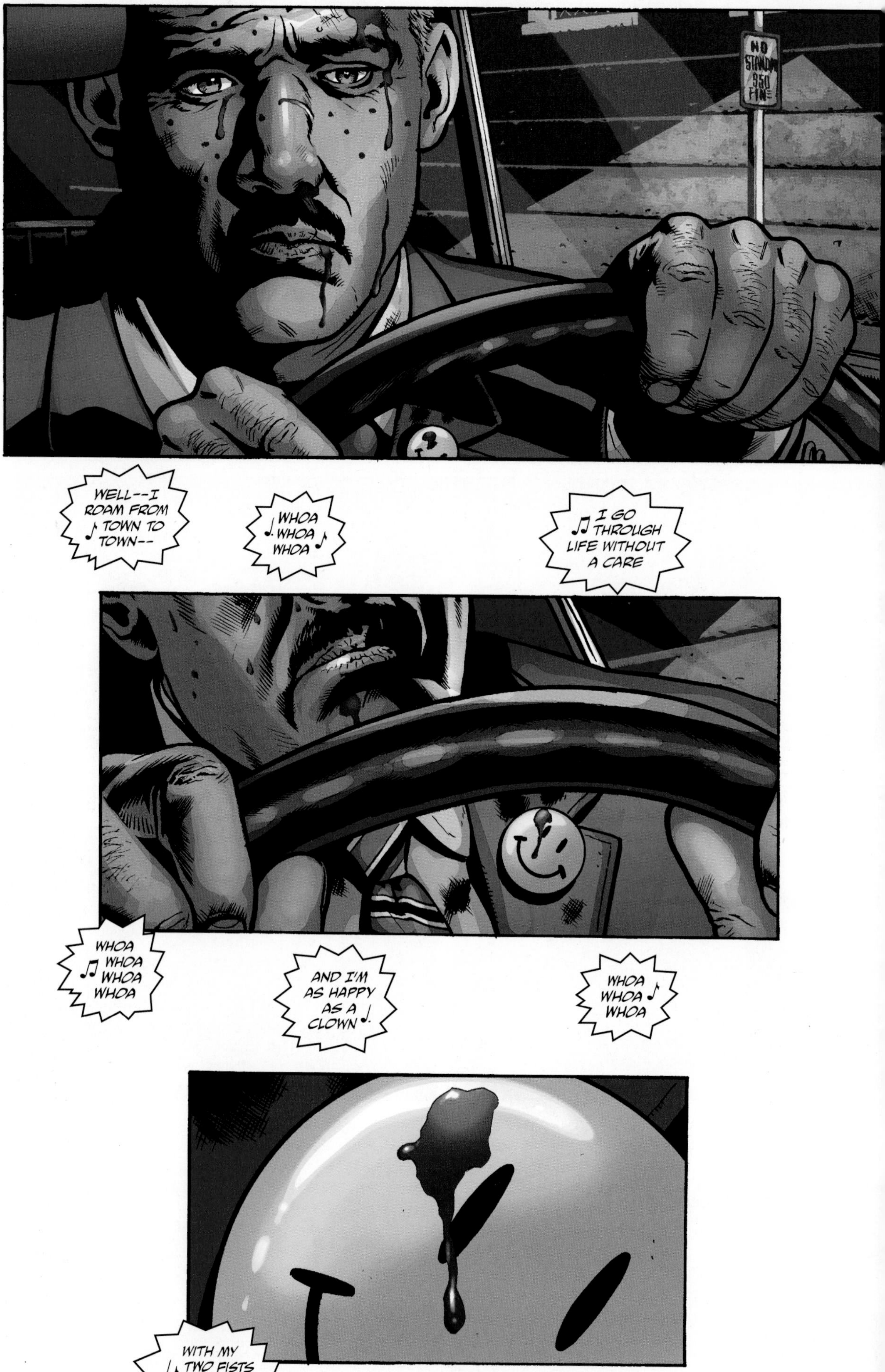
WELL--I ROAM FROM ♪ TOWN TO TOWN--
♩. WHOA WHOA WHOA ♪
♫ I GO THROUGH LIFE WITHOUT A CARE
WHOA ♫ WHOA WHOA WHOA
AND I'M AS HAPPY AS A CLOWN ♩.
WHOA WHOA ♪ WHOA
WITH MY ♪♪ TWO FISTS OF IRON AND I'M GOING NOWHERE
END

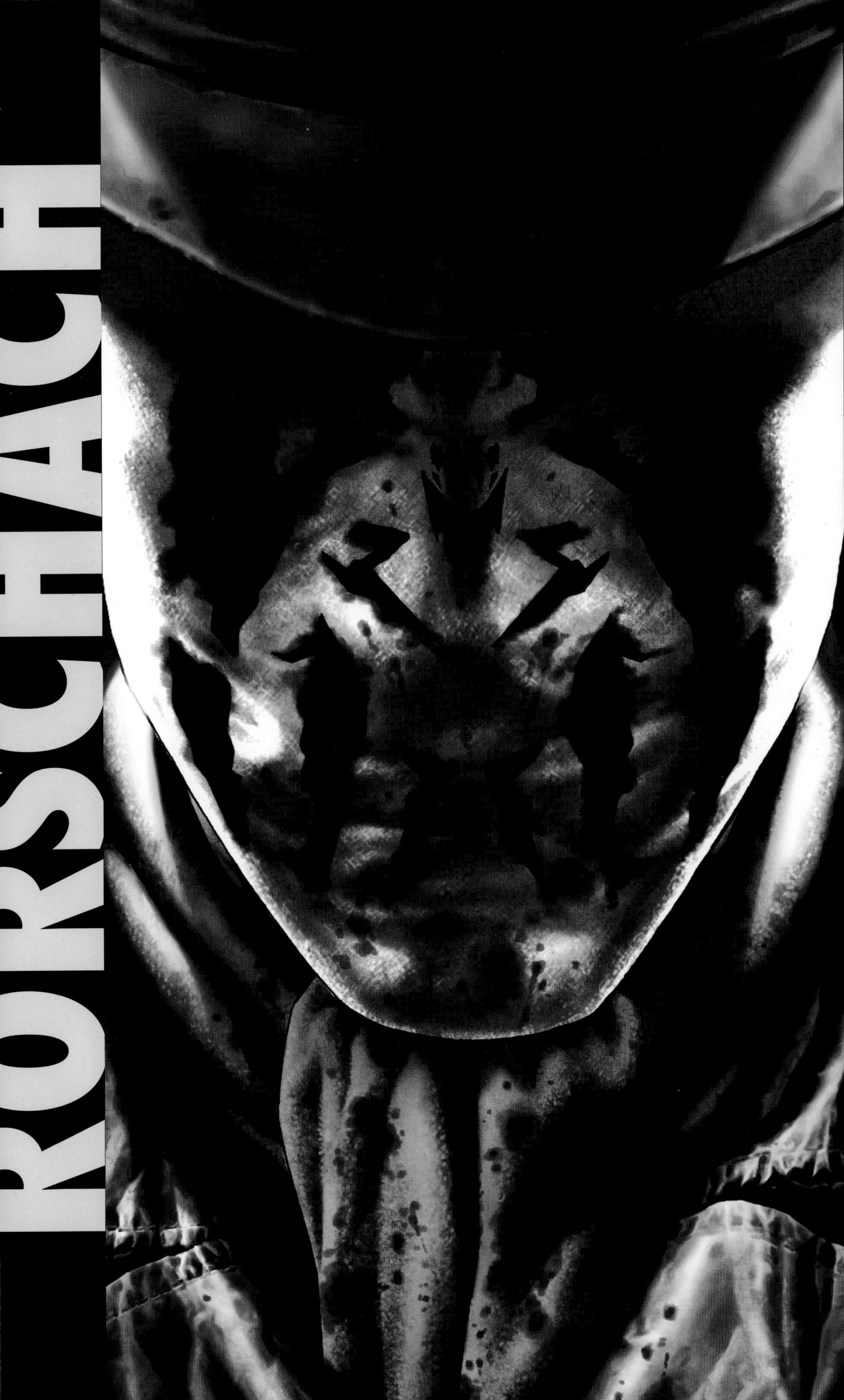
RORSCHACH

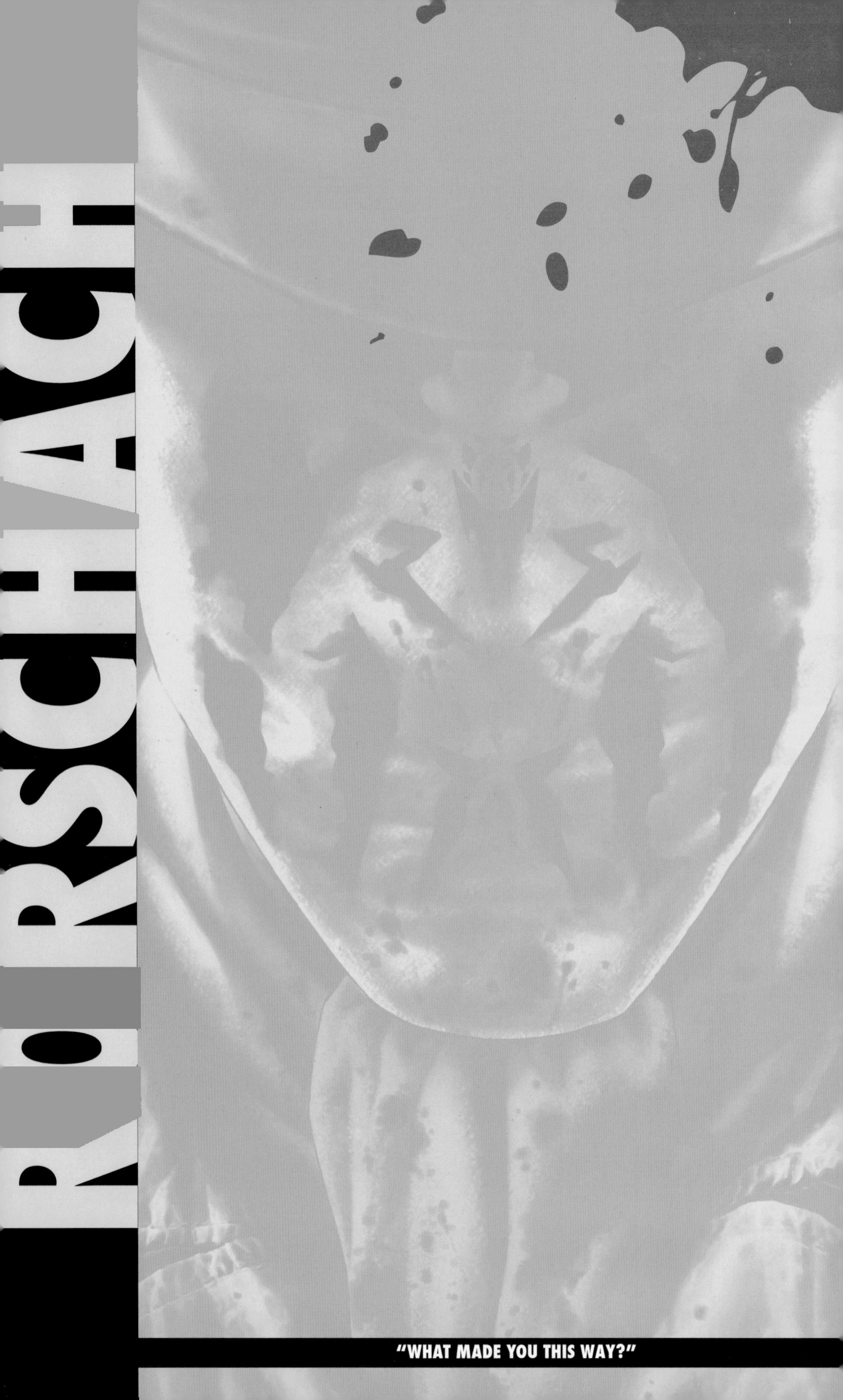
RORSCHACH
"WHAT MADE YOU THIS WAY?"

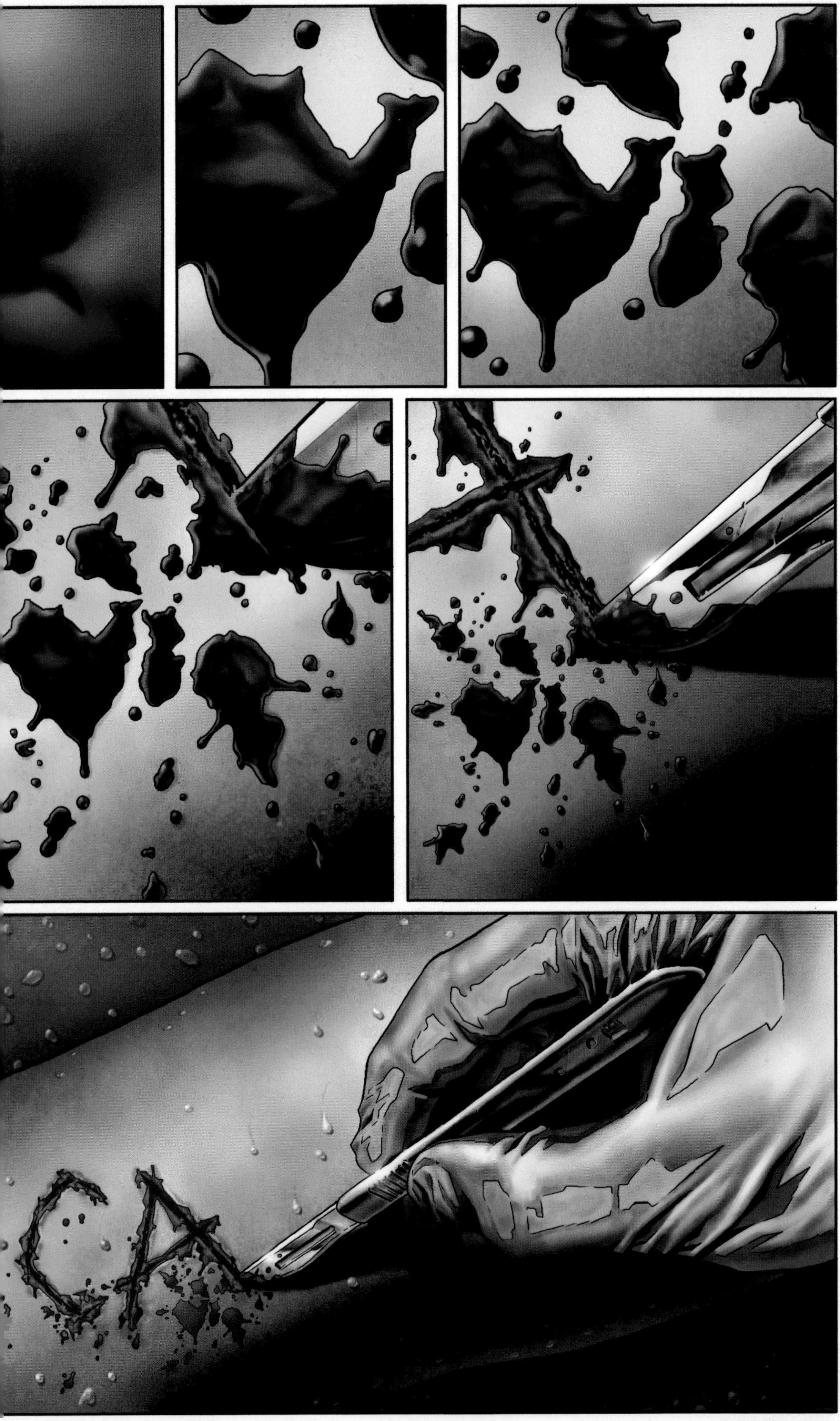
CA

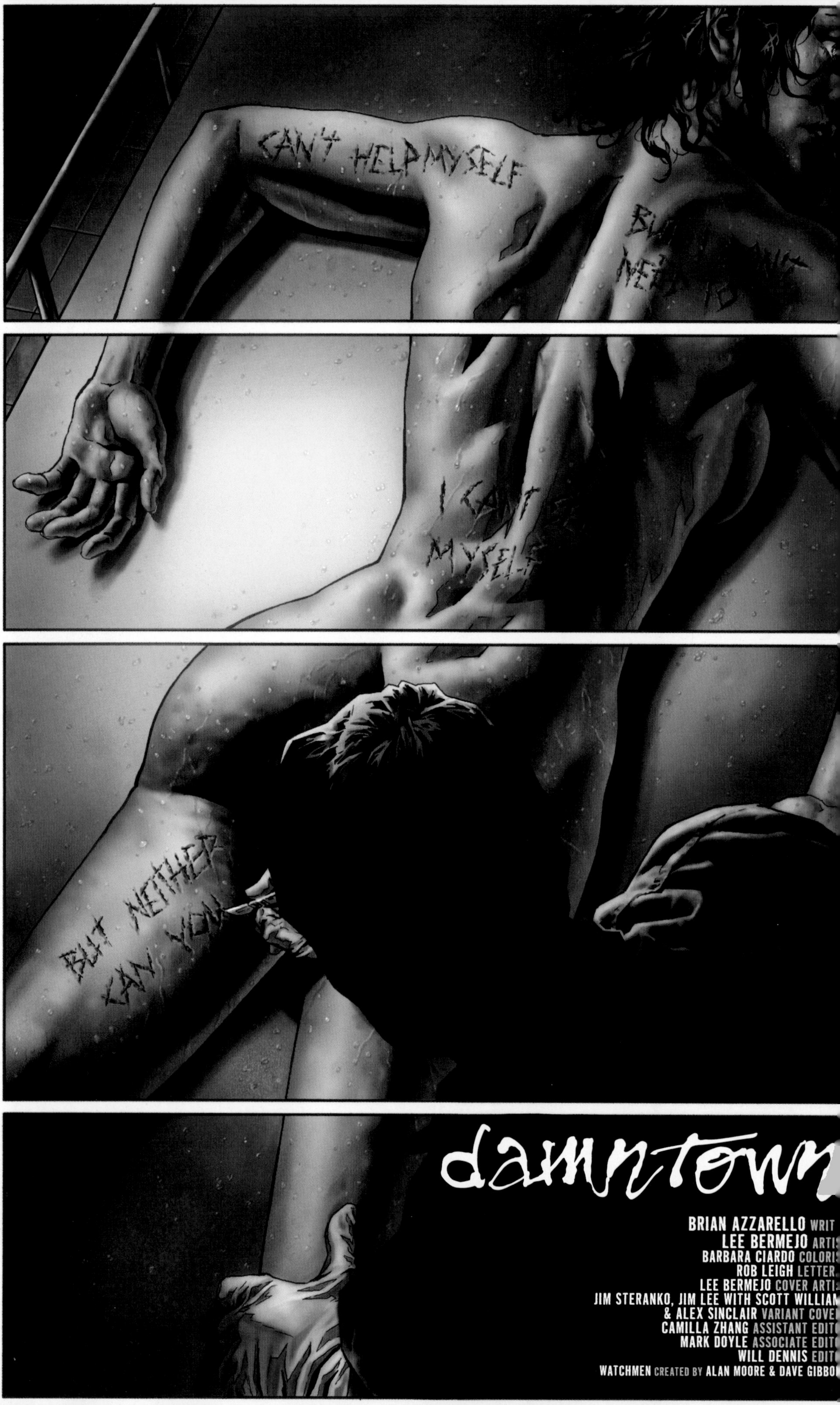
I CAN'T HELP MYSELF
BUT NEITHER CAN YOU
damntown
BRIAN AZZARELLO WRIT
LEE BERMEJO ARTI
BARBARA CIARDO COLORI
ROB LEIGH LETTER
LEE BERMEJO COVER ARTI
JIM STERANKO, JIM LEE WITH SCOTT WILLIAM
& ALEX SINCLAIR VARIANT COVE
CAMILLA ZHANG ASSISTANT EDIT
MARK DOYLE ASSOCIATE EDIT
WILL DENNIS EDIT
WATCHMEN CREATED BY ALAN MOORE & DAVE GIBBO

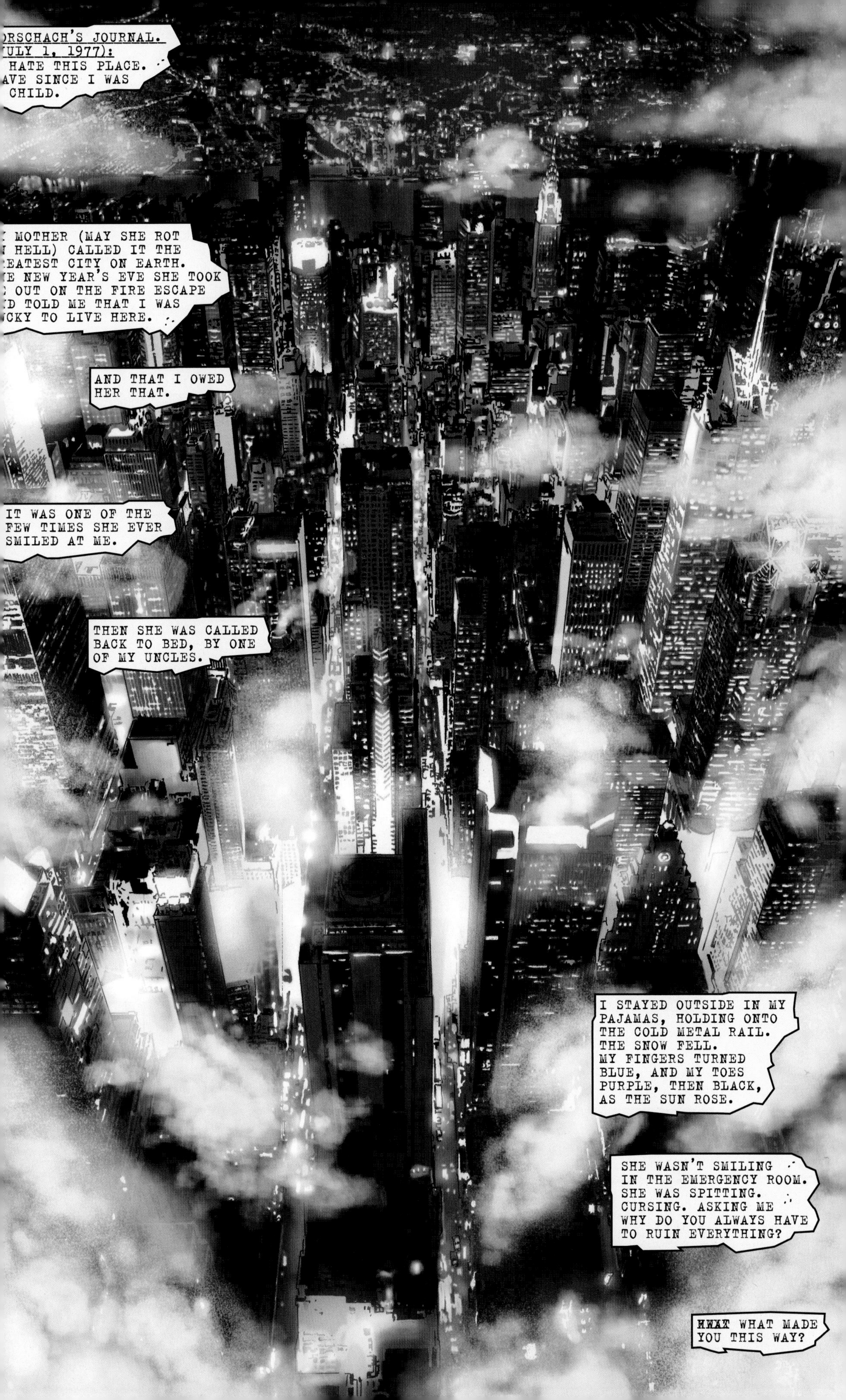
ORSCHACH'S JOURNAL. ULY 1, 1977): HATE THIS PLACE. AVE SINCE I WAS CHILD.
MOTHER (MAY SHE ROT HELL) CALLED IT THE EATEST CITY ON EARTH. E NEW YEAR'S EVE SHE TOOK OUT ON THE FIRE ESCAPE D TOLD ME THAT I WAS CKY TO LIVE HERE.
AND THAT I OWED HER THAT.
IT WAS ONE OF THE FEW TIMES SHE EVER SMILED AT ME.
THEN SHE WAS CALLED BACK TO BED, BY ONE OF MY UNCLES.
I STAYED OUTSIDE IN MY PAJAMAS, HOLDING ONTO THE COLD METAL RAIL. THE SNOW FELL. MY FINGERS TURNED BLUE, AND MY TOES PURPLE, THEN BLACK, AS THE SUN ROSE.
SHE WASN'T SMILING IN THE EMERGENCY ROOM. SHE WAS SPITTING. CURSING. ASKING ME WHY DO YOU ALWAYS HAVE TO RUIN EVERYTHING?
~~HWAT~~ WHAT MADE YOU THIS WAY?

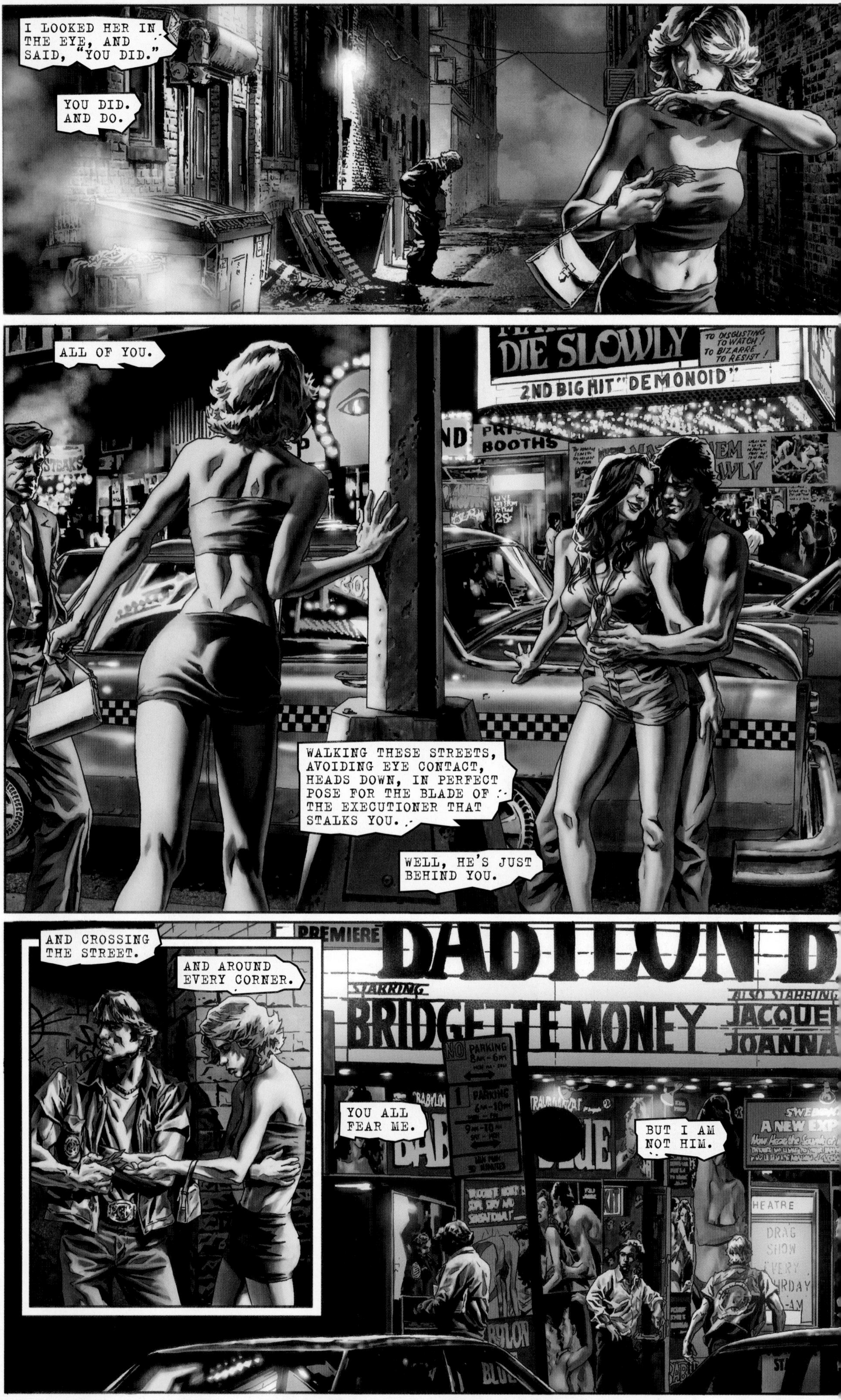
I LOOKED HER IN THE EYE, AND SAID, "YOU DID."
YOU DID. AND DO.
ALL OF YOU.
DIE SLOWLY
TO DISGUSTING TO WATCH! TO BIZARRE TO RESIST!
2ND BIG HIT "DEMONOID"
BOOTHS
WALKING THESE STREETS, AVOIDING EYE CONTACT, HEADS DOWN, IN PERFECT POSE FOR THE BLADE OF THE EXECUTIONER THAT STALKS YOU.
WELL, HE'S JUST BEHIND YOU.
AND CROSSING THE STREET.
AND AROUND EVERY CORNER.
PREMIERE
STARRING
BRIDGETTE MONEY
ALSO STARRING
YOU ALL FEAR ME.
BUT I AM NOT HIM.
DRAG SHOW

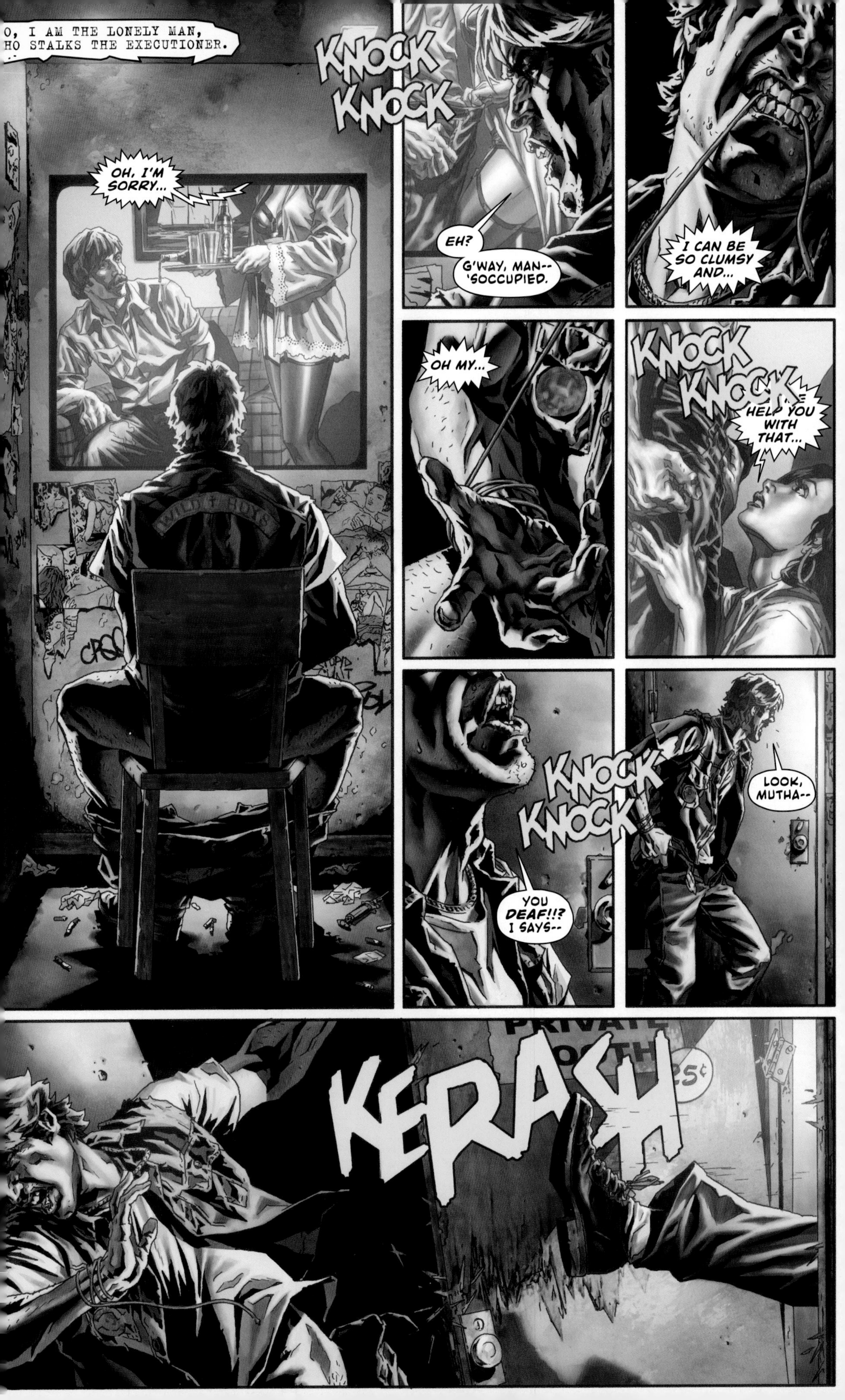
O, I AM THE LONELY MAN,
HO STALKS THE EXECUTIONER.
KNOCK KNOCK
OH, I'M SORRY...
EH?
G'WAY, MAN-- 'SOCCUPIED.
I CAN BE SO CLUMSY AND...
OH MY...
KNOCK KNOCK
HELP YOU WITH THAT...
KNOCK KNOCK
YOU DEAF!!? I SAYS--
LOOK, MUTHA--
KERASH
25¢

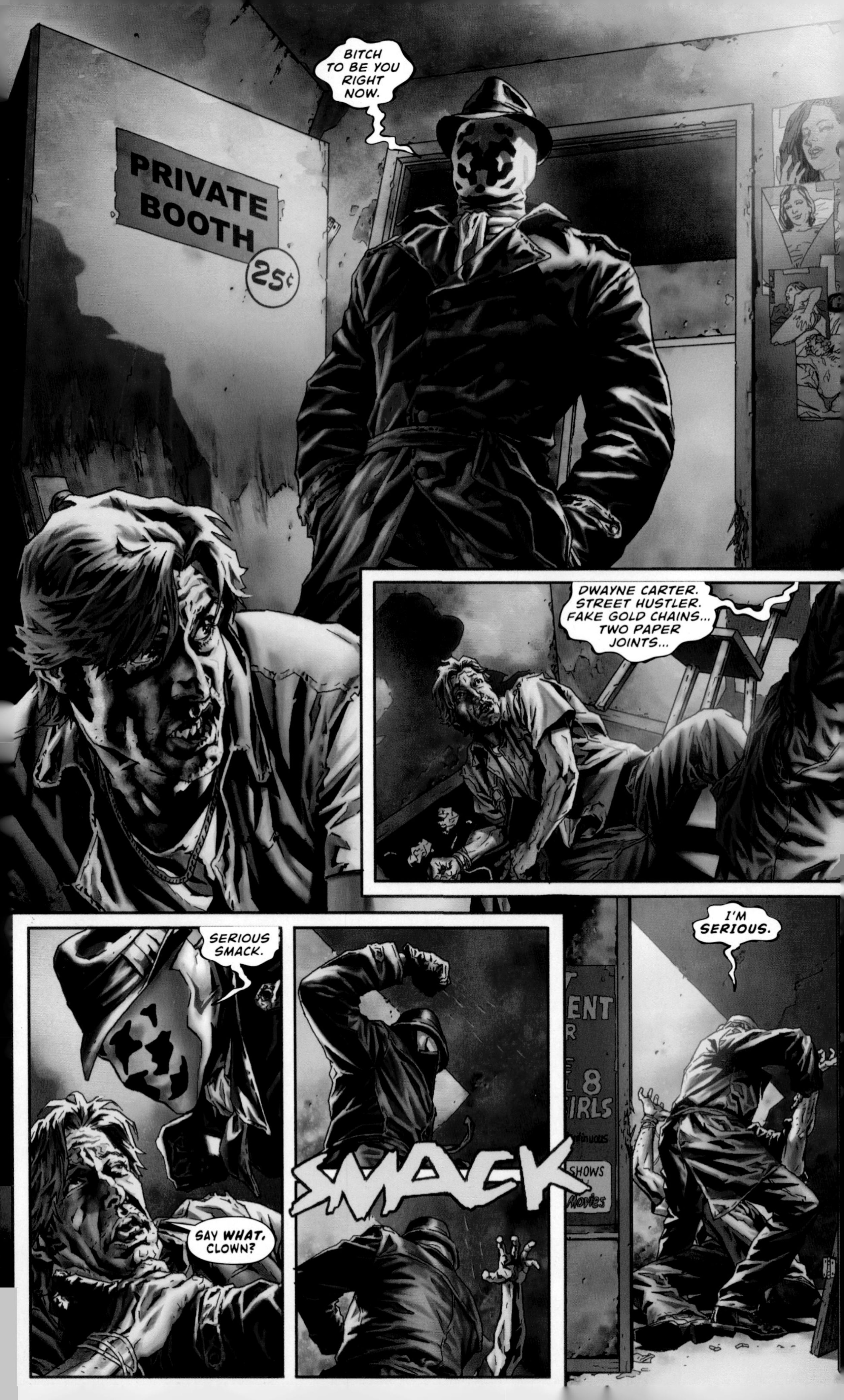
BITCH TO BE YOU RIGHT NOW.
PRIVATE BOOTH
25¢
DWAYNE CARTER. STREET HUSTLER. FAKE GOLD CHAINS... TWO PAPER JOINTS...
SERIOUS SMACK.
SAY WHAT, CLOWN?
SMACK
I'M SERIOUS.

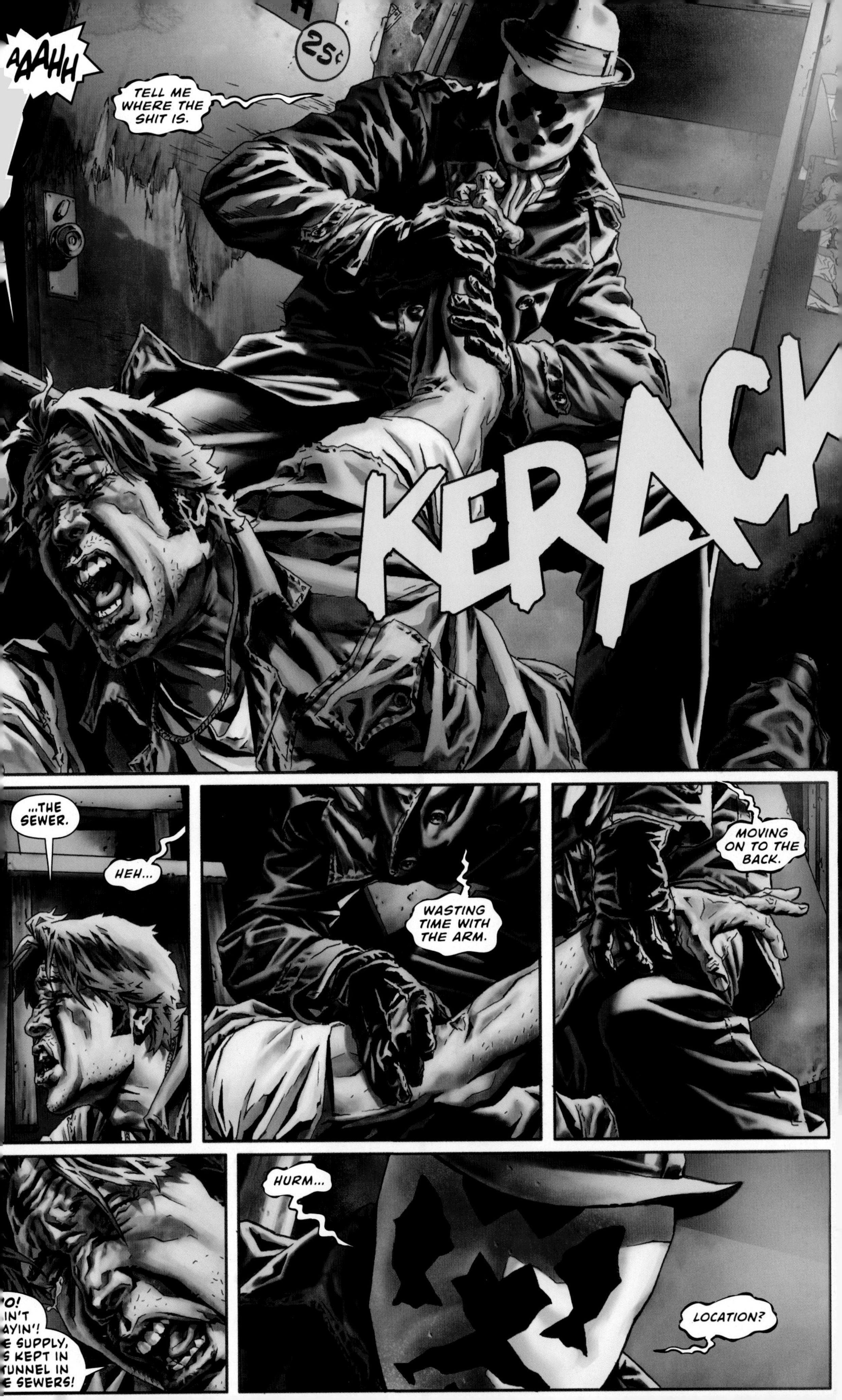
AAAHH
TELL ME WHERE THE SHIT IS.
KERACK
...THE SEWER.
HEH...
WASTING TIME WITH THE ARM.
MOVING ON TO THE BACK.
HURM...
LOCATION?

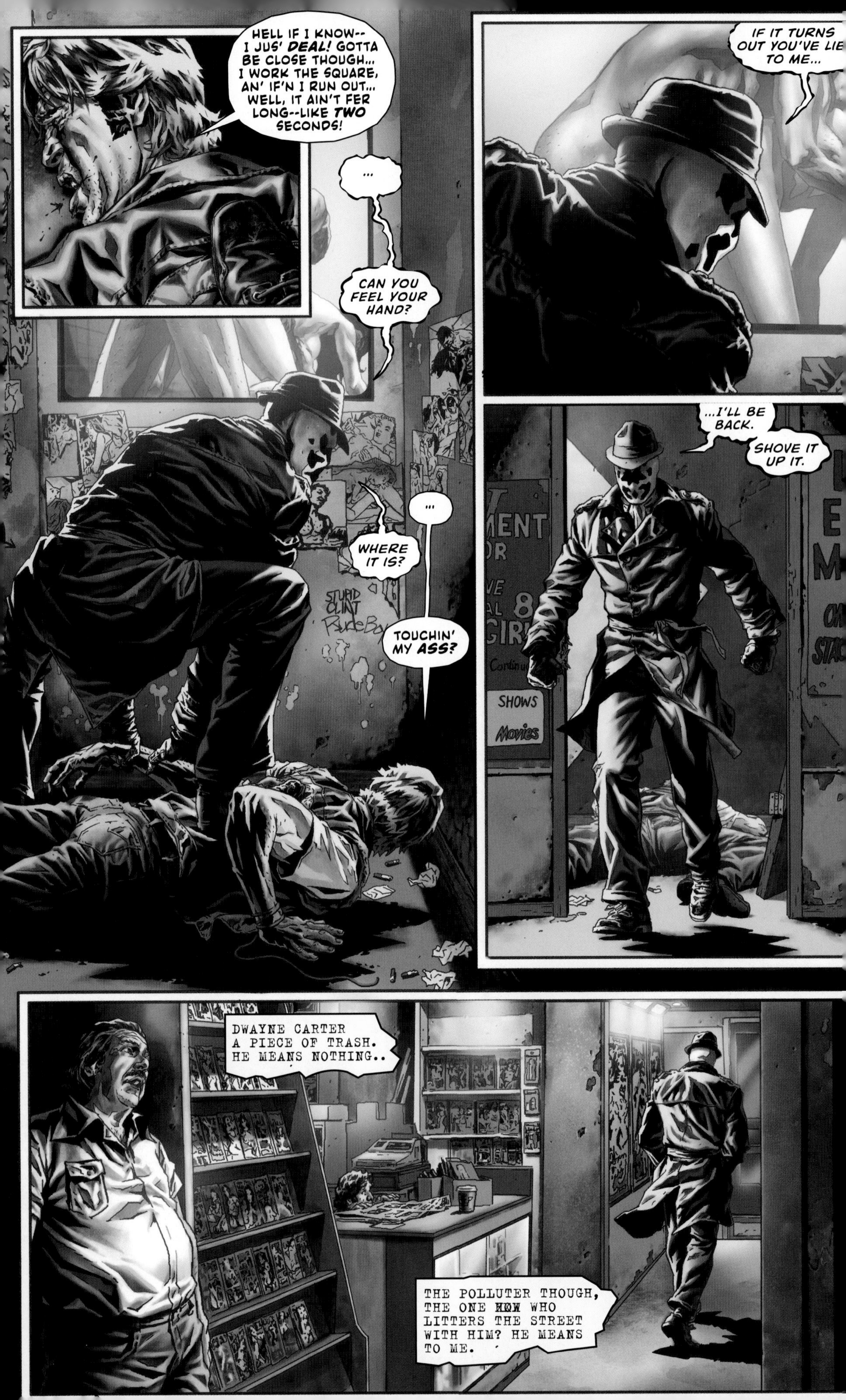
HELL IF I KNOW-- I JUS' DEAL! GOTTA BE CLOSE THOUGH... I WORK THE SQUARE, AN' IF'N I RUN OUT... WELL, IT AIN'T FER LONG--LIKE TWO SECONDS!
...
CAN YOU FEEL YOUR HAND?
...
WHERE IT IS?
TOUCHIN' MY ASS?
STUPID CLINT
RudeBoy
IF IT TURNS OUT YOU'VE LIE TO ME...
...I'LL BE BACK.
SHOVE IT UP IT.
MENT
OR
SHOWS
Movies
DWAYNE CARTER A PIECE OF TRASH. HE MEANS NOTHING..
THE POLLUTER THOUGH, THE ONE HOW WHO LITTERS THE STREET WITH HIM? HE MEANS TO ME.

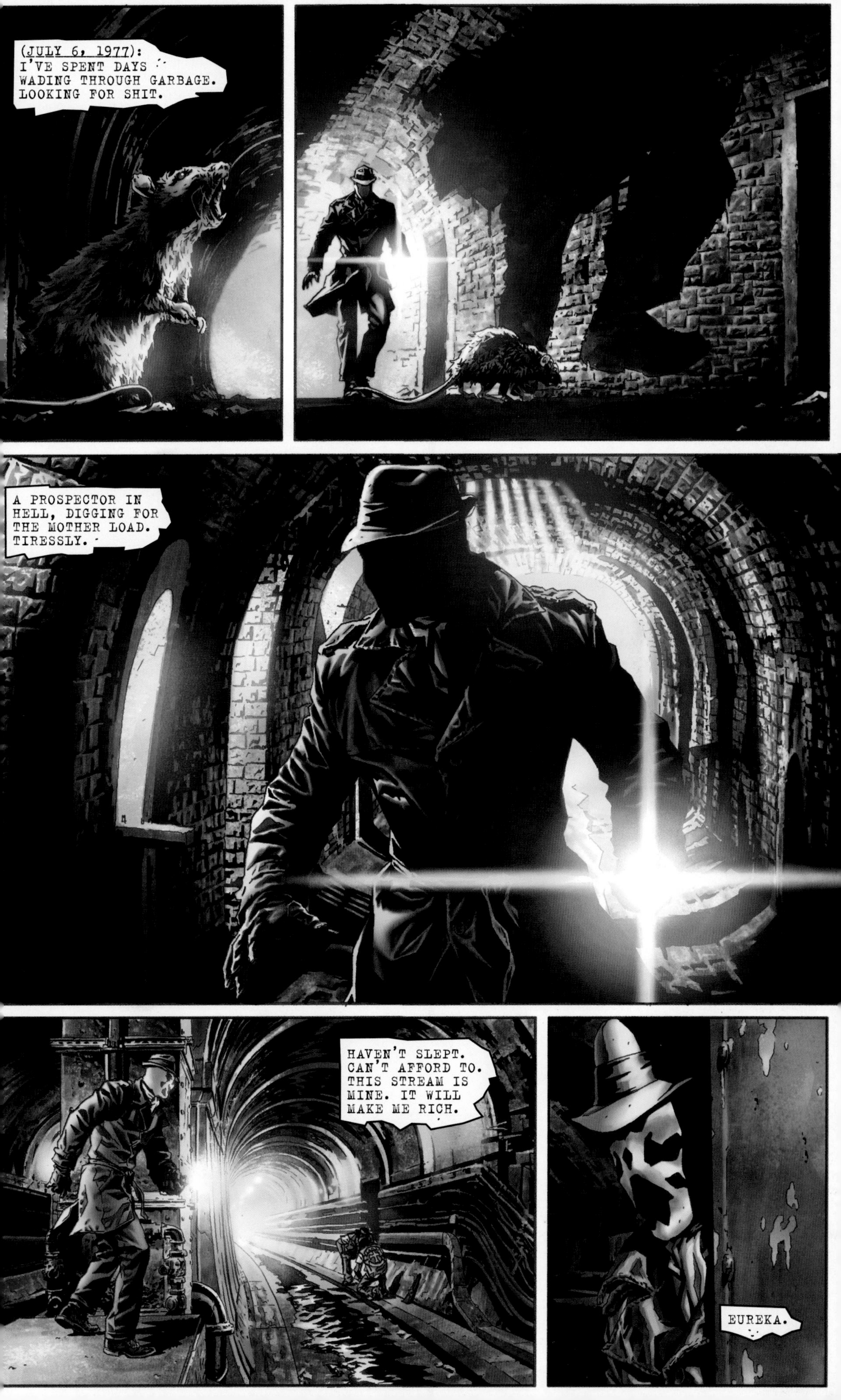
(JULY 6, 1977):
I'VE SPENT DAYS
WADING THROUGH GARBAGE.
LOOKING FOR SHIT.
A PROSPECTOR IN
HELL, DIGGING FOR
THE MOTHER LOAD.
TIRESSLY.
HAVEN'T SLEPT.
CAN'T AFFORD TO.
THIS STREAM IS
MINE. IT WILL
MAKE ME RICH.
EUREKA.

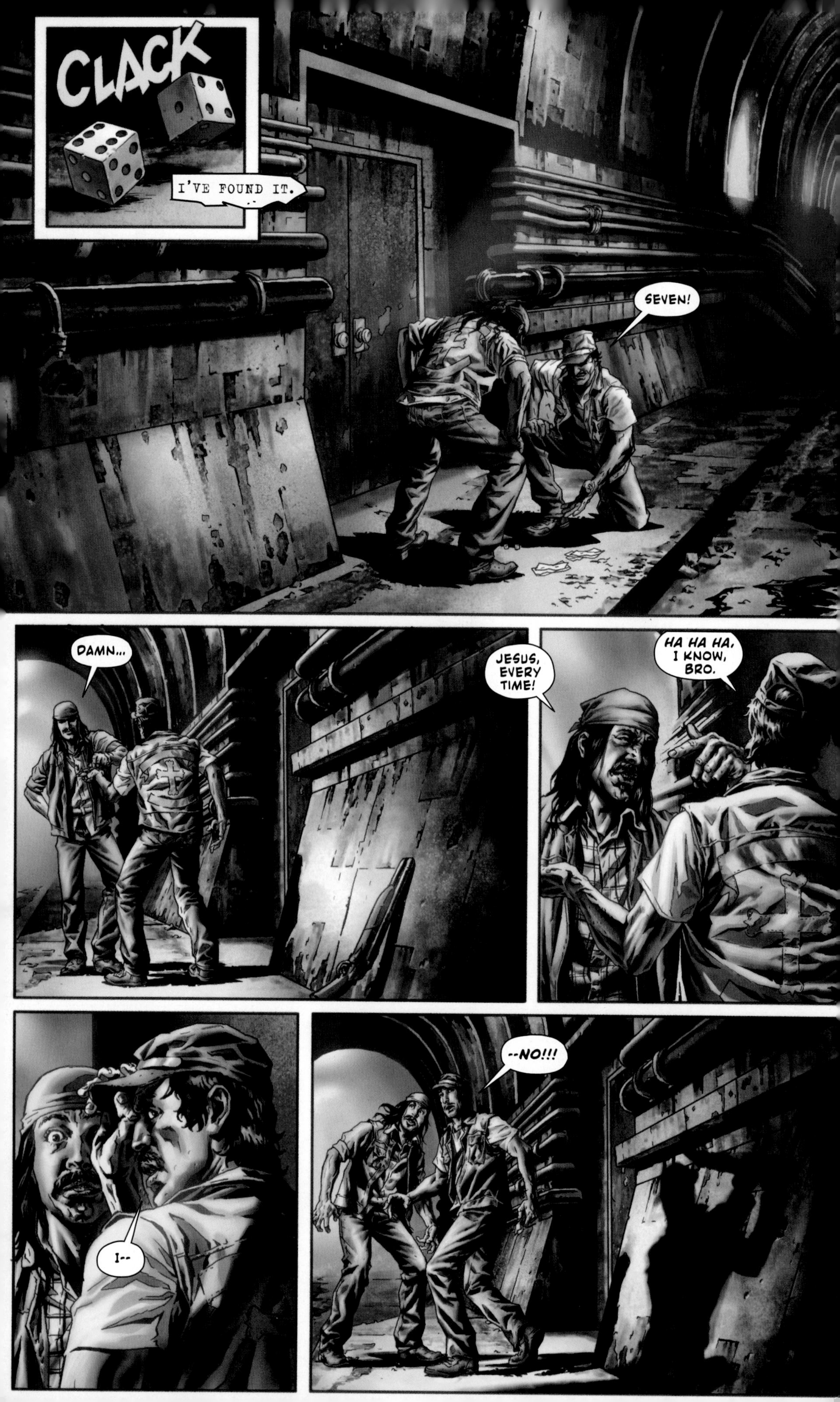
CLACK
I'VE FOUND IT.
SEVEN!
DAMN...
JESUS, EVERY TIME!
HA HA HA, I KNOW, BRO.
I--
--NO!!!

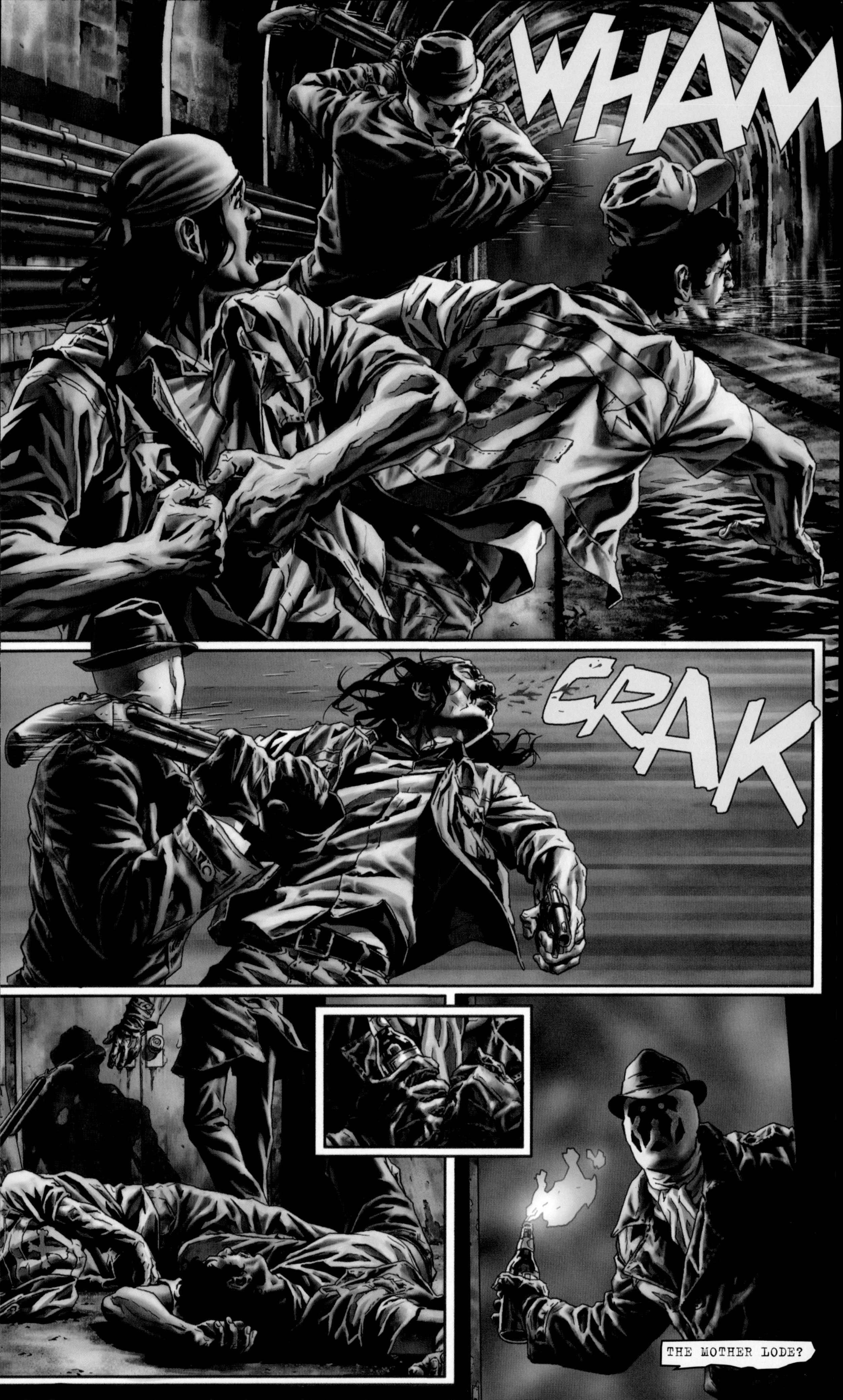
WHAM
CRAK
THE MOTHER LODE?

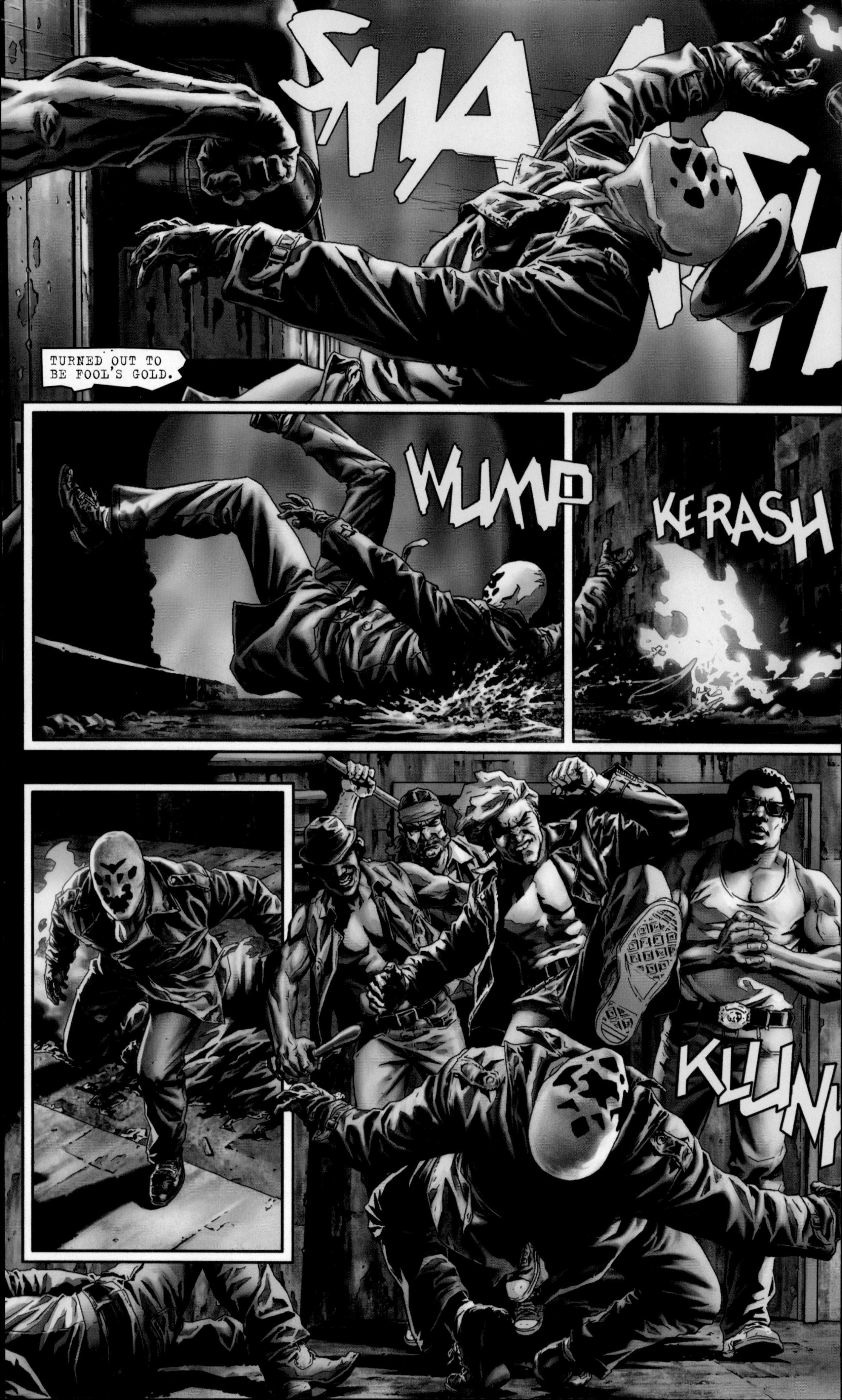

SMAASH
TURNED OUT TO BE FOOL'S GOLD.
WUMP
KE-RASH
KLUN

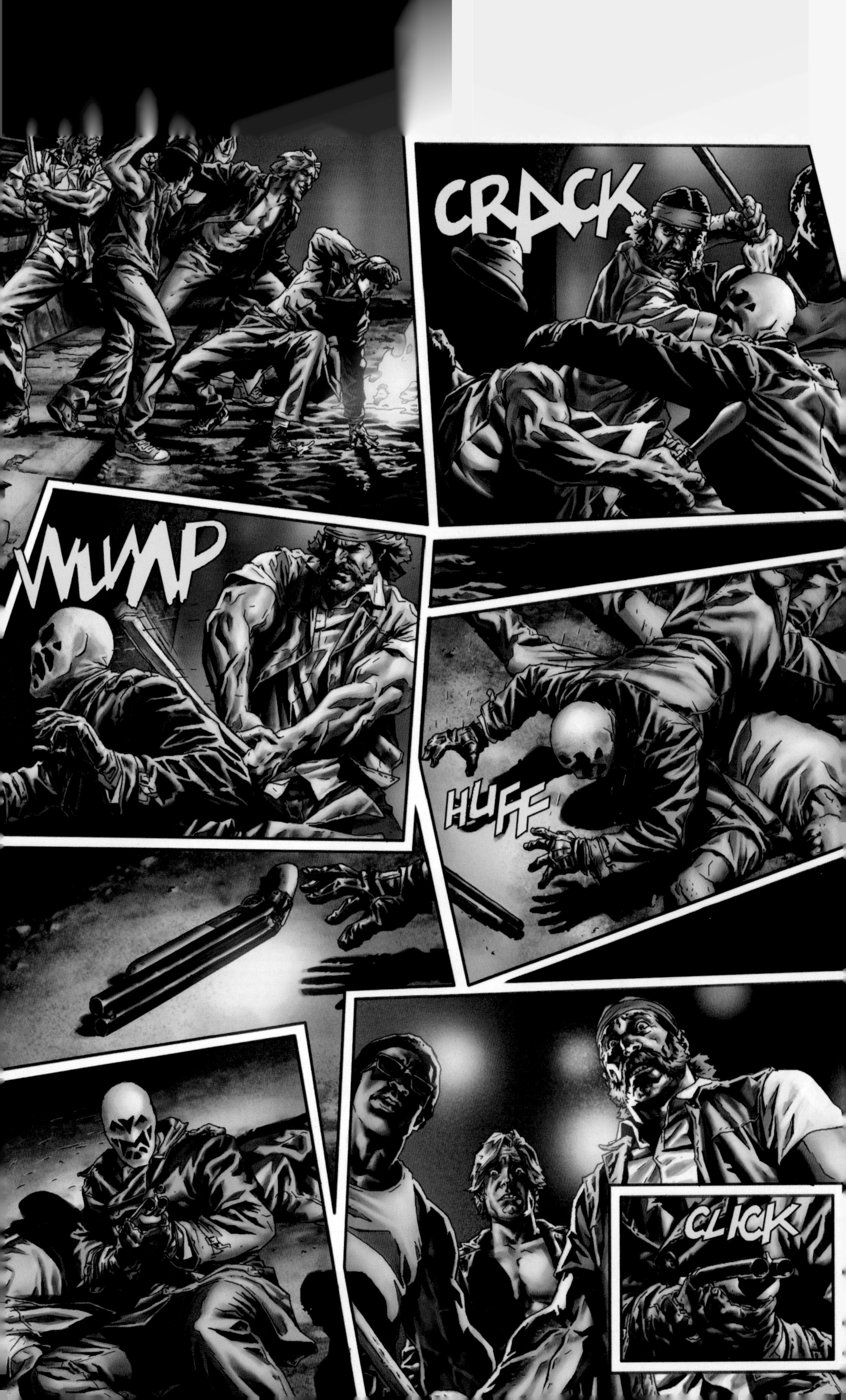
CRACK
WUMP
HUFF
CLICK

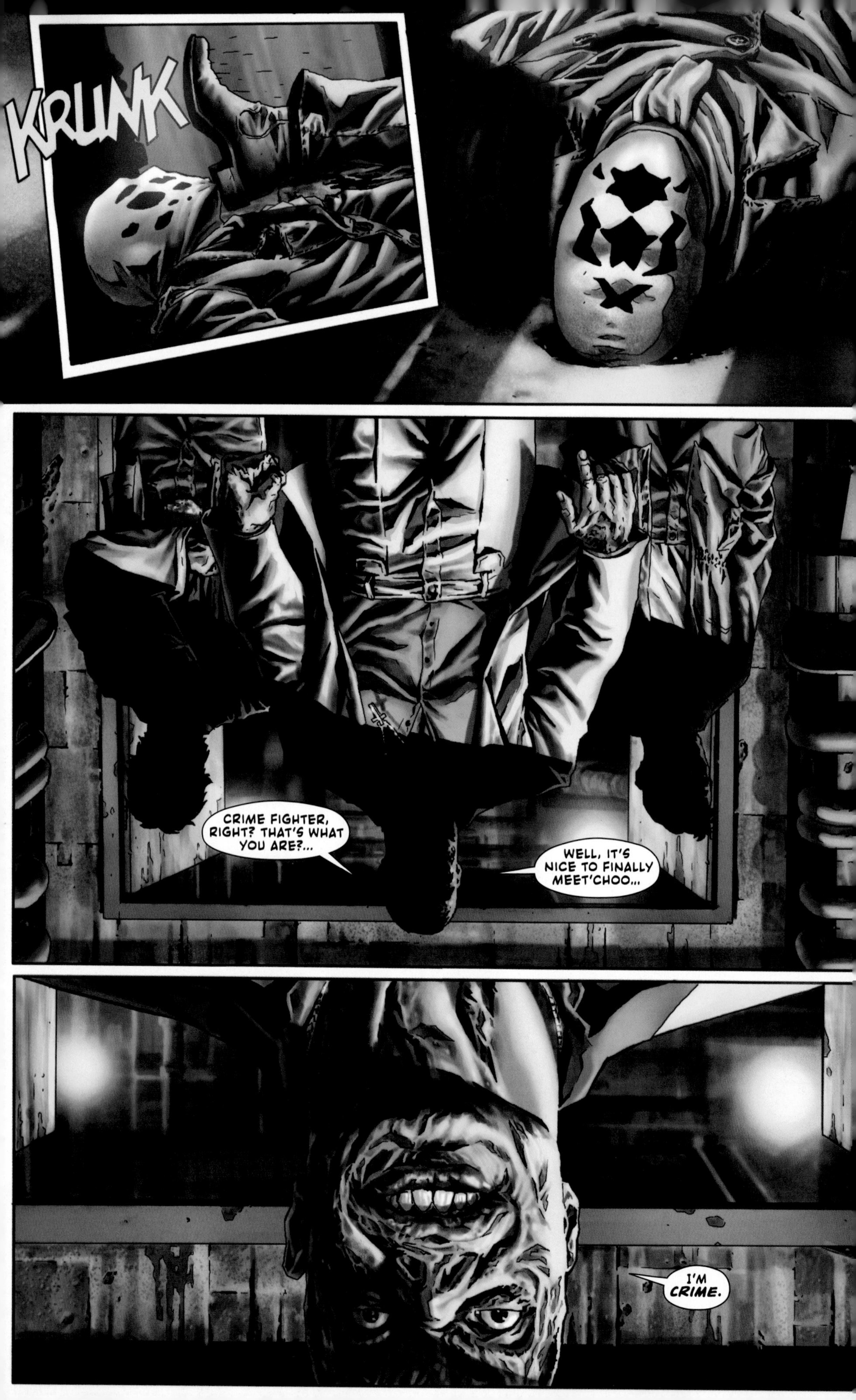
KRUNK
CRIME FIGHTER, RIGHT? THAT'S WHAT YOU ARE?...
WELL, IT'S NICE TO FINALLY MEET'CHOO...
I'M CRIME.

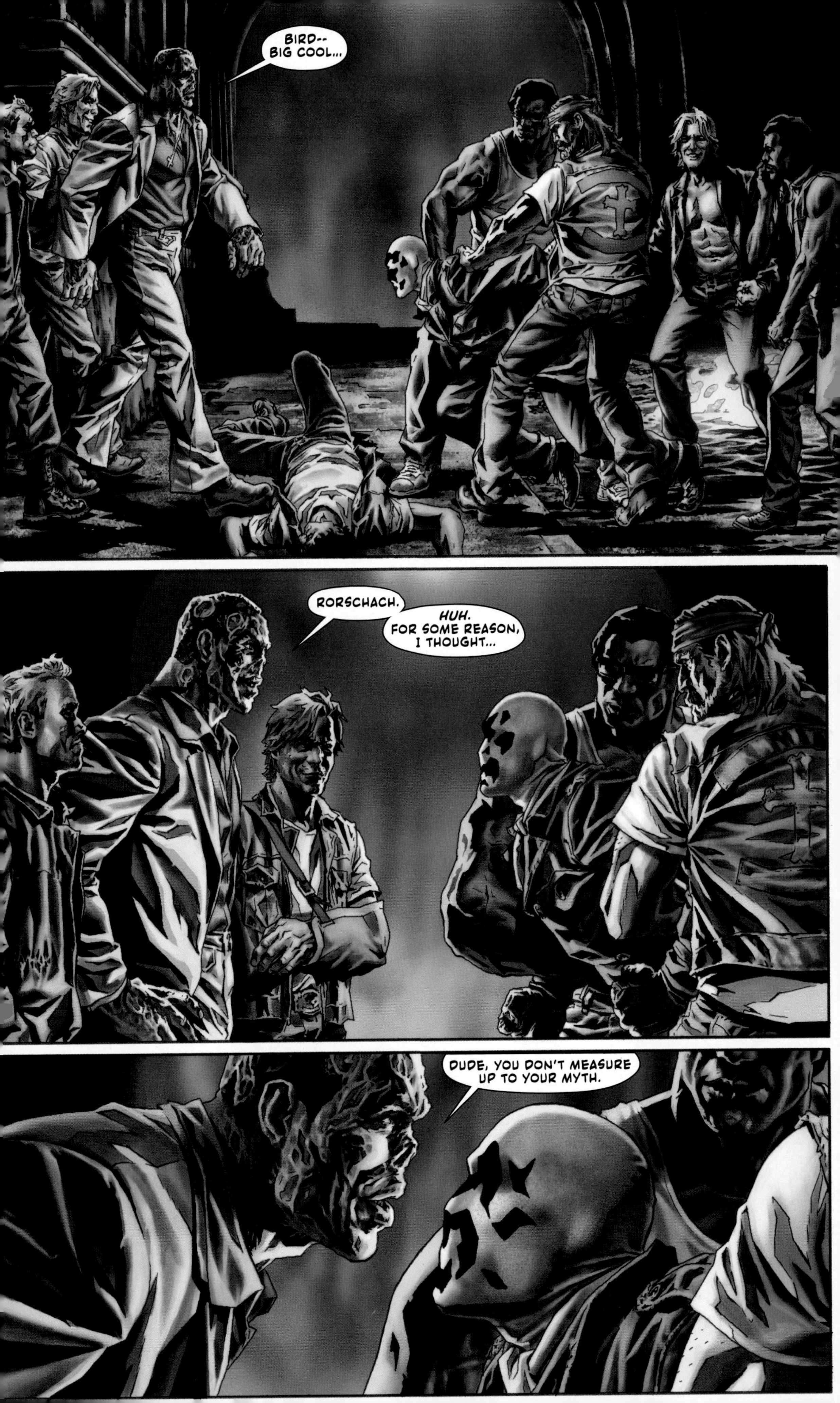
BIRD--
BIG COOL...
RORSCHACH.
HUH.
FOR SOME REASON,
I THOUGHT...
DUDE, YOU DON'T MEASURE
UP TO YOUR MYTH.

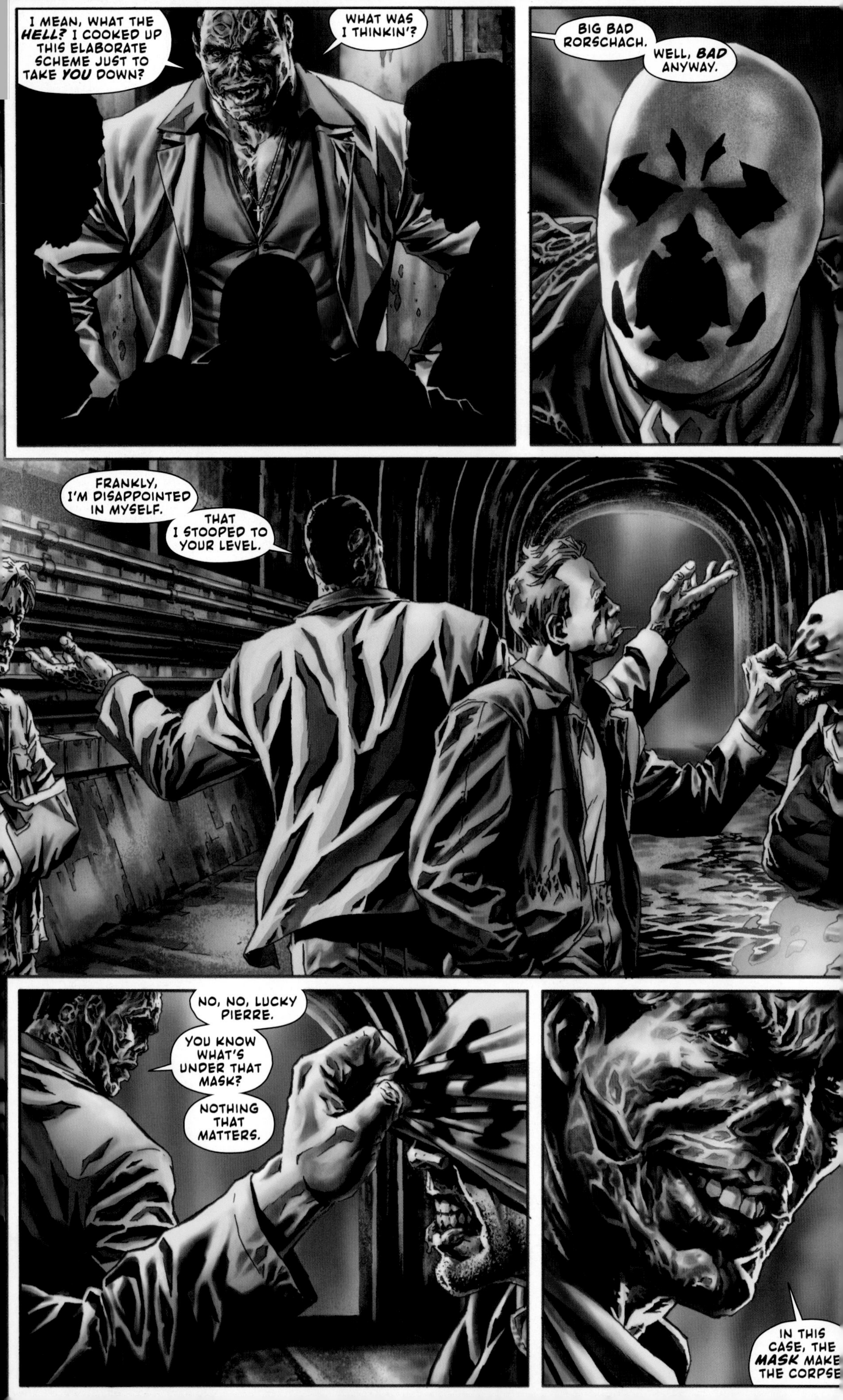
I MEAN, WHAT THE HELL? I COOKED UP THIS ELABORATE SCHEME JUST TO TAKE YOU DOWN?
WHAT WAS I THINKIN'?
BIG BAD RORSCHACH.
WELL, BAD ANYWAY.
FRANKLY, I'M DISAPPOINTED IN MYSELF.
THAT I STOOPED TO YOUR LEVEL.
NO, NO, LUCKY PIERRE.
YOU KNOW WHAT'S UNDER THAT MASK?
NOTHING THAT MATTERS.
IN THIS CASE, THE MASK MAKE THE CORPSE

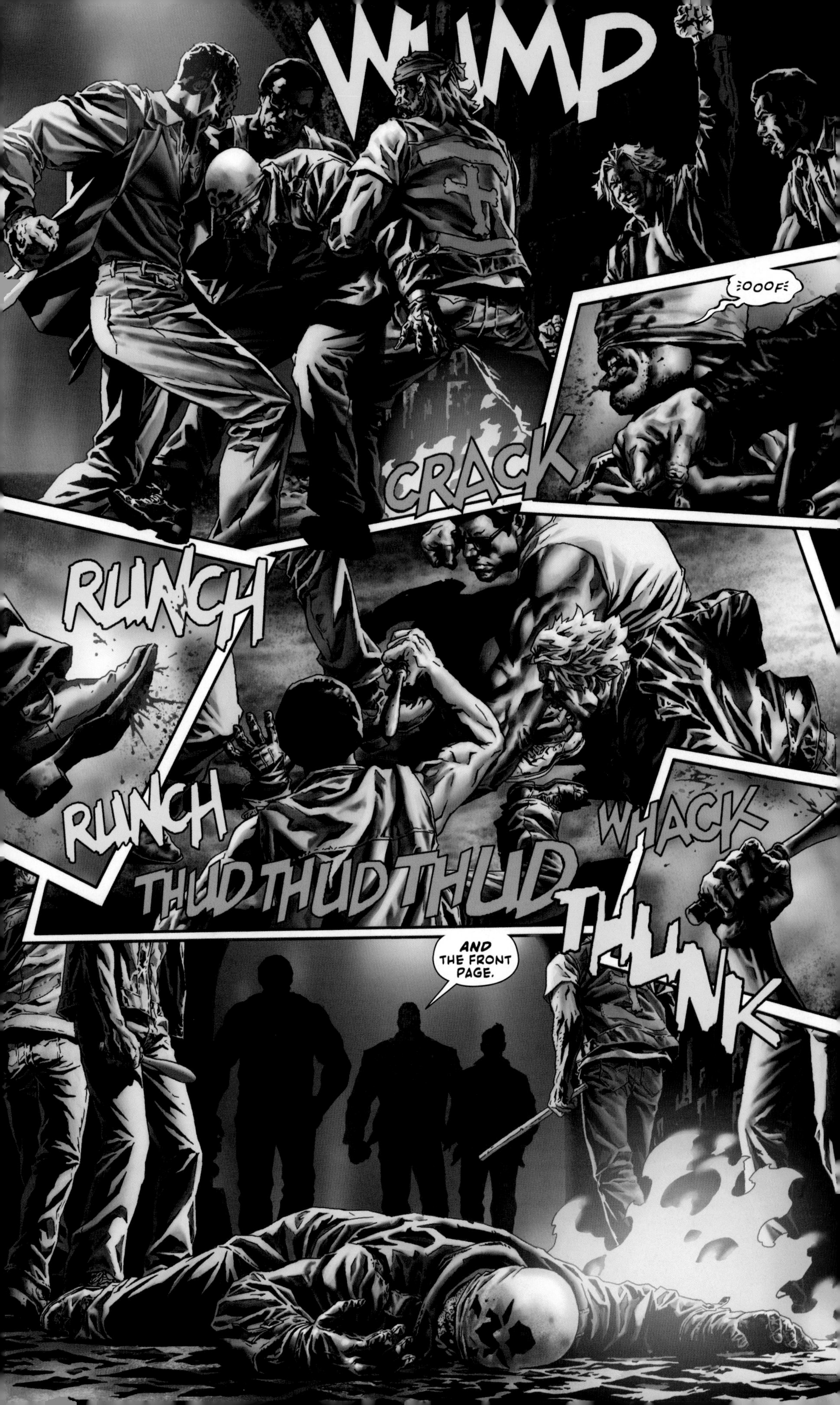
WUMP
OOOF
CRACK
RUNCH
RUNCH
THUD THUD THUD
WHACK
THUNK
AND THE FRONT PAGE.

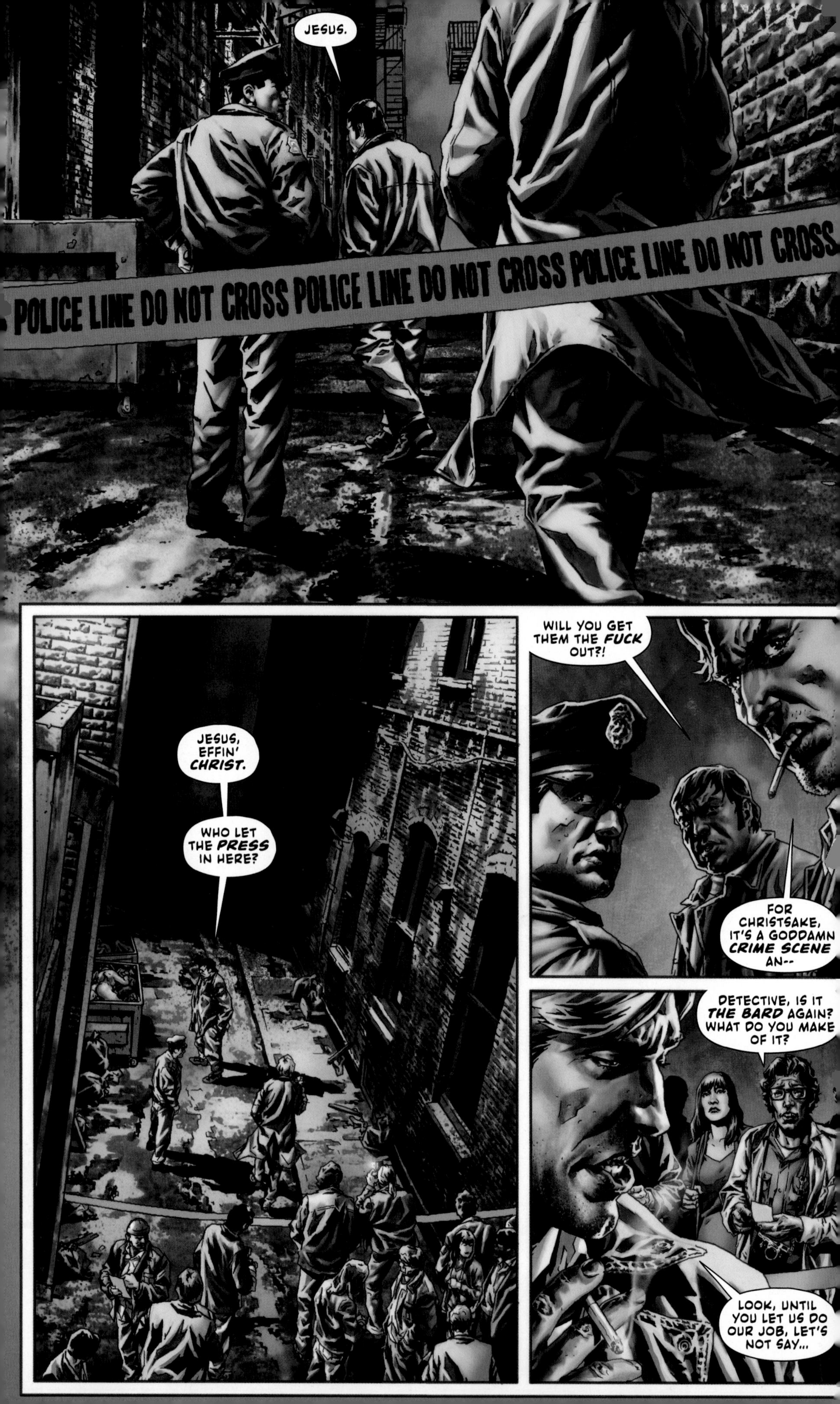
JESUS.
POLICE LINE DO NOT CROSS POLICE LINE DO NOT CROSS POLICE LINE DO NOT CROSS
JESUS, EFFIN' CHRIST.
WHO LET THE PRESS IN HERE?
WILL YOU GET THEM THE FUCK OUT?!
FOR CHRISTSAKE, IT'S A GODDAMN CRIME SCENE AN--
DETECTIVE, IS IT THE BARD AGAIN? WHAT DO YOU MAKE OF IT?
LOOK, UNTIL YOU LET US DO OUR JOB, LET'S NOT SAY...

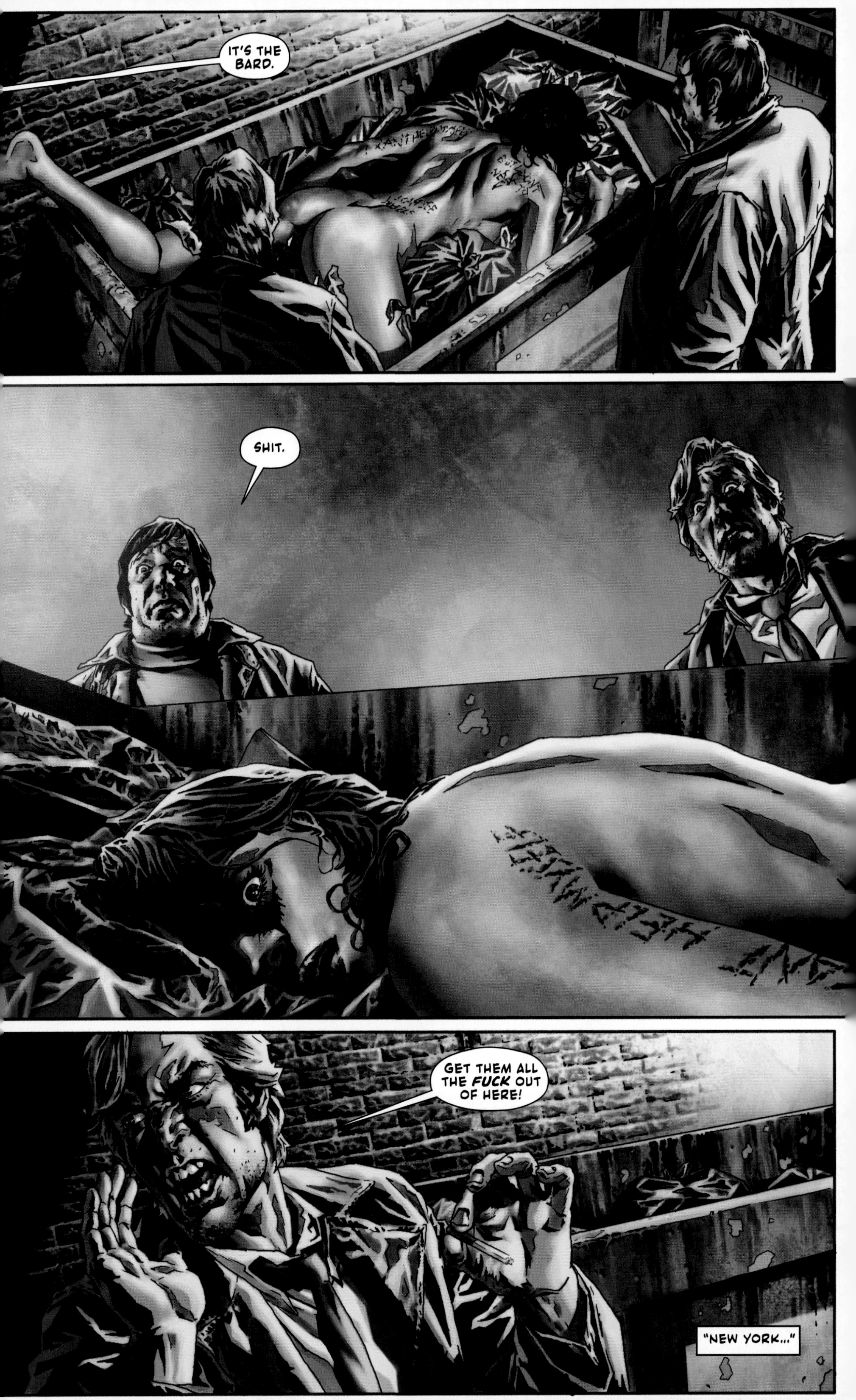
IT'S THE BARD.
SHIT.
GET THEM ALL THE *FUCK* OUT OF HERE!
"NEW YORK..."

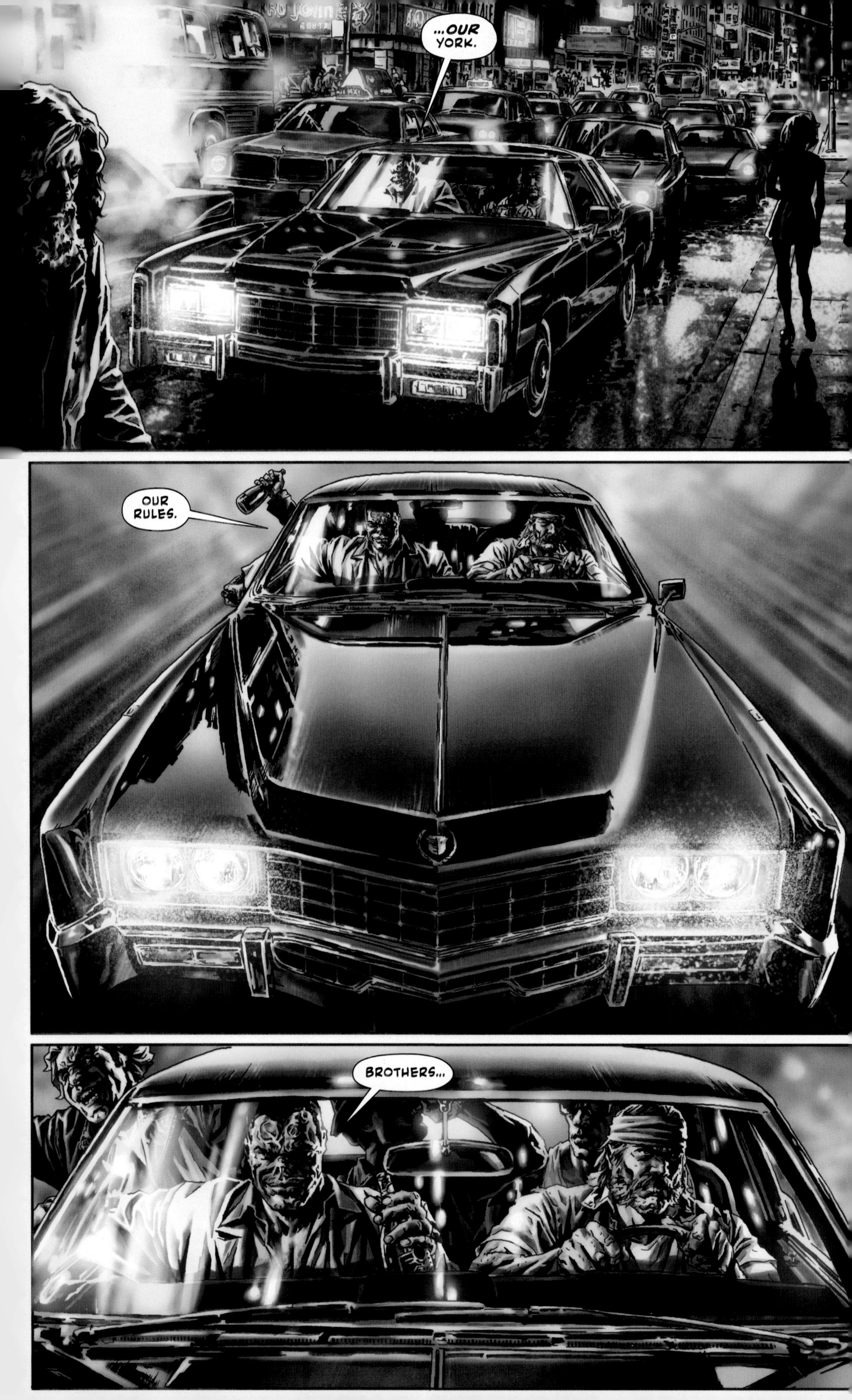
...OUR YORK.
OUR RULES.
BROTHERS...

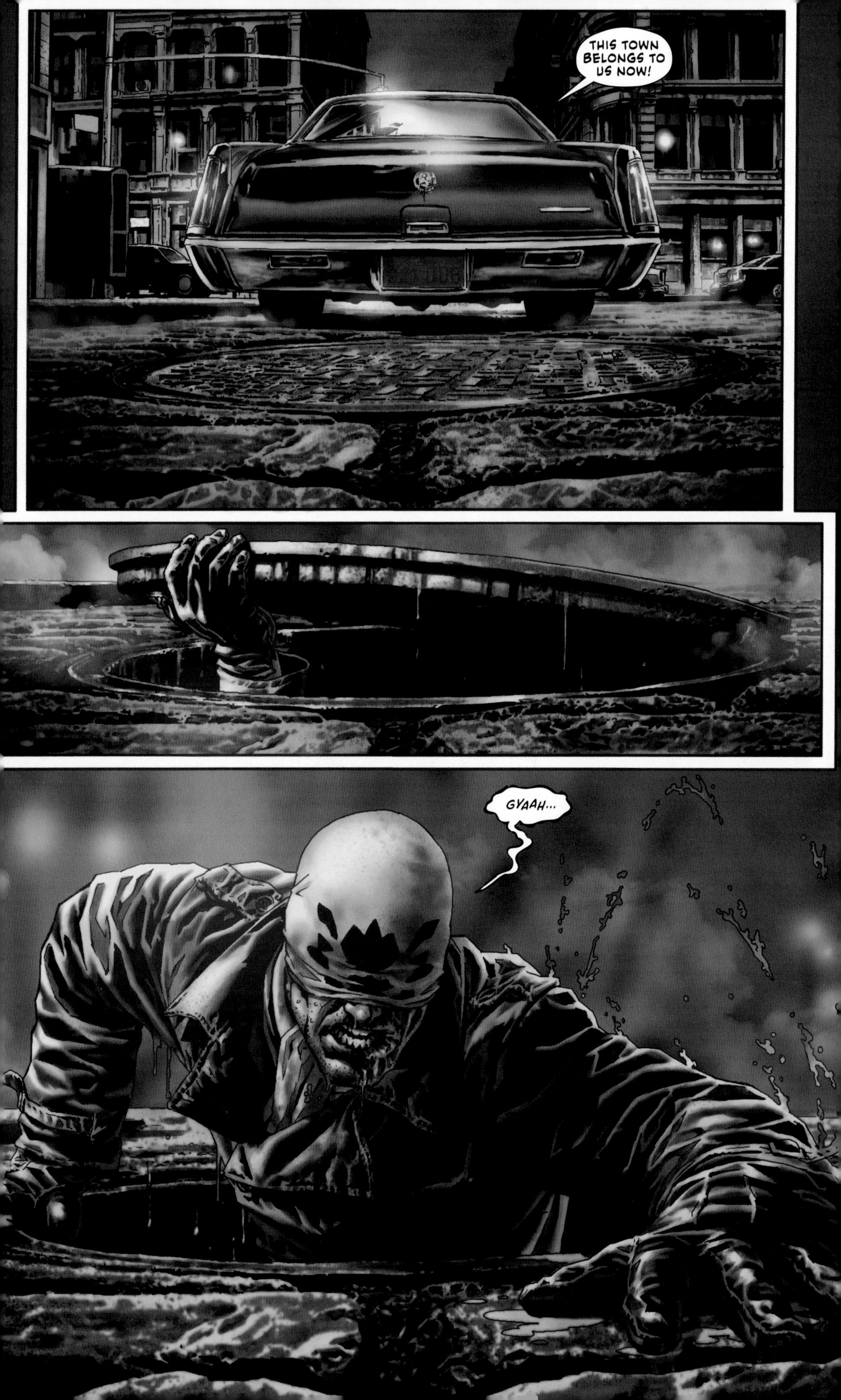
THIS TOWN BELONGS TO US NOW!
GYAAH...

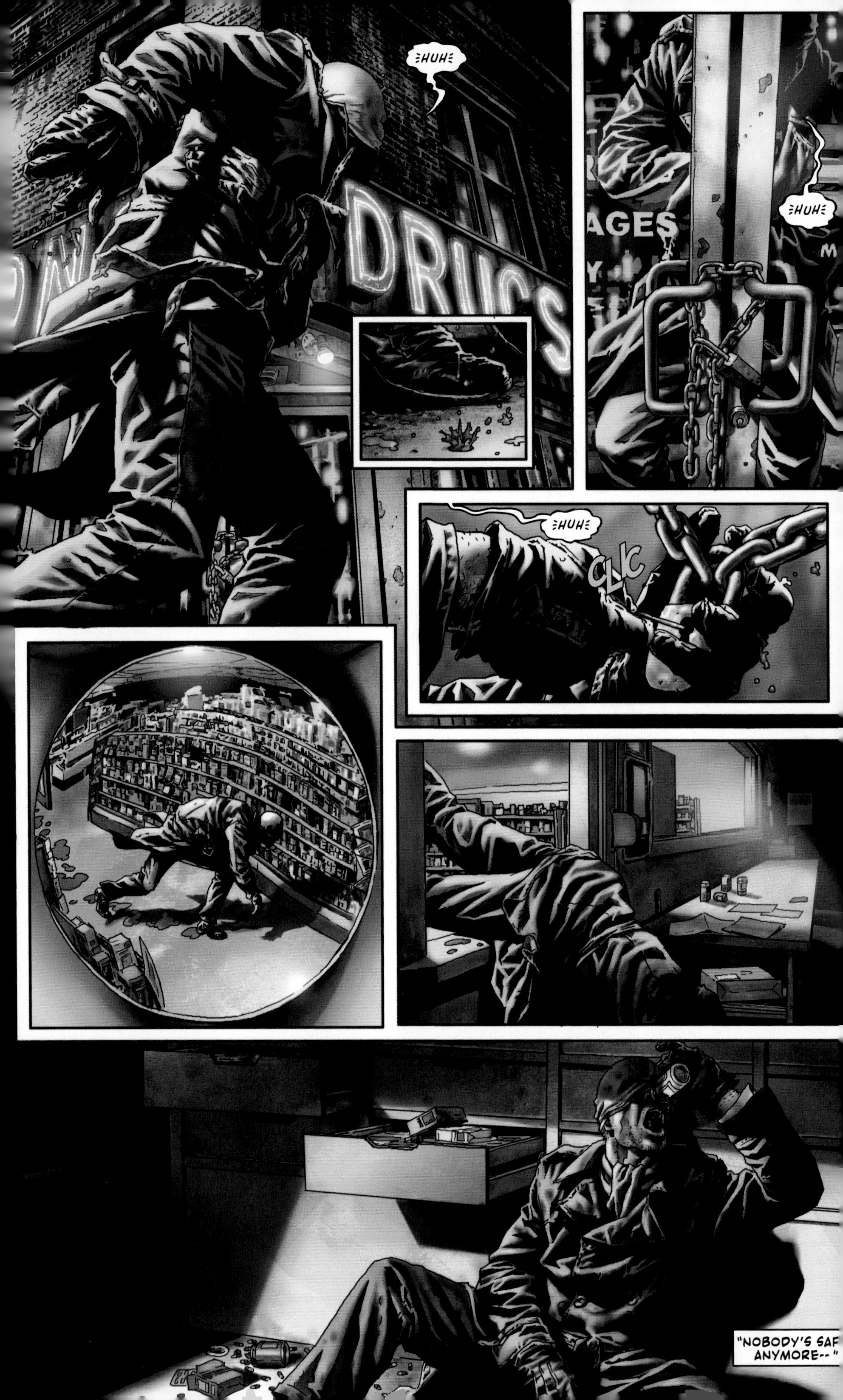

HUH
DRUGS
AGES
HUH
HUH
CLIC
"NOBODY'S SAF
ANYMORE--"

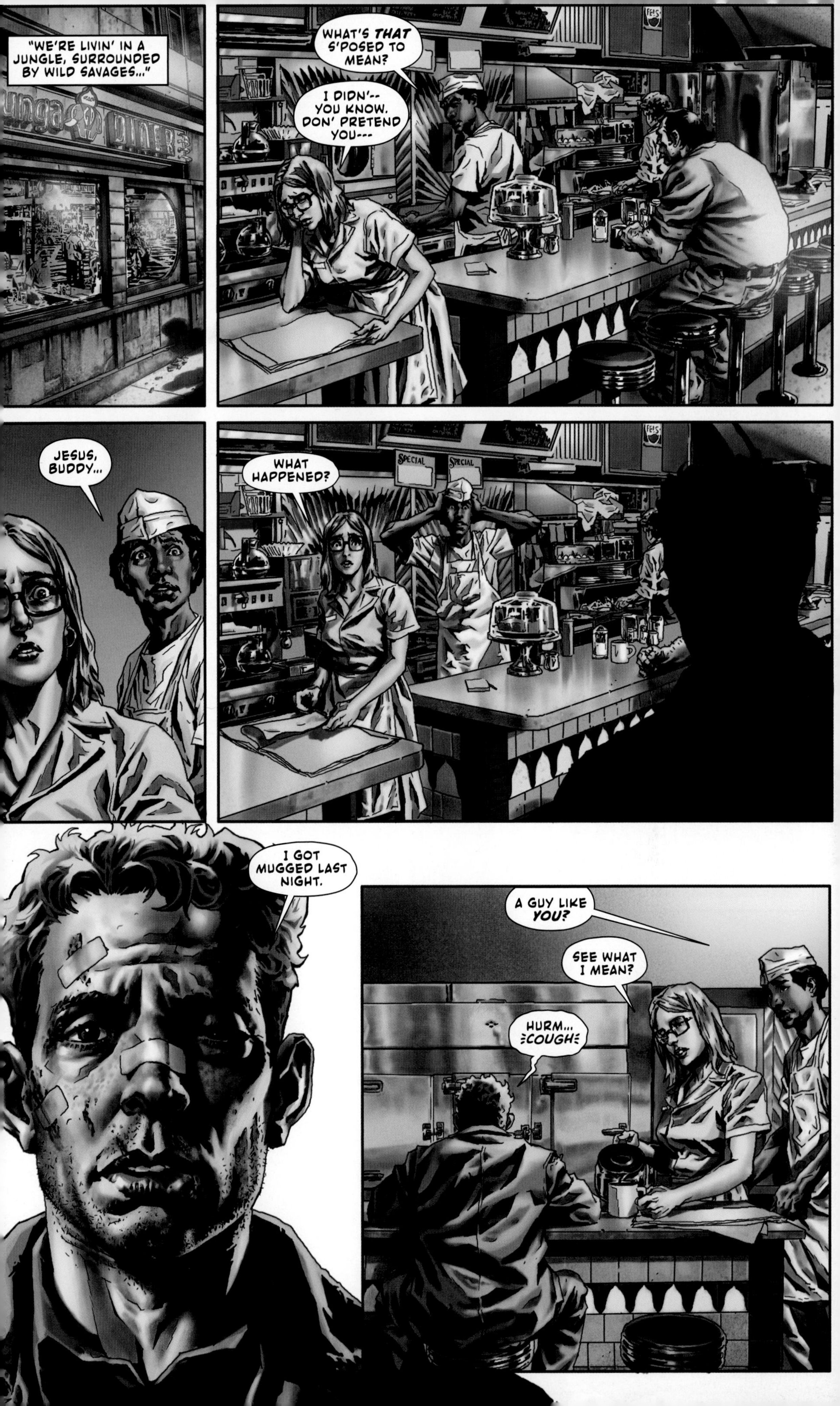
"WE'RE LIVIN' IN A JUNGLE, SURROUNDED BY WILD SAVAGES..."
DINER
WHAT'S THAT S'POSED TO MEAN?
I DIDN'-- YOU KNOW. DON' PRETEND YOU---
JESUS, BUDDY...
WHAT HAPPENED?
SPECIAL
SPECIAL
I GOT MUGGED LAST NIGHT.
A GUY LIKE YOU?
SEE WHAT I MEAN?
HURM... COUGH

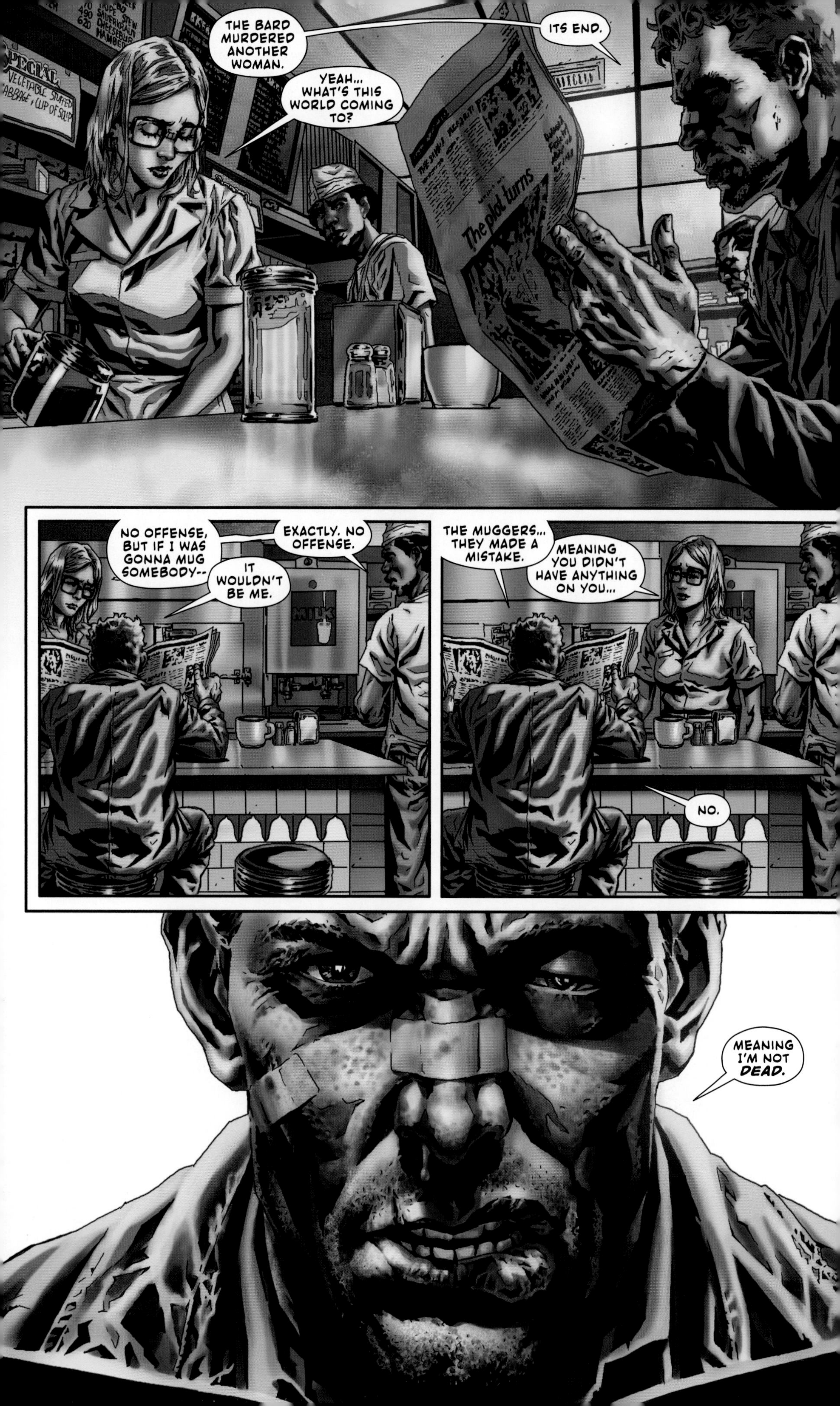
THE BARD MURDERED ANOTHER WOMAN.
ITS END.
YEAH... WHAT'S THIS WORLD COMING TO?
The plot turns
NO OFFENSE, BUT IF I WAS GONNA MUG SOMEBODY--
EXACTLY. NO OFFENSE.
IT WOULDN'T BE ME.
MILK
THE MUGGERS... THEY MADE A MISTAKE.
MEANING YOU DIDN'T HAVE ANYTHING ON YOU...
NO.
MEANING I'M NOT *DEAD.*

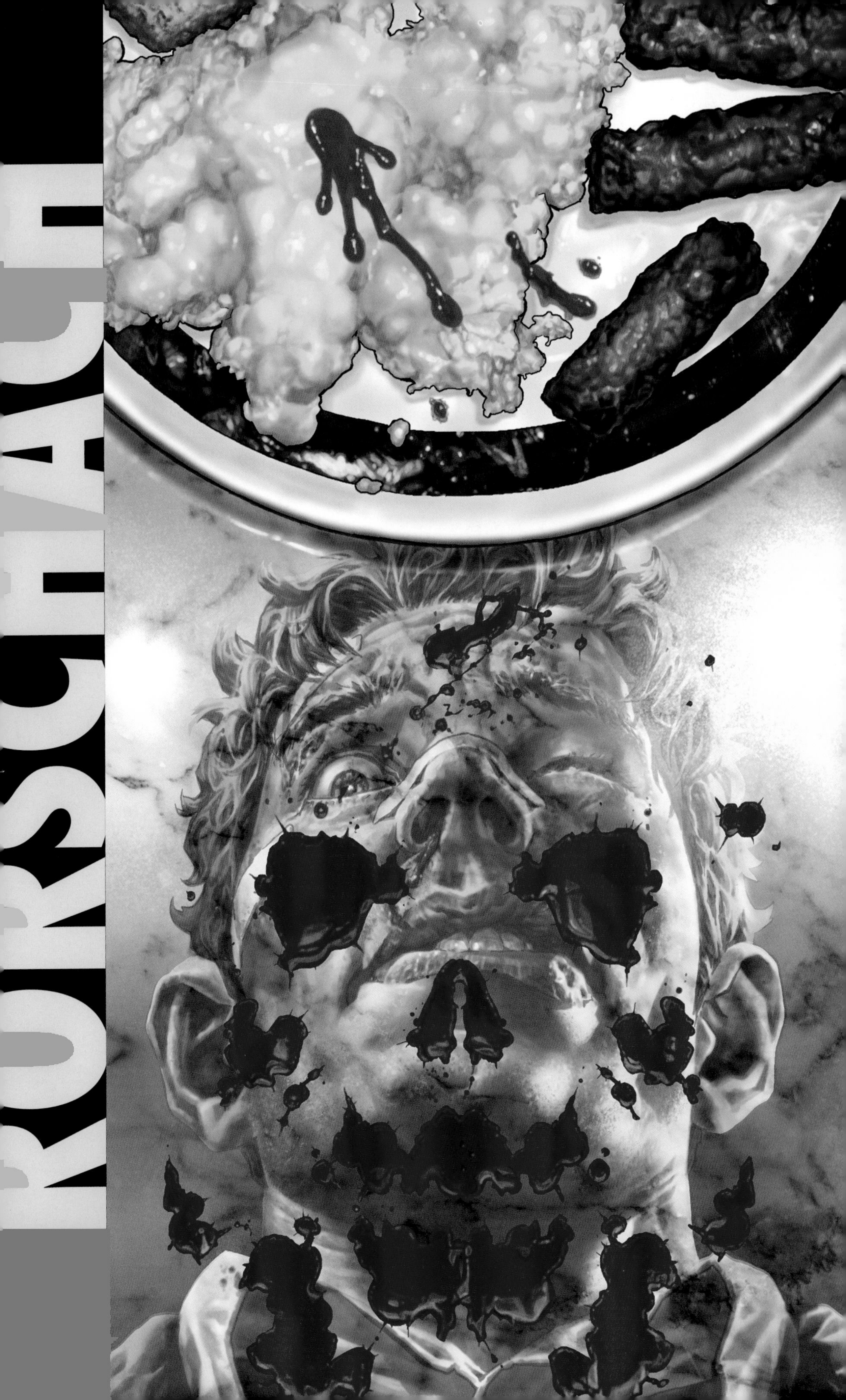
RORSCHACH

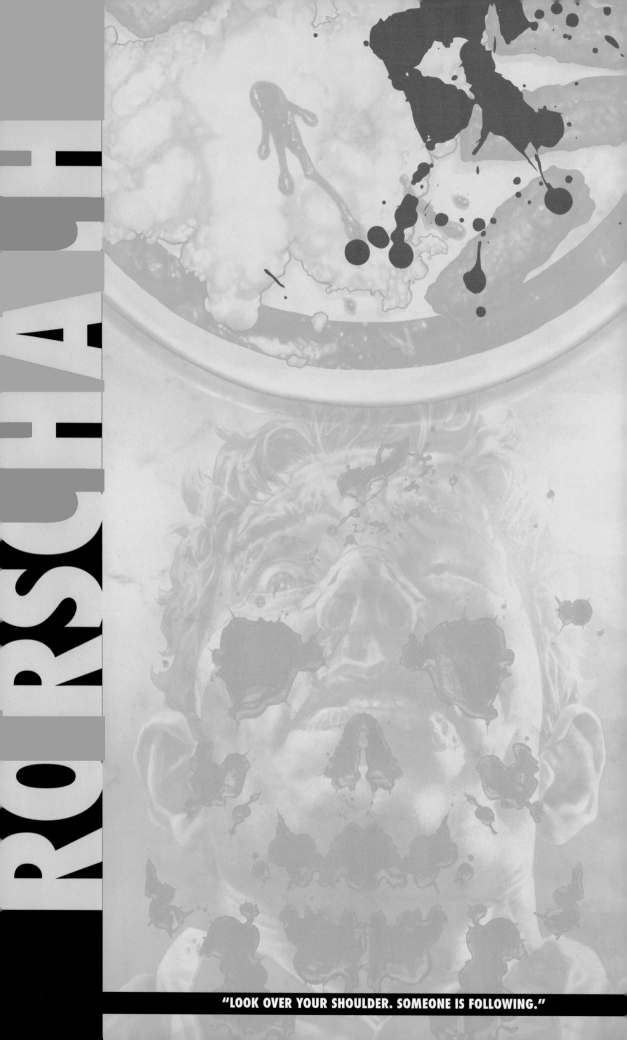

RORSCHACH

"LOOK OVER YOUR SHOULDER. SOMEONE IS FOLLOWING."

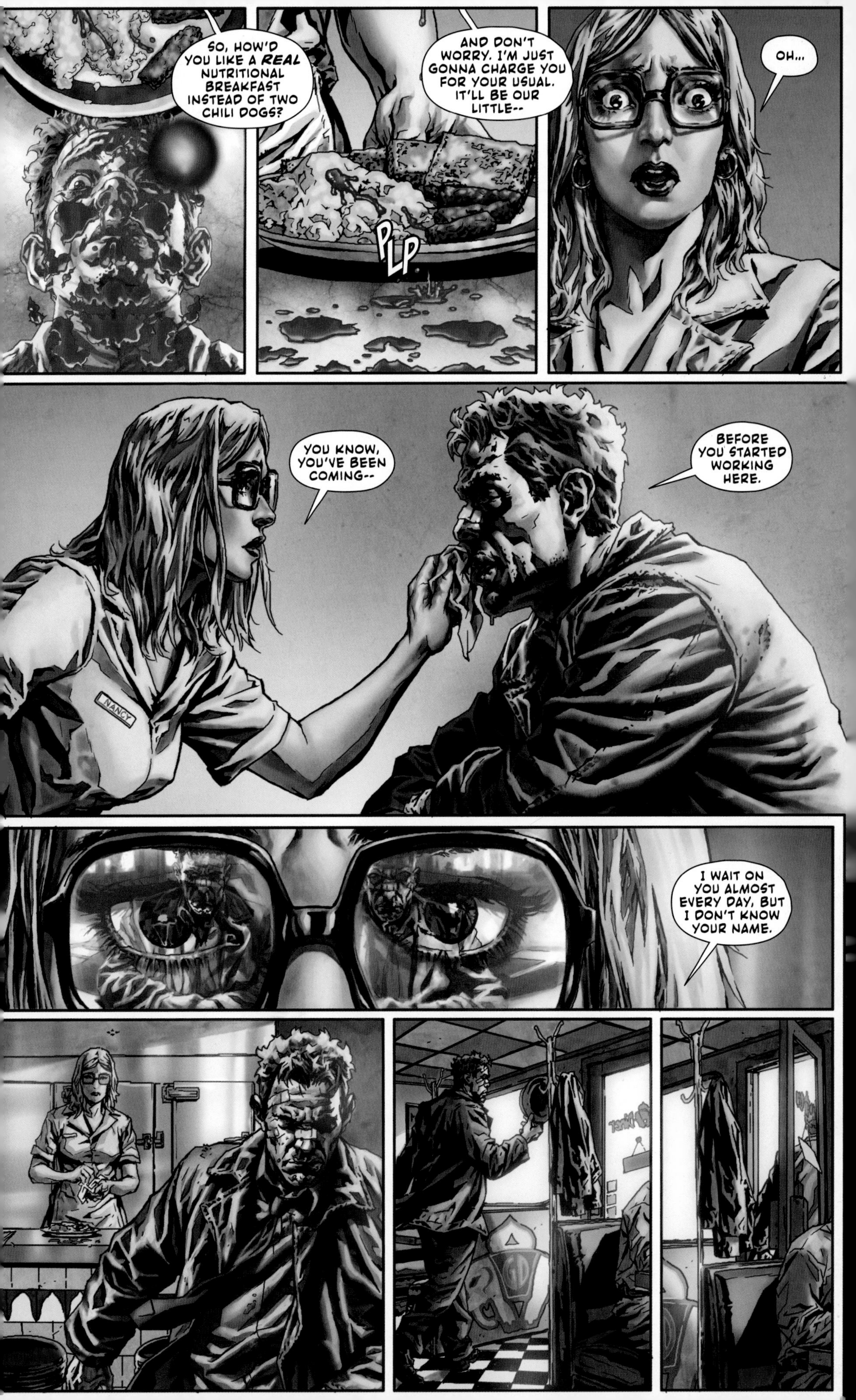
SO, HOW'D YOU LIKE A REAL NUTRITIONAL BREAKFAST INSTEAD OF TWO CHILI DOGS?
AND DON'T WORRY. I'M JUST GONNA CHARGE YOU FOR YOUR USUAL. IT'LL BE OUR LITTLE--
PLP
OH...
YOU KNOW, YOU'VE BEEN COMING--
BEFORE YOU STARTED WORKING HERE.
NANCY
I WAIT ON YOU ALMOST EVERY DAY, BUT I DON'T KNOW YOUR NAME.

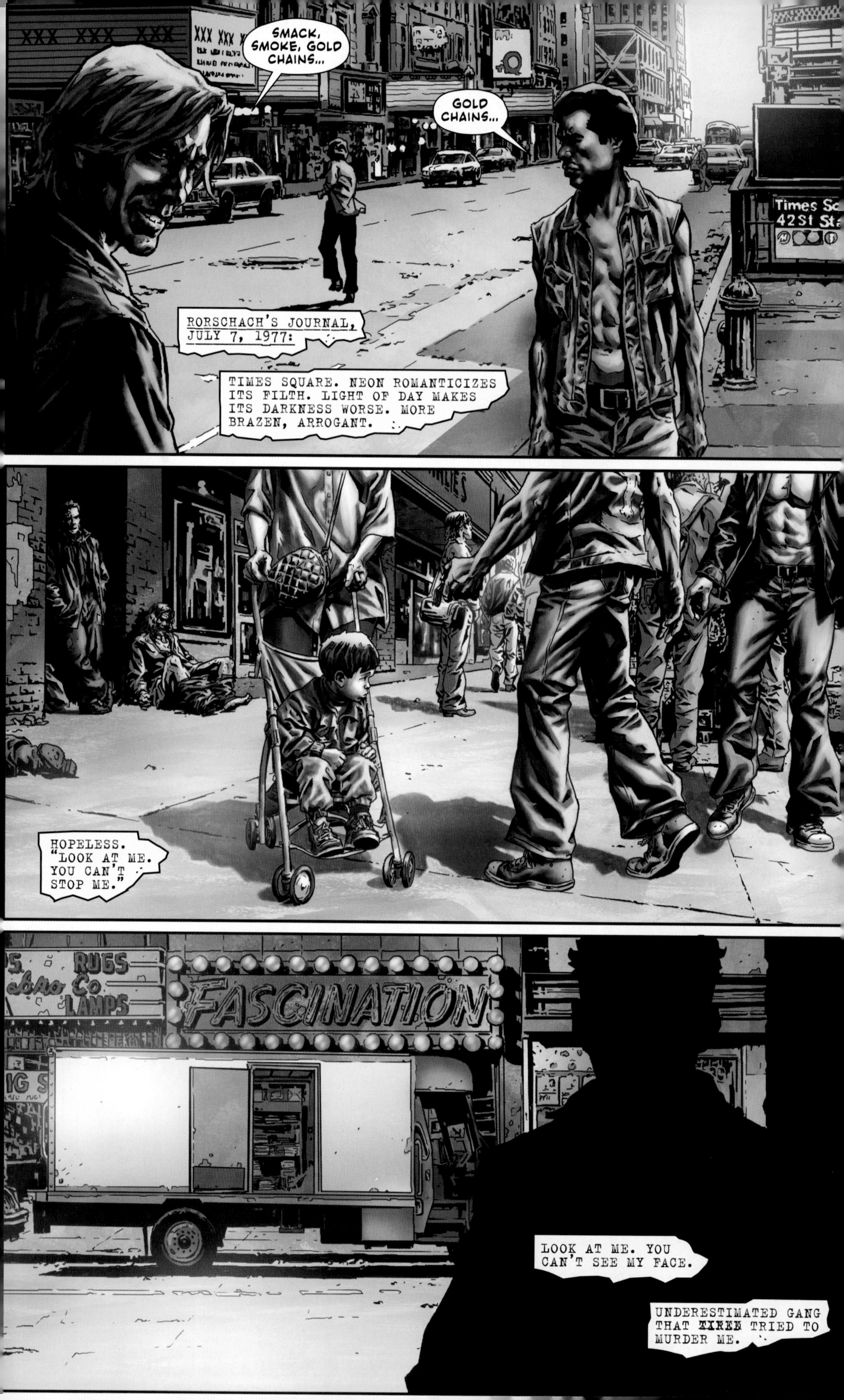
SMACK, SMOKE, GOLD CHAINS...
GOLD CHAINS...
RORSCHACH'S JOURNAL, JULY 7, 1977:
TIMES SQUARE. NEON ROMANTICIZES ITS FILTH. LIGHT OF DAY MAKES ITS DARKNESS WORSE. MORE BRAZEN, ARROGANT.
Times Sq
42 St Sta
HOPELESS. "LOOK AT ME. YOU CAN'T STOP ME."
RUGS
LAMPS
FASCINATION
LOOK AT ME. YOU CAN'T SEE MY FACE.
UNDERESTIMATED GANG THAT TRIED TO MURDER ME.

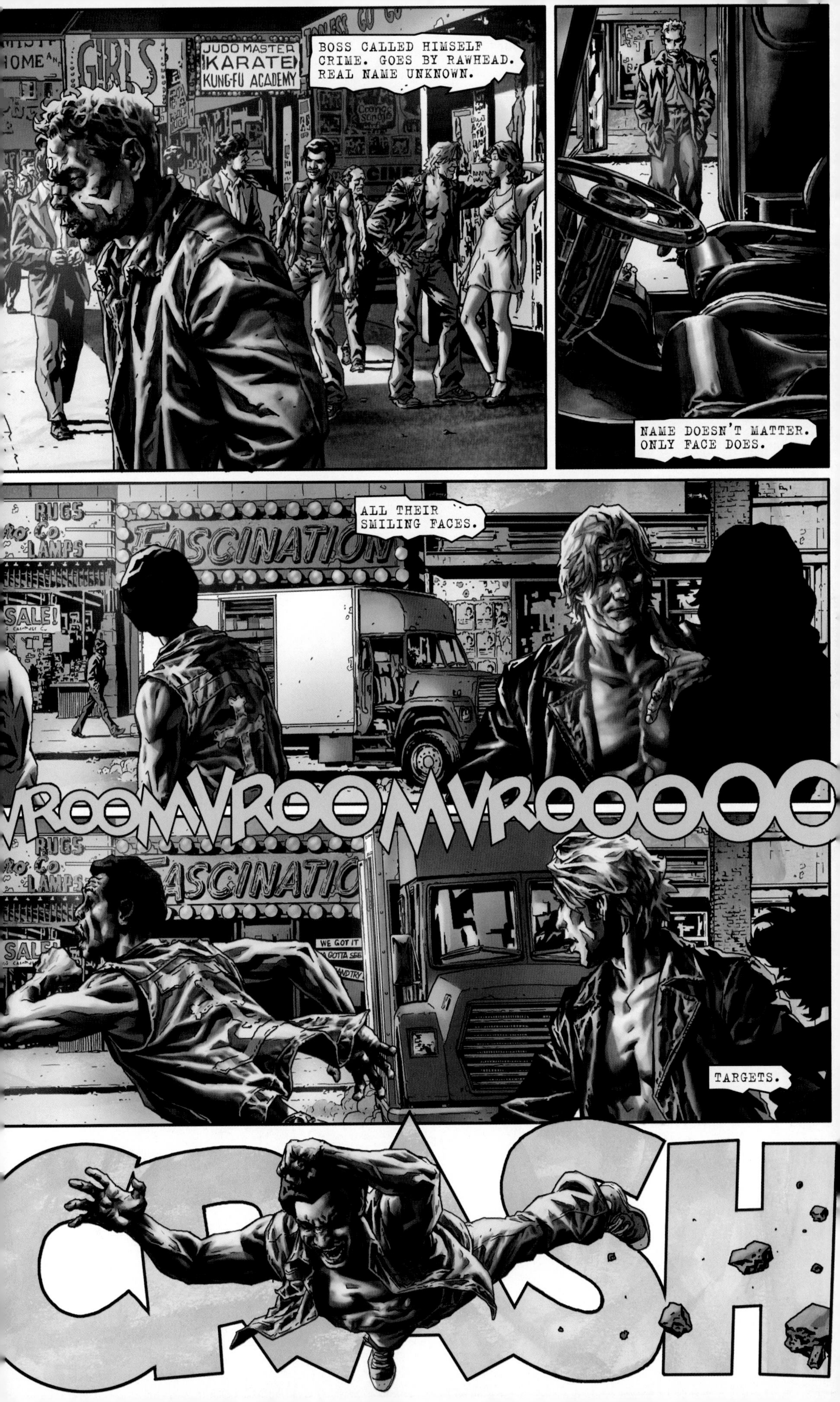

MISTY
HOME
GIRLS
JUDO MASTER KARATE KUNG-FU ACADEMY
BOSS CALLED HIMSELF CRIME. GOES BY RAWHEAD. REAL NAME UNKNOWN.
CINE
NAME DOESN'T MATTER. ONLY FACE DOES.
RUGS
LAMPS
FASCINATION
SALE!
ALL THEIR SMILING FACES.
VROOMVROOMVROOOOOO
WE GOT IT
TARGETS.
CRASH!

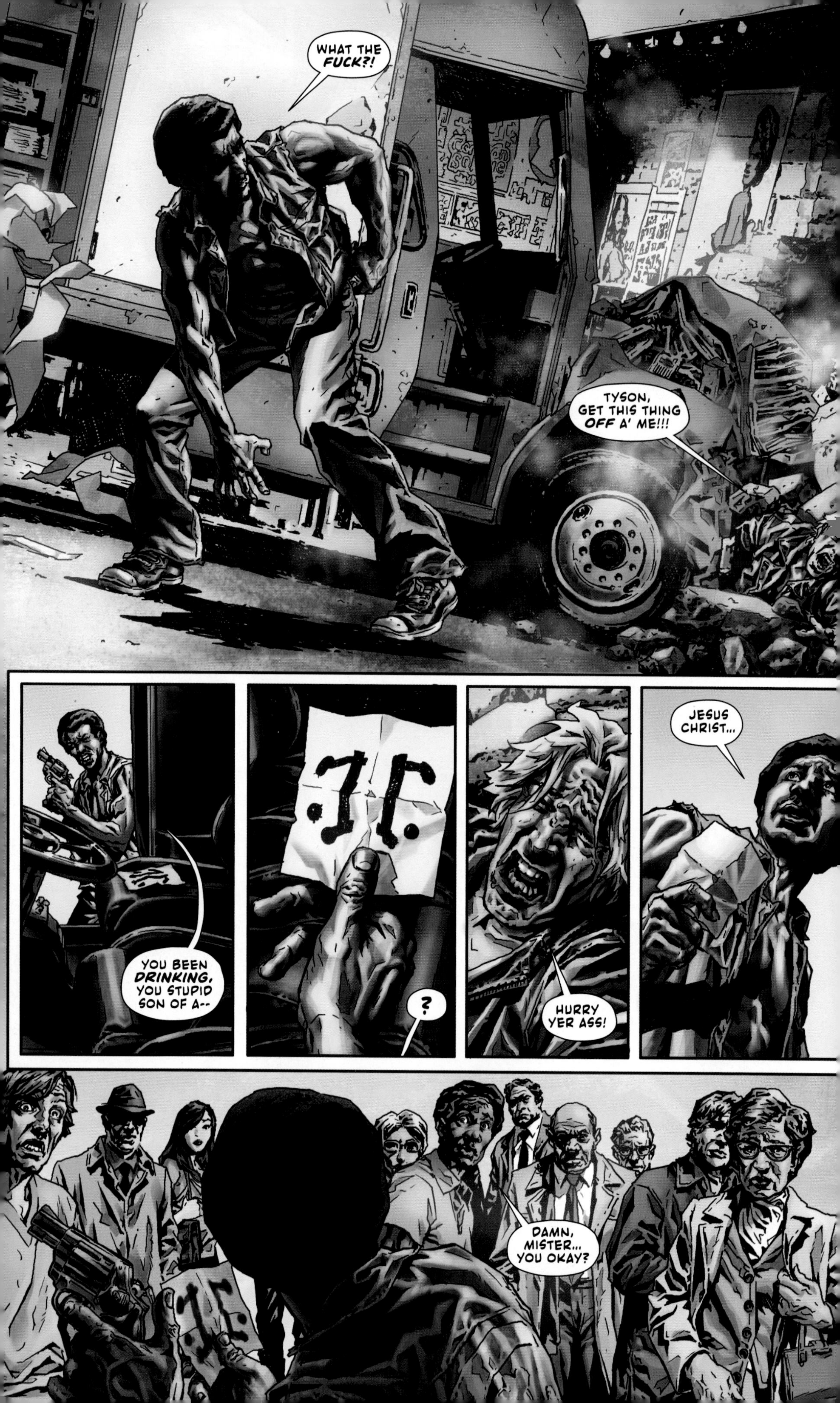
WHAT THE FUCK?!
TYSON, GET THIS THING OFF A' ME!!!
YOU BEEN DRINKING, YOU STUPID SON OF A--
?
HURRY YER ASS!
JESUS CHRIST...
DAMN, MISTER... YOU OKAY?

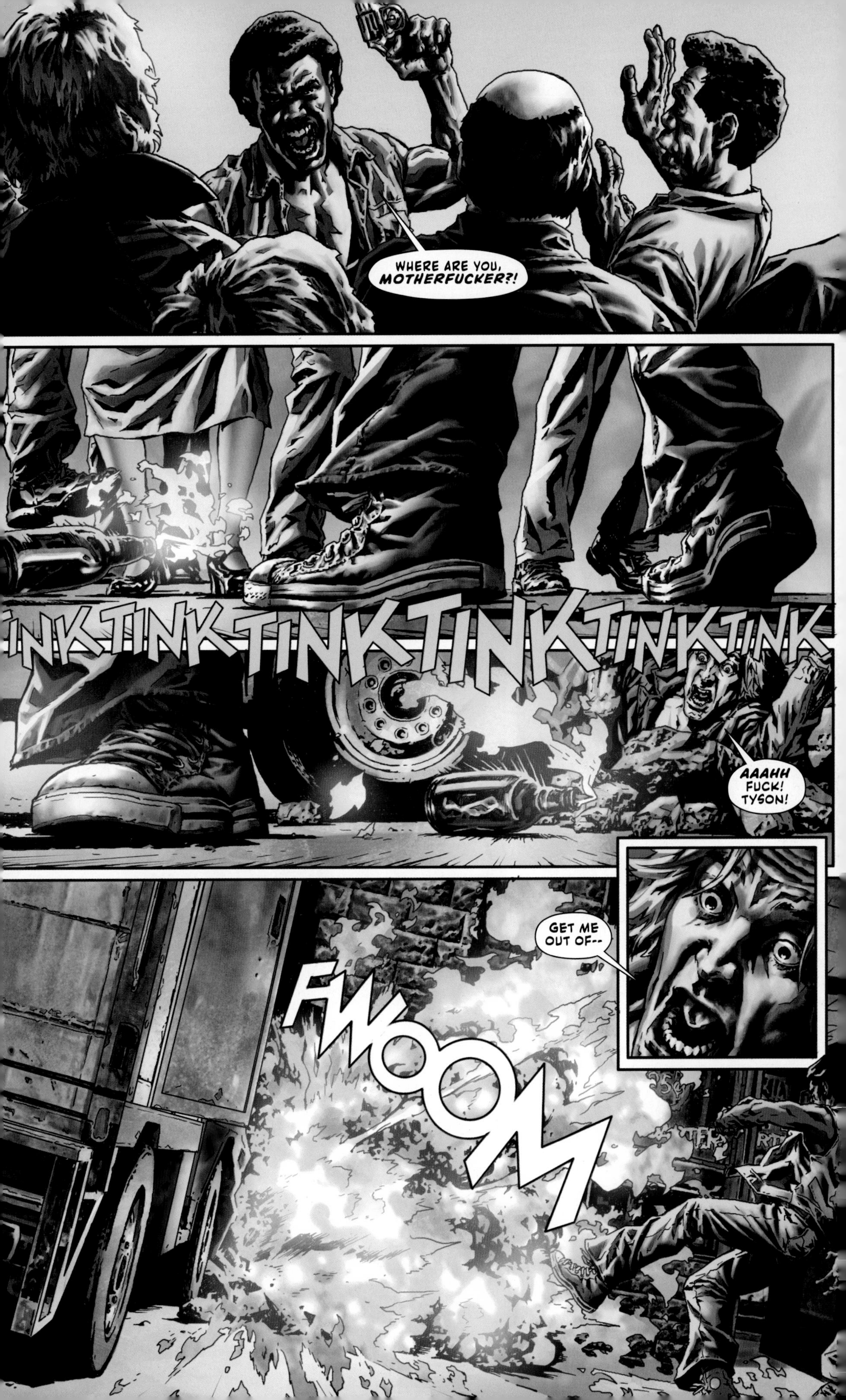
WHERE ARE YOU, MOTHERFUCKER?!
TINKTINKTINKTINKTINKTINK
AAAHH FUCK! TYSON!
GET ME OUT OF--
FWOOM

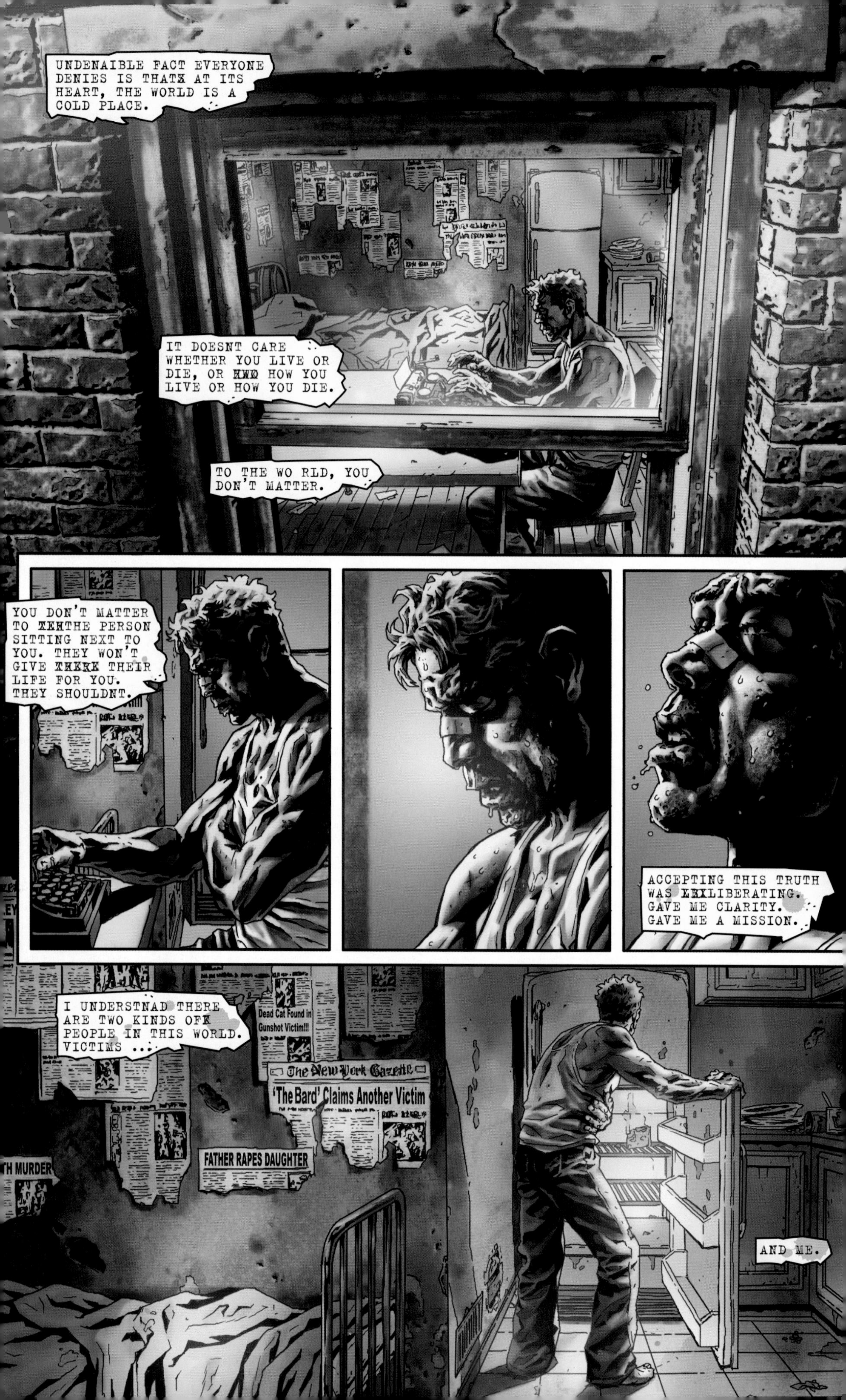
UNDENAIBLE FACT EVERYONE DENIES IS THATX AT ITS HEART, THE WORLD IS A COLD PLACE.
IT DOESNT CARE WHETHER YOU LIVE OR DIE, OR HWO HOW YOU LIVE OR HOW YOU DIE.
TO THE WO RLD, YOU DON'T MATTER.
YOU DON'T MATTER TO TEHTHE PERSON SITTING NEXT TO YOU. THEY WON'T GIVE THERE THEIR LIFE FOR YOU. THEY SHOULDNT.
ACCEPTING THIS TRUTH WAS LEXLIBERATING. GAVE ME CLARITY. GAVE ME A MISSION.
I UNDERSTNAD THERE ARE TWO KINDS OFK PEOPLE IN THIS WORLD. VICTIMS ...
Dead Cat Found in Gunshot Victim!!!
The New York Gazette
'The Bard' Claims Another Victim
TH MURDER
FATHER RAPES DAUGHTER
AND ME.

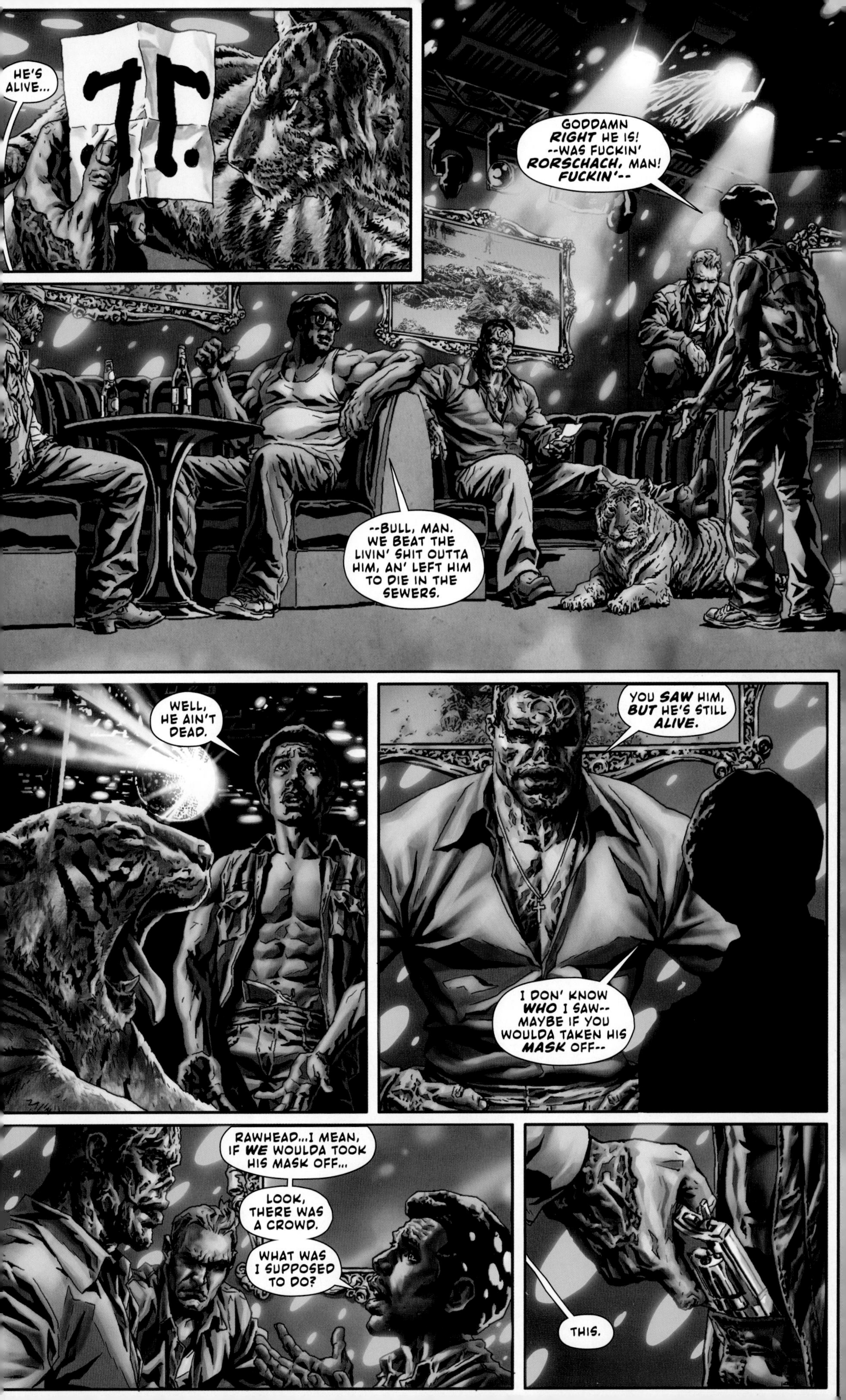
HE'S ALIVE...
GODDAMN RIGHT HE IS! --WAS FUCKIN' RORSCHACH, MAN! FUCKIN'--
--BULL, MAN. WE BEAT THE LIVIN' SHIT OUTTA HIM, AN' LEFT HIM TO DIE IN THE SEWERS.
WELL, HE AIN'T DEAD.
YOU SAW HIM, BUT HE'S STILL ALIVE.
I DON' KNOW WHO I SAW-- MAYBE IF YOU WOULDA TAKEN HIS MASK OFF--
RAWHEAD...I MEAN, IF WE WOULDA TOOK HIS MASK OFF...
LOOK, THERE WAS A CROWD.
WHAT WAS I SUPPOSED TO DO?
THIS.

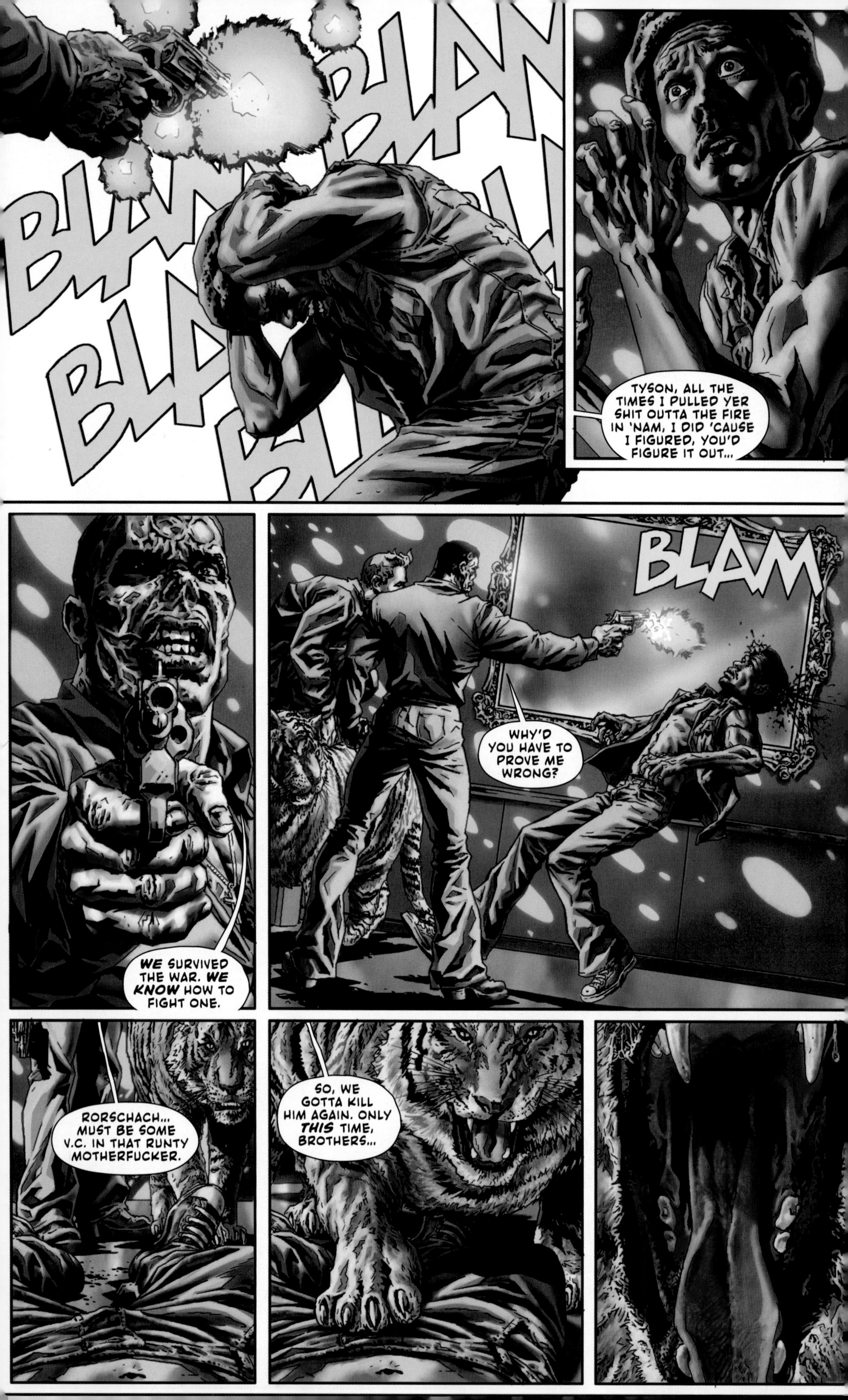
BLAM BLAM
BLAM BLAM
TYSON, ALL THE TIMES I PULLED YER SHIT OUTTA THE FIRE IN 'NAM, I DID 'CAUSE I FIGURED, YOU'D FIGURE IT OUT...
WE SURVIVED THE WAR. WE KNOW HOW TO FIGHT ONE.
BLAM
WHY'D YOU HAVE TO PROVE ME WRONG?
RORSCHACH... MUST BE SOME V.C. IN THAT RUNTY MOTHERFUCKER.
SO, WE GOTTA KILL HIM AGAIN. ONLY THIS TIME, BROTHERS...

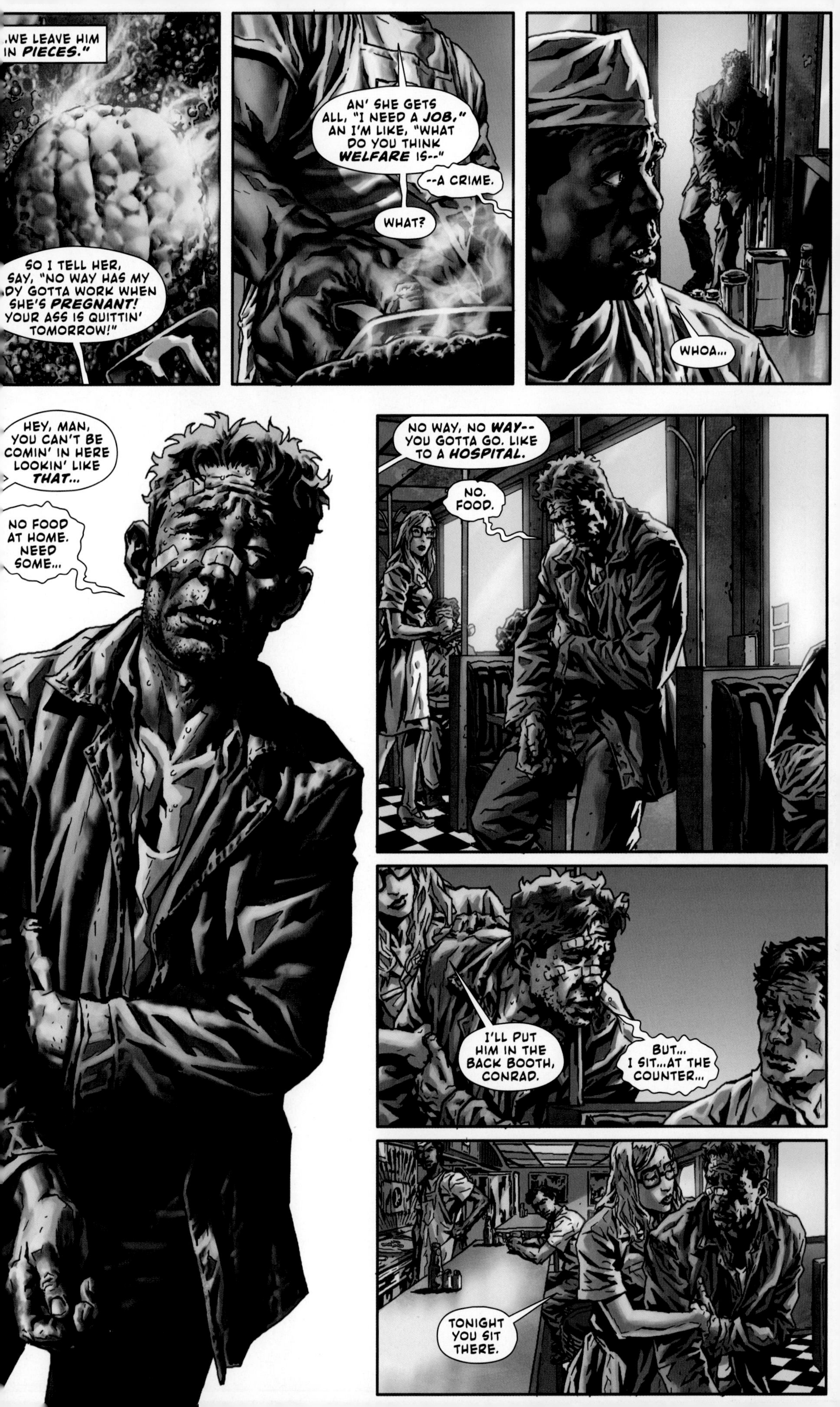
.WE LEAVE HIM IN *PIECES*."
SO I TELL HER, SAY, "NO WAY HAS MY DY GOTTA WORK WHEN SHE'S *PREGNANT!* YOUR ASS IS QUITTIN' TOMORROW!"
AN' SHE GETS ALL, "I NEED A *JOB*," AN I'M LIKE, "WHAT DO YOU THINK *WELFARE* IS--"
--A CRIME.
WHAT?
WHOA...
HEY, MAN, YOU CAN'T BE COMIN' IN HERE LOOKIN' LIKE *THAT*...
NO FOOD AT HOME. NEED SOME...
NO WAY, NO *WAY*-- YOU GOTTA GO. LIKE TO A *HOSPITAL*.
NO. FOOD.
I'LL PUT HIM IN THE BACK BOOTH, CONRAD.
BUT... I SIT...AT THE COUNTER...
TONIGHT YOU SIT THERE.

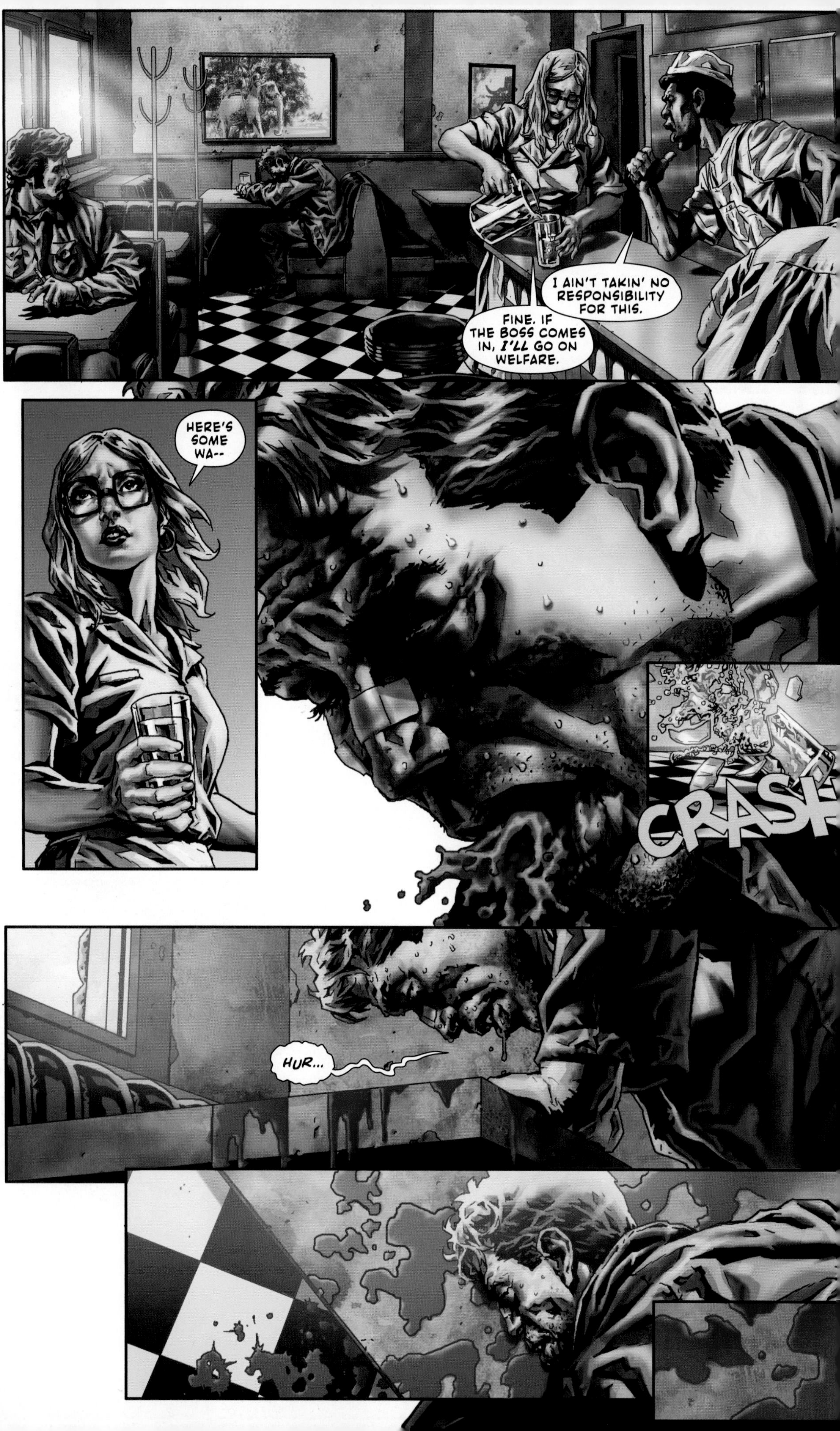
I AIN'T TAKIN' NO RESPONSIBILITY FOR THIS.
FINE. IF THE BOSS COMES IN, I'LL GO ON WELFARE.
HERE'S SOME WA--
CRASH
HUR...

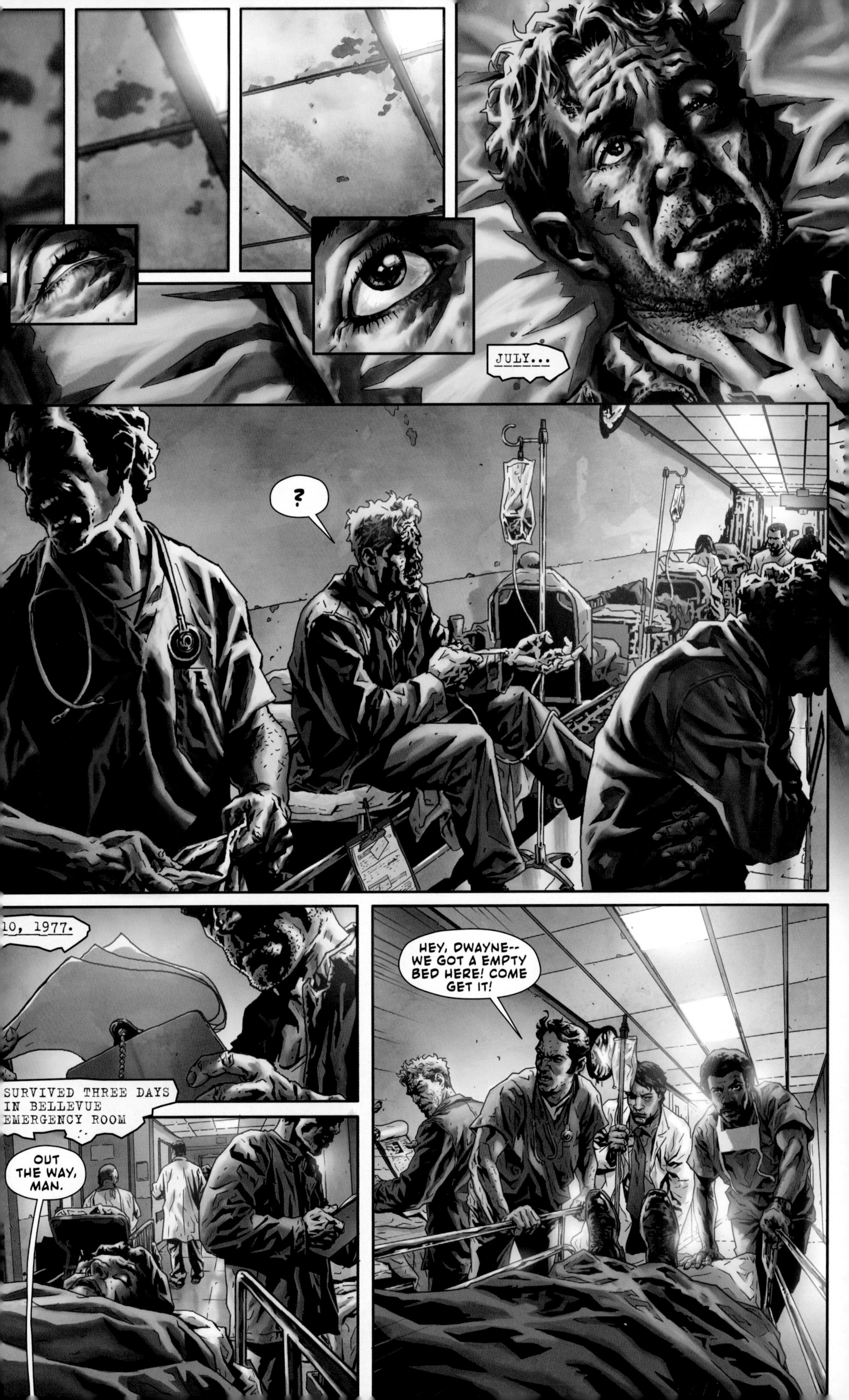
JULY...
?
10, 1977.
SURVIVED THREE DAYS IN BELLEVUE EMERGENCY ROOM
OUT THE WAY, MAN.
HEY, DWAYNE-- WE GOT A EMPTY BED HERE! COME GET IT!

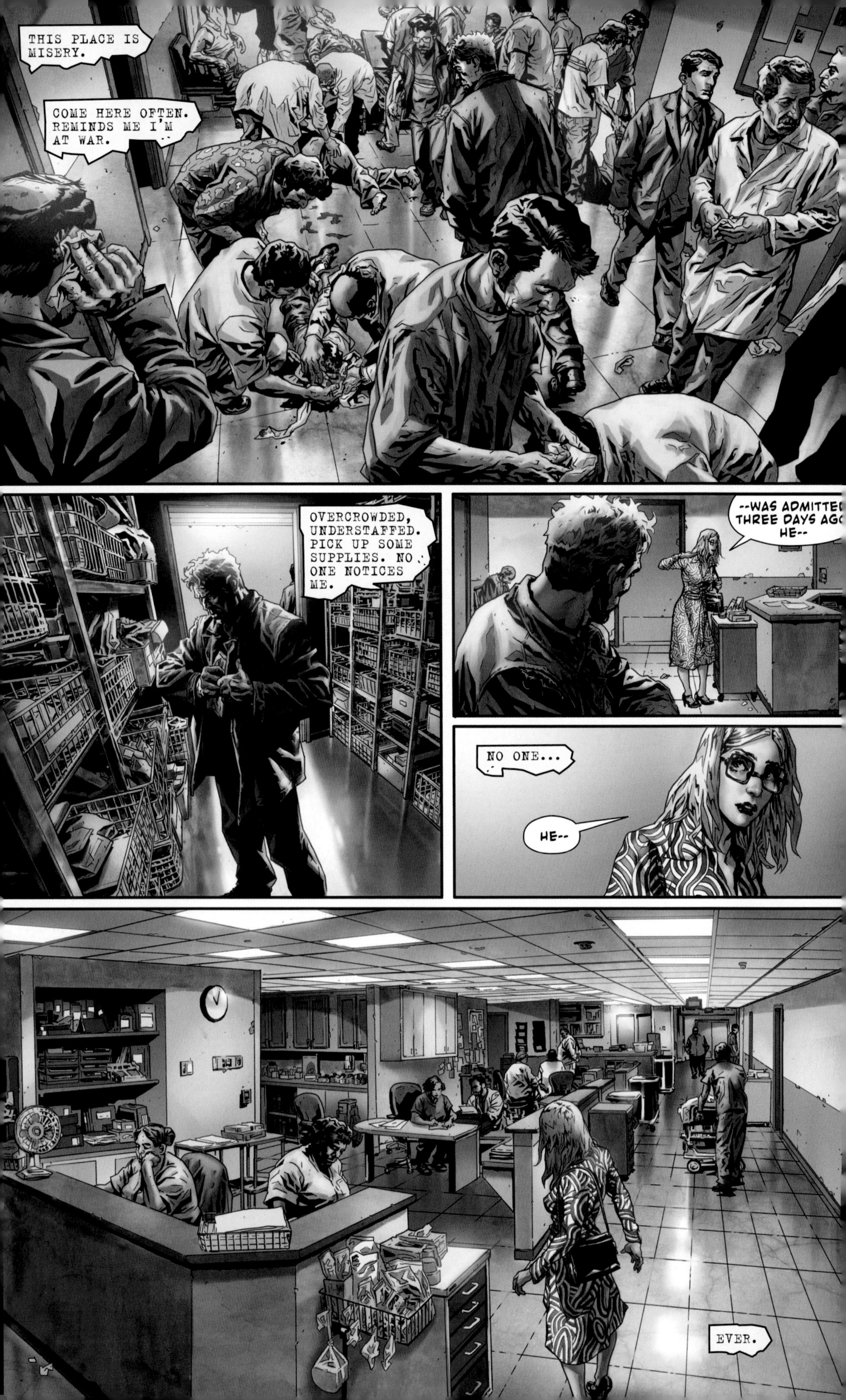
THIS PLACE IS MISERY.
COME HERE OFTEN. REMINDS ME I'M AT WAR.
OVERCROWDED, UNDERSTAFFED. PICK UP SOME SUPPLIES. NO ONE NOTICES ME.
--WAS ADMITTED THREE DAYS AGO HE--
NO ONE...
HE--
EVER.

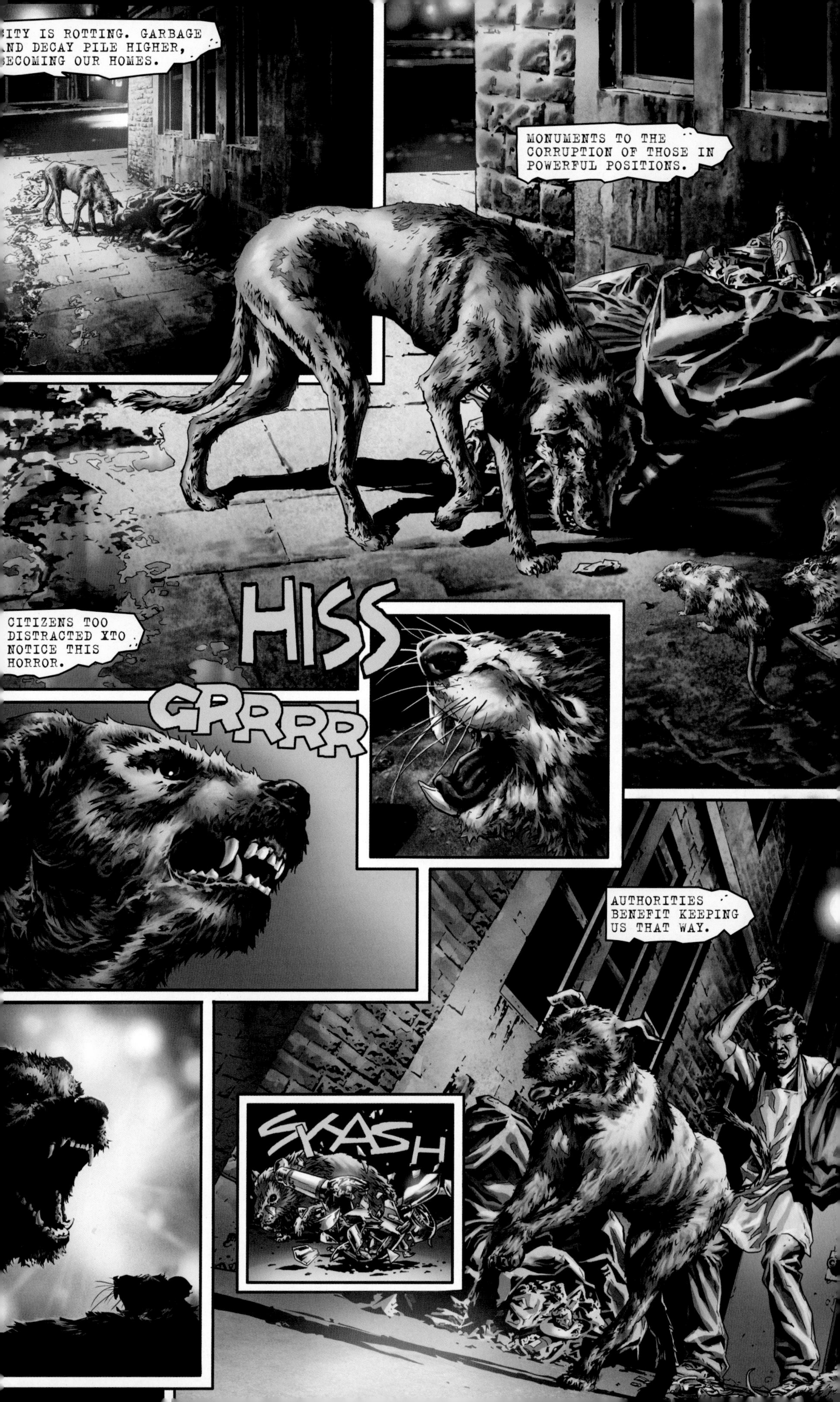

ITY IS ROTTING. GARBAGE
ND DECAY PILE HIGHER,
ECOMING OUR HOMES.
MONUMENTS TO THE
CORRUPTION OF THOSE IN
POWERFUL POSITIONS.
CITIZENS TOO
DISTRACTED XTO
NOTICE THIS
HORROR.
HISS
GRRRR
AUTHORITIES
BENEFIT KEEPING
US THAT WAY.
SMASH

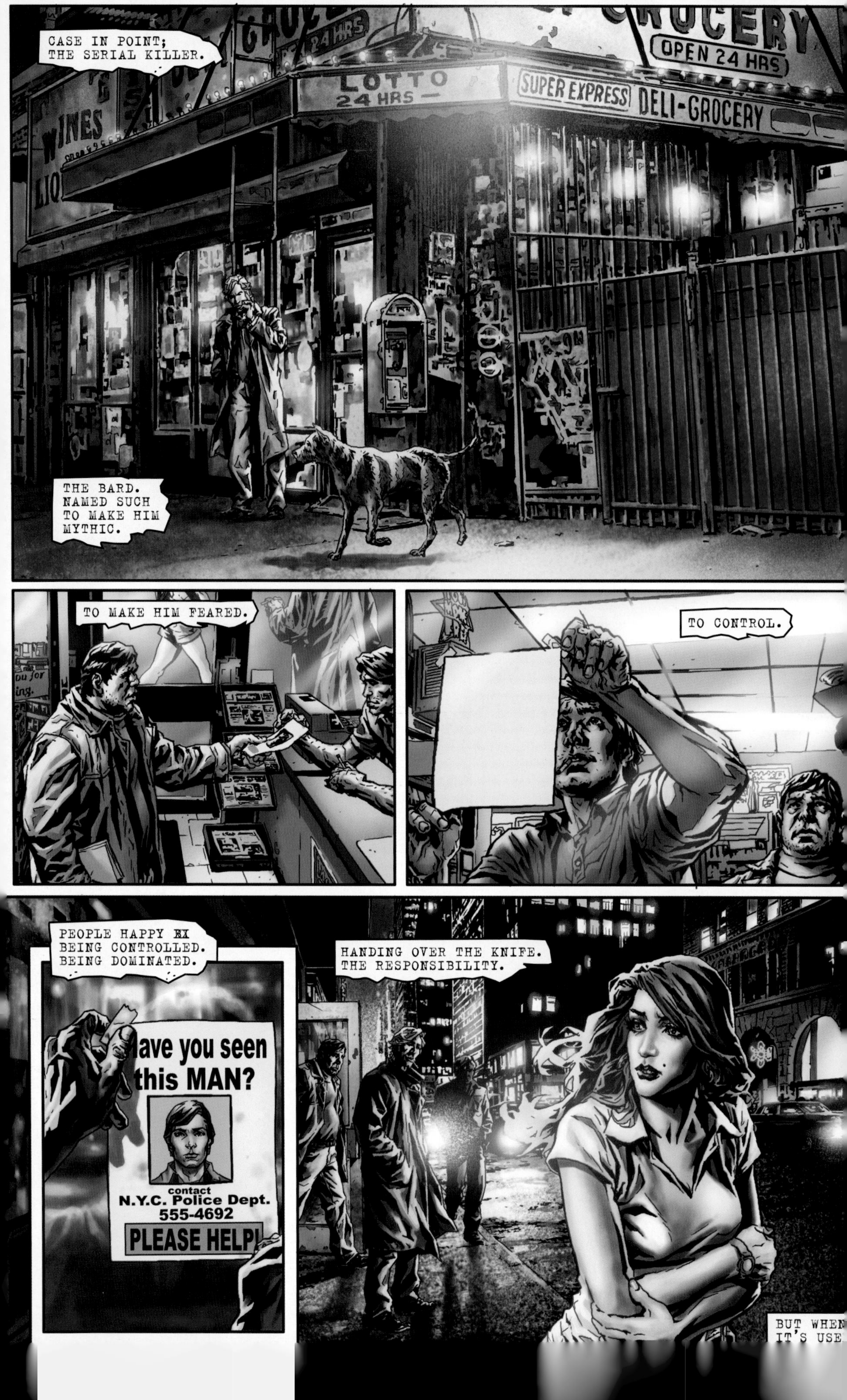

CASE IN POINT; THE SERIAL KILLER.
GROCERY
OPEN 24 HRS
LOTTO 24 HRS
SUPER EXPRESS
DELI-GROCERY
WINES
THE BARD. NAMED SUCH TO MAKE HIM MYTHIC.
TO MAKE HIM FEARED.
TO CONTROL.
PEOPLE HAPPY
BEING CONTROLLED. BEING DOMINATED.
ave you seen this MAN?
contact
N.Y.C. Police Dept.
555-4692
PLEASE HELP!
HANDING OVER THE KNIFE. THE RESPONSIBILITY.
BUT WHEN
IT'S USE

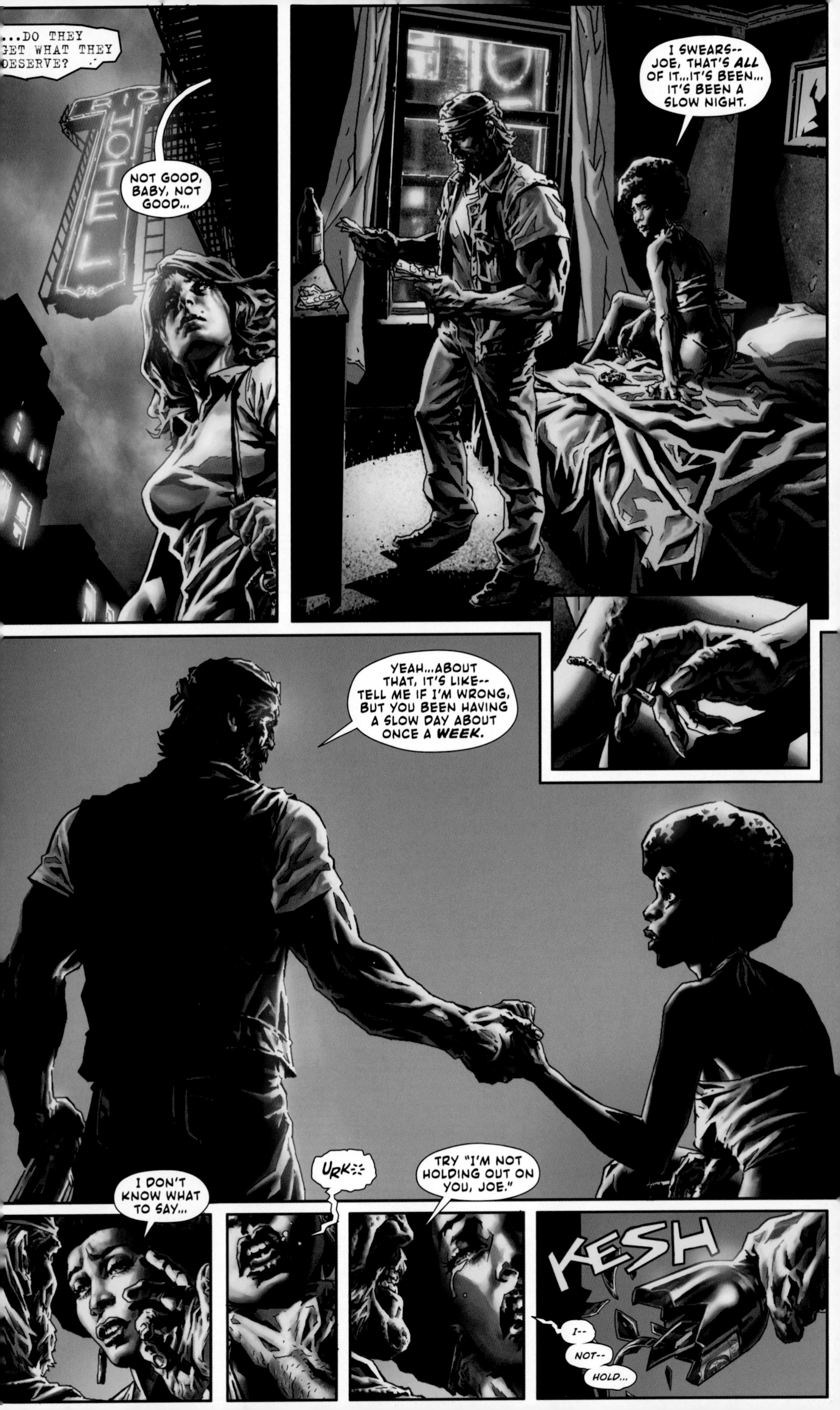
...DO THEY GET WHAT THEY DESERVE?
NOT GOOD, BABY, NOT GOOD...
RIO HOTEL
I SWEARS-- JOE, THAT'S ALL OF IT...IT'S BEEN... IT'S BEEN A SLOW NIGHT.
YEAH...ABOUT THAT, IT'S LIKE-- TELL ME IF I'M WRONG, BUT YOU BEEN HAVING A SLOW DAY ABOUT ONCE A WEEK.
I DON'T KNOW WHAT TO SAY...
URK
TRY "I'M NOT HOLDING OUT ON YOU, JOE."
KESH
I--
NOT--
HOLD...

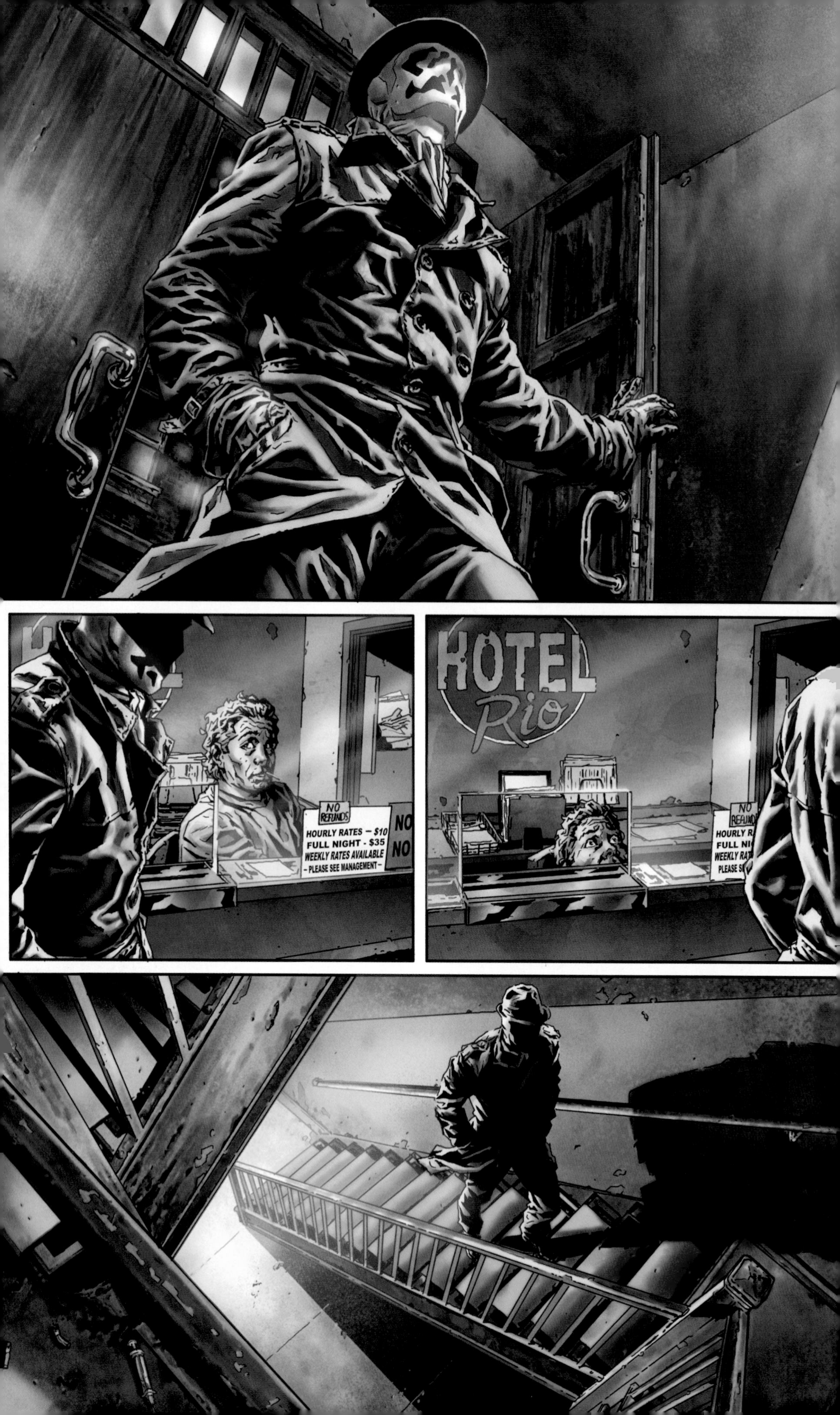
NO REFUNDS
HOURLY RATES — $10
FULL NIGHT - $35
WEEKLY RATES AVAILABLE
- PLEASE SEE MANAGEMENT -
HOTEL Rio

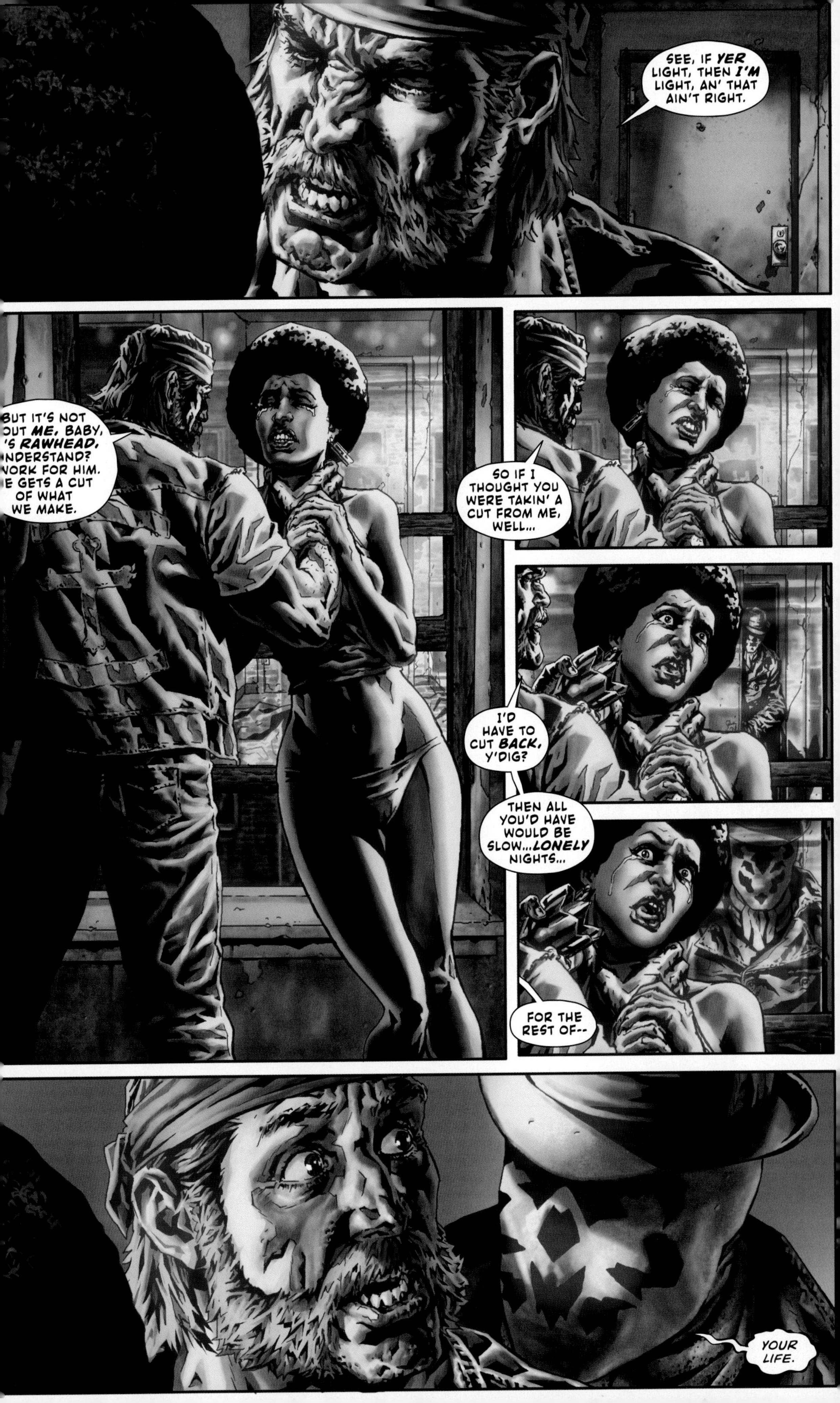
SEE, IF YER LIGHT, THEN I'M LIGHT, AN' THAT AIN'T RIGHT.
BUT IT'S NOT OUT ME, BABY, 'S RAWHEAD, NDERSTAND? WORK FOR HIM. E GETS A CUT OF WHAT WE MAKE.
SO IF I THOUGHT YOU WERE TAKIN' A CUT FROM ME, WELL...
I'D HAVE TO CUT BACK, Y'DIG?
THEN ALL YOU'D HAVE WOULD BE SLOW...LONELY NIGHTS...
FOR THE REST OF--
YOUR LIFE.

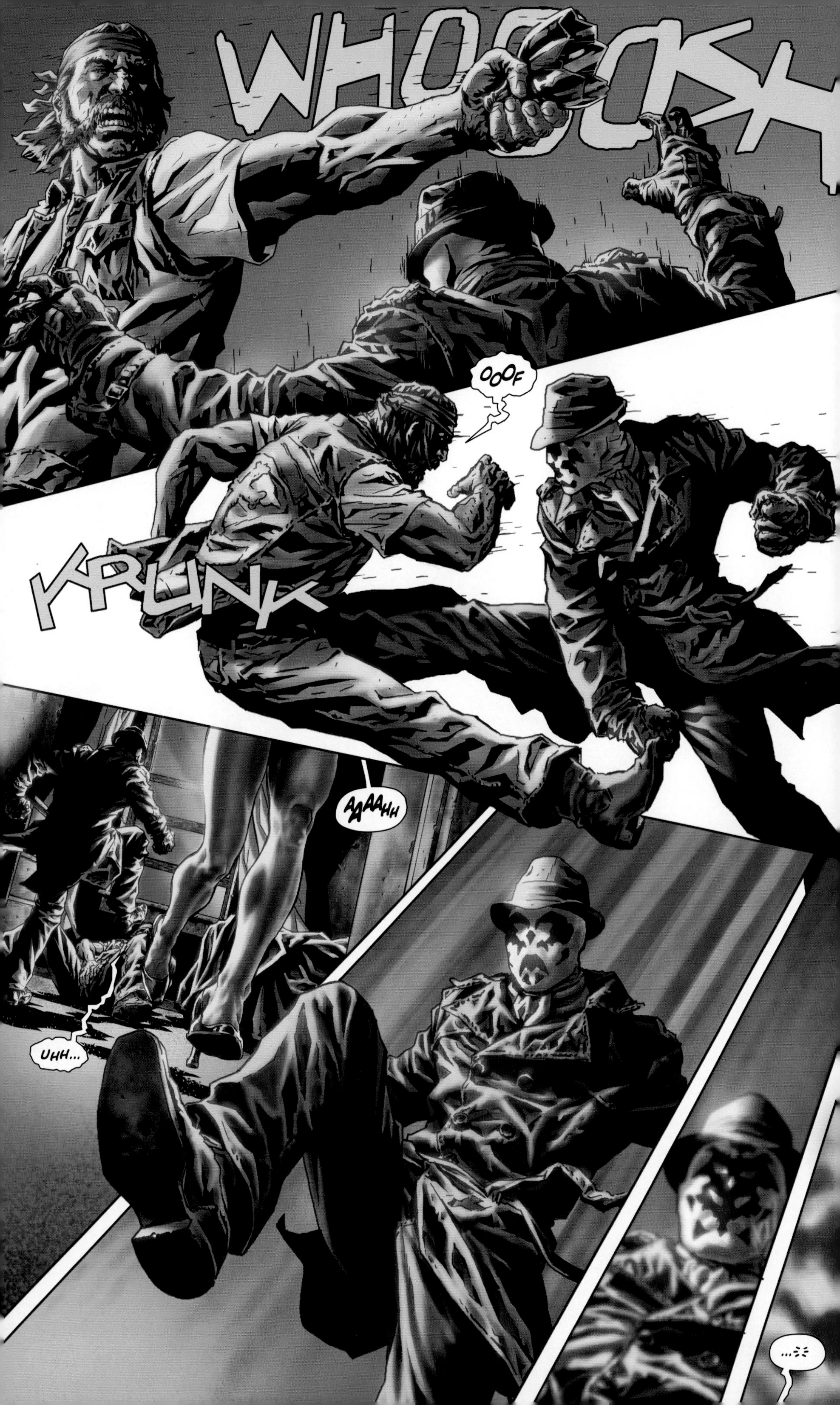
WHOOOSH
OOOF
KRUNK
AAAAHH
UHH...
...!

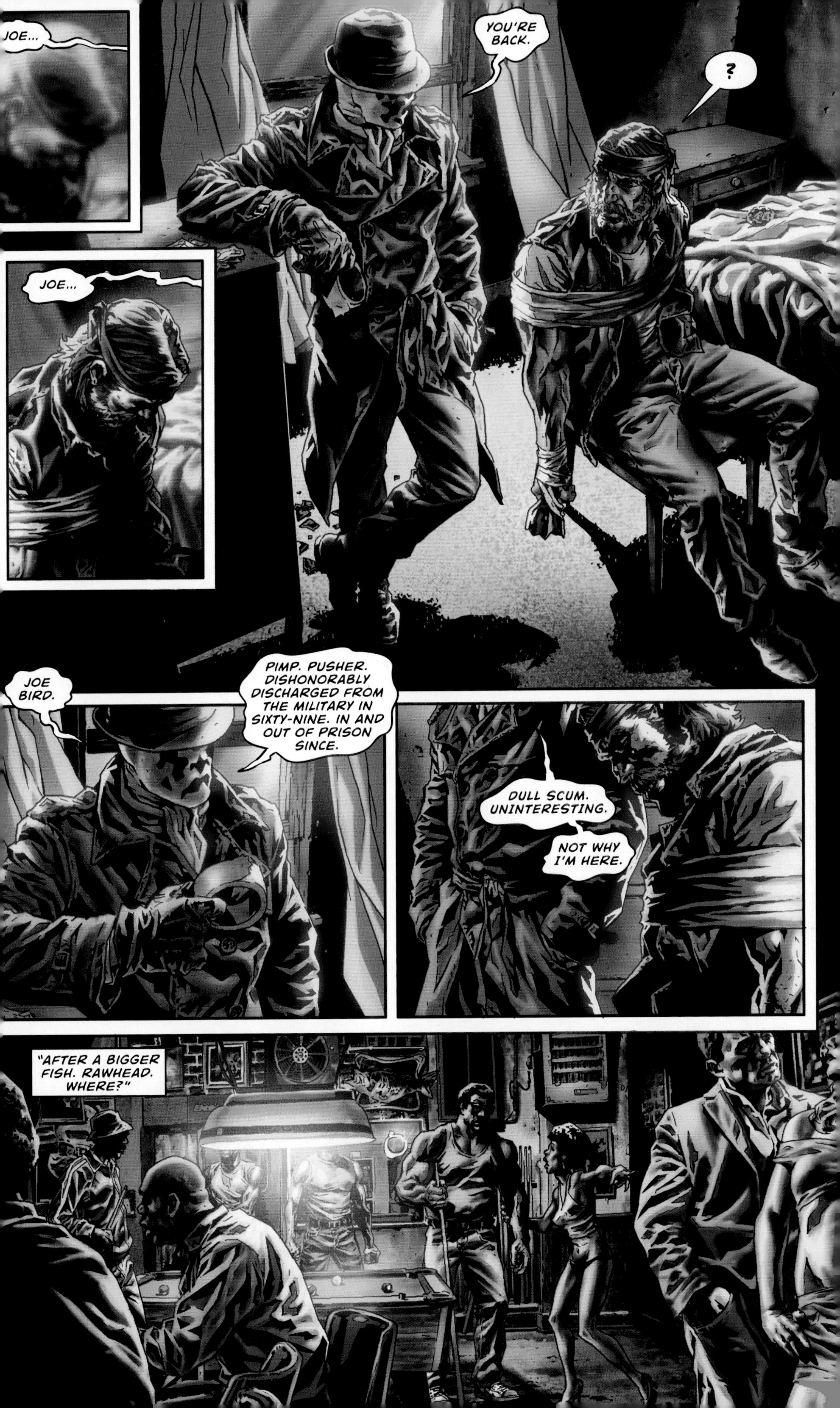
JOE...
JOE...
YOU'RE BACK.
?
JOE BIRD.
PIMP. PUSHER. DISHONORABLY DISCHARGED FROM THE MILITARY IN SIXTY-NINE. IN AND OUT OF PRISON SINCE.
DULL SCUM. UNINTERESTING.
NOT WHY I'M HERE.
"AFTER A BIGGER FISH. RAWHEAD. WHERE?"

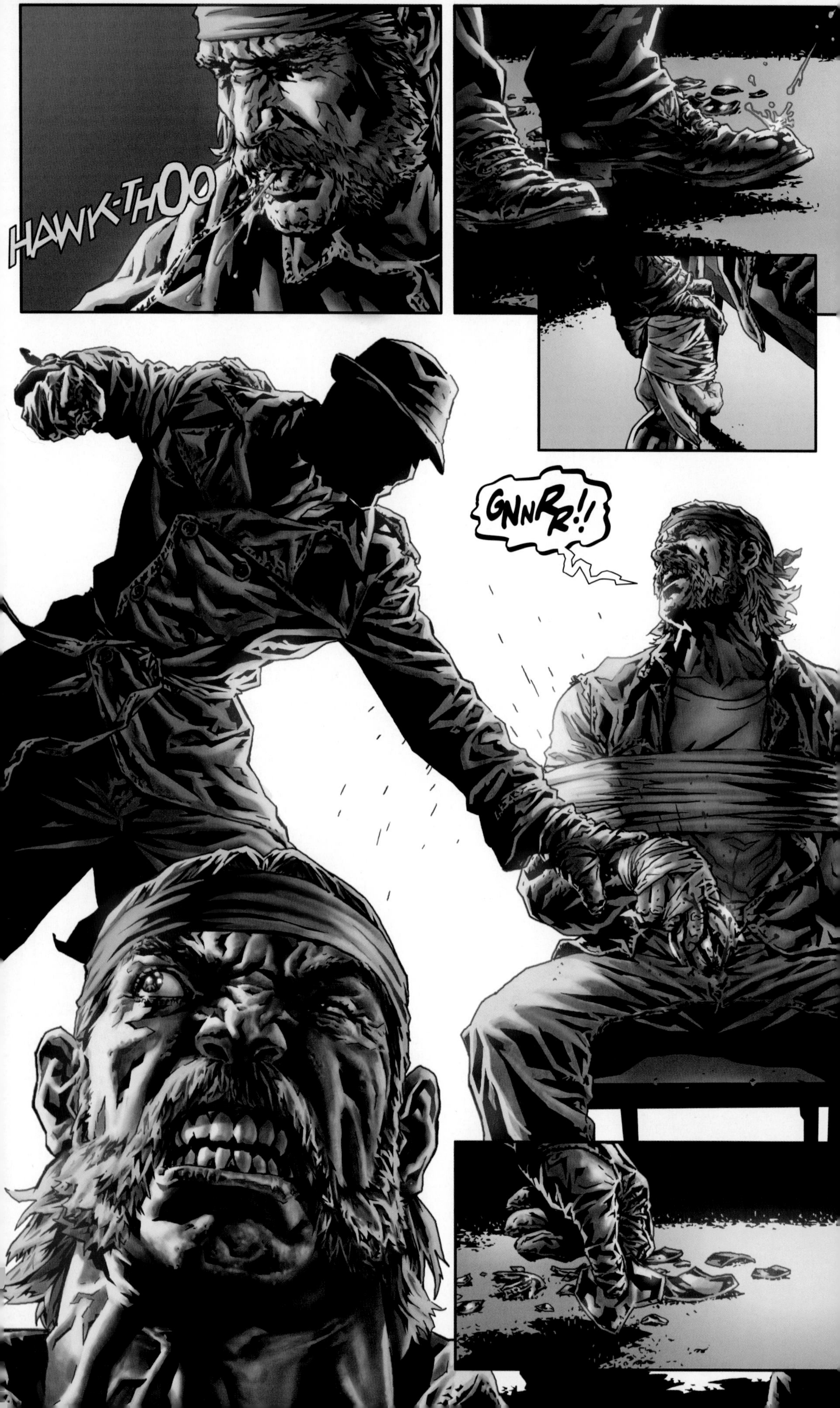
HAWK-THOO
GNNRR!!

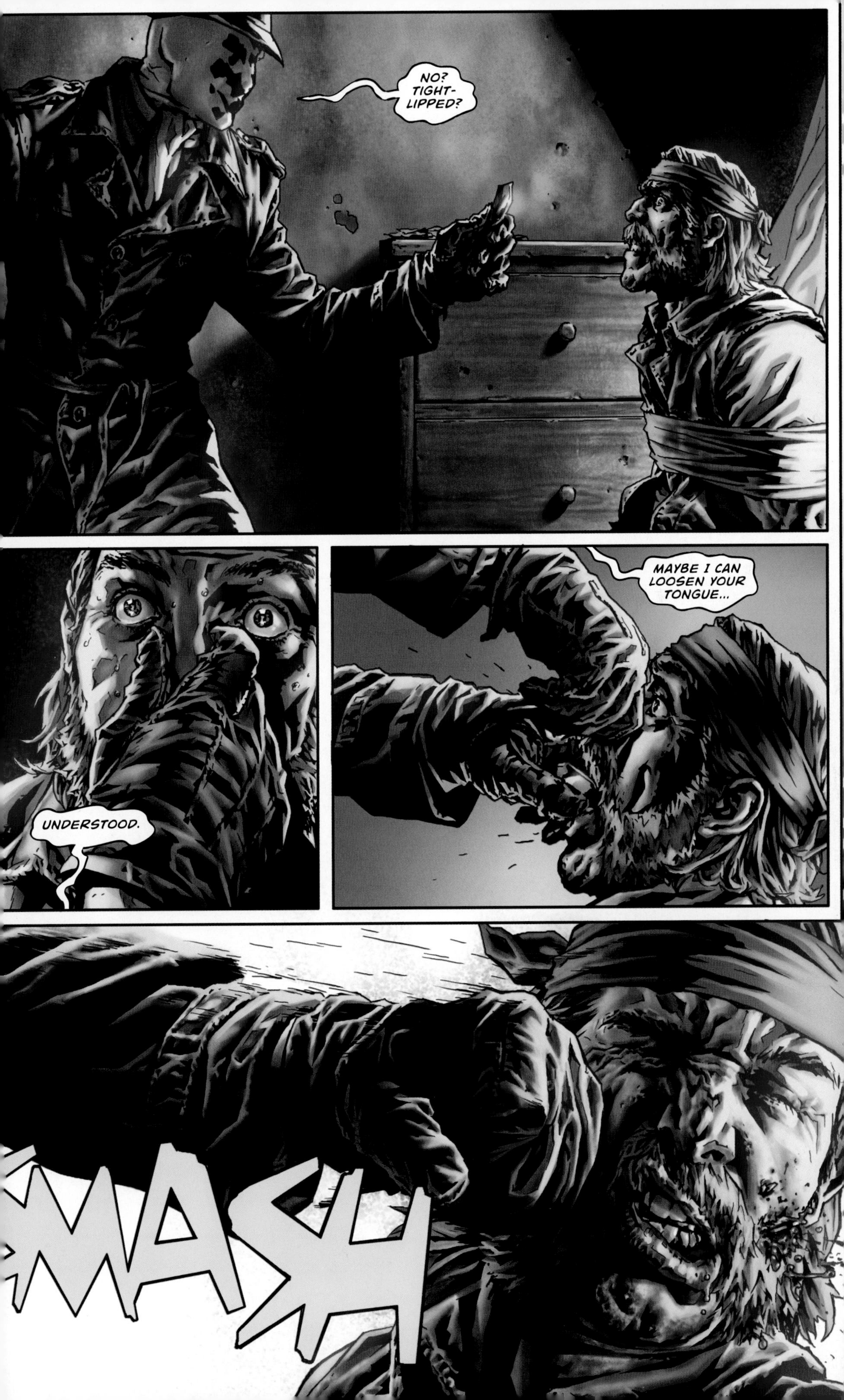
NO? TIGHT-LIPPED?
UNDERSTOOD.
MAYBE I CAN LOOSEN YOUR TONGUE...
MASH

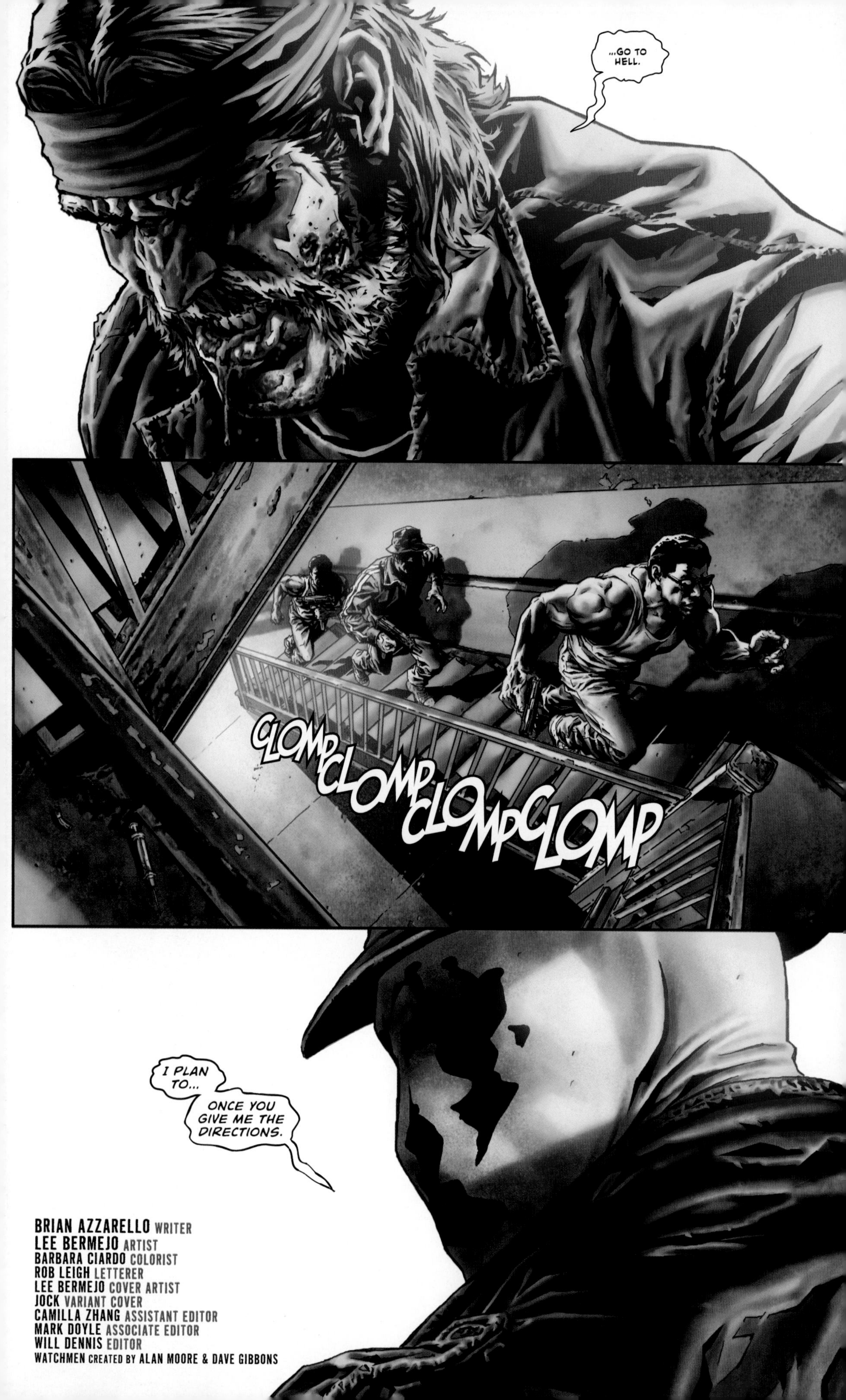
...GO TO HELL.
CLOMPCLOMPCLOMPCLOMP
I PLAN TO...
ONCE YOU GIVE ME THE DIRECTIONS.
BRIAN AZZARELLO WRITER
LEE BERMEJO ARTIST
BARBARA CIARDO COLORIST
ROB LEIGH LETTERER
LEE BERMEJO COVER ARTIST
JOCK VARIANT COVER
CAMILLA ZHANG ASSISTANT EDITOR
MARK DOYLE ASSOCIATE EDITOR
WILL DENNIS EDITOR
WATCHMEN CREATED BY ALAN MOORE & DAVE GIBBONS

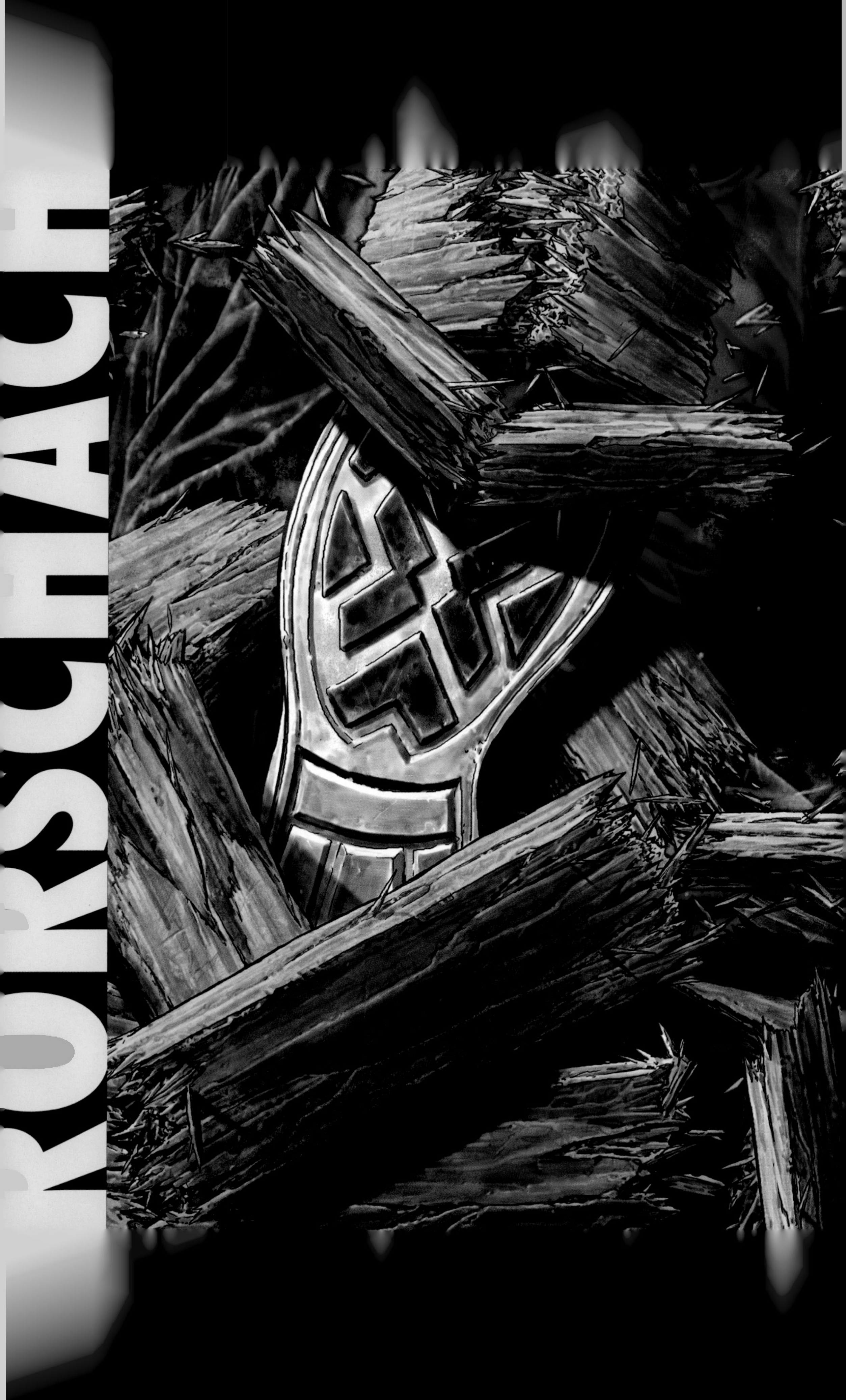
RORSCHACH

RORSCHACH

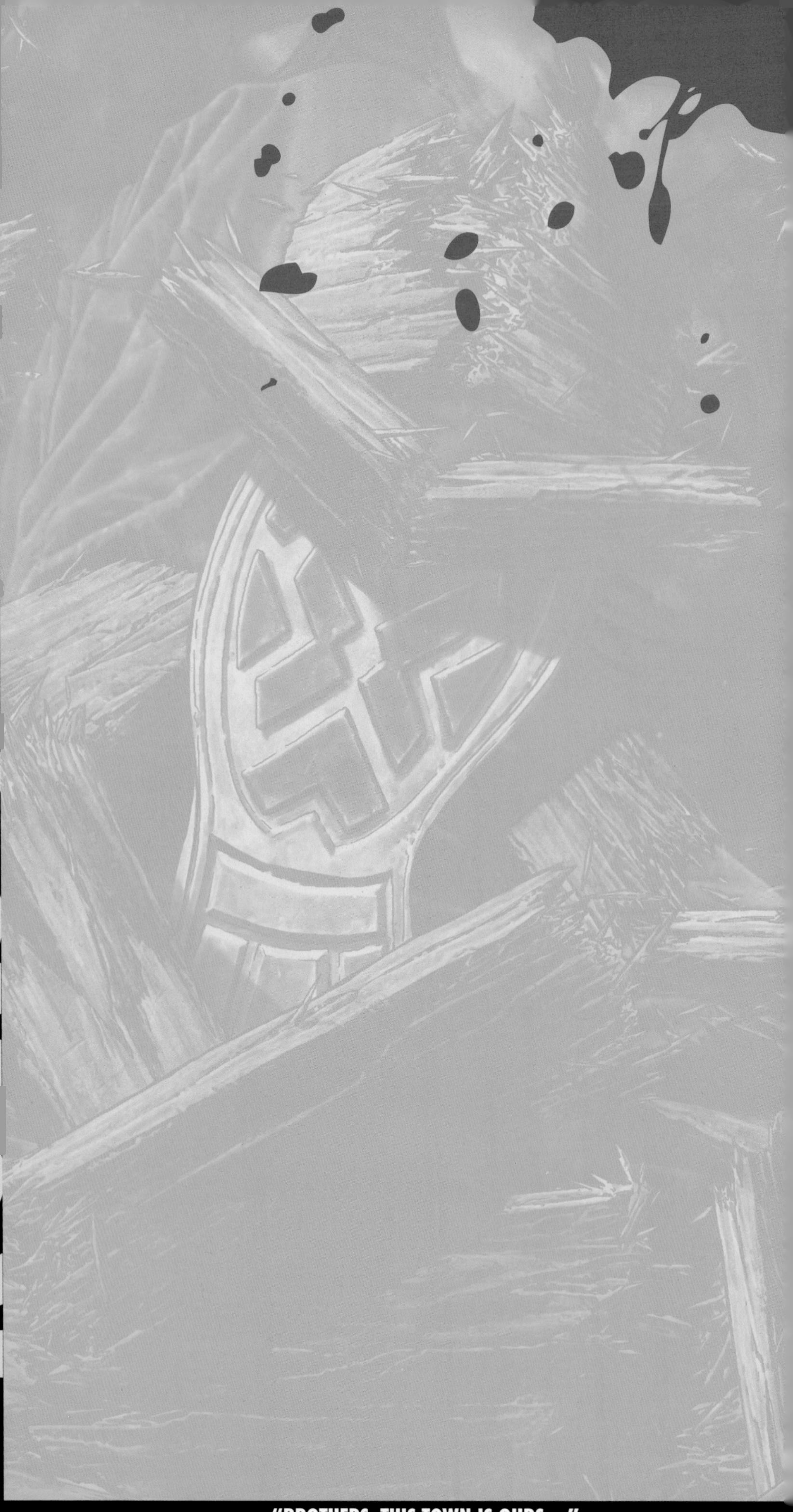

"BROTHERS, THIS TOWN IS OURS..."

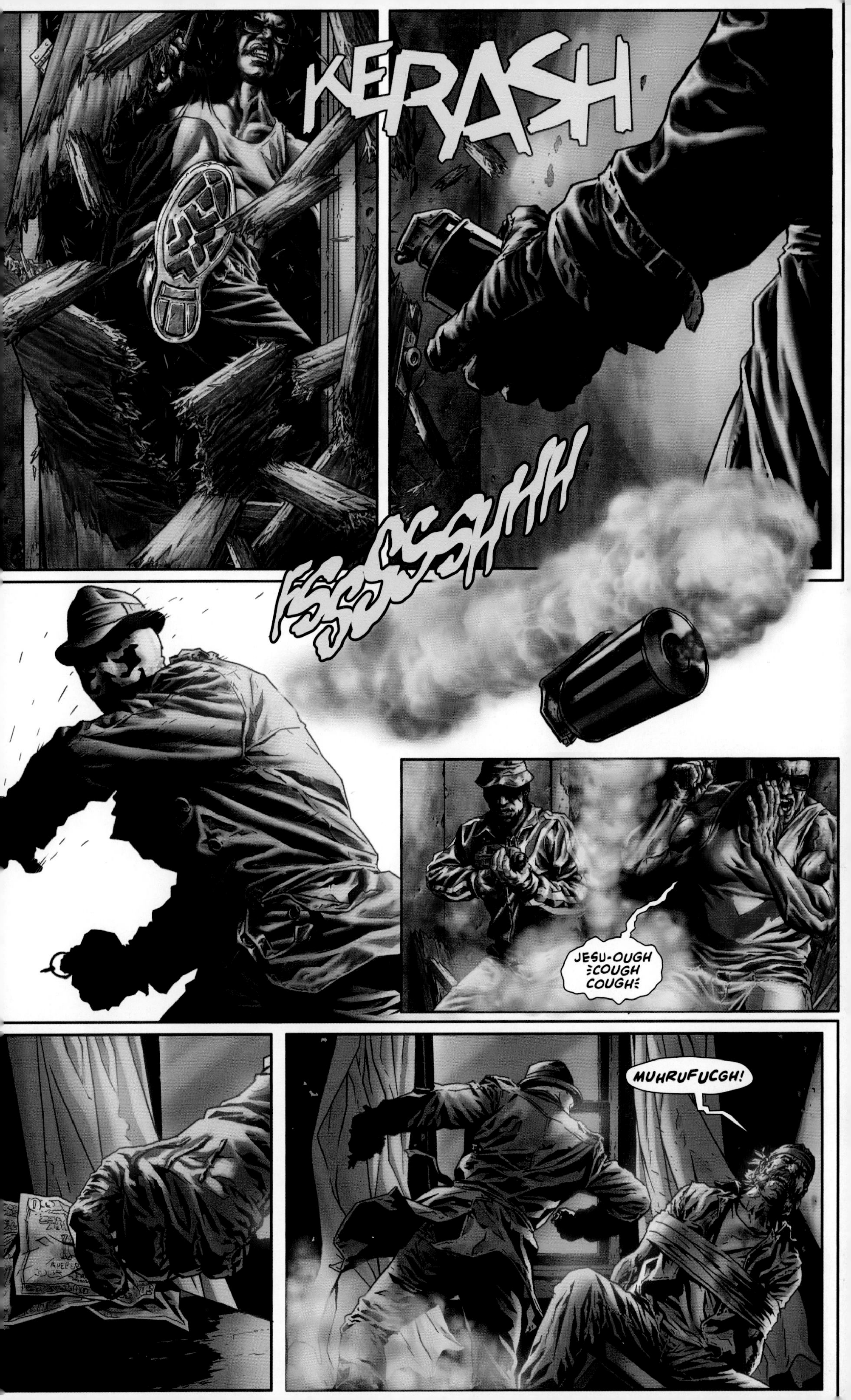
KERASH
FSSSSSHHH
JESU-OUGH
COUGH
COUGH
MUHRUFUCGH!

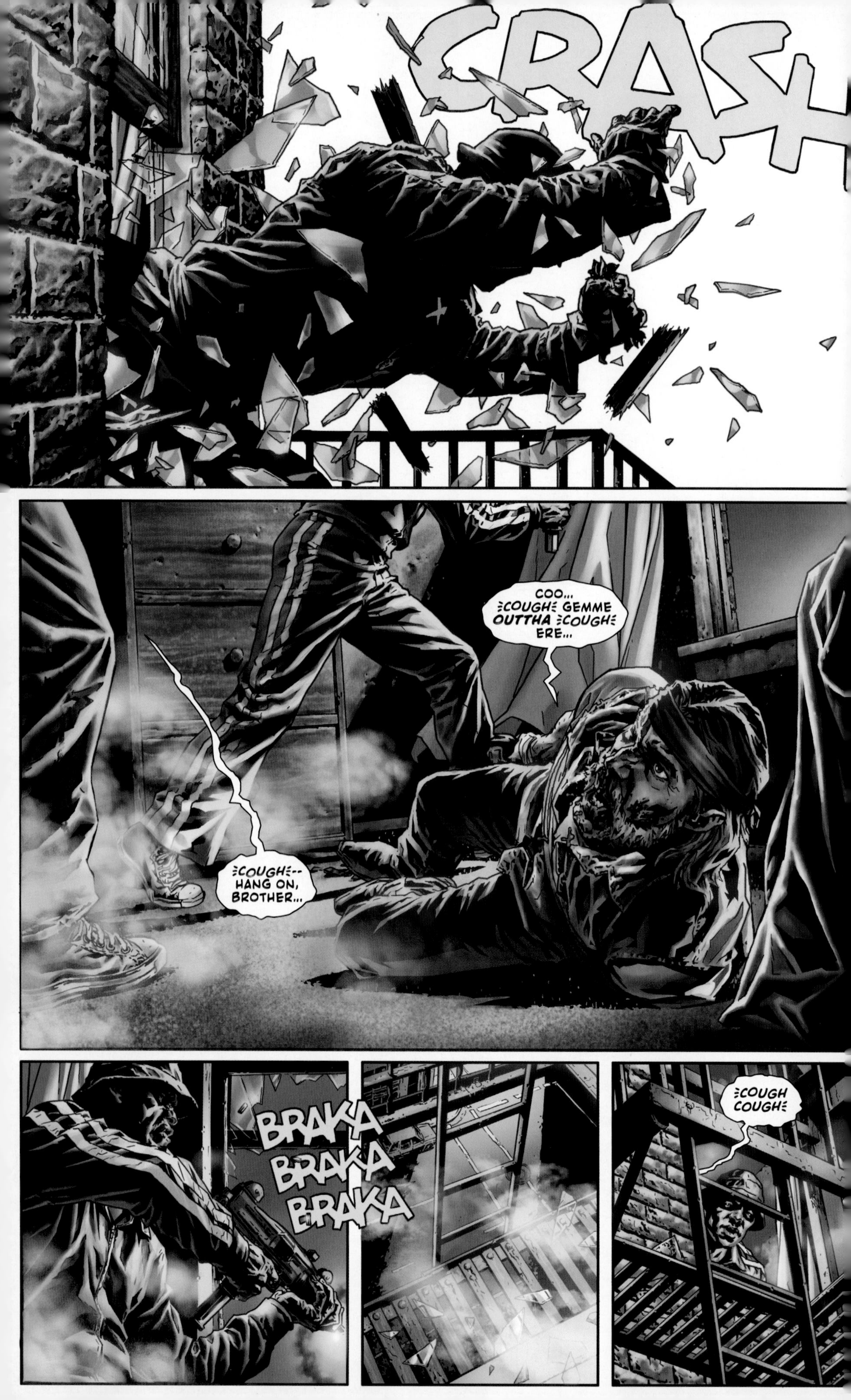
CRASH
COO... ≷COUGH≶ GEMME OUTTHA ≷COUGH≶ ERE...
≷COUGH≶-- HANG ON, BROTHER...
BRAKA
BRAKA
BRAKA
≷COUGH COUGH≶

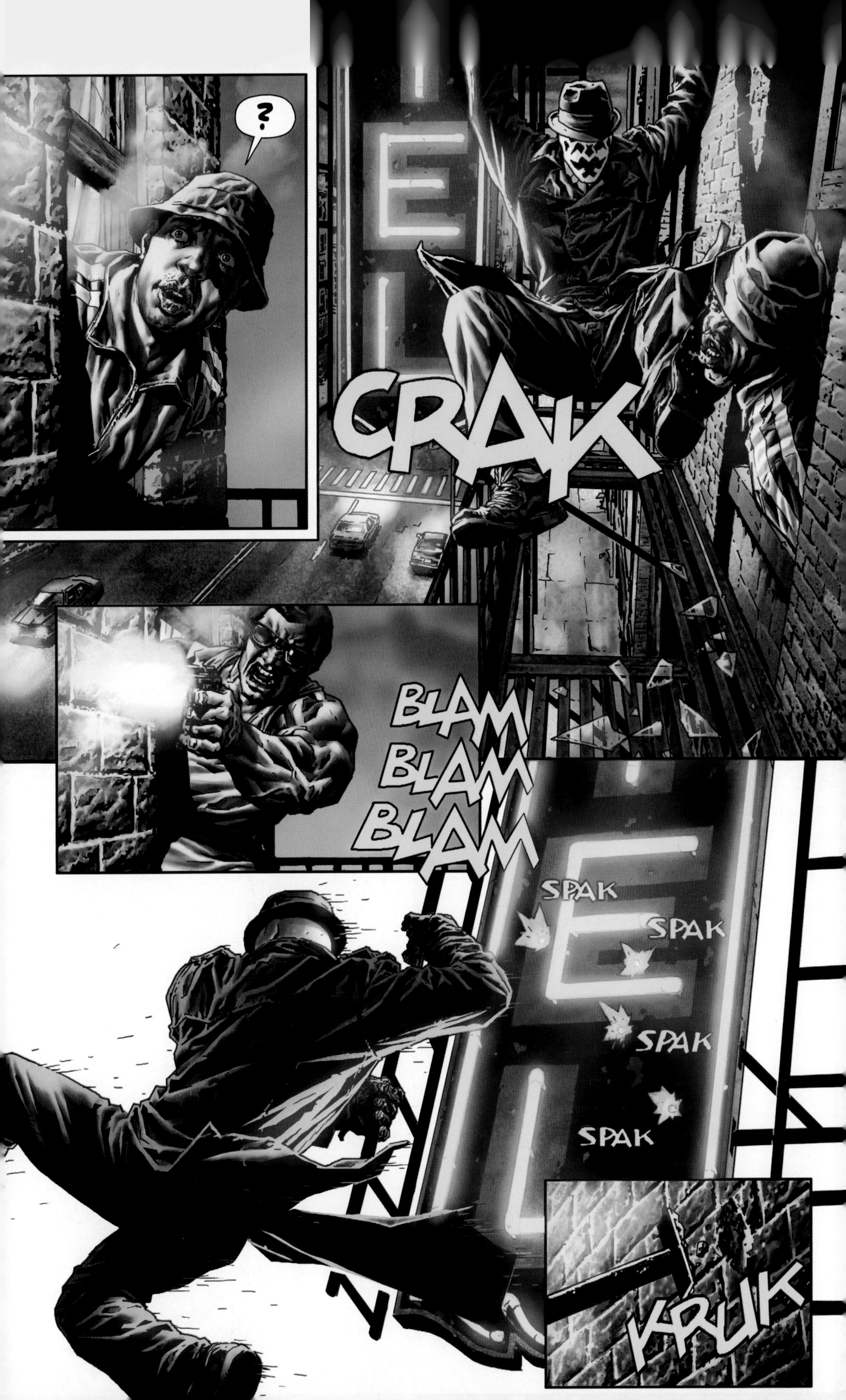
?
CRAK
BLAM
BLAM
BLAM
SPAK
SPAK
SPAK
SPAK
KRUK

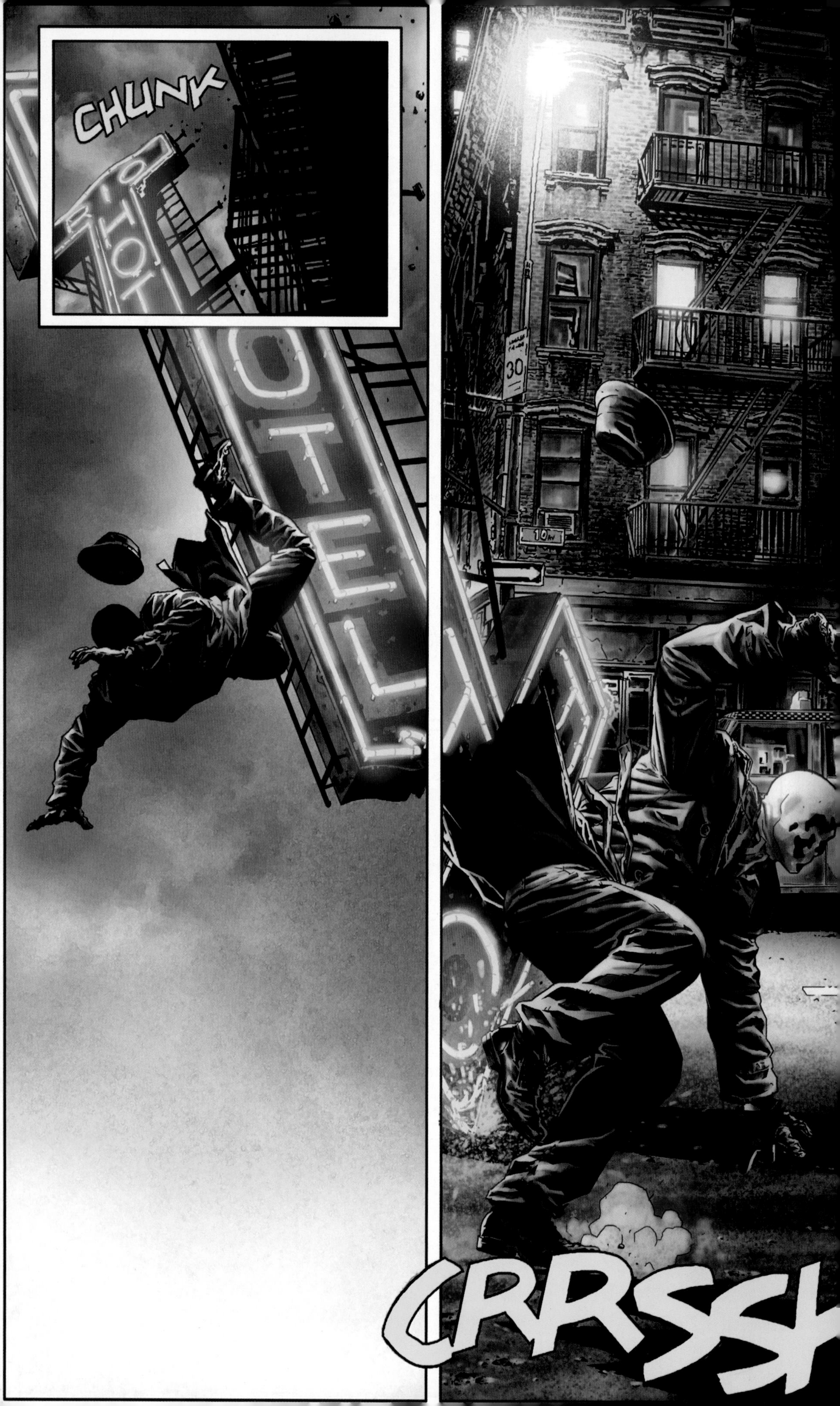
CHUNK
CRRSSH

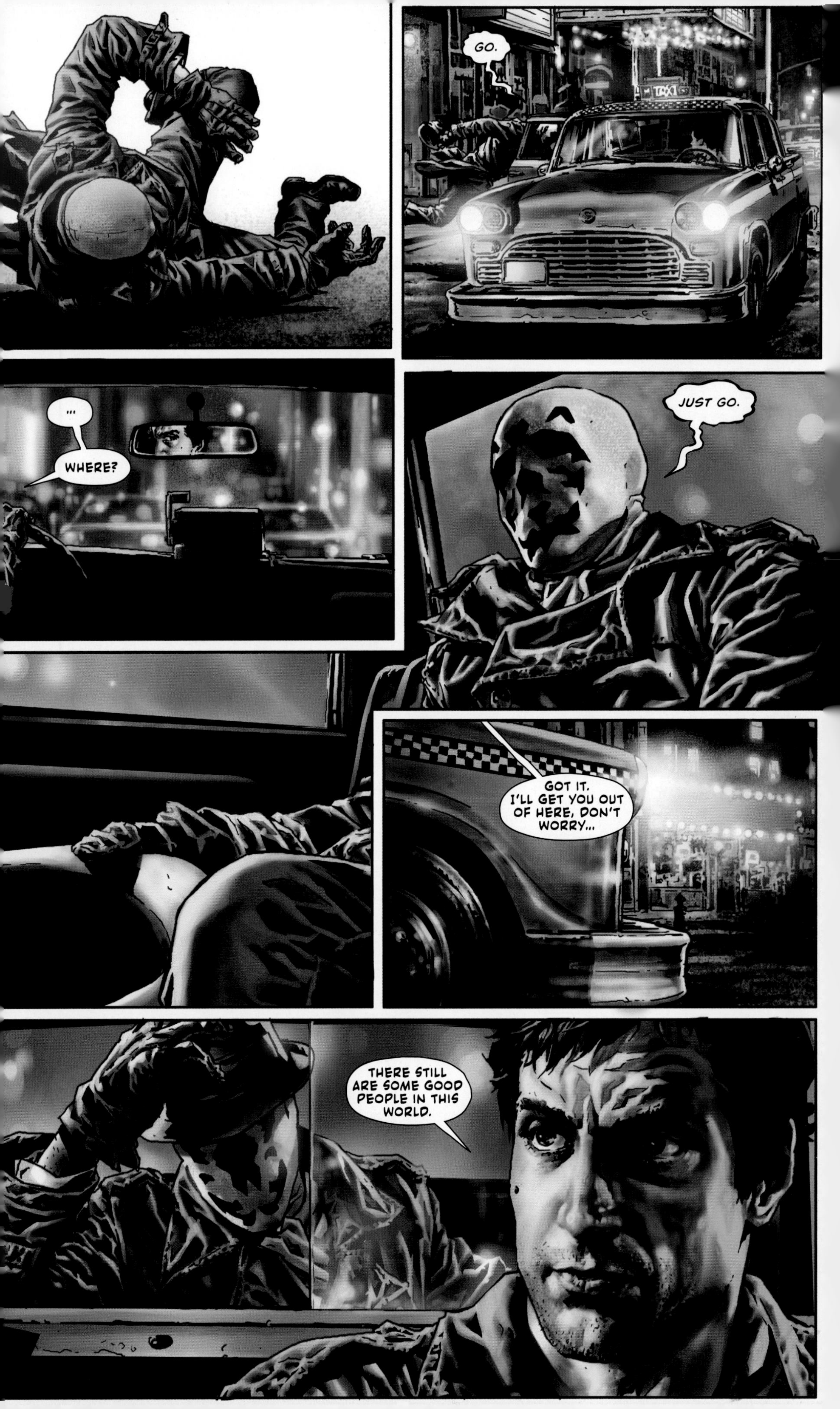
GO.
...
WHERE?
JUST GO.
GOT IT. I'LL GET YOU OUT OF HERE, DON'T WORRY...
THERE STILL ARE SOME GOOD PEOPLE IN THIS WORLD.

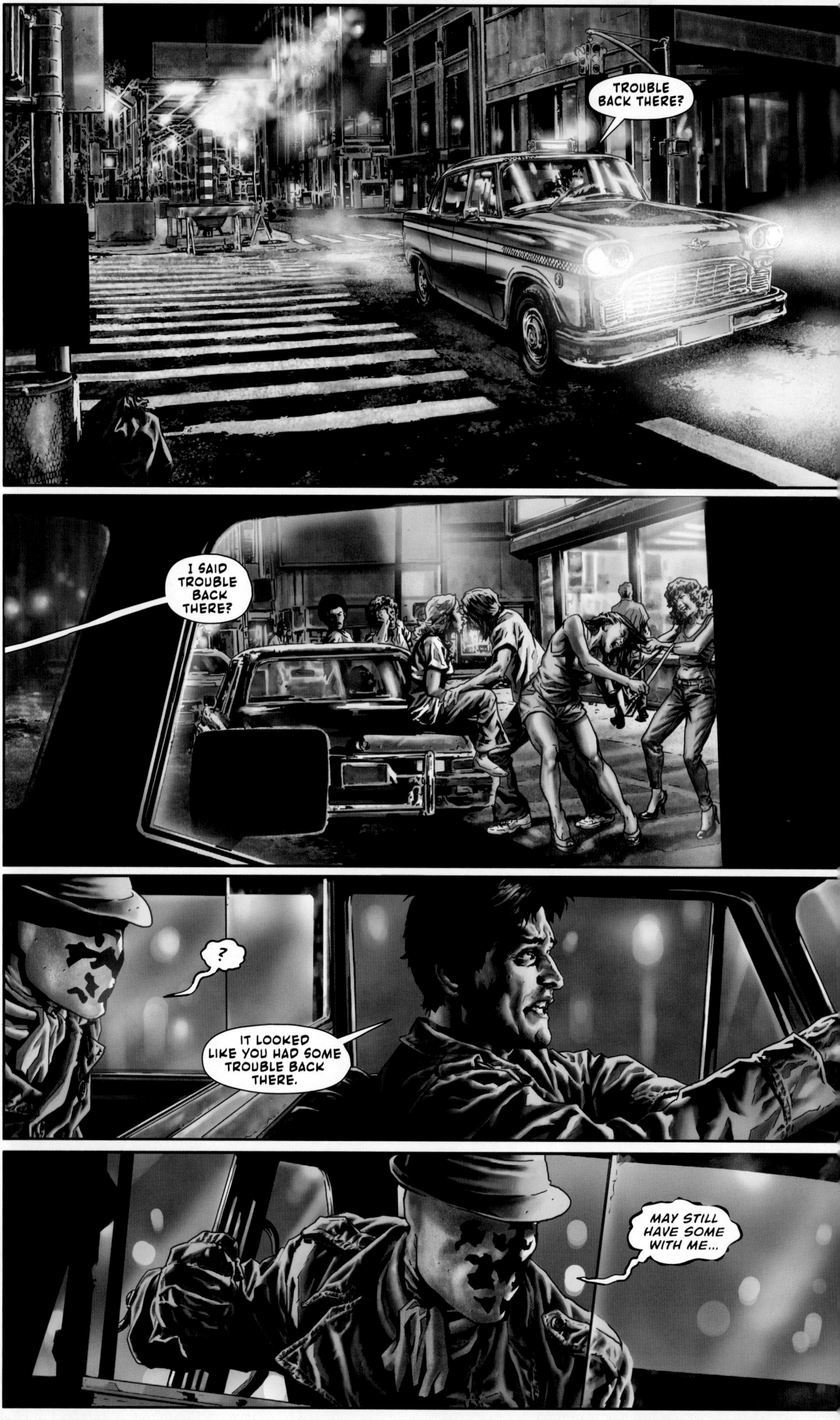
TROUBLE BACK THERE?
I SAID TROUBLE BACK THERE?
?
IT LOOKED LIKE YOU HAD SOME TROUBLE BACK THERE.
MAY STILL HAVE SOME WITH ME...

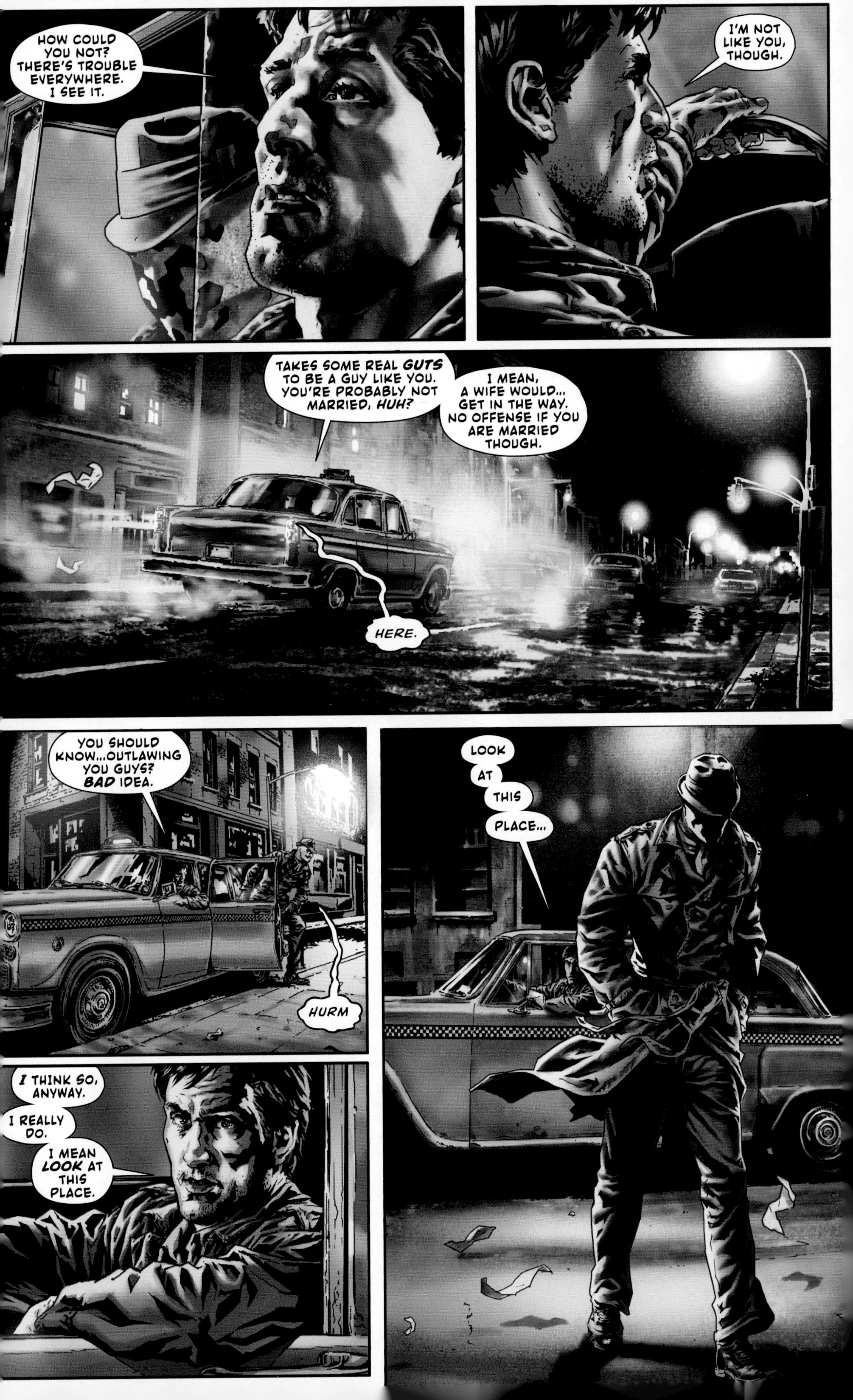
HOW COULD YOU NOT? THERE'S TROUBLE EVERYWHERE. I SEE IT.
I'M NOT LIKE YOU, THOUGH.
TAKES SOME REAL GUTS TO BE A GUY LIKE YOU. YOU'RE PROBABLY NOT MARRIED, HUH?
I MEAN, A WIFE WOULD... GET IN THE WAY. NO OFFENSE IF YOU ARE MARRIED THOUGH.
HERE.
YOU SHOULD KNOW...OUTLAWING YOU GUYS? BAD IDEA.
HURM
I THINK SO, ANYWAY.
I REALLY DO.
I MEAN LOOK AT THIS PLACE.
LOOK
AT
THIS
PLACE...

"...IT'S A SHAME WHAT WE'VE LET IT BECOME."

I'M NOT A MONSTER

INNOCENT A CHILD

YOUR FUTURE REFLECTED

GROWING UP TO SERVE

HEY, LOOK WHO IT IS!

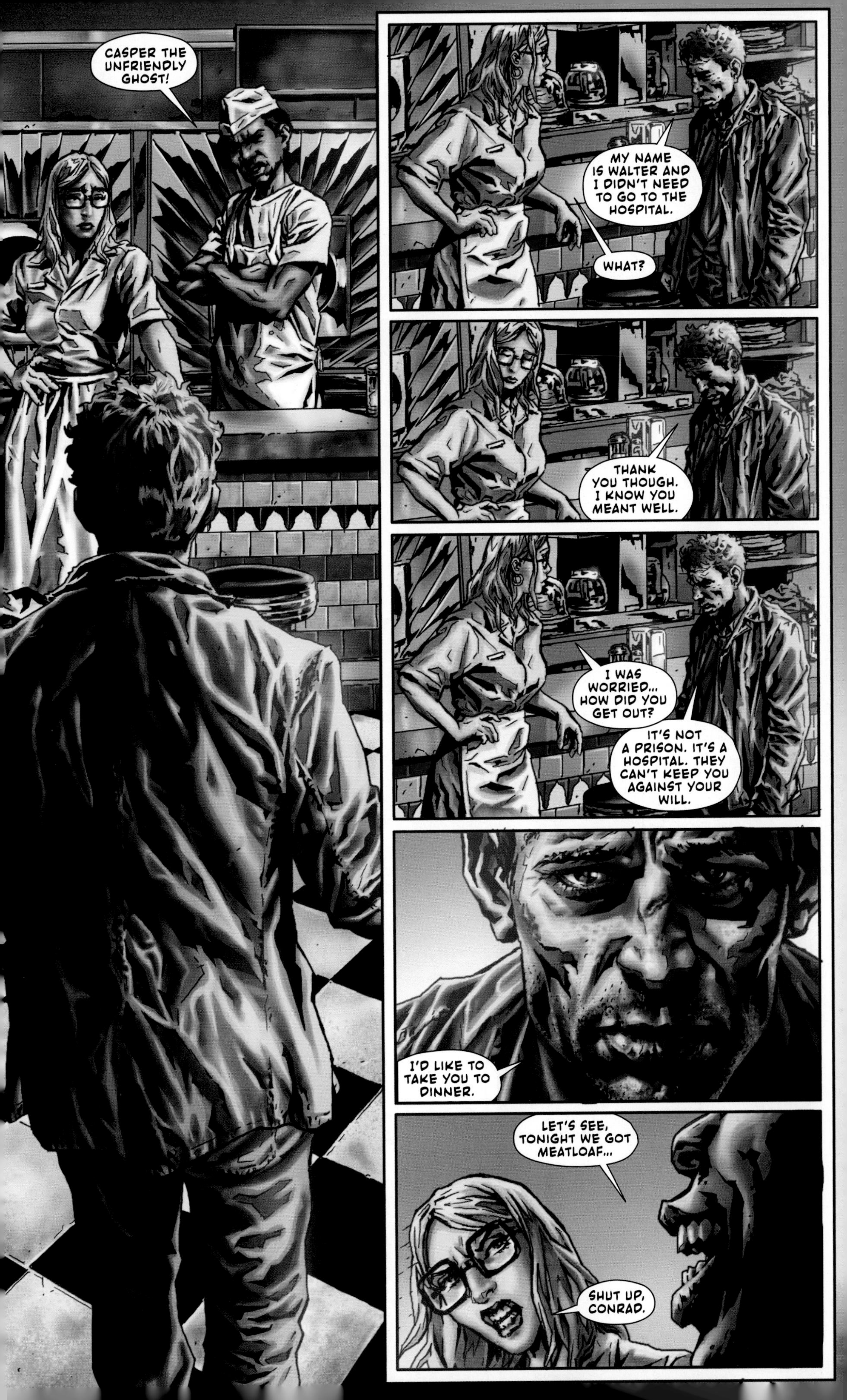
CASPER THE UNFRIENDLY GHOST!
MY NAME IS WALTER AND I DIDN'T NEED TO GO TO THE HOSPITAL.
WHAT?
THANK YOU THOUGH. I KNOW YOU MEANT WELL.
I WAS WORRIED... HOW DID YOU GET OUT?
IT'S NOT A PRISON. IT'S A HOSPITAL. THEY CAN'T KEEP YOU AGAINST YOUR WILL.
I'D LIKE TO TAKE YOU TO DINNER.
LET'S SEE, TONIGHT WE GOT MEATLOAF...
SHUT UP, CONRAD.

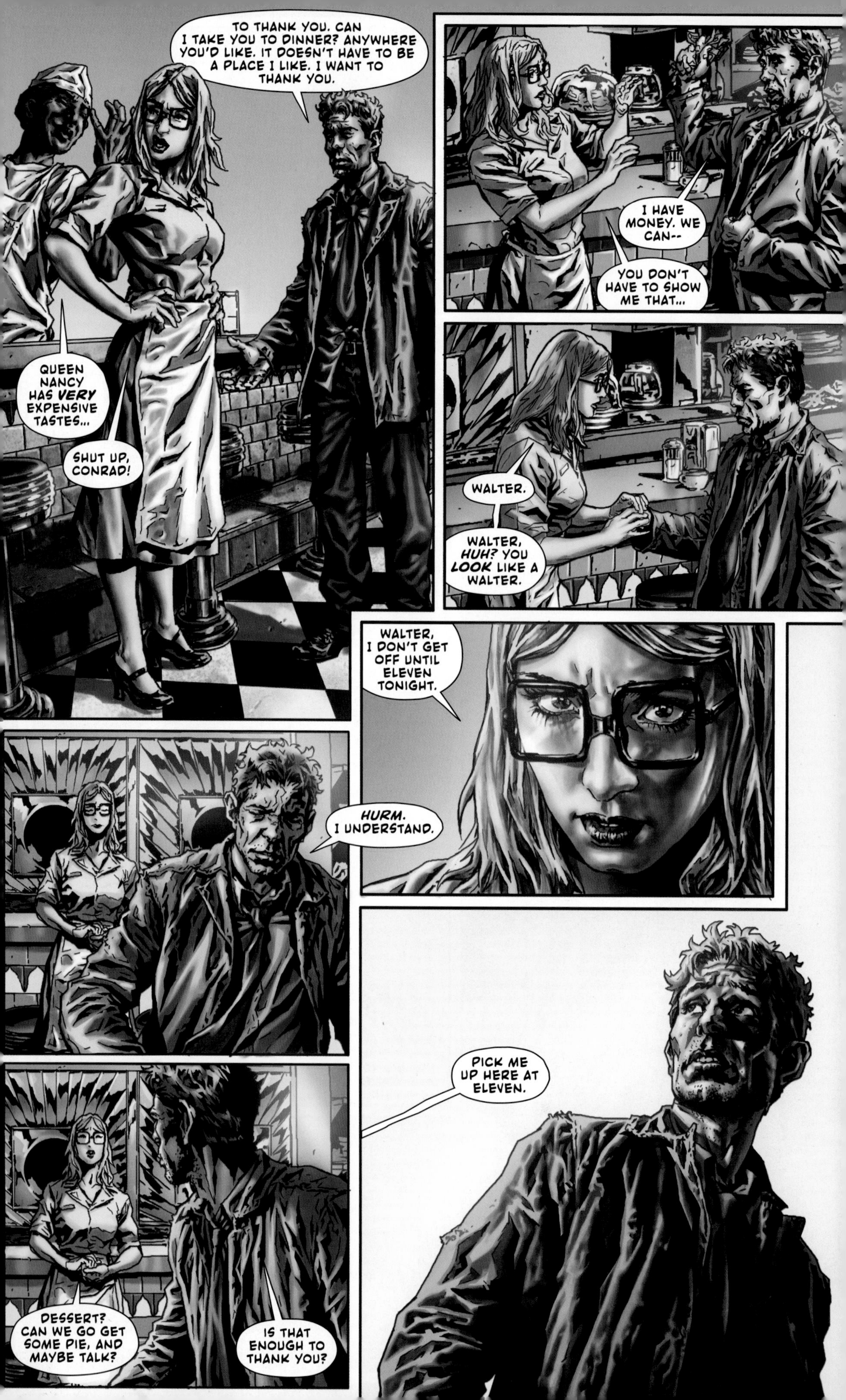
TO THANK YOU. CAN I TAKE YOU TO DINNER? ANYWHERE YOU'D LIKE. IT DOESN'T HAVE TO BE A PLACE I LIKE. I WANT TO THANK YOU.
QUEEN NANCY HAS *VERY* EXPENSIVE TASTES...
SHUT UP, CONRAD!
I HAVE MONEY. WE CAN--
YOU DON'T HAVE TO SHOW ME THAT...
WALTER.
WALTER, *HUH?* YOU *LOOK* LIKE A WALTER.
WALTER, I DON'T GET OFF UNTIL ELEVEN TONIGHT.
HURM. I UNDERSTAND.
DESSERT? CAN WE GO GET SOME PIE, AND MAYBE TALK?
IS THAT ENOUGH TO THANK YOU?
PICK ME UP HERE AT ELEVEN.

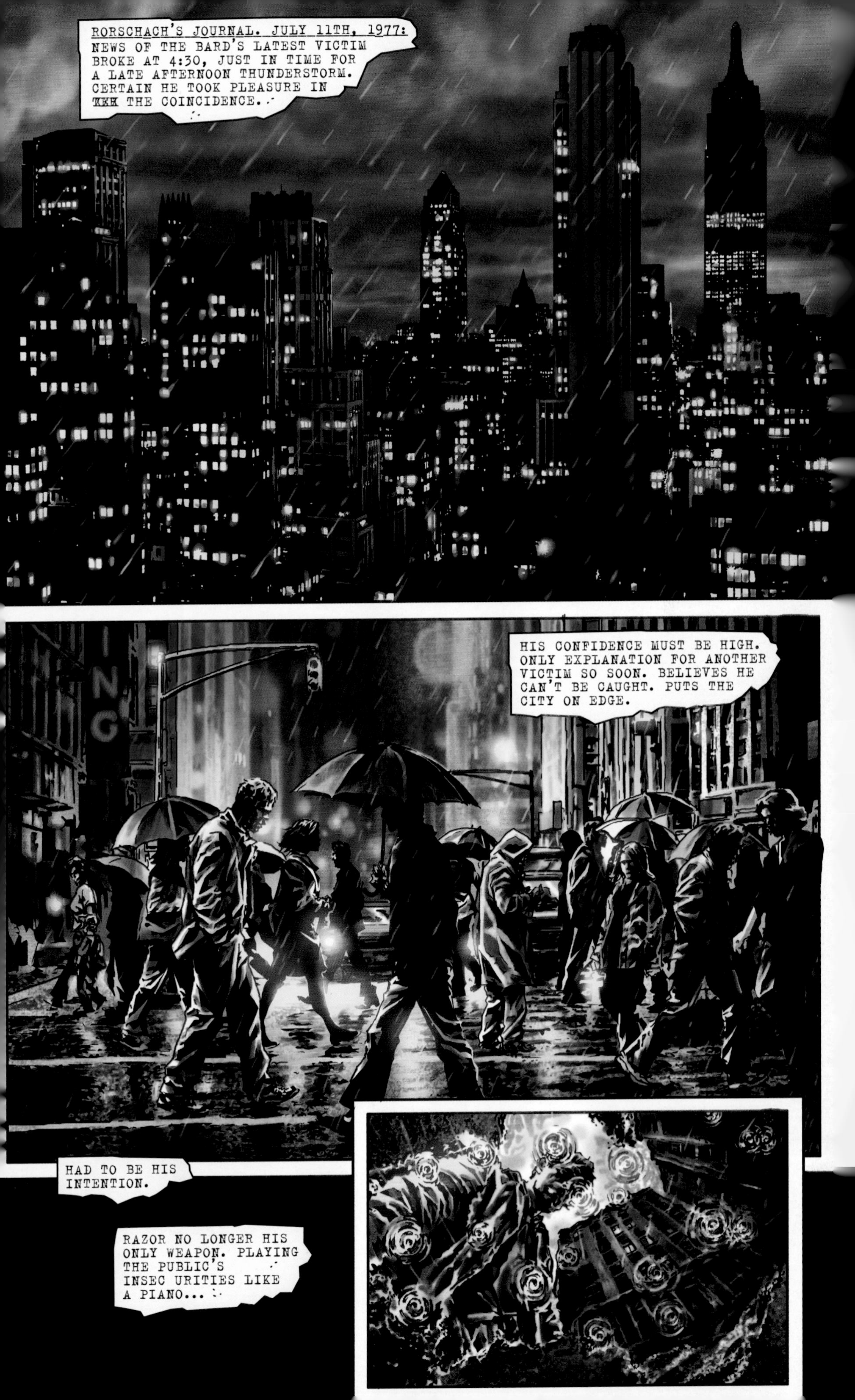
RORSCHACH'S JOURNAL. JULY 11TH, 1977: NEWS OF THE BARD'S LATEST VICTIM BROKE AT 4:30, JUST IN TIME FOR A LATE AFTERNOON THUNDERSTORM. CERTAIN HE TOOK PLEASURE IN THE COINCIDENCE...
HIS CONFIDENCE MUST BE HIGH. ONLY EXPLANATION FOR ANOTHER VICTIM SO SOON. BELIEVES HE CAN'T BE CAUGHT. PUTS THE CITY ON EDGE.
HAD TO BE HIS INTENTION.
RAZOR NO LONGER HIS ONLY WEAPON. PLAYING THE PUBLIC'S INSEC URITIES LIKE A PIANO...

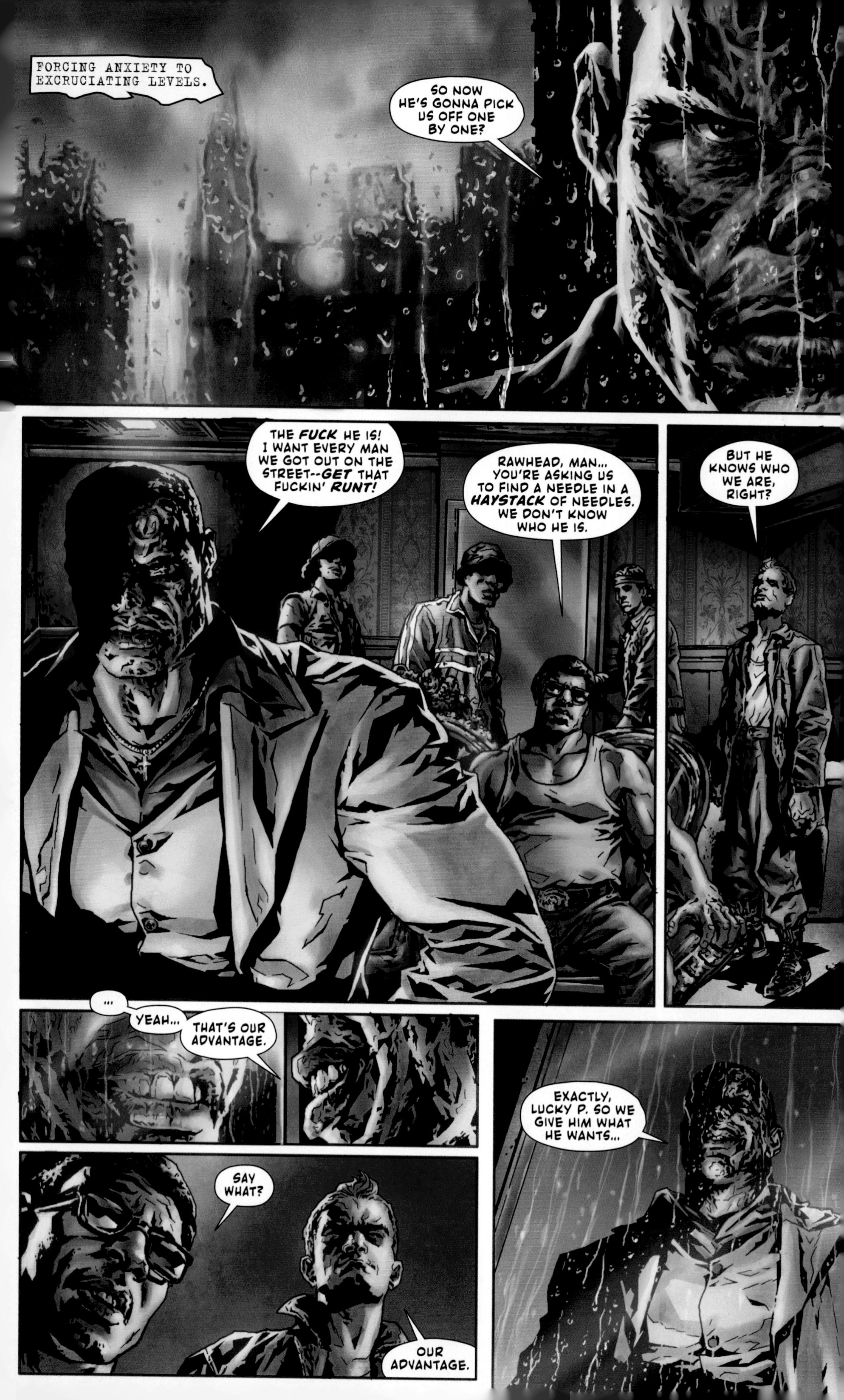
FORCING ANXIETY TO EXCRUCIATING LEVELS.
SO NOW HE'S GONNA PICK US OFF ONE BY ONE?
THE FUCK HE IS! I WANT EVERY MAN WE GOT OUT ON THE STREET--GET THAT FUCKIN' RUNT!
RAWHEAD, MAN... YOU'RE ASKING US TO FIND A NEEDLE IN A HAYSTACK OF NEEDLES. WE DON'T KNOW WHO HE IS.
BUT HE KNOWS WHO WE ARE, RIGHT?
...
YEAH...
THAT'S OUR ADVANTAGE.
SAY WHAT?
OUR ADVANTAGE.
EXACTLY, LUCKY P. SO WE GIVE HIM WHAT HE WANTS...

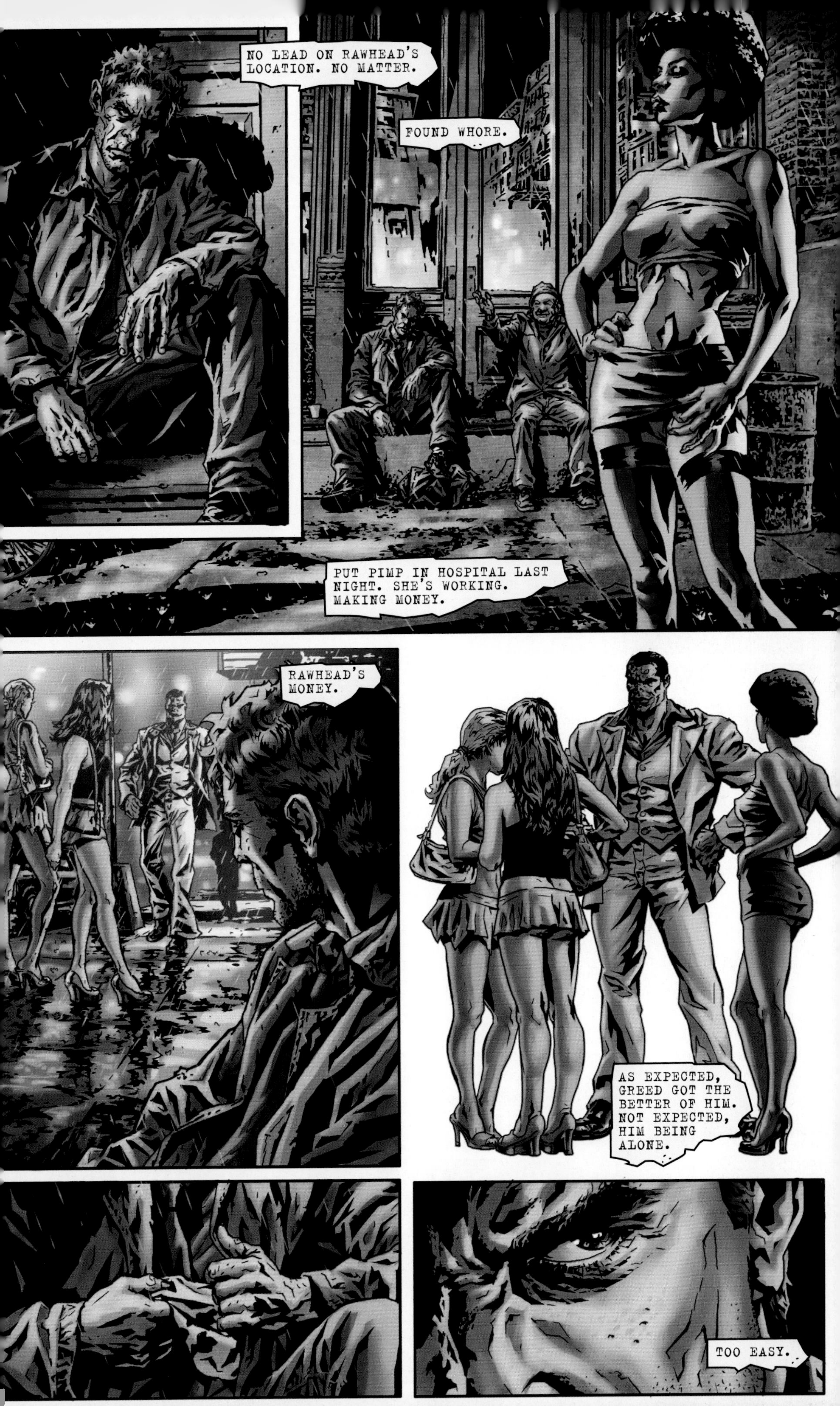
NO LEAD ON RAWHEAD'S LOCATION. NO MATTER.
FOUND WHORE.
PUT PIMP IN HOSPITAL LAST NIGHT. SHE'S WORKING. MAKING MONEY.
RAWHEAD'S MONEY.
AS EXPECTED, GREED GOT THE BETTER OF HIM. NOT EXPECTED, HIM BEING ALONE.
TOO EASY.

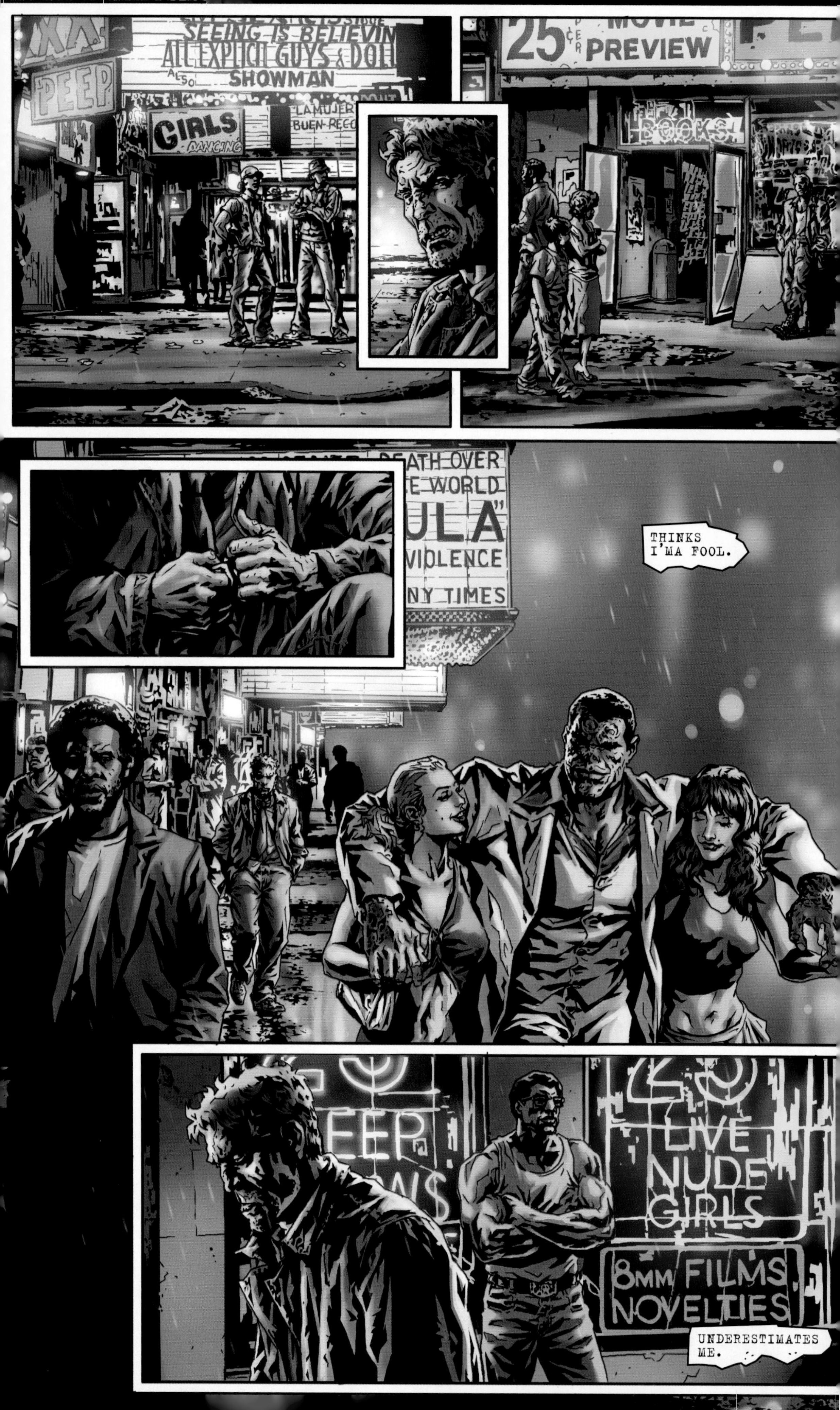

SEEING IS BELIEVIN
ALL EXPLICIT GUYS & DOLL
SHOWMAN
PEEP
GIRLS
DANCING
25¢ PER
PREVIEW
BOOKS
DEATH OVER
WORLD
ULA"
VIOLENCE
NY TIMES
THINKS I'MA FOOL.
LIVE NUDE GIRLS
8MM FILMS
NOVELTIES
UNDERESTIMATES ME.

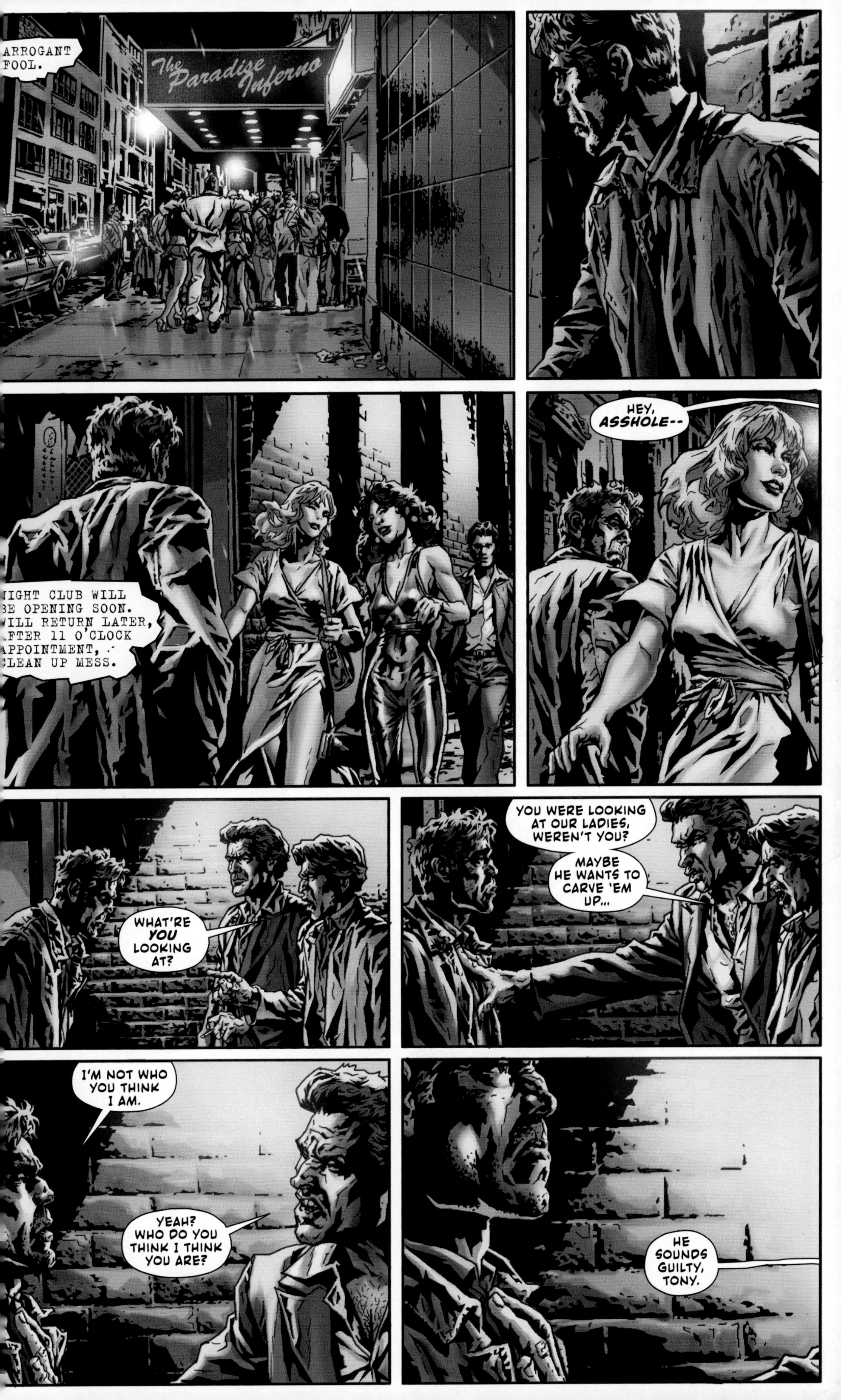
ARROGANT
FOOL.
The Paradise Inferno
NIGHT CLUB WILL
BE OPENING SOON.
WILL RETURN LATER,
AFTER 11 O'CLOCK
APPOINTMENT,
CLEAN UP MESS.
HEY,
ASSHOLE--
WHAT'RE
YOU
LOOKING
AT?
YOU WERE LOOKING
AT OUR LADIES,
WEREN'T YOU?
MAYBE
HE WANTS TO
CARVE 'EM
UP...
I'M NOT WHO
YOU THINK
I AM.
YEAH?
WHO DO YOU
THINK I THINK
YOU ARE?
HE
SOUNDS
GUILTY,
TONY.

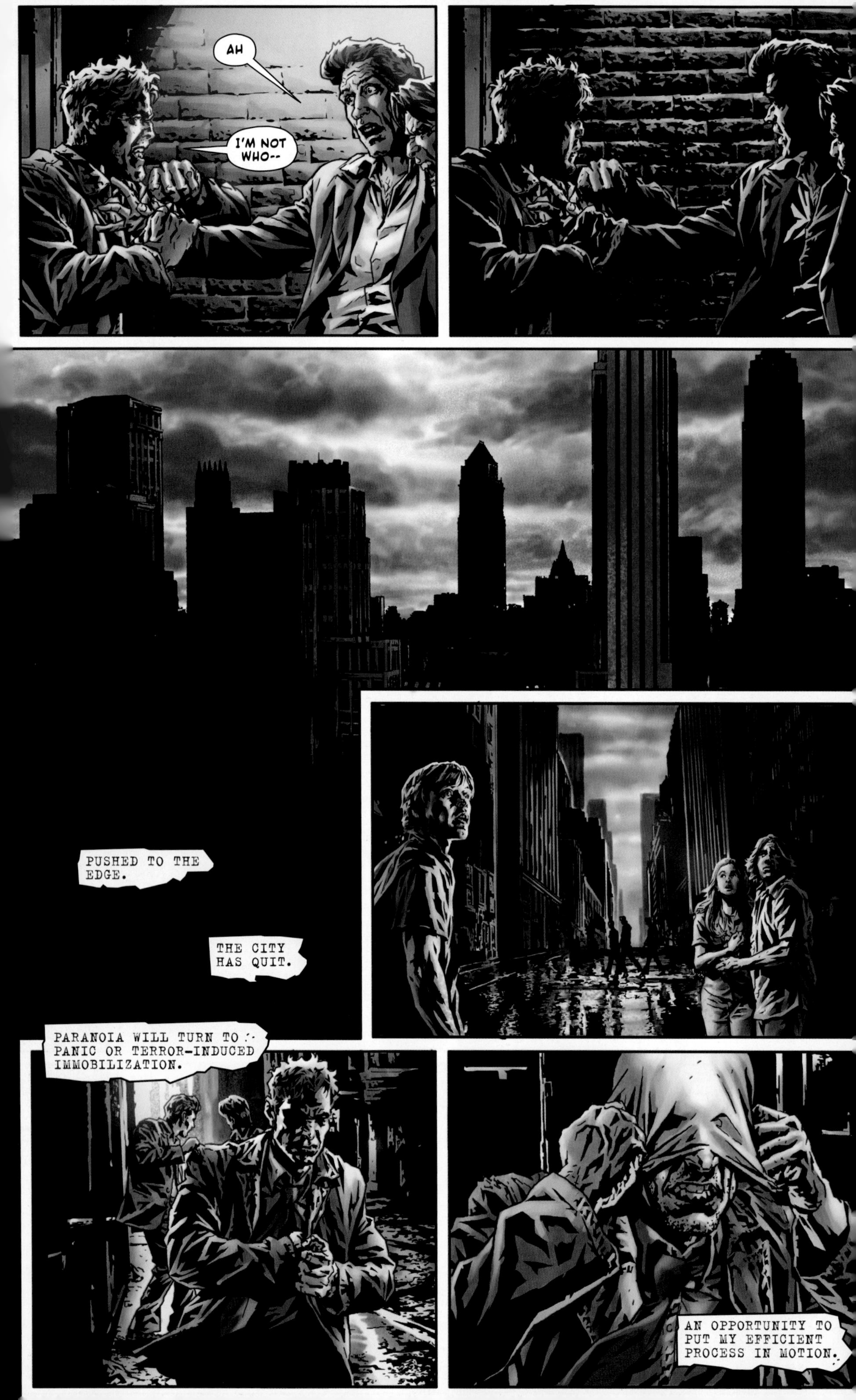
AH
I'M NOT WHO--
PUSHED TO THE EDGE.
THE CITY HAS QUIT.
PARANOIA WILL TURN TO PANIC OR TERROR-INDUCED IMMOBILIZATION.
AN OPPORTUNITY TO PUT MY EFFICIENT PROCESS IN MOTION.

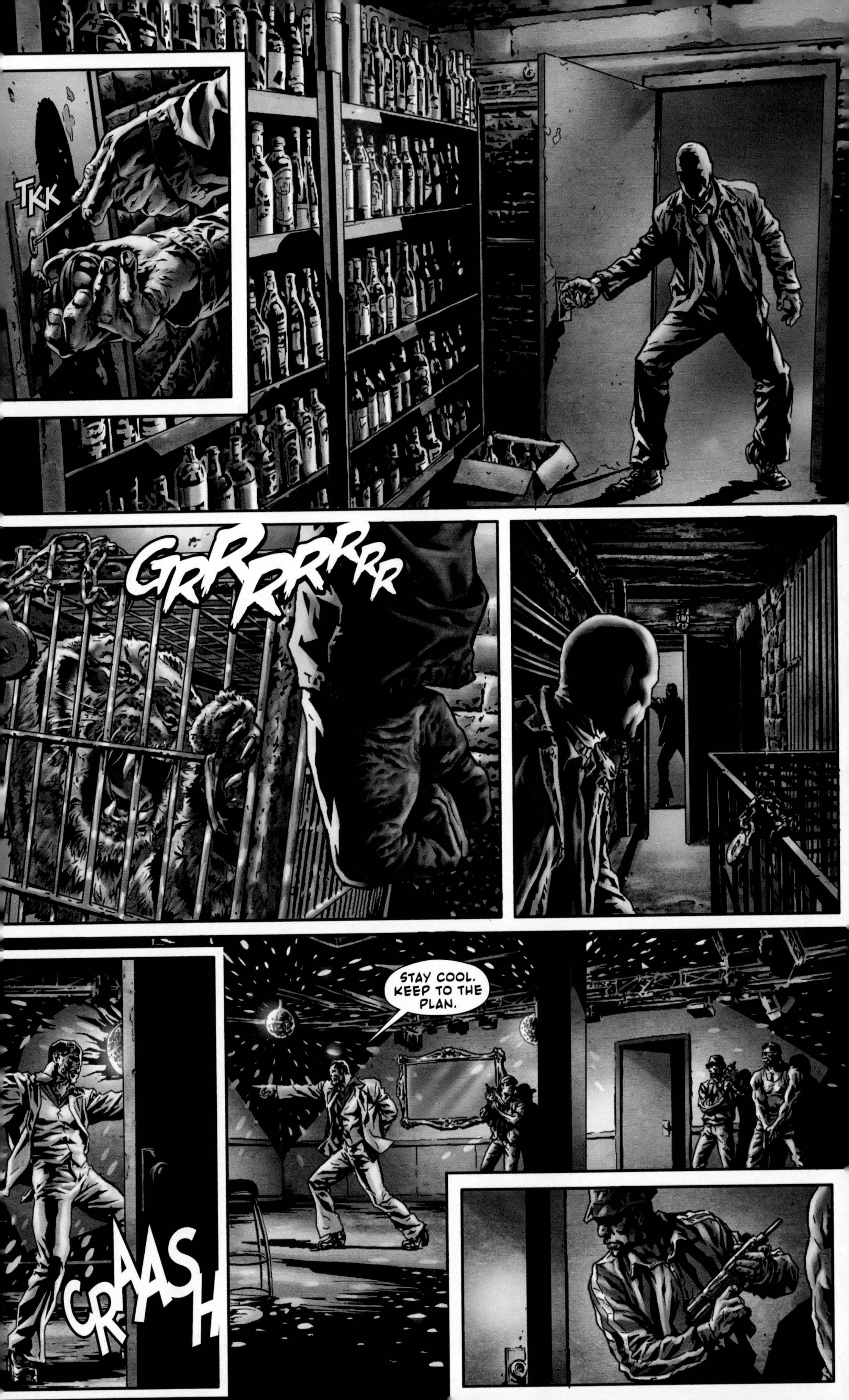
TKK
GRRRRRRR
STAY COOL. KEEP TO THE PLAN.
CRAASH

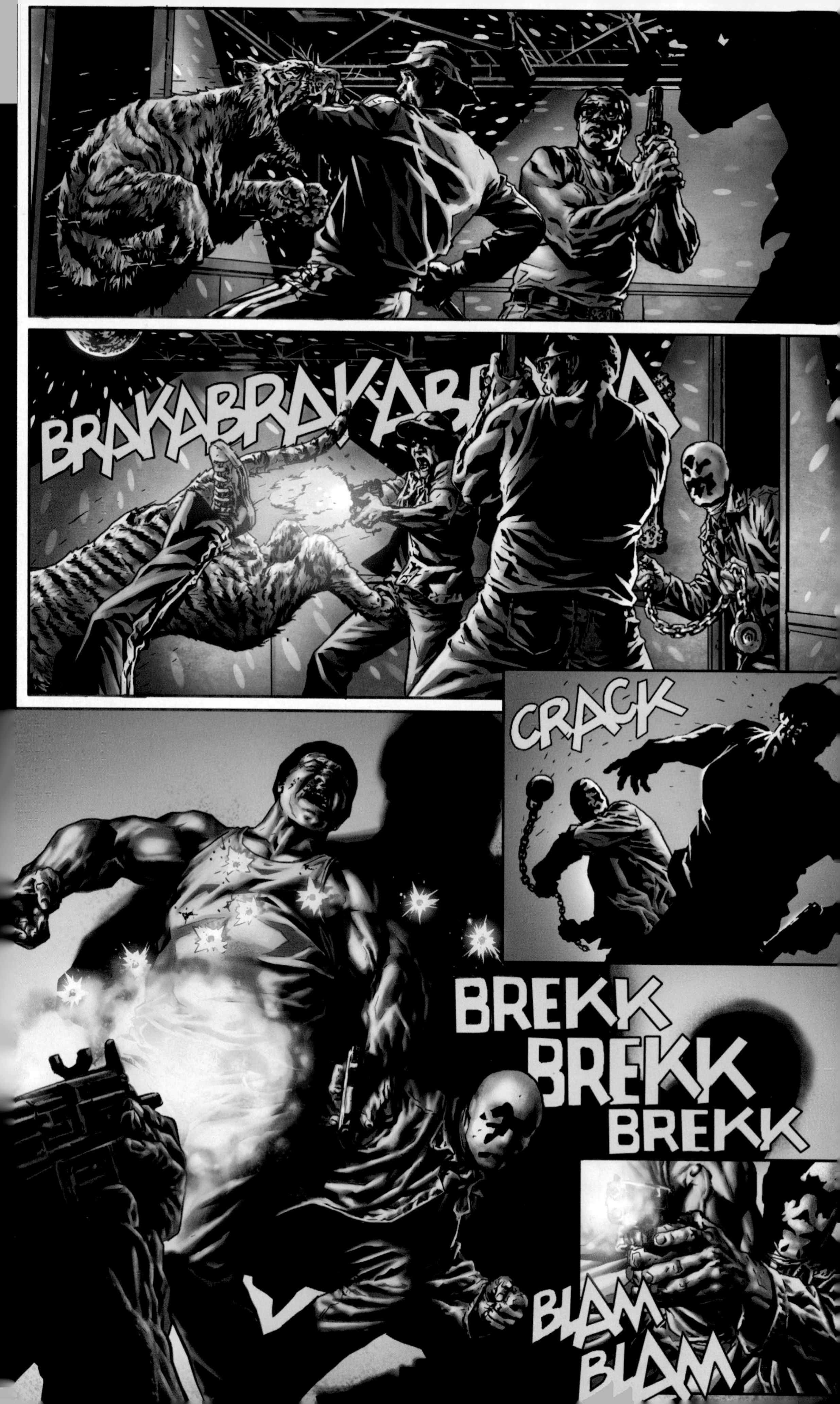
BRAKABRAKABRAKA
CRACK
BREKK
BREKK
BREKK
BLAM
BLAM

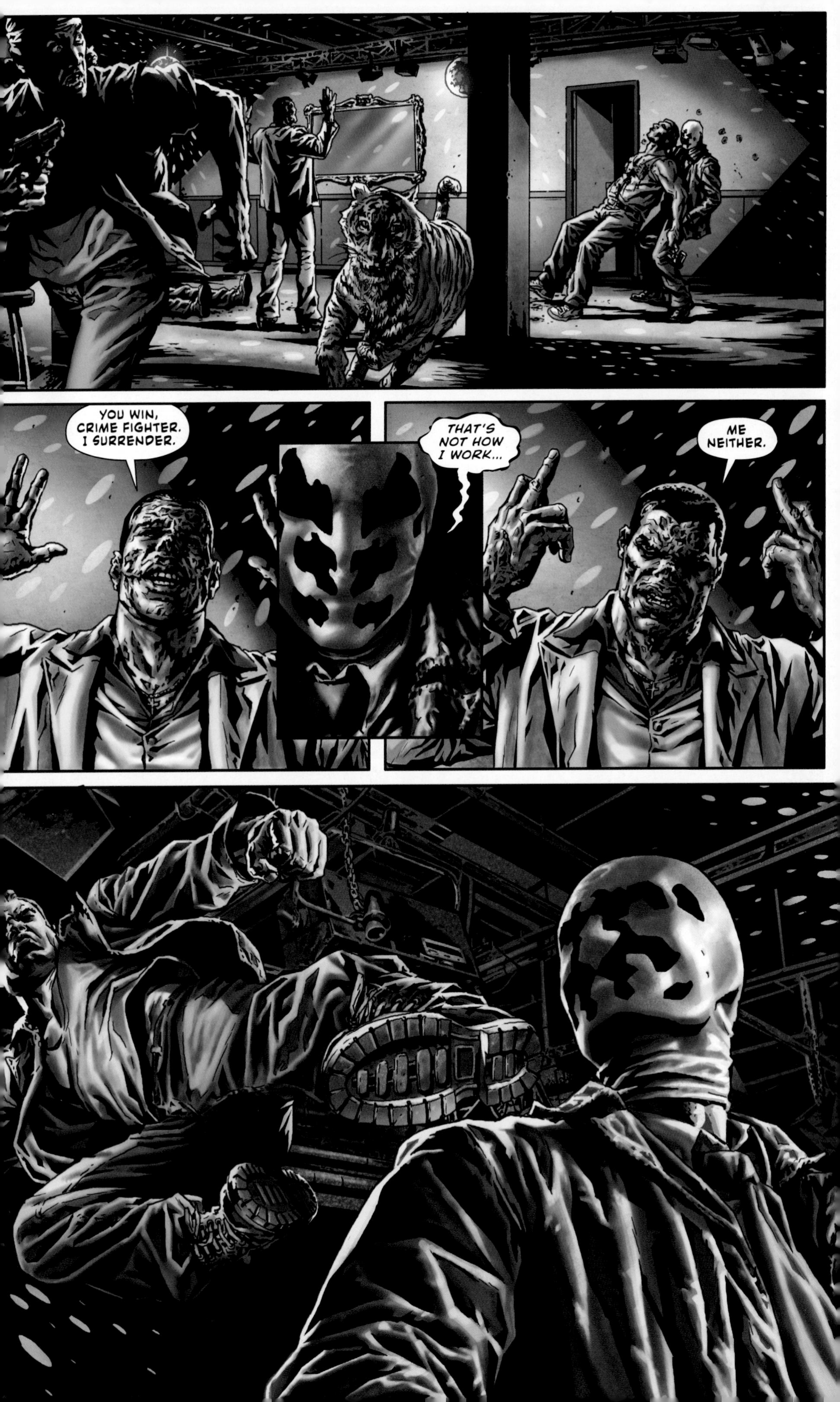
YOU WIN, CRIME FIGHTER. I SURRENDER.
THAT'S NOT HOW I WORK...
ME NEITHER.

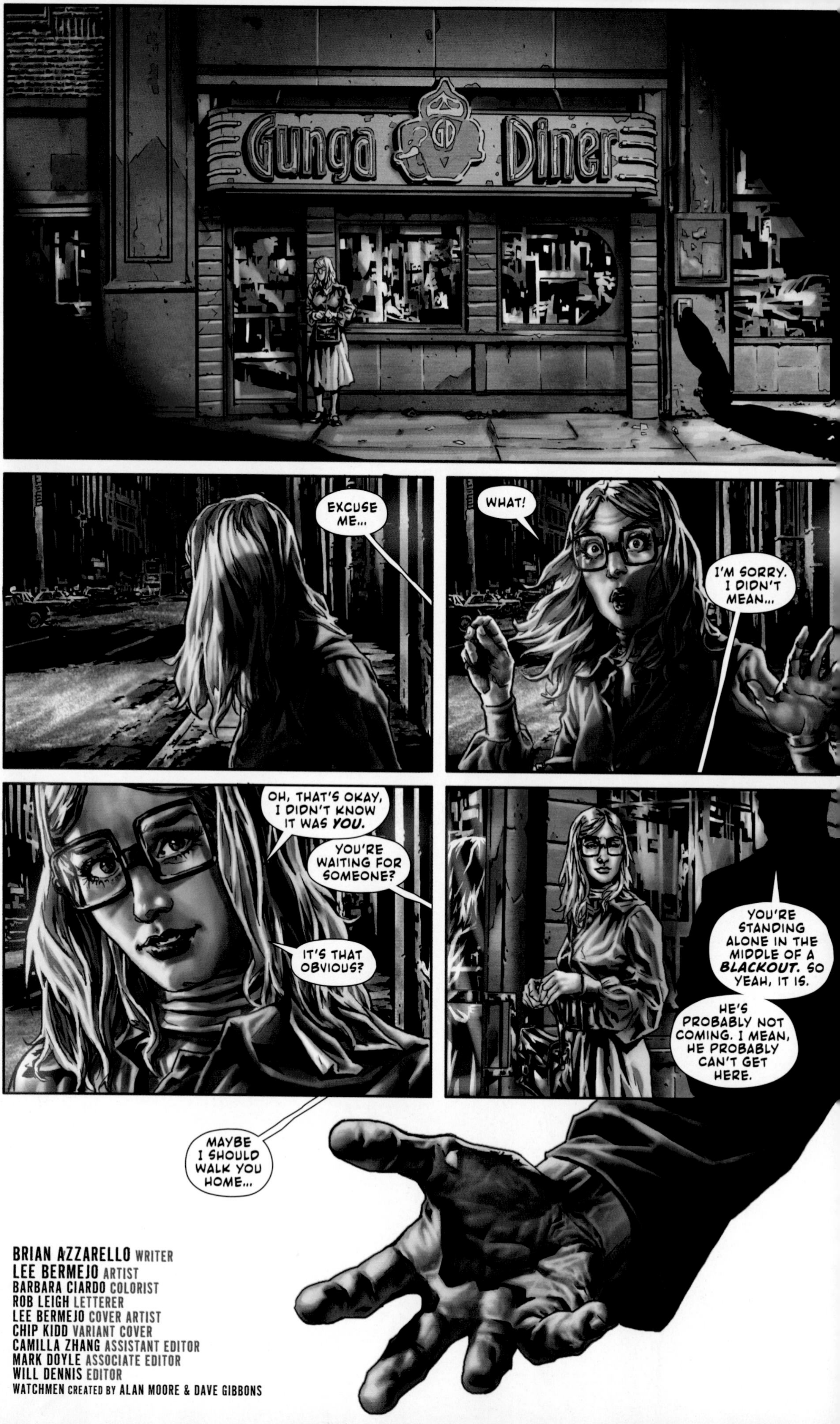
Gunga GD Diner
EXCUSE ME...
WHAT!
I'M SORRY. I DIDN'T MEAN...
OH, THAT'S OKAY, I DIDN'T KNOW IT WAS *YOU.*
YOU'RE WAITING FOR SOMEONE?
IT'S THAT OBVIOUS?
YOU'RE STANDING ALONE IN THE MIDDLE OF A *BLACKOUT.* SO YEAH, IT IS.
HE'S PROBABLY NOT COMING. I MEAN, HE PROBABLY CAN'T GET HERE.
MAYBE I SHOULD WALK YOU HOME...

BRIAN AZZARELLO WRITER
LEE BERMEJO ARTIST
BARBARA CIARDO COLORIST
ROB LEIGH LETTERER
LEE BERMEJO COVER ARTIST
CHIP KIDD VARIANT COVER
CAMILLA ZHANG ASSISTANT EDITOR
MARK DOYLE ASSOCIATE EDITOR
WILL DENNIS EDITOR
WATCHMEN CREATED BY ALAN MOORE & DAVE GIBBONS

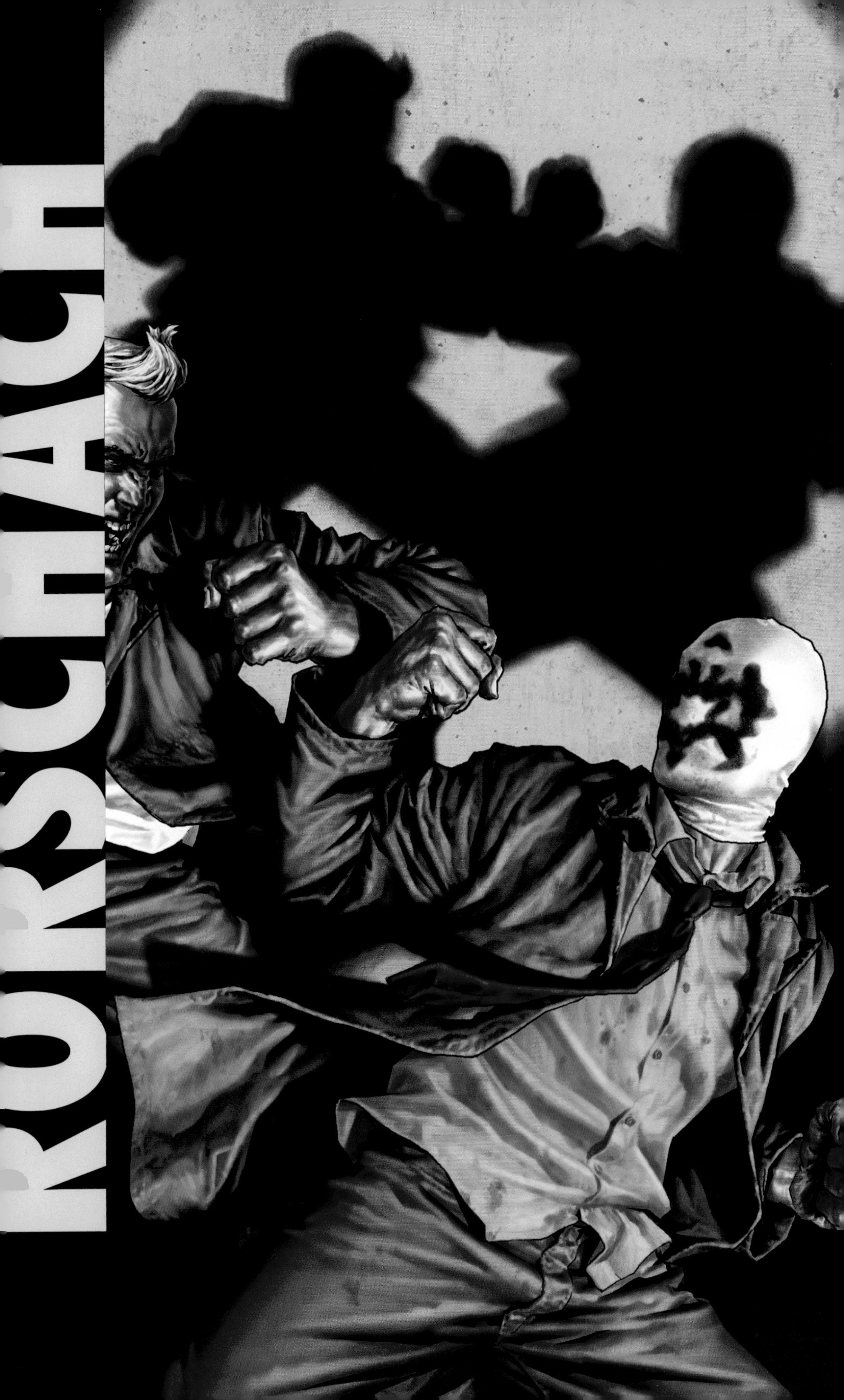
RORSCHACH

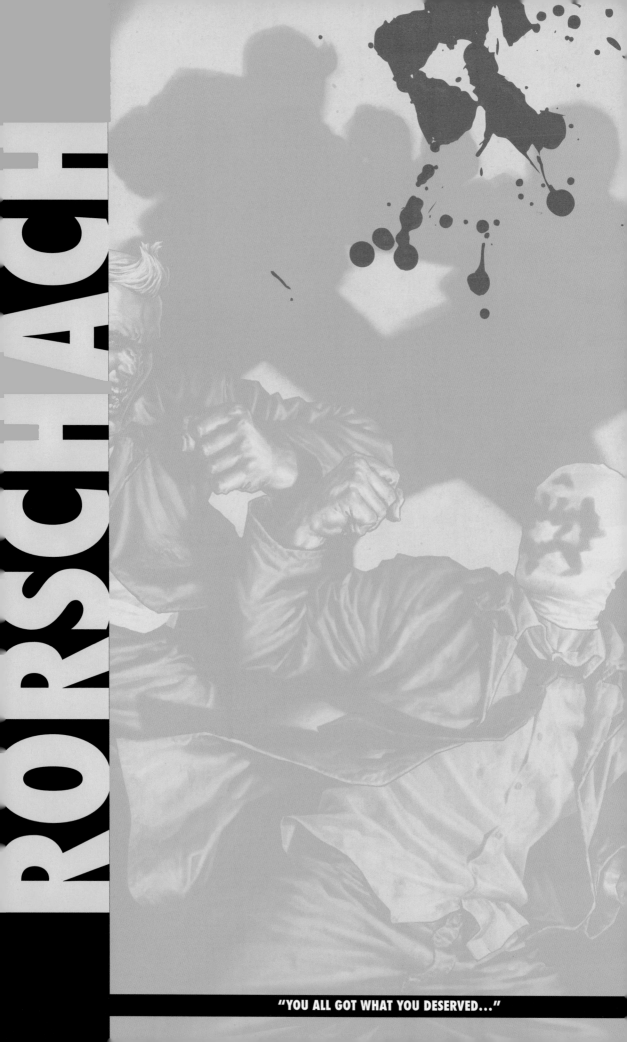

RORSCHACH

"YOU ALL GOT WHAT YOU DESERVED..."

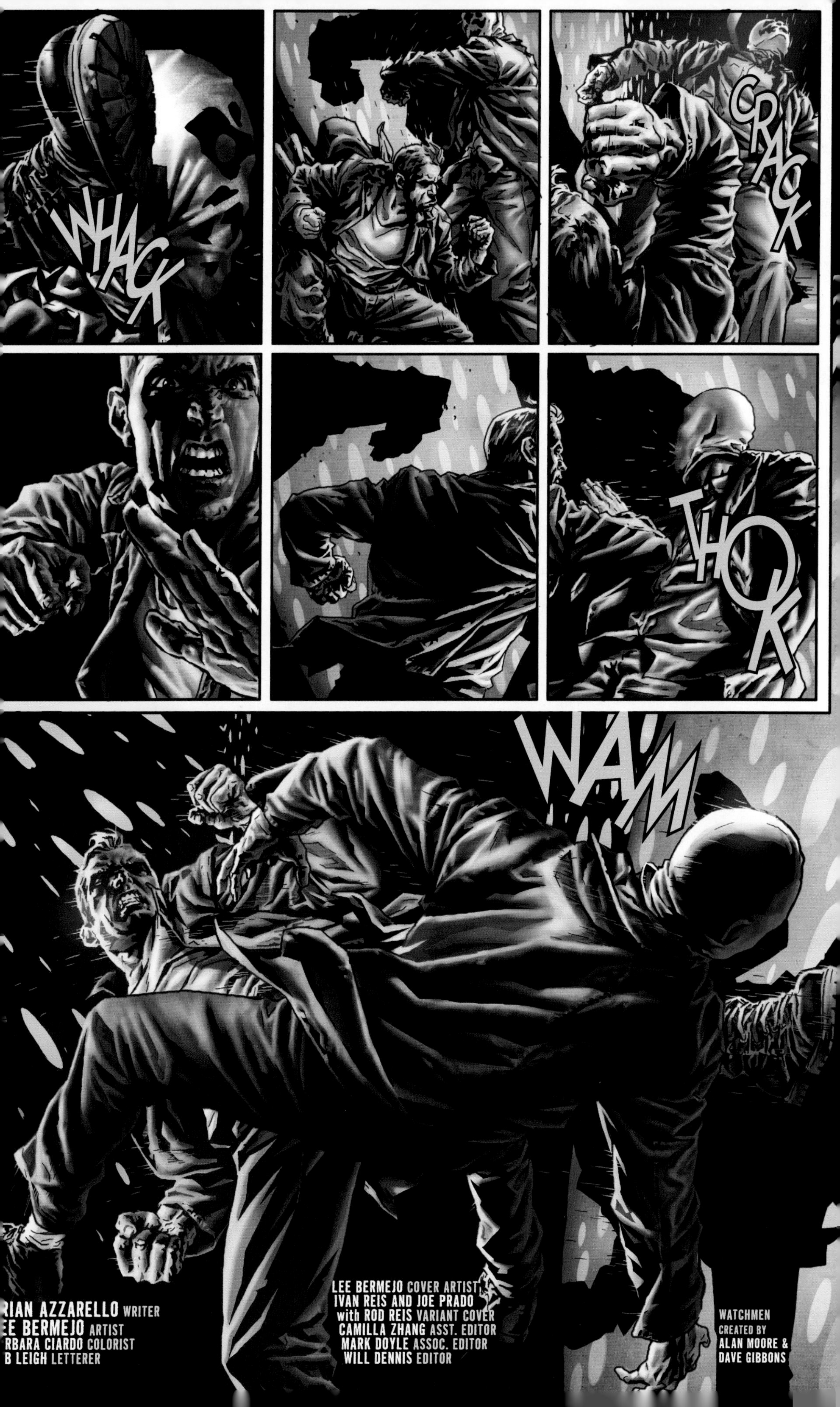
WHACK
CRACK
THOK
WAM
RIAN AZZARELLO WRITER
EE BERMEJO ARTIST
RBARA CIARDO COLORIST
B LEIGH LETTERER
LEE BERMEJO COVER ARTIST
IVAN REIS AND JOE PRADO
with ROD REIS VARIANT COVER
CAMILLA ZHANG ASST. EDITOR
MARK DOYLE ASSOC. EDITOR
WILL DENNIS EDITOR
WATCHMEN
CREATED BY
ALAN MOORE &
DAVE GIBBONS

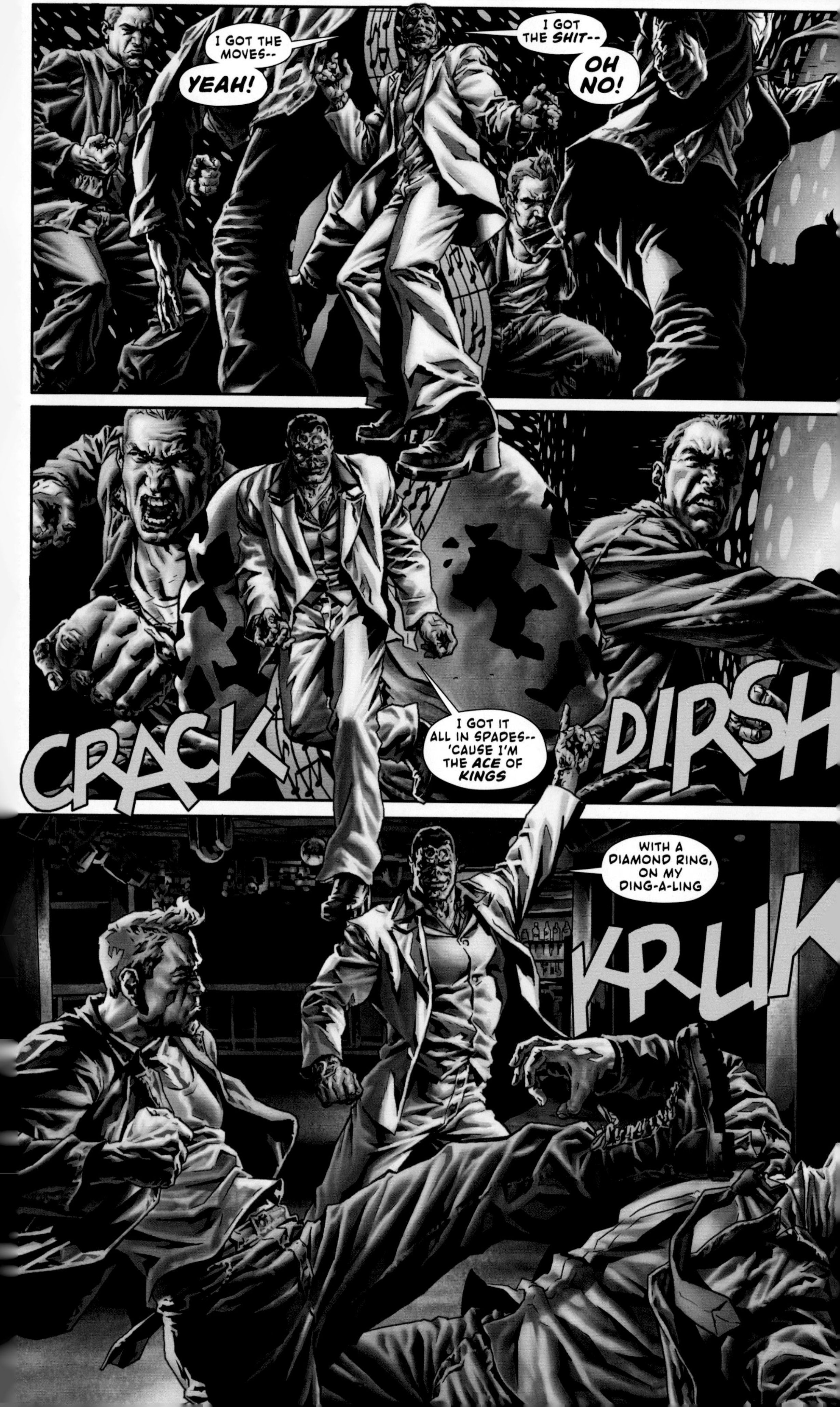
I GOT THE MOVES--
YEAH!
I GOT THE SHIT--
OH NO!
I GOT IT ALL IN SPADES--'CAUSE I'M THE ACE OF KINGS
CRACK
DIRSH
WITH A DIAMOND RING, ON MY DING-A-LING
KRUK

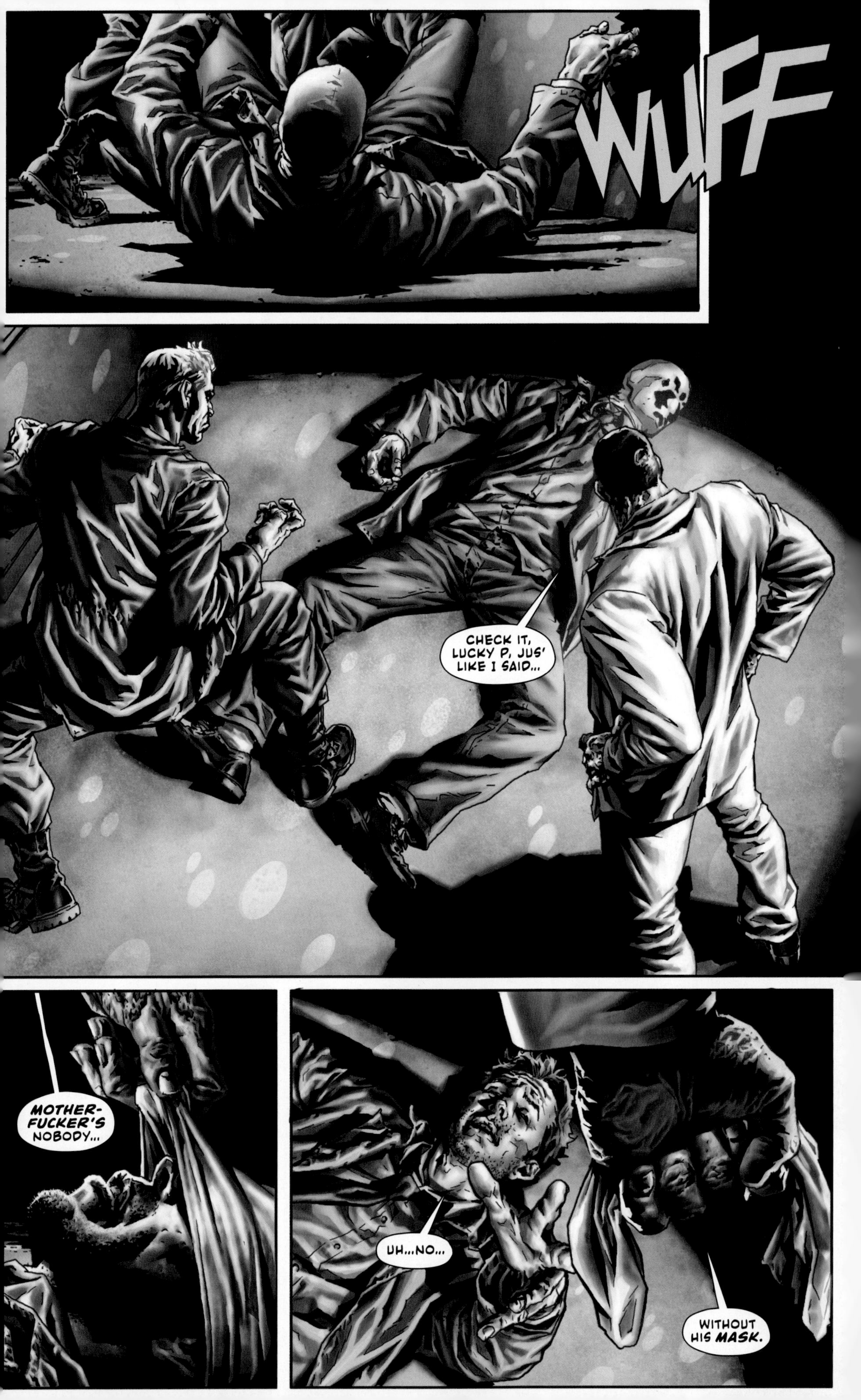
WUFF
CHECK IT, LUCKY P, JUS' LIKE I SAID...
MOTHER-FUCKER'S NOBODY...
UH...NO...
WITHOUT HIS MASK.

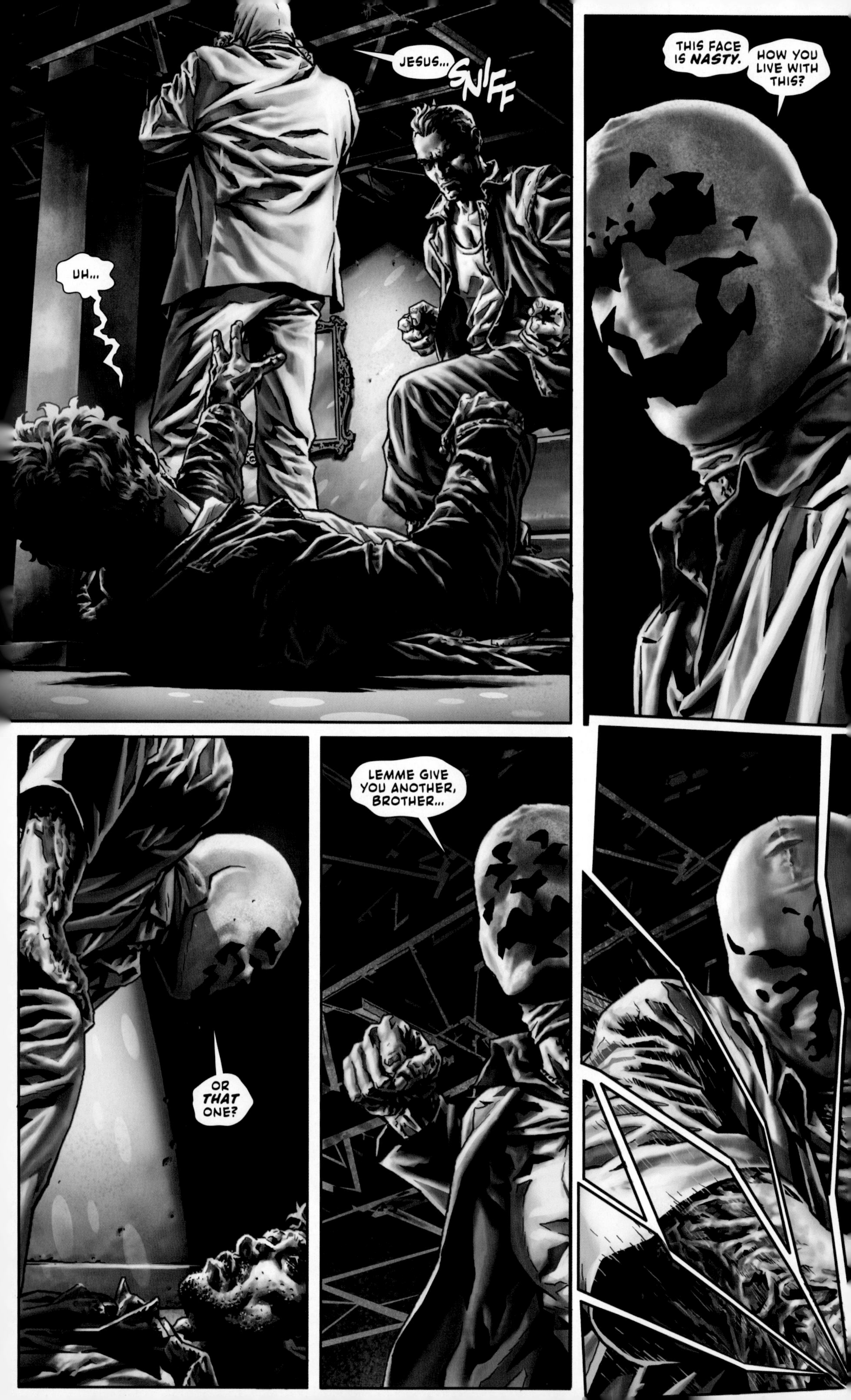
JESUS...
SNIFF
UH...
THIS FACE IS NASTY.
HOW YOU LIVE WITH THIS?
OR THAT ONE?
LEMME GIVE YOU ANOTHER, BROTHER...

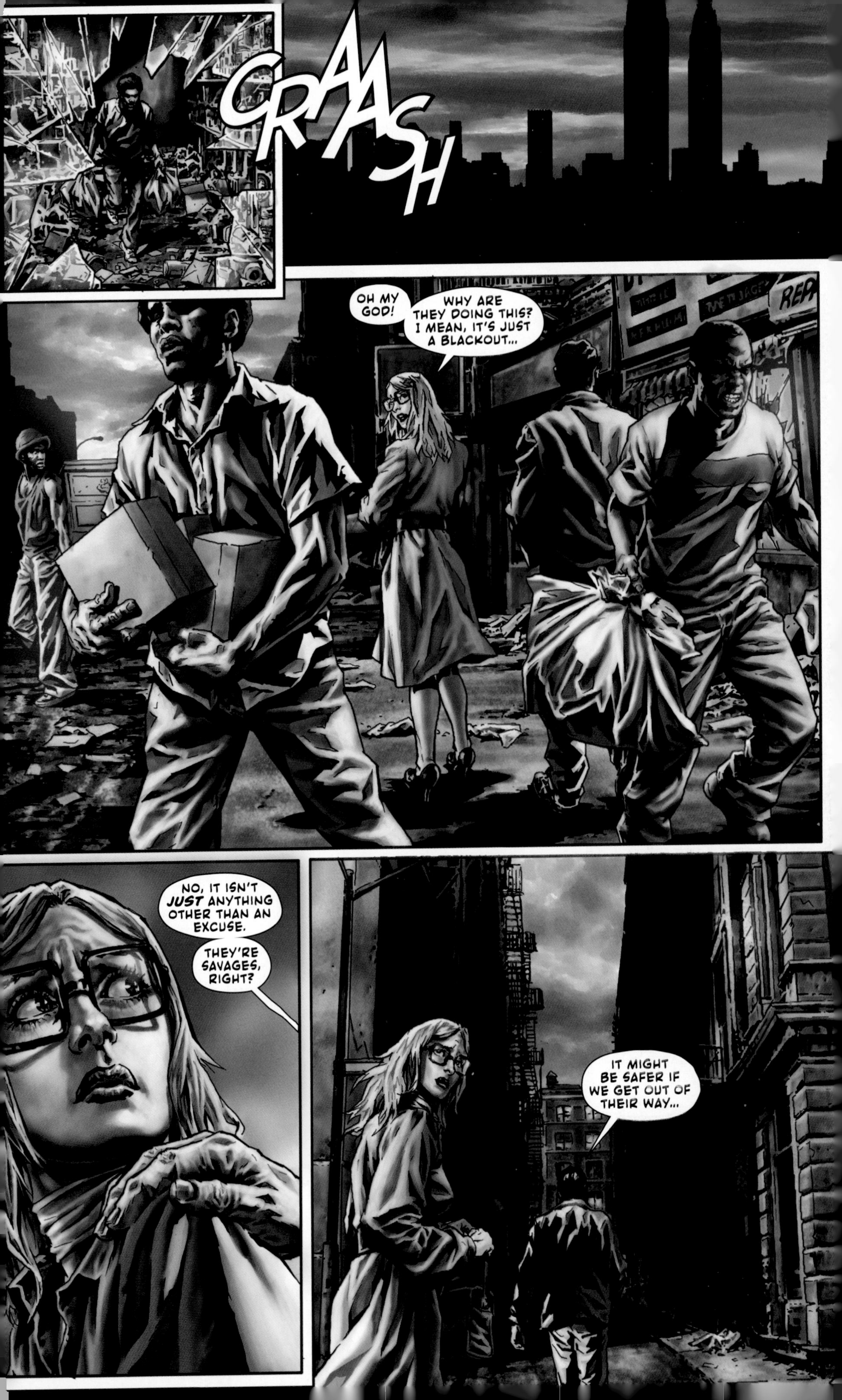
CRAASH
OH MY GOD!
WHY ARE THEY DOING THIS? I MEAN, IT'S JUST A BLACKOUT...
NO, IT ISN'T JUST ANYTHING OTHER THAN AN EXCUSE.
THEY'RE SAVAGES, RIGHT?
IT MIGHT BE SAFER IF WE GET OUT OF THEIR WAY...

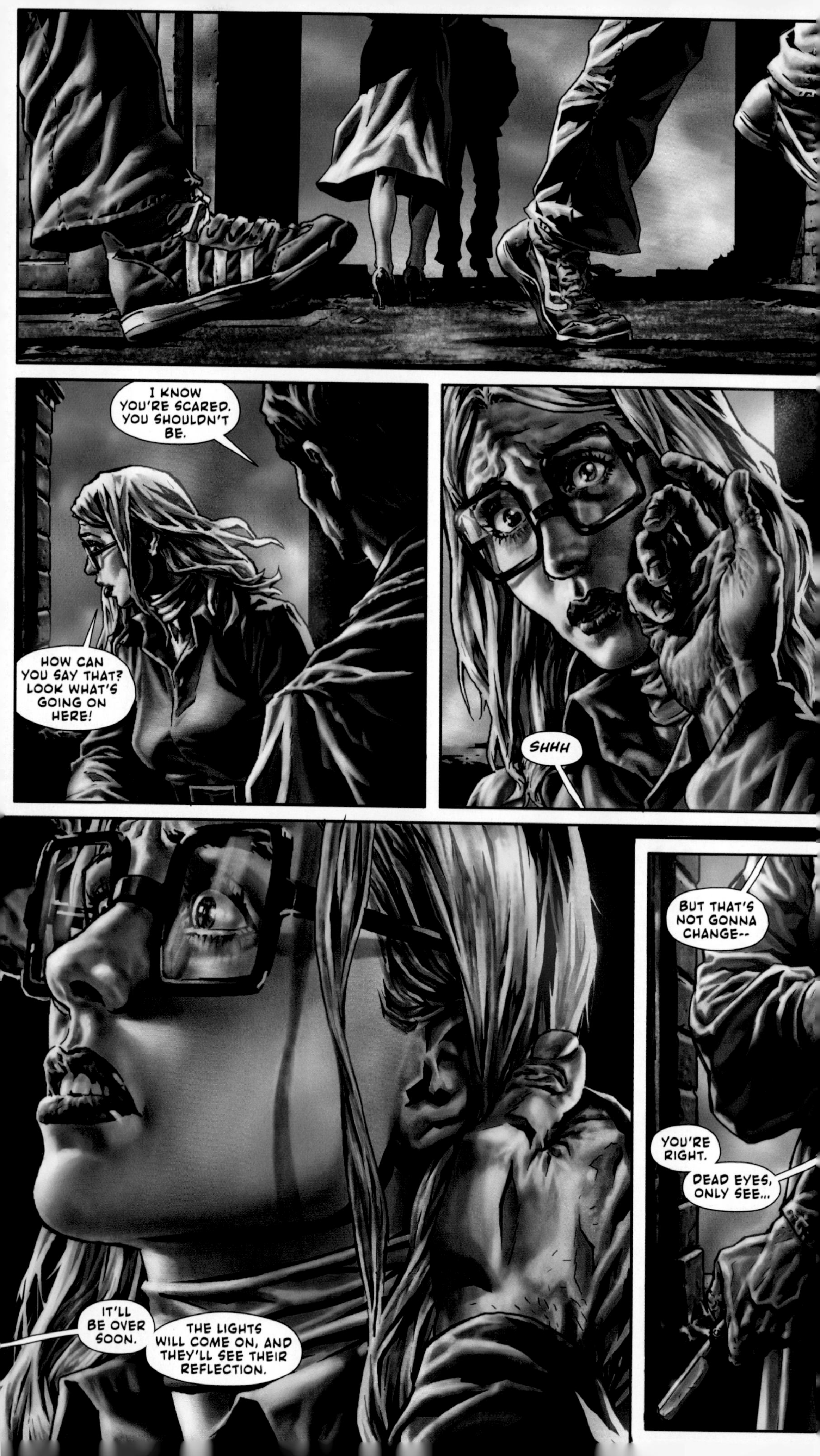
I KNOW YOU'RE SCARED. YOU SHOULDN'T BE.
HOW CAN YOU SAY THAT? LOOK WHAT'S GOING ON HERE!
SHHH
IT'LL BE OVER SOON.
THE LIGHTS WILL COME ON, AND THEY'LL SEE THEIR REFLECTION.
BUT THAT'S NOT GONNA CHANGE--
YOU'RE RIGHT.
DEAD EYES, ONLY SEE...

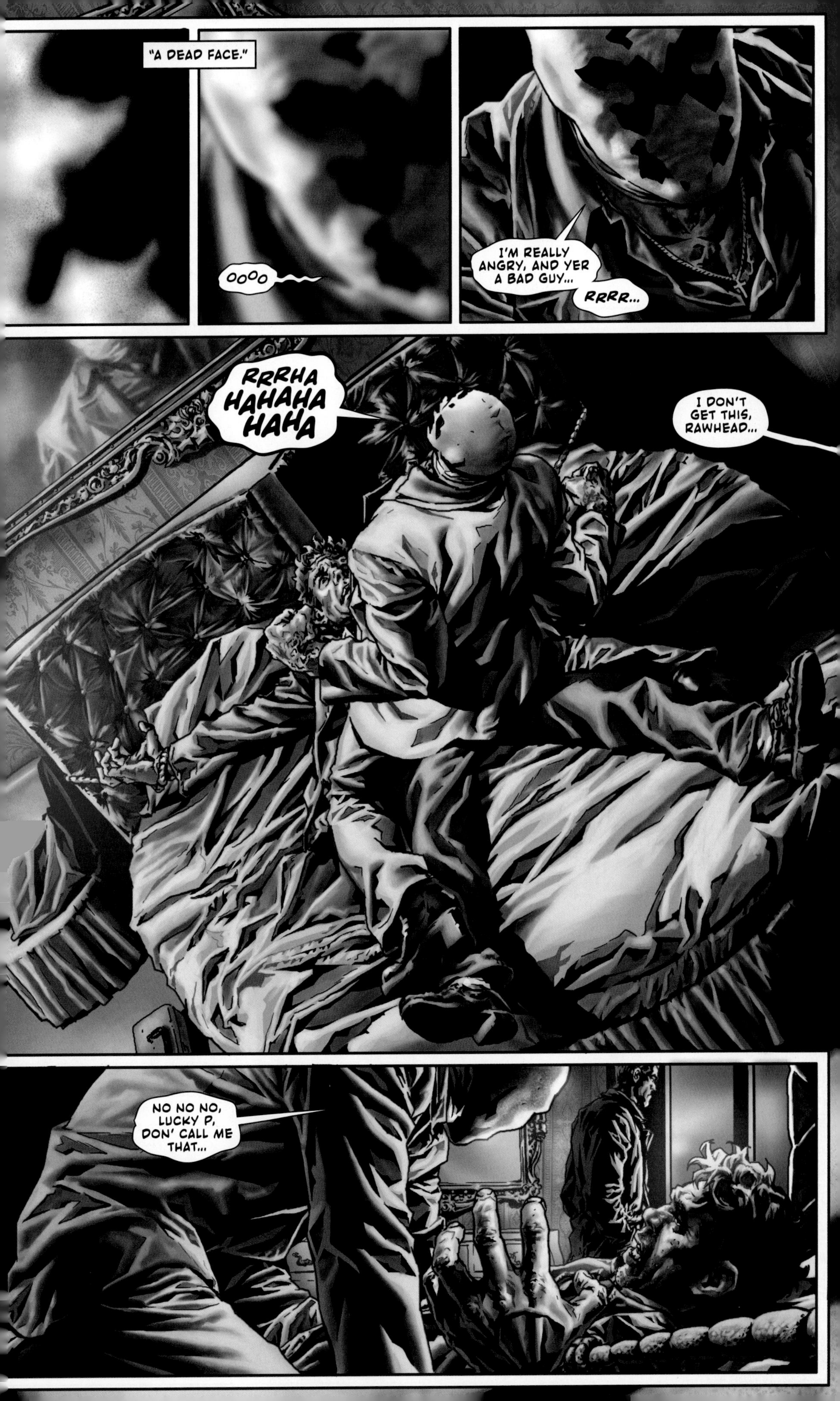
"A DEAD FACE."
OOOO
I'M REALLY ANGRY, AND YER A BAD GUY...
RRRR...
RRRHA HAHAHA HAHA
I DON'T GET THIS, RAWHEAD...
NO NO NO, LUCKY P, DON' CALL ME THAT...

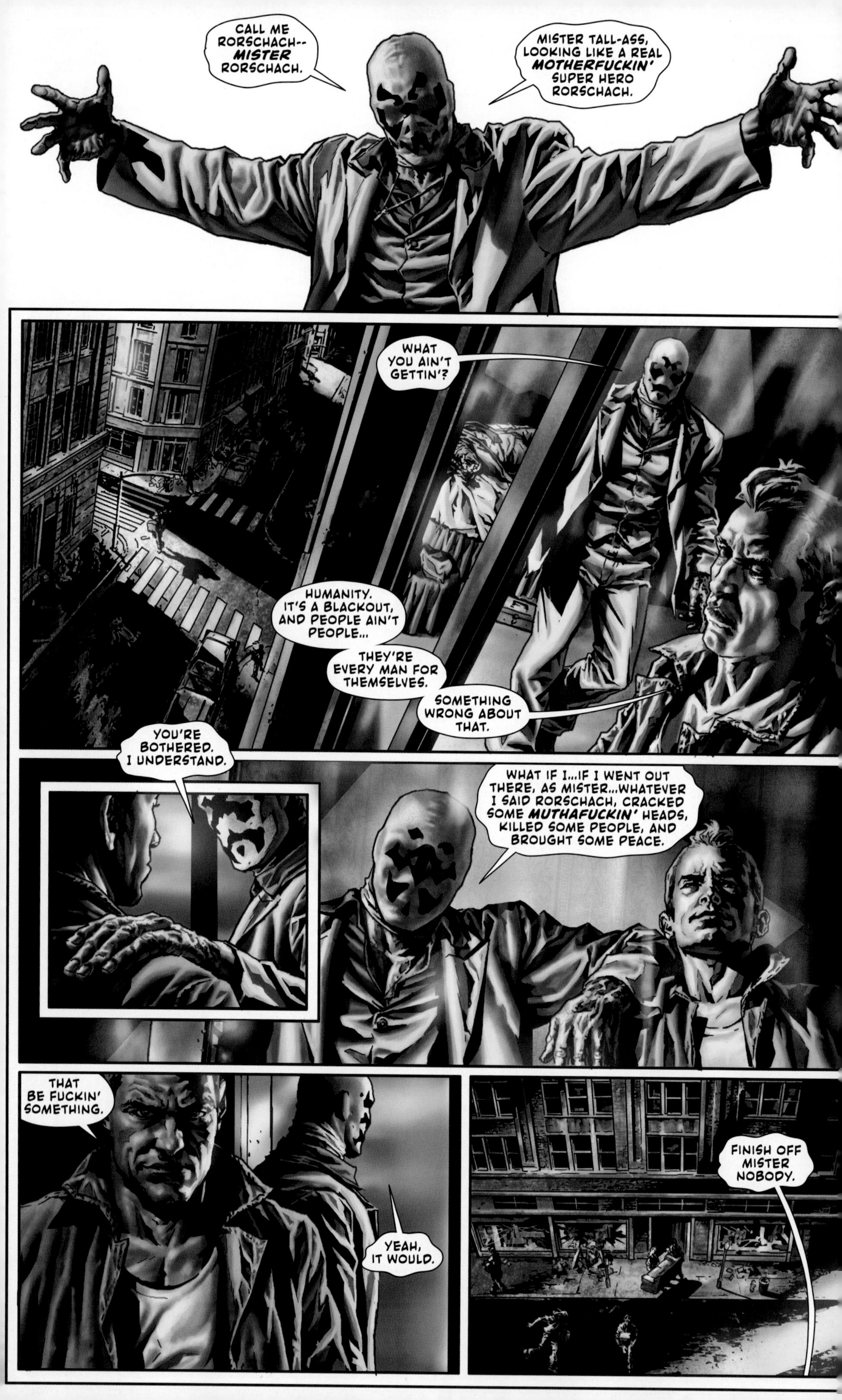
CALL ME RORSCHACH-- MISTER RORSCHACH.
MISTER TALL-ASS, LOOKING LIKE A REAL MOTHERFUCKIN' SUPER HERO RORSCHACH.
WHAT YOU AIN'T GETTIN'?
HUMANITY. IT'S A BLACKOUT, AND PEOPLE AIN'T PEOPLE...
THEY'RE EVERY MAN FOR THEMSELVES.
SOMETHING WRONG ABOUT THAT.
YOU'RE BOTHERED. I UNDERSTAND.
WHAT IF I...IF I WENT OUT THERE, AS MISTER...WHATEVER I SAID RORSCHACH, CRACKED SOME MUTHAFUCKIN' HEADS, KILLED SOME PEOPLE, AND BROUGHT SOME PEACE.
THAT BE FUCKIN' SOMETHING.
YEAH, IT WOULD.
FINISH OFF MISTER NOBODY.

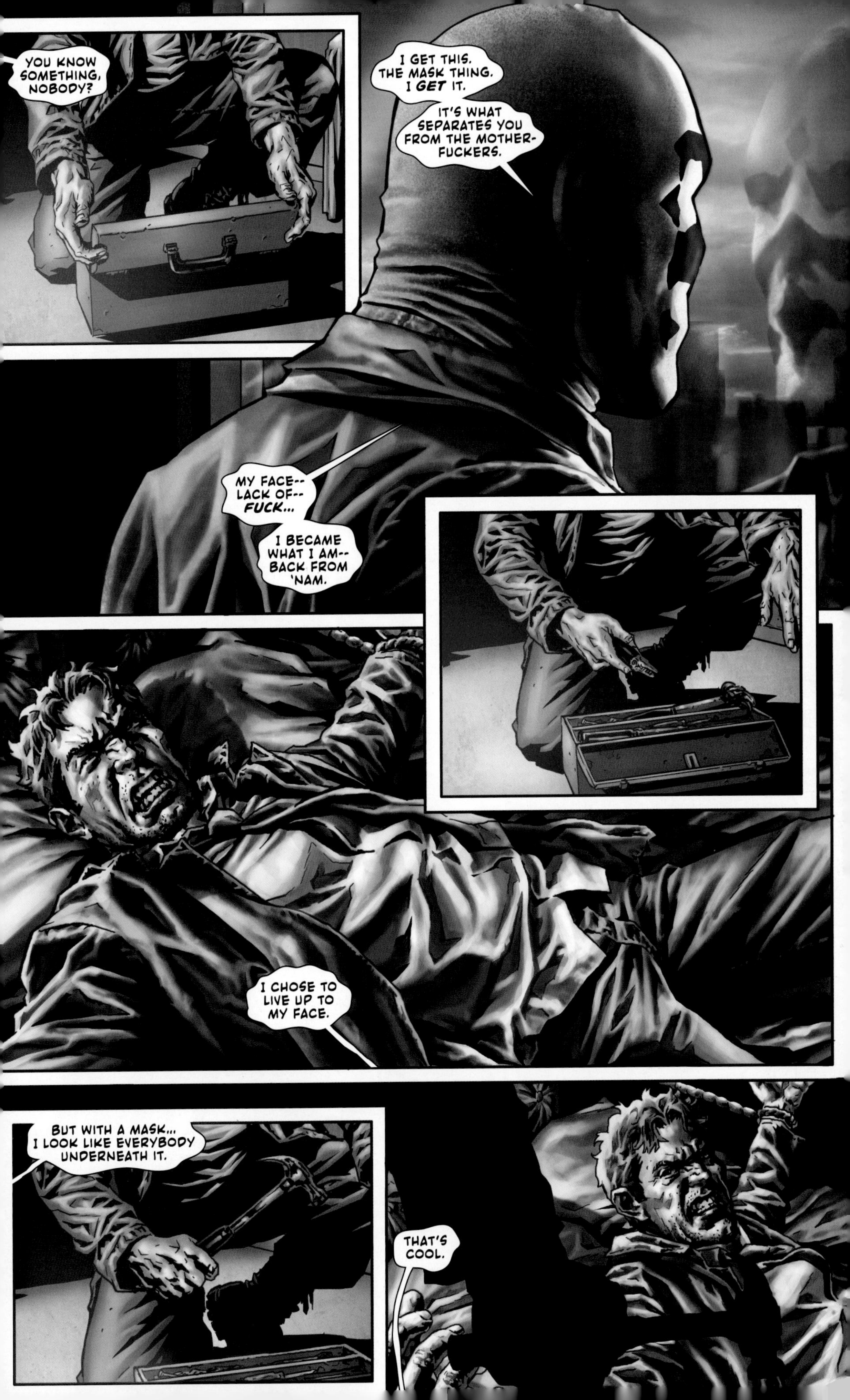

YOU KNOW SOMETHING, NOBODY?
I GET THIS. THE MASK THING. I **GET** IT.
IT'S WHAT SEPARATES YOU FROM THE MOTHER-FUCKERS.
MY FACE-- LACK OF-- **FUCK...**
I BECAME WHAT I AM-- BACK FROM 'NAM.
I CHOSE TO LIVE UP TO MY FACE.
BUT WITH A MASK... I LOOK LIKE EVERYBODY UNDERNEATH IT.
THAT'S COOL.

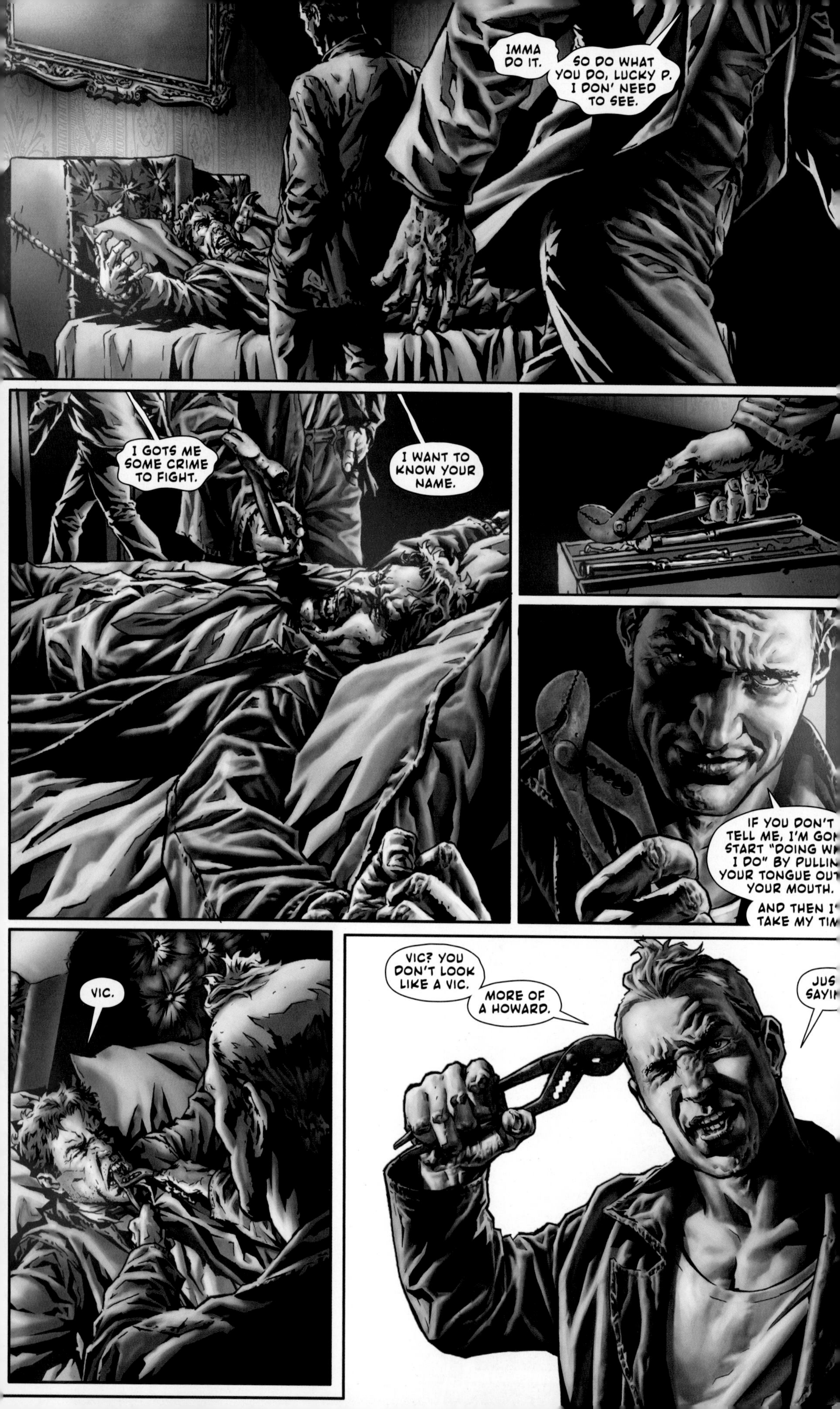
IMMA DO IT.
SO DO WHAT YOU DO, LUCKY P. I DON' NEED TO SEE.
I GOTS ME SOME CRIME TO FIGHT.
I WANT TO KNOW YOUR NAME.
IF YOU DON'T TELL ME, I'M GO START "DOING W I DO" BY PULLIN YOUR TONGUE OUT YOUR MOUTH.
AND THEN I TAKE MY TIM
VIC.
VIC? YOU DON'T LOOK LIKE A VIC.
MORE OF A HOWARD.
JUS SAYI

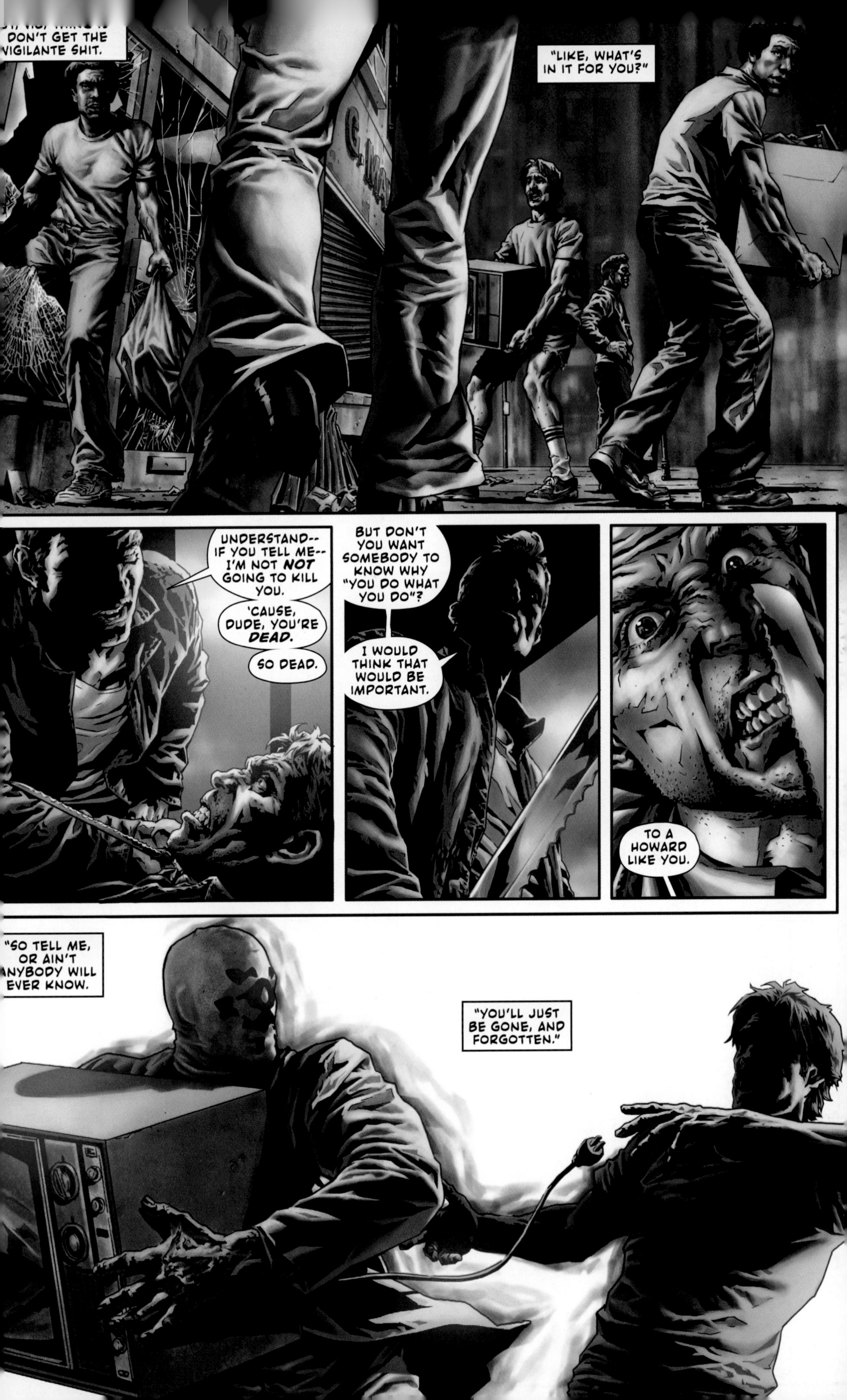
DON'T GET THE
VIGILANTE SHIT.
"LIKE, WHAT'S IN IT FOR YOU?"
UNDERSTAND-- IF YOU TELL ME-- I'M NOT NOT GOING TO KILL YOU.
'CAUSE, DUDE, YOU'RE DEAD.
SO DEAD.
BUT DON'T YOU WANT SOMEBODY TO KNOW WHY "YOU DO WHAT YOU DO"?
I WOULD THINK THAT WOULD BE IMPORTANT.
TO A HOWARD LIKE YOU.
"SO TELL ME, OR AIN'T NYBODY WILL EVER KNOW.
"YOU'LL JUST BE GONE, AND FORGOTTEN."

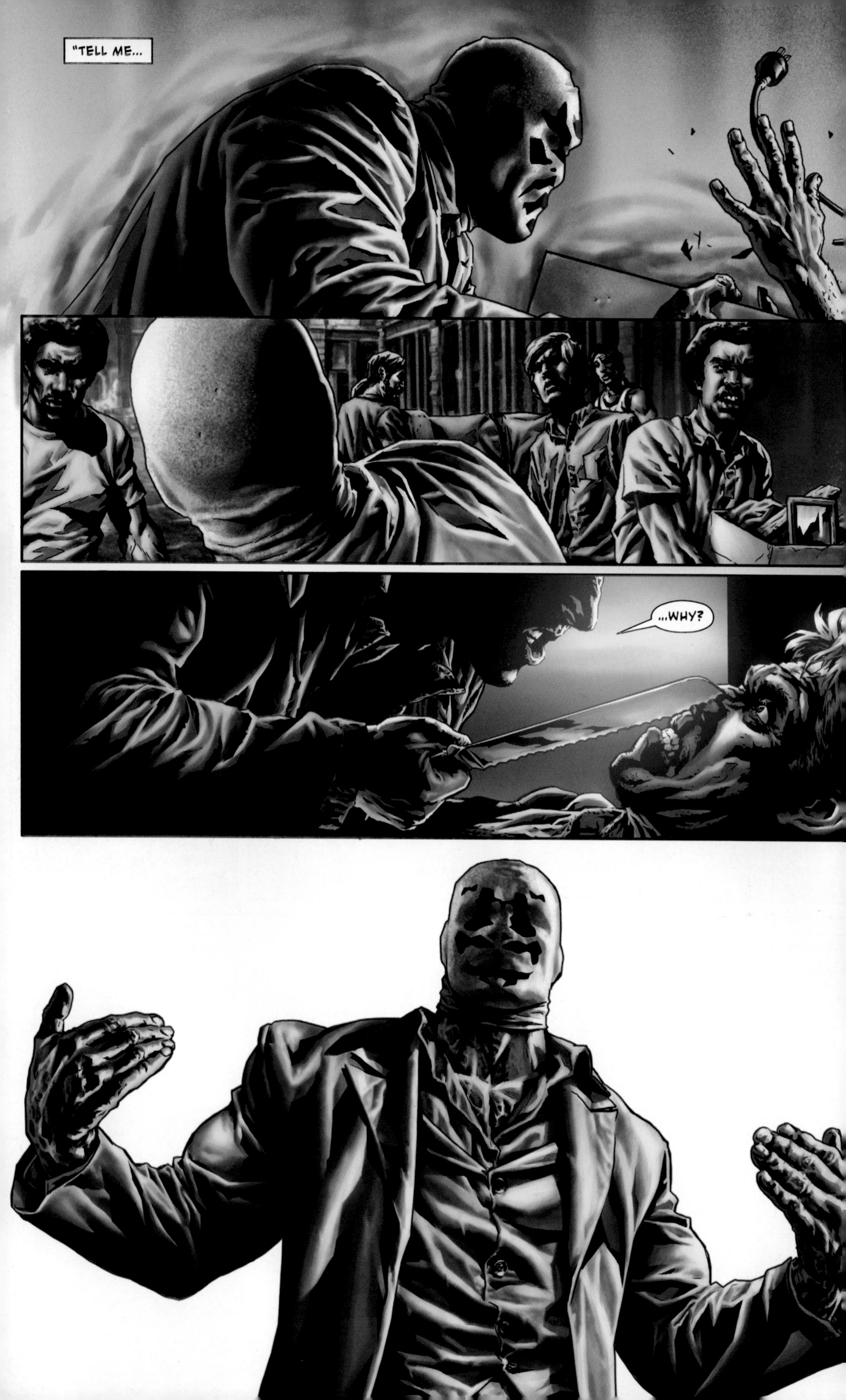

"TELL ME...
...WHY?

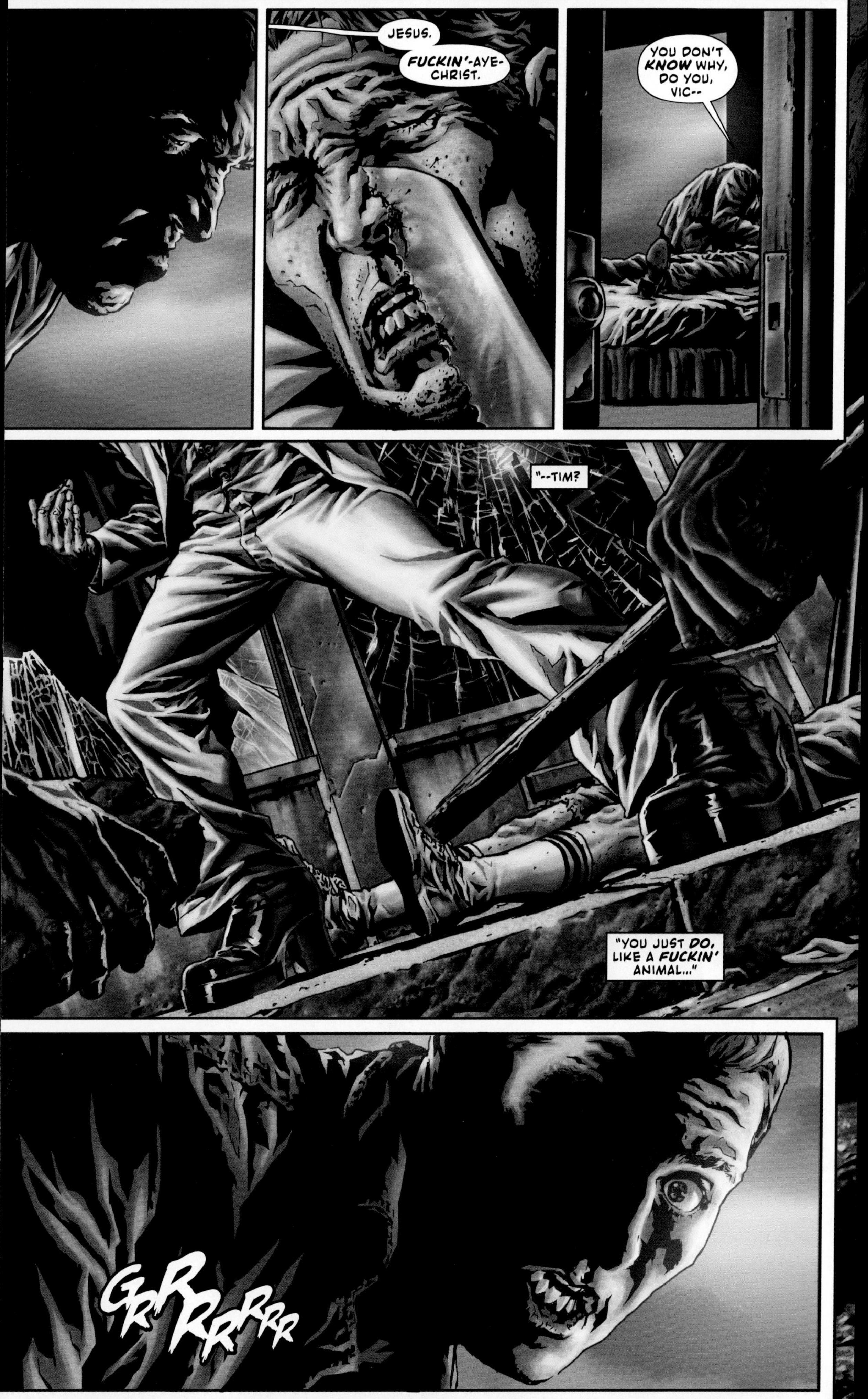
JESUS.
FUCKIN'-AYE-CHRIST.
YOU DON'T KNOW WHY, DO YOU, VIC--
"--TIM?
"YOU JUST DO, LIKE A FUCKIN' ANIMAL..."
GRRRRRRR

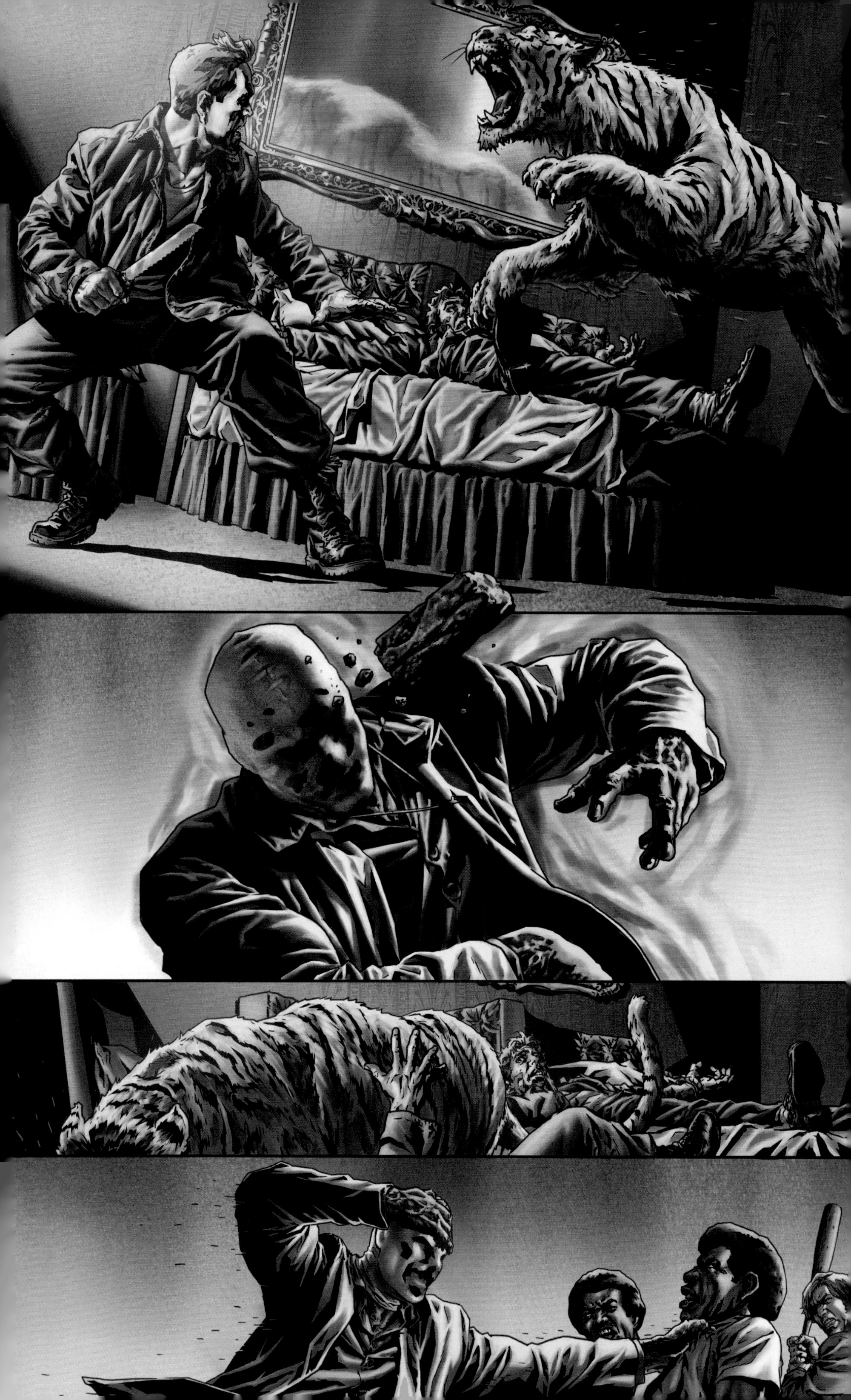

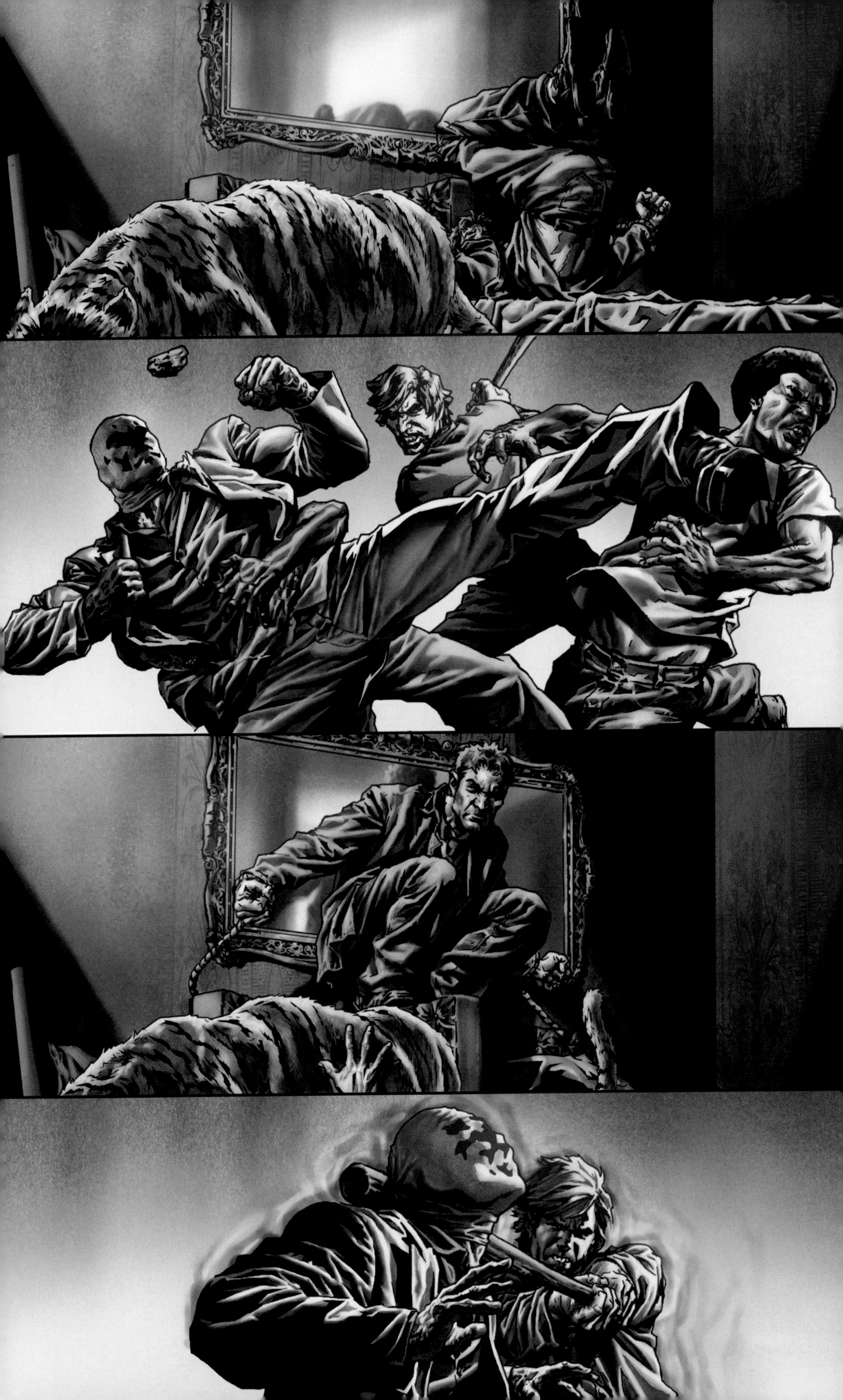

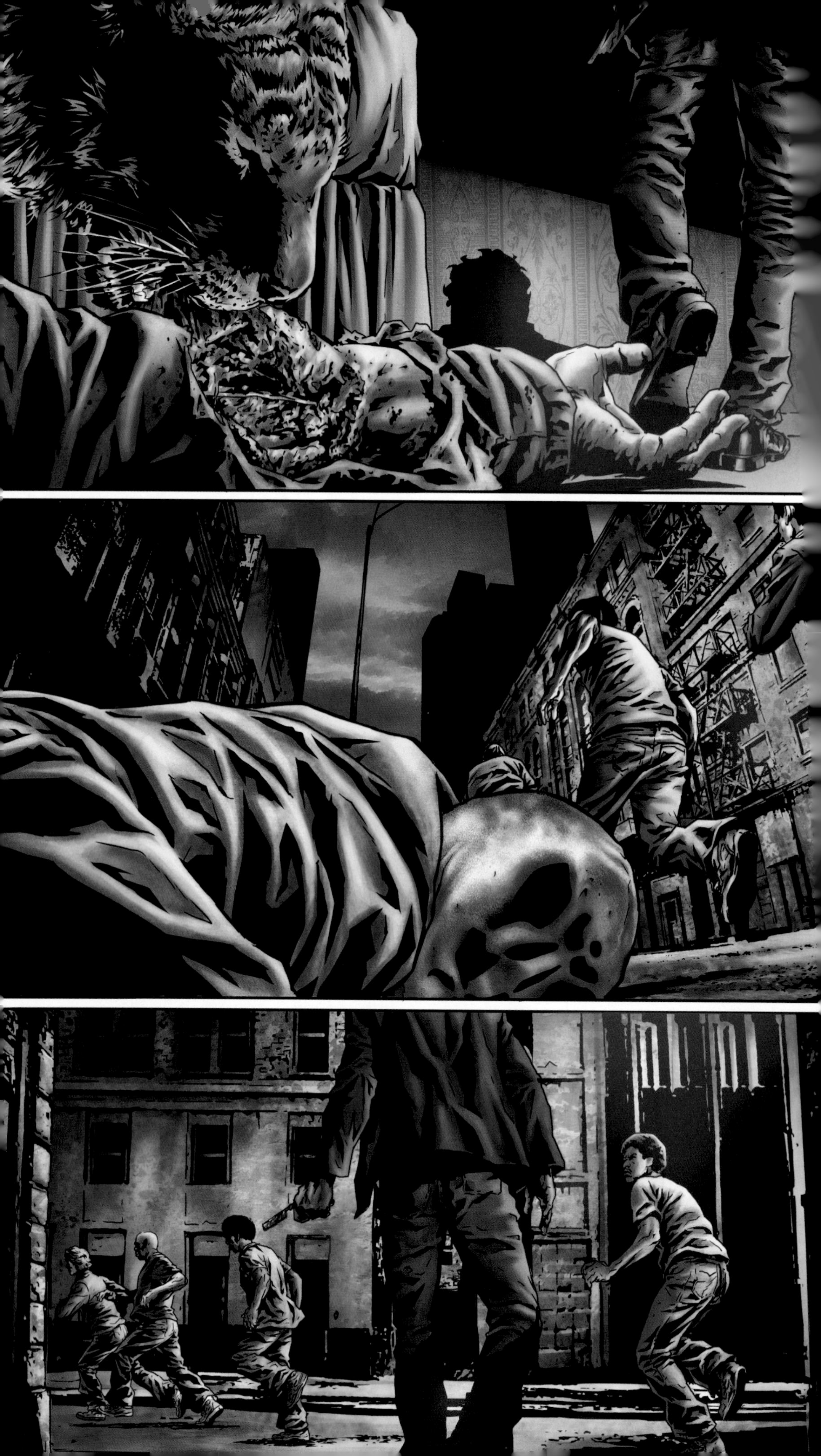

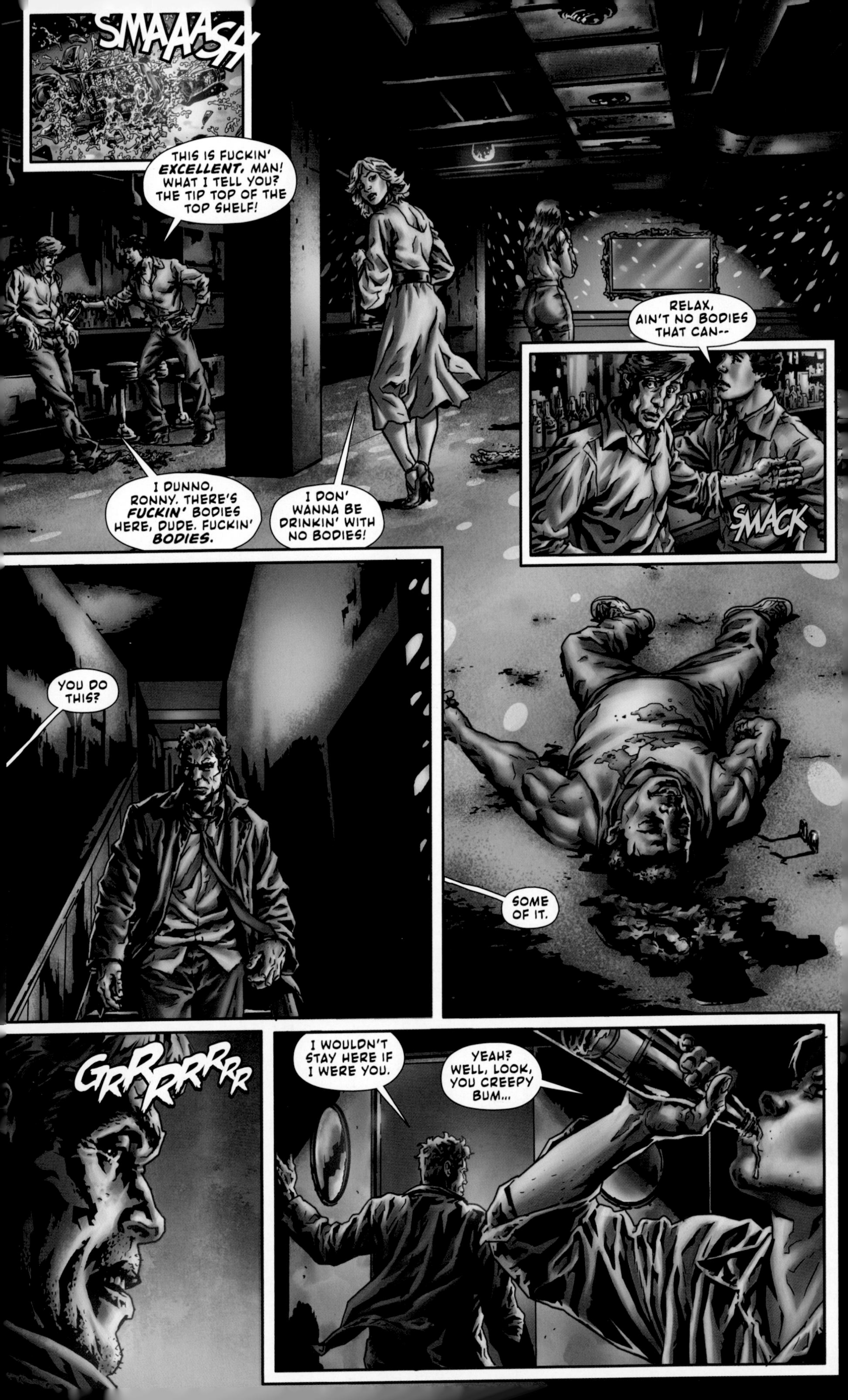
SMAAASH
THIS IS FUCKIN' EXCELLENT, MAN! WHAT I TELL YOU? THE TIP TOP OF THE TOP SHELF!
I DUNNO, RONNY. THERE'S FUCKIN' BODIES HERE, DUDE. FUCKIN' BODIES.
I DON' WANNA BE DRINKIN' WITH NO BODIES!
RELAX, AIN'T NO BODIES THAT CAN--
SMACK
YOU DO THIS?
SOME OF IT.
GRRRRRRR
I WOULDN'T STAY HERE IF I WERE YOU.
YEAH? WELL, LOOK, YOU CREEPY BUM...

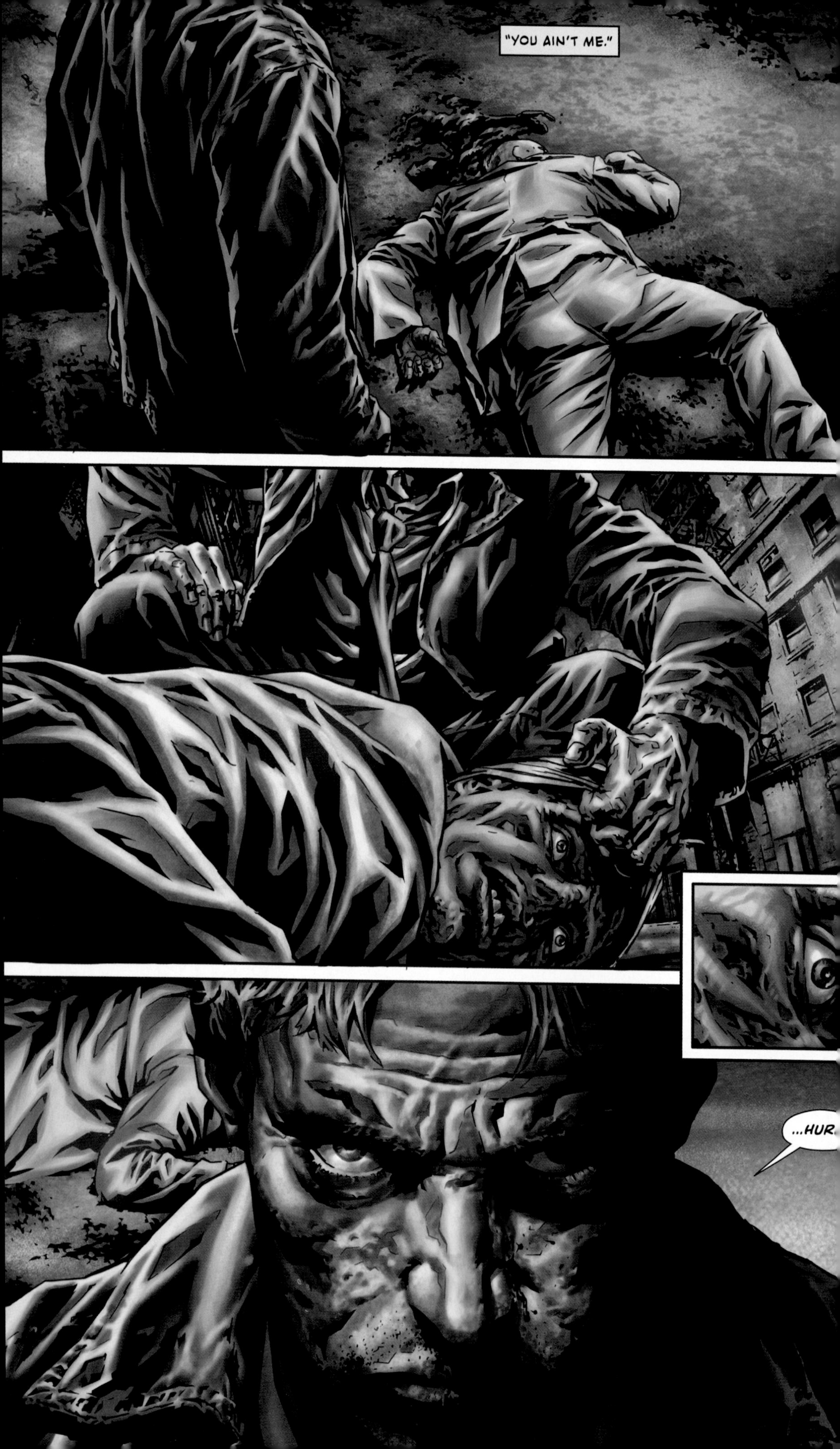
"YOU AIN'T ME."
...HUR

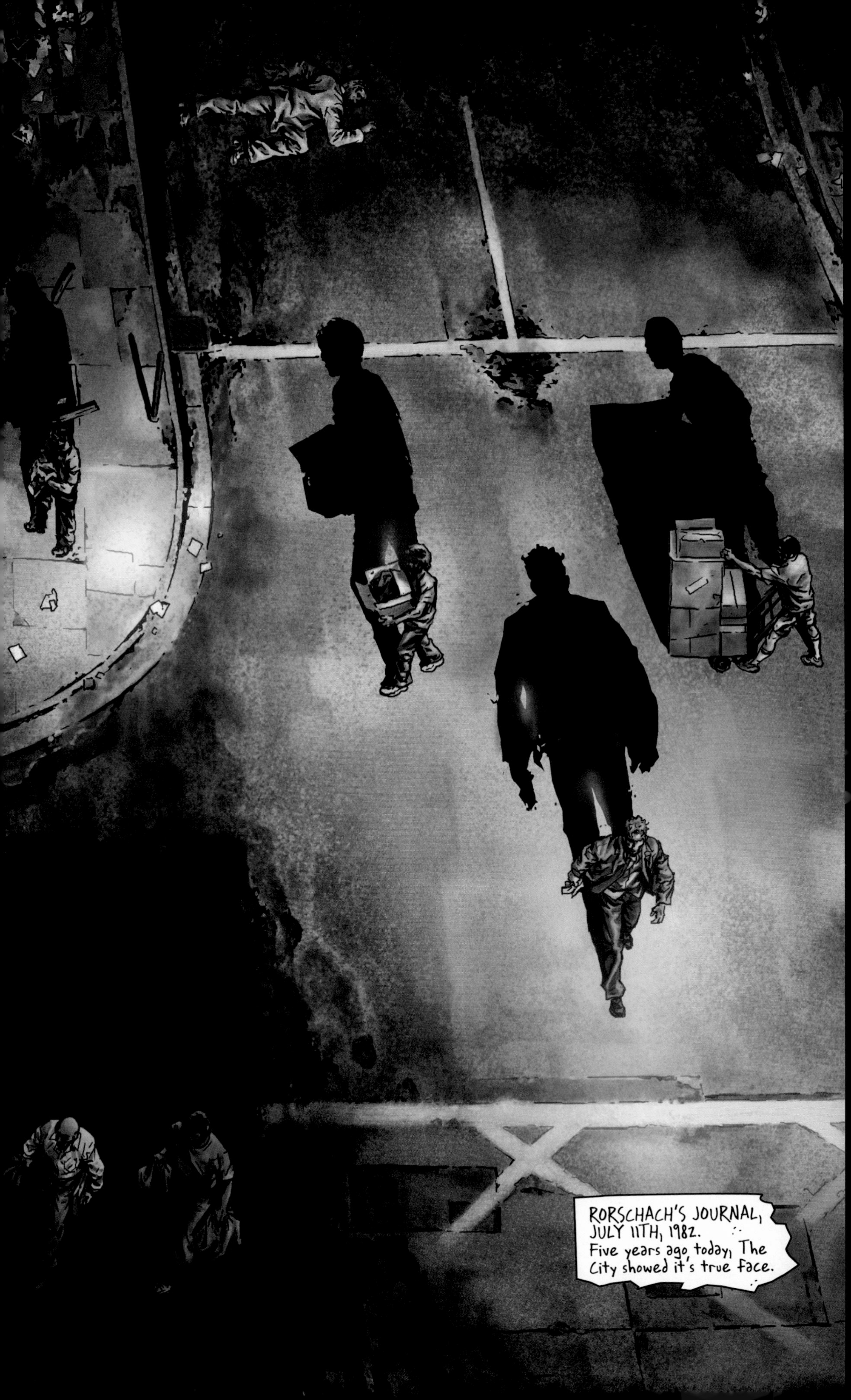
RORSCHACH'S JOURNAL, JULY 11TH, 1982.
Five years ago today, The City showed it's true Face.

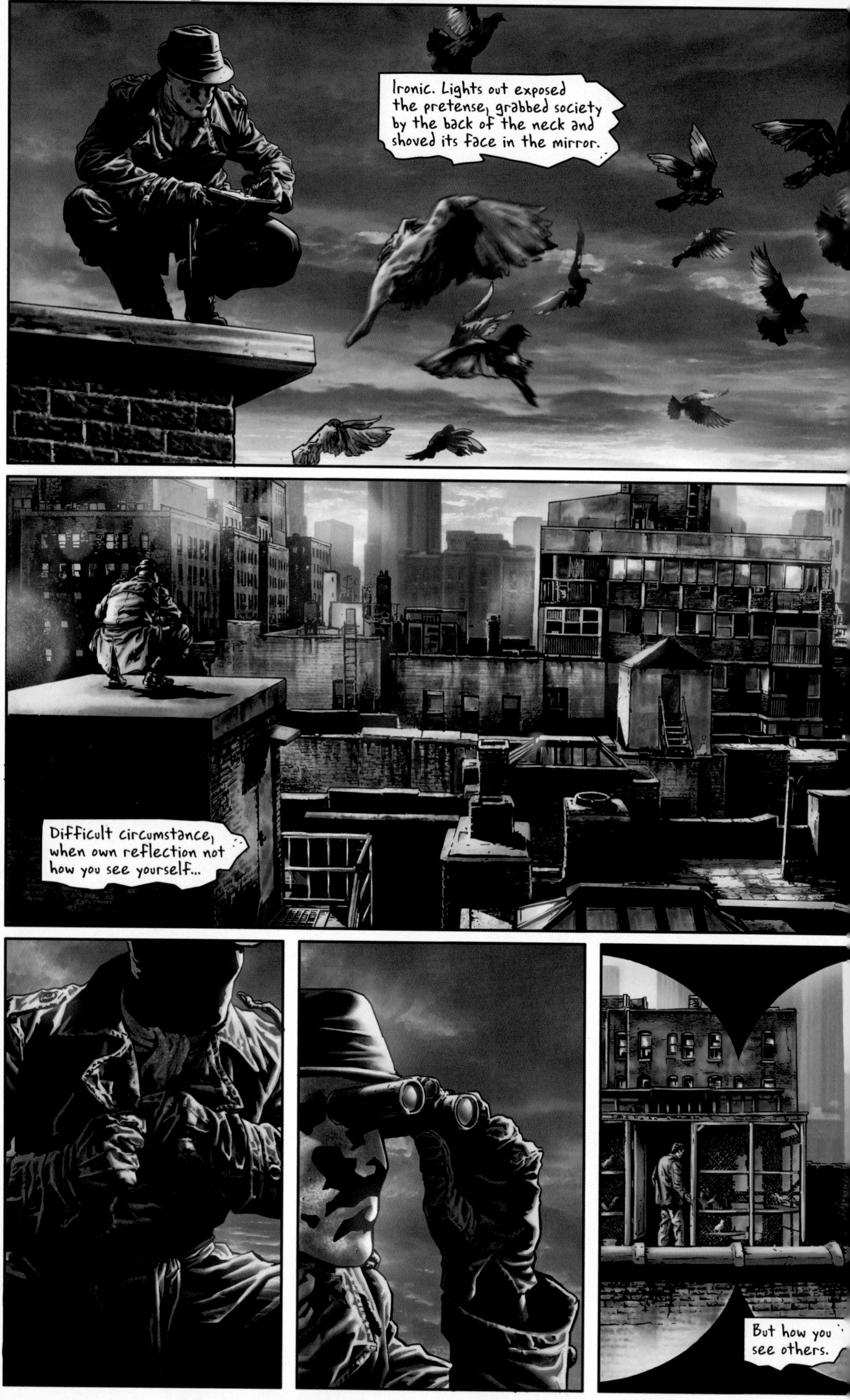
Ironic. Lights out exposed the pretense, grabbed society by the back of the neck and shoved its face in the mirror.
Difficult circumstance, when own reflection not how you see yourself...
But how you see others.

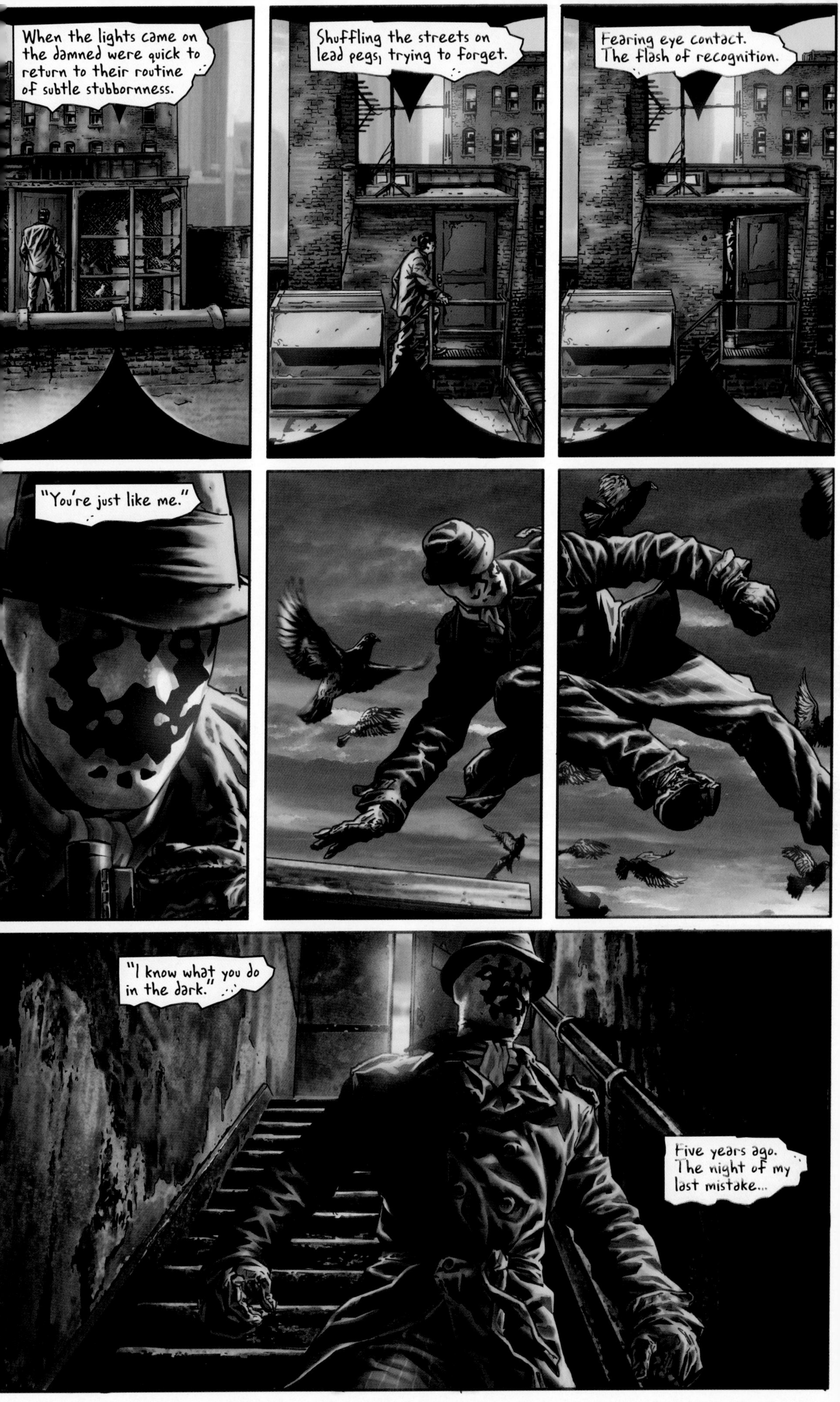
When the lights came on the damned were quick to return to their routine of subtle stubbornness.
Shuffling the streets on lead pegs, trying to forget.
Fearing eye contact. The flash of recognition.
"You're just like me."
"I know what you do in the dark."
Five years ago. The night of my last mistake...

The Bard made his first.

Despite having her throat slit, his victim survived.

In the dark, acting out in the open, Ronald James Randall got sloppy.

Victim identified him.

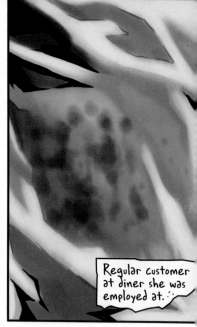

Regular customer at diner she was employed at.

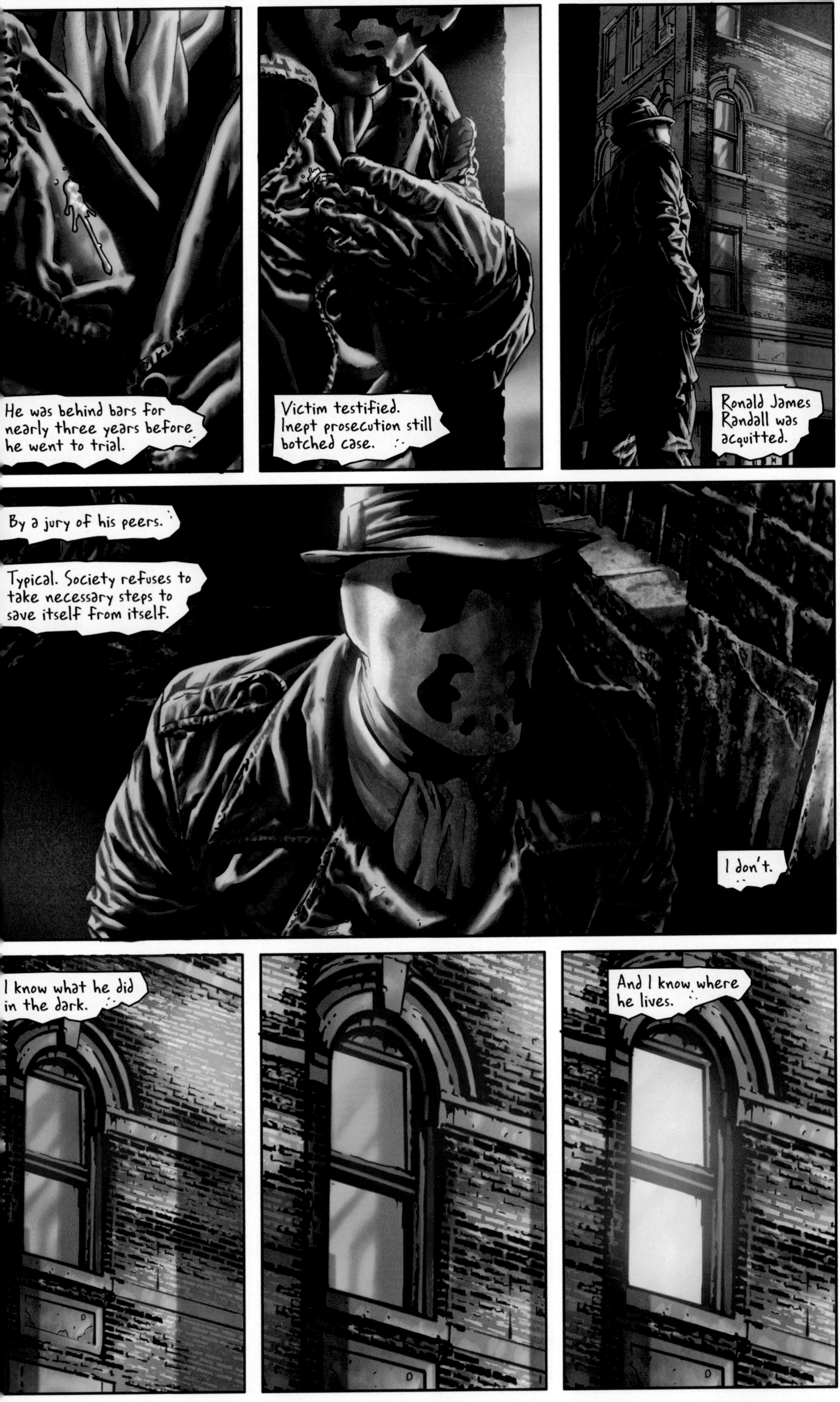
He was behind bars for nearly three years before he went to trial.
Victim testified. Inept prosecution still botched case.
Ronald James Randall was acquitted.
By a jury of his peers.
Typical. Society refuses to take necessary steps to save itself from itself.
I don't.
I know what he did in the dark.
And I know where he lives.

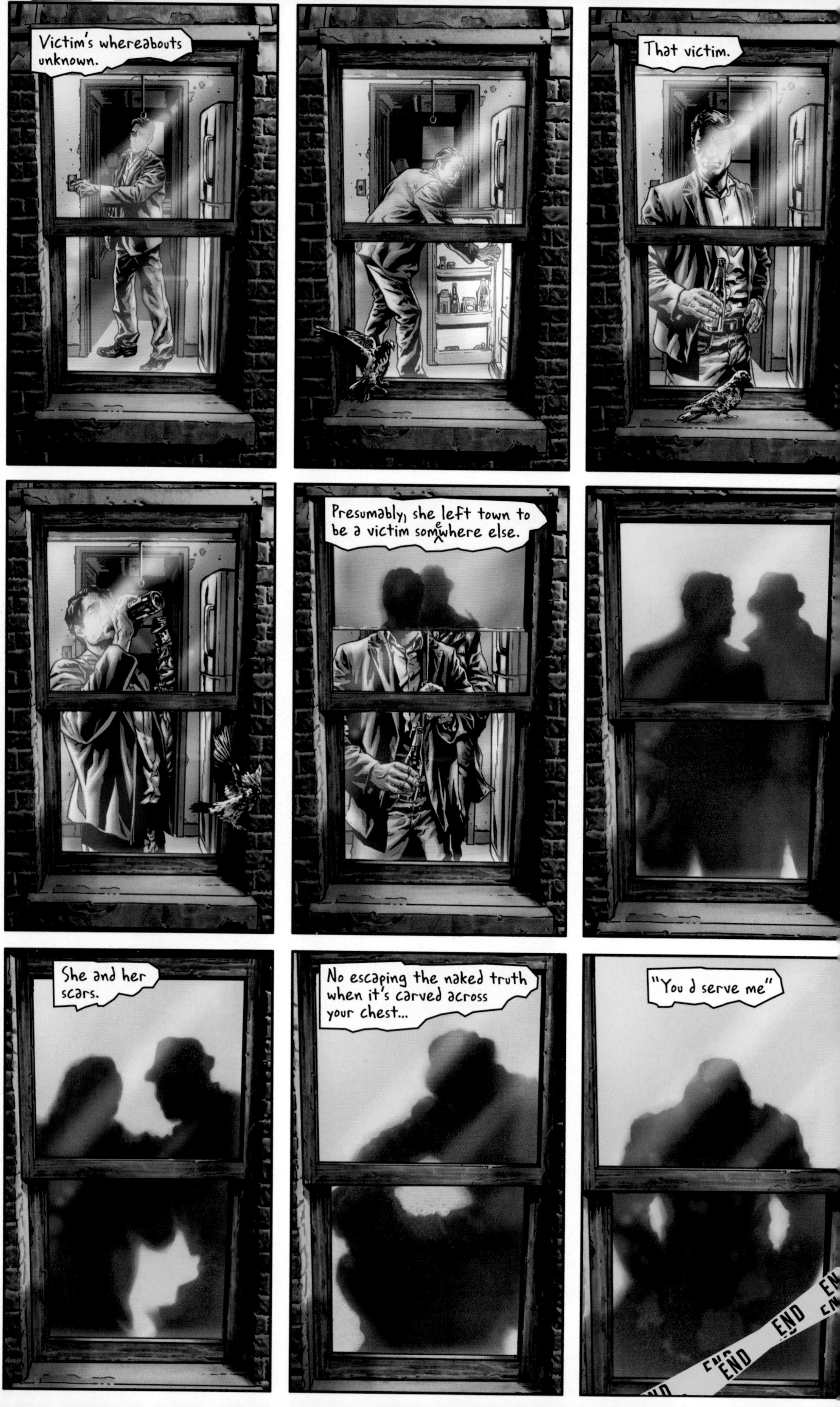
Victim's whereabouts unknown.
That victim.
Presumably, she left town to be a victim somewhere else.
She and her scars.
No escaping the naked truth when it's carved across your chest...
"You d serve me"
END

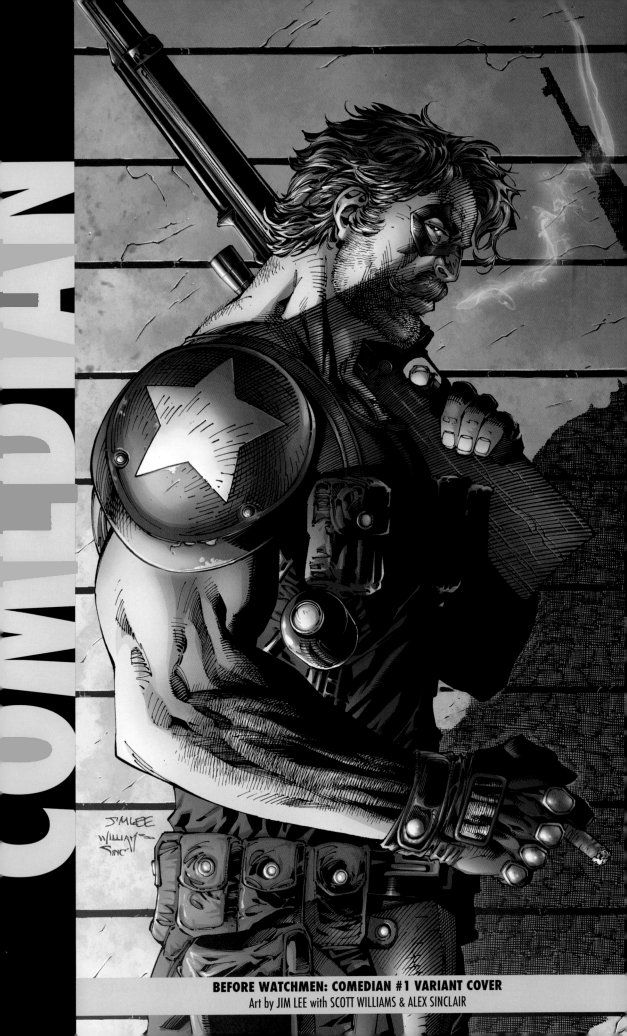

COMEDIAN

BEFORE WATCHMEN: COMEDIAN #1 VARIANT COVER
Art by JIM LEE with SCOTT WILLIAMS & ALEX SINCLAIR

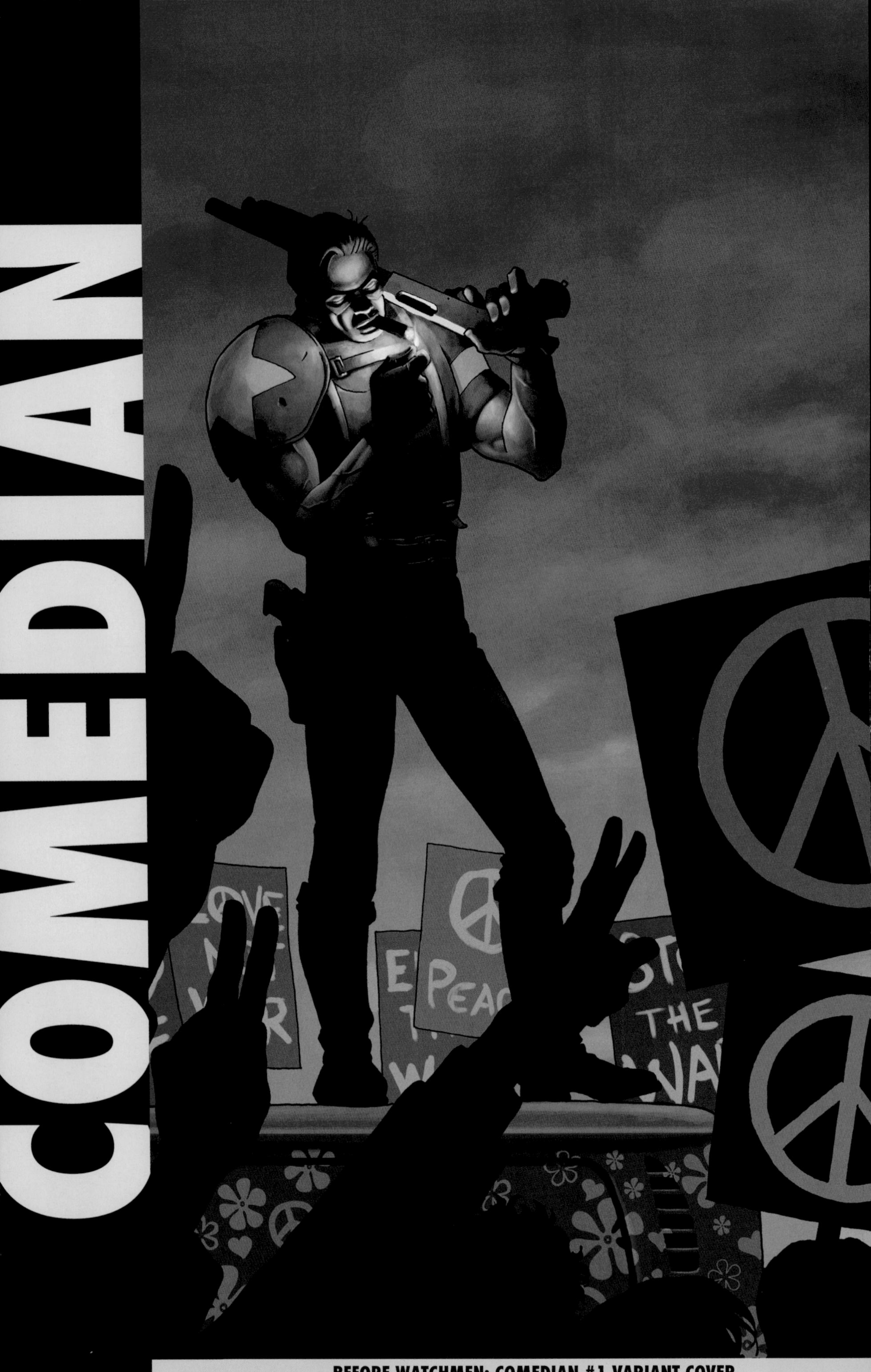
COMEDIAN
THE

BEFORE WATCHMEN: COMEDIAN #1 VARIANT COVER
Art by EDUARDO RISSO

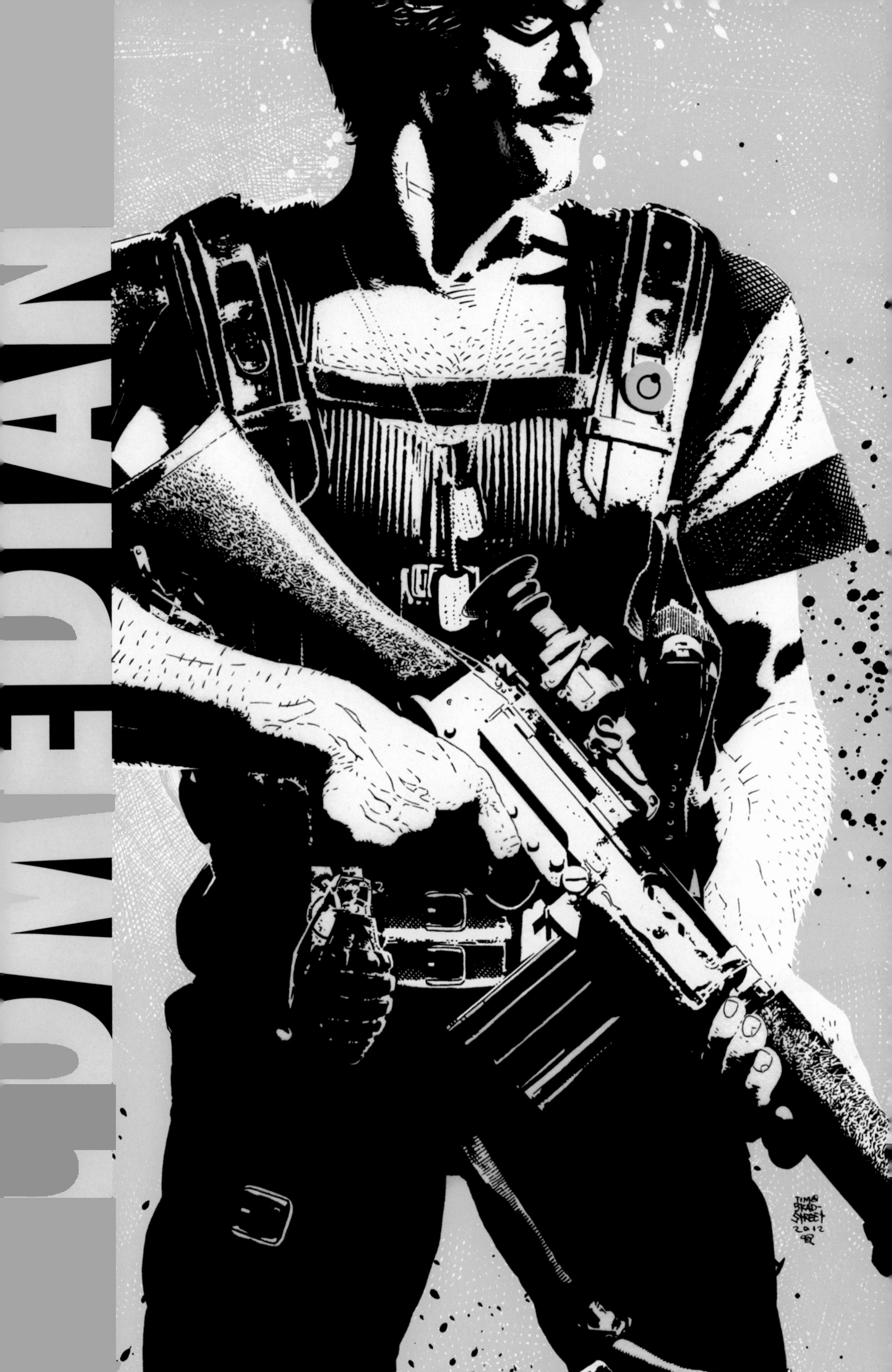
COMEDIAN
TIM BRADSTREET 2012

BEFORE WATCHMEN: COMEDIAN #2 VARIANT COVER

Art by TIM BRADSTREET

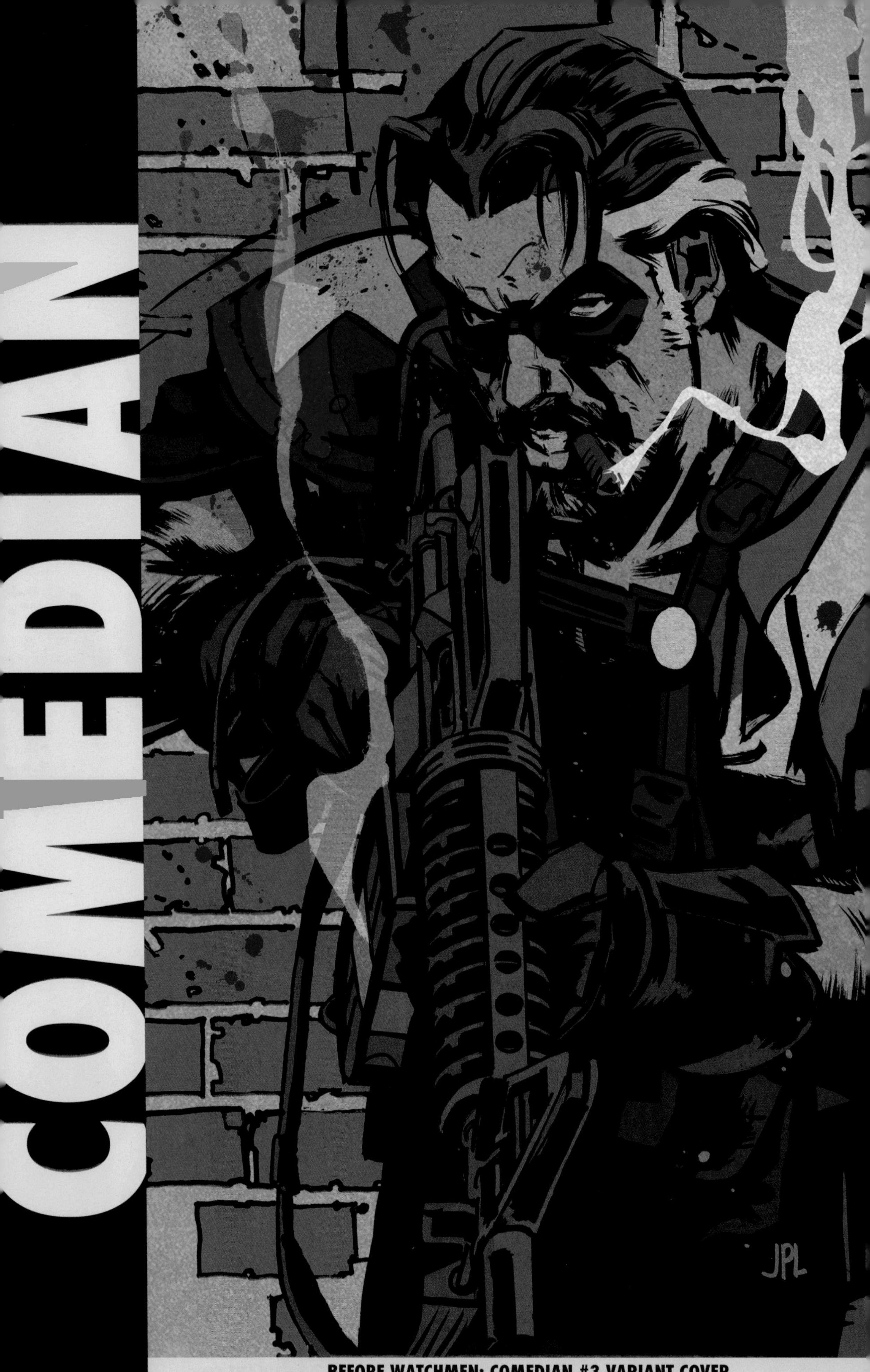
COMEDIAN
JPL

BEFORE WATCHMEN: COMEDIAN #3 VARIANT COVER
Art by JOHN PAUL LEON

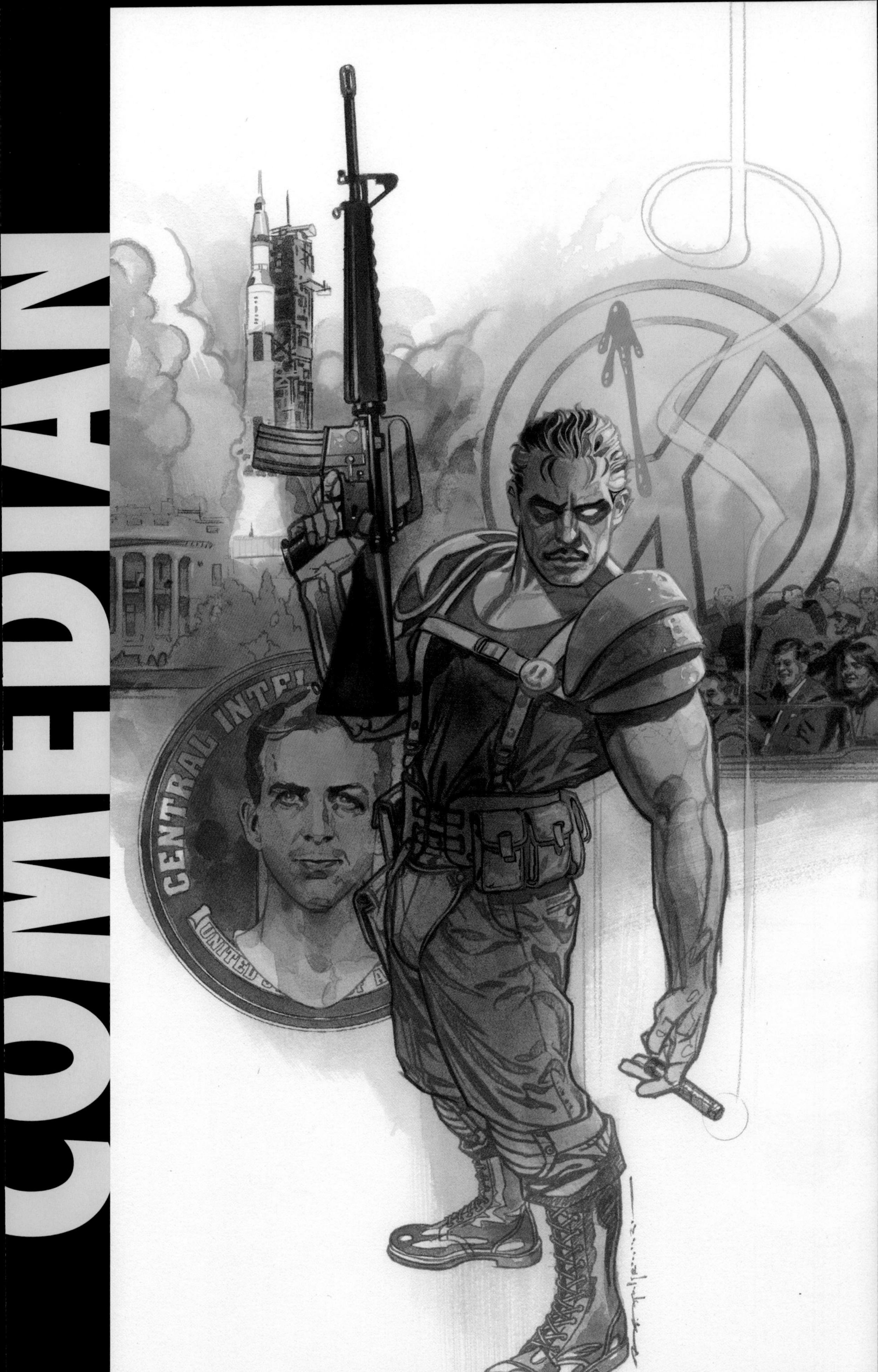
COMEDIAN
CENTRAL

BEFORE WATCHMEN: COMEDIAN #4 VARIANT COVER
Art by BRIAN STELFREEZE

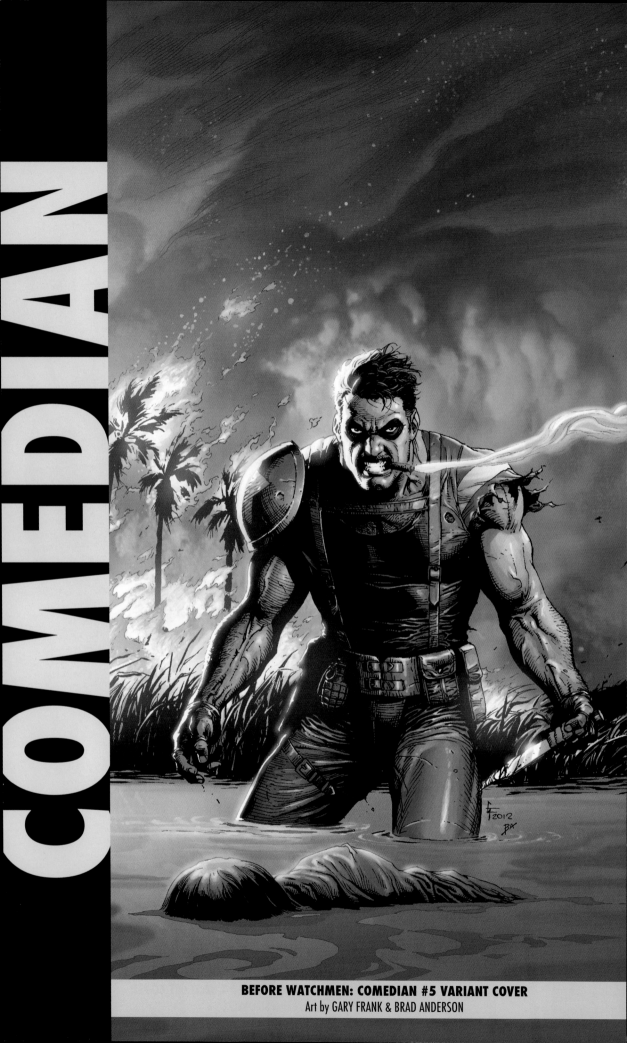

BEFORE WATCHMEN: COMEDIAN #5 VARIANT COVER
Art by GARY FRANK & BRAD ANDERSON

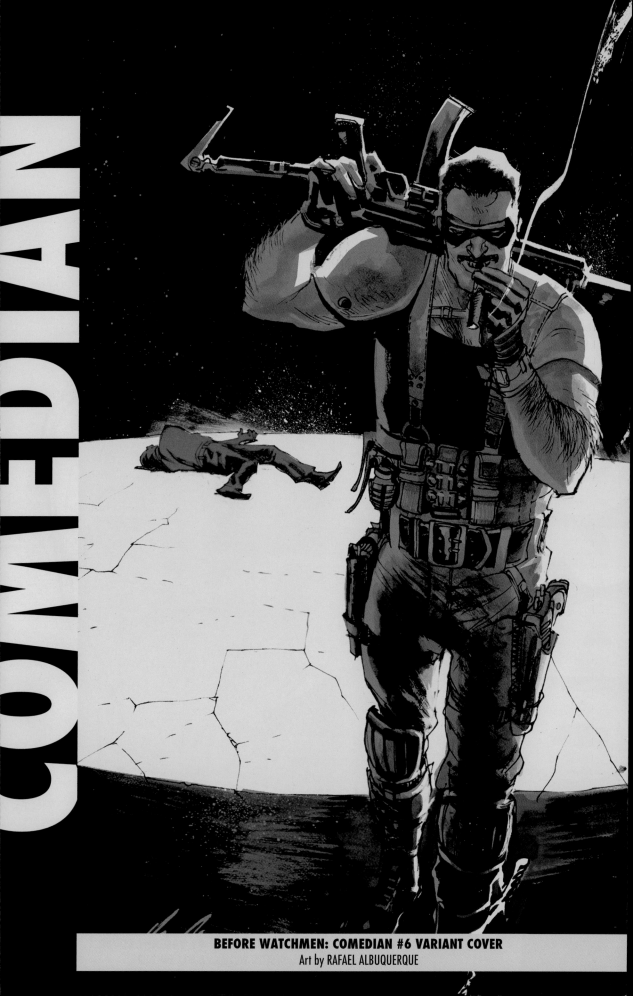

BEFORE WATCHMEN: COMEDIAN #6 VARIANT COVER
Art by RAFAEL ALBUQUERQUE

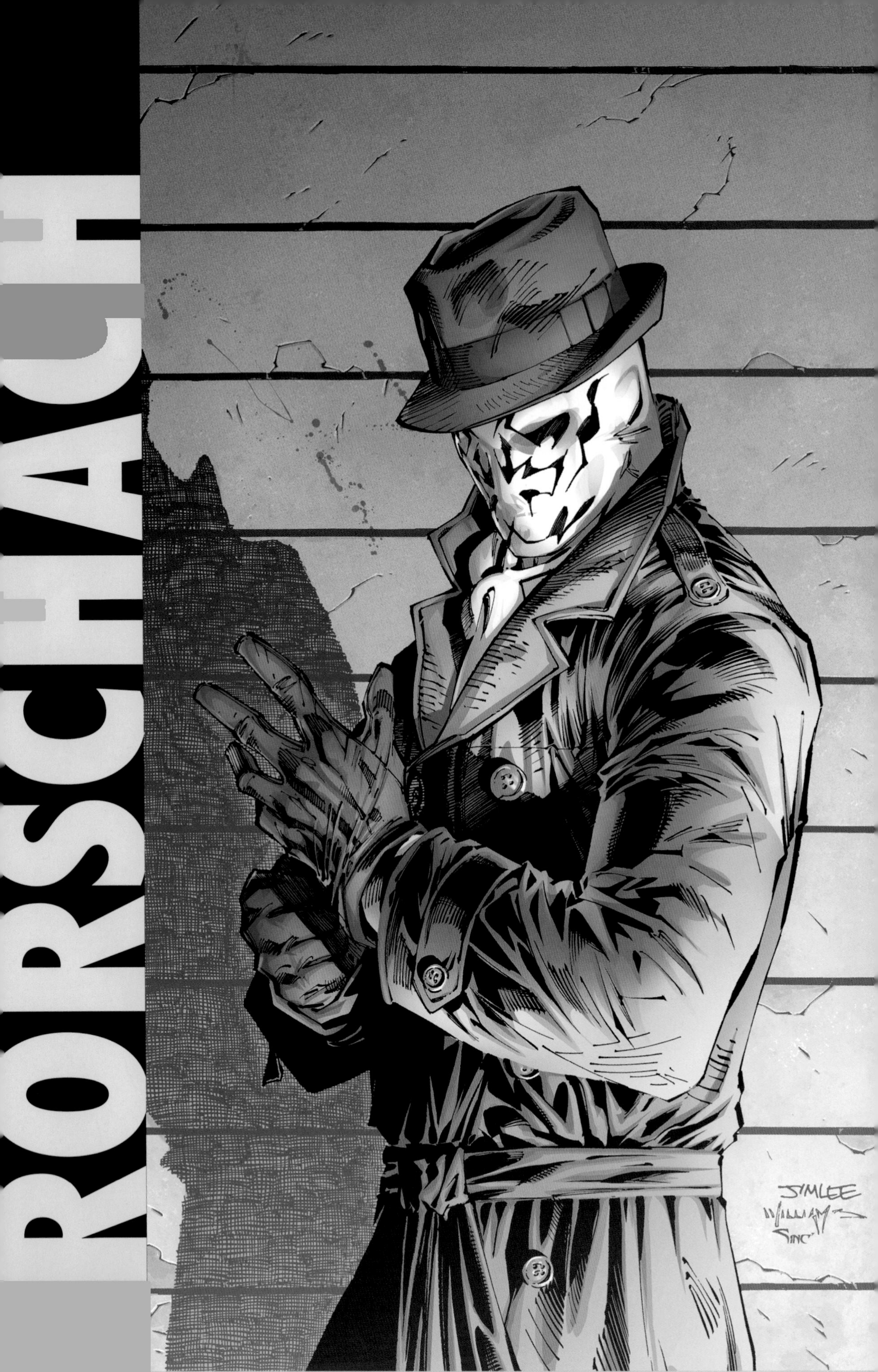
RORSCHACH

BEFORE WATCHMEN: RORSCHACH #1 VARIANT COVER

Art by JIM LEE with SCOTT WILLIAMS & ALEX SINCLAIR

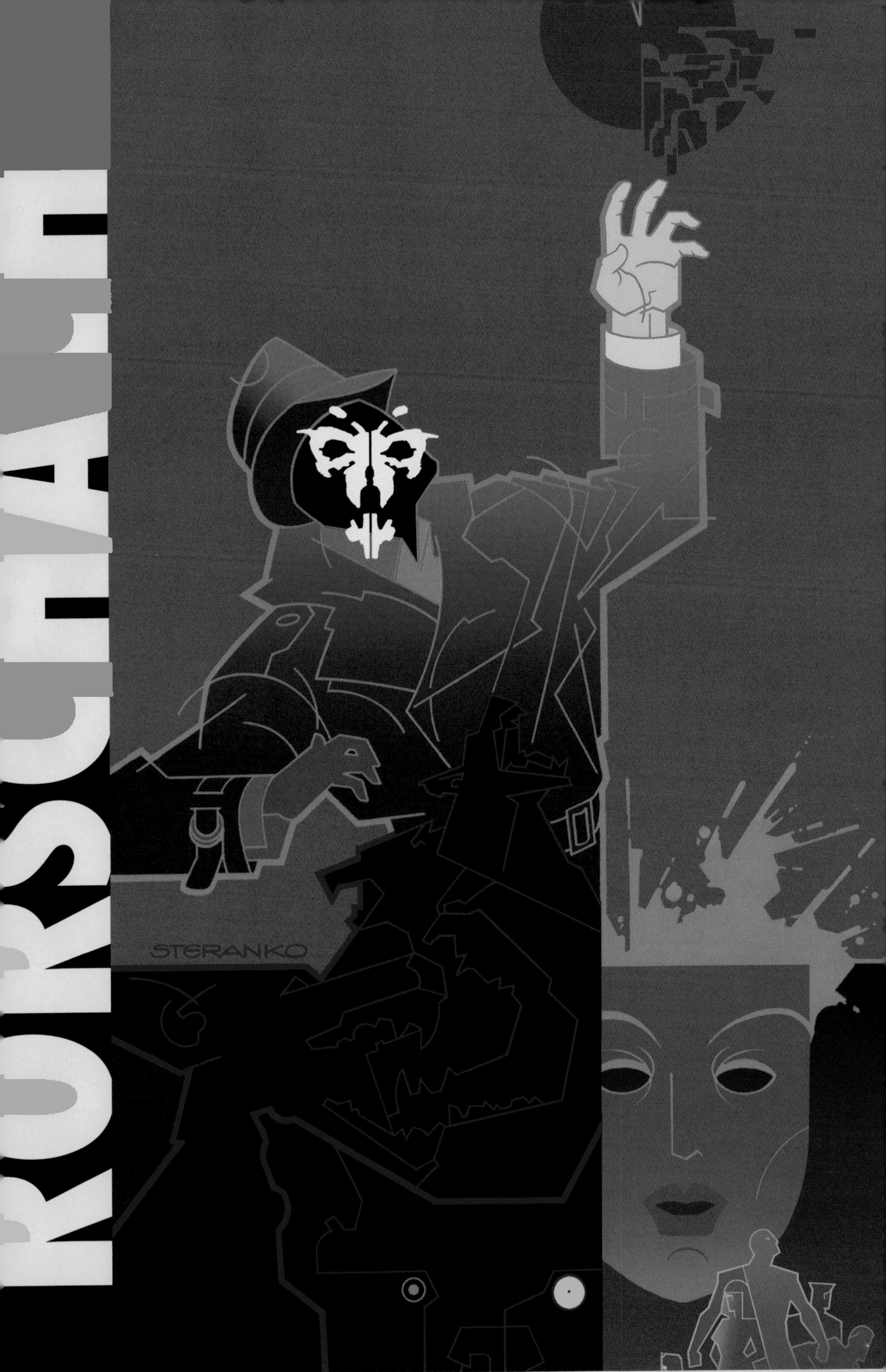
RORSCHACH
STERANKO

BEFORE WATCHMEN: RORSCHACH #1 VARIANT COVER
Art by JIM STERANKO

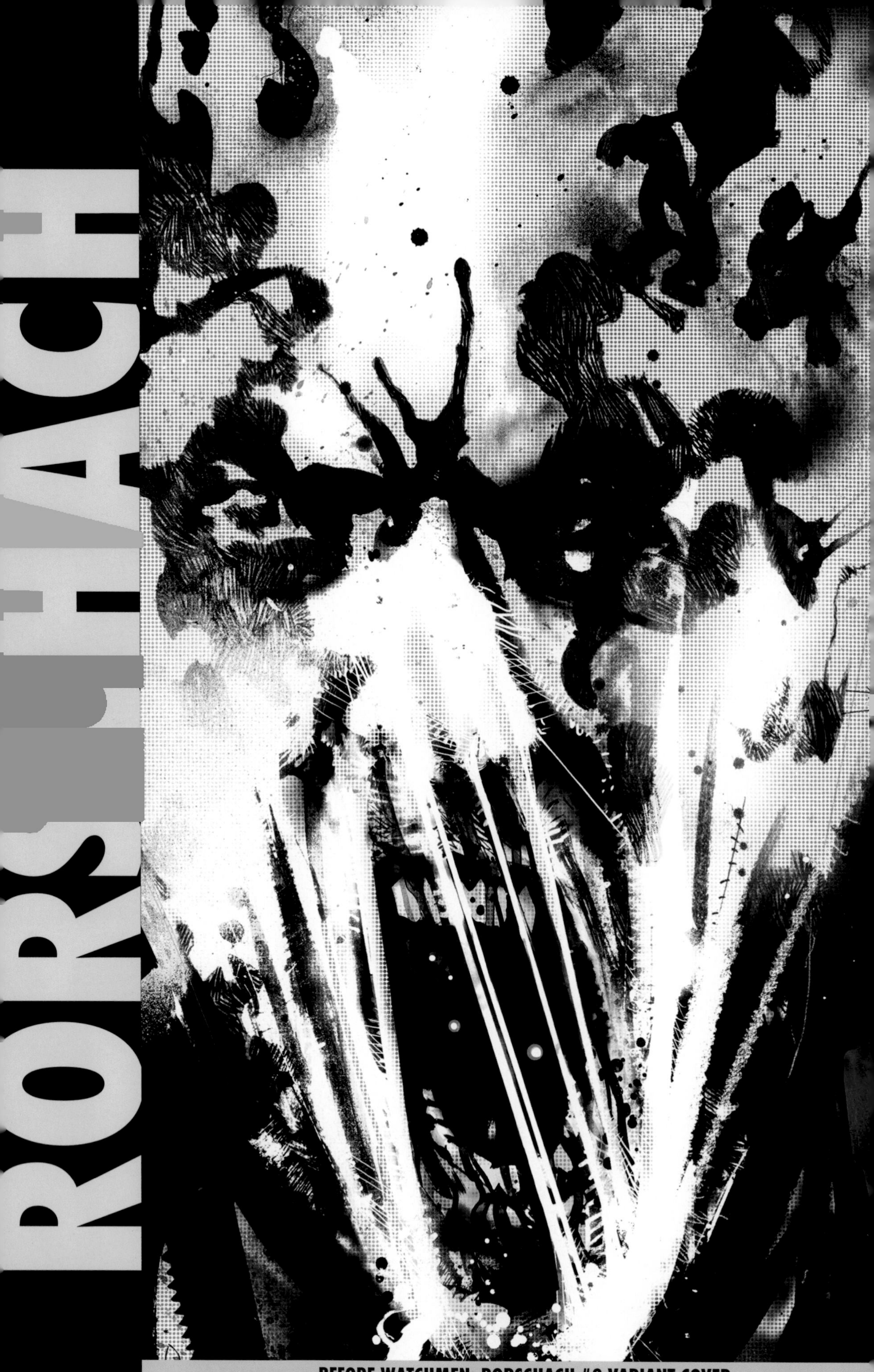
RORSCHACH

BEFORE WATCHMEN: RORSCHACH #2 VARIANT COVER
Art by JOCK

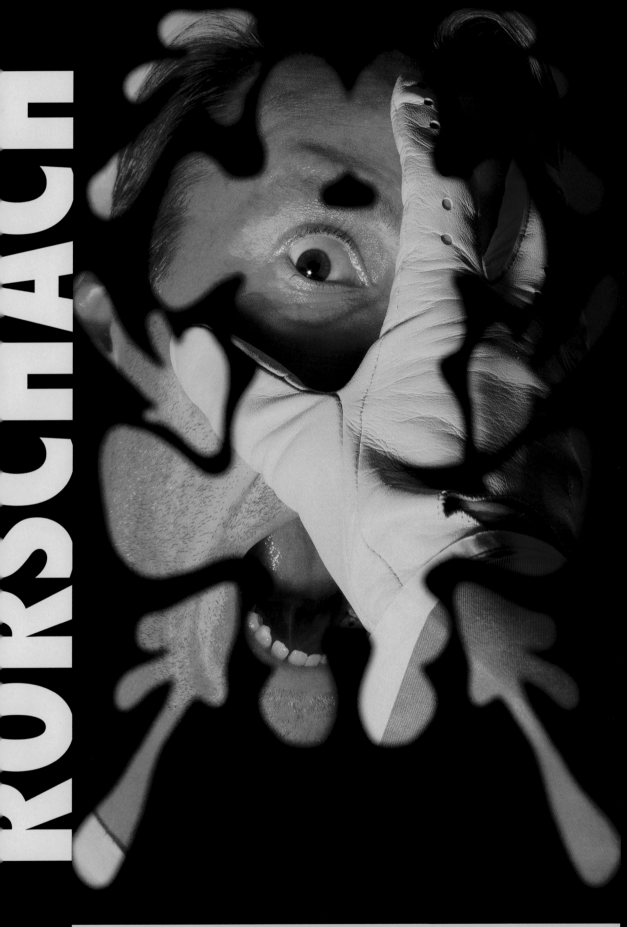

RORSCHACH

BEFORE WATCHMEN: RORSCHACH #3 VARIANT COVER
Art by CHIP KIDD

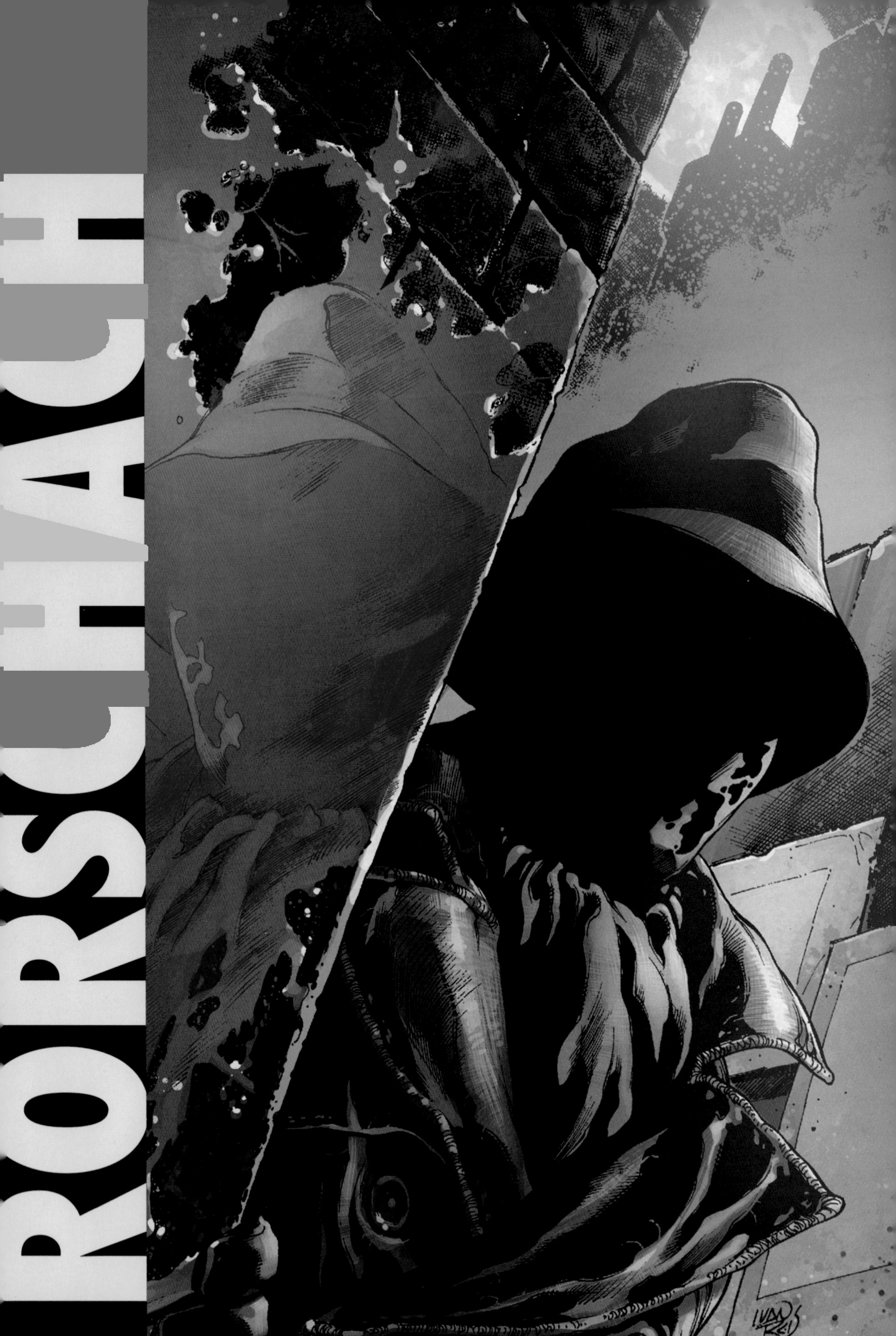
RORSCHACH

BEFORE WATCHMEN: RORSCHACH #4 VARIANT COVER
Art by IVAN REIS & JOE PRADO with ROD REIS

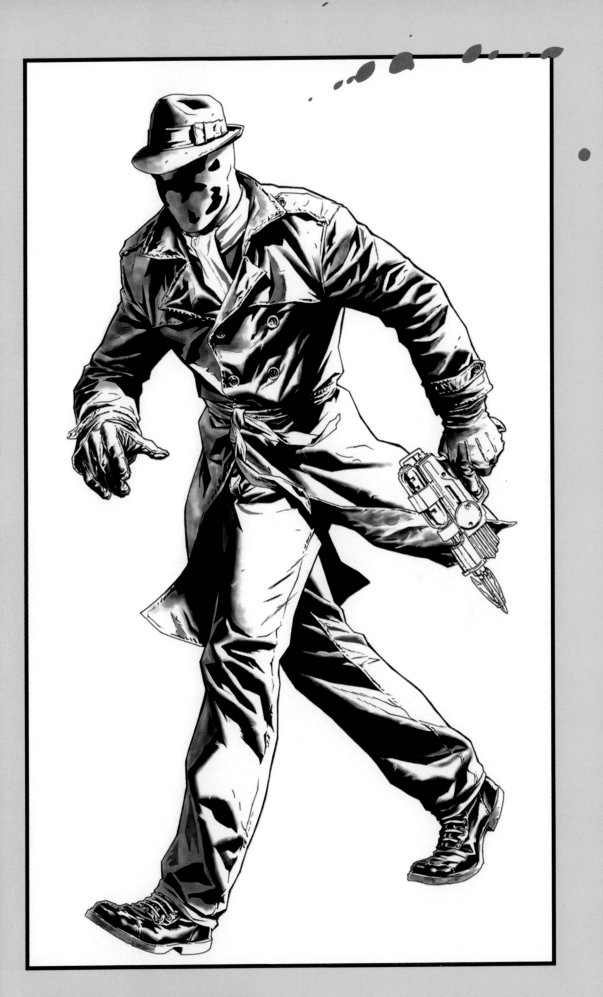

Rorschach statue design by **LEE BERMEJO**

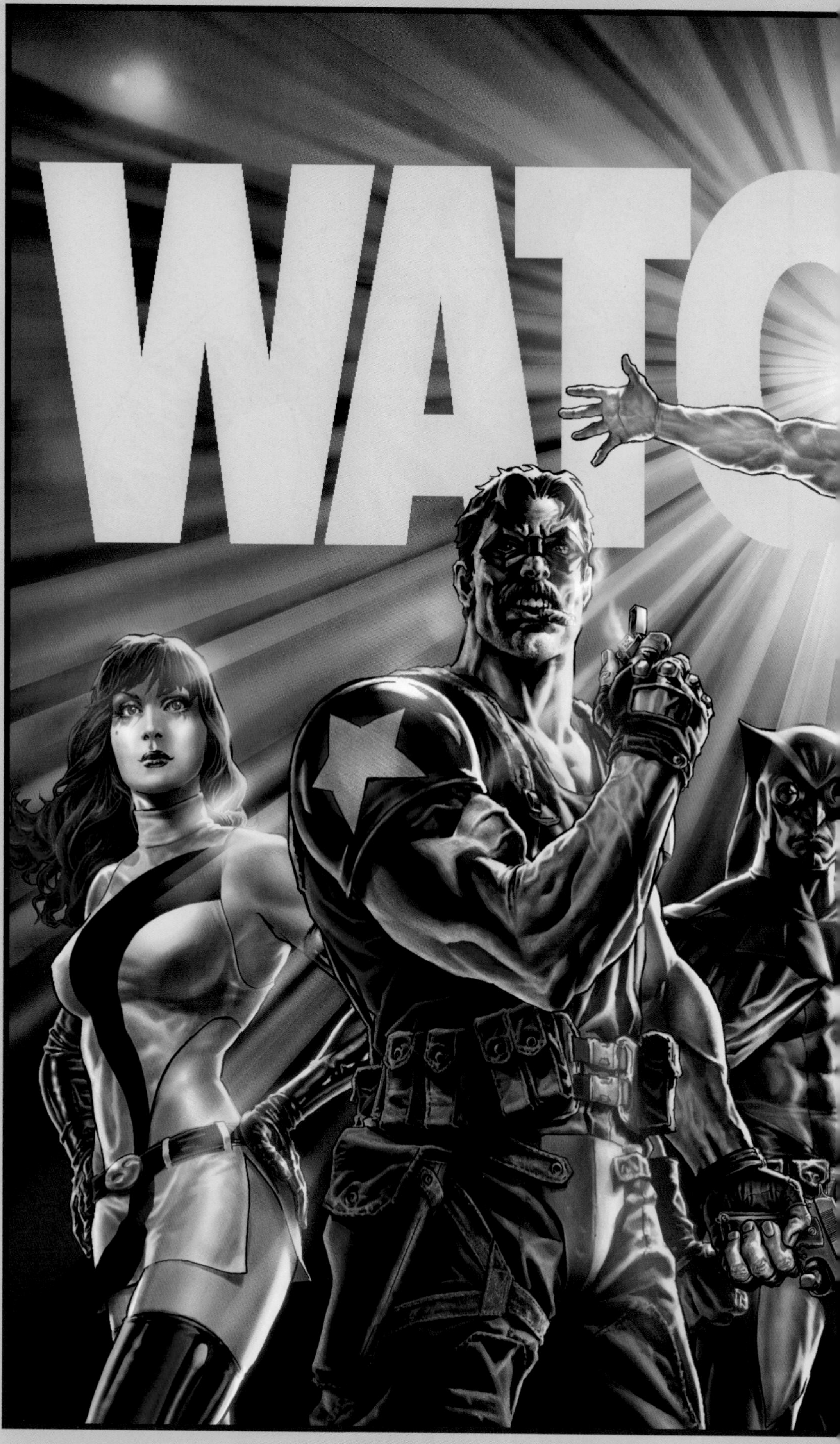
WATC

Before Watchmen promotional poster art by LEE BERMEJO

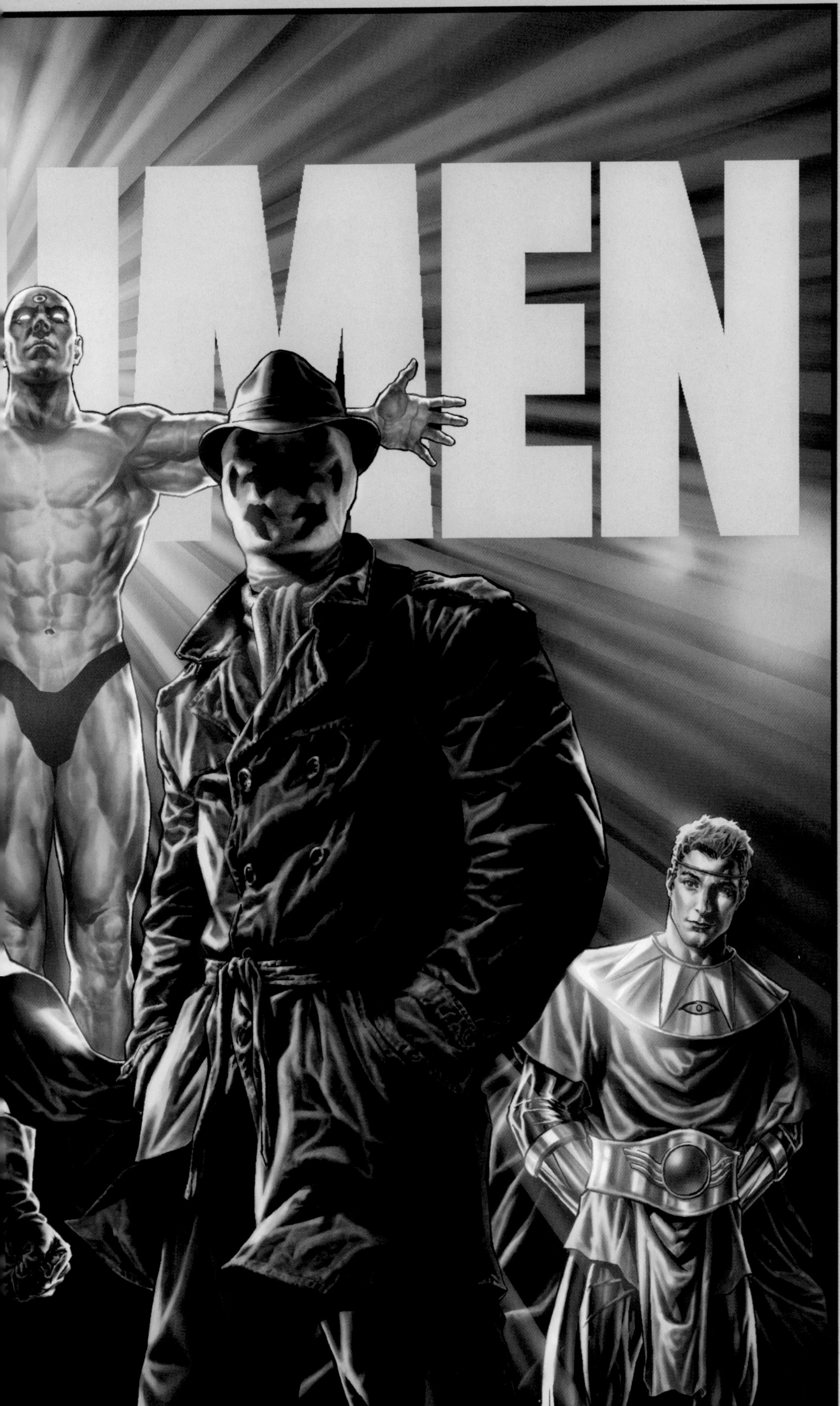
MEN

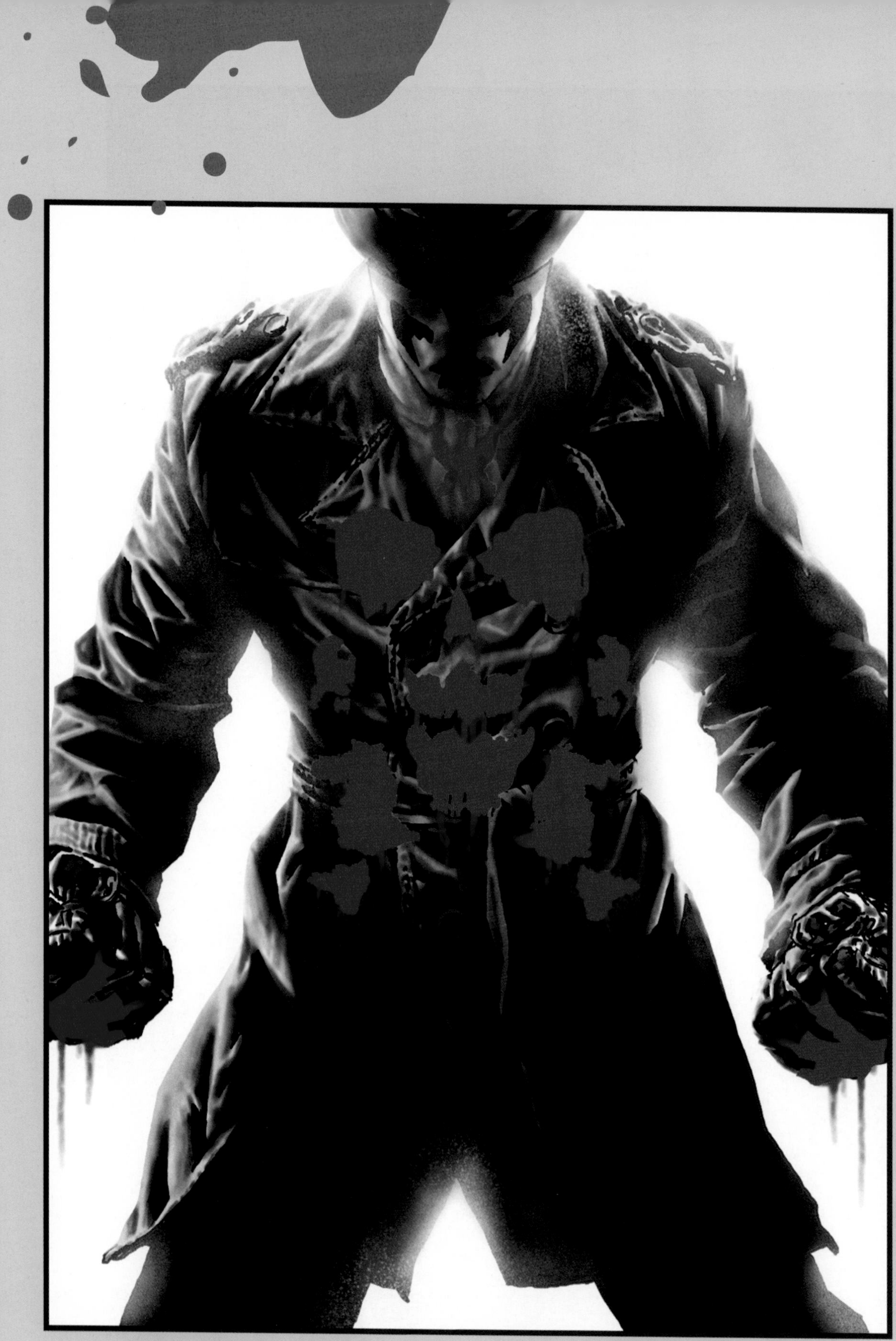

Cover sketch to Before Watchmen: Rorschach #1 by LEE BERMEJO

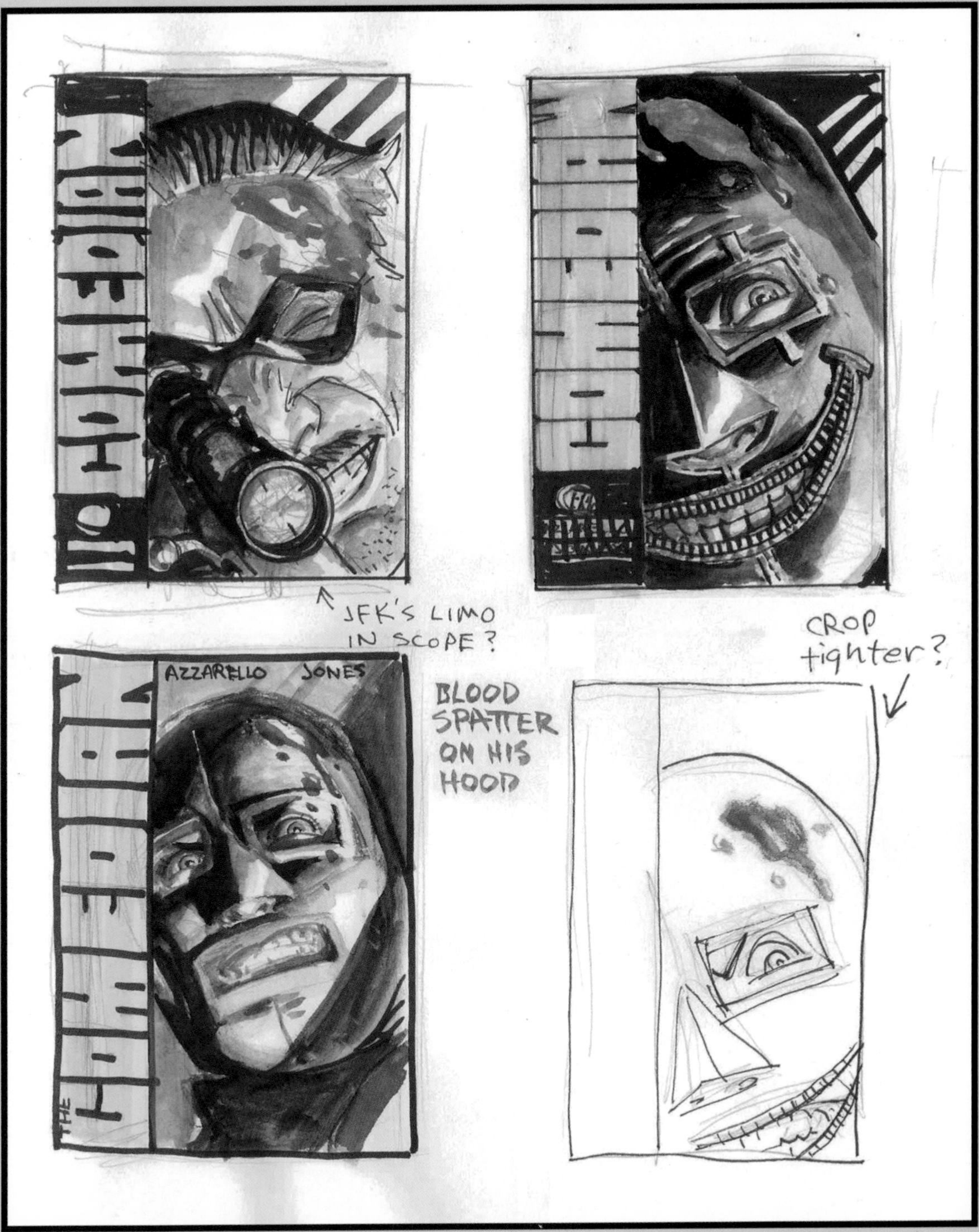
JFK'S LIMO IN SCOPE?
AZZARELLO JONES
THE
BLOOD SPATTER ON HIS HOOD
CROP tighter?

Cover sketch to Before Watchmen: Comedian #4 by J.G. JONES

masked version
cigar
TWO GUNS
VIETNAM ERA COMEDIAN
M-60
Lighting cigar w/ Molatov cocktail
Grenades/ pistols
Fatigues instead of leather pants
shin guards over Trench boots

COMEDIAN

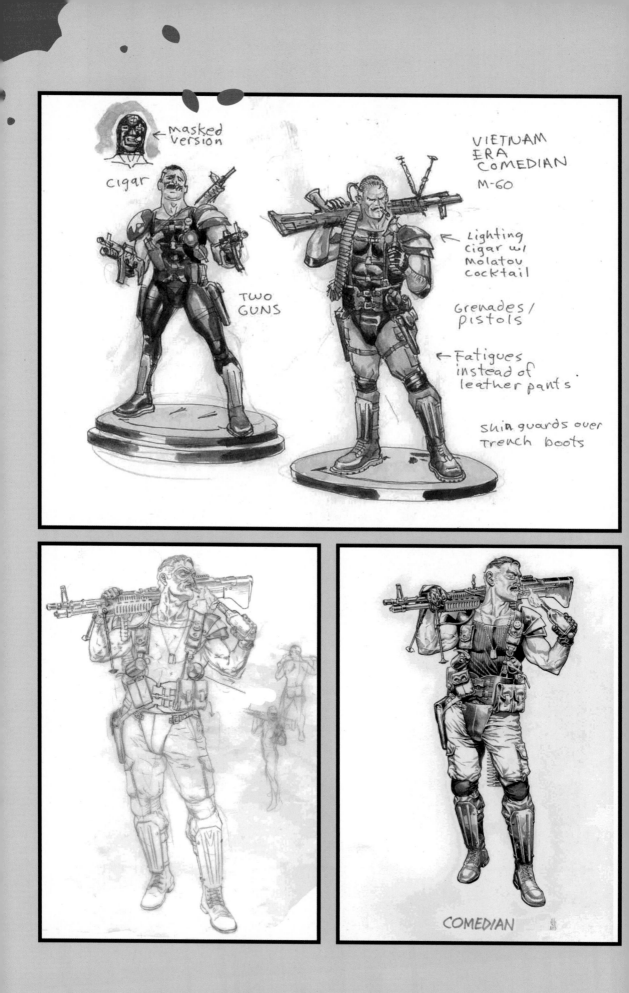

Comedian statue design by J.G. JONES

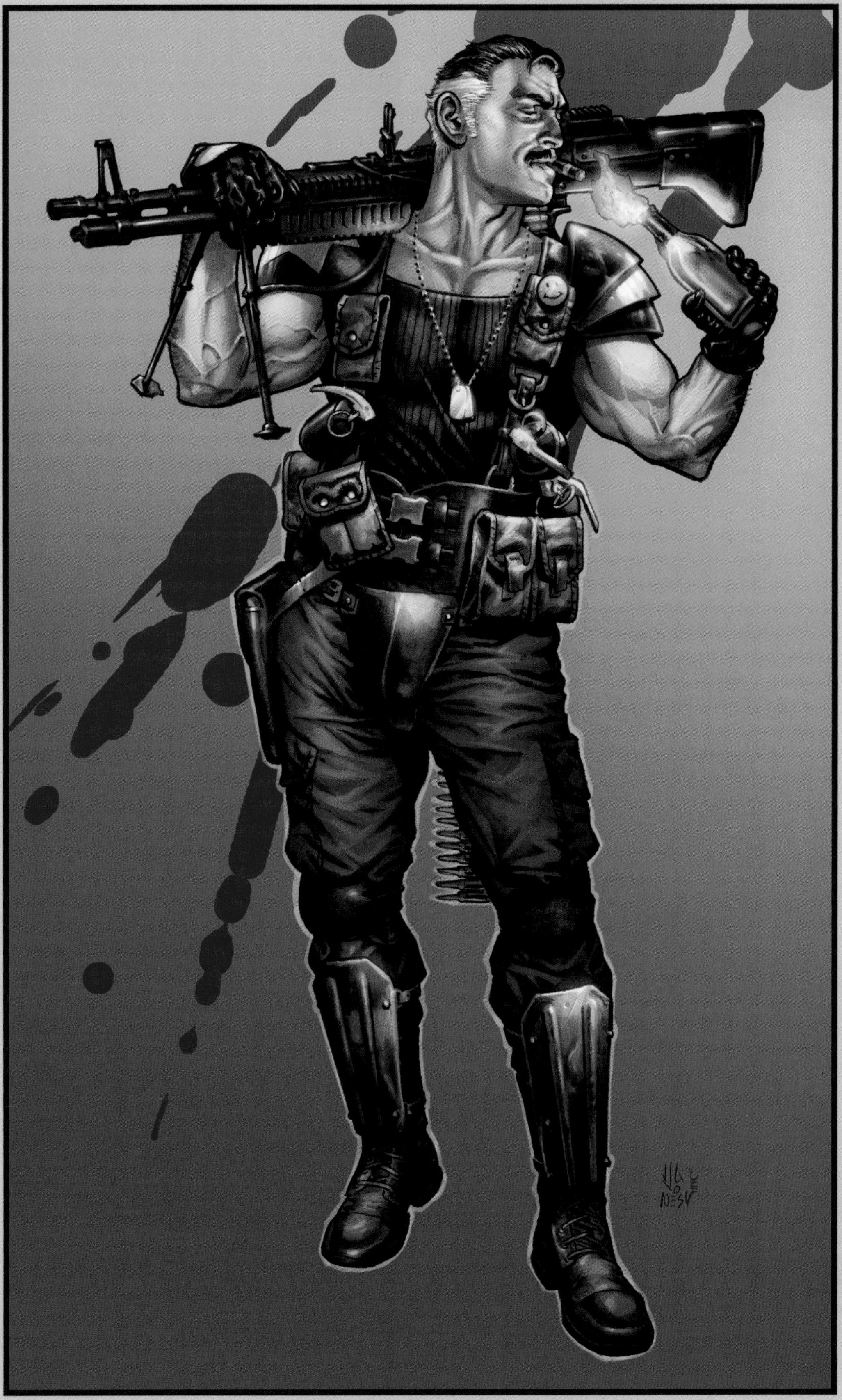

Comedian statue design by J.G. JONES with ALEX SINCLAIR

BIOGRAPHIES

BRIAN AZZARELLO has been writing comics professionally since the mid-1990s. He is the author of JONNY DOUBLE, BATMAN: BROKEN CITY and the Harvey and Eisner Award-winning 100 BULLETS, all created in collaboration with artist Eduardo Risso. *The New York Times* best-selling author's other work for DC includes the titles HELLBLAZER and LOVELESS (both with Marcelo Frusin), SUPERMAN: FOR TOMORROW (with Jim Lee), JOKER and LUTHOR (both with Lee Bermejo), SGT. ROCK: BETWEEN HELL AND A HARD PLACE (with Joe Kubert), FILTHY RICH (with Victor Santos), and most recently the all-new ongoing series WONDER WOMAN (with Cliff Chiang). He also wrote the Richard Corben-illustrated graphic novels *Cage* and *Banner* for Marvel Comics. Azzarello lives in Chicago with his wife, artist Jill Thompson, and twitters only when he has something to say..

J.G. JONES was an even-tempered lad as a child. Always a good kid; he was a country boy with a smile on his face and dirt between his toes. No one is quite sure where it all went wrong.

He somehow got involved in the high-stakes world of big-money comic books. It started simply enough. Some older kid slipped him his first comic at the schoolyard or maybe he just tried it to be cool. Before you know it, he was pulled into the dark underbelly of the Big City, swapping comic illustrations (*Marvel Boy*, *Wanted*) for paychecks.

Time and again he tried to break the mesmerizing pull, and finally seemed close to making a clean break. Then came the siren song of 52. One last hit before quitting. One last roll for the big score, and another year disappeared.

LEE BERMEJO began drawing comics in 1997 for WildStorm Studios in San Diego at age 19. He collaborated with acclaimed writer Brian Azzarello on the graphic novels JOKER and LUTHOR, and worked with writer John Arcudi on the Superman feature in WEDNESDAY COMICS. He has also worked on HELLBLAZER with writer Mike Carey and GLOBAL FREQUENCY with writer Warren Ellis. Bermejo has illustrated covers for the line of Vertigo Crime graphic novels, beginning with FILTHY RICH, written by Brian Azzarello, and DARK ENTRIES, written by Ian Rankin. He has written and illustrated The New York Times best-selling book, BATMAN: NOEL. Currently he is illustrating BEFORE WATCHMEN: RORSHACH, written by Brian Azzarello. Bermejo has lived in Italy since 2003.

RORSCHACH'S

(JULY 1, 19

I HATE THIS
HAVE SINCE
A CHILD.